THE PROS

THE PROSE READER

Essays for Thinking, Reading, and Writing

SIXTH EDITION

Kim Flachmann
Michael Flachmann

California State University
Bakersfield

Upper Saddle River, New Jersey 07458

Library of Congress Cataloging-in-Publication Data

The prose reader: essays for thinking, reading, and writing / [compiled by] Kim
Flachmann, Michael Flachmann.—6th ed.
    p. cm.
  Includes bibliographical references and index.
  ISBN 0-13-029325-3
    1. College readers. 2. English language—Rhetoric—Problems, exercises, etc. 3. Report
writing—Problems, exercises, etc. I. Flachmann, Kim. II. Flachmann, Michael.
  PE1417 .p847 2001
  808'.0427—dc21

                                     2001021247

VP/Editor in Chief: Leah Jewell
Acquisitions Editor: Corey Good
Editorial Assistant: Jennifer Collins
VP/Director of Production
  and Manufacturing: Barbara Kittle
Project Manager: Maureen Richardson
Senior Managing Editor: Mary Rottino
Manufacturing Manager: Nick Sklitsis
Prepress and Manufacturing Buyer: Mary Ann Gloriande
Creative Design Director: Leslie Osher
Interior Design: Anne Nieglos
Cover Design: Bruce Kenselaar
Cover Art: Kerne Erickson/KE Visuals
Image Specialist: Beth Boyd
Manager, Rights & Permissions: Kay Dellosa
Director, Image Resource Center: Melinda Reo
Director of Marketing: Beth Gillett Mejia
Senior Marketing Manager: Brandy Dawson
Marketing Assistant: Christine Moodie

Credits appear on pp. 674–677, which constitute a continuation of the copyright page.

This book was set in 11/13 Bembo by Pine Tree Composition and was printed
and bound by R. R. Donnelley & Sons Company. The cover was printed by
Jaguar Graphics.

Printed in the United States of America

10 9 8 7 6 5 4 3 2 1

ISBN 0-13-029325-3
ISBN 0-13-041634-7 (Instructor's Edition)

Prentice-Hall International (UK) Limited, *London*
Prentice-Hall of Australia Pty. Limited, *Sydney*
Prentice-Hall Canada Inc., *Toronto*
Prentice-Hall Hispanoamericana, S.A., *Mexico*
Prentice-Hall of India Private Limited, *New Delhi*
Prentice-Hall of Japan, Inc., *Tokyo*
Pearson Education Asia Pte. Ltd., *Singapore*
Editora Prentice-Hall do Brasil, Ltda., *Rio de Janeiro*

For Frank and Jo Marschel,
our constant inspiration

RHETORICAL TABLE OF CONTENTS

5 DIVISION/CLASSIFICATION: *Finding Categories*   **272**

Do handguns make our society a safer place? Bronwyn Jones provides a surprising answer to this controversial question.

Controversial author Shelby Steele examines the extent to which affirmative action programs perpetuate the "cultural myth of black inferiority."

What's your opinion in the debate over immigration in America? Peter Salins offers some intriguing facts and figures to help clarify the issue.

Can you imagine a time in the future when no one will be able to read this sentence? Geoffrey Meredith and Kevin Kelly can. What will happen to our world when "text is toast"?

With the ethics of journalists at an all-time low, should we begin to reevaluate the constitutional guarantee of freedom of the press? Mario Cuomo and John Merrill square off over this controversial issue.

---

11 Essays on Thinking, Reading, and Writing   609

THEMATIC TABLE OF CONTENTS

BEHAVIORAL SCIENCE

BUSINESS

CHICANO AND LATIN AMERICAN STUDIES

ECONOMICS

PREFACE

The Prose Reader is based on the assumption that lucid writing follows lucid thinking, whereas poor written work is almost inevitably the product of foggy, irrational thought processes. As a result, our primary purpose in this book, as in the first five editions, is to help students *think* more clearly and logically—both in their minds and on paper.

Furthermore, we believe that college students should be able to think, read, and write on three increasingly difficult levels:

1. *Literal—characterized by a basic understanding of words and their meanings;*
2. *Interpretive—consisting of a knowledge of linear connections between ideas and an ability to make valid inferences based on those ideas; and*
3. *Critical—the highest level, distinguished by the systematic investigation of complex ideas and by the analysis of their relationship to the world around us.*

To demonstrate the vital interrelationship between reader and writer, our text provides your students with prose models intended to inspire their own thinking and writing. Although studying rhetorical strategies is certainly not the only way to approach writing, it is a productive means of helping students become better writers. These essays are intended to encourage your students to improve their writing through a partnership with some of the best examples of professional prose available today. Just as musicians and athletes richly benefit from studying the techniques of the foremost people in their fields, your students will grow in spirit and language use from their collaborative work with the excellent writers in this collection.

HOW THE TEXT WORKS

Each chapter of *The Prose Reader* begins with an explanation of a single rhetorical technique. These explanations are divided into six sections that progress from the effect of this technique on our daily lives to its integral role in the writing process. Also in each introduction, we include a student paragraph and a student essay featuring each particular rhetorical strategy under discussion. The essay is highlighted by annotations and underlining to illustrate how to write that type of essay and to help bridge the gap between student writing and the professional selections that follow. After each essay, the student writer has drafted a personal note with some useful advice for other student writers.

The essays that follow each chapter introduction are selected from a wide variety of well-known contemporary authors. Needless to say, "pure" rhetorical types rarely exist, of course, and when they do, the result often seems artificial. Therefore, although each essay in this collection focuses on a single rhetorical mode as its primary strategy, other strategies are always simultaneously at work. These selections concentrate on one primary technique at a time in much the same way a well-arranged photograph highlights a certain visual detail, though many other elements function in the background to make the picture an organic whole.

Before each reading selection, we offer some material to focus your students' attention on a particular writer and topic before they begin reading the essay. This "prereading" segment begins with biographical information about the author and ends with a number of questions to whet the reader's appetite for the essay that follows. This section is intended to help your students discover interesting relationships among ideas in their reading and then anticipate various ways of thinking about and analyzing the essay. The prereading questions forecast not only the content of the essay, but also the questions and writing assignments that follow.

The questions after each reading selection are designed as guides for thinking about the essay. These questions are at the heart of the relationship represented in this book among thinking, reading, and writing. They are divided into four interrelated sections that move your students smoothly from a literal understanding of what they have just read, to interpretation, and finally to analysis.

After your students have studied the different techniques at work in a reading selection, a specific essay assignment lets them practice all these skills in unison and encourages them to discover even more secrets about the intricate and exciting details of effective communication. Three "Ideas for Discussion/Writing" topics are preceded by "prewriting" questions to help your students generate new ideas. Most of these topics specify a purpose and an audience so that your students can focus their writing as precisely as possible. The word *essay* (which comes from the Old French *essai,* meaning a "try" or an "attempt") is an appropriate label for these writing assignments, because they all ask your students to wrestle with an idea or problem and then *attempt* to give shape to their conclusions in some effective manner. Such "exercises" can be equated with the development of athletic ability: The essay itself demonstrates that your students can put together all the various skills they have learned; it proves they can actually play the "sport" of writing.

WHAT REMAINS THE SAME?

▶ The Prose Reader *is still organized according to the belief that our mental abilities are logically sequential.*

In other words, students cannot read or write analytically before they are able to perform well on the literal and interpretive levels. Accordingly, the book progresses from selections that require predominantly literal skills (*Description, Narration,* and *Example*) through readings involving more interpretation (*Process Analysis, Division/Classification, Comparison/Contrast,* and *Definition*) to essays that demand a high degree of analytical thought (*Cause/ Effect* and *Argument/Persuasion*). Depending on your curriculum and the caliber of your students, these rhetorical modes can, of course, be studied in any order.

▶ The Prose Reader *provides two Tables of Contents.*

First, the book contains a Rhetorical Table of Contents, which includes a one- or two-sentence synopsis of the selection so you can peruse the list quickly and decide which essays to assign. An alternate Thematic Table of Contents lists selections by academic discipline.

▶ *The chapter introductions are filled with several types of useful information about each rhetorical mode.*

Each of the nine rhetorical divisions in the text is introduced by an explanation of how to think, read, and write in that particular mode. Although each chapter focuses on one rhetorical strategy, students are continually encouraged to examine ways in which other modes help support each essay's main intentions.

▶ *Two separate student writing samples are featured in each chapter introduction.*

The chapter introductions contain a sample student paragraph and a complete student essay that illustrate each rhetorical pattern. After each essay, the student writer has provided a thorough analysis, explaining the most enjoyable, exasperating, or noteworthy aspects of writing that particular essay. We have found that this combination of student essays and commentaries makes the professional selections easier for students to read and more accessible as models of thinking and writing.

▶ *This edition includes user-friendly checklists at the end of each chapter introduction.*

These checklists summarize the information in the chapter introduction and serve as references for the students in their own writing tasks. Students should be directed to these lists as early in the course as possible.

▶ *We precede each reading selection with thorough biographical information on the author and provocative prereading questions on the subject of the essay.*

Because our own experience suggests that students often produce their best writing when they are personally involved in the topics of the essays they read and in the human drama surrounding the creation of those essays, the biographies explain the real experiences from which each essay emerged, and the prereading questions ("Preparing to Read") help students focus on the purpose, audience, and subject of the essay. The prereading material also foreshadows the questions and writing assignments that follow each selection. Personalizing this preliminary material encourages students to identify with both the author of an essay and its subject matter, thereby engaging the students' attention and energizing their responses to the selections they read.

▶ *The essays in* The Prose Reader *continue to represent a wide range of topics.*

As in the past, the essays in this edition were selected on the basis of five important criteria: (1) high interest level, (2) currency in the field, (3) moderate length, (4) readability, and (5) broad subject variety. Together, they portray the universality of human experience as expressed through the viewpoints of men and women, many different ethnic and racial groups, and a variety of ages and social classes. The essay topics in this volume include such provocative subjects as discrimination, ethnic identity, job opportunities, aging, war, the media, women's roles, prison life, time management, euthanasia, romantic relationships, family values, immigration, physical handicaps, reading, and the writing process itself.

▶   *The Argument and Persuasion section (Chapter 9) includes three essays on a variety of topics and two sets of opposing-viewpoint essays.*

The essays in Chapter 9 are particularly useful for helping your students refine their critical thinking skills in preparation for longer, more sustained papers on a single topic. The first three essays in this chapter encourage students to grapple with provocative issues that make a crucial difference in how we all live. Then the two sets of opposing viewpoint essays help the students see coherent arguments at work from two different perspectives on a single issue. The argumentative essays cover such timely topics as gun control, affirmative action, and immigration; the opposing viewpoint essays are on the relationship between computers and books and on freedom of the press.

▶   *"Documented Essays: Reading and Writing from Sources" (Chapter 10) features research papers throughout the college curriculum.*

These essays demonstrate the two most common documentation styles—Modern Language Association (MLA) and American Psychological Association (APA). By including documented essays, we intend to clarify some of the mysteries connected with research and documentation and to provide interesting material for creating longer and more elaborate writing assignments. These essays cover the history of war and the relationship between personal appearance and delinquency. We offer a full range of apparatus for these selections, and we provide at the end of each selection a list of Further Reading on each subject and suggested topics for longer, more sophisticated essays and research papers.

▶ *This edition offers four progressively more sophisticated types of questions at the end of each selection.*

These questions are designed to help students move sequentially from various literal-level responses to interpretation and analysis; they also help reveal both the form and content of the essays so your students can cultivate a similar balance in their own writing.

1. *Understanding Details—questions that test the students' literal and interpretive understanding of what they have read;*
2. *Analyzing Meaning—questions that require students to analyze various aspects of the essay;*
3. *Discovering Rhetorical Strategies—questions that investigate the author's rhetorical strategies in constructing the essay;*
4. *Making Connections—questions that ask students to find thematic and rhetorical connections among essays they have read.*

▶ *The writing assignments ("Ideas for Discussion/ Writing") are preceded by Preparing to Write questions.*

These questions are designed to encourage students to express their feelings, thoughts, observations, and opinions on various topics. Questions about their own ideas and experiences help students produce writing that corresponds as closely as possible to the way they think.

▶ *The writing assignments seek to involve students in realistic situations.*

They often provide a specific purpose and audience for the essay topic. In this manner, student writers are drawn into rhetorical scenes that carefully focus their responses to a variety of questions or problems. These prompts are designed for use inside or outside the classroom.

▶ *The book concludes with a glossary of composition terms (along with examples and page references from the text) and an index of authors and titles.*

The glossary provides not only definitions of composition terms but also examples of these terms from this book and their page numbers. The index lists both the author and title of each essay in the book. Both the glossary and the index serve as excellent reference tools for your students as they progress through the material in the text.

WHAT IS NEW?

We have made several changes in the sixth edition of *The Prose Reader* that represent the responses of instructors from many different types of colleges and universities throughout the United States:

▶ *The sixth edition of* The Prose Reader *contains fifteen new essays.*

We have updated some of the selections, added new authors, and introduced many new topics, such as nature, self-esteem, language, gang violence, e-mail, memory, romantic love, guidelines for arguing, gun control, books and computers, writing, and technology.

▶ *This edition makes an even stronger commitment to cultural and gender diversity.*

Although multicultural and women's issues have always been well represented in *The Prose Reader,* in this edition we have included even more essays by women and ethnic-minority authors, among them Susan Austin, Sandra Cisneros, Amy Tan, Brent Staples, Phyllis Schneider, Lois Smith Brady, Mary Roach, Bronwyn Jones, and Diane Russo Cody.

▶ *This edition includes a new set of writing assignments at the end of each chapter.*

These assignments are divided into two categories, offering (1) more practice in a specific rhetorical mode and (2) a focus on interesting contemporary topics regardless of rhetorical mode. In this way, you have a variety of prompts to choose from if you want your students to have further writing experience at any time.

▶ *We have completely renovated our popular "Thinking, Reading, and Writing" section (Chapter 11).*

This chapter now includes essays on one writer's passion for his craft, listening, reading fiction, writing in the professional world, the death of reading, writing as a moral act, and writing and technology. In addition to demonstrating all the rhetorical modes at work, these essays provide a strong conclusion to the theoretical framework of this text by focusing intently on the interrelationships among thinking, reading, and writing.

WHAT SUPPLEMENTS ARE AVAILABLE?

Available with *The Prose Reader* is a thorough **Annotated Instructor's Edition** designed to help make your life in the classroom a little easier. We have filled the margins of the **AIE** with many different kinds of supplementary material, including instructor comments on teaching the different rhetorical modes, provocative quotations, background information about each essay, definitions of terms that may be unfamiliar to your students, a list of related readings from this text that can profitably be taught together, innovative teaching ideas, detailed answers to the questions that follow each selection, additional essay topics, and various revising strategies.

In addition to the *Annotated Instructor's Edition,* we have created the **Instructor's Resource Manual with Quiz Book.** In it, we identify and discuss some of the most widely used theoretical approaches to the teaching of composition; we then offer innovative options for organizing your course, specific suggestions for the first day of class, a summary of the advantages and disadvantages of using different teaching strategies, and several successful techniques for responding to student writing. Next, we provide two objective quizzes for each essay to help you monitor your students' mastery of the selection's vocabulary and content. This supplement ends with three additional professional essays (two opposing-viewpoint essays and one documented essay), a series of student essays (one for each rhetorical strategy featured in the text) followed by the student writer's comments, and an annotated bibliography of books and articles about thinking, reading, and writing.

Also available with *The Prose Reader* is a companion website (**www.prenhall.com/flachmann**) that offers an extensive collection of additional resources for every essay in the text for both the student and the instructor. This website allows students to get additional reinforcement for the text material and provides an easy way for the instructors to integrate the World Wide Web into their courses. The site includes

▶ *author biographies with contextual links,*

▶ *online vocabulary comprehension quizzes for every selection, with instant scoring,*

▶ *pre-reading and post-reading assignments that foster critical thinking for every essay,*

▶ *dynamic web links that provide a valuable source of additional information about the essay topics,*

▶ *communication tools such as chat rooms and message boards to facilitate online collaboration and communication,*

▶ *built-in routing that gives students the ability to forward essay responses and graded quizzes to their instructors, and*

▶ *a faculty module that includes an Instructor's Resource Manual with additional Quizzes*

Finally, we offer an online service called **www.turnitin.com.** This online service makes it easy for instructors to find out if students are copying their assignments from the Internet and is now free to instructors using *The Prose Reader.* In addition to helping educators easily identify instances of Web-based student plagiarism, Turnitin.com also offers a digital archiving system and an online peer review service. To use this service, instructors simply set up a "drop box" at the Turnitin.com website where their students submit papers. Turnitin.com then checks each submission against millions of possible online sources. Within 24 hours, teachers receive a customized, color-coded "Originality Report," complete with live links to suspect Internet locations, for each submitted paper. To access the site for free, instructors must visit the site via the faculty resources section of the Flachmann website at www.prenhall.com/flachmann.

This entire instructional package, available to you free of charge, is intended to help your students discover what they want to say and to assist them in shaping their ideas into a coherent form, thereby encouraging their intelligent involvement in the complex and exciting world around them.

ACKNOWLEDGMENTS

We are pleased to acknowledge the kind assistance and support of a number of people who have helped us put together this sixth edition of *The Prose Reader*. For creative encouragement and editorial guidance at Prentice Hall, we thank Phil Miller, President of Humanities and Social Sciences; Leah Jewell, AVP/Editor in Chief; Corey Good, Acquisitions Editor; Jennifer Collins, Editorial Assistant; Beth Gillett Mejia, AVP/Director of Marketing; Brandy Dawson, Senior Marketing Manager; Christine Moodie, Marketing Assistant; Senior Managing Editor, Mary Rottino; and Maureen Richardson, Senior Project Manager.

For reviews of the manuscript at various stages of completion, we are grateful to Janice Jones, Kent State University, Kent, Ohio; Lyle W. Morgan II, Pittsburgh State University, Pittsburgh, Pennsylvania; Carolyn D. Coward, Shelby State Community College, Memphis, Tennessee; Teresa Purvis, Lansing Community College, Lansing, Michigan; Gena E. Christopher, Jacksonville State University, Jacksonville, Florida; Donnie Yeilding, Central Texas College, Killeen, Texas; Steve Katz, State Technical Institute, Memphis, Tennessee; Craig Howard White, University of Houston, Clear Lake, Houston, Texas; Judith Dan, Boston University, Boston, Massachusetts; Arlie R. Peck, University of Rio Grande, Rio Grande, Ohio; Barbara Smith, Iona College, New Rochelle, New York; Vermell Blanding, Hostos Community College, Bronx, New York; Nancy G. Wright, Austin Peay State University, Clarksville, Tennessee; Paula Miller, Azusa Pacific University, Azusa, California; Paul Kistel, Pierce College, Tacoma, Washington; Christopher Belcher, Community College of Allegheny County, Pittsburgh, Pennsylvania; Helen F. Maxon, Southwestern Oklahoma State University, Oklahoma City, Oklahoma; Geoffrey C. Goodale, University of Massachusetts at Boston, Boston, Massachusetts; Martha Bergeron, Vance-Granville Community College, Henderson, North Carolina; Jan LaFever, Friends University, Wichita, Kansas; Virginia Leonard, West Liberty State College, Wichita, Kansas; Melissa A. Bruner, Southwestern Oklahoma State University, West Liberty, Virginia; James Zarzana, Southwest State University, Marshall, Minnesota; Terrence Burke, Cuyahoga Community College, Cleveland, Ohio; Ellen Dugan-Barrette, Brescia College, Owensboro, Kentucky; Lewis Emond, Dean

Junior College, Franklin, Massachusetts; Jay Jernigan, Eastern Michigan University, Ypsilanti, Michigan; Nellie McCrory, Gaston College, Dallas, North Carolina; Leslie Shipp, Clark County Community College, Henderson, Nevada; William F. Sutlife, Community College of Allegheny County, Monroeville, Pennsylvania; Maureen Aitkn, University of Michigan; Mickie R. Braswell, Lenoir Community College; Judith Burnham, Tulsa Community College; Charles H. Cole, Carl Albert State College; Todd Lieber, Simpson College; Bill Marsh, National University; Felicia S. Pattison, Sterling College; Dianne Peich, Delaware County Community College; K. Siobhan Wright, Carroll Community College; and Melody Ziff, Northern Virginia Community College Annandale.

Several writing instructors across the United States have been kind enough to help shape *The Prose Reader* over the course of its development by responding to specific questions about their teaching experiences with the book: Charles Bordogna, Bergen Community College, Paramus, New Jersey; Mary G. Marshall and Eileen M. Ward, College of DuPage, Glen Ellyn, Illinois; Michael J. Huntington and Judith C. Kohl, Dutchess Community College, Poughkeepsie, New York; Ted Johnston, El Paso County Community College, El Paso, Texas; Koala C. Hartnett, Rick James Mazza, and William H. Sherman, Fairmont State College, Fairmont, West Virginia; Miriam Dick and Betty Krasne, Mercy College, Dobbs Ferry, New York; Elvis Clark, Mineral Area College, Flat River, Missouri; Dayna Spencer, Pittsburg State University, Pittsburg, Kansas; James A. Zarzana, Southwest State University, Marshall, Minnesota; Susan Reinhart Schneling and Trudy Vanderback, Vincennes University, Vincennes, Indiana; Carmen Wong, Virginia Commonwealth University, Richmond, Virginia; John W. Hattman and Virginia E. Leonard, West Liberty State College, West Liberty, West Virginia; Jonathan Alexander, Widener University, Chester, Pennsylvania; Jo Ann Pevoto, College of the Mainland, Texas; Anita Pandey, University of Illinois at Urbana-Champaign, Illinois; Leaf Seligman, University of New Hampshire, Durham, New Hampshire; Arminta Baldwin, West Virginia Wesleyan College, Buckhannon, West Virginia; Joaquim Mendes, New York Institute of Technology, Old Westbury, New York; and Sandra R. Woods, Fairmont State College, Fairmont, West Virginia.

For student essays and writing samples, we thank Rosa Marie Augustine, Donel Crow, Dawn Dobie, Gloria Dumler, Jeff Hicks, Julie Anne Judd, Judi Koch, Dawn McKee, Paul Newberry, Joanne Silva-Newberry, JoAnn Slate, Peggy Stuckey, and Jan Titus.

We also want to thank four very special colleagues for serving as consultants and research assistants throughout the creation of this edition: Monique Idoux, Matt Woodman, Brad Ruff, and Elizabeth Baldridge. And for coordinating our department responsibilities in such a way that *The Prose Reader, sixth edition,* could become a reality, we are grateful to our chair, Victor Lasseter.

In preparing our *Annotated Instructor's Edition,* we owe special gratitude to Cheryl Smith, who revised and recast instructional material for this edition, and to the following writing instructors who have contributed their favorite techniques for teaching various rhetorical strategies: Mary P. Boyles, Pembroke State University; Terrence W. Burke, Cuyahoga Community College; Mary Lou Conlin, Cuyahoga Community College; Ellen Dugan-Barrette, Brescia College; Janet Eber, County College of Morris; Louis Emond, Dean Junior College; Peter Harris, West Virginia Institute of Technology, Montgomery; Jay Jernigan, Eastern Michigan University; Judith C. Kohl, Dutchess Community College; Joanne H. McCarthy, Tacoma Community College; Anthony McCrann, Peru State College; Nellie McCrory, Gaston College; Alan Price, Pennsylvania State University—Hazelton; Patricia A. Ross, Moorpark College; Leslie Shipp, Clark County Community College; Rodney Simard (deceased), California State University, San Bernardino; Elizabeth Wahlquist, Brigham Young University; John White, California State University, Fullerton; and Ted Wise, Porterville College.

We are also grateful to Kathryn Benander, who revised the *Instructor's Resource Manual with Quiz Book.* For this edition, however, she had the company of a new baby to help her stay awake and meet the difficult deadlines.

Cheryl Smith and Kathryn Benander not only helped revise our supplements for *The Prose Reader,* but they also served as research and editorial consultants throughout the entire project. Their work and opinions were invaluable.

Our final and most important debt is to our children, Christopher and Laura, who have always inspired us to be good teachers.

THE PROSE READER

INTRODUCTION

Thinking, Reading, and Writing

Have you ever had trouble expressing your thoughts? If so, you're not alone. Many people have this difficulty—especially when they are asked to write their thoughts down. The good news is that this "ailment" can be cured. We've learned over the years that the more clearly students think about the world around them, the more easily they can express their ideas through written and spoken language. As a result, this textbook intends to improve your writing by helping you think clearly, logically, and critically about important ideas and issues that exist in our world today. You will learn to reason, read, and write about your environment in increasingly complex ways, moving steadily from a simple, literal understanding of topics to interpretation and analysis.

Part of becoming a better writer involves understanding that reading and writing are companion activities that engage people in the creation of thought and meaning—either as readers interpreting a text or as writers constructing one. Clear thinking, then, is the pivotal point that joins together these two efforts. Although studying the rhetorical strategies presented in *The Prose Reader* is certainly not the only way to approach writing, it does provide a productive means of helping students improve their abilities to think, read, and write. Inspired by the well-crafted prose models in this text and guided by carefully worded questions, you can actually raise the level of your thinking skills while improving your reading and writing abilities on three progressively more difficult levels:

1. *The literal level* is the foundation of all human understanding; it entails knowing the meanings of words—individually and in relation to one another. In order for someone to comprehend the sentence "You must exercise your brain to reach your full mental potential" on the literal level, for example, that person would have to know the definitions of all the words in the sentence and understand the way those words work together to make meaning.

2. *Interpretation* requires the ability to make associations between details, draw inferences from pieces of information, and reach conclusions about the material. An interpretive understanding of the sample sentence in level 1 might be translated into the following thoughts: "Exercising the brain sounds a bit like exercising the body. I wonder if there's any correlation between the two. If the brain must be exercised, it is probably made up of muscles, much like the body is." None of these particular "thoughts" is made explicit in the sentence, but each is suggested in one way or another.

3. *Thinking, reading, and writing critically*, the most sophisticated form of rational abilities, involves a type of mental activity that is crucial for successful academic and professional work. A critical analysis of our sample sentence might proceed in the following way: "This sentence is talking to me. It actually addresses me with the word *you*. I wonder what *my* mental potential is. Will I be able to reach it? Will I know when I attain it? Will I be comfortable with it? I certainly want to reach this potential, whatever it is. Reaching it will undoubtedly help me succeed scholastically and professionally. The brain is obviously an important tool for helping me achieve my goals in life, so I want to take every opportunity I have to develop and maintain this part of my body." Students who can take an issue or idea apart in this fashion and understand its various components more thoroughly after reassembling them are rewarded intrinsically with a clearer knowledge of life's complexities and the ability to generate creative, useful ideas. They are also rewarded extrinsically with good grades

and are more likely to win responsible jobs with higher pay, because their understanding of the world around them is perceptive and they are able to apply this understanding effectively to their professional and personal lives.

In this textbook, you will learn to think critically by reading essays written by intelligent, interesting authors and by writing your own essays on a variety of topics. The next several pages offer guidelines for approaching the thinking, reading, and writing assignments in this book. These suggestions should also be useful to you in your other courses.

THINKING CRITICALLY

Recent psychological studies have shown that "thinking" and "feeling" are complementary operations. All of us have feelings that are automatic and instinctive. To feel pride after winning first place at a track meet, for example, or to feel anger at a spiteful friend is not behavior we have to study and master; such emotions come naturally to human beings. Thinking, on the other hand, is much less spontaneous than feeling; research suggests that study and practice are required for sustained mental development.

Thinking critically involves grappling with the ideas, issues, and problems that surround you in your immediate environment and in the world at large. It does not necessarily entail finding fault, which you might naturally associate with the word *critical*, but rather suggests continually questioning and analyzing the world around you. Thinking critically is the highest form of mental activity that human beings engage in; it is the source of success in college and in our professional and personal lives. Fortunately, all of us can learn how to think more critically.

Critical thinking means taking apart an issue, idea, or problem; examining its various parts; and reassembling the topic with a fuller understanding of its intricacies. Implied in this explanation is the ability to see the topic from one or more new perspectives. Using your mind in this way will help you find solutions to difficult problems, design creative plans of action, and ultimately live a life consistent with your opinions on important issues that we all must confront daily.

Since critical or analytical thinking is one of the highest forms of mental activity, it requires a great deal of concentration and practice. Once you have actually felt how your mind works and processes information at this level, however, recreating the experience is somewhat like riding a bicycle: you will be able to do it naturally, easily, and skillfully whenever you want to.

Our initial goal, then, is to help you think critically when you are required to do so in school, on the job, or in any other area of your life. If this form of thinking becomes a part of your daily routine, you will quite naturally be able to call upon it whenever you need it.

Working with the rhetorical modes is an effective way to achieve this goal. With some guidance, each rhetorical pattern can provide you with a mental workout to prepare you for writing and critical thinking in the same way that physical exercises warm you up for various sports. Just as in the rest of the body, the more exercise the brain gets, the more flexible it becomes and the higher the levels of thought it can attain. Through these various guided thinking exercises, you can systematically strengthen your ability to think analytically.

As you move through the following chapters, we will ask you to isolate each rhetorical mode—much like isolating your abs, thighs, and biceps in a weight-lifting workout—so that you can concentrate on these thinking patterns one at a time. Each rhetorical pattern we study will suggest slightly different ways of seeing the world, processing information, and solving problems. Each offers important ways of thinking and making sense of our immediate environment and the larger world around us. Looking closely at rhetorical modes or specific patterns of thought helps us discover how our minds work. In the same fashion, becoming more intricately aware of our thought patterns lets us improve our basic thinking skills as well as our reading and writing abilities. Thinking critically helps us discover fresh insights into old ideas, generate new thoughts, and see connections between related issues. It is an energizing mental activity that puts us in control of our lives and our environment rather than leaving us at the mercy of our surroundings.

Each chapter introduction provides three exercises specifically designed to help you focus in isolation on a particular pattern of thought. While you are attempting to learn what each pattern feels like in your head, use your imagination to play with these exercises on as many different levels as possible.

When you practice each of the rhetorical patterns of thought, you should be aware of building on your previous thinking skills. As the book progresses, the rhetorical modes become more complex and require a higher degree of concentration and effort. Throughout the book, therefore, you should keep in mind that ultimately you want to let these skills accumulate into a full-powered, well-developed ability to process the world around you—including reading, writing, seeing, and feeling—on the most advanced analytical level you can master.

READING CRITICALLY

Reading critically begins with developing a natural curiosity about an essay and nurturing that curiosity throughout the reading process. To learn as much as you can from an essay, you should first study any preliminary material you can find, then read the essay to get a general overview of its main ideas, and finally read the selection again to achieve a deeper understanding of its content. The three phases of the reading process explained next—preparing to read, reading, and rereading—will help you develop this "natural curiosity" so you can approach any reading assignment with an active, inquiring mind.

Preparing to Read

Focusing your attention is an important first stage in both the reading and the writing processes. In fact, learning as much as you can about an essay and its "context" (the circumstances surrounding its development) before you begin reading can help you move through the essay with an energetic, active mind and then reach some degree of analysis before writing on the assigned topics. In particular, knowing where an essay was first published, studying the writer's background, and doing some preliminary thinking on the subject of a reading selection will help you understand the writer's ideas and form some valid opinions of your own.

As you approach any essay, you should concentrate on four specific areas that will begin to give you an overview of the material you are about to read. We will use an essay by Lewis Thomas to demonstrate these techniques.

1. *Title.* A close look at the title will usually provide important clues about the author's attitude toward the topic, the author's

stand on an issue, or the mood of an essay. It can also furnish you with a sense of audience and purpose.

To Err Is Human

From this title, for example, we might infer that the author will discuss errors, human nature, and the extent to which mistakes influence human behavior. The title is half of a well-known proverbial quotation (Alexander Pope's "To err is human, to forgive, divine"), so we might speculate further that the author has written an essay intended for a well-read audience interested in the relationship between errors and humanity. After reading only four words of the essay—its title—you already have a good deal of information about the subject, its audience, and the author's attitude toward both.

2. *Synopsis.* The Rhetorical Table of Contents in this text contains a synopsis of each essay, very much like the following, so that you can find out more specific details about its contents before you begin reading.

> Physician Lewis Thomas explains how we can profit from our mistakes—especially if we trust human nature. Perhaps someday, he says, we can apply this same principle to the computer and magnify the advantages of these errors.

From this synopsis, we learn that Thomas's essay will be an analysis of human errors and of the way we can benefit from those errors. The synopsis also tells us the computer has the potential to magnify the value of our errors.

3. *Biography.* Learning as much as you can about the author of an essay will generally stimulate your interest in the material and help you achieve a deeper understanding of the issues to be discussed. From the biographies in this book, you can learn, for example, whether a writer is young or old, conservative or liberal, open- or close-minded. You might also discover if the essay was written at the beginning, middle, or end of the author's career or how well versed the writer is on the topic. Such information will

invariably help you reach a fuller, more thorough understanding of a selection's ideas, audience, and logical structure.

LEWIS THOMAS   (1913–1993)

Lewis Thomas was a physician who, until his death in 1993, was president emeritus of the Sloan-Kettering Cancer Center and scholar-in-residence at the Cornell University Medical Center in New York City. A graduate of Princeton University and Harvard Medical School, he was formerly head of pathology and dean of the New York University-Bellevue Medical Center and dean of the Yale Medical School. In addition to having written over two hundred scientific papers on virology and immunology, he authored many popular scientific essays, some of which have been collected in *Lives of a Cell* (1974), *The Medusa and the Snail* (1979), *Late Night Thoughts on Listening to Mahler's Ninth Symphony* (1983), *Etcetera, Etcetera* (1990), and *The Fragile Species* (1992). The memoirs of his distinguished career have been published in *The Youngest Science: Notes of a Medicine Watcher* (1983). Thomas liked to refer to his essays as "experiments in thought": "Although I usually think I know what I'm going to be writing about, what I'm going to say, most of the time it doesn't happen that way at all. At some point, I get misled down a garden path. I get surprised by an idea that I hadn't anticipated getting, which is a little bit like being in a laboratory."

As this information indicates, Thomas is a prominent physician who has published widely on scientific topics. We know that he considers his essays "experiments in thought," which makes us expect a relaxed, spontaneous treatment of his subjects. From this biography, we can also infer that he is a leader in the medical world and that, because of the positions he has held, he is well respected in his professional life. Last, we can speculate that he has a clear sense of his audience because he is able to present difficult concepts in clear, everyday language.

4. *Preparing to read.* One other type of preliminary material will broaden your overview of the topic and enable you to approach the essay with an active, thoughtful mind. The "Preparing to Read" sections following the biographies are intended to focus your attention and stimulate your curiosity before you begin the essay. They will also get you ready to form your own opinions on the essay and its topic as you read. Keeping a journal to respond to these questions is an excellent idea, because you will then have a record of your thoughts on various topics related to the reading selection that follows.

Preparing to Read

The following essay, which originally appeared in the *New England Journal of Medicine* (January 1976), illustrates the clarity and ease with which Thomas explains complex scientific topics. As you prepare to read this essay, take a few moments to think about the role mistakes play in our lives: What are some memorable mistakes you have made? Did you learn anything important from any of these errors? Do you make more or fewer mistakes than other people you know? Do you see any advantages to making mistakes? Any disadvantages?

Discovering where, why, and how an essay was first written will provide you with a context for the material you are about to read: Why did the author write this selection? Where was it first published? Who was the author's original audience? This type of information enables you to understand the circumstances surrounding the development of the selection and to identify any topical or historical references the author makes. All the selections in this textbook were published elsewhere first—in another book, a journal, or a magazine. The author's original audience, therefore, consisted of the readers of that particular publication.

From the sample "Preparing to Read" material, we learn that Thomas's essay "To Err Is Human" was originally published in the *New England Journal of Medicine*, a prestigious periodical read principally by members of the scientific community. Written early in 1976, the article plays upon its audience's growing fascination with computers and with the limits of artificial intelligence—subjects just as timely today as they were in the mid-1970s.

The questions here prompt you to consider your own ideas, opinions, or experiences in order to help you generate thoughts on the topic of errors in our lives. These questions are, ideally, the last step in preparing yourself for the active role you should play as a reader.

Reading

People read essays in books, newspapers, magazines, and journals for a great variety of reasons. One reader may want to be stimulated intellectually, whereas another seeks relaxation; one person reads to keep up with the latest developments in his or her profession, whereas the next wants to learn why a certain event happened or how something can be done; some people read in order to be challenged by new ideas, whereas others find comfort principally in printed material that supports their own moral, social, or political opinions. The essays in this textbook fulfill all these expectations in different ways. They have been chosen, however, not only for these reasons, but for an additional, broader purpose: Reading them can help make you a better writer.

Every time you read an essay in this book, you will also be preparing to write your own essay concentrating on the same rhetorical pattern. For this reason, as you read you should pay careful attention to both the content (subject matter) and the form (language, sentence structure, organization, and development of ideas) of each essay. You will also see how effectively experienced writers use particular rhetorical modes (or patterns of thought) to organize and communicate their ideas. Each essay in this collection features one dominant pattern that is generally supported by several others. In fact, the more aware you are of each author's writing techniques, the more rapidly your own writing process will mature and improve.

The questions before and after each essay teach you a way of reading that can help you discover the relationship of a writer's ideas to one another as well as to your own ideas. These questions can also help clarify for you the connection between the writer's topic, his or her style or manner of expression, and your own composing process. In other words, the questions are designed to help you understand and generate ideas, then discover various choices the writers make in composing their essays, and finally realize the freedom you have to make related choices in your own writing. Such an approach to the process of reading takes some of the mystery out of reading and writing and makes them manageable tasks at which anyone can become proficient.

Three general guidelines, each of which is explained below in detail, will help you develop your own system for reading and responding to what you have read:

1. Read the essay to get an overall sense of it.
2. Summarize the essay.
3. Read the questions and assignments that follow the essay.

Guideline 1. First, read the essay to get an overall sense of it in relation to its title, purpose, audience, author, and publication information. Write (in the margins, on a separate piece of paper, or in a journal) your initial reactions, comments, and personal associations.

To illustrate, on the following pages is the Thomas essay with a student's comments in the margins, showing how the student reacted to the essay upon reading it for the first time.

LEWIS THOMAS   (1913–1993)

To Err Is Human

Boy is this true (margin note)

Everyone must have had at least one personal experience with a computer error by this time. Bank balances are suddenly reported to have jumped from $379 into the millions, appeals for charitable contributions are mailed over and over to people with crazy sounding names at your address, <u>department stores send the wrong bills</u>, utility companies write that they're turning everything off, that sort of thing. If you manage to get in touch with someone and complain, you then get instantaneously typed, guilty letters from the same computer, saying, "Our computer was in error, and an adjustment is being made in your account." 1

Last spring this happened to me. (margin note)

exactly (margin note)

These are supposed to be the sheerest, blindest accidents. Mistakes are not believed to be part of the normal behavior of a good machine. If things go wrong, it must be a personal, human error, the result of fingering, tampering, a button getting stuck, someone hitting the wrong key. The computer, at its normal best, is infallible. 2

How can this be? (margin note)

I wonder whether this can be true. After all, the whole point of computers is that they represent an extension of the human brain, vastly improved upon but nonetheless human, <u>superhuman</u> maybe. A good computer can think clearly and quickly enough to beat you at chess, and some of them have even been programmed to write obscure verse. They can do anything we can do, and more besides. 3

In what way? (margin note)

Can this be proven? (margin note)

It is not yet known whether a computer has its own consciousness, and it would be 4

In what way?

hard to find out about this. When you walk into one of those great halls now built for the huge machines, and stand listening, it is easy to imagine that the faint, distant noises are the sound of thinking, and the turning of the spools gives them the look of wild creatures rolling their eyes in the effort to concentrate, choking with information. <u>But real thinking, and dreaming, are other matters</u>.

I expected this essay to be so much more stuffy than it is. I can even understand it.

On the other hand, the evidences of something like an unconscious, equivalent to ours, are all around, in every mail. As extensions of the human brain, they have been constructed with the same property of error, spontaneous, uncontrolled, and rich in possibilities.

5

good, clear comparison for the general reader

so true

great image

<u>Mistakes are at the very base of human thought</u>, embedded there, feeding the structure like <u>root nodules</u>. If we were not provided with the knack of being wrong, we could never get anything useful done.

6

I don't understand this

I agree! This is how we learn

We think our way along by choosing between right and wrong alternatives, and the wrong choices have to be made as frequently as the right ones. We get along in life this way. We are built to make mistakes, coded for error.

We learn, as we say, <u>by "trial and error."</u> Why do we always say that? Why not "trial and rightness" or "trial and triumph"? The old phrase puts it that way because that is, in real life, the way it is done.

7 *?*

Another effective comparison for the general reader

A good laboratory, like a good bank or a corporation or government, has to run like a computer. Almost everything is done flawlessly, by the book, and all the numbers add up to the predicted sums. The days go by. And then, if it is a <u>lucky</u> day, and a

8

<u>lucky</u> laboratory, somebody makes a mistake: the wrong buffer, something in one of the blanks, a decimal misplaced in reading counts, the warm room off by a degree and a half, a mouse out of his box, or just a misreading of the day's protocol. Whatever, when the results come in, something is obviously screwed up, and <u>then the action can begin</u>.

Isn't this a contradiction?

What?

The misreading is not the important error; <u>it opens the way</u>. The next step is the crucial one. If the investigator can bring himself to say, "But even so, look at that!" then the new finding, whatever it is, is ready for snatching. What is needed, for progress to be made, is <u>the move based on error</u>.

aha!

9

Whenever new kinds of thinking are about to be accomplished, or new varieties of music, there has to be an argument beforehand. With two sides debating in the same mind, haranguing, there is an amiable understanding that one is right and the other wrong. Sooner or later the thing is settled, but there can be no action at all if there are not the two sides, and the argument. <u>The hope is in the faculty of wrongness</u>, the tendency toward error. The capacity to leap across mountains of information to land lightly on the wrong side represents the highest of human endowments.

10

interesting idea

I believe Thomas here because of his background

It may be that this is a uniquely human gift, perhaps even stipulated in our genetic instructions. Other creatures do not seem to have DNA sequences for making mistakes as a routine part of daily living, certainly not for programmed error as a guide for action.

11

Could this be related to the human ability to think critically?

We are at our human finest, <u>dancing</u> <u>with our minds</u>, when there are more choices than two. Sometimes there are ten, even twenty different ways to go, all but one bound to be wrong, and the richness of selection in such situations can lift us onto totally new ground. This process is called exploration and is based on human fallibility. If we had only a single center in our brains, capable of responding only when a correct decision was to be made, instead of the jumble of different, credulous, easily conned clusters of neurones that provide for being flung off into blind alleys, up trees, down dead ends, out into blue sky, along wrong turnings, around bends, we could only stay the way we are today, stuck fast.

<u>The lower animals do not have this</u> <u>splendid freedom.</u> They are limited, most of them, to absolute infallibility. Cats, for all their good side, never make mistakes. <u>I</u> <u>have never seen a maladroit, clumsy, or</u> <u>blundering cat.</u> Dogs are sometimes fallible, occasionally able to make charming minor mistakes, but they get this way by trying to mimic their masters. <u>Fish are flawless in</u> <u>everything they do.</u> Individual cells in a tissue are mindless machines, perfect in their performance, as absolutely inhuman as bees.

We should have this in mind as we become dependent on more complex computers for the arrangement of our affairs. Give the computers their heads, I say; let them go their way. If we can learn to do this, turning our heads to one side and wincing while the work proceeds, the possibilities for the future of mankind, and computerkind, are limitless. <u>Your average</u> <u>good computer can make calculations in an</u>

Margin annotations:

12
nice mental image

Yes, but this is so frustrating

This is a great sentence— it has a lot of feeling

I love the phrase "splendid freedom"

13
See ¶ 11

look up "maladroit"

I never thought of mistakes this way

I like this idea

14

so true

Thomas makes our technology sound really exciting

<u>instant which would take a lifetime of slide rules for any of us.</u> Think of what we could gain from the near infinity of precise, <u>machine-made miscomputation</u> which is now so easily within our grasp. We would begin the solving of some of our hardest problems. How, for instance, should we go about organizing ourselves for social living on a planetary scale, now that we have become, as a plain fact of life, a single community? We can assume, as a working hypothesis, that all the right ways of doing this are unworkable. What we need, then, for moving ahead, is a set of wrong alternatives much longer and more interesting than the short list of mistaken courses that any of us can think up right now. We need, in fact, an infinite list, and when it is printed out we need the computer to turn on itself and select, at random, the next way to go. If it is a big enough mistake, we could find ourselves on a new level, stunned, out in the clear, ready to move again.

yes

We need to program computers to make deliberate mistakes so they can help our natural human tendency to learn thru error

Not a contradiction after all.

So mistakes have value!

Guideline 2. *After you have read the essay for the first time, summarize its main ideas in some fashion.* The form of this task might be anything from a drawing of the main ideas as they relate to one another to a succinct written summary. You could draw a graph or map of the topics in the essay (in much the same way that a person would draw a map of an area for someone unfamiliar with a particular route); outline the ideas to get an overview of the piece; or summarize the ideas to check your understanding of the main points of the selection. Any of these tasks can be completed from your original notes and underlining. Each will give you a slightly more thorough understanding of what you have read.

Guideline 3. *Next, read the questions and assignments following the essay to help focus your thinking for the second reading.* Don't answer the questions at this time; just read them to make sure you are picking up the main ideas from the selection and thinking about relevant connections among those ideas.

Rereading

Following your initial reading, read the essay again, concentrating this time on how the author achieved his or her purpose. The temptation to skip this stage of the reading process is often powerful, but this second reading is crucial to your development as a critical reader in all of your courses. This second reading could be compared to seeing a good movie for the second time: The first viewing would provide you with a general understanding of the plot, the characters, the setting, and the overall artistic accomplishment of the director; during the second viewing, however, you would undoubtedly notice many more details and see their specific contributions to the artistic whole. Similarly, the second reading of an essay allows a much deeper understanding of the work under consideration and prepares you to analyze the writer's ideas.

You should also be prepared to do some detective work at this point and look closely at the assumptions the essay is based on: For example, how does the writer move from idea to idea in the essay? What hidden assertions lie behind these ideas? Do you agree or disagree with these assertions? Your assessment of these unspoken assumptions will often play a major role in your critical response to an essay. In the case of Thomas's essay, do you accept the unspoken connection he makes between the workings of the human brain and the computer? What parts of the essay hinge upon your acceptance of this connection? What other assumptions are fundamental to Thomas's reasoning? If you accept his thinking along the way, you are more likely to agree with the general flow of Thomas's essay. If you discover a flaw in his premises or assumptions, your acceptance of his argument will start to break down.

Next, answer the questions that follow the essay. The "Understanding Details" questions will help you understand and remember what you have read on both the literal and the interpretive levels. Some of the questions ask you to restate various important points the author makes (literal); others help you see relationships between the different ideas presented (interpretive).

Understanding Details

Literal   1. According to Thomas, in what ways are computers and humans similar? In what ways are they different?

Lit/Interp   2. In what ways do we learn by "trial and error"? Why is this a useful way to learn?

Interpretive   3. What does Thomas mean by the statement, "If we were not provided with the knack of being wrong, we could never get anything useful done" (paragraph 6)?

Interpretive   4. According to Thomas, in what important way do humans and "lower" animals differ? What does this comparison have to do with Thomas's main line of reasoning?

The "Analyzing Meaning" questions require you to analyze and evaluate some of the writer's ideas in order to form valid opinions of your own. These questions demand a higher level of thought than the previous set and help you prepare more specifically for the discussion/writing assignments that follow the questions.

Analyzing Meaning

Analytical   1. What is Thomas's main point in this essay? How do the references to computers help him make this point?

Analytical   2. In paragraph 10, Thomas explains that an argument must precede the beginning of something new and different. Do you think this is an accurate observation? Explain your answer.

Analytical   3. Why does Thomas perceive human error as such a positive quality? What does "exploration" have to do with this quality (paragraph 12)?

Analytical   4. What could we gain from "the near infinity of precise, machine-made miscomputation" (paragraph 14)? In what ways would our civilization advance?

The "Discovering Rhetorical Strategies" questions ask you to look closely at what strategies the writer uses to develop his or her thesis and how those strategies work. The questions address important features of the writer's composing process, such as word choice, use of detail, transitions, statement of purpose, organization of ideas, sentence structure, and paragraph development. The intent of these questions is to raise various elements of the composing process to the conscious level so you can use them in creating your own essays. If you are able to understand and describe what choices a writer makes to create certain effects in his or her prose, you are more likely to be able to discover the range of choices available to you as you write, and you will also become more aware of your ability to control your readers' thoughts and feelings.

Discovering Rhetorical Strategies

1.   Thomas begins his essay with a list of experiences most of us have had at one time or another. Do you find this an effective beginning? Why or why not?
2.   Which main points in his essay does Thomas develop in most detail? Why do you think he chooses to develop these points so thoroughly?
3.   Explain the simile Thomas uses in paragraph 6: "Mistakes are at the very base of human thought, embedded there, feeding the structure like root nodules." Is this comparison between "mistakes" and "root nodules" useful in this context? Why or why not? Find another simile or metaphor in this essay, and explain how it works.
4.   What principal rhetorical strategies does Thomas use to make his point? Give examples of each from the essay.

A final set of questions, "Making Connections," asks you to consider the essay you have just read in reference to other essays in the book. Your instructor will assign these questions according to the essays you have read. The questions may have you compare the writers' treatment of an idea, the authors' style of writing, the difference in their opinions, or the similarities between their views of the world. Such questions will help you see connections in your own life—not only in your reading and your immediate environment, but also in the larger world around you. These questions, in particular, encourage you to move from specific references in the selections to a broader range of issues and circumstances that affect your daily life.

Making Connections

1.   Kimberly Wozencraft ("Notes from the Country Club") and Judith Wallerstein and Sandra Blakeslee ("Second Chances for Children of Divorce") refer both directly and indirectly to learning from mistakes. Would Lewis Thomas agree with their approach to this topic? In what ways do these authors think alike about the benefits of making errors? In what ways do they differ on the topic? Explain your answer.

2.   Lewis Thomas, Geoffrey Meredith ("The Demise of Writing"), and Keven Kelly ("Will We Still Turn Pages") all discuss technology from different perspectives. In what ways are their ideas related? How are they different?

3.   According to Thomas, humans are complex organisms with a great deal of untapped potential. Maya Angelou ("New Directions") and Barbara Ehrenreich ("The Ecstasy of War") also comment on the uniqueness of human beings. In what ways do these three writers agree or disagree with each other on the intelligence and resourcefulness of human beings? To what extent would each author argue that humans use their mental capacities wisely and completely? Explain your answer.

Because checklists can provide a helpful method of reviewing important information, we offer here a series of questions that represent the three stages of reading just discussed. All these guidelines can be generalized into a checklist for reading any academic assignment in any discipline.

READING INVENTORY

Preparing to Read

Title

✓ What can I infer from the title of the essay about the author's attitude toward the subject or the general tone of the essay?

✓ Who do I think is the author's audience? What is the principal purpose of the essay?

Synopsis

✓ What is the general subject of the essay?

✓ What is the author's approach to the subject?

Biography

✓ What do I know about the author's age, political stance, general beliefs?

✓ How qualified is the author to write on this subject?

✓ When did the author write the essay? Under what conditions? In what context?

✓ Where was the essay first published?

Content

✓ What would I like to learn about this topic?

✓ What are some of my opinions on this subject?

Reading

✓ What are my initial reactions, comments, and personal associations in reference to the ideas in this essay?

✓ What are the essay's main ideas?

✓ Did I read the questions and assignments following the essay?

Rereading

✓ How does the author achieve his or her purpose in this essay?

✓ What assumptions underlie the author's reasoning?

✓ Do I have a clear literal understanding of this essay? What words do I need to look up in a dictionary?

✓ Do I have a solid interpretive understanding of this essay? Do I understand the relationship among ideas? What conclusions can I draw from this essay?

✓ Do I have an accurate analytical understanding of this essay? Which ideas can I take apart, examine, and put back together again? What is my evaluation of this material?

✓ Do I understand the rhetorical strategies the writer uses and the way they work? Can I explain the effects of these strategies?

WRITING CRITICALLY

The last stage of responding to the reading selections in this text offers you various "Ideas for Discussion/Writing" that will allow you to demonstrate the different skills you have learned in each chapter. You will be most successful if you envision each writing experience as an organic process that follows a natural cycle of prewriting, writing, and rewriting.

Preparing to Write

The prewriting phase involves exploring a subject, generating ideas, selecting and narrowing a topic, analyzing an audience, and developing a purpose. Preceding the writing assignments are "Preparing to Write" questions you should respond to before trying to structure your thoughts into a coherent essay. These questions will assist you in generating new thoughts on the topics and may even stimulate new approaches to old ideas. Keeping a journal to respond to these questions is an excellent technique, because you will then have a record of your opinions on various topics related to the writing assignments that follow. No matter what format you use to answer these questions, the activity of prewriting generally continues in various forms throughout the writing process.

Preparing to Write

Write freely about an important mistake you have made: How did the mistake make you feel? What (if anything) did you learn from this mistake? What did you fail to learn that you should have learned? Did this mistake have any positive impact on your life? What were its negative consequences? How crucial are mistakes in our lives?

Responses to these questions can be prompted by a number of different "invention" techniques and carried out by you individually, with another student, in small groups, or as a class project. Invention strategies can help you generate responses to these questions and discover related ideas through the various stages of writing your papers. Because you will undoubtedly vary your approach to different assignments, you should be familiar with the following choices available to you:

Brainstorming.   The basis of brainstorming is free association. Ideally, you should get a group of students together and bounce ideas, words, and thoughts off of one another until they begin to cluster around related topics. If you don't have a group of students handy, brainstorm by yourself or with a friend. In a group of students or with a friend, the exchange of thoughts usually starts orally but should transfer to paper when your ideas begin to fall into related categories. When you brainstorm by yourself, however, you should write down everything that comes to mind. The act of recording your ideas in this case becomes a catalyst for other thoughts; you are essentially setting up a dialogue with yourself on paper. Then, keep writing down words and phrases that occur to you until they begin to fall into logical subdivisions or until your new ideas come to an end.

Freewriting.   Freewriting means writing to discover what you want to say. Set a time limit of about ten minutes, and just write by free association. Write about what you are seeing, feeling, touching, thinking; write about having nothing to say; recopy the sentence you just wrote—anything. Just keep writing on paper or on a computer. After you have generated some material, locate an idea that is central to your writing assignment, put it at the top of another page, and start freewriting again, letting your thoughts take shape around this central idea. This second type of preparation is called *focused freewriting* and is especially valuable when you already have a specific topic.

Journal Entries. Journal entries are much like freewriting, except you have some sense of an audience—probably either your instructor or yourself. In a journal, anything goes. You can respond to the "Preparing to Write" questions, jot down thoughts, paste up articles that spark your interest, write sections of dialogue, draft letters (the kind you never send), record dreams, or make lists. The possibilities are unlimited. An excellent way of practicing writing, the process of keeping a journal is also a wonderful means of dealing with new ideas—a way of fixing them in your mind and making them yours.

Direct Questions. This technique involves asking a series of questions useful in any writing situation to generate ideas, arrange thoughts, or revise prose. One example of this strategy is to use the inquiries journalists rely on to check the coverage in their articles:

Who:	*Who played the game?*
	Who won the game?
What:	*What kind of game was it?*
	What happened in the game?
Why:	*Why was the game played?*
Where:	*Where was the game played?*
When:	*When was the game played?*
How:	*How was the game played?*

If you ask yourself questions of this type on a specific topic, you will begin to produce thoughts and details that will undoubtedly be useful to you in the writing assignments that follow.

Clustering. Clustering is a method of drawing or mapping your ideas as fast as they come into your mind. Put a word, phrase, or sentence in a circle in the center of a blank page. Then put every new idea that comes to you in a circle and show its relationship to a previous thought by drawing a line to the circle containing the original thought. You will probably reach a natural stopping point for this exercise in two to three minutes.

Although you can generate ideas in a number of different ways, the main principle behind the "Preparing to Write" questions in this text is to encourage you to do what is called *expressive writing* before you tackle any writing assignment. This is writing based on your feelings, thoughts, experiences, observations, and opinions. The process of answering questions about your own ideas and experiences makes you "think on paper," enabling you to surround yourself with your own thoughts and opinions. From this reservoir, you can then choose the ideas you want to develop into an essay and begin writing about them one at a time.

As you use various prewriting techniques to generate responses to the "Preparing to Write" questions, you should know that these responses can (and probably will) appear in many different forms. You can express yourself in lists, outlines, random notes, sentences and paragraphs, charts, graphs, or pictures—whatever keeps the thoughts flowing smoothly and productively. One of our students used a combination of brainstorming and clustering to generate the following thoughts in response to the prewriting exercise following the Thomas essay:

Brainstorming

Mistakes:

    happen when I'm in a hurry
    make me feel stupid
    love
    relationships
    trip back East
    pride
    going in circles
    Bob
    learned a lot about people
    people aren't what they seem
    getting back on track
    parents
    corrections
    learning from mistakes
    I am a better person

my values are clear
mistakes help us change
painful
helpful
valuable

Clustering

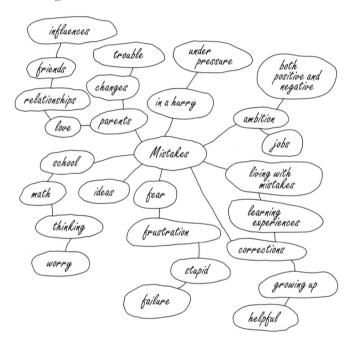

From the free-flowing thoughts you generate, you need to decide what to write about and how to limit your subject to a manageable length. Our student writer chose topic 2 from the "Choosing a Topic" list after the essay (see page 28). Her initial responses to the prewriting questions helped her decide to write on "A Time I Got Lost." She then generated more focused ideas and opinions in the form of a journal entry. It is printed here just as she wrote it, errors and all.

Journal Entry

The craziest mistake I think I ever made was on a trip I took
recently—I was heading to the east coast from California and reached

Durham, North Carolina. I was so excited because I was going to get to see the Atlantic Ocean for the first time in my life and Durham was one of my last tlandmarks before I reached the sea. In Durham I was going to have to change from a northeast direction to due east.

When I got there the highway was under construction. I took the detour, but got all skrewed up till I realized that I had gone the wrong direction. By this time I was lost somewhere in downtown Durham and didn't know which way was east. I stoped and asked a guy at a gas station and he explained how to get back on the east-bound highway. The way was through the middle of town. By the time I got to where I was supposed to turn right I could only turn left. So I started left and then realized I couldn't turn back the other way! I made a couple of other stops after that, and one jerk told me I "just couldn't get there from here." Eventually I found a truck driver heading toward the same eastbound highway, and he told me to follow him. An hour and forty minutes after reaching Durham's city limits I finally managed to leave going east. I felt as if I had spent an entire month there!

The thing I learned from this was just how egocentric I am. I would not have made this error if I had not been so damn cocky about my sense of direction. My mistake was made worse because I got flustered and didn't listen to the directions clearly. I find that the reason I most often make a mistake is because I don't listen carefully to instructions. This has been a problem all my life.

After I got over feeling really dum I decided this kind of thing was not going to happen again. It was too much a waste of time and gas, so I was going to be more careful of road signs and directions.

This all turned out to be a positive experience though. I learned that there are lots of friendly, helpful people. It was kind of reassuring to know that other folks would help you if you just asked.

I feel this and other mistakes are crucial not only to my life but to my personal growth in general. It is the making of mistakes that helps people learn where they are misdirecting their energies. I think mistakes can help all of us learn to be more careful about some part of our lives. This is why mistakes are crucial. Otherwise, we would continue in the same old rut and never improve.

This entry served as the foundation upon which the student built her essay. Her next step was to consider *audience* and *purpose* (which are usually specified in the writing assignments in this text). The first of these features identifies the person or group of people you will address in your essay. The second is a declaration of your principal reason for writing the essay, which usually takes the form of a thesis statement (the statement of purpose or the controlling idea of an essay). Together these pieces of information consciously or subconsciously help you make most of the decisions you are faced with as you write: what words to choose, what sentence structures to use, what order to present ideas in, which topics to develop, and which to summarize. Without a doubt, the more you know about your audience (age, educational background, likes, dislikes, biases, political persuasion, and social status) and your purpose (to inform, persuade, and/or entertain), the easier the writing task will be. In the rough draft and final draft of the essay in the section that follows, the student knew she was writing to a senior English class at her old high school in order to convince them that mistakes can be positive factors in their lives. This clear sense of audience and purpose helped her realize she should use fairly advanced vocabulary, call upon a variety of sentence structures, and organize her ideas chronologically to make her point most effectively to her intended audience.

At this stage of the writing process, some people benefit from assembling their ideas in the form of an outline. Others use an outline as a check on their logic and organization after the first draft has been written. Whether your outlines are informal (a simple list) or more structured, they can help you visualize the logical relationship of your ideas to each other. We recommend using a rough outline throughout the prewriting and writing stages to ensure that your work will be carefully and tightly organized. Your outline, however, should be adjusted to your draft as it develops.

Writing

The writing stage asks you to draft an essay based upon the prewriting material you have assembled. Because you have already made the important preliminary decisions regarding your topic, your audience, and your purpose, the task of actually writing the essay should follow naturally. (Notice we did not say this task should necessarily be easy—just natural.) At this stage, you should look upon your essay as a way of solving a problem or answering a question: The problem/question is posed in your writing assignment, and the solution/answer is your essay. The three "Choosing a Topic" assignments that follow the prewriting questions in the text require you to consider issues related to the essay you just read. Although they typically ask you to focus on one rhetorical pattern, they draw on many rhetorical strategies (as do all writing assignments in the text) and require you to support your statements with concrete examples. These assignments refer to the Lewis Thomas essay and emphasize the use of example, his dominant rhetorical strategy.

Choosing a Topic

1. You have decided to write an editorial for your local newspaper concerning the impact of computers on our lives. Cite specific experiences you have had with computers to help make your main point.
2. You have been invited back to your high school to make a speech to a senior English class about how people can learn from their mistakes. Write your speech in the form of an essay explaining what you learned from a crucial mistake you have made. Use examples to show these students that mistakes can be positive factors in their lives.
3. In an essay for your writing class, explain one specific human quality. Use Thomas's essay as a model. Cite examples to support your explanation.

The following essay is our student's first-draft response to topic 2. After writing her journal entry, the student drafted a tentative thesis statement: "I know there are positive changes that can come from making a mistake because I recently had an opportunity to learn some valuable lessons from one of my errors." This statement helped the student writer further develop and organize her ideas as she focused finally on one well-chosen example to illustrate her thesis. At this point, the thesis is simply the controlling idea around which the other topics take shape; it is often revised several times before the final draft.

First Draft: A Time I Got Lost

Parents and teachers frequently pressure us to avoid committing errors. Meanwhile, our friends laugh at us when we make mistakes. With all these different messages, it is hard for us to think of mistakes as positive events. But if any of you take the time to think about what you have learned from mistakes, I bet you will realize all the good things that have come from these events. I know there are positive changes that can come from making a mistake because I recently had an opportunity to learn some valuable lessons in this way.

While traveling back east this last summer, I made the mistake of turning west on an interstate detour in order to reach the Atlantic Ocean. The adventure took me into the heart of Durham, North Carolina, where I got totally lost. I had to get directions several times until two hours later I was going in the right direction. As I was driving out of town, I realized that although I had made a dumb mistake, I had learned a great deal. Overall, the detour was actually a positive experience.

The first thing I remember thinking after I had gotten my wits together was that I had definitely learned something from making the mistake. I had the opportunity to see a new city, filled with new people—3,000 miles from my own hometown, but very much like it. I also became aware that the beach is not always toward the west, as it is in

California. The entire experience was like getting a geography lesson firsthand.

As this pleasant feeling began to grow, I came to another realization. I was aware of how important other people can be in making a mistake into a positive experience. My first reaction was "Oh no, someone is going to know I made a mistake!" But the amazing part about this mistake was how supportive everyone was. The townspeople had been entirely willing to help someone they did not know. This mistake helped me learn that people tend to be nicer than I had imagined.

The final lesson I learned from getting lost in Durham was how to be more cautious about my actions so as not to repeat the same mistake. It was this internalization of all the information I gleaned from making the mistake that I see as the most positive part of the experience. I realized that in order to avoid such situations in the future I would have to be less egocentric in my decisions and more willing to listen to directions from other people. I needed to learn that my set way of doing things was not always the best way. If I had not made the mistake, I would not have been aware of my other options.

By making this mistake I learned that there is a more comprehensive manner of looking at the world. In the future, if we could all stop after making a mistake and ask ourselves, "What can I learn from this?" we would be less critical of ourselves and have a great many more positive experiences. If I were not able to make mistakes, I would probably not be able to expand my knowledge of my environment, my sense of others, and my understanding of myself.

Rewriting

The rewriting stage includes revising, editing, and proofreading. The first of these activities, *revising*, actually takes place during the entire writing process as you change words, recast sentences, and move whole paragraphs from one place to another. Making these linguistic and organizational choices means you will also be constantly adjusting your content to your purpose (what you want to accomplish) and your audience (the readers) in much the same way you alter your speech to communicate more effectively in response to the gestures, eye movements, or facial expressions of your listener. Revising is literally the act of "reseeing" your essay, looking at it through your readers' eyes to determine whether or not it achieves its purpose. As you revise, you should consider matters of both content and form. *In content*, do you have an interesting, thought-provoking title for your essay? Do you think your thesis statement will be clear to your audience? Does your introduction capture the readers' attention? Is your treatment of your topic consistent throughout the essay? Do you support your assertions with specific examples? Does your conclusion sum up your main points? *In form*, is your essay organized effectively? Do you use a variety of rhetorical strategies? Are your sentence structure and vocabulary varied and interesting?

If you compose on a computer, you will certainly reap the benefits as you revise. Computers remove much of the drudgery of rewriting and retyping your drafts. In writing, you may not make as many major revisions as necessary because of the length of time needed to rewrite the material. Computers allow you to move paragraphs or whole sections of your paper from one position to another by pressing a few keys. Without the manual labor of cutting and pasting, you can immediately see if the new organization will improve the logic and coherence of your paper. You may then remove repetitions or insert words and sentences that will serve as the transitions between sections.

You should also consider the value of the graphic design options available on computer software, because the way you present your papers generally affects how your instructor evaluates them. If they are clearly laid out without coffee stains or paw prints from your dog, you have a better chance of being taken seriously than if they are sloppily done. A computer can help in this regard, giving you access to boldface type, italics, boxes, bullets, and graphs of all sorts and letting you make a new copy if you do have an unexpected encounter with a coffee cup or a frisky dog.

Editing entails correcting mistakes in your writing so that your final draft conforms to the conventions of standard written English. Correct punctuation, spelling, and mechanics will help you make your points and will encourage your readers to move smoothly through your essay from topic to topic. At this stage, you should be concerned about such matters as whether your sentences are complete, whether your punctuation is correct and effective, whether you have followed conventional rules for using mechanics, and whether the words in your essay are spelled correctly.

Proofreading involves reading over your entire essay, slowly and carefully, to make certain you have not allowed any errors to slip into your draft. (Most college instructors don't look upon errors as kindly as Thomas does.) In general, good writers try to let some time elapse between writing the final draft and proofreading it (at least a few hours, perhaps a day or so). Otherwise, they find themselves proofreading their thoughts rather than their words. Some writers even profit from proofreading their papers backward—a technique that allows them to focus on individual words and phrases rather than on entire sentences.

Because many writers work well with checklists, we present here a set of guidelines that will help you review the entire writing process.

WRITING INVENTORY

Preparing to Write

- ✓ Have I explored the prewriting questions through brainstorming, freewriting, journal entries, direct questions, or clustering?
- ✓ Do I understand my topic or assignment?
- ✓ Have I narrowed my topic adequately?
- ✓ Do I have a specific audience for my essay? Do I know their likes and dislikes? Their educational level? Their knowledge of the subject?
- ✓ Do I have a clear and precise purpose for my essay?

Writing

✓ Can I express my topic as a problem or question?

✓ Is my essay a solution or an answer to that problem or question?

Rewriting

Revising the Content

✓ Does my essay have a clear, interesting title?

✓ Will my statement of purpose (or thesis) be clear to my audience?

✓ Will the introduction make my audience want to read the rest of my essay?

✓ Have I included enough details to prove my main points?

✓ Does my conclusion sum up my central points?

✓ Will I accomplish my purpose with this audience?

Revising the Form

✓ Have I organized my ideas as effectively as possible for this audience?

✓ Do I use appropriate rhetorical strategies to support my main point?

✓ Is my sentence structure varied and interesting?

✓ Is my vocabulary appropriate for my topic, my purpose, and my audience?

✓ Do I present my essay as effectively as possible, including useful graphic design techniques on the computer, if appropriate?

Editing and Proofreading

✓ Have I written complete sentences throughout my essay?

✓ Have I used punctuation correctly and effectively (check especially the use of commas, apostrophes, colons, and semicolons)?

✓ Have I followed conventional rules for mechanics (capitalization, underlining or italics, abbreviations, and numbers)?

✓ Are all the words in my essay spelled correctly? (Use a dictionary or a spellchecker when in doubt.)

Following is the student's revised draft of her essay on making mistakes in life. The final draft of this typical freshman essay (written to high school seniors, as the assignment specifies) represents the entire writing process at work. We have made notes in the margin to highlight various effective elements in her essay, and we have underlined substantial changes in words and phrases from earlier drafts.

Mistakes and Maturity

Catchy title; good change from first draft

Rapport with audience and point of view established

Parents and teachers frequently harp on us to correct our errors. Meanwhile, our friends laugh at us when we make mistakes. With all these negative messages, most of us have a hard time believing that problems can be positive experiences. But if we take the time to think about what we have learned from various blunders, we will realize all the good that has come from these events. I know making mistakes can have positive results because I recently learned several valuable lessons from one unforgettable experience.

Clear, stimulating introduction for high school seniors

Revised thesis statement

While I was traveling on the east coast last summer, I made the mistake of turning west on an interstate detour in an attempt to reach the Atlantic Ocean. This adventure took me into the center of Durham, North Carolina, where I became totally lost, bewildered, and angry at myself. I had to ask for directions several times until two hours later, when I finally found the correct highway toward the ocean. As I was driving out of town, I realized that although I had made

Good brief summary of complex experience (see notes from Preparing to Write)

Background information

Good details

a "dumb" mistake, I had actually learned a great deal. Overall, my adventure had been quite positive.

First topic (topics are in chrono- logical order)

The first insight I remember having after my wits returned was that <u>I had definitely learned more about United States geography from making this mistake.</u> I had become intimately acquainted with a town 3,000 miles from home that greatly resem- bled my own city, and I had become aware that the beach is not always toward the west, as it is in California. I had also met some pleasant strangers. <u>Looking at my confusion as a learning experience encour- aged me to have positive feelings about the mistake.</u>

Adequate number of examples

Nice close to this paragraph

As I relaxed and let this happy feeling grow, I came to another realization. <u>I be- came aware of how important other people can be in turning a mistake into a positive event.</u> Although my first reaction had been "Oh, no! Someone is going to know I'm lost," I was amazed by how supportive other people were during my panic and embarrassment. From an old man swinging on his front porch to an elementary school boy crossing the street with his bright blue backpack, I found that the townspeople of Durham were entirely willing to help someone they did not even know. <u>I realized that people in general are nicer than I had previously thought.</u>

Second topic

Clear explanation with details

Good summary statement

The final lesson I learned from making this mistake was <u>how to be more cautious about my future decisions.</u> This insight was, in fact, the most positive part of the entire experience. What I realized I must do to prevent similar errors in the future was to relax, not be so bullheaded in my decisions,

Third topic

Specific details

and be more willing to listen to directions from other people. <u>I might never have had these positive realizations if I had not made this mistake.</u>

<small>Good summary statement</small>

<small>Clear transition statement</small>   Thus, <u>by driving in circles for two hours, I developed a more comprehensive way of looking at the world.</u> If I were unable to make mistakes, I probably would not have had this chance to <u>learn about my environ-ment, improve my impressions of strangers,</u> and <u>reconsider the egocentric way in which I act in certain situations.</u> Perhaps there's a lesson here for all of us. Instead of criticiz-ing ourselves unduly, if each one of us could pause after we make an error and ask, "How can I profit from this?," <u>we would realize that mistakes can often be turned into positive events that will help us be-come more confident and mature.</u>

<small>Good summary of three topics without being repetitive</small>

<small>Concluding statement applicable to all readers</small>

<small>Nicely focused concluding remark</small>

As these various drafts of the student paper indicate, the essay assignments in this book encourage you to transfer to your own writing your understanding of how form and content work to-gether. If you use the short-answer questions after each reading selection as a guide, the writing assignments will help you learn how to give shape to your own ideas and to gain control of your readers' thoughts and feelings. In essence, they help you recognize the power you have through language over your life and your en-vironment.

CONCLUSION

As you approach the essays in this text, remember that both reading and writing function most efficiently as processes of dis-covery. Through them, you educate and expand your own mind and the minds of your readers. They can provide a powerful means of discovering new information or clarifying what you al-ready know. Reading and writing lead to understanding. And just as you can discover how to read through writing, so too can you become more aware of the details of the writing process through reading. We hope your time spent with this book is both pleasant and profitable as you refine your ability to discover and express effectively the good ideas within yourself.

1

DESCRIPTION

Exploring Through the Senses

All of us use description in our daily lives. We might, for example, try to convey the horrors of a recent history exam to our parents, help a friend visualize someone we met on vacation, or describe an automobile accident for a police report. Whatever our specific purpose, description is fundamental to the act of communication: We give and receive descriptions constantly, and our lives are continually affected by this simple yet important rhetorical technique.

DEFINING DESCRIPTION

Description may be defined as the act of capturing people, places, events, objects, and feelings in words so that a reader (or listener) can visualize and respond to them. Unlike narration, which traditionally presents events in a clear time sequence, description essentially suspends its objects in time, making them exempt from the limits of chronology. Narration tells a story, while pure description contains no action or time. Description is one of our primary forms of self-expression; it paints a verbal picture that helps the reader understand or share a sensory experience through the process of "showing" rather than "telling." *Telling* your friends, for example, that "the campgrounds were filled with friendly, happy activities" is not as engaging as *showing* them by saying, "The campgrounds were alive with the smell of spicy baked beans, the sound of high-pitched laughter, and the sight of happy families sharing the warmth of a fire." Showing your readers helps them understand your experience through as many senses as possible.

Descriptions fall somewhere between two extremes: (1) totally objective reports (with no trace of opinions or feelings), such as we might find in a dictionary or an encyclopedia, and (2) very subjective accounts, which focus almost exclusively on personal impressions. The same horse, for instance, might be described by one writer as "a large, solid-hoofed herbivorous mammal having a long mane and a tail" (objective) and by another as "a magnificent and spirited beast flaring its nostrils in search of adventure" (subjective). Most descriptive writing, however, falls somewhere between these two extremes: "a large, four-legged beast in search of adventure."

Objective description is principally characterized by its impartial, precise, and emotionless tone. Found most prominently in technical and scientific writing, such accounts might include a description of equipment to be used in a chemistry experiment, the results of a market survey for a particular consumer product, or a medical appraisal of a heart patient's physical symptoms. In situations like these, accurate, unbiased, and easily understandable accounts are of the utmost importance.

Subjective description, in contrast, is intentionally created to produce a particular response in the reader or listener. Focusing on feelings rather than on raw data, it tries to activate as many senses as possible, thereby leading the audience to a specific conclusion or state of mind. Examples of subjective descriptions are a parent's disapproving comments about one of your friends, a professor's glowing analysis of your most recent "A" paper, or a basketball coach's critique of the team's losing effort in last night's big game.

In most situations, the degree of subjectivity or objectivity in a descriptive passage depends to a large extent upon the writer's purpose and intended audience. In the case of the heart patient mentioned above, the person's physician might present the case in a formal, scientific way to a group of medical colleagues; in a personal, sympathetic way to the invalid's spouse; and in financial terms to a number of potential contributors in order to solicit funds for heart disease research.

The following paragraph describes one student's fond memories of visiting "the farm." As you read it, notice the writer's use of subjective description to communicate to her readers the multitude of contradictory feelings she connects with this rural retreat.

> *The shrill scream of the alarm shatters a dream. This is the last day of my visit to the place I call "the farm," an old ramshackle house in the country owned by one of my aunts. I want to go out once more in the peace of the early morning, walk in the crisp and chilly fields, and breathe the sweet air. My body feels jarred as my feet hit the hard-packed clay dirt. I tune out my stiff muscles and cold arms and legs and instead focus on two herons playing hopscotch on the canal bank: Every few yards I walk toward them, they fly one over the other an almost equal distance away from me. A killdeer with its piercing crystalline cry dips its body as it flies low over the water, the tip of its wing leaving a ring to reverberate outward. The damp earth has a strong, rich, musky scent. To the east, dust rises, and for the first time I hear the clanking and straining of a tractor as it harrows smooth the soil before planting. A crop duster rises close by just as it cuts off its release of spray, the acrid taste of chemical filtering down through the air. As the birds chatter and peck at the fields, I reluctantly return to my life in the city.*

THINKING CRITICALLY BY USING DESCRIPTION

Each rhetorical mode in this book gives us new insight into the process of thinking by providing different options for arranging our thoughts and our experiences. The more we know about these options, the more conscious we become of how our minds operate and the better chance we have to improve and refine our thinking skills. (For a more thorough definition of the term "rhetorical mode," see the glossary at the end of this book.)

As you examine description as a way of thinking, consider it in isolation for a moment—away from the other rhetorical modes. Think of it as a muscle you can isolate and strengthen on its own in a weight-training program before you ask it to perform together with other muscles. By isolating description, you will learn more readily what it entails and how it functions as a critical-thinking tool. In the process, you will also strengthen your knowledge of how to recognize and use description more effectively in your reading, in your writing, and in your daily life.

Just as you exercise to strengthen muscles, so too will you benefit from doing exercises to improve your skill in using descriptive techniques. As you have learned, description depends to a great extent on the keenness of your senses. So as you prepare to read and write descriptive essays, do the following tasks so that you can first learn what the process of description feels like in your own head. Really use your imagination to play with these exercises on as many different levels as possible. Also write when you are asked to do so. The combination of thinking and writing is often especially useful when you practice your thinking skills.

1. Make a list of five descriptive words you would use to trigger each of the following senses: taste, sight, hearing, touch, and smell.
2. Find a picture of a person, an animal, a bouquet of flowers, a sunset, or some other still-life portrait. List words you would use to describe this picture to a classmate. Then list a few similes and metaphors that actually describe this still-life. How would your description differ if you were seeing the subject in real life rather than in a picture?
3. Choose an unusual object and brainstorm about its physical characteristics. Then brainstorm about the emotions this object evokes. Why is this object so unusual or special? Compare your two brainstorming results and draw some conclusions about their differences.

READING AND WRITING DESCRIPTIVE ESSAYS

All good descriptions share four fundamental qualities: (1) an accurate sense of audience (who the readers are) and purpose (why the essay was written), (2) a clear vision of the object being described, (3) a careful selection of details that help communicate the author's vision, and (4) a consistent point of view or perspective from which a writer composes. The dominant impression or main effect the writer wishes to leave with a specific audience dictates virtually all of the verbal choices in a descriptive essay. Although description is featured in this chapter, you should also pay close attention to how other rhetorical strategies (such as example, division/classification, and cause/effect) can best support an essay's dominant impression.

How to Read a Descriptive Essay

Preparing to Read.   As you approach the reading selections in this chapter, you should focus first on the author's title and try to make some initial assumptions about the essay that follows: Does Ray Bradbury reveal his attitude toward his subject in the title "Summer Rituals"? Can you guess what the general mood of Kimberly Wozencraft's "Notes from the Country Club" will be? Then scan the essay to discover its audience and purpose: What do you think John McPhee's purpose is in "The Pines"? Whom is Malcolm Cowley addressing in "The View from 80"? What do land and bones have in common in Austin's essay? You should also read the synopsis of each essay in the Rhetorical Table of Contents (on pages vii–xv); these brief summaries will provide you with helpful information at this point in the reading process.

Next, learn as much as you can about the author and the conditions under which the essay was composed, information that is provided in the biographical statement before each essay. For a descriptive essay, the conditions under which the author wrote the essay, coupled with his or her purpose, can be very revealing: When and under what conditions did Kimberly Wozencraft write "Notes from the Country Club"? What was her intention in writing the essay? Can you determine when Malcolm Cowley's piece was written? Does it describe the author's life now or in the past? Learning where the essay was first published will also give you valuable information about its audience.

Last, before you begin to read, try to do some brainstorming on the essay's title. In this chapter, respond to the Preparing to Read questions before each essay, which ask you to begin thinking and writing about the topic under consideration. Then pose your own questions: What are some of the most important rituals in your life (Bradbury)? What would you like to learn from Cowley about the joys and frustrations of being eighty years old? What is one of your favorite places (Austin)?

Reading.   As you read each essay for the first time, jot down your initial reactions to it, and try to make connections and see relationships among the author's biography; the essay's title, purpose, and audience; and the synopsis. In this way, you will create a context or framework for your reading. See if you can figure out, for example, what Bradbury is implying about rituals in general in his essay "Summer Rituals" or why Wozencraft wrote an essay about her experiences in prison. Try to discover what the relationship is between purpose, audience, and publication information in Cowley's essay.

Also determine at this point if the author's treatment of his or her subject is predominantly objective (generally free of emotion) or subjective (heavily charged with emotion). Or perhaps the essay falls somewhere between these two extremes.

In addition, make sure you have a general sense of the dominant impression each author is trying to convey. Such an initial approach to reading these descriptive selections will give you a foundation upon which to analyze the material during your second, more in-depth reading.

Finally, at the end of your first reading, take a look at the questions after each essay to make certain you can answer them. This material will guide your rereading.

Rereading.   As you reread these descriptive essays, you should be discovering exactly what the essay's dominant impression is and how the author created it. Notice each author's careful selection of details and the way in which these details come together to leave you with this impression. Also try to determine how certain details add to and detract from that dominant impression and how the writer's point of view affects it: How does Cowley enable us to identify with his experiences if we have never been 80 years old? How does Austin create a sense of serenity in "Land and Bones"?

Try to find during this reading other rhetorical modes that support the description. Although the essays in this chapter describe various persons, places, or objects, all of the authors call upon other rhetorical strategies (especially example and comparison/contrast) to communicate their descriptions. How do these various rhetorical strategies work together in each essay to create a coherent whole?

Finally, answering the questions after each essay will check your understanding of the author's main points and help you think critically about the essay in preparing for the discussion/ writing assignments that follow.

For an inventory of the reading process, you may want to review the checklists on pages 20–21 of the Introduction.

How to Write a Descriptive Essay

Preparing to Write. Before you choose a writing assignment, use the prewriting questions that follow each essay to help you discover your own ideas and opinions about the general topic of the essay. Next, choose an assignment or read the one assigned to you. Then, just as you do when you read an essay, you should determine the audience and purpose for your description (if these are not specified for you in the assignment). To whom are you writing? And why? Will an impartial, objective report be appropriate, or should you present a more emotional, subjective account to accomplish your task? In assessing your audience, you need to determine what they do and do not know about your topic. This information will help you make decisions about what you are going to say and how you will say it. Your purpose will be defined by what you intend your audience to know, think, or believe after they have read your descriptive essay. Do you want them to make up their own minds about summer rituals or old age, for example, based on an objective presentation of data, or do you hope to sway their opinions through a more subjective display of information? Or perhaps you will decide to blend the two techniques, combining facts and opinions in order to achieve the impression of personal certainty based on objective evidence. What dominant impression do you want to leave with your audience? As you might suspect, decisions regarding audience and purpose are as important to writing descriptions as they are to reading descriptions and will shape your descriptive essay from start to finish.

The second quality of good description concerns the object of your analysis and the clarity with which you present it to the reader. Whenever possible, you should thoroughly investigate the person, place, moment, or feeling you wish to describe, paying particular attention to its effect upon each of your five senses. What can you see, smell, hear, taste, and touch as you examine it? If you want to describe your house, for example, begin by asking yourself a series of pertinent questions: How big is the house? What color is it? How many exterior doors does the house have? How many interior doors? Are any of the rooms wallpapered? If so, what are the color and texture of that wallpaper? How many different shades of paint cover the walls? Which rooms have constant noises (from clocks and other mechanical devices)? Are the kitchen appliances hot or cold to the touch? What is the quietest room in the house? The noisiest? What smells do you notice in the laundry? In the kitchen? In the basement? Most important, do any of these sensory questions trigger particular childhood memories? Although you will probably not use all of these details in your descriptive essay, the process of generating and answering such detailed questions will help reacquaint you with the object of your description as it also assists you in designing and focusing your paper. To help you generate some of these ideas, you may want to review the prewriting techniques introduced on pages 21–27.

Writing.   As you write, you must select the details of your description with great care and precision so that you leave your reader with a specific impression. If, for instance, you want your audience to feel the warmth and comfort of your home, you might concentrate on describing the plush carpets, the big upholstered chairs, the inviting scent of hot apple cider, and the crackling fire. If, on the other hand, you want to gain your audience's sympathy, you might prefer to focus on the sparse austerity of your home environment: the bare walls, the quietness, the lack of color and decoration, the dim lighting, and the frigid temperature. You also want to make sure you omit unrelated ideas, like a conversation between your parents you accidentally overheard. Your careful choice of details will help control your audience's reaction.

To make your impression even more vivid, you might use figurative language to fill out your descriptions. Using words "figuratively" means using them imaginatively rather than literally. The two most popular forms of figurative language are *simile* and *metaphor*. A *simile* is a comparison between two dissimilar objects or ideas introduced by *like* or *as*: "The rocking chairs sounded like crickets" (Bradbury). A *metaphor* is an implied comparison between two dissimilar objects or ideas that is not introduced by *like* or *as*: "Life for younger persons is still a battle royal of each against each" (Cowley). Besides enlivening your writing, figurative language helps your readers understand objects, feelings, and ideas that are complex or obscure by comparing them to those that are more familiar.

The last important quality of an effective descriptive essay is point of view, your physical perspective on your subject. Because the organization of your essay depends on your point of view, you need to choose a specific angle from which to approach your description. If you verbally jump around your home, referring first to a picture on the wall in your bedroom, next to the microwave in the kitchen, and then to the quilt on your bed, no reasonable audience will be able to follow your description. Nor will they want to. If, however, you move from room to room in some logical, sequential way, always focusing on the details you want your readers to know, you will be helping your audience form a clear, memorable impression of your home. Your vision will become their vision. In other words, your point of view plays a part in determining the organization of your description. Working spatially, you could move from side to side (from one wall to another in the rooms we have discussed), from top to bottom (from ceiling to floor), or from far to near (from the farthest to the closest point in a room), or you might progress from large to small objects, from uninteresting to interesting, or from funny to serious. Whatever plan you choose should help you accomplish your purpose with your particular audience.

Rewriting.   As you reread each of your descriptive essays, play the role of your audience and try to determine what dominant impression you receive by the end of your reading.

- Do you communicate the dominant impression you want to convey?
- Do you have a clear point of view on your subject?
- How does the essay make you feel?
- What does it make you think about?
- Which senses does it stimulate?
- Do you use similes or metaphors when appropriate?
- Are you *showing* rather than *telling* in your description?

For additional suggestions on the writing process, you may want to consult the checklists on pages 32–34 of the Introduction.

STUDENT ESSAY: DESCRIPTION AT WORK

In the following essay, a student relives some of her childhood memories through a subjective description of her grandmother's house. As you read it, pay particular attention to the different types of sensual details the student writer chooses to communicate her dominant impression of her grandmother's home. Notice also her use of carefully chosen details to *show* rather than *tell* us about her childhood reminiscences, especially her comparisons, which make the memory as vivid for the reader as it is for the writer.

Grandma's House

Writer's point of view or perspective My most vivid childhood memories are set in my Grandma Goodlink's house, a curious blend of familiar and mysterious treasures. Grandma lived at the end of a dead-end street, in the same house she had lived in since the first day of her marriage. That was half a century and thirteen children ago. A set of crumbly steps made of concrete mixed with gravel led up to her front door. I remember a big gap between the house and the steps, as if someone had not pushed them up close enough to the house. Anyone who looked into the gap **Sight** could see old toys and books that had fallen into the crack behind the steps and had remained there, forever irretrievable. **Dominant impression**

Comparison (simile)

Only a hook-type lock on the front door protected Grandma's many beautiful antiques. Her living room was set up like a church or schoolroom, with an old purple velvet couch against the far wall and two chairs immediately in front of the couch facing the same direction. One-half of the couch was always buried in old clothes, magazines, and newspapers, and a lone shoe sat atop the pile, a finishing touch to some **Comparison (simile)** **Sight** **Sight** bizarre modern sculpture. To one side was an aged and tuneless upright piano with yellowed keys. The ivory overlay was missing so that the wood underneath showed through, and many of the keys made only a muffled and frustrating thump, no matter how hard I pressed them. On the wall facing the piano was the room's only window, draped with yellowed lace curtains. Grandma always left that window open. I remember sitting near it, smelling the rain while the curtains tickled my face.

For no apparent reason, an old curtain hung in the door between the kitchen and the living room. In the kitchen, a large Formica-topped table always held at least a half-dozen varieties of homemade jelly, as well as a loaf of bread, gooseberry pies or cherry pies with the pits left in, boxes of cereal, and anything else not requiring refrigeration, as if the table served as a small, portable pantry. Grandma's kitchen always smelled of toast, and I often wondered—and still do—if she lived entirely on toast. A hole had eaten through the kitchen floor, not just the warped yellow linoleum, but all the way through the floor itself. My sisters and I never wanted to take a bath at Grandma's house, because we discovered that anyone who lay on the floor on his stomach and put one eye to the hole could see the bathtub, which was kept in the musty basement because the upstairs bathroom was too small.

The back bedroom was near the kitchen and adjacent to the basement stairs. I once heard one of my aunts call that room a firetrap, and indeed it was. The room was wallpapered with the old newspapers Grandma liked to collect, and the bed was stacked high with my mother's and aunts' old clothes. There was no space between the

Marginal annotations (left): Comparison (metaphor), Sight, Sound, Smell, Smell, Smell, Sight

Marginal annotations (right): Sound, Sight, Sight, Touch, Sight, Taste, Comparison (simile), Sight, Sight, Sight

furniture in that room, only a narrow path against one wall leading to the bed. A sideboard was shoved against the opposite wall; a sewing table was pushed up against the sideboard; a short chest of drawers lay against the sewing table; and so on. But no one could identify these pieces of forgotten furniture without digging through the sewing patterns, half-made dresses, dishes, and books. Any outsider would just think this was a part of the room where the floor had been raised to about waist-level, so thoroughly was the mass of furniture hidden. | Sight

Stepping off Grandma's sloping back porch was like stepping into an enchanted forest. The grass and weeds were hip-level, with a tiny dirt path leading to nowhere, as if it had lost its way in the jungle. A fancy white fence, courtesy of the neighbors, bordered the yard in back and vainly attempted to hold in the gooseberries, raspberries, and blackberries that grew wildly along the side of Grandma's yard. Huge crabapple, cherry, and walnut trees shaded the house and hid the sky. I used to stand under them and look up, pretending to be deep in a magic forest. The ground was cool and damp under my bare feet, even in the middle of the day, and my head would fill with the sweet fragrance of mixed spring flowers and the throaty cooing of doves I could never find but could always hear. But, before long, the wind would shift, and the musty aroma of petroleum from a nearby refinery would jerk me back to reality.

Comparison (simile) · *Comparison (simile)* · *Sight* · *Sight* · *Sight* · *Touch* · *Smell* · *Sound* · *Smell*

Grandma's house is indeed a place of wonderful memories. Just as her decaying concrete steps store the treasures of many lost childhoods, her house still stands, guarding the memories of generations of children and grandchildren.

Dominant impression rephrased

Student Writer's Comments

Writing this descriptive essay was easy and enjoyable for me—once I got started. I decided to write about my grandmother's house because I knew it so well, but I had trouble coming up with the impression I wanted to convey to my readers. I have so many recollections of this place I didn't know which set of memories would be most interesting to others. So I began by brainstorming, forcing myself to think of images from all five senses.

After I had accumulated plenty of images, which triggered other memories I had completely forgotten, I began to write. I organized my essay spatially as if I were walking through Grandma's house room by room. But I let my senses lead the way. Before I started writing, I had no idea how many paragraphs I would have, but as I meandered through the house recording my memories of sights, smells, sounds, tastes, and textures, I ended up writing one paragraph on each room, plus one for the yard. For this assignment, I wrote the three paragraphs about the inside of the house first; then, the introduction started to take shape in my head, so I got it down; and last, I wrote the paragraph on the backyard and my conclusion. Finally, my "dominant impression" came to me: This is a house that guards the memories of many generations. My grandmother has always lived in this house, and my mother has her own set of memories associated with this place too.

This focus for my paper made the revising process fairly easy, as I worked on the entire essay with a specific purpose in mind. Previously, my biggest problem had been that I had too many scattered memories and realized I had to be more selective. Once I had my dominant impression, I knew which images to keep and which to drop from my draft. Also, as I reworked my essay, I looked for ways to make my description more exciting and vivid for the reader—as if he or she were right there with me. To accomplish this, I explained some special features of my grandma's house by comparing them with items the reader would most likely be familiar with. I also worked, at this point, on making one paragraph flow into another by adding transitions that would move the reader smoothly from one group of ideas to the next. "Only a hook-type lock on the front door" got my readers into the living room. The old curtain between the kitchen and the living room moved my essay out of the living room and into the kitchen. I started my third paragraph about the indoors by saying "The back bedroom was near the kitchen and adjacent to the basement stairs" so my readers could get their bearings in relation to other parts of the house they had already been introduced to. Finally, I was satisfied that my essay was a clear, accurate description of my view of my grandma's house. My brother might have a completely different set of memories, but this was my version of a single generation of impressions organized, finally, into one coherent essay.

SOME FINAL THOUGHTS ON DESCRIPTION

Because description is one of the most basic forms of verbal communication, you will find descriptive passages in most of the reading selections throughout this textbook. Description provides us with the means to capture our audience's attention and clarify certain points in all of our writing. The examples chosen for the following section, however, are predominantly descriptive—the main purpose in each being to involve the readers' senses as vividly as possible. As you read through each of these essays, try to determine its intended audience and purpose, the object of the description, the extent to which details are included or excluded, and the author's point of view. Equipped with these four areas of reference, you can become an increasingly sophisticated reader and writer of descriptive prose.

DESCRIPTION IN REVIEW

Reading Descriptive Essays

Preparing to Read

- ✓ What assumptions can you make from the essay's title?
- ✓ Can you guess what the general mood of the essay is?
- ✓ What is the essay's purpose and audience?
- ✓ What does the synopsis in the Rhetorical Table of Contents tell you about the essay?

✓ What can you learn from the author's biography?

✓ Can you guess what the author's point of view toward the subject is?

✓ What are your responses to the Preparing to Read questions?

Reading

✓ Is the essay predominantly objective or subjective?

✓ What dominant impression is the author trying to convey?

✓ Did you preview the questions that follow the essay?

Rereading

✓ How does the author create the essay's dominant impression?

✓ What other rhetorical modes does the author use to support the essay's purpose?

✓ What are your responses to the questions after the essay?

Writing Descriptive Essays

Preparing to Write

✓ What are your responses to the Preparing to Write questions?

✓ What is your purpose? Will you be primarily objective or subjective?

✓ Who is your audience?

✓ What is the dominant impression you want to convey?

✓ Do you know the object of your description well?

Writing

✓ Do the details you are choosing support your dominant impression?

✓ Do you use words literally and figuratively?

✓ What is your point of view toward your subject?

✓ Do you *show* rather than *tell* your dominant impression?

Rewriting

✓ Do you communicate the dominant impression you want to convey?

✓ Do you have a clear point of view on your subject?

✓ How does the essay make you feel?

✓ What does it make you think about?

✓ Which senses does it stimulate?

✓ Do you use similes or metaphors when appropriate?

✓ Are you *showing* rather than *telling* your description?

RAY BRADBURY   (1920–   )

Summer Rituals

Ray Bradbury is one of America's best-known and most loved writers of science fiction. His extensive publications include such popular novels as *The Martian Chronicles* (1950), *The Illustrated Man* (1951), *Fahrenheit 451* (1953), *Dandelion Wine* (1957), and *Something Wicked This Way Comes* (1962). He has also written dozens of short stories, poems, essays, plays, and radio and movie scripts (including the screenplay of John Huston's film version of *Moby Dick*). As a child, he escaped his strict Baptist upbringing through a steady diet of Jules Verne, H. G. Wells, and Edgar Rice Burroughs, along with Buck Rogers and Prince Valiant comic books: "I was a sucker for lies, beautiful, fabulous lies, which instruct us to better our lives as a result, but which don't tell the truth." A frequent theme in his many novels is the impact of science on humanity: "My stories are intended," he claims, "as much to forecast how to prevent dooms, as to predict them." Bradbury's more recent publications include *The Last Circus* (1981), *The Complete Poems of Ray Bradbury* (1982), *The Love Affair* (1983), *Dinosaur Tales* (1983), *A Memory for Murder* (1984), *Forever and the Earth* (1984), *Death Is a Lonely Business* (1985), *The Toynbee Convector* (1989), *A Day in the Life of Hollywood* (1992), *Quicker Than the Eye* (1996), *Driving Blind* (1998), and *From the Dust Returned* (2000). The author lives in Cheviot Hills, California, where he enjoys painting and making ceramics.

Preparing to Read

"Summer Rituals," an excerpt from *Dandelion Wine*, describes the comfortable ceremony of putting up a front-porch swing in early summer. Focusing on the perceptions of Douglas, a young boy, the essay clearly sets forth the familiar yet deeply significant rhythms of life in a small town. Before you read this selection, take a few moments to consider the value of ritual in your own life: Can you think of any activities that you and your family have elevated to the level of ceremonial importance? What about holidays? Birthdays? Sporting events? Spring cleaning? When do these activities take place? Do the same people participate in them every year? Why do you repeat these rituals? What purpose do they have for you? For others whom you know? For society in general?

Yes, summer was rituals, each with its natural time and 1 place. The ritual of lemonade or ice-tea making, the ritual of wine, shoes, or no shoes, and at last, swiftly following the others, with quiet dignity, the ritual of the front-porch swing.

On the third day of summer in the late afternoon Grandfather 2 reappeared from the front door to gaze serenely at the two empty eye rings in the ceiling of the porch. Moving to the geranium-pot-lined rail like Ahab surveying the mild day and the mild-looking sky, he wet his finger to test the wind, and shucked his coat to see how shirt sleeves felt in the westering hours. He acknowledged the salutes of other captains on yet other flowered porches, out themselves to discern the gentle ground swell of weather, oblivious to their wives chirping or snapping like fuzzball hand dogs hidden behind black porch screens.

"All right, Douglas, let's set it up." 3

In the garage they found, dusted, and carried forth the how- 4 dah, as it were, for the quiet summer-night festivals, the swing chair which Grandpa chained to the porch-ceiling eyelets.

Douglas, being lighter, was first to sit in the swing. Then, after 5 a moment, Grandfather gingerly settled his pontifical weight beside the boy. Thus they sat, smiling at each other, nodding, as they swung silently back and forth, back and forth.

Ten minutes later Grandma appeared with water buckets and 6 brooms to wash down and sweep off the porch. Other chairs, rockers and straight-backs, were summoned from the house.

"Always like to start sitting early in the season," said Grandpa, 7 "before the mosquitoes thicken."

About seven o'clock you could hear the chairs scraping back 8 from the tables, someone experimenting with a yellow-toothed piano, if you stood outside the dining-room window and listened. Matches being struck, the first dishes bubbling in the suds and tinkling on the wall racks, somewhere, faintly, a phonograph playing. And then as the evening changed the hour, at house after house on the twilight streets, under the immense oaks and elms,

on shady porches, people would begin to appear, like those figures who tell good or bad weather in rain-or-shine clocks.

Uncle Bert, perhaps Grandfather, then Father, and some of the   9
cousins; the men all coming out first into the syrupy evening,
blowing smoke, leaving the women's voices behind in the cool-
ing-warm kitchen to set their universe aright. Then the first male
voices under the porch brim, the feet up, the boys fringed on the
worn steps or wooden rails where sometime during the evening
something, a boy or a geranium pot, would fall off.

At last, like ghosts hovering momentarily behind the door   10
screen, Grandma, Great-grandma, and Mother would appear, and
the men would shift, move, and offer seats. The women carried
varieties of fans with them, folded newspapers, bamboo whisks, or
perfumed kerchiefs, to start the air moving about their faces as
they talked.

What they talked of all evening long, no one remembered next   11
day. It wasn't important to anyone what the adults talked about; it
was only important that the sounds came and went over the delicate ferns that bordered the porch on three sides; it was only important that the darkness filled the town like black water being
poured over the houses and that the cigars glowed and that the
conversations went on and on. The female gossip moved out, disturbing the first mosquitoes so they danced in frenzies on the air.
The male voices invaded the old house timbers; if you closed
your eyes and put your head down against the floor boards you
could hear the men's voices rumbling like a distant, political
earthquake, constant, unceasing, rising or falling a pitch.

Douglas sprawled back on the dry porch planks, completely   12
contented and reassured by these voices, which would speak on
through eternity, flow in a stream of murmurings over his body,
over his closed eyelids, into his drowsy ears, for all time. The
rocking chairs sounded like crickets, the crickets sounded like
rocking chairs, and the moss-covered rain barrel by the diningroom window produced another generation of mosquitoes to
provide a topic of conversation through endless summers ahead.

Sitting on the summer-night porch was so good, so easy and so   13
reassuring that it could never be done away with. These were rituals that were right and lasting; the lighting of pipes, the pale
hands that moved knitting needles in the dimness, the eating of
foil-wrapped, chill Eskimo Pies, the coming and going of all the

people. For at some time or other during the evening, everyone visited here; the neighbors down the way, the people across the street; Miss Fern and Miss Roberta humming by in their electric runabout, giving Tom or Douglas a ride around the block and then coming up to sit down and fan away the fever in their cheeks; or Mr. Jonas, the junkman, having left his horse and wagon hidden in the alley, and ripe to bursting with words, would come up the steps looking as fresh as if his talk had never been said before, and somehow it never had. And last of all, the children, who had been off squinting their way through a last hide-and-seek or kick-the-can, panting, glowing, would sickle quietly back like boomerangs along the soundless lawn, to sink beneath the talking talking talking of the porch voices which would weigh and gentle them down. . . .

Oh, the luxury of lying in the fern night and the grass night   14
and the night of susurrant, slumbrous voices weaving the dark together. The grownups had forgotten he was there, so still, so quiet Douglas lay, noting the plans they were making for his and their own futures. And the voices chanted, drifted, in moonlit clouds of cigarette smoke while the moths, like late appleblossoms come alive, tapped faintly about the far street lights, and the voices moved on into the coming years. . . .

UNDERSTANDING DETAILS

1. What are the main similarities and differences between Douglas and Grandfather in this essay? How are their views of the world the same? How are their views different?

2. From the scattered details you have read in this essay, describe Douglas's house. How large do you think the front porch is? What color is the house? How many trees and shrubs surround it? What part of your description is based on facts in the essay? What part comes from inferences you have made on your own?

3. How do the men differ from the women in this excerpt? Divide a piece of paper into two columns; then list as many qualities of each gender as you can find. (For example, the narrator hears the men's voices "rumbling" like an "earthquake"; in contrast, the women move like "ghosts," their gossip "disturbing the . . . mosquitoes.") What other descriptive differences

can you find between the men and women? What conclusions can you draw from these differences?

4. How did the conversation blend with the surroundings in Bradbury's description?

ANALYZING MEANING

1. A "ritual" may be briefly defined as "a customarily repeated act that expresses a system of values." Using this definition, explain why the ritual of the front-porch swing is important to Douglas's family. What feelings or implicit values lie behind this particular ritual?

2. What other rituals are mentioned in this essay? How are they related to the front-porch swing? To summer? To Douglas and his family?

3. Bradbury helps us feel the comfort, warmth, and familiarity of the scene depicted in this essay through the use of a number of original descriptive details: for example, "summer-night festivals," "yellow-toothed piano," "rain-or-shine clocks," "syrupy evening," and "foil-wrapped, chill Eskimo Pies." Find at least five other descriptive words or phrases, and explain how each enables us to identify with the characters and situations in this story. Which of the five senses does each of these details arouse in the reader?

4. In what ways do you think Douglas was "completely contented and reassured" (paragraph 12) by the voices around him? Why did Douglas feel this contentment would last "for all time" (paragraph 12)?

DISCOVERING RHETORICAL STRATEGIES

1. Some of the author's sentences are very long and involved, whereas others are quite short. What effects do these changes in sentence length have on you as a reader? Give a specific example of a shift in length from one sentence to another and explain its effect.

2. This descriptive essay is filled with many interesting similes (comparisons using the words *like* or *as*) and metaphors (comparisons without *like* or *as*). For example, Grandfather standing

on the front porch looks *like* Ahab, the possessed sea captain from Herman Melville's epic novel *Moby Dick* (paragraph 2). Later, Bradbury uses a metaphor to focus his readers on "the night of susurrant, slumbrous voices weaving the dark together" (paragraph 14). Find at least one other comparison, either a simile or a metaphor, and explain how it works within the context of its sentence or paragraph. What type of comparison is being made (a simile or a metaphor)? What do we learn about the object being described (for example, Grandfather or the night) through its association with the other reference (Ahab or voices weaving the dark together)?

3. What is the point of view of the author in this selection? Would the essay be more effective if it were reported from the standpoint of Douglas? Of Grandfather? Of the women? Why or why not? How does the author's point of view help Bradbury organize his description? Should the fact that Bradbury's middle name is Douglas have any bearing on our interpretation of this story?

4. Although Bradbury draws mainly on description to write this essay, what other rhetorical strategies work together to help the reader grasp the full effect of "Summer Rituals"? Give examples of each strategy.

MAKING CONNECTIONS

1. For Douglas, hanging the porch swing was an important yearly ritual. What rituals can you find in the childhoods of Russell Baker ("The Saturday Evening Post") and/or Eudora Welty ("Listening")? What specific meanings did these rituals have within each author's family?

2. Compare and contrast Bradbury's neighborhood with that of Robert Ramirez ("The Barrio"). Which neighborhood would you feel most comfortable in? Why would you feel comfortable there?

3. Which author's relationship with his/her parents was most like your own: Ray Bradbury's, Russell Baker's ("The Saturday Evening Post"), or Sandra Cisneros's ("Only daughter")? How did each of these children relate differently to his or her parents?

IDEAS FOR DISCUSSION/WRITING

Preparing to Write

List some of the most important rituals in your life: How many times a year do these rituals occur? What purpose do they serve? How do rituals help create a strong social framework in your life? In your friends' lives? In society in general?

Choosing a Topic

1. Write a descriptive essay about a ritual that is significant in your life, addressing it to someone who has never experienced that particular activity. Include the people involved and the setting. Try to use all five senses in your description.
2. Choose a ritual that is part of your family life, and write an essay describing your feelings about this ceremonial event. Address it to someone outside your family. Use similes and metaphors to make your description as vivid as possible.
3. Explain to someone visiting the United States for the first time the value of a particular tradition in American society. Then help this person understand the importance of that tradition in your life.

Before beginning your essay, you might want to consult the checklists on pages 51–53.

KIMBERLY WOZENCRAFT   (1954–   )

Notes from the Country Club

Kimberly Wozencraft grew up in Dallas, Texas, and dropped out of college when she was twenty-one to become a police officer. Her first assignment, prior to training at the police academy, was a street-level undercover narcotics investigation. Like many narcotics agents, Wozencraft became addicted to drugs, which impaired her judgment and resulted in a 1981 conviction for violating the civil rights of a reputed child pornographer. After serving an eighteen-month sentence in the Federal Correctional Institution at Lexington, Kentucky, she moved to New York City, where she has lived since her release. She holds a Master of Fine Arts degree from Columbia University, and her essays, poems, and short stories have appeared in a variety of magazines, including *Northwest Review, Quarto, Big Wednesday,* and *Witness.* Her first novel, *Rush,* was made into a movie in 1992, and her most recent book, *The Catch,* was published by Doubleday in 1998.

Preparing to Read

Originally published in *Witness,* "Notes from the Country Club" was selected for inclusion in *The Best American Essays of 1988,* edited by Annie Dillard. Through carefully constructed prose, the author describes her prison environment and the anxiety caused by living for more than a year in such an alien, difficult place. As you prepare to read this essay, take a moment to think about your own behavior in difficult situations: What kind of person do you become? How do you act toward other people? How is this behavior different from the way you usually act? How do you know when you're in a difficult situation? What do you generally do to relieve the tension?

They had the Haitians up the hill, in the "camp" section where they used to keep the minimum security cases. The authorities were concerned that some of the Haitians might be diseased, so they kept them isolated from the main coed prison population by lodging them in the big square brick building surrounded by eight-foot chain-link with concertina wire on top. We were not yet familiar with the acronym AIDS.

One or two of the Haitians had drums, and in the evenings 2 when the rest of us were in the Big Yard, the drum rhythms carried over the bluegrass to where we were playing gin or tennis or softball or just hanging out waiting for dark. When they really got going some of them would dance and sing. Their music was rhythmic and beautiful, and it made me think of freedom.

There were Cubans loose in the population, spattering their 3 guttural Spanish in streams around the rectangular courtyard, called Central Park, at the center of the prison compound. These were Castro's Boat People, guilty of no crime in this country, but requiring sponsors before they could walk the streets as free people.

Walking around the perimeter of Central Park was like taking 4 a trip in microcosm across the United States. Moving leftward from the main entrance, strolling along under the archway that covers the wide sidewalk, you passed the doorway to the Women's Unit, where I lived, and it was how I imagined Harlem to be. There was a white face here and there, but by far most of them were black. Ghetto blasters thunked out rhythms in the sticky evening air, and folks leaned against the window sills, smoking, drinking Cokes, slinking, and nodding. Every once in a while a joint was passed around, and always there was somebody pinning, checking for hacks on patrol.

Past Women's Unit was the metal door to the Big Yard, the 5 main recreation area of three or four acres, two sides blocked by the building, two sides fenced in the usual way—chain-link and concertina wire.

Past the Big Yard you entered the Blue Ridge Mountains, a 6 sloping grassy area on the edge of Central Park, where the locals, people from Kentucky, Tennessee, and the surrounding environs, sat around playing guitars and singing, and every once in a while passing around a quart of hooch. They make it from grapefruit juice and a bit of yeast smuggled out of the kitchen. Some of the inmates who worked in Cable would bring out pieces of a black foam rubber substance and wrap it around empty Cremora jars to make thermos jugs of sorts. They would mix the grapefruit juice and yeast in the containers and stash them in some out-of-the-way spot for a few weeks until presto! you had hooch, bitter and tart and sweet all at once, only mildly alcoholic, but entirely suitable for evening cocktails in Central Park.

Next, at the corner, was the Commissary, a tiny store tucked 7 inside the entrance to Veritas, the second women's unit. It wasn't much more than a few shelves behind a wall of Plexiglas, with a constant line of inmates spilling out of the doorway. They sold packaged chips, cookies, pens and writing paper, toiletries, some fresh fruit, and the ever-popular ice cream, sold only in pints. You had to eat the entire pint as soon as you bought it, or else watch it melt, because there weren't any refrigerators. Inmates were assigned one shopping night per week, allowed to buy no more than seventy-five dollars' worth of goods per month, and were permitted to pick up a ten-dollar roll of quarters if they had enough money in their prison account. Quarters were the basic spending unit in the prison; possession of paper money was a shippable offense. There were vending machines stocked with junk food and soda, and they were supposedly what the quarters were to be used for. But we gambled, we bought salami or fried chicken sneaked out by the food service workers, and of course people sold booze and drugs. The beggars stood just outside the Commissary door. Mostly they were Cubans, saying, "Oyez! Mira! Mira! Hey, Poppy, one quarter for me. One cigarette for me, Poppy?"

There was one Cuban whom I was specially fond of. His name 8 was Shorty. The name said it. He was only about five-two, and he looked just like Mick Jagger. I met him in Segregation, an isolated section of tiny cells where prisoners were locked up for having violated some institutional rule or another. They tossed me in there the day I arrived; again the authorities were concerned, supposedly for my safety. I was a police woman before I became a convict, and they weren't too sure that the other inmates would like that. Shorty saved me a lot of grief when I went into Seg. It didn't matter if you were male or female there, you got stripped and handed a tee shirt, a pair of boxer shorts and a set of Peter Pans—green canvas shoes with thin rubber soles designed to prevent you from running away. As if you could get past three steel doors and a couple of hacks just to start with. When I was marched down the hall between the cells, the guys started whistling and hooting, and they didn't shut up even after I was locked down. They kept right on screaming until finally I yelled out, "Yo no comprendo!" and they all moaned and said, "Another . . . Cuban," and finally got quiet. Shorty was directly across from me, I could see his eyes through the rectangular slot in my cell door. He rattled off a paragraph or two of Spanish, all of which was lost on me, and I said quietly, "Yo no comprendo bien español. Yo soy de Texas, yo hablo inglés?" I could tell he was smiling by the squint of his eyes, and he just said, "Bueno." When the hacks came around to take us out for our mandatory hour of recreation, which consisted of standing around in the Rec area while two guys shot a game of pool on the balcony above the gym, Shorty slipped his hand into mine and smiled up at me until the hack told him to cut it out. He knew enough English to tell the others in Seg that I was not really Spanish, but he kept quiet about it, and they left me alone.

Beyond the Commissary, near the door to the dining hall, was   9
East St. Louis. The prison had a big portable stereo system which they rolled out a few times a week so that an inmate could play at being a disc jockey. They had a good-sized collection of albums, and there was usually some decent jazz blasting out of there. Sometimes people danced, unless there were uptight hacks on duty to tell them not to.

California was next. It was a laid back kind of corner near the   10
doors to two of the men's units. People stood around and smoked hash or grass or did whatever drugs happened to be available and there was sometimes a sort of slow-motion game of handball going on. If you wanted drugs, this was the place to come.

If you kept walking, you would arrive at the Power Station,   11
the other southern corner where the politicos-gone-wrong congregated. It might seem odd at first to see these middle-aged government mavens standing around in their Lacoste sport shirts and Sans-a-belt slacks, smoking pipes or cigars and waving their arms to emphasize some point or other. They kept pretty much to themselves and ate together at the big round tables in the cafeteria, sipping cherry Kool-Aid and pretending it was Cabernet Sauvignon.

That's something else you had to deal with—the food. It was   12
worse than elementary school steam table fare. By the time they finished cooking it, it was tasteless, colorless, and nutritionless. The first meal I took in the dining room was lunch. As I walked toward the entry, a tubby fellow was walking out, staggering re-

ally, rolling his eyes as though he were dizzy. He stopped and leaned over, and I heard someone yell, "Watch out, he's gonna puke!" I ducked inside so as to miss the spectacle. They were serving some rubbery, faint pink slabs that were supposed to be ham, but I didn't even bother to taste mine. I just slapped at it a few times to watch the fork bounce off and then ate my potatoes and went back to the unit.

Shortly after that I claimed that I was Jewish, having gotten the   13
word from a friendly New York lawyer who was in for faking some of his clients' immigration papers. The kosher line was the only way to get a decent meal in there. In fact, for a long time they had a Jewish baker from Philadelphia locked up, and he made some truly delicious cream puffs for dessert. They sold for seventy-five cents on the black market, but once I had established myself in the Jewish community, I got them as part of my regular fare. They fed us a great deal of peanut butter on the kosher line; every time the "goyim" got meat, we got peanut butter, but that was all right with me. Eventually I was asked to light the candles at the Friday evening services, since none of the real Jewish women bothered to attend. I have to admit that most of the members of our little prison congregation were genuine *alter kokers*, but some of them were amusing. And I enjoyed learning first hand about Judaism. The services were usually very quiet, and the music, the ancient intoning songs, fortified me against the screeching pop-rock vocal assaults that were a constant in the Women's Unit. I learned to think of myself as the *shabot shiksa*, and before my time was up, even the rabbi seemed to accept me.

I suppose it was quite natural that the Italians assembled just   14
"down the street" from the offending ex-senators, judges, and power brokers. Just to the left of the main entrance. The first night I made the tour, a guy came out of the shadows near the building and whispered to me. "What do you need, sweetheart? What do you want, I can get it. My friend Ahmad over there, he's very rich, and he wants to buy you things. What'll it be, you want some smoke, a few ludes, vodka, cigarettes, maybe some kosher salami fresh from the kitchen? What would you like?" I just stared at him. The only thing I wanted at that moment was out, and even Ahmad's millions, if they existed at all, couldn't do that. The truth is, every guy I met in there claimed to be wealthy, to have been locked up for some major financial crime. Had I

taken all of them up on their offers of limousines to pick me up at the front gate when I was released and take me to the airport for a ride home in a private Lear jet, I would have needed my own personal cop out front just to direct traffic.

Ahmad's Italian promoter eventually got popped for zinging the cooking teacher one afternoon on the counter in the home economics classroom, right next to the new Cuisinart. The assistant warden walked in on the young lovebirds, and before the week was up, even the Cubans were walking around singing about it. They had a whole song down, to the tune of "Borracho Me Acosté a Noche." 15

At the end of the tour, you would find the jaded New Yorkers, sitting at a picnic table or two in the middle of the park, playing gin or poker and bragging about their days on Madison Avenue and Wall Street, lamenting the scarcity of good deli, even on the kosher line, and planning where they would take their first real meal upon release. 16

If you think federal correctional institutions are about the business of rehabilitation, drop by for an orientation session one day. There at the front of the classroom, confronting rows of mostly black faces, will be the warden, or the assistant warden, or the prison shrink, pacing back and forth in front of the blackboard and asking the class, "Why do you think you're here?" This gets a general grumble, a few short, choked laughs. Some well-meaning soul always says it—rehabilitation. 17

"Nonsense!" the lecturer will say. "There are several reasons for locking people up. Number one is incapacitation. If you're in here, you can't be out there doing crime. Secondly, there is deterrence. Other people who are thinking about doing crime see that we lock people up for it and maybe they think twice. But the real reason you are here is to be punished. Plain and simple. You done wrong, now you got to pay for it. Rehabilitation ain't even part of the picture. So don't be looking to us to rehabilitate you. Only person can rehabilitate you is you. If you feel like it, go for it, but leave us out. We don't want to play that game." 18

So that's it. You're there to do time. I have no misgivings about why I went to prison. I deserved it. I was a cop; I got strung out on cocaine; I violated the rights of a pornographer. My own drug use as an undercover narcotics agent was a significant factor in my crime. But I did it, and I deserved to be punished. 19

Most of the people I met in Lexington, though, were in for drugs, and the majority of them hadn't done anything more than sell an ounce of cocaine or a pound of pot to some apostle of the law.

It seems lately that almost every time I look at the *New York* 20 *Times* op-ed page, there is something about the drug problem. I have arrested people for drugs, and I have had a drug problem myself. I have seen how at least one federal correctional institution functions. It does not appear that the practice of locking people up for possession or distribution of an insignificant quantity of a controlled substance makes any difference at all in the amount of drug use that occurs in the United States. The drug laws are merely another convenient source of political rhetoric for aspiring officeholders. Politicians know that an antidrug stance is an easy way to get votes from parents who are terrified that their children might wind up as addicts. I do not advocate drug use. Yet, having seen the criminal justice system from several angles, as a police officer, a court bailiff, a defendant, and a prisoner, I am convinced that prison is not the answer to the drug problem, or for that matter to many other white-collar crimes. If the taxpayers knew how their dollars were being spent inside some prisons, they might actually scream out loud.

There were roughly 1,800 men and women locked up in Lex, 21 at a ratio of approximately three men to every woman, and it did get warm in the summertime. To keep us tranquil they devised some rather peculiar little amusements. One evening I heard a commotion on the steps at the edge of Central Park and looked over to see a rec specialist with three big cardboard boxes set up on the plaza, marked 1, 2, and 3. There were a couple of hundred inmates sitting at the bottom of the steps. Dennis, the rec specialist, was conducting his own version of the television game show *Let's Make a Deal!* Under one of the boxes was a case of soda, under another was a racquetball glove, and under a third was a fly swatter. The captive contestant picked door number 2, which turned out to contain the fly swatter, to my way of thinking the best prize there. Fly swatters were virtually impossible to get through approved channels, and therefore cost as much as two packs of cigarettes on the black market.

Then there was the Annual Fashion Show, where ten or twenty 22 inmates had special packages of clothing sent in, only for the one evening, and modeled them on stage while the baddest drag queen in the compound moderated and everyone else ooohed and aah-hed. They looked good up there on stage in Christian Dior and Ralph Lauren instead of the usual fatigue pants and white tee shirts. And if such activities did little to prepare inmates for a pro-ductive return to society, well, at least they contributed to the fan-tasyland aura that made Lexington such an unusual place.

I worked in Landscape, exiting the rear gate of the compound   23 each weekday morning at about nine after getting a half-hearted frisk from one of the hacks on duty. I would climb on my tractor to drive to the staff apartment complex and pull weeds or mow the lawn. Landscape had its prerogatives. We raided the gardens regularly and at least got to taste fresh vegetables from time to time. I had never eaten raw corn before, but it could not have tasted better. We also brought in a goodly supply of real vodka, and a bit of hash now and then, for parties in our rooms after lights out. One guy strapped a six-pack of Budweiser to his arms with masking tape and then put on his prison-issue Army field jacket. When he got to the rear gate, he raised his arms straight out at shoulder level, per instructions, and the hack patted down his torso and legs, never bothering to check his arms. The inmate had been counting on that. He smiled at the hack and walked back to his room, a six-pack richer.

I was fortunate to be working Landscape at the same time as   24 Horace, a fellow who had actually lived in the city of Lexington before he was locked up. His friends made regular deliveries of as-sorted contraband, which they would stash near a huge elm tree near the outer stone fence of the reservation. Horace would drive his tractor over, make the pickup, and the rest of us would carry it, concealed, through the back gate when we went back inside for lunch or at the end of the day. "Contraband" included every-thing from drugs to blue eye shadow. The assistant warden be-lieved that female inmates should wear no cosmetics other than what she herself used—a bit of mascara and a light shade of lip-stick. I have never been a plaything of Fashion, but I did what I could to help the other women prisoners in their never-ending quest for that Cover Girl look.

You could depend on the fact that most of the hacks would   25 rather have been somewhere else, and most of them really didn't care *what* the inmates did, as long as it didn't cause any commo-tion. Of course, there were a few you had to look out for. The captain in charge of security was one of them. We tried a little experiment once, after having observed that any time he saw someone laughing, he took immediate steps to make the inmate and everyone around him acutely miserable. Whenever we saw him in the area, we immediately assumed expressions of intense unhappiness, even of despair. Seeing no chance to make anyone more miserable than they already appeared to be, the captain left us alone.

Almost all of the female hacks, and a good number of the males, had outrageously large derrières, a condition we inmates referred to as "the federal ass." This condition may have resulted from the fact that most of them appeared, as one inmate succinctly described it, simply to be "putting in their forty a week to stay on the government teat." Employment was not an easy thing to find in Kentucky.

Despite the fact that Lexington is known as a "country club" prison, I must admit that I counted days. From the first moment that I was in, I kept track of how many more times I would have to watch the sun sink behind eight feet of chain-link, of how many more days I would have to spend eating, working, playing, and sleeping according to the dictates of a "higher authority." I don't think I can claim that I was rehabilitated. If anything I underwent a process of dehabilitation. What I learned was what Jessica Mitford tried to tell people many years ago in her book *Kind and Usual Punishment.* Prison is a business, no different from manufacturing tires or selling real estate. It keeps people employed, and it provides cheap labor for NASA, the U.S. Postal Service, and other governmental or quasi-governmental agencies. For a short time, before I was employed in Landscape, I worked as a finisher of canvas mailbags, lacing white rope through metal eyelets around the top of the bags and attaching clamps to the ropes. I made one dollar and fourteen cents for every one hundred that I did. If I worked very hard, I could do almost two hundred a day.

It's not about justice. If you think it's about justice, look at the newspapers and notice who walks. Not the little guys, the guys doing a tiny bit of dealing or sniggling a little on their income tax, or the woman who pulls a stunt with welfare checks because her husband has skipped out and she has no other way to feed her kids. I do not say that these things are right. But the process of selective prosecution, the "making" of cases by D.A.s and police departments, and the presence of some largely unenforceable statutes currently on the books (it is the reality of "compliance": no law can be forced on a public which chooses to ignore it; hence, selective prosecution) make for a criminal justice system which cannot realistically function in a fair and equitable manner. Criminal justice—I cannot decide if it is the ultimate oxymoron or a truly accurate description of the law enforcement process in America.

In my police undercover capacity, I have sat across the table   29
from an armed robber who said, "My philosophy of life is slit thy neighbor's throat and pimp his kids." I believe that the human animals who maim and kill people should be dealt with, as they say, swiftly and surely. But this business of locking people up, at enormous cost, for minor, nonviolent offenses does not truly or effectively serve the interest of the people. It serves only to promote the wasteful aspects of the federal prison system, a system that gulps down tax dollars and spews up *Let's Make a Deal!*

I think about Lexington almost daily. I will be walking up   30
Broadway to shop for groceries, or maybe riding my bike in the original Central Park, and suddenly I'm wondering who's in there now, at this very moment, and for what inane violations, and what they are doing. Is it chow time, is the Big Yard open, is some inmate on stage in the auditorium singing "As Time Goes By" in a talent show? It is not a fond reminiscence or a desire to be back in the Land of No Decisions. It is an awareness of the waste. The waste of tax dollars, yes, but taxpayers are used to that. It is the unnecessary trashing of lives that leaves me uneasy. The splitting of families, the enforced monotony, the programs which purport to prepare an inmate for re-entry into society but which actually succeed only in occupying a few more hours of the inmate's time behind the walls. The nonviolent offenders, such as small-time drug dealers and the economically deprived who were driven to crime out of desperation, could remain in society under less costly supervision, still undergoing "punishment" for their crime, but at least contributing to rather than draining the resources of society.

Horace, who was not a subtle sort of fellow, had some tee   31
shirts made up. They were delivered by our usual supplier out in Landscape, and we wore them back in over our regular clothes. The hacks tilted their heads when they noticed, but said nothing.

On the front of each shirt was an outline of the state of Kentucky, and above the northwest corner of the state were the words "Visit Beautiful Kentucky!" Inside the state boundary were:

- Free Accommodations
- Complimentary Meals
- Management Holds Calls
- Recreational Exercise

In small letters just outside the southwest corner of the state was: "Length of Stay Requirement." And in big letters across the bottom:

Take Time to Do Time
F.C.I. Lexington

I gave mine away on the day I finished my sentence. It is a   32
time-honored tradition to leave some of your belongings to friends who have to stay behind when you are released. But you must never leave shoes. Legend has it that if you do, you will come back to wear them again.

UNDERSTANDING DETAILS

1. Draw Lexington prison and put the names on the sections of the facility. Then, describe each section in your own words.
2. Why was walking around the outside of Central Park "like taking a trip in microcosm across the United States" (paragraph 4)? Give examples to explain your answer.
3. Why was Wozencraft especially fond of Shorty? What secret did they share at the beginning of the author's prison term?
4. Does the author feel she had been unfairly punished by being sent to prison? What had she done wrong?

ANALYZING MEANING

1. What was Wozencraft's attitude toward other people in Lexington prison? Why do you think she felt this way? What types of relationships did she have with inmates and staff members?
2. Why does the author say, "If the taxpayers knew how their dollars were being spent inside some prisons, they might actu-

ally scream out loud" (paragraph 20)? What exactly is she referring to? What is she implying? Give some examples.

3. Why do you think Lexington is known as a "country club" prison? What features of the prison might have brought about its nickname?

4. Wozencraft feels strongly that people who perform minor, nonviolent crimes should not be put in prison. Why does she feel this way? Who should be locked up according to the author? From her point of view, how does rehabilitation take place?

DISCOVERING RHETORICAL STRATEGIES

1. This essay is organized predominantly as a clockwise tour of Lexington prison. How and when does Wozencraft introduce the facts about her own imprisonment and her opinions about the current American system of justice? Explain in as much detail as you can the effect of integrating the guided tour and the related facts and opinions.

2. Wozencraft uses specific prison jargon throughout this essay. In what way does this jargon add to or detract from the essay? What effect would the essay have without this jargon?

3. Wozencraft ends her essay with an explanation of "a time-honored tradition." Is this an effective ending for the piece? Why or why not?

4. Though spatial description is the dominant rhetorical strategy the author uses in this essay to accomplish her purpose, what other strategies help make the essay effective? Give examples of these strategies.

MAKING CONNECTIONS

1. If Kimberly Wozencraft, Ellen Goodman ("A Working Community"), and Richard Rodriguez ("The Fear of Losing a Culture") were discussing the importance of belonging to a "community," which author would argue most strongly that community is a positive force in our lives? Explain your answer.

2. Malcolm Cowley ("The View from 80"), Harold Krents ("Darkness at Noon"), and the terminally ill in "Accidents, Suicide, and Euthanasia" (Sherwin Nuland) all feel imprisoned

in much the same way Wozencraft does in her essay. In what way is each of these authors "confined?" Have you ever felt imprisoned for any reason? Why? How did you escape?

3. What would Wozencraft, Germaine Greer ("A Child Is Born"), and/or William Ouchi ("Japanese and American Workers: Two Casts of Mind") have to say about the importance of relying on other people to help endure difficult or challenging situations? How much do you rely on friends and relatives in your own life? How comfortable are you with these relationships?

IDEAS FOR DISCUSSION/WRITING

Preparing to Write

Write freely about your memories of a recent difficult or awkward situation in your life: What were the circumstances? What did you do? What did others do? How did you relate to others in this situation? Why was the situation so difficult? How did you get out of it?

Choosing a Topic

1. Write an essay describing for your peers a difficult or awkward situation you have been in recently. Why was it awkward? Explain the specific circumstances so that your classmates can clearly imagine the setting and the difficulty or problem. Then, discuss your reaction to the situation.

2. A friend of yours has just been sentenced to prison for one year. Write a letter to this person describing what you think his or her biggest adjustments will be.

3. Wozencraft describes many problems within the prison system. With these problems in mind, write a letter to the editor of your local newspaper discussing whether prisons actually rehabilitate criminals. Use examples from Wozencraft's essay to help make your point.

Before beginning your essay, you might want to consult the checklists on pages 51–53.

The Pines

The range of subjects investigated by author John McPhee is quite astounding. In his twenty books and numerous articles, he has written about sports, food, art, geology, geography, science, history, education, and a variety of other topics. One of the most famous of these "non-fictional, book-length narratives," as he calls them, is *A Sense of Where You Are* (1965), a study of former basketball great Bill Bradley; another is *Levels of the Game* (1969), a chronicle of the epic 1968 U.S. Open semifinal tennis match between Arthur Ashe and Clark Graebner. Most of McPhee's essays have appeared first in the *New Yorker*, a prestigious literary magazine for which he has been a staff writer since 1965. His more recent publications include *In Suspect Terrain* (1983), *La Place de la Concorde Suisse* (1984), *Table of Contents* (1985), *Rising from the Plains* (1986), *The Control of Nature* (1989), *Looking for a Ship* (1990), *Assembling California* (1993), *The Ransom of Russian Art* (1994), *The Second John McPhee Reader* (1996), *Irons in the Fire* (1997), and *Annals of the Former World* (1998), which was awarded the Pulitzer Prize in 1999. "What all these pieces of writing have in common," according to the author, "is that they are about real people and real places. All the different topics are just milieus in which to sketch people and places." McPhee lives in New Jersey near Princeton University, where he teaches a seminar entitled "The Literature of Fact." His hobbies include going on long bike rides, fishing for shad and pickerel, and skiing.

Preparing to Read

The following essay, "The Pines," is a small section from a longer piece called *The Pine Barrens* (1968), which describes a remote wilderness in southern New Jersey. Like many of McPhee's narrative essays, "The Pines" is structured around a single colorful character—in this case, Fred Brown, a talkative backwoods native whose simple surroundings and quaint mannerisms speak well for the solitary life. In contrast, Brown's friend Bill Wasovwich is almost painfully shy; he is a person (like McPhee himself, some critics tell us) who speaks little, listens intently, and observes the world around him with great care. Both men worry openly about the encroaching civilization that threatens their unique way of life. As you prepare to read this essay, think for a moment about the different types of people you know: Do you have talkative friends? Quiet friends? Which type of person is most appealing to you? Which type are you? Have you ever lived in the woods? What are the principal advantages of living in a rural environment rather than in a big city? What are the disadvantages?

Fred Brown's house is on an unpaved road that curves along   1
the edge of a wide cranberry bog. What attracted me to it
was the pump that stands in his yard. It was something of a wonder that I noticed the pump, because there were, among other things, eight automobiles in the yard, two of them on their sides and one of them upside down, all ten years old or older. Around the cars were old refrigerators, vacuum cleaners, partly dismantled radios, cathode-ray tubes, a short wooden ski, a large wooden mallet, dozens of cranberry picker's boxes, many tires, an orange crate dated 1946, a cord or so of firewood, mandolins, engine heads, and maybe a thousand other things. The house itself, two stories high, was covered with tarpaper that was peeling away in some places, revealing its original shingles, made of Atlantic white cedar from the stream courses of the surrounding forest. I called out to ask if anyone was home, and a voice inside called back, "Come in. Come in. Come on the hell in."

I walked through a vestibule that had a dirt floor, stepped up   2
into a kitchen, and went on into another room that had several overstuffed chairs in it and a porcelain-topped table, where Fred Brown was seated, eating a pork chop. He was dressed in a white sleeveless shirt, ankle-top shoes, and undershorts. He gave me a cheerful greeting and, without asking why I had come or what I wanted, picked up a pair of khaki trousers that had been tossed onto one of the overstuffed chairs and asked me to sit down. He set the trousers on another chair, and he apologized for being in the middle of his breakfast, explaining that he seldom drank much but the night before he had had a few drinks and this had caused his day to start slowly. "I don't know what's the matter with me, but there's got to be something the matter with me, because drink don't agree with me anymore," he said. He had a raw onion in one hand, and while he talked he shaved slices from the onion

and ate them between bites of the chop. He was a muscular and well-built man, with short, bristly white hair, and he had bright, fast-moving eyes in a wide-open face. His legs were trim and strong, with large muscles in the calves. I guessed that he was about sixty, and for a man of sixty he seemed to be in remarkably good shape. He was actually seventy-nine. "My rule is: Never eat except when you're hungry," he said, and he ate another slice of the onion.

In a straight-backed chair near the doorway to the kitchen sat a   3 young man with long black hair, who wore a visored red leather cap that had darkened with age. His shirt was coarse-woven and had eyelets down a V neck that was laced with a thong. His trousers were made of canvas, and he was wearing gum boots. His arms were folded, his legs were stretched out, he had one ankle over the other, and as he sat there he appeared to be sighting carefully past his feet, as if his toes were the outer frame of a gun-sight and he could see some sort of target in the floor. When I had entered, I had said hello to him, and he had nodded without looking up. He had a long, straight nose and high cheekbones, in a deeply tanned face that was, somehow, gaunt. I had no idea whether he was shy or hostile. Eventually, when I came to know him, I found him to be as shy a person as I have ever had a chance to know. His name is Bill Wasovwich, and he lives alone in a cabin about half a mile from Fred. First his father, then his mother left him when he was a young boy, and he grew up depending on the help of various people in the pines. One of them, a cranberry grower, employs him and has given him some acreage, in which Bill is building a small cranberry bog of his own, "turfing it out" by hand. When he is not working in the bogs, he goes roaming, as he puts it, setting out cross-country on long, looping journeys, hiking about thirty miles in a typical day, in search of what he calls "events"—surprising a buck, or a gray fox, or perhaps a poacher or a man with a still. Almost no one who is not native to the pines could do this, for the woods have an undulating same-ness, and the understory—huckleberries, sheep laurel, sweet fern, high-bush blueberry—is often so dense that a wanderer can walk in a fairly tight circle and think that he is moving in a straight line. State forest rangers spend a good part of their time finding hikers and hunters, some of whom have vanished for days. In his long, pathless journeys, Bill always emerges from the woods near his cabin—and about when he plans to. In the fall, when thousands of hunters come into the pines, he sometimes works as a guide. In the evenings, or in the daytime when he is not working or roaming, he goes to Fred Brown's house and sits there for hours. The old man is a widower whose seven children are long since gone from Hog Wallow, and he is as expansively talkative and worldly as the young one is withdrawn and wild. Although there are fifty-three years between their ages, it is obviously fortunate for each of them to be the other's neighbor.

That first morning, while Bill went on looking at his out-   4
stretched toes, Fred got up from the table, put on his pants, and said he was going to cook me a pork chop, because I looked hungry and ought to eat something. It was about noon, and I was even hungrier than I may have looked, so I gratefully accepted his offer, which was a considerable one. There are two or three small general stores in the pines, but for anything as fragile as a fresh pork chop it is necessary to make a round trip from Fred's place of about fifty miles. Fred went into the kitchen and dropped a chop into a frying pan that was crackling with hot grease. He has a fairly new four-burner stove that uses bottled gas. He keeps water in a large bowl on a table in the kitchen and ladles some when he wants it. While he cooked the meat, he looked out a window through a stand of pitch pines and into the cranberry bog. "I saw a big buck out here last night with velvet on his horns," he said. "Them horns is soft when they're in velvet." On a nail high on one wall of the room that Bill and I were sitting in was a large meat cleaver. Next to it was a billy club. The wall itself was papered in a flower pattern, and the wallpaper continued out across the ceiling and down the three other walls, lending the room something of the appearance of the inside of a gift box. In some parts of the ceiling, the paper had come loose. "I didn't paper this year," Fred said. "For the last couple months, I've had sinus." The floor was covered with old rugs. They had been put down in random pieces, and in some places as many as six layers were stacked up. In winter, when the temperature approaches zero, the worst cold comes through the floor. The only source of heat in the house is a wood-burning stove in the main room. There were seven calendars on the walls, all current and none with pictures of nudes. Fading into pastel on one wall was a rotogravure photograph of President and Mrs. Eisenhower. A framed poem read:

God hath not promised
Sun without rain
Joy without sorrow
Peace without pain.

Noticing my interest in all this, Fred reached into a drawer and   5
showed me what appeared to be a postcard. On it was a photograph of a woman, and Fred said with a straight face that she was
his present girl, adding that he meets her regularly under a juniper
tree on a road farther south in the pines. The woman, whose appearance suggested strongly that she had never been within a great
many miles of the Pine Barrens, was wearing nothing at all.

I asked Fred what all those cars were doing in his yard, and he   6
said that one of them was in running condition and the rest were
its predecessors. The working vehicle was a 1956 Mercury. Each
of the seven others had at one time or another been his best car,
and each, in turn, had lain down like a sick animal and had died
right there in the yard, unless it had been towed home after a
mishap elsewhere in the pines. Fred recited, with affection, the
history of each car. Of one old Ford, for example, he said, "I
upset that up to Speedwell in the creek." And of an even older
car, a station wagon, he said, "I busted that one up in the snow. I
met a car on a little hill, and hit the brake, and hit a tree." One of
the cars had met its end at a narrow bridge about four miles from
Hog Wallow, where Fred had hit a state trooper, head on.

The pork was delicious and almost crisp. Fred gave me a potato   7
with it and a pitcher of melted grease from the frying pan to pour
over the potato. He also handed me a loaf of bread and a dish of
margarine, saying, "Here's your bread. You can have one piece or
two. Whatever you want."

Fred apologized for not having a phone, after I asked where I   8
would have to go to make a call, later on. He said, "I don't have
no phone because I don't have no electric. If I had electric, I
would have had a phone in here a long time ago." He uses a
kerosene lamp, a propane lamp, and two flashlights.

He asked where I was going, and I said that I had no particular   9
destination, explaining that I was in the pines because I found it
hard to believe that so much unbroken forest could still exist so
near the big Eastern cities, and I wanted to see it while it was still

there. "Is that so?" he said, three times. Like many people in the pines, he often says things three times. "Is that so? Is *that* so?"

I asked him what he thought of a plan that has been developed   10
by Burlington and Ocean Counties to create a supersonic jetport in the pines, connected by a spur of the Garden State Parkway to a new city of two hundred and fifty thousand people, also in the pines.

"They've been talking about that for three years, and they've   11
never given up," Fred said.

"It'd be the end of these woods," Bill said. This was the first   12
time I heard Bill speak. I had been there for an hour, and he had not said a word. Without looking up, he said again, "It'd be the end of these woods, I can tell you that."

Fred said, "They could build ten jetports around me. I wouldn't   13
give a damn."

"You ain't going to be around very long," Bill said to him. "It   14
would be the end of these woods."

Fred took that as a fact, and not as an insult. "Yes, it would be   15
the end of these woods," he said. "But there'd be people here you could do business with."

Bill said, "There ain't no place like this left in the country, I   16
don't believe—and I travelled around a little bit, too."

Eventually, I made the request I had intended to make when I   17
walked in the door. "Could I have some water?" I said to Fred. "I have a jerry can, and I'd like to fill it at the pump."

"Hell, yes," he said. "That isn't my water. That's God's water.   18
That right, Bill?"

"I *guess* so," Bill said, without looking up. "It's good water, I   19
can tell you that."

"That's God's water," Fred said again. "Take all you want."   20

UNDERSTANDING DETAILS

1. What attracted McPhee to Fred Brown's house? In what ways is this object representative of Fred's yard? Of Fred's life?
2. What other things are in Fred's front yard? What does this collection of junk say about Fred and his lifestyle?
3. In paragraph 3, McPhee comments that, despite the wide difference in age between Fred and Bill, "it is obviously fortunate

for each of them to be the other's neighbor." In what ways do the two characters need each other?

4. Describe in your own words the inside of Fred's house. Which details does McPhee stress in his description? Why does he focus on these and not on others?

ANALYZING MEANING

1. Why is McPhee visiting "the pines"? What do you think his opinion of "the pines" is? What specific references reveal his opinions?
2. Why does Bill go "roaming"? What do you think the purpose of these journeys is?
3. Why does Bill believe a jetport would be "the end of these woods" (paragraph 12)? Why do you think these were the first words Bill had spoken since the author arrived? Explain your answer.
4. Why do you think McPhee ends this piece with several references to God? How does the dialogue about "God's water" help us understand Fred and Bill even more specifically?

DISCOVERING RHETORICAL STRATEGIES

1. Which senses does McPhee concentrate on most in this description? Choose one paragraph to analyze. In one column, write down all the senses the description arouses; in another, record the words and phrases that activate these senses.
2. What "tone" or "mood" is McPhee trying to create in this excerpt? Is he successful? Explain your answer.
3. What is the author's "point of view" in this essay? How would the method of description change if the story were told from Fred's vantage point? From Bill's? How does this particular point of view help the author organize his description?
4. McPhee relies heavily on description to make his point. What other rhetorical modes support this narrative essay? Give examples of each of these modes from the essay.

MAKING CONNECTIONS

1. How does the friendship between Fred and Bill described in McPhee's essay differ from friendships in Kimberly Wozen-craft's "Notes from the Country Club" and/or Robert

Ramirez's "The Barrio"? Which friendships are stronger in your opinion? Explain your answer.

2. Compare and contrast McPhee's concern about preserving the environment with similar feelings of Susan Austin ("Land and Bones"). How are they similar? How are they different?

3. In McPhee's essay, how does Fred Brown feel about the uses and abuses of technology? Would Geoffrey Meredith ("The Demise of Writing") or Mitchell Stephens ("The Death of Reading") agree with him? Explain your answer.

IDEAS FOR DISCUSSION/WRITING

Preparing to Write

Write freely about someone you know who represents a specific personality "type": What distinguishes this type from other types you know? What do people of this type have in common? What are their looks, values, needs, desires, living conditions, and so on? What do you have in common with the type of person you have just described? How are you different?

Choosing a Topic

1. Give a name (either real or fictitious) to the person you have just described in the prewriting exercise, and write an essay depicting the house, apartment, or room in which this person lives. Try to make your description as vivid and as well organized as McPhee's portrait of Fred Brown. Imagine that the audience for your description is someone who has never met this person and has never seen where the person lives.

2. Write an essay describing for your classmates some of the "junk" you have collected over the years. Why are certain items junk to some people and treasures to others? What makes the things you are describing special to you?

3. Describe the inside of your house, apartment, or room, explaining to your class what the decorations say about you as a person. If someone in your class were to see where you live, could he or she make any accurate deductions about your political, social, or moral values based upon the contents and arrangement of the place you call "home"?

Before beginning your essay, you might want to consult the checklists on pages 51–53.

The View from 80

Malcolm Cowley had a long and distinguished career as a literary historian, critic, editor, and poet. After receiving his bachelor's degree at Harvard, he served in the American Ambulance Corps during World War I, then pursued graduate studies in literature at the University of Montpellier in France. In 1929, he became associate editor of *The New Republic*, presiding over the magazine's literary department for the next fifteen years. Perhaps his most important book of literary criticism is *Exile's Return* (1934), a study of the "lost generation" of expatriate Americans living in Paris in the 1920s, which included Ernest Hemingway, Ezra Pound, F. Scott Fitzgerald, and Hart Crane. Cowley returned to the same topic in 1973 with *A Second Flowering: Works and Days of the Lost Generation*. He also published editions of such authors as Hemingway, William Faulkner, Nathaniel Hawthorne, Walt Whitman, and Fitzgerald; two collections of his own poetry, *Blue Juniata* (1929) and *The Dry Season* (1941); and numerous other translations, editions, and books of criticism. His most recent publications include *The Flower and the Leaf: A Contemporary Record of American Writing Since 1941* (1985) and *Conversations with Malcolm Cowley* (1986). Asked the secret of his amazing productivity, Cowley replied: "Writers often speak of 'saving their energy,' as if each man were given a nickel's worth of it, which he is at liberty to spend. To me, the mind of the poet resembles Fortunatus' purse: The more spent, the more it supplies."

Preparing to Read

The following essay was originally commissioned by *Life* magazine (1978) for inclusion in a series of articles on aging. Cowley later converted the piece into the first chapter of a book with the same title: *The View from 80* (1980). Through a combination of vivid personal experience and well-researched documentation, the author crafted an essay that helps us experience what life is like for an eighty-year-old man. As you prepare to read Cowley's description of "the country of age," take some time to think about age in general: How many people over the age of sixty do you know? Over the age of seventy? How do they behave? Do you think these older people see themselves in the same way you see them? Do you think they consider themselves "old"? What clues remind them of their advancing age? What events and attitudes remind you of your age? In what ways will you be different than you are now when you reach the age of eighty?

They gave me a party on my 80th birthday in August 1978. First there were cards, letters, telegrams, even a cable of congratulation or condolence; then there were gifts, mostly bottles; there was catered food and finally a big cake with, for some reason, two candles (had I gone back to very early childhood?). I blew the candles out a little unsteadily. Amid the applause and clatter I thought about a former custom of the Northern Ojibwas when they lived on the shores of Lake Winnipeg. They were kind to their old people, who remembered and enforced the ancient customs of the tribe, but when an old person became decrepit, it was time for him to go. Sometimes he was simply abandoned, with a little food, on an island in the lake. If he deserved special honor, they held a tribal feast for him. The old man sang a death song and danced, if he could. While he was still singing, his son came from behind and brained him with a tomahawk.

That was quick, it was dignified, and I wonder whether it was any more cruel, essentially, than some of our civilized customs or inadvertencies in disposing of the aged. I believe in rites and ceremonies. I believe in big parties for special occasions such as an 80th birthday. It is a sort of belated bar mitzvah, since the 80-year-old, like a Jewish adolescent, is entering a new stage of life; let him (or her) undergo a *rite de passage*, with toasts and a cantor. Seventy-year-olds, or septuas, have the illusion of being middle-aged, even if they have been pushed back on a shelf. The 80-year-old, the octo, looks at the double-dumpling figure and admits that he is old. The last act has begun, and it will be the test of the play.

To enter the country of age is a new experience, different from what you supposed it to be. Nobody, man or woman, knows the country until he has lived in it and has taken out his citizenship papers. Here is my own report, submitted as a road map and guide to some of the principal monuments.

The new octogenarian feels as strong as ever when he is sitting   4
back in a comfortable chair. He ruminates, he dreams, he remembers. He doesn't want to be disturbed by others. It seems to him
that old age is only a costume assumed for those others; the true,
the essential self is ageless. In a moment he will rise and go for a
ramble in the woods, taking a gun along, or a fishing rod, if it is
spring. Then he creaks to his feet, bending forward to keep his
balance, and realizes that he will do nothing of the sort. The body
and its surroundings have their messages for him, or only one
message: "You are old." Here are some of the occasions on which
he receives the message:

- when it becomes an achievement to do thoughtfully, step by
  step, what he once did instinctively
- when his bones ache
- when there are more and more little bottles in the medicine
  cabinet, with instructions for taking four times a day
- when he fumbles and drops his toothbrush (butterfingers)
- when his face has bumps and wrinkles, so that he cuts himself
  while shaving (blood on the towel)
- when year by year his feet seem farther from his hands
- when he can't stand on one leg and has trouble pulling on his
  pants
- when he hesitates on the landing before walking down a flight
  of stairs
- when he spends more time looking for things misplaced than
  he spends using them after he (or more often his wife) has
  found them
- when he falls asleep in the afternoon
- when it becomes harder to bear in mind two things at once
- when a pretty girl passes him in the street and he doesn't turn
  his head
- when he forgets names, even of people he saw last month
  ("Now I'm beginning to forget nouns," the poet Conrad
  Aiken said at 80)
- when he listens hard to jokes and catches everything but the
  snapper

- when he decides not to drive at night anymore
- when everything takes longer to do—bathing, shaving, getting dressed or undressed—but when time passes quickly, as if he were gathering speed while coasting downhill. The year from 79 to 80 is like a week when he was a boy.

Those are some of the intimate messages. "Put cotton in your ears and pebbles in your shoes," said a gerontologist, a member of that new profession dedicated to alleviating all maladies of old people except the passage of years. "Pull on rubber gloves. Smear Vaseline over your glasses, and there you have it: instant aging." Not quite. His formula omits the messages from the social world, which are louder, in most cases, than those from within. We start by growing old in other people's eyes, then slowly we come to share their judgment. 5

I remember a morning many years ago when I was backing out of the parking lot near the railroad station in Brewster, New York. There was a near collision. The driver of the other car jumped out and started to abuse me; he had his fists ready. Then he looked hard at me and said, "Why, you're an old man." He got back into his car, slammed the door, and drove away, while I stood there fuming. "I'm only 65," I thought. "He wasn't driving carefully. I can still take care of myself in a car, or in a fight, for that matter." 6

My hair was whiter—it may have been in 1974—when a young woman rose and offered me her seat in a Madison Avenue bus. That message was kind and also devastating. "Can't I even stand up?" I thought as I thanked her and declined the seat. But the same thing happened twice the following year, and the second time I gratefully accepted the offer, though with a sense of having diminished myself. "People are right about me," I thought while wondering why all those kind gestures were made by women. Do men now regard themselves as the weaker sex, not called upon to show consideration? All the same it was a relief to sit down and relax. 7

A few days later I wrote a poem, "The Red Wagon," that belongs in the record of aging: 8

> For his birthday they gave him a red express wagon
> with a driver's high seat and a handle that steered.

His mother pulled him around the yard.
"Giddyap," he said, but she laughed and went off
to wash the breakfast dishes.

"I wanta ride too," his sister said,
and he pulled her to the edge of a hill.
"Now, sister, go home and wait for me,
but first give a push to the wagon."
He climbed again to the high seat,
this time grasping that handle-that-steered.

The red wagon rolled slowly down the slope,
then faster as it passed the schoolhouse
and faster as it passed the store,
the road still dropping away.
Oh, it was fun.
But would it ever stop?
Would the road always go downhill?
The red wagon rolled faster.
Now it was in strange country.
It passed a white house he must have dreamed about,
deep woods he had never seen,
a graveyard where, something told him, his sister
was buried.

Far below
the sun was sinking into a broad plain.

The red wagon rolled faster.
Now he was clutching the seat, not even trying to steer.
Sweat clouded his heavy spectacles.
His white hair streamed in the wind.

Even before he or she is 80, the aging person may undergo an-   9
other identity crisis like that of adolescence. Perhaps there had
also been a middle-aged crisis, the male or the female menopause,
but the rest of adult life he had taken himself for granted, with his
capabilities and failings. Now, when he looks in the mirror, he
asks himself, "Is this really me?"—or he avoids the mirror out of
distress at what it reveals, those bags and wrinkles. In his new

•

makeup he is called upon to play a new role in a play that must be improvised. André Gide, that long-lived man of letters, wrote in his journal, "My heart has remained so young that I have the continual feeling of playing a part, the part of the 70-year-old that I certainly am; and the infirmities and weaknesses that remind me of my age act like a prompter, reminding me of my lines when I tend to stray. Then, like the good actor I want to be, I go back into my role, and I pride myself on playing it well."

In his new role the old person will find that he is tempted by   10
new vices, that he receives new compensations (not so widely known), and that he may possibly achieve new virtues. Chief among these is the heroic or merely obstinate refusal to surrender in the face of time. One admires the ships that go down with all flags flying and the captain on the bridge.

Among the vices of age are avarice, untidiness, and vanity, which   11
last takes the form of a craving to be loved or simply admired. Avarice is the worst of those three. Why do so many old persons, men and women alike, insist on hoarding money when they have no prospect of using it and even when they have no heirs? They eat the cheapest food, buy no clothes, and live in a single room when they could afford better lodging. It may be that they regard money as a form of power; there is a comfort in watching it accumulate while other powers are dwindling away. How often we read of an old person found dead in a hovel, on a mattress partly stuffed with bankbooks and stock certificates! The bankbook syndrome, we call it in our family, which has never succumbed.

Untidiness we call the Langley Collyer syndrome. To explain,   12
Langley Collyer was a former concert pianist who lived alone with his 70-year-old brother in a brownstone house on upper Fifth Avenue. The once fashionable neighborhood had become part of Harlem. Homer, the brother, had been an admiralty lawyer, but was now blind and partly paralyzed; Langley played for him and fed him on buns and oranges, which he thought would restore Homer's sight. He never threw away a daily paper because Homer, he said, might want to read them all. He saved other things as well and the house became filled with rubbish from roof to basement. The halls were lined on both sides with bundled newspapers, leaving narrow passageways in which Langley had devised booby traps to catch intruders.

On March 21, 1947, some unnamed person telephoned the   13
police to report that there was a dead body in the Collyer house.
The police broke down the front door and found the hall impass-
able; then they hoisted a ladder to a second-story window. Behind it Homer was lying on the floor in a bathrobe; he had
starved to death. Langley had disappeared. After some delay, the
police broke into the basement, chopped a hole in the roof, and
began throwing junk out of the house, top and bottom. It was 18
days before they found Langley's body, gnawed by rats. Caught in
one of his own booby traps, he had died in a hallway just outside
Homer's door. By that time the police had collected, and the Department of Sanitation had hauled away, 120 tons of rubbish, including, besides the newspapers, 14 grand pianos and the parts of
a dismantled Model T Ford.

Why do so many old people accumulate junk, not on the scale   14
of Langley Collyer, but still in a dismaying fashion? Their tables
are piled high with it, their bureau drawers are stuffed with it,
their closet rods bend with the weight of clothes not worn for
years. I suppose that the piling up is partly from lethargy and
partly from feeling that everything once useful, including their
own bodies, should be preserved. Others, though not so many,
have such a fear of becoming Langley Collyers that they strive to
be painfully neat. Every tool they own is in its place, though it
will never be used again; every scrap of paper is filed away in alphabetical order. At last their immoderate neatness becomes another vice of age, if a milder one.

The vanity of older people is an easier weakness to explain, and   15
to condone. With less to look forward to, they yearn for recognition of what they have been: the reigning beauty, the athlete, the
soldier, the scholar. It is the beauties who have the hardest time. A
portrait of themselves at twenty hangs on the wall, and they try to
resemble it by making an extravagant use of creams, powder, and
dyes. Being young at heart, they think they are merely revealing
their essential persons. The athletes find shelves for their silver trophies, which are polished once a year. Perhaps a letter sweater lies
wrapped in a bureau drawer. I remember one evening when a no-
longer athlete had guests for dinner and tried to find his sweater.
"Oh, that old thing," his wife said. "The moths got into it, and I
threw it away." The athlete sulked, and his guests went home early.

But there are also pleasures of the body, or the mind, that are   16
enjoyed by a greater number of older persons. Those pleasures include some that younger people find hard to appreciate. One of
them is simply sitting still, like a snake on a sunwarmed stone,
with a delicious feeling of indolence that was seldom attained in
earlier years. A leaf flutters down; a cloud moves by inches across
the horizon. At such moments the older person, completely relaxed, has become a part of nature—and a living part, with blood
coursing through his veins. The future does not exist for him. He
thinks, if he thinks at all, that life for younger persons is still a battle royal of each against each, but that now he has nothing more
to win or lose. He is not so much above as outside the battle, as if
he had assumed the uniform of some small neutral country, perhaps Liechtenstein or Andorra. From a distance he notes that
some of the combatants, men or women, are jostling ahead—but
why do they fight so hard when the most they can hope for is a
longer obituary? He can watch the scrounging and gouging, he
can hear the shouts of exultation, the moans of the gravely
wounded, and meanwhile he feels secure; nobody will attack him
from ambush.

Age has other physical compensations besides the nirvana of   17
dozing in the sun. A few of the simplest needs become a pleasure
to satisfy. When an old woman in a nursing home was asked what
she really liked to do she answered in one word: "Eat." She might
have been speaking for many of her fellows. Meals in a nursing
home, however badly cooked, serve as climactic moments of the
day. The physical essence of the pensioners is being renewed at an
appointed hour; now they can go back to meditating or to watching TV while looking forward to the next meal. They can also
look forward to sleep, which has become a definite pleasure, not
the mere interruption it once had been.

Here I am thinking of old persons under nursing care. Others   18
ferociously guard their independence, and some of them suffer
less than one might expect from being lonely and impoverished.
They can be rejoiced by visits and meetings, but they also have
company inside their heads. Some of them are busiest when their
hands are still. What passes through the minds of many is a stream
of persons, images, phrases, and familiar tunes. For some that
stream has continued since childhood, but now it is deeper; it is

their present and their past combined. At times they conduct silent dialogues with a vanished friend, and these are less tiring—often more rewarding—than spoken conversations. If inner resources are lacking, old persons living alone may seek comfort and a kind of companionship in the bottle. I should judge from the gossip of various neighborhoods that the outer suburbs from Boston to San Diego are full of secretly alcoholic widows. One of those widows, an old friend, was moved from her apartment into a retirement home. She left behind her a closet in which the floor was covered wall to wall with whiskey bottles. "Oh, those empty bottles!" she explained. "They were left by a former tenant."

Not whiskey or cooking sherry but simply giving up is the 19 greatest temptation of age. It is something different from a stoical acceptance of infirmities, which is something to be admired.

The givers-up see no reason for working. Sometimes they lie 20 in bed all day when moving about would still be possible, if difficult. I had a friend, a distinguished poet, who surrendered in that fashion. The doctors tried to stir him to action, but he refused to leave his room. Another friend, once a successful artist, stopped painting when his eyes began to fail. His doctor made the mistake of telling him that he suffered from a fatal disease. He then lost interest in everything except the splendid Rolls-Royce, acquired in his prosperous days, that stood in the garage. Daily he wiped the dust from its hood. He couldn't drive it on the road any longer, but he used to sit in the driver's seat, start the motor, then back the Rolls out of the garage and drive it in again, back twenty feet and forward twenty feet; that was his only distraction.

I haven't the right to blame those who surrender, not being 21 able to put myself inside their minds or bodies. Often they must have compelling reasons, physical or moral. Not only do they suffer from a variety of ailments, but also they are made to feel that they no longer have a function in the community. Their families and neighbors don't ask them for advice, don't really listen when they speak, don't call on them for efforts. One notes that there are not a few recoveries from apparent senility when that situation changes. If it doesn't change, old persons may decide that efforts are useless. I sympathize with their problems, but the men and women I envy are those who accept old age as a series of challenges.

For such persons, every new infirmity is an enemy to be outwit-   22
ted, an obstacle to be overcome by force of will. They enjoy each
little victory over themselves, and sometimes they win a major success. Renoir was one of them. He continued painting, and magnif-
icently, for years after he was crippled by arthritis; the brush had to
be strapped to his arm. "You don't need your hand to paint," he
said. Goya was another of the unvanquished. At 72 he retired as an
official painter of the Spanish court and decided to work only for
himself. His later years were those of the famous "black paintings"
in which he let his imagination run (and also of the lithographs, then
a new technique). At 78 he escaped a reign of terror in Spain by fleeing to Bordeaux. He was deaf, and his eyes were failing; in order to
work he had to wear several pairs of spectacles, one over another,
and then use a magnifying glass; but he was producing splendid
work in a totally new style. At 80 he drew an ancient man propped
on two sticks, with a mass of white hair and beard hiding his face and
with the inscription "I am still learning."

"Eighty years old!" the great Catholic poet Paul Claudel wrote   23
in his journal. "No eyes left, no ears, no teeth, no legs, no wind!
And when all is said and done, how astonishingly well one does
without them!"

UNDERSTANDING DETAILS

1. Name five ways, according to Cowley, that people begin to
   realize they are "old." How did Cowley himself learn that he
   was old?
2. List three vices of old age, and explain them as Cowley sees
   them.
3. What are three compensations of advancing age? In what ways
   are these activities pleasurable?
4. What does Cowley mean in paragraph 15 by "the vanity of
   older people"? How do older people manifest this vanity?

ANALYZING MEANING

1. What does the wagon symbolize in the author's poem about
   aging (paragraph 8)? What purpose does this poem serve in
   the essay?

2. For older people, what is the value of the conversations, images, friends, relatives, and melodies that pass through their minds? How might the elderly use these distractions constructively?
3. According to this essay, what qualities characterize those people who "surrender" (paragraph 21) to old age and those who "accept old age as a series of challenges" (paragraph 21)? Why do you think Cowley has more respect for the latter group?
4. What is Cowley's general attitude toward "the country of age"? Why does he feel that way about this stage of life?

DISCOVERING RHETORICAL STRATEGIES

1. After reading this essay, try to summarize in a single word or phrase Cowley's impressions of old age. How does this dominant impression help the author organize the many different details presented in his essay?
2. Why did Cowley include the reference to the Ojibwas at the end of the first paragraph? What effect does that anecdote have on our sympathies as readers?
3. Cowley uses a number of distinct metaphors in describing old age. He equates being old, for example, with acting out a certain "role" in life. He also portrays aging as a "rite of passage," a "challenge," and an "unfamiliar country" through which we must travel. In what sense is each of these metaphors appropriate? How does each help us understand the process of growing old?
4. Cowley uses language to describe a state of being that most of us are not familiar with yet. What other rhetorical strategies does he call upon to make his descriptive essay effective? Give examples of each.

MAKING CONNECTIONS

1. What are the primary differences among the "ageism" recounted by Malcolm Cowley, the racism explained by Lewis Sawaquat ("For My Indian Daughter"), and/or the sexism described by Sandra Cisneros ("Only daughter") and Judy Brady ("Why I Want a Wife")? Is one of these "isms" more dangerous than the others? Have you ever experienced any of these types of prejudice?

2. Compare and contrast the weaknesses of old age depicted in Cowley's essay with those portrayed by the grandfather in Ray Bradbury's "Summer Rituals" or by Fred Brown in John McPhee's "The Pines." Do you know anyone in his or her eighties? How does that person act? How do you think you will behave when you are that old?

3. How is Cowley's description of the "identity crisis" many older people go through similar to the identity crisis Lewis Sawaquat ("For My Indian Daughter") suffered when he discovered his Native American heritage and Richard Rodriguez ("The Fear of Losing a Culture") went through when he immigrated to America? Have you ever gone through an identity crisis? How did you resolve it? Was your crisis like those described by Cowley, Sawaquat, or Rodriguez in any way?

IDEAS FOR DISCUSSION/WRITING

Preparing to Write

Write freely about your impressions of one or more older people in your life: Who are they? What characteristics do they share? How are they different from each other? Different from you? Similar to you? How do you know they are "old"?

Choosing a Topic

1. Cowley explains at the outset of his essay that "the country of age is a new experience, different from what you supposed it to be. Nobody, man or woman, knows the country until he has lived in it and has taken out his citizenship papers" (paragraph 3). Interview an older person to discover his or her view of "the country of age." Then write an essay for your peers describing that person's opinions.

2. In his essay, Cowley describes the signals he receives from his body and his environment that tell him he is "old." What messages did you receive when you were young that indicated you were a "child"? What messages do you receive now that remind you of your present age? How are these messages different from those you received when you were a child? Describe these signals in a well-developed essay addressed to your classmates.

3. Do you think that Americans treat their aged with enough respect? Explain your answer in detail to an older person. Describe various situations that support your opinion.

Before beginning your essay, you might want to consult the checklists on pages 51–53.

SUSAN AUSTIN   (1961-   )

Land and Bones

Born in the scenic Monterey coastal area of California, Susan Austin moved frequently during her youth because her father was in the military. After graduating from high school in the San Francisco Bay area, she earned a B.S. at Texas A&M University in Wildlife and Fishery Science, then began a diverse series of jobs working as a field biologist on remote atolls in the Northwestern Hawaiian Islands chain, a fisheries observer monitoring Japanese catches in the Bering Sea, a carpenter's helper, and a species preservation specialist working with bald eagles and red-tailed hawks in Idaho. She became interested in writing as a career after taking a children's literature class and publishing several natural history articles for young readers. Currently an MFA student in fiction and poetry at the James A. Michener Center for Writers at the University of Texas at Austin, she explains that she has recently and unexpectedly "fallen in love with language," which allows her to express herself in new and exciting ways. A hiker, mountain bike enthusiast, and a cross-country skier, she admits that she is "not your classic writer," having come late to the profession from an entirely different background. Her advice to college students is to "let your mind be like Wyoming: an open range for ideas. And above all, read good literature." Since Austin herself has now returned to the world of a college student, she hopes her ex-ample will serve as an inspiration to everyone using *The Prose Reader*.

Preparing to Read

In the following selection, Austin describes "hard winters" in North Dakota. As you prepare to read Austin's description, take a few moments to think about a location in nature that is particularly memorable for you: What physical characteristics does this place have? Do you find it pleasant or unpleasant? Are you happy or sad when you think about it? What are some sights, smells, tastes, sounds, or textures you associate with this location? What other associations do you have with this place?

T he snow drifts onto the roof on the north side of the 1 cabin. The fire crackles hot. I plug the notebook computer into the two deep cycle batteries with an automobile adapter then sit in the big chair and put my feet up on the bed, so the winter air that rises between the floorboards doesn't chill my toes.

Two brothers, Karl and Miles, built this fourteen by twenty- 2 eight foot cabin in 1906. The logs they hewed by hand. No family here to tell their stories. The last old-timer who knew the brothers talks about courting in the heart of winter on a horse-drawn sleigh. She sings, "Sleigh bells ring, are you list'nin'?" She says lips were too cold to form a kiss. Hard winters are what all the old-timers talk about.

Greg's mother knows of winter not so far from here. She 3 comes from Dakota pioneers. In the winter of 1922, in Bathgate, North Dakota, her mother, Mary Jane McAulay, went next door to a ladies' party. A flurry of snow drifting like soft down feathers became a blizzard. Francis McAulay went out in the storm to help his Mary Jane home, leaving their three small children behind. He didn't know that Mary Jane was already on her way, guided by the picket fence that separated the two houses. Francis floundered for hours as snow lifted from old drifts and made new ones in his path.

Lost to the fence, to the house, and to Mary Jane, he vowed 4 that if he got home and found his family safe, they would never spend another winter in North Dakota. The following year, before the days turned cold and the light dimmed early, Francis McAulay moved his family to Kelso, Washington.

I wonder sometimes what the brothers who built this cabin 5 might have thought of my computer. Greg's mother said, "I'm almost sure they wouldn't have been envious." I don't think so either. The brothers carved a field and hewed a cabin and didn't ask for much more. They farmed with a horse-drawn plow long after motorized tractors tilled the neighbor's land. In 1954, when the horses were too old to work and the brothers too old to train a new team, they bought a used '53 Ford tractor. They shortened the tongues and replaced the hitches on the drill. The new Ford pulled the old farm equipment through the soil. Sentinels, now the drills, their rust polished smooth by weather, stand at the edge of the fields alongside piles of hand-picked stone.

What am I envious of? I don't need flush toilets, electric lights,   6
or a plowed road in winter. All things that do not exist at the old
boys' cabin.

I'm envious of the brothers, of this land as they knew it. Peo-   7
ple ask, "What's the hardest part of living out here?" Acre by
acre, season by season, realtor by realtor: "Watching it go," I
answer.

Come winter, when Greg and I are dwarfed by the mountains   8
and a quarter section of deep snow fields, edged into the forest, I
like to believe that only the weather can change the homestead,
wear it to dust by wind and rain and snow. First the brittle chink-
ing will fall out in places and the wind will bore wider holes.
Then snow piles inside in drifts; rain seeps and blows through.
The wood will rot and the cabin will become a marmot house,
with straw and fuzz from our winter hats matted in mouse nests.
The foundation may settle too much in a fast spring melt, and the
cabin will lean to the north, then topple by wind. Bare bones
bleached and scattered, like the cow moose who lay down in the
aspen grove, leaving last year's young to fend off winter-starved
coyotes just two weeks before the snow eased. The calf was smart
to leave the rot of its mother. Coyotes and ravens and one bald
eagle finished her off, scattered the bones.

One winter I went to the outer banks of North Carolina to re-   9
mind myself how the ocean eats up roads, clears and dumps sand
where it pleases, untamed. When I was a child, I walked to the
beach on toughened feet with tar babies smeared in patches on
my soles. I usually brought something, towel or surfboard,
dropped or dragged, catching on sea grass and dried fence slats.
When I was this child, I knew the tide and the surf just by the
sound of the waves, by their lazy roll or thunder as they broke at
the wet sand, and the ground shuddered under my tarred feet.

I have taken this new land into my bones. How did it happen?   10
I walked a lot at first across the open fields, down along the gul-
lies, the creek bottoms, into the woods. I watched, listened. Then
a new sense seeped in. And one winter night I found my way
home by the feel of the land.

I had driven to the end of the plowed road and parked next to   11
the dovetailed pine granary. I was tired and warm for a moment. I

thought I would stay there, curled on the truck seat, and sleep. But the cold quickly chilled my blood. I lifted the pack to my back and gathered the energy I needed to ski the two and a half miles home.

Under a new moon, dense fog meeting snow, I skied into the   12 colder air that settles in the creek bottom. I felt my way along the road, cut drifts that soften into low hills on either side. The sharp corner of the dugway reminded me of the etched curve of Greg's hip. Instead of hurrying to his warm covers, I lingered. The scent of moose lingered, too, on the still air. Coyotes sang. When the coyotes quieted, I heard the faint hoot of a great horned owl.

Across the flat upper field, I wandered off track, circled the   13 chicken coop and the dog's shed. Then I reached out into the fog and touched the sawdust and splinter chink and hand-hewn logs of the cabin. Out of absolute darkness I finally felt what the old boys must have known—the dips and contours and flat reaches, with no other guidance than the familiar sway of the land through their bones.

UNDERSTANDING DETAILS

1. What does the phrase "land and bones" refer to in this essay? Look especially at the last sentence.
2. List two sights, two smells, two tastes, two sounds, and two textures that Austin recalls from her experiences in North Dakota. How do these sensual details help the reader experience the place the author describes?
3. In what ways is this place beautiful? In what ways is it stark?
4. What is Austin's dominant impression?

ANALYZING MEANING

1. Why does North Dakota hold special memories for the author? Explain your answer.
2. What significance does the snow have in Austin's memory?
3. Why did Francis McAulay vow that he would never spend another winter in North Dakota?
4. What does Austin mean when she says, "I like to believe that only the weather can change the homestead" (paragraph 8)?

DISCOVERING RHETORICAL STRATEGIES

1. This descriptive essay contains several different characters. What is the narrator's relationship to each of them? Why do you think Austin brings each into her description?
2. Using vivid details throughout her description, the narrator engages our senses as often as possible. Reread paragraph 12. Then list in one column all the senses mentioned and, in another, the words that arouse those senses.
3. How does Austin use words and details to change the tone of her writing at key points in this essay?
4. Although this essay moves forward predominantly through description, what other traditional rhetorical modes support Austin's dominant impression? Give examples of each of these modes in the essay.

MAKING CONNECTIONS

1. Examine the "sense of place" described by Susan Austin, John McPhee ("The Pines"), Robert Ramirez ("The Barrio"), and Ellen Goodman ("A Working Community"). Which of these authors feels most connected to his or her special place? Which is the least connected? Why?
2. Compare and contrast the way the following authors use description in their essays: Susan Austin, Ray Bradbury ("Summer Rituals"), and Kimberly Wozencraft ("Notes from the Country Club"). Which essay seems most "real" to you? Why?
3. Both Susan Austin and Annie Dillard ("Living Like Weasels") have an acute reverence for nature. Both, we might say, "feel it in their bones." Which author would you most like to spend a day with touring the territory she describes in her essay? Why is this author (and this particular place) especially appealing to you?

IDEAS FOR DISCUSSION/WRITING

Preparing to Write

Write freely for a few minutes about a place that is special to you: What are some of the strongest memories of the sights, smells, tastes, sounds, and textures you associate with this place?

Who else knows about this place? What are your feelings about it?

Choosing a Topic

1. Based on your sensory memories, write a descriptive essay about this special place for a friend of yours who has never been there. Decide on a dominant impression you want to communicate to your friend and a perspective that will help create that impression.
2. Describe for your classmates your favorite game. How many can play? What are the rules? When is the game most exciting? Why do you like this game?
3. Using your imagination, travel back in time to a particular moment or event in your past. Write an essay describing in detail what you were seeing, smelling, tasting, hearing, and touching at that time in your life. Where were you? How old were you? What was happening at this precise moment in your past? What exactly were you doing? How did you feel while you were engaged in this activity? Who else was in the scene with you? Did you feel safe? Secure? Happy? Sad? Anxious to escape? Free?

Before beginning your essay, you might want to consult the checklists on pages 51–53.

CHAPTER WRITING ASSIGNMENTS
Practicing Description

1. Write a spatial description of your home by exploring its basic sections or rooms. What does your home reveal about you as a person? About your family?
2. Think about the extent to which influences such as family, education, and community have contributed to the person you are today. Describe the kind of person you are and the sources of a few of your most important qualities.
3. Consider the health of the environment in your immediate community (air, noise, landscape). Describe an environmental problem you have observed. Be sure to provide examples of the problem you are describing.

Exploring Ideas

1. Discuss a cultural icon (like a rock star or a prominent building) and what it represents about the culture you are describing. How did this person or object become an icon in its culture? What biases or ideals does it express? How do people outside this culture view it?
2. Think about the ways people's physical surroundings (office, weather, house, apartment) affect them. Discuss one important way these surroundings have influenced someone's behavior. Provide examples in your discussion that explore the relationship between various features in your surroundings and the manner in which people react to them.
3. In your opinion, how well are elderly people treated in America? Write an essay describing the level of respect older people get in American society. Use examples of people you know to support your ideas.

2

NARRATION

Telling a Story

A good story is a powerful method of getting someone's attention. The excitement that accompanies a suspenseful ghost story, a lively anecdote, or a vivid joke easily attests to this fact. In fact, narration is one of the earliest verbal skills we all learn as children, providing us with a convenient, logical, and easily understood means of sharing our thoughts with other people. Storytelling is powerful because it offers us a way of dramatizing our ideas so that others can identify with them.

DEFINING NARRATION

Narration involves telling a story that is often based on personal experience. Stories can be oral or written, real or imaginary, short or long. A good story, however, always has a point or purpose. It can be the dominant mode (as in a novel or short story), supported by other rhetorical strategies, or it can serve the purpose of another rhetorical mode (as in a persuasive essay, a historical survey, or a scientific report).

In its subordinate role, narration can provide examples or explain ideas. If asked why you are attending college, for instance, you might turn to narration to make your answer clear, beginning with a story about your family's hardships in the past. The purpose of telling such a story would be to show your listeners how important higher education is to you by encouraging them to understand and identify with your family history.

Unlike description, which generally portrays people, places, and objects in *space*, narration asks the reader to follow a series of actions through a particular *time* sequence. Description, however, often complements the movement of narration, though. People must be depicted, for instance, along with their relationships to one another, before their actions can have any real meaning for us; similarly, places must be described so that we can picture the setting and understand the activities in a specific scene. The organization of the action and the time spent on each episode in a story should be based principally on a writer's analysis of the interests and needs of his or her audience.

To be most effective, narration should prolong the exciting parts of a story and shorten the routine facts that simply move the reader from one episode to another. If you were robbed on your way to work, for example, a good narrative describing the incident would concentrate on the traumatic event itself rather than on such mundane and boring details as what you had for breakfast and what clothes you had put on prior to the attack. Finally, just like description, narration *shows* rather than *tells* its purpose to the audience. The factual statement "I was robbed this morning" could be made much more vivid and dramatic through the addition of some simple narration: "As I was walking to work at 7:30 A.M., a huge and angry-looking man ran up to me, thrust a gun into the middle of my stomach, and took my money, my new wristwatch, all my credit cards, and my pants—leaving me penniless and embarrassed."

The following paragraph written by a student recounts a recent parachuting experience. As you read this narrative, notice especially the writer's use of vivid detail to *show* rather than *tell* her message to the readers.

I have always needed occasional "fixes" of excitement in my life, so when I realized one spring day that I was more than ordinarily bored, I made up my mind to take more than ordinary steps to relieve that boredom. I decided to go parachuting. The next thing I knew, I was stuffed into a claustrophobically small plane with five other terrified people, rolling down a bumpy, rural runway, droning my way to 3,500 feet and an exhilarating experience. Once over the jump area, I waited my turn, stepped onto the strut, held my breath, and then kicked off into the cold, rushing air as my heart pounded heavily. All I could think was, "I hope this damn parachute opens!" The sensation of falling backward through space was unfamiliar and disconcerting till my chute opened with a loud "pop," momentarily pulling me upward toward the distant sky. After several minutes of floating downward, I landed rudely on the hard ground. Life, I remembered happily, could be awfully exciting, and a month later, when my tailbone had stopped throbbing, I still felt that way.

THINKING CRITICALLY BY USING NARRATION

Rhetorical modes offer us different ways of perceiving reality. Narration is an especially useful tool for sequencing or putting details and information in some kind of logical order, usually chronological. Working with narration helps us see clear sequences separate from all other mental functions.

Practicing exercises in narrative techniques can help you see clear patterns in topics you are writing about. Although narration is usually used in conjunction with other rhetorical modes, we are going to isolate it here so you can appreciate its specific mechanics separate from other mental activities. If you feel the process of narration in your head, you are more likely to understand exactly what it entails and thus to use it more effectively in reading other essays and in organizing and writing your own essays.

For the best results, we will once again do some warm-up exercises to make your sequencing perceptions as accurate and successful as possible. In this way, you will actually learn to feel how your mind works in this particular mode and then be more aware of the thinking strategies available to you in your own reading and writing. As you become more conscious of the mechanics of the individual rhetorical modes, you will naturally become more adept at combining them to accomplish the specific purpose and the related effect you want to create.

The following exercises, which require a combination of thinking and writing skills, will help you practice this particular strategy in isolation. Just as in a physical workout, we will warm up your mental capabilities one by one as if they were muscles that can be developed individually before being used together in harmony.

1. Make a chronological list of the different activities you did yesterday, from waking in the morning to sleeping at night. Randomly pick two events from your day, and treat them as the highlights of your day. Now write freely for five minutes, explaining the story of your day and emphasizing the importance of these two highlights.
2. Recall an important event that happened to you between the ages of five and ten. Brainstorm about how this event made you feel at the time it happened. Then brainstorm about how this event makes you feel now. What changes have you discovered in your view of this event?
3. Create a myth or story that illustrates a belief or idea that you think is important. You might begin with a moral that you believe in and then compose a story that "teaches" or demonstrates that moral.

READING AND WRITING NARRATIVE ESSAYS

To read a narrative essay most effectively, you should spend your time concentrating on the writer's main story line and use of details. To create an effective story, you have some important decisions to make before you write and certain variables to control as you actually draft your narrative.

During the prewriting stage, you need to generate ideas and choose a point of view through which your story will be presented. Then, as you write, the preliminary decisions you have made regarding the selection and arrangement of your details (especially important in a narrative) will allow your story to flow more easily. Carefully controlled organization, along with appropriate timing and pacing, can influence your audience's reactions in very powerful ways.

How to Read a Narrative Essay

Preparing to Read.   As you prepare to read the narratives in this chapter, try to guess what each title tells you about its essay's topic and about the author's attitude toward that topic: Can you guess, for example, how Lewis Sawaquat feels about his daughter from his title "For My Indian Daughter" or what Maya Angelou's attitude is toward the events described in "New Directions"? Also, scan the essay and read its synopsis in the Rhetorical Table of Contents to help you anticipate as much as you can about the author's purpose and audience.

The more you learn from the biography about the author and the circumstances surrounding the composition of a particular essay, the better prepared you will be to read the essay. For a narrative essay, the writer's point of view or perspective toward the story and its characters is especially significant. From the biographies, can you determine Maya Angelou's attitude toward Annie Johnson's energy and determination in "New Directions" or Russell Baker's opinion of his mother in "The Saturday Evening Post"? Also, what is Cisneros's reason for writing "Only daughter"?

Last, before you begin to read, answer the Preparing to Read questions and then try to generate some of your own inquiries on the general subject of the essay: What do you want to know about being a Native American (Sawaquat)? What childhood experience greatly affected your life (Baker)? What do you think of children in general (Cisneros)?

Reading.   As you read a narrative essay for the first time, simply follow the story line and try to get a general sense of the narrative and of the author's general purpose. Is Baker trying to encourage us all to be writers or simply to help us understand why he writes? Record your initial reactions to each essay as they occur to you. Is Keillor's purpose to make us feel sympathetic or antagonistic toward his childhood memory?

Based on the biographical information preceding the essay and on the essay's tone, purpose, and audience, try to create a context for the narrative as you read. How do such details help you understand your reading material more thoroughly? A first reading of this sort, along with a survey of the questions that follow the essay, will help prepare you for a critical understanding of the material when you read it for the second time.

Rereading.   As you reread these narrative essays, notice the author's selection and arrangement of details. Why does Angelou organize her story one way and Cisneros another? What effect does their organization create?

Also, pay attention to the timing and the pacing of the story line. What do the long descriptions of Annie's plans add to Angelou's "New Directions"? What does the quick pace of Keillor's narrative communicate?

In addition, consider at this point what other rhetorical strategies the authors use to support their narratives. Which writers use examples to supplement their stories? Which use definitions? Which use comparisons? Why do they use these strategies?

Finally, when you answer the questions after each essay, you can check your understanding of the material on different levels before you tackle the discussion/writing topics that follow. For a general checklist of reading guidelines, please see pages 20–21 of the Introduction.

How to Write a Narrative Essay

Preparing to Write.   First, you should answer the prewriting questions to help you generate thoughts on the subject at hand. Next, as in all writing, you should explore your subject matter and discover as many specific details as possible. (See pages 21–27 of the Introduction for a discussion of prewriting techniques.) Some writers rely on the familiar journalistic checklist of Who, What, When, Where, Why, and How to make sure they cover all aspects of their narrative. If you were using the story of a basketball game at your college to demonstrate the team spirit of your school, for example, you might want to consider telling your readers *who* played in the game and/or *who* attended; *what* happened before, during, and after the game; *when* and *where* it took place; *why* it was being played (or *why* these particular teams were playing each other or *why* the game was especially important); and *how* the winning basket was shot. Freewriting or a combination of freewriting and the journalistic questions is another effective way of getting ideas and story details on paper for use in a first draft.

Once you have generated these ideas, you should always let your purpose and audience ultimately guide your selection of details, but the process of gathering such journalistic information gives you some material from which to choose. You will also need to decide whether to include dialogue in your narrative. Again, the difference here is between *showing* and *telling*: Will your audience benefit from reading what was actually said, word for word, during a discussion, or will a brief description of the conversation be sufficiently effective? In fact, all the choices you make at this stage of the composing process will give you material with which to create emphasis, suspense, conflict, and interest in your subject.

Next, you must decide upon the point of view that will most readily help you achieve your purpose with your specific audience. Point of view includes the (1) person, (2) vantage point, and (3) attitude of your narrator. *Person* refers to who will tell the story: an uninvolved observer, a character in the narrative, or an omniscient (all-seeing) narrator. This initial decision will guide your thoughts on *vantage point*, which is the frame of reference of the narrator: close to the action, far from the action, looking back on the past, or reporting on the present. Finally, your narrator will naturally have an *attitude*, or *personal feeling*, about the subject: accepting, hostile, sarcastic, indifferent, angry, pleased, or any number of similar emotions. Once you adopt a certain perspective in a story, you should follow it for the duration of the narrative. This consistency will bring focus and coherence to your essay.

Writing.   After you have explored your topic and adopted a particular point of view, you need to write a thesis statement and to select and arrange the details of your story coherently so that the narrative has a clear beginning, middle, and end. The most natural way to organize the events of a narrative, of course, is chronologically. In your story about the school basketball game, you would probably narrate the relevant details in the order they occurred (i.e., sequentially, from the beginning of the game to its conclusion). More experienced writers may elect to use flashbacks: An athlete might recall a significant event that happened during the game, or a coach might recollect the contest's turning point. Your most important consideration is that the elements of a narrative essay follow some sort of time sequence, aided by the use of clear and logical transitions (e.g., "then," "next," "at this point," "suddenly") that help the reader move smoothly from one event to the next.

Rewriting.   As you reread the narrative you have written, pretend you are a reader (instead of the writer) and make sure you have told the story from the most effective point of view, considering both your purpose and your audience:

- Is your purpose (or thesis) clearly stated?
- Who is your audience?
- To what extent does this narrator help you achieve your purpose?

Further, as you reread, make certain you can follow the events of the story as they are related:

- Does one event lead naturally to the next?
- Are all the events relevant to your purpose?
- Do you *show* rather than *tell* your message?

For more advice on writing and editing, see pages 32–34.

STUDENT ESSAY: NARRATION AT WORK

The following essay characterizes the writer's mother by telling a story about an unusual family vacation. As you read it, notice that the student writer states her purpose clearly and succinctly in the first paragraph. She then becomes an integral part of her story as she carefully selects examples and details that help convey her thesis.

A Vacation with My Mother

First-person narrator — <u>I</u> had an interesting childhood—not because of where I grew up and not because I ever did anything particularly adventuresome or thrilling. In fact, I don't think my life seemed especially interesting to me at the time. But now, telling friends about my supposedly ordinary childhood, I notice an array of responses ranging from astonishment to hilarity. — General subject

Specific subject — ment to hilarity. <u>The source of their surprise and amusement is my mother—gracious, charming, sweet, and totally out of synchronization with the rest of the world.</u> <u>One strange family trip we took when I was eleven captures the essence of her zaniness.</u> — Thesis statement

My two sets of grandparents lived in Colorado and North Dakota, respectively, and my parents decided we would spend a few weeks driving to those states and seeing all the sights along the relaxed and rambling way. <u>My eight-year-old brother, David, and I had some serious reservations.</u> If Dad had ever had Mom drive him to school, we reasoned, he'd never even consider letting her help drive us anywhere out of town, let alone out of California. If we weren't paying attention, we were as likely to end up at her office or the golf course as we were to arrive at school. Sometimes she'd drop us off at a friend's house to play and then forget where she'd left us. The notion of going on a long trip with her was really unnerving.

<u>How can I explain my mother to a stranger?</u> Have you ever watched reruns of the old *I Love Lucy* with Lucille Ball? I did as a child, and I thought Lucy Ricardo was normal. I lived with somebody a lot like her. Now, Mom wasn't a redhead (not usually, anyway), and Dad wasn't a Cuban nightclub owner, but <u>at home we had the same situation of a loving but bemused husband trying to deal with the off-the-wall logic and enthusiasm of a frequently exasperating wife. We all adored her, but we had to admit it: Mom was a flaky, absentminded, genuine eccentric.</u>

<u>As the first day of our trip approached,</u> David and I reluctantly said good-bye to all of our friends. Who knew if we'd ever see any of them again? Finally, the moment of our departure arrived, and we loaded suitcases, books, games, camping gear, and a tent into the car and bravely drove off. We bravely drove off again two hours later after we'd returned home to get the purse and traveler's checks that Mom had forgotten.

Margin notes:
Narrator's attitude
Examples
Transition
Narrator's vantage point
Transition
Careful selection of details

David and I were always a little nervous when using gas station bathrooms if Mom **Use of** was driving while Dad napped: "You stand **dialogue** outside the door and play lookout while I go, and I'll stand outside the door and play lookout while you go." I had terrible visions: "Honey, where are the kids?" "What?! Oh, gosh . . . I thought they were being **Examples** awfully quiet. Uh . . . Idaho?" We were never actually abandoned in a strange city, but we weren't about to take any chances.

Transition On the fourth or fifth night of the trip, **Passage** we had trouble finding a motel with a va- **of time** cancy. After driving futilely for an hour, Mom suddenly had a great idea: Why didn't we find a house with a likely-looking back- **Example** yard and ask if we could pitch our tent there? To her, the scheme was eminently reasonable. Vowing quietly to each other to hide in the back seat if she did it, David and I groaned in anticipated mortification. To our profound relief, Dad vetoed the idea. Mom never could understand our objections. If a strange family showed up on her front doorstep, Mom would have been delighted. She thinks everyone in the world is as nice as she is. We finally found a vacancy in the next town. David and I were thrilled—the place featured bungalows in the shape of Native-American tepees.

Transition The Native-American motif must have reminded my parents that we had not yet used the brand-new tent, Coleman stove, portable mattress, and other camping gear we had brought. We headed to a national park the next day and found a campsite by a **Chronolog-** lake. It took hours to figure out how to get **Careful** **ical order** the tent up: It was one of those deluxe **of details** models with mosquito-net windows, canvas floors, and enough room for three large families to sleep in. It was after dark before we finally got it erected, and the night had turned quite cold. We fixed a hurried campfire dinner (chicken burned on the outside and raw in the middle) and prepared to go to sleep. That was when we realized that Mom had forgotten to bring along some important pieces of equipment—our sleeping bags. The four of us huddled together on our thin mattresses borrowed from our station-wagon floor. That ended our camping days. Give me a stucco tepee any time.

We drove through several states and saw lots of great sights along the way: the Grand Canyon, Carlsbad Caverns, caves, mountains, waterfalls, even a haunted house. David and I were excited and amazed at all the wonders we found, and Mom was just as enthralled as we were. Her constant pleasure and sense of the world as a beautiful, magical place was infectious. I never realized until I grew up how really childlike—in the best sense of the word—my mother actually is. She is innocent, optimistic, and always ready to be entertained. Looking back on that long-past family vacation, I now realize that my childhood was more special because I grew up with a mother who wasn't afraid to try anything and who taught me to look at the world as a series of marvelous opportunities to be explored. What did it matter that she thought England was bordered by Germany? We were never going to try to drive there. So what if she was always leaving her car keys in the refrigerator or some other equally inexplicable place? In the end, we

Examples (spatial order)

Transition

Narrator's attitude

Examples

Concluding remark always got where we were going—and we generally had a grand time along the way.

Student Writer's Comments

I enjoyed writing about this childhood vacation because of all the memories it brought back. I knew I wanted to write a narrative to explain my mother, and the word *zany* immediately popped into my mind. So I knew what my focus was going to be from the outset. My prewriting started spontaneously as soon as I found this angle. So many thoughts and memories rushed into my head that I couldn't even get to a piece of paper to write them down before I lost some of them. But there were way too many to put into one essay. The hardest part of writing this narrative was trying to decide what material to use and what to leave out. Spending a little more time before writing my first draft proved to be a good investment in this case. I got a clean piece of paper and began freewriting, trying to mold some of my scattered ideas from brainstorming into a coherent, readable form. During this second stage of prewriting, I remembered one special vacation we took that I thought might capture the essence of my mother—and also of my family.

My first draft was about three times the length of this one. My point of view was the innocent participant/observer who came to know and love her mother for her absent-mindedness. I had really developed my thesis from the time I got this writing assignment. And I told my story chronologically except for looking back in the last paragraph when I attempted to analyze the entire experience. I had no trouble *showing* rather than *telling* because all of the details were so vivid to me—as if they had happened yesterday. But that was my downfall. I soon realized that I could not possibly include everything that was on the pages of my first draft.

The process of cranking out my rough draft made my point of view toward life with my mother very clear to me and helped me face the cutting that was ahead of me. I took the raw material of a very lengthy first draft and forced myself to choose the details and examples that best characterized my mother and what life was like growing up under the care of such a lovely but daffy individual. The sense of her being both "lovely" and "daffy" was the insight that helped me the most in revising the content of my essay. I made myself ruthlessly eliminate anything that interfered with the overall effect I was trying to create—from extraneous images and details to words and phrases that didn't contribute to this specific view of my mom.

The final result, according to my classmates, communicated my message clearly and efficiently. The main criticism I got from my class was that I might have cut too much from my first draft. But I think this focused picture with a few highlights conveys my meaning in the best possible way. I offered enough details to *show* rather than *tell* my readers what living with my mother was like, but not too many to bore them. I was also able to take the time in my essay to be humorous now and then ("David and I reluctantly said good-bye to all of our friends. Who knew if we'd ever see any of them again?" and "Give me a stucco tepee any time."), as well as pensive and serious ("I now realize that my childhood was more special because I grew up with a mother who wasn't afraid to try anything and who taught me to look at the world as a series of marvelous opportunities to be explored."). Even though in looking at the essay now I would tamper with a few things, I am generally happy with the final draft. It captures the essence of my mother from my point of view, and it also gave my class a few laughs. Aren't the readers' reactions the ultimate test of a good story?

SOME FINAL THOUGHTS ON NARRATION

Just as with other modes of writing, all decisions regarding narration should be made with a specific purpose and an intended audience constantly in mind. As you will see, each narrative in this section is directed at a clearly defined audience. Notice, as you read, how each writer manipulates the various features of narration so that the readers are simultaneously caught up in the plot and deeply moved to feel, act, think, and believe the writer's personal opinions.

NARRATION IN REVIEW

Reading Narrative Essays

Preparing to Read

- ✓ What assumptions can you make from the essay's title?
- ✓ Can you guess what the author's mood is?
- ✓ What is the essay's purpose and audience?
- ✓ What does the synopsis in the Rhetorical Table of Contents tell you about the essay?
- ✓ What can you learn from the author's biography?
- ✓ Can you guess what the author's point of view toward the subject is?
- ✓ What are your responses to the Preparing to Read questions?

Reading

- ✓ What is the essay's general story line?
- ✓ What is the author's purpose?
- ✓ Did you preview the questions that follow the essay?

Rereading

- ✓ What details did the author choose and how are they arranged?
- ✓ How does the author control the pace of the story?
- ✓ What other rhetorical modes does the author use to support the essay's purpose?
- ✓ What are your responses to the questions after the essay?

Writing Narrative Essays

Preparing to Write

- ✓ What are your responses to the Preparing to Write questions?
- ✓ What is your purpose?
- ✓ Who is your audience?
- ✓ What is your narrator's point of view—including person, vantage point, and attitude toward the subject?

Writing

- ✓ What is your thesis?
- ✓ What details will best support this thesis?
- ✓ How can you arrange these details most effectively?
- ✓ Do you show rather than tell your story?
- ✓ Does your narrative essay follow a time sequence?

Rewriting

- ✓ Is your purpose (or thesis) clearly stated?
- ✓ Who is your audience?
- ✓ To what extent does this narrator help you achieve your purpose?
- ✓ Does one event lead naturally to the next?
- ✓ Are all the events relevant to your purpose?
- ✓ Do you *show* rather than *tell* your message?

LEWIS SAWAQUAT   (1935–   )

For My Indian Daughter

Lewis Sawaquat is a Native American who is now retired from his thirty-year job as a surveyor for the Soil Conservation Service of the United States Department of Agriculture. He was born in Harbor Springs, Michigan, where his great-great-grandfather was the last official "chief" of the region. After finishing high school, Sawaquat entered the army, graduated from Army Survey School, and then completed a tour of duty in Korea. Upon returning to America, he enrolled in the Art Institute of Chicago to study commercial art. Sawaquat now lives in Peshawbestown, Michigan, where his hobbies include gardening, swimming, and walking in the woods. He serves as a pipe carrier and cultural/spiritual adviser to his Ottawa tribe. Recently, he started a consulting firm and travels around the country speaking on Native-American issues. He also plans to write a book entitled *Dreams: The Universal Language*, which will investigate the Native-American approach to dream interpretation. His daughter, Gaia, who is described in the following essay, is now a junior at Yale University. His advice to students using *The Prose Reader* is to "pay attention to life; there's nothing more important to becoming a writer."

Preparing to Read

"For My Indian Daughter" originally appeared in the "My Turn" column of *Newsweek* magazine (September 5, 1983) under the author's former name, Lewis Johnson. In his article, the author speaks eloquently of prejudice, ethnic pride, and growing cultural awareness. Before reading this selection, think for a few minutes about your own heritage: What is your ethnic identity? Are you content with this background? Have you ever gone through an identity crisis? Do you anticipate facing any problems because of your ancestry? If so, how will you handle these problems when they occur?

My little girl is singing herself to sleep upstairs, her voice mingling with the sounds of the birds outside in the old maple trees. She is two, and I am nearly 50, and I am very taken with her. She came along late in my life, unexpected and unbidden, a startling gift.

Today at the beach my chubby-legged, brown-skinned daughter ran laughing into the water as fast as she could. My wife and I laughed watching her, until we heard behind us a low guttural curse and then an unpleasant voice raised in an imitation war whoop.

I turned to see a fat man in a bathing suit, white and soft as a grub, as he covered his mouth and prepared to make the Indian war cry again. He was middle-aged, younger than I, and had three little children lined up next to him, grinning foolishly. My wife suggested we leave the beach, and I agreed.

I knew the man was not unusual in his feelings against Indians. His beach behavior might have been socially unacceptable to more civilized whites, but his basic view of Indians is expressed daily in our small town, frequently on the editorial pages of the county newspaper, as white people speak out against Indian fishing rights and land rights, saying in essence, "Those Indians are taking our fish, our land." It doesn't matter to them that we were here first, that the U.S. Supreme Court has ruled in our favor. It matters to them that we have something they want, and they hate us for it. Backlash is the common explanation of the attacks on Indians, the bumper stickers that say, "Spear an Indian, Save a Fish," but I know better. The hatred of Indians goes back to the beginning when white people came to this country. For me it goes back to my childhood in Harbor Springs, Mich.

Theft. Harbor Springs is now a summer resort for the very affluent, but a hundred years ago it was the Indian village of my Ottawa ancestors. My grandmother, Anna Showanessy, and other Indians like her, had their land there taken by treaty, by fraud, by violence, by theft. They remembered how whites had burned down the village at Burt Lake in 1900 and pushed the Indians out. These were the stories in my family.

When I was a boy, my mother told me to walk down the alleys in Harbor Springs and not to wear my orange football sweater out of the house. This way I would not stand out, not be noticed, and not be a target.

I wore my orange sweater anyway and deliberately avoided the   7
alleys. I was the biggest person I knew and wasn't really afraid. But
I met my comeuppance when I enlisted in the U.S. Army. One
night all the men in my barracks gathered together and, gang-
fashion, pulled me into the shower and scrubbed me down with rough
brushes used for floors, saying, "We won't have any dirty Indians in
our outfit." It is a point of irony that I was cleaner than any of them.
Later in Korea I learned how to kill, how to bully, how to hate Kore-
ans. I came out of the war tougher than ever and, strangely, white.

I went to college, got married, lived in La Porte, Ind., worked   8
as a surveyor and raised three boys. I headed Boy Scout groups,
never thinking it odd when the Scouts did imitation Indian
dances, imitation Indian lore.

One day when I was 35 or thereabouts I heard about an Indian   9
powwow. My father used to attend them and so with great curiosity and a strange joy at discovering a part of my heritage, I decided
the thing to do to get ready for this big event was to have my
friend make me a spear in his forge. The steel was fine and blue
and iridescent. The feathers on the shaft were bright and proud.

In a dusty state fairground in southern Indiana, I found white   10
people dressed as Indians. I learned they were "hobbyists," that is,
it was their hobby and leisure pastime to masquerade as Indians on
weekends. I felt ridiculous with my spear, and I left.

It was years before I could tell anyone of the embarrassment of   11
this weekend and see any humor in it. But in a way it was that
weekend, for all its silliness, that was my awakening. I realized I
didn't know who I was. I didn't have an Indian name. I didn't
speak the Indian language. I didn't know the Indian customs.
Dimly I remembered the Ottawa word for dog, but it was a baby
word, *kahgee*, not the full word, *muhkahgee*, which I was later to
learn. Even more hazily I remembered a naming ceremony (my
own). I remembered legs dancing around me, dust. Where had
that been? Who had I been? "Sawaquat," my mother told me
when I asked, "where the tree begins to grow."

That was 1968, and I was not the only Indian in the country   12
who was feeling the need to remember who he or she was. There
were others. They had powwows, real ones, and eventually I
found them. Together we researched our past, a search that for
me culminated in the Longest Walk, a march on Washington in

1978. Maybe because I now know what it means to be Indian, it surprises me that others don't. Of course there aren't very many of us left. The chances of an average person knowing an average Indian in an average lifetime are pretty slim.

Circle. Still, I was amused one day when my small, four-year-   13
old neighbor looked at me as I was hoeing in my garden and said, "You aren't a real Indian, are you?" Scotty is little, talkative, likable. Finally I said, "I'm a real Indian." He looked at me for a moment and then said, squinting into the sun, "Then where's your horse and feathers?" The child was simply a smaller, whiter version of my own ignorant self years before. We'd both seen too much TV, that's all. He was not to be blamed. And so, in a way, the moronic man on the beach today is blameless. We come full circle to realize other people are like ourselves, as discomfiting as that may be sometimes.

As I sit in my old chair on my porch, in a light that is fading so   14
the leaves are barely distinguishable against the sky, I can picture my girl asleep upstairs. I would like to prepare her for what's to come, take her each step of the way saying, there's a place to avoid, here's what I know about this, but much of what's before her she must go through alone. She must pass through pain and joy and solitude and community to discover her own inner self that is unlike any other and come through that passage to the place where she sees all people are one, and in so seeing may live her life in a brighter future.

UNDERSTANDING DETAILS

1. What is the principal point of this essay by Sawaquat? How many different stories does the author tell to make this point?
2. What does Sawaquat see as the origin of the hatred of Native Americans in the United States?
3. What does Sawaquat learn from his first powwow (paragraphs 9 and 10)?
4. How does Sawaquat discover his original identity? In what way does this knowledge change him?

ANALYZING MEANING

1. Why does Sawaquat begin this essay with the story about his daughter on the beach? How does the story make you feel?

2. Why do thoughts about his daughter prompt Sawaquat's memories of his own identity crisis? What does the author's identity have to do with his daughter?
3. The author calls paragraphs 5–12 "Theft" and paragraphs 13–14 "Circle." Explain these two subtitles from the author's point of view.
4. Why do you think Sawaquat says that his daughter "must pass through pain and joy and solitude and community to discover her own inner self" (paragraph 14)? To what extent do we all need to do this in our lives?

DISCOVERING RHETORICAL STRATEGIES

1. Sawaquat occasionally uses dialogue to help make his points. What does the dialogue add to the various narratives he cites here?
2. Describe as thoroughly as possible the point of view of Sawaquat's narrator. Include in your answer a discussion of person, vantage point, and attitude.
3. Why do you think Sawaquat divides his essay into three sections? Why do you think he spends most of his time on the second section?
4. Although Sawaquat uses primarily narration to advance his point of view, which other rhetorical strategies help support his essay? Give examples of each.

MAKING CONNECTIONS

1. Compare the concern Lewis Sawaquat has for his daughter with that displayed for Russell Baker ("The Saturday Evening Post") by his mother and/or that for Amy Tan ("Mother Tongue") by her mother. Which parent do you think loves his or her child most? On what do you base this conclusion?
2. How strong is Sawaquat's attachment to his Native-American culture? Contrast the passion of his ethnic identity with that demonstrated by Richard Rodriguez ("The Fear of Losing a Culture"), Alice Walker ("Beauty: When the Other Dancer Is the Self"), or Shelby Steele ("Affirmative Action: The Price of Preference").

3. What responsibilities, according to Sawaquat, should parents accept regarding the eventual happiness of their children? Would Bill Cosby ("The Baffling Question") or Michael Dorris ("The Broken Cord") agree with him? Why or why not? To what extent do you agree with Sawaquat?

IDEAS FOR DISCUSSION/WRITING

Preparing to Write

Write freely about your own identity: What is your cultural heritage? How do you fit into your immediate environment? Has your attitude about yourself and your identity changed over the years? Do you know your own inner self? How do you plan to continue learning about yourself?

Choosing a Topic

1. Write a narrative essay that uses one or more stories from your past in order to describe to a group of friends the main features of your identity.

2. Explain to your children (whether real or imaginary) in narrative form some simple but important truths about your heritage. Take care to select your details well, choose an appropriate point of view, and arrange your essay logically so that you keep your readers' interest throughout the essay.

3. Have you recently experienced any social traumas in your life that you would like to prepare someone else for? Write a letter to the person you would like to warn. Use narration to explain the situation, and suggest ways to avoid the negative aspects you encountered.

Before beginning your essay, you might want to consult the checklists on pages 115–116.

MAYA ANGELOU   (1928–   )

New Directions

Maya Angelou was born Marguerite Johnson on April 4, 1928, in St. Louis, Missouri. Nicknamed "Maya" by her brother, she moved with her family to California; then, at age three, she was sent to live with her grandmother in Stamps, Arkansas, where she spent the childhood years later recorded in her autobiographical novel *I Know Why the Caged Bird Sings* (1970). After a brief marriage, she embarked upon an amazingly prolific career in dance, drama, and writing. During the past forty years, Angelou has been at various times a nightclub performer specializing in calypso songs and dances, an actress, a playwright, a civil-rights activist, a newspaper editor, a television writer and producer, a poet, and a screenwriter. She has also written several television specials, including *Three Way Choice* (a five-part miniseries) and *Afro-Americans in the Arts*, both for PBS. Her most recent work has included a BBC-TV documentary entitled *Trying to Make It Home* (1988); a stage production of Errol John's *Moon on a Rainbow Shawl*, which she directed in London (1988); and five novels, *I Shall Not Be Moved* (1990), *Lessons in Living* (1993), *Wouldn't Take Nothing for My Journey Now* (1993), *A Brave and Startling Truth* (1995), and *Phenomenal Woman* (2000). A tall, graceful, and imposing woman, Angelou was once described as conveying "pride without arrogance, self-esteem without smugness."

Preparing to Read

Taken from Angelou's book *Wouldn't Take Nothing for My Journey Now*, the following essay describes how Annie Johnson, a strong and determined woman, found "a new path" in her life. Before you read this essay, take a moment to think about a time you changed directions: What were the circumstances surrounding this change? Why did you make the change? What did you learn from the experience? What alterations would you make if you followed this path again?

In 1903 the late Mrs. Annie Johnson of Arkansas found herself 1
with two toddling sons, very little money, a slight ability to
read and add simple numbers. To this picture add a disastrous
marriage and the burdensome fact that Mrs. Johnson was a Negro.

When she told her husband, Mr. William Johnson, of her dis- 2
satisfaction with their marriage, he conceded that he too found it
to be less than he expected and had been secretly hoping to leave
and study religion. He added that he thought God was calling
him not only to preach but to do so in Enid, Oklahoma. He did
not tell her that he knew a minister in Enid with whom he could
study and who had a friendly, unmarried daughter. They parted
amicably, Annie keeping the one-room house and William taking
most of the cash to carry himself to Oklahoma.

Annie, over six feet tall, big-boned, decided that she would not 3
go to work as a domestic and leave her "precious babes" to anyone else's care. There was no possibility of being hired at the
town's cotton gin or lumber mill, but maybe there was a way to
make the two factories work for her. In her words, "I looked up
the road I was going and back the way I come, and since I wasn't
satisfied, I decided to step off the road and cut me a new path." She
told herself that she wasn't a fancy cook but that she could "mix
groceries well enough to scare hunger away from a starving man."

She made her plans meticulously and in secret. One early 4
evening to see if she was ready, she placed stones in two five-
gallon pails and carried them three miles to the cotton gin. She
rested a little, and then, discarding some rocks, she walked in the
darkness to the saw mill five miles farther along the dirt road. On
her way back to her little house and her babies, she dumped the
remaining rocks along the path.

That same night she worked into the early hours boiling 5
chicken and frying ham. She made dough and filled the rolled-out
pastry with meat. At last she went to sleep.

The next morning she left her house carrying the meat pies, 6
lard, an iron brazier, and coals for a fire. Just before lunch she appeared in an empty lot behind the cotton gin. As the dinner noon
bell rang, she dropped the savors into boiling fat, and the aroma
rose and floated over to the workers who spilled out of the gin,
covered with white lint, looking like specters.

Most workers had brought their lunches of pinto beans and 7
biscuits or crackers, onions and cans of sardines, but they were

tempted by the hot meat pies which Annie ladled out of the fat. She wrapped them in newspapers, which soaked up the grease, and offered them for sale at a nickel each. Although business was slow, those first days Annie was determined. She balanced her appearances between the two hours of activity.

So, on Monday if she offered hot fresh pies at the cotton gin   8 and sold the remaining cooled-down pies at the lumber mill for three cents, then on Tuesday she went first to the lumber mill presenting fresh, just-cooked pies as the lumbermen covered in sawdust emerged from the mill.

For the next few years, on balmy spring days, blistering sum-   9 mer noons, and cold, wet, and wintry middays, Annie never disappointed her customers, who could count on seeing the tall, brown-skin woman bent over her brazier, carefully turning the meat pies. When she felt certain that the workers had become dependent on her, she built a stall between the two hives of industry and let the men run to her for their lunchtime provisions.

She had indeed stepped from the road which seemed to have   10 been chosen for her and cut herself a brand-new path. In years that stall became a store where customers could buy cheese, meal, syrup, cookies, candy, writing tablets, pickles, canned goods, fresh fruit, soft drinks, coal, oil, and leather soles for worn-out shoes.

Each of us has the right and the responsibility to assess the roads   11 which lie ahead, and those over which we have traveled, and if the future road looms ominous or unpromising, and the roads back uninviting, then we need to gather our resolve and, carrying only the necessary baggage, step off that road into another direction. If the new choice is also unpalatable, without embarrassment, we must be ready to change that as well.

UNDERSTANDING DETAILS

1. What path is Annie Johnson following that she dislikes? How does she change this path?
2. Describe Annie physically and mentally in your own words. Use as much detail as possible.
3. Why does Annie carry stones in two five-gallon pails for three miles? What is she trying to accomplish?
4. In what ways does Annie's business grow? How does Annie's personality make this growth possible?

ANALYZING MEANING

1. Why do you think Annie succeeds in her business? What are the main ingredients of her success?
2. In what ways are the details at the beginning of this narrative essay typical of the year 1903?
3. What does Angelou mean when she says, "Each of us has the right and the responsibility to assess the roads which lie ahead, and those over which we have traveled" (paragraph 11)? In what way is this message basic to an understanding of the essay?
4. Explain the title of the essay. Cite specific details from the essay in your explanation.

DISCOVERING RHETORICAL STRATEGIES

1. Angelou writes this narrative essay in a fairly formal style, using multisyllable words (*concede* rather than *yield* or *admit*) and the characters' title and names (Mrs. Annie Johnson instead of Annie Johnson). Why do you think Angelou presents her essay in this way? Describe the tone she maintains throughout the essay.
2. The author uses the metaphor of taking a "new road" to describe Annie Johnson's decision. Is this metaphor effective in your opinion? Why or why not?
3. Over what period of time do you think this story took place? How does the author show her readers that time is passing in this narrative essay?
4. Angelou often ends her essays with lessons that she wants the readers to understand. How does her lesson in the last paragraph of this narrative essay affect the story? Does the story itself go with the lesson? How did you respond to having the author tell you what to think at the end of the story?

MAKING CONNECTIONS

1. In Angelou's essay, Annie Johnson cuts "a new path" for herself by selling food to factory workers. Contrast this sudden change in the direction of her life with similar "new paths" taken by Bill Cosby ("The Baffling Question"), by Brent Staples in "A Brother's Murder," or by female weightlifters in

Gloria Steinem's "The Politics of Muscle." Who do you think had the most difficult transition to make? Explain your answer.

2. If Angelou, Russell Baker ("The Saturday Evening Post"), Sandra Cisneros ("Only daughter"), and Harold Krents ("Darkness at Noon") were discussing the value of persistence and determination in life, which author would argue most strongly for the value of that quality? Why? Would you agree?

3. Food is an important ingredient not only in Angelou's essay, but also in those written by Ray Bradbury ("Summer Rituals"), Kimberly Wozencraft ("Notes From the Country Club"), and Garrison Keillor ("How the Crab Apple Grew"). Which of these most involves the topic of food? Which the least? Which authors use food as a structuring device in their essays?

IDEAS FOR DISCUSSION/WRITING

Preparing to Write

Write freely about all the major changes you have made in your life: Were most of these changes for the best? How did they benefit you? How did they benefit others? Did they hurt anyone? Do you think most people have trouble changing directions in their lives? Why or why not? How might we all improve our attitudes about change?

Choosing a Topic

1. The editor of your school newspaper has asked you to write a narrative essay about an important change you made in your life. The newspaper is running a series of essays about changing directions in life, and the staff has heard that you have a story to tell. Tell your story in essay form to be printed in the school newspaper.

2. Why are major changes so difficult for us to make? Write a narrative essay for your peers to respond to this question. Use characters to dramatize your answer.

3. Decide on an important truth about life, and then write a narrative essay to support that truth. Make the details as vivid as possible.

Before beginning your essay, you might want to consult the checklists on pages 115–116.

RUSSELL BAKER   (1925–   )

The Saturday Evening Post

Russell Baker is one of America's foremost satirists and humorists. Born in Virginia, he grew up in New Jersey and Maryland, graduated from Johns Hopkins University, and then served for two years as a pilot in the U.S. Navy. Following the service, he became a newspaper reporter for the *Baltimore Sun*, which sent him to England as its London correspondent. He subsequently joined the staff of the *New York Times* as a member of its Washington bureau. From 1962 to 1998, he wrote his widely syndicated "Observer" column in the *Times*, which blended wry humor, a keen interest in language, and biting social commentary about the Washington scene. His books include *An American in Washington* (1961), *No Cause for Panic* (1964), and *Poor Russell's Almanac* (1972), plus two collections of early essays, *So This Is Depravity* (1980) and *The Rescue of Miss Yaskell and Other Pipe Dreams* (1983). *Growing Up* (1982), a bestseller vividly recounting his own childhood, earned him the 1983 Pulitzer Prize for biography. His more recent publications include *The Good Times* (1989), which continues his life story from approximately age twenty until he began working for the *New York Times* in the early 1960s; *There's a Country in My Cellar: The Best of Russell Baker* (1990), a collection of his newspaper columns; and *Inventing the Truth: The Art and Craft of Memoir* (1995, with William Zinsser).

Preparing to Read

The following skillfully written essay is an excerpt from Baker's autobiography, *Growing Up*. In it, the author recalls enduring memories from his youth that clearly project the experiences and emotions of his coming of age in 1920s rural Virginia. As you prepare to read this selection, think for a moment about some of your own childhood memories: What were your strengths as a child? Your weaknesses? Have these character traits changed as you've matured? How are you like or unlike various members of your family? How do you react to these similarities and/or differences? What are your main goals in life? How do your character traits affect these goals?

I began working in journalism when I was eight years old. It was my mother's idea. She wanted me to "make something" of myself and, after a levelheaded appraisal of my strengths, decided I had better start young if I was to have any chance of keeping up with the competition.

The flaw in my character which she had already spotted was lack of "gumption." My idea of a perfect afternoon was lying in front of the radio rereading my favorite Big Little Book, *Dick Tracy Meets Stooge Viller*. My mother despised inactivity. Seeing me having a good time in repose, she was powerless to hide her disgust. "You've got no more gumption than a bump on a log," she said. "Get out in the kitchen and help Doris do those dirty dishes."

My sister Doris, though two years younger than I, had enough gumption for a dozen people. She positively enjoyed washing dishes, making beds, and cleaning the house. When she was only seven, she could carry a piece of short-weighted cheese back to the A & P, threaten the manager with legal action, and come back triumphantly with the full quarter-pound we'd paid for and a few ounces extra thrown in for forgiveness. Doris could have made something of herself if she hadn't been a girl. Because of this defect, however, the best she could hope for was a career as a nurse or schoolteacher, the only work that capable females were considered up to in those days.

This must have saddened my mother, this twist of fate that had allocated all the gumption to the daughter and left her with a son who was content with Dick Tracy and Stooge Viller. If disappointed, though, she wasted no energy on self-pity. She would make me make something of myself whether I wanted to or not. "The Lord helps those who help themselves," she said. That was the way her mind worked.

She was realistic about the difficulty. Having sized up the material the Lord had given her to mold, she didn't overestimate what she could do with it. She didn't insist that I grow up to be President of the United States.

Fifty years ago parents still asked boys if they wanted to grow up to be President, and asked it not jokingly but seriously. Many parents who were hardly more than paupers still believed their sons could do it. Abraham Lincoln had done it. We were only sixty-five years from Lincoln. Many a grandfather who walked among us could remember Lincoln's time. Men of grandfatherly

age were the worst for asking if you wanted to grow up to be
President. A surprising number of little boys said yes and meant it.

I was asked many times myself. No, I would say, I didn't want   7
to grow up to be President. My mother was present during one of
these interrogations. An elderly uncle, having posed the usual
question and exposed my lack of interest in the Presidency, asked,
"Well, what *do* you want to be when you grow up?"

I loved to pick through trash piles and collect empty bottles, tin   8
cans with pretty labels, and discarded magazines. The most desirable job on earth sprang instantly to mind. "I want to be a garbage
man," I said.

My uncle smiled, but my mother had seen the first distressing   9
evidence of a bump budding on a log. "Have a little gumption,
Russell," she said. Her calling me Russell was a signal of unhappiness. When she approved of me, I was always "Buddy."

When I turned eight years old she decided that the job of start-   10
ing me on the road toward making something of myself could no
longer be safely delayed. "Buddy," she said one day, "I want you
to come home right after school this afternoon. Somebody's coming, and I want you to meet him."

When I burst in that afternoon, she was in conference in the   11
parlor with an executive of the Curtis Publishing Company. She
introduced me. He bent low from the waist and shook my hand.
Was it true as my mother had told him, he asked, that I longed
for the opportunity to conquer the world of business?

My mother replied that I was blessed with a rare determination   12
to make something of myself.

"That's right," I whispered.   13

"But have you got the grit, the character, the never-say-quit   14
spirit it takes to succeed in business?"

My mother said I certainly did.   15

"That's right," I said.   16

He eyed me silently for a long pause, as though weighing   17
whether I could be trusted to keep his confidence, then spoke man-
to-man. Before taking a crucial step, he said, he wanted to advise me
that working for the Curtis Publishing Company placed enormous
responsibility on a young man. It was one of the great companies of
America. Perhaps the greatest publishing house in the world. I had
heard, no doubt, of the *Saturday Evening Post*?

Heard of it? My mother said that everyone in our house had　18
heard of the *Saturday Post* and that I, in fact, read it with religious
devotion.

Then doubtless, he said, we were also familiar with those two　19
monthly pillars of the magazine world, the *Ladies Home Journal*
and the *Country Gentleman.*

Indeed we were familiar with them, said my mother.　20

Representing the *Saturday Evening Post* was one of the weightiest　21
honors that could be bestowed in the world of business, he said. He
was personally proud of being a part of the great corporation.

My mother said he had every right to be.　22

Again he studied me as though debating whether I was worthy　23
of a knighthood. Finally: "Are you trustworthy?"

My mother said I was the soul of honesty.　24

"That's right," I said.　25

The caller smiled for the first time. He told me I was a lucky　26
young man. He admired my spunk. Too many young men
thought life was all play. Those young men would not go far in
this world. Only a young man willing to work and save and keep
his face washed and his hair neatly combed could hope to come
out on top in a world such as ours. Did I truly and sincerely believe that I was such a young man?

"He certainly does," said my mother.　27

"That's right," I said.　28

He said he had been so impressed by what he had seen of me　29
that he was going to make me a representative of the Curtis Publishing Company. On the following Tuesday, he said, thirty
freshly printed copies of the *Saturday Evening Post* would be delivered at our door. I would place these magazines, still damp with
the ink of the presses, in a handsome canvas bag, sling it over my
shoulder, and set forth through the streets to bring the best in
journalism, fiction, and cartoons to the American public.

He had brought the canvas bag with him. He presented it with　30
reverence fit for a chasuble. He showed me how to drape the sling
over my left shoulder and across the chest so that the pouch lay easily accessible to my right hand, allowing the best in journalism,
fiction, and cartoons to be swiftly extracted and sold to a citizenry
whose happiness and security depended upon us soldiers of the
free press.

The following Tuesday I raced home from school, put the can-   31
vas bag over my shoulder, dumped the magazines in, and, tilting
to the left to balance their weight on my right hip, embarked on
the highway of journalism.

We lived in Belleville, New Jersey, a commuter town at the   32
northern fringe of Newark. It was 1932, the bleakest year of the
Depression. My father had died two years before, leaving us with
a few pieces of Sears, Roebuck furniture and not much else, and
my mother had taken Doris and me to live with one of her
younger brothers. This was my Uncle Allen. Uncle Allen had
made something of himself by 1932. As salesman for a soft-drink
bottler in Newark, he had an income of $30 a week; wore pearl-
gray spats, detachable collars, and a three-piece suit; was happily
married; and took in threadbare relatives.

With my load of magazines I headed toward Belleville Avenue.   33
That's where the people were. There were two filling stations at
the intersection with Union Avenue, as well as an A & P, a fruit
stand, a bakery, a barber shop, Zuccarelli's drugstore, and a diner
shaped like a railroad car. For several hours I made myself highly
visible, shifting position now and then from corner to corner,
from shop window to shop window, to make sure everyone
could see the heavy black lettering on the canvas bag that said THE
SATURDAY EVENING POST. When the angle of the light indicated
it was suppertime, I walked back to the house.

"How many did you sell, Buddy?" my mother asked.   34
"None."   35
"Where did you go?"   36
"The corner of Belleville and Union Avenues."   37
"What did you do?"   38
"Stood on the corner waiting for somebody to buy a *Saturday*   39
Evening Post."
"You just stood there?"   40
"Didn't sell a single one."   41
"For God's sake, Russell!"   42
Uncle Allen intervened. "I've been thinking about it for some   43
time," he said, "and I've about decided to take the *Post* regularly.
Put me down as a regular customer." I handed him a magazine,
and he paid me a nickel. It was the first nickel I earned.

Afterwards my mother instructed me in salesmanship. I would   44
have to ring doorbells, address adults with charming self-

confidence, and break down resistance with a sales talk pointing
out that no one, no matter how poor, could afford to be without
the *Saturday Evening Post* in the home.

I told my mother I'd changed my mind about wanting to suc-   45
ceed in the magazine business.

"If you think I'm going to raise a good-for-nothing," she   46
replied, "you've got another think coming." She told me to hit
the streets with the canvas bag and start ringing doorbells the
instant school was out next day. When I objected that I didn't
feel any aptitude for salesmanship, she asked how I'd like to
lend her my leather belt so she could whack some sense into me.
I bowed to superior will and entered journalism with a heavy
heart.

My mother and I had fought this battle almost as long as I   47
could remember. It probably started even before memory began,
when I was a country child in northern Virginia and my mother,
dissatisfied with my father's plain workman's life, determined that
I would not grow up like him and his people, with calluses on
their hands, overalls on their backs, and fourth-grade educations
in their heads. She had fancier ideas of life's possibilities. Introducing me to the *Saturday Evening Post*, she was trying to wean
me as early as possible from my father's world where men left
with their lunch pails at sunup, worked with their hands until the
grime ate into the pores, and died with a few sticks of mail-order
furniture as their legacy. In my mother's vision of the better life
there were desks and white collars, well-pressed suits, evenings of
reading and lively talk, and perhaps—if a man were very, very
lucky and hit the jackpot, really made something important of
himself—perhaps there might be a fantastic salary of $5,000 a year
to support a big house and a Buick with a rumble seat and a vacation in Atlantic City.

And so I set forth with my sack of magazines. I was afraid of   48
the dogs that snarled behind the doors of potential buyers. I was
timid about ringing the doorbells of strangers, relieved when no
one came to the door, and scared when someone did. Despite my
mother's instructions, I could not deliver an engaging sales pitch.
When a door opened I simply asked, "Want to buy a *Saturday
Evening Post?*" In Belleville few persons did. It was a town of
30,000 people, and most weeks I rang a fair majority of its doorbells. But I rarely sold my thirty copies. Some weeks I canvassed

the entire town for six days and still had four or five unsold magazines on Monday evening; then I dreaded the coming of Tuesday morning, when a batch of thirty fresh *Saturday Evening Posts* was due at the front door.

"Better get out there and sell the rest of those magazines   49
tonight," my mother would say.

I usually posted myself then at a busy intersection where a traf-   50
fic light controlled commuter flow from Newark. When the light turned red, I stood on the curb and shouted my sales pitch at the motorists.

"Want to buy a *Saturday Evening Post?*"   51

One rainy night when car windows were sealed against me, I   52
came back soaked and with not a single sale to report. My mother beckoned to Doris.

"Go back down there with Buddy and show him how to sell   53
these magazines," she said.

Brimming with zest, Doris, who was then seven years old, re-   54
turned with me to the corner. She took a magazine from the bag, and when the light turned red, she strode to the nearest car and banged her small fist against the closed window. The driver, probably startled at what he took to be a midget assaulting his car, lowered the window to stare, and Doris thrust a *Saturday Evening Post* at him.

"You need this magazine," she piped, "and it only costs a   55
nickel."

Her salesmanship was irresistible. Before the light changed half   56
a dozen times, she disposed of the entire batch. I didn't feel hu-miliated. To the contrary. I was so happy I decided to give her a treat. Leading her to the vegetable store on Belleville Avenue, I bought three apples, which cost a nickel, and gave her one.

"You shouldn't waste money," she said.   57

"Eat your apple." I bit into mine.   58

"You shouldn't eat before supper," she said. "It'll spoil your   59
appetite."

Back at the house that evening, she dutifully reported me for   60
wasting a nickel. Instead of a scolding, I was rewarded with a pat on the back for having the good sense to buy fruit instead of candy. My mother reached into her bottomless supply of maxims and told Doris, "An apple a day keeps the doctor away."

By the time I was ten I had learned all my mother's maxims by 61
heart. Asking to stay up past normal bedtime, I knew that a refusal
would be explained with, "Early to bed and early to rise, makes a
man healthy, wealthy, and wise." If I whimpered about having to
get up early in the morning, I could depend on her to say, "The
early bird gets the worm."

The one I most despised was, "If at first you don't succeed, try, try 62
again." This was the battle cry with which she constantly sent me
back into the hopeless struggle whenever I moaned that I had rung
every doorbell in town and knew there wasn't a single potential buyer
left in Belleville that week. After listening to my explanation, she
handed me the canvas bag and said, "If at first you don't succeed...."

Three years in that job, which I would gladly have quit after 63
the first day except for her insistence, produced at least one valuable result. My mother finally concluded that I would never make
something of myself by pursuing a life in business and started considering careers that demanded less competitive zeal.

One evening when I was eleven, I brought home a short 64
"composition" on my summer vacation which the teacher had
graded with an A. Reading it with her own schoolteacher's eye,
my mother agreed that it was top-drawer seventh grade prose and
complimented me. Nothing more was said about it immediately,
but a new idea had taken life in her mind. Halfway through supper she suddenly interrupted the conversation.

"Buddy," she said, "maybe you could be a writer." 65

I clasped the idea to my heart. I had never met a writer, had 66
shown no previous urge to write, and hadn't a notion how to become a writer, but I loved stories and thought that making up
stories must surely be almost as much fun as reading them. Best of
all, though, and what really gladdened my heart, was the ease of
the writer's life. Writers did not have to trudge through the town
peddling from canvas bags, defending themselves against angry
dogs, being rejected by surly strangers. Writers did not have to
ring doorbells. So far as I could make out, what writers did could-
n't even be classified as work.

I was enchanted. Writers didn't have to have any gumption at 67
all. I did not dare tell anybody for fear of being laughed at in the
schoolyard, but secretly I decided that what I'd like to be when I
grew up was a writer.

UNDERSTANDING DETAILS

1. How does Baker's ideal day differ from that of his sister?
2. According to the author's mother, what is the main flaw in his character? How does this flaw eventually affect his choice of a career?
3. Why does Baker feel he has no "aptitude for salesmanship" (paragraph 46)? What has led him to this conclusion?
4. Which of his mother's maxims does the author dislike the most? Explain his reaction.

ANALYZING MEANING

1. Why does Baker begin this selection with a comparison of his personality and his sister's? What does this comparison have to do with the rest of the essay?
2. Why does the author's mother insist that he work for the *Saturday Evening Post*? What does she think he will gain from the experience? What does he actually learn?
3. What "battle" (paragraph 47) have the author and his mother been fighting for as long as he can remember? Who finally wins this battle?
4. Why is Baker so delighted with the idea of becoming a writer when he grows up? How is this notion compatible with his personality?

DISCOVERING RHETORICAL STRATEGIES

1. How does Baker arrange the details in this excerpt? Why do you think he organizes them in this way? How would a different arrangement have changed the essay?
2. Who do you think is Baker's intended audience? Describe them in detail. How did you come to this conclusion?
3. What is the climax of Baker's narrative? How does he lead up to and develop this climactic moment? What stylistic traits tell us that this is the most exciting point in the story?
4. Besides narration, what other rhetorical strategies does Baker draw on to develop his thesis? Give examples of each of these strategies.

MAKING CONNECTIONS

1. Baker insists on the importance of dedicating oneself to a career. Compare and contrast his feelings on this subject with similar sentiments found in essays by Sandra Cisneros ("Only daughter"), William Ouchi ("Japanese and American Workers: Two Casts of Mind"), and Gloria Steinem ("The Politics of Muscle"). How dedicated do you intend to be to your own future career?

2. How is young Russell Baker's naive conception of a writer's "easy" life different from the views on writing expressed by Paul Roberts ("How to Say Nothing in Five Hundred Words"), Natalie Goldbert ("The Rules of Writing Practice"), or Kurt Vonnegut ("How to Write with Style")? Which of these authors would argue most fervently that writing is "hard" work? How do you feel about the process of writing? Is it easy or hard for you? Explain your answer.

3. Baker's mother had a strong influence on him as he grew up. Would Germaine Greer ("A Child Is Born") argue that Mrs. Baker was typical of American mothers, or would Greer assert that she was more like a non-Western mother in her influence over her son? How much control has your own mother had over your upbringing? Are you pleased with the amount of influence she has had over you? Explain your answer.

IDEAS FOR DISCUSSION/WRITING

Preparing to Write

Write freely about yourself in relation to your aspirations: What type of person are you? What do you think about? What are your ideals? Your hopes? Your dreams? Your fears? What do you enjoy doing in your spare time? How are you different from other members of your family? Is anyone in your family a model for you? How have members of your immediate family affected your daily life—past and present? Your career goals? How do you anticipate your family will affect your future?

Choosing a Topic

1. Write a narrative essay introducing yourself to your English class. To explain and define your identity, include descriptions of family members whenever appropriate.

2. Write a narrative that helps explain to a friend how you got involved in a current interest. To expand upon your narrative, refer whenever possible to your long-term goals and aspirations.
3. Ten years from now, your local newspaper decides to devote an entire section to people getting started in careers. You are asked to submit the story of how you got involved in your profession (whatever it may be). Write a narrative that might appear in your hometown newspaper ten years from now; be sure to give the article a catchy headline.

Before beginning your essay, you might want to consult the checklists on pages 115–116.

SANDRA CISNEROS   (1954–   )

Only daughter

Born in Chicago, Sandra Cisneros was the Only daughter raised in a family with six brothers. She moved frequently during her childhood, eventually earning a B.A. in English from Loyola University and an M.F.A. in creative writing from the University of Iowa, where she developed her unique voice of a strong and independent working-class, Mexican-American woman. Her first book, *The House on Mango Street* (1984), is a loosely structured series of vignettes focusing upon the isolation and cultural conflicts endured by Latina women in America. Later publications include *My Wicked, Wicked Ways* (1987), *Woman Hollering Creek* (1991), and *The Future is Mestizo: Life Where Cultures Meet* (2000). Critics have described her works of fiction as "poetic": "nearly every sentence contains an explosive sensory image. She gives us unforgettable characters that we want to lift off the page and hang out with for a while." Asked to analyze her writing style, Cisneros has explained that "I am a woman, and I am a Latina. Those are the things that make my writing distinctive. Those are the things that give my writing power. They are the things that give it *sabor* (flavor), that give it *picante* (spice)."

Preparing to Read

"Only daughter," an essay first published in *Glamour*, chronicles one of the author's most memorable experiences on a visit to her parents' home in Chicago. Full of family history, the story uses the reunion as a forum for Cisneros's observations about life in a Mexican family. As you prepare to read this essay, take a few moments to consider the many social and cultural influences that shape your life: What is your family like? What activities do you enjoy? Have you ever felt that your family didn't accept these activities? Have you ever been angry at the extent to which social or cultural pressures have governed your life? How did you react to these forces? Can you think of a specific situation in which you overcame social or cultural differences? What was the result?

Once, several years ago, when I was just starting out my writing career, I was asked to write my own contributor's note for an anthology. I wrote: "I am the only daughter in a family of six sons. *That* explains everything."

Well, I've thought that ever since, and yes, it explains a lot to me, but for the reader's sake I should have written: "I am the only daughter in a *Mexican* family of six sons." Or even: "I am the only daughter of a Mexican father and a Mexican-American mother." Or: "I am the only daughter of a working-class family of nine." All of these had everything to do with who I am today.

I was/am the only daughter and *only* a daughter. Being an only daughter in a family of six sons forced me by circumstance to spend a lot of time by myself because my brothers felt it beneath them to play with a *girl* in public. But that aloneness, that loneliness, was good for a would-be writer—it allowed me time to think and think, to imagine, to read and prepare myself.

Being only a daughter for my father meant my destiny would lead me to become someone's wife. That's what he believed. But when I was in the fifth grade and shared my plans for college with him, I was sure he understood. I remember my father saying, *"Que bueno, mi'ja,* that's good." That meant a lot to me, especially since my brothers thought the idea hilarious. What I didn't realize was that my father thought college was good for girls—good for finding a husband. After four years in college and two more in graduate school, and still no husband, my father shakes his head even now and says I wasted all that education.

In retrospect, I'm lucky my father believed daughters were meant for husbands. It meant it didn't matter if I majored in something silly like English. Alter all, I'd find a nice professional eventually, right? This allowed me the liberty to putter about embroidering my little poems and stories without my father interrupting with so much as a "What's that you're writing?"

But the truth is, I wanted him to interrupt. I wanted my father to understand what it was I was scribbling, to introduce me as "My only dauther, the writer." Not as "This is my only daughter. She teaches." *Es maestra*—teacher. Not even *profesora.*

In a sense, everything I have ever written has been for him, to win his approval even though I know my father can't read English words, even though my father's only reading includes the brown-ink *Esto* sports magazines from Mexico City and the bloody *¡Alarma!* magazines that feature yet another sighting of *La Virgen de Gaudalupe* on a tortilla or a wife's revenge on her philandering husband by bashing his skull in with a *molcajete* (a kitchen mortar made of volcanic rock). Or the *fotonovelas,* the little picture paperbacks with tragedy and trauma erupting from the characters' mouths in bubbles.

A father represents, then, the public majority. A public who is 8 disinterested in reading, and yet one whom I am writing about and for, and privately trying to woo.

When we were growing up in Chicago, we moved a lot be- 9 cause of my father. He suffered bouts of nostalgia. Then we'd have to let go of our flat, store the furniture with mother's relatives, load the station wagon with baggage and bologna sandwiches and head south. To Mexico City.

We came back, of course. To yet another Chicago flat, another 10 Chicago neighborhood, another Catholic school. Each time, my father would seek out the parish priest in order to get a tuition break, and complain or boast: "I have seven sons."

He meant *siete hijos,* seven children, but he translated it as 11 "sons." "I have seven sons." To anyone who would listen. The Sears Roebuck employee who sold us the washing machine. The short-order cook where my father ate his ham-and-eggs breakfasts. "I have seven sons." As if he deserved a medal from the state.

My papa. He didn't mean anything by the mistranslation, I'm 12 sure. But somehow I could feel myself being erased. I'd tug my father's sleeve and whisper: "Not seven sons. Six! and one *daughter.*"

When my oldest brother graduated from medical school, he 13 fulfilled my father's dream that we study hard and use this—our heads, instead of this—our hands. Even now my father's hands are thick and yellow, stubbed by a history of hammer and nails and twine and coils and springs. "Use this," my father said, tapping his head, "and not this," showing us those hands. He always looked tired when he said it.

Wasn't college an investment? And hadn't I spent all those 14 years in college? And if I didn't marry, what was it all for? Why would anyone go to college and then choose to be poor? Especially someone who has always been poor.

Last year, after ten years of writing professionally, the financial   15
rewards started to trickle in. My second National Endowment for
the Arts Fellowship. A guest professorship at the University of
California, Berkeley. My book, which sold to a major New York
publishing house.

At Christmas, I flew home to Chicago. The house was throb-   16
bing, same as always; hot *tamales* and sweet *tamales* hissing in my
mother's pressure cooker, and everybody—my mother, six brothers, wives, babies, aunts, cousins—talking too loud and at the
same time, like in a Fellini film, because that's just how we are.

I went upstairs to my father's room. One of my stories had just   17
been translated into Spanish and published in an anthology of Chicano writing, and I wanted to show it to him. Ever since he recovered from a stroke two years ago, my father likes to spend his leisure
hours horizontally. And that's how I found him, watching a Pedro
Infante movie on Galavision and eating rice pudding.

There was a glass filmed with milk on the bedside table. There   18
were several vials of pills and balled Kleenex. And on the floor,
one black sock and a plastic urinal that I didn't want to look at
but looked at anyway. Pedro Infante was about to burst into song,
and my father was laughing.

I'm not sure if it was because my story was translated into Span-   19
ish, or because it was published in Mexico, or perhaps because the
story dealt with Tepeyac, the *colonia* my father was raised in and
the house he grew up in, but at any rate, my father punched the
mute button on his remote control and read my story.

I sat on the bed next to my father and waited. He read it very   20
slowly. As if he were reading each line over and over. He laughed
at all the right places and read lines he liked out loud. He pointed
and asked questions: "Is this So-and-so?" "Yes," I said. He kept
reading.

When he was finally finished, after what seemed like hours, my   21
father looked up and asked: "Where can we get more copies of
this for the relatives?"

UNDERSTANDING DETAILS

1. How many children are in Cisneros's family? How many are boys?
2. Why does Cisneros's father always say he has seven sons? Why is this detail significant?
3. Why did Cisneros's father let her go to college? Explain your answer.
4. What are the differences in the way the author's father views his sons and his daughter?

ANALYZING MEANING

1. What does Cisneros mean when she says, "I am the only daughter and only a daughter" (paragraph 2)?
2. What does her cultural heritage have to do with the fact that she is the only daughter?
3. Why does Cisneros write for her father even though he can't read English?
4. Why was her father's reaction to her story published in Spanish "the most wonderful" (paragraph 22) thing that happened to her last year? Why is her father's opinion so important to her?

DISCOVERING RHETORICAL STRATEGIES

1. From what point of view does Cisneros write this narrative essay? How does this particular point of view help us understand her attitude toward the experience?
2. In writing this essay, Cisneros is making a comment about families in general and Mexican families in particular. What is her ultimate message? What details help you understand this message? Does the fact that she doesn't capitalize "daughter" in her title have anything to do with this message?
3. How does Cisneros organize the details of this narrative? Is this the most effective order for what she is trying to say?
4. Although Cisneros's essay is primarily narrative, what other rhetorical strategies does she use to make her point? Give examples of each.

MAKING CONNECTIONS

1. In "Only daughter," Sandra Cisneros describes the importance of her father's support of and appreciation for her writing career. Compare and contrast the theme of family support described by Sandra Cisneros, Russell Baker ("The Saturday Evening Post"), Germaine Greer ("A Child Is Born"), and Mary Pipher ("Beliefs about Families"). Which author would argue that support from one's family is most crucial to our development as a person? Why?

2. Both Sandra Cisneros and Amy Tan ("Mother Tongue") became extremely successful writers in English, while speaking another language at home as they grew up. Can you find any other common denominators in the experiences of these two authors that account for their current skill in using the English language?

3. Compare and contrast the use of examples in the essays by Sandra Cisneros, Harold Krentz ("Darkness at Noon"), and Brent Staples ("A Brother's Murder"). Which essay is most densely packed with examples? Which uses example most effectively? Which least effectively? Why?

IDEAS FOR DISCUSSION/WRITING

Preparing to Write

Write freely about a time in your life when you did not fit in with your own family: What were the circumstances? How did you feel? What were your alternatives? Did you take any action? What were the motivating forces for this action? Were you satisfied with the outcome? How do you feel about this experience now?

Choosing a Topic

1. Write a narrative essay telling your classmates about a time you did not fit in. Make a special effort to communicate your feelings regarding this experience. Remember to choose your details and point of view with an overall purpose in mind.

2. What is America's system of social classes? Where do you fit into the structure? Does our system allow for much mobility between classes? Write a narrative essay for your classmates explaining your understanding of the American class system. Use yourself and/or a friend as an example.

3. Explain in a coherent essay written for the general public why you think we are all sometimes motivated by cultural or personal influences beyond our control. Refer to the Cisneros essay or to experiences of your own to support your explanation.

Before beginning your essay, you might want to consult the checklists on pages 115–116.

GARRISON KEILLOR   (1942–   )

How the Crab Apple Grew

Best known for his creation of the Peabody Award-winning radio program *A Prairie Home Companion*, Garrison Keillor, a native of Anoka, Minnesota, began his career as a radio announcer and producer during his student days at the University of Minnesota. His show features an eclectic mix of traditional jazz and folk music, supplemented by Keillor's rambling, nostalgic, and often hilarious anecdotes about the zany inhabitants of the fictitious small town of Lake Wobegon, Minnesota. Chief among its residents are Father Emil, the local priest who blesses small animals on the lawn of Our Lady of Perpetual Responsibility Church; Dorothy, the garrulous owner of the Chatterbox Cafe; and Dr. Nute, a retired dentist who coaxes trout toward his fishing lure by intoning, "Open wide . . . this may sting a bit." Keillor—a tall, soft-spoken man who often performs in a tuxedo, high-top sneakers, red socks, and red suspenders—even has a pseudosponsor for the show: Powdermilk Biscuits, "a whole-wheat treat that gives shy people the strength to do what has to be done." Thus far, Keillor's monologues have spawned a number of short stories published in the *New Yorker* and several books, including *Happy to Be Here: Stories and Comic Pieces* (1982), *Lake Wobegon Days* (1985), *Leaving Home* (1987), *We Are Still Married* (1989), *WLT: A Radio Romance* (1992), *The Book of Guys* (1993), *Wobegon Boy* (1997), and *Me: By Jimmy "Big Boy" Valente As Told to Garrison Keillor* (1999).

Preparing to Read

Taken from *Leaving Home*, this graceful and humorous story is a masterful demonstration by Keillor of how to write a narrative essay. As you prepare to read this selection, take a few minutes to think about various items in your life (in your backyard, in your house, at school, at a friend's) that have special meaning to you: What are these items? Why is each of them significant? How do other people relate to these items? In what ways do your surroundings tell different stories about you? What items in your life bring complete stories to your mind? What are some of these stories?

I t has been a quiet week in Lake Wobegon. It was warm and sunny on Sunday, and on Monday the flowering crab in the Dieners' backyard burst into blossom. Suddenly, in the morning, when everyone turned their backs for a minute, the tree threw off its bathrobe and stood trembling, purple, naked, revealing all its innermost flowers. When you saw it standing where weeks before had been a bare stick stuck in the dirt, you had to stop; it made your head spin.

Becky Diener sat upstairs in her bedroom and looked at the tree. She was stuck on an assignment from Miss Melrose for English, a 750-word personal essay, "Describe your backyard as if you were seeing it for the first time." After an hour she had thirty-nine words, which she figured would mean she'd finish at 1:45 P.M. Tuesday, four hours late, and therefore would get an F even if the essay was great, which it certainly wasn't.

How can you describe your backyard as if you'd never seen it? If you'd never seen it, you'd have grown up someplace else, and wouldn't be yourself; you'd be someone else entirely, and how are you supposed to know what that person would think?

She imagined seeing the backyard in 1996, returning home from Hollywood. "Welcome Becky!" said the big white banner across McKinley Street as the pink convertible drove slowly along, everyone clapping and cheering as she cruised by, Becky Belafonte the movie star, and got off at her old house. "Here," she said to the reporters, "is where I sat as a child and dreamed my dreams, under this beautiful flowering crab. I dreamed I was a Chinese princess." Then a reporter asked, "Which of your teachers was the most important to you, encouraging you and inspiring you?" And just then she saw an old woman's face in the crowd, Miss Melrose pleading, whispering, "Say me, oh please, say me," and Becky looked straight at her as she said, "Oh, there were so many, I couldn't pick out one, they were all about the same, you know. But perhaps Miss—Miss—oh, I can't remember her name—she taught English, I think—Miss Milross? She was one of them. But there were so many."

She looked at her essay. "In my backyard is a tree that has always been extremely important to me since I was six years old when my dad came home one evening with this bag in the trunk and he said, 'Come here and help me plant this'—"

She crumpled the sheet of paper and started again.

"One evening when I was six years old, my father arrived   7
home as he customarily did around 5:30 or 6:00 P.M. except this
evening he had a wonderful surprise for me, he said, as he led me
toward the car.

"My father is not the sort of person who does surprising things   8
very often so naturally I was excited that evening when he said he
had something for me in the car, having just come home from
work where he had been. I was six years old at the time."

She took out a fresh sheet. "Six years old was a very special age   9
for me and one thing that made it special was when my dad and I
planted a tree together in our backyard. Now it is grown and
every spring it gives off large purple blossoms. . . ."

The tree was planted by her dad, Harold, in 1976, ten years   10
after he married her mother, Marlys. They grew up on Taft
Street, across from each other, a block from the ballfield. They
liked each other tremendously, and then they were in love, as
much as you can be when you're so young. Thirteen and fourteen years old and sixteen and seventeen: they looked at each
other a lot. She came and sat in his backyard to talk with his
mother and help her shell peas but really to look at Harold as he
mowed the lawn, and then he disappeared into the house and she
sat waiting for him, and of course he was in the kitchen looking
out at her. It's how we all began, when our parents looked at each
other, as we say, "when you were just a gleam in your father's
eye," or your mother's, depending on who saw who first.

Marlys was long-legged, lanky, had short black hair and sharp   11
eyes that didn't miss anything. She came over to visit the Dieners
every chance she got. Her father was a lost cause, like the Confederacy, like the search for the Northwest Passage. He'd been
prayed for and suffered for and fought for and spoken for, by people who loved him dearly, and when all was said and done, he just
reached for the gin bottle and said, "I don't know what you're
talking about," and he didn't. He was a sore embarrassment to
Marlys, a clown, a joke, and she watched Harold for evidence
that he wasn't similar. One night she dropped in at the Dieners'
and came upon a party where Harold, now nineteen, and his
friends were drinking beer by the pail. Harold flopped down on his
back and put his legs in the air and a pal put a lit match up to
Harold's rear end and blue flame came out like a blowtorch, and
Marlys went home disgusted and didn't speak to him for two years.

Harold went crazy. She graduated from high school and started   12
attending dances with a geography teacher named Stu Jasperson,
who was tall and dark-haired, a subscriber to *Time* magazine, educated at Saint Cloud Normal School, and who flew a red Piper
Cub airplane. Lake Wobegon had no airstrip except for
Tollerud's pasture, so Stu kept his plane in Saint Cloud. When he
was en route to and from the plane was almost the only time
Harold got to see Marlys and try to talk sense into her. But she
was crazy about Stu the aviator, not Harold the hardware clerk,
and in an hour Stu came buzzing overhead doing loops and dives
and dipping his wings. Harold prayed for him to crash. Marlys
thought Stu was the sun and the moon; all Harold could do was
sit and watch her, in the backyard, staring up, her hand shielding
her eyes, saying, "Oh, isn't he marvelous?" as Stu performed aer-
ial feats and then shut off the throttle and glided overhead singing
"Vaya con Dios" to her. "Yes, he is marvelous," said Harold,
thinking, "DIE DIE DIE."

That spring, Marlys was in charge of the Sweethearts Banquet   13
at the Lutheran church. Irene Holm had put on a fancy winter
Sweethearts Banquet with roast lamb, and Marlys wanted to top
her and serve roast beef with morel mushrooms, a first for a
church supper in Lake Wobegon. Once Irene had referred to
Marlys's dad as a lush.

Morel mushrooms are a great delicacy. They are found in the   14
wild by people who walk fifteen miles through the woods to get
ten of them and then never tell the location to a soul, not even on
their deathbeds to a priest. So Marlys's serving them at the banquet would be like putting out emeralds for party favors. It would
blow Irene Holm out of the water and show people that even if
Marlys's dad was a lush, she was still someone to be reckoned
with.

Two men felt the call to go and search for morels: Harold put   15
on his Red Wing boots and knapsack and headed out one
evening with a flashlight. He was in the woods all night. Morels
are found near the base of the trunk of a dead elm that's been
dead three years, which you can see by the way moonlight doesn't
shine on it, and he thought he knew where some were, but
around midnight he spotted a bunch of flashlights behind him, a
posse of morelists bobbing along on his trail, so he veered off and
hiked five miles in the wrong direction to confuse them, and by

then the sun was coming up so he went home to sleep. He woke at 2:00 P.M., hearing Stu flying overhead, and in an instant he knew. Dead elms! Of course! Stu could spot them from the air, send his ground crew to collect them for Marlys, and the Sweethearts Banquet would be their engagement dinner.

Stu might have done just that, but he wanted to put on a show   16
and land the Cub in Lake Wobegon. He circled around and around, and came in low to the west of town, disappearing behind the trees. "He's going to crash!" cried Marlys, and they all jumped in their cars and tore out, expecting to find the young hero lying bloody and torn in the dewy grass, with a dying poem on his lips. But there he was standing tall beside the craft, having landed successfully in a field of spring wheat. They all mobbed around him, and he told how he was going up to find the morels and bring them back for Marlys.

There were about forty people there. They seemed to enjoy it,   17
so he drew out his speech, talking about the lure of aviation and his boyhood and various things so serious that he didn't notice Harold behind him by the plane or notice the people who noticed what Harold was doing and laughed. Stu was too inspired to pay attention to the laughter. He talked about how he once wanted to fly to see the world but once you get up in the air you can see that Lake Wobegon is the most beautiful place of all, a lot of warm horse manure like that, and then he gave them a big manly smile and donned his flying cap and scarf and favored them with a second and third smile and a wave, and he turned and there was Harold to help him into the cockpit.

"Well, thanks," said Stu, "mighty kind, mighty kind." Harold   18
jumped to the propeller and threw it once and twice, and the third time the engine fired, and Stu adjusted the throttle, checked the gauges, flapped the flaps, fit his goggles, and never noticed the ground was wet and his wheels were sunk in. He'd parked in a wet spot, and then during his address someone had gone around and made it wetter, so when Stu pulled back on the throttle the Cub just sat, and he gave it more juice and she creaked a little, and he gave it more and the plane stood on its head with its tail in the air and dug in.

It pitched forward like the *Titanic*, and the propeller in the mud   19
sounded like he'd eaten too many green apples. The door opened and Stu climbed out, trying to look dignified and studious as he

tilted eastward and spun, and Harold said, "Stu, we didn't say we wanted those mushrooms sliced."

Harold went out that afternoon and collected five hundred morel mushrooms around one dead elm tree. Marlys made her mark at the Sweethearts dinner, amazing Irene Holm, who had thought Marlys was common. Harold also brought out of the woods a bouquet of flowering crab apple and asked her to marry him, and eventually she decided to.

The tree in the backyard came about a few years afterward. They'd been married awhile, had two kids, and some of the gloss had worn off their life, and one afternoon, Harold, trying to impress his kids and make his wife laugh, jumped off the garage roof, pretending he could fly, and landed wrong, twisting his ankle. He lay in pain, his eyes full of tears, and his kids said, "Oh poor Daddy, poor Daddy," and Marlys said, "You're not funny, you're ridiculous."

He got up on his bum ankle and went in the woods and got her a pint of morels and a branch from the flowering crab apple. He cut a root from another crab apple and planted the root in the ground. "Look, kids," he said. He sharpened the branch with his hatchet and split the root open and stuck the branch in and wrapped a cloth around it and said, "Now, there, that will be a tree." They said, "Daddy, will that really be a tree?" He said, "Yes." Marlys said, "Don't be ridiculous."

He watered it and tended it and, more than that, he came out late at night and bent down and said, "GROW. GROW. GROW." The graft held, it grew, and one year it was interesting, and the next it was impressive and then wonderful, and finally it was magnificent. It's the most magnificent thing in the Dieners' backyard. Becky finished writing 750 words late that night and lay down to sleep. A backyard is a novel about us, and when we sit there on a summer day, we hear the dialogue and see the characters.

UNDERSTANDING DETAILS

1. Where does this narrative essay take place? Describe this particular place in detail. What one word might characterize this setting?
2. Why is Becky worried about this particular assignment?

3. How many false starts does Becky make when she is trying to write this essay? What causes those false starts?
4. Explain the rivalry between Harold and Stu. What do they both want?

ANALYZING MEANING

1. How are the tree and Becky's writing assignment related?
2. Why does Marlys finally marry Harold?
3. What can you learn about writing from Becky's approach to this essay? How does she finally get started? How does she keep her essay going? How does she keep it focused? What truths from this experience can you apply to your own writing?
4. What does Keillor mean when he says, "A backyard is a novel about us, and when we sit there on a summer day, we hear the dialogue and see the characters" (paragraph 23)?

DISCOVERING RHETORICAL STRATEGIES

1. Keillor starts many of his narratives with "It has been a quiet week in Lake Wobegon." What effect does this beginning have on the rest of the essay?
2. What metaphor or comparison does Keillor use to explain in the beginning of his essay that the tree has bloomed? How effective is this opening? Explain your answer.
3. What does this particular crab apple symbolize? Explain your answer in detail.
4. How appropriate is the title of this essay? What are some other possible titles?

MAKING CONNECTIONS

1. Imagine that Paul Roberts ("How to Say Nothing in Five Hundred Words") has just read Keillor's essay about the courtship of Harold and Marlys Diener. What grade do you think he would give the paper in a college composition class? What comments would he have for its author?
2. Compare and contrast Keillor's technique of recalling the past in this essay with similar recollections in Ray Bradbury's

"Summer Rituals," Russell Baker's "The Saturday Evening Post," and Phyllis Schneider's "Memory: Tips You'll Never Forget." Which author's technique of historical reporting seems most vivid and convincing to you? Explain why.

3. Throughout his essay, Keillor mentions a number of details that will strike most readers as funny. How is Keillor's use of humor different from that of Bill Cosby ("The Baffling Question"), Jessica Mitford ("Behind the Formaldehyde Curtain"), Judy Brady ("Why I Want a Wife"), or Mary Roach ("Meet the Bickersons")? Which of these essays do you find most entertaining? Explain your answer.

IDEAS FOR DISCUSSION/WRITING

Preparing to Write

Write freely about various symbols in your life or your family's life: What are these symbols? What do they represent? Which of the symbols remind you of various relationships within your family? Which of these symbols are positive? Which are negative? Which symbols remind you of important stories about yourself or other family members? Why are these stories important? What makes specific family stories so important?

Choosing a Topic

1. Write a narrative essay introducing yourself to your English class through a special item in your life. To explain and define your identity, include your relationship to this item in your essay.

2. Write a narrative essay that explains how your parents met. What were the highlights of this meeting? Where did it lead? What is their relationship like now?

3. Your school newspaper is running a series of articles on symbols in our lives. You have been asked to submit a narrative essay on the item that best represents you as a student in college. What is this item? How does it represent you? Shape your answers to these questions into a narrative essay.

Before beginning your essay, you might want to consult the checklists on pages 115–116.

CHAPTER WRITING ASSIGNMENTS

Practicing Narration

1. Think of a story that is often repeated by your family members because of its special significance or its humor. Retell the story to an audience who does not know your family, and explain to your readers the story's significance.

2. What has been the most challenging and life-changing event in your life? Remember this event as clearly as you can by noting special details on scratch paper. Write an essay that describes what led up to this event, what happened, and how you reacted to the event. Explain why this experience was so challenging and/or life-changing.

3. Think of a time when you received a very special gift. Tell the story of how you received this gift, who gave it to you, and why it was memorable. For a more sophisticated approach, try to think of gifts that are not material or tangible objects, but rather intangible qualities or concepts (such as love, life, and happiness).

Exploring Ideas

1. Write an essay that identifies the most important qualities in a friend. Explain how each quality is important to a meaningful and fulfilling friendship.

2. Cut an advertisement out of a magazine or newspaper. Examine its "story" and the way the advertiser is selling the product. Write an essay that discusses the effect of advertising on individuals and on American society. How honest or believable should advertising be? What are our expectations for advertising?

3. Describe a time when you quit a job or hobby that others thought you should continue. Discuss the principal features of this activity, your frustration with them, and the main aspects of the job or hobby that others valued. In retrospect, do you think you made a wise decision?

3

EXAMPLE

Illustrating Ideas

Citing an example to help make a point is one of the most instinctive techniques we use in communication. If, for instance, you state that being an internationally ranked tennis player requires constant practice, a friend might challenge that assertion and ask what you mean by "constant practice." When you respond "at least three hours a day," your friend might ask for more specific proof. At this stage in the discussion, you could offer the following illustrations to support your statement: When not on tour, Venus Williams practices three hours per day; Pete Sampras, four hours; and Martina Hingis, five hours. Your friend's doubt will have been answered through your use of examples.

DEFINING EXAMPLES

Well-chosen examples and illustrations are an essay's building blocks. They are drawn from your experience, your observations, and your reading. They help you *show* rather than *tell* what you mean, usually by supplying concrete details (references to what we can see, smell, taste, hear, or touch) to support abstract ideas (such as faith, hope, understanding, and love), by providing specifics

("I like chocolate") to explain generalizations ("I like sweets"), and by giving definite references ("Turn left at the second stoplight") to clarify vague statements ("Turn in a few blocks"). Though illustrations take many forms, writers often find themselves indebted to description or narration (or some combination of the two) in order to supply enough relevant examples to achieve their rhetorical intent.

As you might suspect, examples are important ingredients in producing exciting, vivid prose. Just as crucial is the fact that carefully chosen examples often encourage your readers to feel one way or another about an issue being discussed. If you tell your parents, for instance, that living in a college dormitory is not conducive to academic success, they may doubt your word, perhaps thinking that you are simply attempting to coerce money out of them for an apartment. You can help dispel this notion, however, by giving them specific examples of the chaotic nature of dorm life: the party down the hall that broke up at 2:00 A.M. when you had a chemistry exam that same morning at 8 o'clock; the stereo next door that seems to be stuck on its highest decibel level at all hours of the day and night; and the new "friend" you recently acquired who thinks you are the best listener in the world—especially when everyone else has the good sense to be asleep. After such a detailed and well-documented explanation, your parents could hardly deny the strain of this difficult environment on your studies. Examples can be very persuasive.

The following paragraphs written by a student use examples to explain how the writer reacts to boredom in his life. As you read this excerpt, notice how the writer shows rather than tells the readers how he copes with boredom by providing exciting details that are concrete, specific, and definite:

We all deal with boredom in our own ways. Unfortunately, most of us have to deal with it far too often. Some people actually seek boredom. Being bored means that they are not required to do anything; being boring means that no one wants anything from them. In short, these people equate boredom with peace and relaxation. But for the rest of us, boredom is not peaceful. It produces anxiety.

Most people deal with boredom by trying to distract themselves from boring circumstances. Myself, I'm a reader. At the breakfast table over a boring bowl of cereal, I read the cereal box, the milk carton, the

Example 157

wrapper on the bread. (Have you ever noticed how many of those ingredients are unpronounceable?) Waiting in a doctor's office, I will gladly read weekly news magazines of three years ago, a book for five-year-olds, advertisements for drugs, and even the physician's odd-looking diplomas on the walls. Have you ever been so bored you were reduced to reading through all the business cards in your wallet? Searching for names similar to yours in the phone book? Browsing through the National Enquirer *while waiting in the grocery line? At any rate, that's my recipe for beating boredom. What's yours?*

THINKING CRITICALLY BY USING EXAMPLE

Working with examples gives you yet another powerful way of processing your immediate environment and the larger world around you. It involves a manner of thinking that is completely different from description and narration. Using examples to think critically means seeing a definite order in a series of specific, concrete illustrations related in some way that may or may not be immediately obvious to your readers.

Isolating this rhetorical mode involves playing with related details in such a way that they create various patterns that relay different messages to the reader. Often, the simple act of arranging examples helps both the reader and the writer make sense of an experience or idea. In fact, ordering examples and illustrations in a certain way may give one distinct impression, while ordering them in another way may send a completely different message. Each pattern creates a different meaning and, as a result, an entirely new effect.

With examples, more than with description and narration, patterns need to be discovered in the context of the topic, the writer's purpose, and the writer's ultimate message. Writers and readers of example essays must make a shift from chronological to logical thinking. A writer discussing variations in faces, for example, would be working with assorted memories of people, incidents, and age differences. All of these details will eventually take shape in some sort of statement about faces, but these observations would probably not follow a strictly chronological sequence.

The exercises here will help you experience the mental differences among the rhetorical modes we have studied so far and will also prepare you to make sense of details and examples through careful arrangement and rearrangement of them in your essay. In addition, these exercises will continue to give you more information about your mind's abilities and range.

1. For each sentence below, provide two to three examples that would illustrate the generalization:
   a. I really liked (disliked) some of the movies released this year.
   b. Many career opportunities await a college graduate.
   c. Some companies make large sums of money by selling products with the names of professional sports teams on them.
2. Give an example (as specific as possible) of each item listed here: car, pizza, song, musician, event, friend, emotion, vacation, plant.
3. Jot down five examples of a single problem on campus that bothers you. First, arrange these examples in an order that would convince the president of your school that making some changes in this area would create a more positive learning environment. Second, organize your five examples in such a way that they would convince your parents that the learning environment at your current school cannot be salvaged and you should immediately transfer to another school.

READING AND WRITING ESSAYS THAT USE EXAMPLES

A common criticism of college-level writers is that they often base their essays on unsupported generalizations, such as "All sports cars are unreliable." The guidelines discussed in this introduction will help you avoid this problem and use examples effectively to support your ideas.

As you read the essays in this chapter, take time to notice the degree of specificity the writers use to make various points. To a certain extent, the more examples you use in your essays, the clearer your ideas will be and the more your readers will understand and be interested in what you are saying.

Notice also that these writers know when to stop—when "more" becomes too much and boredom sets in for the reader. Most college students err by using too few examples, however, so we suggest that, when in doubt about whether or not to include another illustration, you should go ahead and add one.

Example   159

How to Read an Essay that Uses Examples

Preparing to Read.   Before you begin reading the essays in this chapter, take some time to think about each author's title: What can you infer about Bill Cosby's attitude toward having children from his title "The Baffling Question"? What do you think is Fred Pelka's view of the sick in American society? In addition, try to discover the writer's audience and purpose at this point in the reading process; scanning the essay and surveying its synopsis in the Rhetorical Table of Contents will provide you with useful information for this task.

Also important as you prepare to read is information about the author and about how a particular essay was written. Most of this material is furnished for you in the biography preceding each essay. From it, you might learn why Harold Krents is qualified to write about blindness or why Brent Staples published "A Brother's Murder."

Finally, before you begin to read, take time to answer the Preparing to Read questions and to make some associations with the general subject of the essay: What do you know about health chauvinism (Fred Pelka)? What are some of your thoughts on bilingualism (Amy Tan)?

Reading.   As you first read these essays, record any ideas that come to mind. Make associations freely with the content of each essay, its purpose, its audience, and the facts about its publication. For example, try to learn why Cosby writes about having children or why Krents titles his essay "Darkness at Noon." At this point, you will probably be able to make some pretty accurate guesses about the audience each author is addressing. Creating a context for your reading—including the writer's qualifications; the essay's tone, purpose, and audience; and the publication data—is an important first step toward being able to analyze your reading material in any mode.

Finally, after you have read an essay in this section once, preview the questions after the selection before you read it again. Let these questions focus your attention for your second reading.

Rereading.   As you read the essays in this chapter for a second time, focus on the examples each writer uses to make his or her point: How relevant are these examples to the thesis and purpose of each essay? How many examples do the writers use? Do they vary the length of these examples to achieve different goals? Do the authors use examples their readers can easily identify with and understand? How are these examples organized in each case? Does this arrangement support each writer's purpose? For example, how relevant are Cosby's examples to his central idea? How many examples does Pelka use to make each point? Does Krents vary the length of each of his examples to accomplish different purposes? How does Tan organize her examples? Does this arrangement help her accomplish her purpose? In what way? Does Staples use examples that everyone can identify with? How effective are his examples?

As you read, consider also how other rhetorical modes help each writer accomplish his or her purpose. What are these modes? How do they work along with examples to help create a coherent essay?

Last, answering the questions after each essay will help you check your grasp of its main points and will lead you from the literal to the analytical level in preparation for the discussion/writing assignments that follow.

For a thorough summary of reading tasks, you might want to consult the checklists on pages 20–21 of the Introduction.

How to Write an Essay that Uses Examples

Preparing to Write.   Before you can use examples in an essay, you must first think of some. One good way to generate ideas is to use some of the prewriting techniques explained in the Introduction (pages 21–27) as you respond to the Preparing to Write questions that appear before the writing assignments for each essay. You should then consider these thoughts in conjunction with the purpose and audience specified in your chosen writing assignments. Out of these questions should come a number of good examples for your essay.

Writing.   In an example essay, a thesis statement or controlling idea will help you begin to organize your paper. (See page 28 for more information on thesis statements.) Examples become the primary method of organizing an essay when they actually guide the readers from point to point in reference to the writer's thesis

Example   161

statement. The examples you use should always be relevant to the thesis and purpose of your essay. If, for instance, the person talking about tennis players cited the practice schedules of only unknown players, her friend certainly would not be convinced of the truth of her statement about how hard internationally ranked athletes work at their game. To develop a topic principally with examples, you can use one extended example or several shorter examples, depending on the nature and purpose of your assertion. If you are attempting to prove that Americans are more health conscious now than they were twenty years ago, citing a few examples from your own neighborhood will not provide enough evidence to be convincing. If, however, you are simply commenting on a neighborhood health trend, you can legitimately refer to these local cases. Furthermore, always try to find examples with which your audience can identify so that they can follow your line of reasoning. If you want your parents to help finance an apartment, citing instances from the lives of current rock stars will probably not prove your point because your parents may not sympathize with these particular role models.

The examples you choose must also be arranged as effectively as possible to encourage audience interest and identification. If you are using examples to explain the imaginative quality of Disneyland, for instance, the most logical approach would probably be to organize your essay by degrees (i.e., from least to most imaginative or most to least original). But if your essay uses examples to help readers visualize your bedroom, a spatial arrangement of the details (moving from one item to the next) might be easiest for your readers to follow. If the subject is a series of important events, like graduation weekend, the illustrations might most effectively be organized chronologically. As you will learn from reading the selections that follow, the careful organization of examples leads quite easily to unity and coherence in your essays. *Unity* is a sense of wholeness and interrelatedness that writers achieve by making sure all their sentences are related to the essay's main idea; *coherence* refers to logical development in an essay, with special attention to how well ideas grow out of one another as the essay develops. Unity and coherence produce good writing—and that, of course, helps foster confidence and accomplishment in school and in your professional life.

Rewriting. As you reread your example essays, look closely at the choice and arrangement of details in relation to your purpose and audience:

- Have you included enough examples to develop each of your topics adequately?
- Are the examples you have chosen relevant to your thesis?
- Have you arranged these examples in a logical manner that your audience can follow?

For more detailed information on writing, see the checklists on pages 32–34 of the Introduction.

STUDENT ESSAY: EXAMPLES AT WORK

In the following essay, a student uses examples to explain and analyze her parents' behavior as they prepare for and enjoy their grandchildren during the Christmas holidays. As you read it, study the various examples the student writer uses to convince us that her parents truly undergo a transformation each winter.

Mom and Dad's Holiday Disappearing Act

General topic

Often during the winter holidays, people find surprises: Children discover the secret contents of brightly wrapped packages that have teased them for weeks; cooks are astonished by the wealth of smells and memories their busy kitchens can bring about; workaholics stumble upon the true joy of a few days' rest. My surprise over the past few winters has been the personality transformation my parents go through around mid-December as they change from Dad and Mom into Poppa and Granny. Yes, they become grandparents and are completely different from the people I know the other eleven and a half months of the year.

Background information

Thesis statement

The first sign of my parents' metamorphosis is the delight they take in visiting toy and children's clothing stores. These two

Details to capture holiday spirit

First point

Example   163

people, who usually despise anything having to do with shopping malls, become

Examples relevant to thesis

crazed consumers. While they tell me to budget my money and shop wisely, they are buying every doll, dump truck, and velvet outfit in sight. And this is only the beginning of the holidays!

Transition   When my brother's children arrive, Poppa and Granny come into full form. First they throw out all ideas about a balanced diet for the grandkids. While we   Second point were raised in a house where everyone had to take two bites of broccoli, beets, or liver (foods that appeared quite often on our table despite constant groaning), the grandchildren never have to eat anything that does not appeal to them. Granny carries   Humorous examples marshmallows in her pockets to bribe the   (organized from littlest ones into following her around the   particular house, while Poppa offers "surprises" of   to general) candy and cake to them all day long. Boxes of chocolate-covered cherries disappear while the bran muffins get hard and stale. The kids love all the sweets, and when the sugar revs up their energy levels, Granny and Poppa can always decide to leave and do a bit more shopping or go to bed while my brother and sister-in-law try to deal with their supercharged, hyperactive kids.

Transition   Once the grandchildren have arrived, Granny and Poppa also seem to forget all of   Third point the responsibility lectures I so often hear in my daily life. If little Tommy throws a fit at a friend's house, he is "overwhelmed by the number of adults"; if Mickey screams at his sister during dinner, he is "developing his own personality"; if Nancy breaks Granny's vanity mirror (after being told twice to put it down), she is "just a curious child." But, if I track mud into the house while helping to unload groceries, I become "careless"; if I scold one of the grandkids for tearing pages out of my calculus book, I am "impatient." If a grandchild talks back to her mother, Granny and Poppa chuckle at her spirit. If I mumble one word about all of this doting, Mom and Dad have a talk with me about petty jealousies.

Examples in the form of comparison

When my nieces and nephews first started appearing at our home for the holidays a few years ago, I probably was jealous, and I complained a lot. But now I spend more time simply sitting back and watching Mom and Dad change into what we call the "Incredible Huggers." They enjoy their time with these grandchildren so much that I easily forgive them their Granny and Poppa faults.

Tranisition to conclusion

Writer's attitude

I believe their personality change is due to the lack of responsibility they feel for the grandkids: In their role as grandparents, they don't have to worry about sugar causing cavities or temporary failures of self-discipline turning into lifetime faults. Those problems are up to my brother and sister-in-law. All Granny and Poppa have to do is enjoy and love their grandchildren. They have all the fun of being parents without any of the attendant obligations. And you know what? I think they've earned the right to make this transformation—at least once a year.

Writer's analysis of situation

Specific reference to intro- duction

Concluding remark

Student Writer's Comments

To begin this essay, I listed examples of my parents' antics during the Christmas holidays as parents and as grandparents and then tried to figure out how these examples illustrated patterns of behavior. Next, I scratched out an outline pairing my parents' actions with what I thought were the causes of those

Example   165

actions. But once I sat down to write, I was completely stumped. I had lots of isolated ideas and saw a few patterns, but I had no notion of where this essay was going.

I thought I might put the theory that writing is discovery to the ultimate test and sit down to write out a very rough first draft. I wanted the introduction to be humorous, but I also wanted to maintain a dignified tone (so I wouldn't sound like a whiny kid!). I was really having trouble getting started. I decided to write down *anything* and then come back to the beginning later on. All of the examples and anecdotes were swimming around in my head wanting to be committed to paper. But I couldn't make sense of many of them, and I still couldn't see where I was headed. I found I needed my thesaurus and dictionary from the very beginning; they helped take the pressure off me to come up with the perfect word every time I was stuck. As I neared the middle of the paper, the introduction popped into my head, so I jotted down my thoughts and continued with the flow of ideas I needed for the body of my essay.

Writing my conclusion forced me to put my experiences with my parents into perspective and gave me an angle for revising the body of my essay. But my focus didn't come to me until I began to revise my entire paper. At that point, I realized I had never really tried to analyze how I felt toward my parents or why they acted as they do during the Christmas holidays. I opened the conclusion with "I believe their [my parents'] personality change is due to" and sat in one place until I finished the statement with a reason that made sense out of all these years of frustration. It finally came to me: They act the way they do during the holidays because they don't have primary responsibility for their grandkids. It's a role they have never played before, and they are loving it. (Never mind how it is affecting me!) This basic realization led me to new insights about the major changes they go through during the holidays and ended up giving me a renewed appreciation of their behavior. I couldn't believe the sentence I wrote to close the essay: "I think they've earned the right to make this transformation—at least once a year." Holy cow! Writing this essay actually brought me to a new understanding of my parents.

Revising was a breeze. I felt as if I had just been through a completely draining therapy session, but I now knew what I thought of this topic and where my essay was headed. I dropped irrelevant examples, reorganized other details, and tightened up some of the explanations so they set up my conclusion more clearly. Both my parents and I were delighted with the results.

SOME FINAL THOUGHTS ON EXAMPLES

Although examples are often used to supplement and support other methods of development—such as cause/effect, comparison/contrast, and process analysis—the essays in this section focus principally on examples. A main idea is expressed in the introduction of each, and the rest of the essay provides examples to bolster that contention. As you read these essays, pay close attention to each author's choice and arrangement of examples; then try to determine which organizational techniques are most persuasive for each specific audience.

EXAMPLE IN REVIEW

Reading Example Essays

Preparing to Read

- ✓ What assumptions can you make from the essay's title?
- ✓ Can you guess what the general mood of the essay is?
- ✓ What is the essay's purpose and audience?
- ✓ What does the synopsis in the Rhetorical Table of Contents tell you about the essay?
- ✓ What can you learn from the author's biography?
- ✓ Can you guess what the author's point of view toward the subject is?
- ✓ What are your responses to the Preparing to Read questions?

Reading

- ✓ What general message is the author trying to convey?
- ✓ Did you preview the questions that follow the essay?

Example   167

Rereading

- ✓ What examples help the author communicate the essay's general message?
- ✓ How are these examples organized?
- ✓ What other rhetorical modes does the author use to support the essay's purpose?
- ✓ What are your responses to the questions after the essay?

Writing Example Essays

Preparing to Write

- ✓ What are your responses to the Preparing to Write questions?
- ✓ What is your purpose?
- ✓ Who is your audience?
- ✓ What is the message you want to convey?

Writing

- ✓ What is your thesis or controlling idea?
- ✓ Do the examples you are choosing support this thesis?
- ✓ Are these examples arranged as effectively as possible?
- ✓ What is your point of view toward your subject?
- ✓ How do you achieve unity and coherence in your example essay?

Rewriting

- ✓ Have you included enough examples to develop each of your topics adequately?
- ✓ Are the examples you have chosen relevant to your thesis?
- ✓ Have you arranged these examples in a logical manner that your audience can follow?

The Baffling Question

Comedian, actor, recording artist, and author Bill Cosby is undoubtedly one of America's best-loved entertainers. From his beginnings on the *I Spy* television series through his *Fat Albert* years and his work on *Sesame Street*, his eight Grammy awards for comedy albums, his commercials for everything from Kodak film to Jell-O pudding, his portrayal of the affable obstetrician Cliff Huxtable on his immensely popular *Cosby Show*, and his latest role in *Kids Say the Darndest Things*, he has retained his public persona of an honest and trustworthy storyteller intrigued by the ironies in our everyday lives. "When I was a kid," he has explained, "I always used to pay attention to things that other people didn't even think about. I'd remember funny happenings, just little trivial things, and then tell stories about them later. I found I could make people laugh, and I enjoyed doing it because it gave me a sense of security. I thought that if people laughed at what you said, that meant they liked you." After a series of hit movies in the 1970s, Cosby returned to prime-time television in 1984 because of his concern about his family's viewing habits: "I got tired of seeing TV shows that consisted of a car crash, a gunman, and a hooker talking to a Black pimp. It was cheaper to do a series than to throw out my family's six television sets." At the peak of its success, *The Cosby Show* was seen weekly by over sixty million viewers. Cosby's publications include *You Are Somebody Special* (1978), *Fatherhood* (1986), *Time Flies* (1988), and *Love and Marriage* (1989). He lives with his wife, Camille, in Los Angeles, where he relaxes by playing an occasional game of tennis.

Preparing to Read

The following selection is from one of Cosby's six books, *Fatherhood*, which details the joys and frustrations of raising children. Before reading this piece, pause to consider the effect parenthood has had or might have on your life: How did/would you make the decision whether to have children? What variables were/would be involved in this decision? What are/would be some of the difficulties involved in raising children? Some of the joys?

How did your parents react to you when you were a child? What memories do you have of your own childhood?

So you've decided to have a child. You've decided to give up 1 quiet evenings with good books and lazy weekends with good music, intimate meals during which you finish whole sentences, sweet private times when you've savored the thought that just the two of you and your love are all you will ever need. You've decided to turn your sofas into trampolines and to abandon the joys of leisurely contemplating reproductions of great art for the joys of frantically coping with reproductions of yourselves. Why? 2

Poets have said the reason to have children is to give yourself 3 immortality; and I must admit I did ask God to give me a son because I wanted someone to carry on the family name. Well, God did just that, and I now confess that there have been times when I've told my son not to reveal who he is.

"You make up a name," I've said. "Just don't tell anybody 4 who you are."

Immortality? Now that I have had five children, my only hope 5 is that they all are out of the house before I die.

No, immortality was not the reason why my wife and I pro- 6 duced these beloved sources of dirty laundry and ceaseless noise. And we also did not have them because we thought it would be fun to see one of them sit in a chair and stick out his leg so that another one of them running by was launched like Explorer I. After which I said to the child who was the launching pad, "Why did you do that?"

"Do what?" he replied. 7

"Stick out your leg." 8

"Dad, I didn't know my leg was going out. My leg, it does that 9 a lot."

If you cannot function in a world where things like this are 10 said, then you better forget about raising children and go for daffodils.

My wife and I also did not have children so they could yell at 11 each other all over the house, moving me to say, "What's the problem?"

"She's waving her foot in my room," my daughter replied.   12

"And something like that *bothers* you?"   13

"Yes, I don't *want* her foot in my room."   14

"Well," I said, dipping into my storehouse of paternal wisdom,   15
"why don't you just close the door?"

"Then I can't see what she's doing!"   16

Furthermore, we did not have the children because we   17
thought it would be rewarding to watch them do things that
should be studied by the Menninger Clinic.

"Okay," I said to all five one day, "go get into the car."   18

All five then ran to the same car door, grabbed the same han-   19
dle, and spent the next few minutes beating each other up. Not
one of them had the intelligence to say, "Hey, *look*. There are
three more doors." The dog, however, was already inside.

And we did not have the children to help my wife develop   20
new lines for her face or because she had always had a desire to
talk out loud to herself: "Don't tell *me* you're *not* going to do
something when I tell you to move!" And we didn't have children so I could always be saying to someone, "Where's my
change?"

Like so many young couples, my wife and I simply were un-   21
able to project. In restaurants we did not see the small children
who were casting their bread on the water in the glasses the
waiter had brought; and we did not see the mother who was fasting because she was both cutting the food for one child while
pulling another from the floor to a chair that he would use for
slipping to the floor again. And we did not project beyond those
lovely Saturdays of buying precious little things after leisurely
brunches together. We did not see that *other* precious little things
would be coming along to destroy the first batch.

UNDERSTANDING DETAILS

1. According to Cosby, exactly what is "the baffling question"?
   Why is this question "baffling"?
2. If everyone felt as Cosby does about raising children, what
   kinds of people would have children?
3. List three important issues that Cosby believes couples should
   consider before they have children.

4. From Cosby's point of view, in what important ways do children change a couple's life?

ANALYZING MEANING

1. Why do you think Cosby focuses on the problems children create in a couple's life? What effect does this approach have on his main point?
2. What does Cosby mean when he says, "You've decided . . . to abandon the joys of leisurely contemplating reproductions of great art for the joys of frantically coping with reproductions of yourselves" (paragraph 1)? Whom is he addressing?
3. Following Cosby's logic, why did he and his wife have children? What examples lead you to this conclusion?
4. In what way is the last sentence in this essay a good summary statement? What specific thoughts does it summarize?

DISCOVERING RHETORICAL STRATEGIES

1. How does the first paragraph set the tone for the rest of the essay?
2. Cosby's primary strategy in this essay is irony. That is, he suggests reasons for having children by listing reasons *not* to have children. What effect is this approach likely to have on his readers?
3. How does Cosby use specific examples to create humor? Is his humor effective? Explain your answer.
4. Cosby is a master of choosing vivid examples to make his point. What other rhetorical strategies does Cosby use to develop his essay? Give examples of each.

MAKING CONNECTIONS

1. Compare Bill Cosby's comments about raising children with those made by Germaine Greer in "A Child Is Born." To what extent is the behavior of Cosby's children typically "American" according to Greer's description of Western society?
2. How seriously does Cosby intend his readers to take his "advice" about not having children? Do you see any connection between his point of view and that expressed by Judy Brady in

"Why I Want a Wife"? How do both of these essays work through the rhetorical device of "irony" (that is, saying the opposite of what we really mean)? Which essay is most effective? Explain your answer.

3. Contrast Cosby's rapport with his children with the parent–child relationships depicted in Lewis Sawaquat's "For My Indian Daughter," Sandra Cisneros's "Only daughter," or Michael Dorris's "The Broken Cord." Which parents do you think love their children most? Why do you believe this is true?

IDEAS FOR DISCUSSION/WRITING

Preparing to Write

Write freely about the art of parenthood: From your observations or experience, what are some of the principal problems and joys of parenthood? How is being a parent different from baby-sitting? What pleasant baby-sitting experiences have you had? What unpleasant experiences? What kind of child were you? What specific memories lead you to this conclusion?

Choosing a Topic

1. Write an essay for the general public explaining one particular problem or joy of parenthood. In your essay, mimic Cosby's humorous approach to the topic. Use several specific examples to make your point.

2. Write an editorial for your local newspaper on your own foolproof techniques for doing one of the following: (a) baby-sitting, (b) raising children, or (c) becoming a model child. Use specific examples to explain your approach.

3. Interview one or two relatives who are older than you; ask them about the type of child you were. Have them recall some particularly memorable details that characterized your behavior. Then, write an essay explaining their predominant impressions of you. Use examples to support these impressions.

Before beginning your essay, you might want to consult the checklists on pages 166–167.

Hating the Sick: Health Chauvinism and Its Cure

Fred Pelka was born on Long Island, New York, in 1954 and earned his B.A. in English from State University of New York Buffalo in 1976. He held a variety of odd jobs until 1983, when he became a writer, which he describes as "the oddest job of all." His freelance work has appeared in the *Boston Globe*, the *Christian Science Monitor*, *Mothering*, *Poets and Writers*, the *Three-penny Review*, and a number of other periodicals. He is currently a contributing editor to *On the Issues: The Progressive Women's Quarterly* in New York City and also to *Mainstream: Magazine of the Able-Disabled* in San Diego. His first book, *A Companion to the Disability Rights Movement*, was published by ABCCLIO in 1997. In his opinion, men and women with disabilities are "the most oppressed people on the planet," and the disability movement "is one of the most important civil rights movements in the last hundred years." In his spare time, Pelka enjoys traveling "as cheaply as possible." Recent favorite destinations have included Reykjavik, Iceland; Zagreb, Croatia; and the Colville National Forest in Washington. His advice to student writers using *The Prose Reader* is "to read as much as possible, and then choose the writers you love, living and dead, to be your inspiration and mentors."

Preparing to Read

"Hating the Sick: Health Chauvinism and Its Cure," which originally appeared in *The Humanist* (July/August 1994), argues that most people are prejudiced to some degree against the sick and disabled. The author cites various examples of abusive behavior to prove his point. As you prepare to read this essay, take a few moments to consider your own feelings and reactions to those who are less fortunate than you: To what extent does discrimination play a part in your reaction? Have you ever experienced prejudice? Have any of your friends experienced it? Do you think bigotry exists in other areas of life in today's society? If so, which areas of life seem most troubled? Which are least so? What can be done to relieve hatred toward the sick and disabled? How would you go about making your ideas a reality?

Nothing comes to an individual that he has not summoned. . . . A person's external circumstances do fit their level of internal spiritual development.

Eileen Gardner

A couple of years back, I went to see a midnight screening 1 of *The Rocky Horror Picture Show*. Determined to do my share at this audience-participation event, I threw rice during the marriage scene, squirted water during the rain scene, and shouted the appropriate responses at this or that bit of dialogue.

Near the end of the film, one of the characters, a professorial 2 type in a wheelchair, was confronted by Riff Raff, a hunchback from Transsexual Transylvania armed with a silver ray-gun. A theatergoer behind me—far gone in excitement or intoxication—stood up, shaking his fist, and screamed, "Kill that fucking cripple!" The rest of the audience cheered.

I was stunned. Turning, I saw something on the man's face be- 3 yond simple amusement. I saw anger. I saw contempt. I saw hatred.

We live in a health chauvinist society—a culture that often re- 4 gards the disabled and ill as morally inferior to those who are able-bodied and healthy. Just as our culture often blames rape survivors for their victimization and poor people for their poverty, we all receive messages, both subtle and overt, that people with disabilities are "different," that sickness and disability are caused by sin, bad karma, or negative emotions.

Consider an article by Catherine Ponder called "Forgiveness Is 5 Healing," which appeared in the winter 1991 issue of *Spirit of Change*, a New Age journal specializing in features on holistic healing, childhood mystical experiences, Feldenkrais, and so on. The article is an excerpt from Ponder's mid-1960s book *The Dynamic Laws of Healing*, which, according to the editors of *Spirit of Change*, demonstrates how "by forgiving the roots of our disease, we regain perfect health." Together with Eileen Gardner's comment, cited above, it is one of the most succinct statement's of health chauvinism I've seen.

Ponder's piece begins with a parable in which two people talk   6
about a third person's illness (as is usually the case, at no time is
the person with the disability allowed to speak for herself):

> A puzzled lady said to a friend, "I cannot understand it. I have
> the nicest neighbor who is dying of cancer. It seems so unfair,
> because this is one of the kindest, gentlest people I know."
>
> The friend replied, "She may seem kind and gentle, but if
> she is dying of cancer, then there is some old negative emotion
> that is literally consuming the cells of her body. There is proba-
> bly someone she hates."

"Later," Ponder tells us, "the mystery was cleared up. The one
in doubt reported, 'You were right. I learned quite by accident
that this neighbor has a relative whom she violently hates. They
have not spoken in thirty years.'" The article goes on to describe
another woman who "discovered a lump on her breast. Instead of
frantically rushing out to negatively discuss it with others, she decided to analyze the situation and pray for guidance. . . . She realized that a hard condition in the body indicates a corresponding
hard condition of the mind." The story ends with the woman
eventually curing her cancer through daily meditation, which
presumably softened her mind.

"If you have a problem," Ponder concludes, "you have some-   7
thing to forgive. If you experience pain, you need to forgive."

This notion of disability as a sign of moral failure, a mark of   8
evil, is apparent even in our fairy tales and children's stories,
where the villain is often someone with an obvious physical disability or "deformity"—a child-eating dwarf or monster or giant,
a Rumpelstilskin or a Captain Hook. Leslie Fiedler, in *Freaks:
Myths and Images of the Secret Self,* points out how "*monster* is the
oldest word in our tongue for human anomalies."

Our contemporary movies and literature continue this theme.   9
Freddy Krueger—the mutilated child molester in the *Nightmare on
Elm Street* slasher series—is a perfect example of this correlation
between evil and physical deformity. Not only does he have
razor-extended fingernails (an update on Captain Hook) but the
layers of scar tissue on his face show us just how evil he really is.
Scar tissue, says Susana Kaysen in *Girl Interrupted*, is not just the
natural consequence of trauma to tissue. "It shields and disguises

what's beneath. That's why we grow it; we have something to hide." *Mainstream* magazine, a disability-rights monthly published in San Diego, recently ran a cover story on "the new black-face"—how Hollywood generally hires able-bodied actors and actresses to pretend they're disabled. Most of these characters—from Richard Dreyfuss in *Whose Life Is It, Anyway?* to Al Pacino in *Scent of a Woman*—are portrayed as embittered and emotionally stunted, unattractive people who need their able-bodied friends to straighten them out. A "Star Trek: Deep Space Nine" episode featured a disabled woman whose maladjusted anger and bitterness were soothed by the ministrations of her non-disabled doctor.

Hollywood's image of disability mirrors what the religious   10 community has been telling us for millennia. Eileen Gardner's statement didn't come out of a vacuum; she identified herself as a born-again Christian, and her sentiments place her in the mainstream of fundamentalist Christian thought. For every message in the Bible that tells us the rain falls on the just and the unjust alike, there are multiple stories of illness and disability—especially mental illness or disability—being caused by demonic possession and cast out by the righteous and godly (and non-disabled). Jesus may tell us in John 9:1 that blindness is not caused by sin, but he also cures mental illness by casting "unclean spirits" out of the sufferer and into a herd of swine. And Fiedler points out that, although dwarfs, for example, were sometimes elevated to high office in the Roman Catholic church, there was also an injunction in Leviticus forbidding them to serve at the altar.

"In Biblical times," writes Kathi Wolfe in "The Bible and Dis-   11 abilities: From 'Healing' to the 'Burning Bush'" (*Disability Rag*, September/October 1993), "many thought that disabilities were caused by sin. People with disabilities were outcasts, ignored by their families and neighbors—often left alone to beg. The Bible was influenced by this context in its portrayal of disabled people."

"We all know that sin is evil," writes R. Randolph Cooper, in   12 "Healing: The Visible Sign of a Whole Ministry." Cooper is a contributor to *Sharing: A Journal of Christian Healing*, published by the Order of St. Luke the Physician, which describes itself as an "interdenominational, international" organization "dedicated to Christian healing." "Likewise, sickness is evil, and our deliverance from sickness is as real and necessary to our salvation as is our deliverance from sin." Cooper first qualifies this by saying that "sickness is merely a manifestation of evil (not my evil, but the presence of evil at work in the world)." In the next sentence, however, he emphasizes that "*to be forgiven and to be healed are exactly the same* —healing brings forgiveness, and forgiveness brings healing." And so the Christian Cooper reaches exactly the same conclusion as the New Age Ponder.

Conversely, some fundamentalist Christians see the alleged   13 powers of faith-healers as proof of a direct hotline to divinity. Take as an example erstwhile presidential candidate Pat Robertson. When he isn't railing about feminists trying to turn women into lesbians, child murderers, and witches, he's bestowing his spiritual largesse on (generally anonymous) people with disabilities. These quotes are taken from one of his "700 Club" broadcasts: "We come up against cancer and declare it gone in the name of Jesus! High blood pressure, give way. . . . The sinus cavities must he opened up. . . ."

"Sickness," writes the Reverend Mark A. Pearson of the Order   14 of St. Luke, "comes from a misuse of human free will as expressed in sin. . . . If I abuse my body, which is the Temple of God, if I harbor bitterness or anger, if I refuse to forgive, some kind of sickness will likely occur." The Reverend Rufus J. Womble, also of the Order, writes of the ill and disabled "surrendering to illness and defeat, without realizing in the slightest degree that they have yielded to evil."

This condemnation of people with disabilities is by no means   15 limited to Christians or to Western cultures. James I. Charlton, in "Religion and Disability: A World View" (*Disability Rag,* September/October 1993), quotes disability activists from Zimbabwe, Malaysia, and Indonesia as saying that their religious traditions also regard disability as "divine punishment." Upon his retirement, the head of the Spastic Society of Britain was asked if he could envision the day when a person with spasticity would head that charity. "That'd be like putting dogs and cats in charge of the Humane Society," he quipped, as quoted in the November/December 1993 issue of *Mouth: The Voice of Disability Rights.*

The social and individual acceptance of health chauvinism   16 serves a number of purposes. First, it mitigates any responsibility those of us who aren't ill or disabled might feel toward those who are. Not only are the disabled different, but they are to blame for that difference, and they have thus placed themselves outside the circle of our compassion. We need not worry about discriminating against them in the workplace or slashing funds for Medicaid or rehabilitation or independent-living services. If we do decide to help "the less fortunate," health chauvinism allows us to adopt a stance of moral superiority—of pity, charity, and "forgiveness."

Health chauvinism also undercuts any critique of a social sys-   17
tem that oppresses people with disabilities, who commonly report that it is society's reaction to their disability—in the form of attitudinal barriers, job and school and housing discrimination, and lack of accessible transportation and public facilities—rather than the disability itself, that is their greatest problem. "The problem with blindness or mobility impairment or hearing impairment is every bit as much what society as a whole refuses to accommodate," Dr. Irving Zola, chair of sociology at Brandeis University, told the *Boston Globe* in April 1993. "If you individualize it, if it's only my personal character, my God, we don't have to do anything. We don't have to make ramps to make buildings accessible. We don't have to change. It's not our attitudes—it's that *he's* so screwed up."

It's also worth noting here that blaming cancer or other ill-   18
nesses on bad feelings lets other possible culprits off the hook—for instance, the nuclear power industry, chemical pollutants in our food and our environment, and so on. Again, health chauvinism works to prop up the status quo, to undermine voices for radical change.

Second, health chauvanism serves to protect the temporarily   19
well and able-bodied from the fear of the unknown or unmanageable. Since we cannot predict, with any certainty, who will develop leukemia or liver cancer or multiple sclerosis, none of us knows if and when we or a loved one might be stricken. Not to worry: Eileen Gardner, Pat Robertson, *Spirit of Change*, and the Order of St. Luke all have the answer. If cancer is caused by bad feelings, or by being bad, we all can avoid it by following the right rules. Thus, a collateral benefit for the healthy is that health chauvinism allows them to feel good about themselves. After all, if illness or disability are caused by sin or bad thoughts or wrong living, then the fact that I'm healthy must mean I'm a pretty swell person. This works fine and goes a long way toward helping you keep your peace of mind—until the day you come down with cancer.

This isn't to say that there is no link between attitude or emo- 20
tions and health, or that certain behaviors—cigarette smoking, for
example, or heavy drug or alcohol use—aren't self-destructive.
But such behaviors aren't *sinful*, nor are they purely questions
of attitude; nor do they explain the majority of illnesses and
disabilities.

Finally, health chauvinism serves to divide the disabled from 21
other disenfranchised groups, as the comments of Norfolk
County District Attorney William Delahunt make clear. Last year,
a 76-year-old Quincy, Massachusetts, woman—a resident of a
public-housing project for elders and people with disabilities—
was raped in her apartment. Though the police had no suspect
and no evidence whatsoever that anyone living in the building
had committed the crime, the DA nevertheless concluded that the
assailant was a mentally ill resident and that "you just can't mix"
the mentally ill with the elderly. Quincy Public Housing Director
Jake Comer went even further, calling for a cap on the number of
disabled people in elderly/disabled housing, and telling the press
that the elderly have to live in fear of the mentally disabled. All of
this, even though, according to Stephen E. Collins at the Alliance
for the Mentally Ill of Massachusetts, "study after study has shown
that the population of persons with mental illness is less violent
than the general population. In fact, the mentally ill are more
likely to be victims of crime than perpetrators."

It's no coincidence that the two examples in Ponder's article 22
on how "negative emotions" and "hard feelings" cause illness are
women. Women are generally more likely than men to be
blamed for their own illness or disability. We can trace this at least
as far back as the creation myth of Adam and Eve, where the pain
of childbirth—and the death that often resulted from it—were
blamed on women's sinfulness, on their status as "daughters of
Eve." Health chauvinism and sexism go hand in hand, from the
contempt with which the medical profession has traditionally
treated "women's problems" (such as menstruation and menopause) to the use of diagnoses such as "hysteria" and "depression"
to brush off any malady or disability the male-dominated medical
profession cannot immediately explain or treat.

"There's a tradition in psychiatry," says Dr. Miriam Greenspan, 23
author of *A New Approach to Women and Therapy,* "of diagnosing

women with any kind of physical complaint as having 'hysteria.'
Recently it's been changed to 'depression.'"

Here's what the thirteenth edition of the *Merck Manual*, the   24
bible of medical definitions, says about "hysteria":

> For the hysterical patient, the sickness role is a preferable alter-
> native to ordinary life. The role of the invalid includes social
> permission to be dependent, and immature personalities who
> cannot satisfy their dependency needs in adult relationships
> may seek the special attention and compassion given to a sick
> person.

How far is this, really, from the Order of St. Luke's Reverend
Rufus J. Womble when he writes,

> One question the sick should face is—do you really want to be
> well, regardless of how desperately ill you may be? Do you re-
> ally want to give up your grumbling and other poisonous sins?
> Do you want to come out into the world and accept your full
> responsibility or do you want to continue your sheltered life?

Womble's notion that people with disabilities lead "sheltered"
lives is far off the mark. John Winske, director of the Massachusetts Coalition of Citizens with Disabilities, cites a national
unemployment rate of 65 to 70 percent for people with disabilities seeking work. He points out that housing, job, and social
discrimination against people with disabilities has been so preva-
lent that federal legislation was required to address the problen.
(Indeed, at one time a Chicago city ordinance made it illegal for
anyone who was "in any way deformed so as to be an unsightly
or disgusting object" to appear in public.) And Dr. Sandra Cole in
Disability, Sexuality, and Abuse points out that the incidence of
physical and sexual abuse of disabled people is apparently far
higher than that of the general public.

Health chauvinism, like other prejudices, generally gets worse   25
with hard economic times, and that certainly seems to be the case
today. In Germany, skinheads are targeting people with disabilities as well as *Auslanders*. "Violence Against Disabled People in
Germany," a report prepared in 1993 by German disability-rights
advocate Ottmar Miles-Paul and Dinah Radtke, documents how

a blind man was beaten to death in Siegen, how deaf students were attacked and beaten in Halle, and how a wheelchair user in Hannover committed suicide after he'd been spat upon by school children and then pushed down the stairs of a subway station. During these attacks, the assailants were heard to say, "Under Hitler you would have been gassed." The reference is to the Nazis' T4 program, under which tens of thousands of severely disabled and mentally ill Germans were murdered in the early 1940s through lethal injections or in gas vans and gas chambers. According to Hannah Arendt in *Eichmann in Jerusalem*, some of the techniques developed in this war of extermination against what Hitler called "useless eaters" were later used during the Final Solution.

Closer to home, Barbara Faye Waxman, project director for   26 ADA training for the Los Angeles Regional Family Planning Council, has written on hatred as the "unacknowledged dimension in violence against disabled people." Waxman has recommended that the federal government begin tracking hate crimes against people with disabilities. In an article in the fall 1991 issue of *Sexuality and Disability,* she cites the case of Cary Dickenson, whom she believes was targeted by his assailants because of his multiple disabilities, murdered, and then stuffed into the trash at a southern California library. James Lundvall, a Denver man with paraplegia, was hospitalized in a coma after vandals set fire to the wheelchair ramp to his house—twice within 48 hours. Two-and-a-half-year-old Eric Bernstein was shot to death by his mother when he wouldn't respond to treatment for his multiple disabilities. "It has not yet occurred to the authorities," Waxman writes, "that these overt acts were hate crimes."

The traditional explanation of why people with disabilities are   27 so often the victims of abuse has been that they are more vulnerable than the general population and, thus, easier targets. Waxman believes otherwise:

> While it is certainly true that society places disabled people in highly vulnerable situations, the contention that vulnerability is the primary explanation for disability-related violence is too superficial. Rather, *hatred is the primary cause, and vulnerabilty only provides an opportunity for offenders to express their hatred.* Indeed, people who are respected and considered an equal are not generally abused. [emphasis added]

Our collective response to AIDS is ample indication that health   28
chauvinism can have devastating consequences—and not only for
the currently disabled. Pat Buchanan, speaking for homophobes
everywhere, declared the epidemic to be "nature's" response to
homosexuality, as if the epidemic was some divine retribution for
the "sin" of being gay. That sentiments like these are linked in
fundamental ways to the oppression of people with disabilities has
been acknowledged by members of both the disability and the
HIV/AIDS communities. The founding of the HIV/Disability
Alliance in Boston is a recognition that the two groups have common interests and in many ways share a common oppression.

To end health chauvinism, we must first recognize it for what   29
it is: a form of bigotry, a category of hate. Giving up this prejudice will be difficult, because it means coming to terms with our
own fragility, our own mortality. It means recognizing that disability and illness are an inevitable part of the human experience.
We are all only one accident, one virus, one bacteria cell away
from being ill or disabled ourselves. The true test of our morality
is how we treat each other in the face of this unalterable reality.

UNDERSTANDING DETAILS

1. What incident at the beginning of the essay shocked the
   writer?
2. What is a "health chauvinist society" (paragraph 4)? What are
   its primary values?
3. What contemporary characters portray deformity in their physical appearance?
4. According to Pelka, how does the Bible depict disabled people?

ANALYZING MEANING

1. In what ways does society believe that "sickness is merely a
   manifestation of evil" (paragraph 12)?
2. In what ways do "health chauvinism and sexism go hand in
   hand" (paragraph 22)? Explain your answer.
3. How is society's general reaction to AIDS related to health
   chauvinism? Can you offer some examples that support the author's theory about their connection?
4. Why does Pelka call health chauvinism "a form of bigotry"
   (paragraph 29)?

DISCOVERING RHETORICAL STRATEGIES

1. List the author's main points in this essay. Why does he choose to deal with these topics in this particular order?
2. What examples does Pelka use to support each of his main points? Outline the essay to show how the examples work.
3. Describe Pelka's intended audience in as much detail as possible. Why do you think he has aimed his essay at this particular group?
4. Besides examples, what other rhetorical strategies does Pelka draw upon to make his statement about health chauvinism in the United States? Give examples of each.

MAKING CONNECTIONS

1. Imagine that Shelby Steele ("Affirmative Action: The Price of Preference") has just read Pelka's essay. Would he agree or disagree with Pelka's principal argument that health chauvinism is a form of prejudice? Explain your answer.
2. Lewis Sawaquat ("For My Indian Daughter"), Harold Krents ("Darkness at Noon"), Rosenbaum and Chesney-Lind ("Appearance and Delinquency: A Research Note"), and Pelka all approach bigotry in different ways. Which author's argument do you find most convincing? Explain your reasoning.
3. Compare and contrast Pelka's use of examples with the examples provided by Bill Cosby ("The Baffling Question") and/or by Harold Krents ("Darkness at Noon"). Whose explanation is most interesting? Explain your answer.

IDEAS FOR DISCUSSION/WRITING

Preparing to Write

Write freely about the response of contemporary society to illness and disability in general: In what areas of our society have disabled rights advanced most dramatically? Where has their advancement been least dramatic? Why do you think disabled Americans have had more success in some areas than in others? How does prejudice prevent the sick and disabled from making social and economic progress? Which aspects of American life are most blatantly prejudiced against the sick and disabled? Which are least prejudiced? How do you account for this difference?

Choosing a Topic

1. Using many examples to support his argument, Pelka claims in his essay that health chauvinism is pervasive in American society. From your view of the world, write an example essay explaining to your friends another social problem that is also widespread in American society.

2. As a college student, you see many events every day that could qualify as hate crimes. Write an essay for your school newspaper entitled "Hating the _____." Fill in the blank, and then, through carefully chosen examples, explain to the college community the extent of the hatred you have identified.

3. The Americans with Disabilities Act (ADA) went into effect in 1991. It was designed to protect the rights of people with disabilities, making public places more accessible for those with disabilities. Have you noticed a change in accessibility for the disabled in public places over the last five years? Direct your comments to the general public, and use examples to support your opinion.

Before beginning your essay, you might want to consult the checklists on pages 166–167.

HAROLD KRENTS   (1944–1987)

Darkness at Noon

Raised in New York City, Harold Krents earned a B.A. and a law degree at Harvard, studied at Oxford University, worked as a partner in a Washington, D.C., law firm, was the subject of a longrunning Broadway play, and wrote a popular television movie—all despite the fact that he was born blind. His "1-A" classification by a local draft board, which doubted the severity of his handicap, brought about the 1969 Broadway hit play *Butterflies Are Free* by Leonard Gershe. Krents once explained that he was merely the "prototype" for the central character: "I gave the story its inspiration—the play's plot is not my story; its spirit is." In 1972 Krents wrote *To Race the Wind*, which was made into a CBS-TV movie in 1980. During his career as a lawyer, Krents worked hard to expand legal protection for the handicapped and fought to secure their right to equal opportunity in the business world. He died in 1987 of a brain tumor.

Preparing to Read

In the following article, originally published in *The New York Times* (1978), the author gives examples of different kinds of discrimination he has suffered because of his blindness. As you prepare to read this essay, take a few minutes to think about disabilities or handicaps in general: Do you have a disability? If so, how are you treated by others? How do you feel others respond to your handicap? Do you know someone else who has a disability? How do you respond to that person? How do you think he or she wants to be treated? To what extent do you think disabilities should affect a person's job opportunities? What can be done to improve society's prejudices against the disabled?

B lind from birth, I have never had the opportunity to see   1
myself and have been completely dependent on the image
I create in the eye of the observer. To date it has not been
narcissistic.

There are those who assume that since I can't see, I obviously   2
also cannot hear. Very often people will converse with me at the

top of their lungs, enunciating each word very carefully. Conversely, people will also often whisper, assuming that since my eyes don't work, my ears don't either.

For example, when I go to the airport and ask the ticket agent   3
for assistance to the plane, he or she will invariably pick up the phone, call a ground hostess and whisper: "Hi, Jane, we've got a 76 here." I have concluded that the word "blind" is not used for one of two reasons: Either they fear that if the dread word is spoken, the ticket agent's retina will immediately detach, or they are reluctant to inform me of my condition of which I may not have been previously aware.

On the other hand, others know that of course I can hear, but   4
believe that I can't talk. Often, therefore, when my wife and I go out to dinner, a waiter or waitress will ask Kit if *"he* would like a drink" to which I respond that "indeed *he* would."

This point was graphically driven home to me while we were   5
in England. I had been given a year's leave of absence from my Washington law firm to study for a diploma in law degree at Oxford University. During the year I became ill and was hospitalized. Immediately after admission, I was wheeled down to the X-ray room. Just at the door sat an elderly woman—elderly I would judge from the sound of her voice. "What is his name?" the woman asked the orderly who had been wheeling me.

"What's your name?" the orderly repeated to me.   6

"Harold Krents," I replied.   7

"Harold Krents," he repeated.   8

"When was he born?"   9

"When were you born?"   10

"November 5, 1944," I responded.   11

"November 5, 1944," the orderly intoned.   12

This procedure continued for approximately five minutes at   13
which point even my saint-like disposition deserted me. "Look," I finally blurted out, "this is absolutely ridiculous. Okay, granted I can't see, but it's got to have become pretty clear to both of you that I don't need an interpreter."

"He says he doesn't need an interpreter," the orderly reported   14
to the woman.

The toughest misconception of all is the view that because I   15
can't see, I can't work. I was turned down by over forty law firms

because of my blindness, even though my qualifications included a cum laude degree from Harvard College and a good ranking in my Harvard Law School class.

The attempt to find employment, the continuous frustration of   16 being told that it was impossible for a blind person to practice law, the rejection letters, not based on my lack of ability but rather on my disability, will always remain one of the most disillusioning experiences of my life.

I therefore look forward to the day, with the expectation that it   17 is certain to come, when employers will view their handicapped workers as a little child did me years ago when my family still lived in Scarsdale.

I was playing basketball with my father in our backyard accord-   18 ing to procedures we had developed. My father would stand beneath the hoop, shout, and I would shoot over his head at the basket attached to our garage. Our next-door neighbor, aged five, wandered over into our yard with a playmate. "He's blind," our neighbor whispered to her friend in a voice that could be heard distinctly by Dad and me. Dad shot and missed; I did the same. Dad hit the rim; I missed entirely; Dad shot and missed the garage entirely. "Which one is blind?" whispered back the little friend.

I would hope that in the near future when a plant manager   19 is touring the factory with the foreman and comes upon a handicapped and nonhandicapped person working together, his comment after watching them work will be, "Which one is disabled?"

UNDERSTANDING DETAILS

1. According to Krents, what are three common misconceptions about blind people?
2. What important details did you learn about Krents's life from this essay? How does he introduce this information?
3. In what ways was Krents frustrated in his search for employment? Was he qualified for the jobs he sought? Why or why not?
4. What attitude toward the handicapped does Krents look forward to in the future?

ANALYZING MEANING

1. What does Krents mean when he says that his self-image gained through the eyes of others "has not been narcissistic" (paragraph 1)? Why do you think this is the case?
2. What is Krents's attitude toward his handicap? What parts of his essay reveal that attitude?
3. How do you account for the reactions to his blindness that Krents tells about in this essay? Are you aware of such behavior in yourself? In others?
4. Do you think we will ever arrive at the point in the working world that Krents describes in the last paragraph? How can we get there? What advantages or disadvantages might accompany such a change?

DISCOVERING RHETORICAL STRATEGIES

1. How does Krents organize the three main points in his essay? Why does he put them in this order? What is the benefit of discussing employment last?
2. Krents often offers specific examples in the form of dialogue or spoken statements. Are these effective ways to develop his main points? Explain your answer.
3. Krents establishes a fairly fast pace in this essay as he discusses several related ideas in a small amount of space. How does he create this sense of speed? What effect does this pace have on his essay as a whole?
4. Although the author's dominant rhetorical mode is example in this essay, what other strategies does he use to develop his ideas? Give examples of each of these strategies.

MAKING CONNECTIONS

1. Compare the employment discrimination faced by Krents because of his blindness with the racial and social discrimination suffered by Lewis Sawaquat ("For My Indian Daughter") and Franklin Zimring ("Confessions of an Ex-Smoker"). Which person has been treated most unfairly by society? Explain your answer.

2. How similar is Krents's use of humor to that of Russell Baker ("The Saturday Evening Post") and Bill Cosby ("The Baffling Question")? Which author do you find most amusing? Why? Is humor used in a different way in Krents's essay than it is in the Cosby essay? If so, how?

3. How many examples does Krents use in his essay? Does Krents use more or fewer examples per page than Bill Cosby ("The Baffling Question") or Fred Pelka ("Hating the Sick: Health Chauvinism and Its Cure")? How does the number of examples affect the believability of each author's argument?

IDEAS FOR DISCUSSION/WRITING

Preparing to Write

Write freely about disabilities: If you are disabled, what is your response to the world? Why do you respond the way you do? How does society respond to you? Are you pleased or not with your relationship to society in general? If you are not disabled, what do you think your attitude would be if you were disabled? How do you respond to disabled people? To what extent does your response depend upon the disability? Are you satisfied with your reaction to other people's disabilities? Are you prejudiced in any way against people with disabilities? Do you think our society as a whole demonstrates any prejudices toward the disabled? If so, how can we correct these biases?

Choosing a Topic

1. As a reporter for your campus newspaper, you have been assigned to study and write about the status of services for the disabled on your campus. Is your school equipped with parking for the handicapped? A sufficient number of ramps for wheelchairs? Transportation for the handicapped? Other special services for the handicapped? Interview some disabled students to get their views on these services. Write an example essay for the newspaper, explaining the situation.

2. With your eyes closed, take a walk through a place that you know well. How does it feel to be nearly sightless? What senses begin to compensate for your loss of vision? Write an essay for

your classmates detailing your reactions. Use specific examples to communicate your feelings.

3. Do you have any phobias or irrational fears that handicap you in any way? Write a letter to a friend explaining one of these "handicaps" and your method of coping with it.

Before beginning your essay, you might want to consult the checklists on pages 166–167.

AMY TAN   (1952–   )

Mother Tongue

In a very short time, Amy Tan has established herself as one of the foremost Chinese-American writers. Her first novel, *The Joy Luck Club* (1989), which was praised as "brilliant . . . a jewel of a book" by *The New York Times Book Review*, focuses on the lives of four Chinese women in pre-1949 China and their American-born daughters in modern-day California. Through a series of vignettes, Tan weaves together the dreams and sorrows of these mothers and daughters as they confront oppression in China and equally difficult cultural challenges in the new world of the United States. Like the protagonists in *The Joy Luck Club*, Tan's parents, a Baptist minister and a licensed vocational nurse, emigrated to America shortly before Tan's birth. She showed an early talent for writing when, at age eight, she won an essay contest (and a transistor radio) with a paper entitled "Why I Love the Library." Following the tremendous success of her first novel, Tan apparently had great difficulty writing her second book, *The Kitchen God's Wife* (1991). As she was working on it, she began grinding her teeth, which resulted in two broken molars and a sizable dental bill. "I am glad that I shall never again have to write a second book," the author has confessed. "Actually, I cannot recall any writer—with or without a splashy debut—who said the second book came easily." Successful film and stage adaptations of *The Joy Luck Club* in 1993 were followed by *The Chinese Siamese Cat* (1994), *The Hundred Secret Senses* (1995), *The Year of No Flood* (1996), and *The Bonesetter's Daughter* (2001).

Preparing to Read

In the following essay, originally published in *The Threepenny Review*, Amy Tan explains the different "Englishes" she learned to use in her youth. As you prepare to read this essay, take a few minutes to think about the different varieties of English that you use: How do you change your use of English when you relay the same message to different people? Why do you make these changes? Do you feel as if you do well in English class? On English tests? Do your test scores represent your true abilities in

English? In Math? How could you become an even better writer
and speaker of English than you already are?

I am not a scholar of English or literature. I cannot give you
much more than personal opinions on the English language
and its variations in this country or others.   1

I am a writer. And by that definition, I am someone who has   2
always loved language. I am fascinated by language in daily life. I
spend a great deal of my time thinking about the power of language—the way it can evoke an emotion, a visual image, a complex idea, or a simple truth. Language is the tool of my trade. And
I use them all—all the Englishes I grew up with.

Recently, I was made keenly aware of the different Englishes I do   3
use. I was giving a talk to a large group of people, the same talk I
had already given to half a dozen other groups. The nature of the
talk was about my writing, my life, and my book, *The Joy Luck Club*.
The talk was going along well enough, until I remembered one
major difference that made the whole talk sound wrong. My mother
was in the room. And it was perhaps the first time she had heard me
give a lengthy speech, using the kind of English I have never used
with her. I was saying things like, "The intersection of memory
upon imagination" and "There is an aspect of my fiction that relates
to thus-and-thus"—a speech filled with carefully wrought grammatical phrases, burdened, it suddenly seemed to me, with nominalized
forms, past perfect tenses, conditional phrases, all the forms of standard English that I had learned in school and through books, the
forms of English I did not use at home with my mother.

Just last week, I was walking down the street with my mother,   4
and I again found myself conscious of the English I was using, the
English I do use with her. We were talking about the price of
new and used furniture and I heard myself saying this: "Not waste
money that way." My husband was with us as well, and he didn't
notice any switch in my English. And then I realized why. It's because over the twenty years we've been together I've often used
the same kind of English with him, and sometimes he even uses it
with me. It has become our language of intimacy, a different sort
of English that relates to family talk, the language I grew up with.

So you'll have some idea of what this family talk I heard sounds   5
like, I'll quote what my mother said during a recent conversation

which I videotaped and then transcribed. During this conversation, my mother was talking about a political gangster in Shanghai who had the same last name as her family's, Du, and how the gangster in his early years wanted to be adopted by her family, which was rich by comparison. Later, the gangster became more powerful, far richer than my mother's family, and one day showed up at my mother's wedding to pay his respects. Here's what she said in part:

"Du Yusong having business like fruit stand. Like of the street kind. He is Du like Du Zong—but not Tsung-ming Island people. The local people call putong, the river east side, he belong to that side local people. That man want to ask Du Zong father take him in like become own family. Du Zong father wasn't look down on him, but didn't take seriously, until that man big like become a mafia. Now important person, very hard to inviting him. Chinese way, came only to show respect, don't stay for dinner. Respect for making big celebration, he shows up. Mean gives lots of respect. Chinese custom. Chinese social life that way. If too important won't have to stay too long. He come to my wedding. I didn't see, I heard it. I gone to boy's side, they have YMCA dinner, Chinese age I was nineteen." 6

You should know that my mother's expressive command of English belies how much she actually understands. She reads the *Forbes* report, listens to *Wall Street Week,* converses daily with her stockbroker, reads all of Shirley MacLaine's books with ease—all kinds of things I can't begin to understand. Yet some of my friends tell me they understand 50 percent of what my mother says. Some say they understand 80 to 90 percent. Some say they understand none of it, as if she were speaking pure Chinese. But to me, my mother's English is perfectly clear, perfectly natural. It's my mother tongue. Her language, as I hear it, is vivid, direct, full of observation and imagery. That was the language that helped shape the way I saw things, expressed things, made sense of the world. 7

Lately, I've been giving more thought to the kind of English my mother speaks. Like others, I have described it to people as "broken" or fractured" English. But I wince when I say that. It has always bothered me that I can think of no way to describe it other than "broken," as if it were damaged and needed to be fixed, as if it lacked a certain wholeness and soundness. I've heard other terms used, "limited English," for example. But they seem 8

just as bad, as if everything is limited, including people's perceptions of the limited English speaker.

I know this for a fact, because when I was growing up, my   9
mother's "limited" English limited *my* perception of her. I was
ashamed of her English. I believed that her English reflected the
quality of what she had to say. That is, because she expressed
them imperfectly, her thoughts were imperfect. And I had plenty
of empirical evidence to support me: the fact that people in department stores, at banks, and at restaurants did not take her seriously, did not give her good advice, pretended not to understand
her, or even acted as if they did not hear her.

My mother has long realized the limitations of her English as   10
well. When I was fifteen, she used to have me call people on the
phone and pretend I was she. In this guise, I was forced to ask for
information or even to complain and yell at people who had been
rude to her. One time it was a call to her stockbroker in New
York. She had cashed out her small portfolio, and it just so happened we were going to go to New York the next week, our very
first trip outside California. I had to get on the phone and say in an
adolescent voice that was not very convincing, "This is Mrs. Tan."

And my mother was standing in the back whispering loudly,   11
"Why he don't send me check, already two weeks late. So mad
he lie to me, losing my money."

And then I said in perfect English, "Yes, I'm getting rather   12
concerned. You had agreed to send the check two weeks ago, but
it hasn't arrived."

Then she began to talk more loudly. "What he want, I come   13
to New York tell him front of his boss, you cheating me?" And I
was trying to calm her down, make her be quiet, while telling the
stockbroker, "I can't tolerate any more excuses. If I don't receive
the check immediately, I am going to have to speak to your manager when I'm in New York next week." And sure enough, the
following week there we were in front of this astonished stockbroker, and I was sitting there red-faced and quiet, and my
mother, the real Mrs. Tan, was shouting at his boss in her impec-
cable broken English.

We used a similar routine just five days ago, for a situation that   14
was far less humorous. My mother had gone to the hospital for an
appointment, to find out about a benign brain tumor a CAT scan
had revealed a month ago. She said she had spoken very good

English, her best English, no mistakes. Still, she said, the hospital did not apologize when they said they had lost the CAT scan and she had come for nothing. She said they did not seem to have any sympathy when she told them she was anxious to know the exact diagnosis, since her husband and son had both died of brain tumors. She said they would not give her any more information until the next time and she would have to make another appointment for that. So she said she would not leave until the doctor called her daughter. She wouldn't budge. And when the doctor finally called her daughter, me, who spoke in perfect English—lo and behold—we had assurances the CAT scan would be found, promises that a conference call on Monday would be held, and apologies for any suffering my mother had gone through for a most regrettable mistake.

I think my mother's English almost had an effect on limiting   15
my possibilities in life as well. Sociologists and linguists probably will tell you that a person's developing language skills are more influenced by peers. But I do think that the language spoken in the family, especially in immigrant families which are more insular, plays a large role in shaping the language of the child. And I believe that it affected my results on achievement tests, IQ tests, and the SAT. While my English skills were never judged as poor, compared to math, English could not be considered my strong suit. In grade school I did moderately well, getting perhaps B's, sometimes B-pluses, in English and scoring perhaps in the sixtieth or seventieth percentile on achievement tests. But those scores were not good enough to override the opinion that my true abilities lay in math and science, because in those areas I achieved A's and scored in the ninetieth percentile or higher.

This was understandable. Math is precise; there is only one   16
correct answer. Whereas, for me at least, the answers on English tests were always a judgment call, a matter of opinion and personal experience. Those tests were constructed around items like fill-in-the-blank sentence completion, such as "Even though Tom was _____, Mary thought he was _____."
And the correct answer always seemed to be the most bland combinations of thoughts, for example, "Even though Tom was shy, Mary thought he was charming," with the grammatical structure "even though" limiting the correct answer to some sort of semantic opposites, so you wouldn't get answers like, "Even though

Tom was foolish, Mary thought he was ridiculous." Well, according to my mother, there were very few limitations as to what Tom could have been and what Mary might have thought of him. So I never did well on tests like that.

The same was true with word analogies, pairs of words in which you were supposed to find some sort of logical, semantic relationship—for example, "*Sunset* is to *nightfall* as _____ is to _____." And here you would be presented with a list of four possible pairs, one of which showed the same kind of relationship: *red* is to *stoplight, bus* is to *arrival, chills* is to *fever, yawn* is to *boring*. Well, I could never think that way. I knew what the tests were asking, but I could not block out of my mind the images already created by the first pair, "*sunset* is to *nightfall*"—and I would see a burst of colors against a darkening sky, the moon rising, the lowering of a curtain of stars. And all the other pairs of words—red, bus, stoplight, boring—just threw up a mass of confusing images, making it impossible for me to sort out something as logical as saying: "A sunset precedes nightfall" is the same as "a chill precedes a fever." The only way I would have gotten that answer right would have been to imagine an associative situation, for example, my being disobedient and staying out past sunset, catching a chill at night, which turns into feverish pneumonia as punishment, which indeed did happen to me.

I have been thinking about all this lately, about my mother's English, about achievement tests. Because lately I've been asked, as a writer, why there are not more Asian Americans represented in American literature. Why are there few Asian Americans enrolled in creative writing programs? Why do so many Chinese students go into engineering? Well, these are broad sociological questions I can't begin to answer. But I have noticed in surveys—in fact, just last week—that Asian students, as a whole, always do significantly better on math achievement tests than in English. And this makes me think that there are other Asian-American students whose English spoken in the home might also be described as "broken" or "limited." And perhaps they also have teachers who are steering them away from writing and into math and science, which is what happened to me.

Fortunately, I happen to be rebellious in nature and enjoy the challenge of disproving assumptions made about me. I became an English major my first year in college, after being enrolled as pre-

17

18

19

med. I started writing nonfiction as a freelancer the week after I was told by my former boss that writing was my worst skill and I should hone my talents toward account management.

But it wasn't until 1985 that I finally began to write fiction.   20
And at first I wrote using what I thought to be wittily crafted sentences, sentences that would prove I had mastery over the English language. Here's an example from the first draft of a story that later made its way into *The Joy Luck Club,* but without this line: "That was my mental quandary in its nascent state." A terrible line, which I can barely pronounce.

Fortunately, for reasons I won't get into today, I later decided I   21
should envision a reader for the stories I would write. And the reader I decided upon was my mother, because these were stories about mothers. So with this reader in mind—and in fact she did read my early drafts—I began to write stories using all the Englishes I grew up with: the English I spoke to my mother, which for lack of a better term might be described as "simple"; the English she used with me, which for lack of a better term might be described as "broken"; my translation of her Chinese, which could certainly be described as "watered down"; and what I imagined to be her translation of her Chinese if she could speak in perfect English, her internal language, and for that I sought to preserve the essence, but neither an English nor a Chinese structure. I wanted to capture what language ability tests can never reveal: her intent, her passion, her imagery, the rhythms of her speech, and the nature of her thoughts.

Apart from what any critic had to say about my writing, I knew   22
I had succeeded where it counted when my mother finished reading my book and gave me her verdict: "So easy to read."

UNDERSTANDING DETAILS

1. What do you think is Tan's main reason for writing this essay?
2. What are the four "Englishes" that Tan grew up with? Explain each in your own words.
3. What is Tan referring to when she uses the term "mother tongue"?
4. How did Tan feel about her mother's "limited English" in the past?

ANALYZING MEANING

1. How did Amy Tan become a writer? In what way did her rebellious nature help her make this decision?
2. How do all the Englishes Tan grew up with help her as a writer? Explain your answer.
3. What relationship does Tan see between achievement test scores and actual abilities?
4. Why did Tan choose her mother as the audience she envisions when she writes?

DISCOVERING RHETORICAL STRATEGIES

1. Why does Tan actually quote some of her mother's language early in her essay? What effect does this example have on you as a reader?
2. List Tan's main points in this essay. Why do you think she deals with these topics in this particular order?
3. Describe Tan's intended audience in as much detail as possible. Why do you think she aims her essay at this particular group?
4. What other rhetorical strategies does Tan use to help make her point? Give examples of each of these strategies.

MAKING CONNECTIONS

1. Compare and contrast Amy Tan's relationship with her mother and the parent-child relationships examined in the following essays: Lewis Sawaquat's "For My Indian Daughter," Russell Baker's "The Saturday Evening Post," Bill Cosby's "The Baffling Question," Wallerstein and Blakeslee's "Second Chances for Children of Divorce," and Germaine Greer's "A Child Is Born."
2. In her essay, Tan describes her love of English and her avocation as a writer despite her relatively weak performance on English achievement tests as a child. Examine the manner in which other people exceeded the expectations placed on them as expressed in Maya Angelou's "New Directions," Russell Baker's "The Saturday Evening Post," Harold Krents's "Darkness at Noon," and Alice Walker's "Beauty: When the Other Dancer Is the Self."

3. Discuss the theme of "the limitations of language" as it appears in the following essays: Amy Tan's "Mother Tongue," Paul Roberts's "How to Say Nothing in Five Hundred Words," Judith Viorst's "The Truth About Lying," Mary Roach's "Meet the Bickersons," and Rita Mae Brown's "Writing as a Moral Act."

IDEAS FOR DISCUSSION/WRITING

Preparing to Write

Write freely about your own abilities in English: Do you feel you use more than one version of English? How does your oral English differ from your written English? Is English your first language? What do you think of yourself as a writer? As a reader? How well do you perform on English achievement tests?

Choosing a Topic

1. As a college student, you see different people approaching their writing assignments in different ways every day. Some students get right down to work. Others procrastinate until the last minute. Some write in spurts until they have finished the task. Write an essay for your school newspaper explaining your observations about the different ways people write. Use carefully chosen examples to illustrate your observations. You might even want to interview some of your peers about their writing rituals.

2. You have been asked to respond to a national survey on the role of education in our lives. The organization conducting the survey wants to know the extent to which education has helped or hindered you in achieving your goals. In a well-developed essay written for a general audience, explain the benefits and liabilities of education in your life at present. Use specific examples to develop your essay.

3. In her essay, Tan refers to the fact that her teachers steered her "away from writing and into math and science" (paragraph 18) primarily because of her test scores. But she believes her test scores were not an accurate measurement of her ability in English because of her background in the language. Do you think test scores are ever used inappropriately to advise students? Or do you think these scores are the best way we currently have

to measure ability and aptitude? Direct your comments to the general public, and use several specific examples to support your opinion.

Before beginning your essay, you might want to consult the checklists on pages 166–167.

A Brother's Murder

Brent Staples is one of nine children born to a truck driver and a housewife in Chester, Pennsylvania, a factory town fifteen miles south of Philadelphia. He holds a Ph.D. in psychology from the University of Chicago and a Doctorate of Humane Letters from Mount St. Mary's College. His memoir, *Parallel Time: Growing Up in Black and White*, was published by Pantheon Books in 1994. It was a finalist for the *Los Angeles Times* Book Award and a winner of the Annisfield Wolff Award, which had been previously won by James Baldwin, Ralph Ellison, and Zora Neale Hurston. A past editor of the *New York Times* Book Review section and an assistant metropolitan editor, Staples currently writes on politics and culture for the *Times* editorial page. He is an avid gardener and is especially fond of roses. He advises college writers that "ninety percent of writing is rewriting. The simple declarative sentence is your best friend in the world."

Preparing to Read

"A Brother's Murder" was first published in an anthology of African-American writing entitled *Bearing Witness*. In this emotional account of his brother's death, Staples realizes many important truths about the role of violence among African-American men. Before reading this essay, think for a few moments about violence in general: From your observations, which kinds of people are most violent? Why do these people use violence? What do you think is the cause of most violent acts? In your opinion, why is the crime rate so high in American society today? Can we do anything to reduce this crime rate? What are some of your constructive suggestions for controlling violence today?

It has been more than two years since my telephone rang with the news that my younger brother Blake—just 22 years old—had been murdered. The young man who killed him was only 24. Wearing a ski mask, he emerged from a car, fired six times at close range with a massive .44 Magnum, then fled. The   1 two had once been inseparable friends. A senseless rivalry—beginning, I think, with an argument over a girlfriend—escalated from posturing, to threats, to violence, to murder. The way the two were living, death could have come to either of them from anywhere. In fact, the assailant had already survived multiple gunshot wounds from an incident much like the one in which my brother lost his life.

As I wept for Blake, I felt wrenched backward into events and circumstances that had seemed light-years gone. Though a decade apart, we both were raised in Chester, Pennsylvania, an angry, heavily black, heavily poor, industrial city southwest of Philadelphia. There, in the 1960s, I was introduced to mortality, not by the old and failing, but by beautiful young men who lay wrecked after sudden explosions of violence. The first, I remember from my 14th year—Johnny, brash lover of fast cars, stabbed to death two doors from my house in a fight over a pool game. The next year, my teen-age cousin, Wesley, whom I loved very much, was shot dead. The summers blur. Milton, an angry young neighbor, shot a crosstown rival, wounding him badly. William, another teen-age neighbor, took a shotgun blast to the shoulder in some urban drama and displayed his bandages proudly. His brother, Leonard, severely beaten, lost an eye and donned a black patch. It went on.

I recall not long before I left for college, two local Vietnam veterans—one from the Marines, one from the Army—arguing fiercely, nearly at blows about which outfit had done the most in the war. The most killing, they meant. Not much later, I read in a magazine article that set that dispute in a context. In the story, a noncommissioned officer—a sergeant, I believe—said he would pass up any number of affluent, suburban-born recruits to get hard-core soldiers from the inner city. They jumped into the rice paddies with "their manhood on their sleeves," I believe he said. These two items—the veterans arguing and the sergeant's words—still characterize for me the circumstances under which black men in their teens and 20's kill one another with such frequency. With a touchy paranoia born of living battered lives, they are desperate to be *real* men. Killing is only *machismo* taken to the extreme. Incursions to be punished by death were many and minor, and they remain so: they include stepping on the wrong toe, literally; cheating in a drug deal; simply saying "I dare you" to someone holding a gun; crossing territorial lines in a gang dispute. My brother grew up to wear his manhood on his sleeve. And when he died, he was in that group—black, male, and in its teens and early 20's—that is far and away the most likely to murder or be murdered.

I left the East Coast after college, spent the mid- and late- 4 1970's in Chicago as a graduate student, taught for a time, then became a journalist. Within 10 years of leaving my hometown, I was overeducated and "upwardly mobile," ensconced on a quiet, tree-lined street where voices raised in anger were scarcely ever heard. The telephone, like some grim umbilical, kept me connected to the old world with news of deaths, imprisonings, and misfortune. I felt emotionally beaten up. Perhaps to protect my self, I added a psychological dimension to the physical distance I had already achieved. I rarely visited my hometown. I shut it out.

As I fled the past, so Blake embraced it. On Christmas of 1983, 5 I traveled from Chicago to a black section of Roanoke, Virginia, where he then lived. The desolate public housing projects, the hopeless, idle young men crashing against one another—these reminded me of the embittered town we'd grown up in. It was a place where once I would have been comfortable, or at least sure of myself. Now, hearing of my brother's forays into crime, his scrapes with police and street thugs, I was scared, unsteady on foreign terrain.

I saw Blake's romance with the street life, and the hustler 6 image had flowered dangerously. One evening that late December, standing in some Roanoke dive among drug dealers and grim, hair-trigger losers, I told him I feared for his life. He had affected the image of the tough he wanted to be. But behind the dark glasses and the swagger, I glimpsed the baby-faced toddler I'd once watched over. I nearly wept. I wanted desperately for him to live. The young think themselves immortal, and a dangerous light shone in his eyes as he spoke laughingly of making fools of the policemen who had raided his apartment looking for drugs. He cried out as I took his right hand. A line of stitches lay between the thumb and index finger. Kickback from a shotgun, he explained, nothing serious. Gunplay had become part of his life.

I lacked the language simply to say: Thousands have lived this 7 for you and died. I fought the urge to lift him bodily and shake him. This place and the way you are living smells of death to me,

I said. Take some time away, I said. Let's go downtown tomorrow and buy a plane ticket anywhere, take a bus trip, anything to
get away and cool things off. He took my alarm casually. We
arranged to meet the following night—an appointment he would
not keep. We embraced as though through glass. I drove away.

As I stood in my apartment in Chicago holding the receiver   8
that evening in February 1984, I felt as though part of my soul
had been cut away. I questioned myself then, and I still do. Did I
not reach back soon or earnestly enough for him? For weeks I
awoke crying from a recurrent dream in which I chased him, ur-
gently trying to get him to read a document I had, as though
reading it would protect him from what had happened in waking
life. His eyes shining like black diamonds, he smiled and danced
just out of my grasp. When I reached for him, I caught only the
space where he had been.

UNDERSTANDING DETAILS

1. What does Staples mean when he refers to his brother's death
   by saying, "The way the two were living, death could have
   come to either of them from anywhere" (paragraph 1)?
2. What stages did Staples's brother and his murderer go through
   before Blake was killed?
3. Why do you think Staples wrote this essay? What is his main
   point?
4. What did Staples learn about African-American males by examining his brother's life?

ANALYZING MEANING

1. In what ways does Brent Staples's brother represent an important segment of the African-American male population?
2. Why did Staples create a distance between his present life and
   his past?
3. What examples does Staples use to prove his theory that
   "killing is only *machismo* taken to the extreme" (paragraph 3)?
   Do you agree with this conclusion? Can you think of any examples that demonstrate the opposite position?
4. What was "Blake's romance with the street life" (paragraph 5)?

DISCOVERING RHETORICAL STRATEGIES

1. Describe in as much detail as possible Staples's intended audience. Why do you think he aims his essay at this particular group?
2. In what way does Staples's recurring dream (paragraph 8) symbolize the author's relationship with his brother? How does this final paragraph sum up Staples's feelings about the plight of African-American males in American society today?
3. In paragraph 7, Staples uses a simile (a special comparison between two unlike items, using "like" or "as"): "We embraced as though through glass." This image adds an extra dimension to Staples's description. Find another simile in this essay, and explain its effect on you.
4. This essay progresses most obviously through the use of examples. What other rhetorical strategies support this dominant mode? In what ways do they add to Staples's main point?

MAKING CONNECTIONS

1. Through hard work and a college education, Brent Staples was able to rise above the violent environment that contributed to his brother's death. Examine each of the following essays, and explain how the central characters escaped their own difficult environments: Maya Angelou's "New Directions," Harold Krents's "Darkness at Noon," and Wallerstein and Blakeslee's "Second Chances for Children of Divorce."
2. Compare and contrast Staples's comments about violence with opinions on the topic voiced by Kimberly Wozencraft's "Notes from the Country Club," Sherwin Nuland's "Accidents, Suicide, and Euthanasia," Bruce Catton's "Grant and Lee: A Study in Contrasts," Stephen King's "Why We Crave Horror Movies," and Barbara Ehrenreich's "The Ecstasy of War."
3. How do Brent Staples's comments about the community in which his brother lived differ from the sense of "community" in the following essays: Germaine Greer's "A Child Is Born," William Ouchi's "Japanese and American Workers: Two Casts of Mind," Robert Ramirez's "The Barrio," and Ellen Goodman's "A Working Community"?

IDEAS FOR DISCUSSION/WRITING

Preparing to Write

Write freely about your view of violence in American society today: What is the source of most of this violence? How can we control violence in American society? Why do you think violence is increasing? How else might we channel our innate violent reactions? What other suggestions do you have for reducing violent crimes today?

Choosing Your Topic

1. Write an essay for a college-educated audience based on one of the following statements: "Current pressure in contemporary society causes most of the violence today" or "People's natural instincts cause most of the violence in contemporary society."

2. Interview some people about how they manage their anger: What do they do when they get mad? How do they control their reactions? Have they ever become violent? Then write an essay for the students in your English class explaining your findings.

3. According to Staples, the military frame of mind—the urge to kill—is at the heart of "the circumstances under which black men in their teens and 20's kill one another with such frequency" (paragraph 3). Do you agree or disagree with this statement? Write a well-developed essay, using examples from your experience, to support your opinion.

Before beginning your essay, you might want to consult the checklists on pages 166–167.

CHAPTER WRITING ASSIGNMENTS

Practicing Example

1. Think about some qualities that irritate you in other people's behavior (such as how someone drives, how someone talks on the phone, or how someone laughs). In an essay, use examples to explain a behavior that irritates you and the reason it bothers you so much.

2. Think about all the different roles people play, such as father, teacher, big brother, or sister. Who in your experience provides the best example of how this "role" should be performed? Write an essay that explains why this person is the best example of this role.

3. What do you do best as a writer? Which parts of the writing process do you seem to deal with most successfully? Taking examples from your own writing, compose an essay that discusses your strengths as a writer.

Exploring Ideas

1. Should America as a country promote the use of a single national language, or should we instead acknowledge and encourage the use of multiple languages? Write an essay that explores the advantages and/or disadvantages of either single or multiple languages in American society. As you write, use specific examples to support your position.

2. In what ways do all forms of the media use stereotypes? Choose a specific "type" (such as liberal, conservative, radical, athlete), and, using as many specific examples as possible, explain how the media help or hinder our understanding of a certain personality or issue.

3. Discuss a time when someone embarrassed you publicly. Describe what happened and how it affected you. What, if anything, did you learn from the experience?

4

PROCESS ANALYSIS
Explaining Step by Step

Human nature is characterized by the perpetual desire to understand and analyze the process of living well. The bestseller list is always crowded with books on how to know yourself better, how to be assertive, how to become famous, how to avoid a natural disaster, or how to be rich and happy—all explained in three easy lessons. Open almost any popular magazine, and you will find numerous articles on how to lose weight, how elections are run in this country, how to dress for success, how a political rally evolved, how to gain power, or how to hit a successful topspin backhand. People naturally gravitate toward material that tells them how something is done, how something happened, or how something works, especially if they think the information will help them improve their lives in a significant way.

DEFINING PROCESS ANALYSIS

A *process* is a procedure that follows a series of steps or stages; *analysis* involves taking a subject apart and explaining its components in order to better understand the whole. Process analysis, then, explains an action, a mechanism, or an event from beginning to end. It concentrates on either a mental or a physical operation: how to solve a chemistry problem, how to tune up your car, how John F. Kennedy was shot, how the telephone system works. In fact, the explanation of the writing process beginning on page 21 of this book is a good case in point: It divides writing into three interrelated verbal activities and explains how they each work—separately and together.

A process analysis can take one of two forms: (1) It can give directions, thereby explaining how to do something (directive), or (2) it can give information about how something happened or how something works (informative). The first type of analysis gives directions for a task the reader may wish to attempt in the future. Examples include how to make jelly, how to lose weight, how to drive to Los Angeles, how to assemble stereo equipment, how to make money, how to use a microscope, how to knit, how to resuscitate a dying relationship, how to win friends, how to discipline your child, and how to backpack.

The second type of analysis furnishes information about what actually occurred in specific situations or how something works. Examples include how Hiroshima was bombed, how certain Hollywood stars live, how the tax system works, how *Shakespeare in Love* was filmed, how Babe Ruth earned a place in the Baseball Hall of Fame, how gold was first discovered in California, how computers work, how a kibbutz functions, and how the Gulf War began. These subjects and others like them respond to a certain fascination we all have with mastering some processes and understanding the intricate details of others. They all provide us with opportunities to raise our own standard of living, either by helping us directly apply certain processes to our own lives or by increasing our understanding of how our complex world functions.

The following student paragraph analyzes the process of constructing a garden compost pit. Written primarily for people who might wish to make such a pit, this piece is directive rather than informative. Notice in particular the amount of detail the student calls upon to explain each stage of the process and the clear transitions she uses to guide us through her analysis.

No garden is complete without a functioning compost pit. Here's a simple, inexpensive way to make your garbage work for you! To begin with, make a pen out of hog wire or chicken wire, four feet long by eight feet wide by four feet high, splitting it down the middle with another piece of wire so that you end up with a structure that looks like a capital "E" on its side. This is a compost duplex. In the first pen, place a layer of soda ash, just sprinkled on the surface of the dirt. Then, pile an inch or so of leaves, grass clippings, or sawdust on top of the soda ash. You're now ready for the exciting part. Start throwing in all the organic refuse from your kitchen (no meat, bones, or grease, please). After the food is a foot or so deep, throw in a shovelful of steer manure, and cover the entire mess with a thin layer of dirt. Then water it down. Continue this layering process until the pile is three to three-and-a-half feet high. Allow the pile to sit until it decomposes (from one month in warm climates to six months in colder weather). Next, take your pitchfork and start slinging the contents of pen one into pen two (which will land in reverse order, of course, with the top on the bottom and the bottom on the top). This ensures that everything will decompose evenly. Water this down and begin making a new pile in pen one. That's all there is to it! You now have a ready supply of fertilizer for your garden.

THINKING CRITICALLY BY USING PROCESS ANALYSIS

Process analysis embodies clear, careful, step-by-step thinking that takes one of three different forms: chronological, simultaneous, or cyclical. The first follows a time sequence from "first this" to "then that." The second forces you to deal with activities or events that happen or happened at the same time, such as people quietly studying or just getting home from work when the major 1994 earthquake hit Los Angeles. And the third requires you to process information that is continuous, like the rising and setting of the sun. No other thinking pattern will force you to slow down as much as process analysis because the process you are explaining probably won't make any sense if you leave out even the slightest detail.

Good process analysis can truly help your reader see an event in a totally new light. An observer looks at a product already assembled or at a completed event and has no way of knowing without the help of a good process analysis how it got to this final stage. Such an analysis gives the writer or speaker as well as the observer a completely new way of "seeing" the subject in question. Separating process analysis from the other rhetorical modes lets you practice this method of thinking so that you will have a better understanding of the various mental procedures going on in your head. Exercising this possibility in isolation will help you feel its range and its intricacies so that you can become more adept at using it, fully developed, in combination with other modes of thought.

1. List as many examples of each type of process (chronological, simultaneous, and cyclical) that you can think of. Share your list with the class.
2. Write out the process of tying a shoe step by step. Have another person follow your steps exactly to test how well you have analyzed this process.
3. Write a paragraph telling how *not* to do something. Practice your use of humor as a technique for creating interest in the essay by emphasizing the "wrong" way, for example, to wash a car or feed a dog.

READING AND WRITING PROCESS ANALYSIS ESSAYS

Your approach to a process analysis essay should be fairly straightforward. As a reader, you should be sure you understand the author's statement of purpose and then try to visualize each step as you go along. As a writer, you need to adapt the mechanics of the way you normally write to the demands of a process analysis paper, beginning with an interesting topic and a number of clearly explained ideas or stages. As usual, the intended audience determines the choice of words and the degree of detail.

How to Read a Process Analysis Essay

Preparing to Read.   Preparing to read a process analysis essay is as uncomplicated as the essay itself. The title of Edwin Bliss's essay in this chapter, "Managing Your Time," tells us exactly what we are going to learn about. Paul Roberts's essay teaches us "How to Say Nothing in Five Hundred Words." Scanning each selection to assess the author's audience will give you an even better idea of what to expect in these essays, while the synopsis of each in the Rhetorical Table of Contents will help focus your attention on its subject.

Also important as you prepare to read these essays are the qualifications of each author to write on this subject: Has he or she performed the task, worked with the mechanism, or seen the event? Is the writer's experience firsthand? When Edwin Bliss discusses "Managing Your Time," is he writing from his personal experience? What is Jessica Mitford's experience with mortuaries? How does she know what goes on "Behind the Formaldehyde Curtain"? The biography preceding each essay will help you uncover this information and find out other publication details that will encourage you to focus on the material you are about to read.

Finally, before you begin reading, answer the prereading questions, and then do some brainstorming on the subject of the essay: What do you want to know about euthanasia (Sherwin Nuland)? How adept are you with e-mail, and what do you think you can learn about the subject from Mark Hanson?

Reading.   When you read the essays in this chapter for the first time, record your initial reactions to them. Consider the preliminary information you have been studying in order to create a context for each author's composition: What circumstances prompted Mitford's "Behind the Formaldehyde Curtain"? Who do you think is Roberts's target audience in "How to Say Nothing in Five Hundred Words"? Why did Sherwin Nuland write "Accidents, Suicide, and Euthanasia"?

Also determine at this point whether the essay you are reading is *directive* (explaining how to do something) or *informative* (giving information about how something happened or how something works). This fundamental understanding of the author's intentions, along with a reading of the questions following the essay, will prepare you to approach the contents of each selection critically when you read it a second time.

Rereading.   As you reread these process analysis essays, look for an overview of the process at the beginning of the essay so you know where each writer is headed. The body of each essay, then, is generally a discussion of the stages of the process.

This central portion of the essay is often organized *chronologically* (as in Mitford's essay), with clear transitions so that readers can easily follow the writer's train of thought. Other methods of organization are *cyclical* (such as the Nuland essay on euthanasia), describing a process that has no clear beginning or end, and *simultaneous* (such as the essays by Bliss on organizing one's time, by Roberts on writing an essay, and by Hanson on e-mail), in which many activities occur at the same time with a clear beginning and end. Most of these essays discuss the process as a whole at some point. During this second reading, you will also benefit from discovering what rhetorical modes each writer uses to support his or her process analysis and why these rhetorical modes work effectively. What does Bliss's cause/effect reasoning add to his essay on time management? And how do the descriptions in Mitford's essay on mortuaries heighten the horror of the American mortuary business? Do the examples that Hanson gives help explain the process of writing e-mail? How do all the rhetorical modes in each essay help create a coherent whole? After reading each essay for a second time, answer the questions that follow the selection to see if you are understanding your reading material on the literal, interpretive, and analytical levels before you take on the discussion/writing assignments.

For an overview of the entire reading process, you might consult the checklists on pages 20-21 of the Introduction.

How to Write a Process Analysis Essay

Prewriting.   As you begin a process analysis assignment, you first need to become as familiar as you can with the action, mechanism, or event you are going to describe. If possible, try to go through the process yourself at least once or twice. If you can't actually carry out the procedure, going through the process mentally and taking notes is a good alternative. Then, try to read something about the process. After all this preparation (and careful consideration of your audience and purpose), you should be ready to brainstorm, freewrite, cluster, or use your favorite prewriting technique (see pages 21–27 of the Introduction) in response to the prewriting questions before you start composing your paper.

Writing.   The essay should begin with an overview of the process or event to be analyzed. This initial section should introduce the subject, divide it into a number of recognizable steps, and describe the result once the process is complete. Your thesis in a process essay is usually a purpose statement that clearly and briefly explains your approach to the procedure you will discuss: "Building model airplanes can be divided into four basic steps" or "The American courts follow three stages in prosecuting a criminal case."

Next, the directive or informative essay should proceed logically through the various stages of the process, from beginning to end. The parts of a process usually fall nicely into chronological order, supported by such transitions as "at first," "in the beginning," "next," "then," "after that," and "finally." Some processes, however, are either simultaneous, forcing the writer to choose a more complex logical order for the essay (such as classification), or cyclical, requiring the writer to choose a starting point and then explain the cycle stage by stage. Playing the guitar, for example, involves two separate and simultaneous components that must work together: holding the strings against the frets with the fingers of one hand and strumming with the other hand. In analyzing this procedure, you would probably want to describe both parts of the process and then explain how the hands work together to produce music. An example of a cyclical process would be the changing of the seasons. To explain this concept to a reader, you would need to pick a starting point, such as spring, and describe the entire cycle, stage by stage, from that point onward.

In a process paper, you need to be especially sensitive to your intended audience, or they will not be able to follow your explanation. The amount of information, the number of examples and illustrations, and the terms to be defined all depend on the prior knowledge and background of your readers. A writer explaining to a group of amateur cooks how to prepare a soufflé would take an entirely different approach to the subject than he or she would if the audience were a group of bona fide chefs hoping to land jobs in elegant French restaurants. The professional chefs would need more sophisticated and precise explanations than their recreational counterparts, who would probably find such an approach tedious and complicated because of the extraneous details.

The last section of a process analysis paper should consider the process as a whole. If, for example, the writer is giving directions on how to build a model airplane, the essay might end with a good description or drawing of the plane. The informative essay on our legal system might offer a summary of the stages of judging and sentencing a criminal. And the essay on cooking a soufflé might finish with a photograph of the mouth-watering dish.

Rewriting.   In order to revise a process analysis essay, first make sure your main purpose is apparent throughout your paper:

• Have you written a directive or an informative essay?

• Is your purpose statement clear?

Next, you need to determine if your paper is aimed at the proper audience:

• Have you given your readers an overview of the process you are going to discuss?

• Do you go through the process you are explaining step by step?

• At the end of the essay, do you help your readers see the process as a complete entity?

The checklists on pages 32–34 will give you further guidelines for writing, revising, and proofreading.

STUDENT ESSAY: PROCESS ANALYSIS AT WORK

The student essay that follows analyzes the process of using a "home permanent" kit. Notice that, once the student gives an overview of the process, she discusses the steps one at a time, being careful to follow a logical order (in this case, chronological) and to use clear transitions. Then, see how the end of the essay shows the process as a whole.

Follow the Simple Directions

Although fickle hairstylists in Paris and Hollywood decide what is currently "in," many romanticists disregard fashion and yearn for a mane of delicate tendrils. Sharing this urge but resenting the cost, I opted for a "home perm" kit. Any literate person with normal dexterity could follow illustrated directions, I reasoned, and the eight easy steps would energize my limp locks in less than two hours. "Before" and "after"

Purpose statement for informative process analysis

Overview

photos of flawless models showed the metamorphosis one might achieve. Confidently,
I assembled towels, rollers, hair clips, wav-

*First step,
(chronolog
ical order)*

ing lotion, neutralizer, end papers, and a
plastic cap. While shampooing, I chortled
about my ingenuity and economy.

Transition   After towel-drying my hair, I applied the   *Second
step*
gooey, acidic waving lotion thoroughly.
Then I wrapped an end paper around a   *Third step*
parted section and rolled the first curl ("se-
curely but not too tightly"). Despite the reassuring click of the fastened rollers, as I
sectioned each new curl the previous one
developed its own volition and slowly un-
rolled itself. Resolutely, I reapplied waving
lotion and rewound—and rewound—each

Transition   curl. Since my hair was already saturated, I
regarded the next direction skeptically:
"Apply waving lotion to each curl." Faith-   *Fourth step*
fully, however, I complied with the instruc-

Transition   tions. Ignoring the fragile state of the
fastened rollers, I then feigned assurance and   *Fifth step*
enclosed my entire head in a plastic cap. In
forty minutes, chemical magic would occur.

Restless with anticipation, I puttered
about the house; while absorbed in small
chores, I felt the first few drops of lotion escape from the plastic tent. Stuffing wads of
cotton around the cap's edges did not help,
and the small drops soon became rivulets
that left red streaks on my neck and face
and splattered on the floor. (Had I over-
done the waving lotion?) Ammonia fumes
so permeated each room that I was soon
asked to leave. Retreating to the bathroom,
I opened the window and dreamed of frivolous new hairstyles.

Transition   Finally, the waving time had elapsed;
neutralizing was next. I removed my plastic   *Sixth step*

cap, carefully heeding the caution: "Do not disturb curlers as you rinse waving lotion from hair." With their usual impudence, however, all the curlers soon bobbed in the sink; undaunted, I continued. "This next step is critical," warned the instructions. Thinking half-hearted curls were better than no curls at all, I poured the entire bottle of neutralizer on my hair. After a drippy

Transition

Seventh step

ten-minute wait, I read the next step: "Carefully remove rollers." As this advice was superfluous, I moved anxiously to the finale: "Rinse all solution from your hair, and enjoy your curls."

Transition

Eighth step

Final product

Lifting my head from the sink and expecting visions of Aphrodite, I saw instead Medusa's image in the mirror. Limp question-mark spirals fell over my eyes, and each "curl" ended in an explosion of steel-wool frizz. Reflecting on my ineptitude, I knew why the direction page was illustrated only with drawings. After washing a large load of ammonia-scented towels, I took two aspirin and called my hairdresser. Some repair services are cheap at any price.

Concluding remark

Student Writer's Comments

Any person with normal dexterity probably *could* do a successful perm! But I sure had trouble. And I decided I wanted to communicate that trouble within my process analysis essay. When I was given this writing assignment, I knew immediately that I wanted to explain how to do a perm. But I didn't know how to handle the humor that had resulted from my misguided attempt to administer a perm to myself. Part of my response to this assignment resides deep within my personality (I'm a closet comedian), but part of it simply has to do with the relationship between me and permanents (actually, anything having to do with cosmetics). But as I started out on this project, I had no idea if I could mold the comedy into a step-by-step analysis of a process.

First, I went to the store and bought a brand-new home perm, so I could review the guidelines step by step. On a piece of paper, I listed the procedures for giving myself a perm. On another sheet of paper, I wrote down any stories or associations I had with each stage of the process. Some of the notes on the second sheet of paper took the form of full paragraphs, others a list of words and phrases, and still others a combination of lists and full sentences. I found myself laughing aloud at some of the memories the home perm directions triggered.

I knew I was writing a directive essay for someone who might actually want to try a home perm. After making my preliminary lists of ideas, I just let my natural sense of humor direct my writing. My overview and purpose statement came easily. Next, I went through the directions one by one, laughing at myself and the process along the way. Before I knew it, I found myself writing, "After washing a large load of ammonia-scented towels, I took two aspirin and called my hairdresser"— the perfect end, or so I thought, to my comedy of errors. I had written the whole first draft from start to finish without once surfacing for air.

When I reread my draft, I realized that the approach I had taken to this process analysis assignment was a satirical one. It allowed me to go through the proper procedure of giving myself a home perm while simultaneously poking fun at myself along the way. As I revised my essay, I tried to exaggerate some of the humorous sections that demonstrated my ineptness or my failure to follow the directions correctly, hoping they would communicate the true ridiculousness of this entire situation. After omitting some details and embellishing others, I came up with the current last sentence of the essay: "Some repair services are cheap at any price." This new concluding remark took the edge off the whiny tone of the previous sentence and brought the essay to an even lighter close than before. I ended up liking the way the humor worked in the essay, because besides accurately capturing my most recent process analysis experience, it made a potentially dull essay topic rather entertaining. My only problem now is that I'm still not sure I got all the frizz out of my hair!

SOME FINAL THOUGHTS ON PROCESS ANALYSIS

In this chapter, a single process dictates the development and organization of each of the essays that follow. Both directional and informational methods are represented here. Notice in particular the clear purpose statements that set the focus of the essays in each case, as well as the other rhetorical modes (such as narration, comparison/contrast, and definition) that are used to help support the writers' explanations.

PROCESS ANALYSIS IN REVIEW

Reading Process Analysis Essays

Preparing to Read

✓ What assumptions can you make from the essay's title?

✓ Can you guess what the general mood of the essay is?

✓ What is the essay's purpose and audience?

✓ What does the synopsis in the Rhetorical Table of Contents tell you about the essay?

✓ What can you learn from the author's biography?

✓ Can you guess what the author's point of view toward the subject is?

✓ What are your responses to the Preparing to Read questions?

Reading

✓ Is the essay *directive* (explaining how to do something) or *informative* (giving information about how something happened)?

✓ What general message is the author trying to convey?

✓ Did you preview the questions that follow the essay?

Rereading

✓ Does the author furnish an overview of the process?

✓ How is the essay organized—chronologically, cyclically, or simultaneously?

✓ What other rhetorical modes does the author use to support the essay's purpose?

✓ What are your responses to the questions after the essay?

Writing Process Analysis Essays

Preparing to Write

✓ What are your responses to the Preparing to Write questions?

✓ What is your purpose?

✓ Who is your audience?

✓ Are you as familiar as possible with the action, mechanism, or event you are going to explain?

Writing

✓ Do you provide an overview of the process at the beginning of the essay?

✓ Does your first paragraph introduce your subject, divide it into recognizable steps, describe the result once the process is complete, and include a purpose statement?

✓ Is your process analysis essay either directive or informative?

✓ Do you proceed logically through the various steps of the process?

✓ Are the essay's details organized chronologically, simultaneously, or cyclically?

✓ What is your audience's background?

✓ Does your essay end considering the process as a whole?

Rewriting

✓ Have you written a *directive* or an *informative* essay?

✓ Is your purpose statement clear?

✓ Have you given your readers an overview of the process you are going to discuss?

✓ Do you go through the process you are explaining step by step?

✓ At the end of the essay, do you help your readers see the process as a complete entity?

EDWIN BLISS   (1923–   )

Managing Your Time

An internationally known consultant on time-management techniques, Edwin Bliss earned his B.S. and M.S. degrees at the University of Utah, worked as a reporter for the *Columbus Dispatch*, taught journalism at a variety of schools, and was a lobbyist for the National Industrial Council and the U.S. Chamber of Commerce. Not until he became a member of the Washington staff of Senator Wallace F. Bennett, however, did he begin to understand the importance of time management. Since then, Bliss has put his management techniques to work as a consultant for a number of businesses in America and abroad through public seminars sponsored by a company called CareerTrack. "Organizing your time properly is especially important for college students," he claims; "a knowledge of time-management skills can help you avoid writers' block so that you turn your papers in on time." His first book, *Getting Things Done: The ABC's of Time Management*, was published in 1976 (updated and reissued in 1991); his second, *Doing It Now: A Twelve-Step Program for Overcoming Procrastination*, came out in 1983; and his third, *Are Your Employees Stealing You Blind?* (coauthored with Isamu Aoki), appeared in 1993. Bliss currently lives in central California, where he is writing a book on how to operate a small business.

Preparing to Read

In the following essay, which is taken from *Getting Things Done: The ABC's of Time Management*, Bliss offers a number of specific suggestions to help you organize your time more efficiently. Before reading his essay, take a few minutes to think about how you arrange your days: How carefully do you schedule your time? Do you make lists of things you want to do every day? Do you usually accomplish more or less than you wanted to in a typical day? How well do you concentrate on a single activity? Are you able to say *no* to events you don't want to participate in? How much do you procrastinate? Are all aspects of your life in a healthy balance (e.g., work, recreation, school, and family)? If not, what could you do to create a more balanced life for yourself?

I first became interested in the effective use of time when I was   1
an assistant to a U.S. Senator. Members of Congress are faced
with urgent and conflicting demands on their time—for committee work, floor votes, speeches, interviews, briefings, correspondence, investigations, constituents' problems, and the need to
be informed on a wide range of subjects. The more successful
Congressmen develop techniques for getting maximum benefit
from minimum investments of time. If they don't, they don't
return.

Realizing that I was not one of those who use time effectively,   2
I began to apply in my own life some of the techniques I had observed. Here are ten I have found most helpful.

Plan.   You need a game plan for your day. Otherwise, you'll   3
allocate your time according to whatever happens to land on your
desk. And you will find yourself making the fatal mistake of dealing primarily with problems rather than opportunities. Start each
day by making a general schedule, with particular emphasis on the
two or three major things you would like to accomplish—including things that will achieve long-term goals. Remember, studies
prove what common sense tells us: The more time we spend
planning a project, the less total time is required for it. Don't let
today's busywork crowd planning-time out of your schedule.

Concentrate.   Of all the principles of time management,   4
none is more basic than concentration. People who have serious
time-management problems invariably are trying to do too many
things at once. The amount of time spent on a project is not what
counts: It's the amount of *uninterrupted* time. Few problems can
resist an all-out attack; few can be solved piecemeal.

Take Breaks.   To work for long periods without taking a   5
break is not an effective use of time. Energy decreases, boredom
sets in, and physical stress and tension accumulate. Switching for a
few minutes from a mental task to something physical—isometric
exercises, walking around the office, even changing from a sitting
position to a standing position for a while—can provide relief.

Merely resting, however, is often the best course, and you   6
should not think of a "rest" break as poor use of time. Not only
will being refreshed increase your efficiency, but relieving tension
will benefit your health. Anything that contributes to health is
good time management.

Avoid Clutter. Some people have a constant swirl of papers   7
on their desks and assume that somehow the most important matters will float to the top. In most cases, however, clutter hinders
concentration and can create tension and frustration—a feeling of
being "snowed under."

Whenever you find your desk becoming chaotic, take time out   8
to reorganize. Go through all your papers (making generous use
of the wastebasket) and divide them into categories: (1) Immediate action, (2) Low priority, (3) Pending, (4) Reading material.
Put the highest priority item from your first pile in the center of
your desk, then put everything else out of sight. Remember, you
can think of only one thing at a time, and you can work on only
one task at a time, so focus all your attention on the most important one. A final point: Clearing the desk completely, or at least
organizing it, each evening should be standard practice. It gets the
next day off to a good start.

Don't Be a Perfectionist. There is a difference between   9
striving for excellence and striving for perfection. The first is at-
tainable, gratifying, and healthy. The second is often unattainable,
frustrating, and neurotic. It's also a terrible waste of time. The
stenographer who retypes a lengthy letter because of a trivial
error, or the boss who demands such retyping, might profit from
examining the Declaration of Independence. When the inscriber
of that document made two errors of omission, he inserted the
missing letters between the lines. If this is acceptable in the document that gave birth to American freedom, surely it would be acceptable in a letter that will be briefly glanced at en route to
someone's file cabinet or wastebasket?

Don't Be Afraid to Say No. Of all the time-saving tech-   10
niques ever developed, perhaps the most effective is frequent use
of the word *no*. Learn to decline, tactfully but firmly, every request that does not contribute to your goals. If you point out that
your motivation is not to get out of work but to save your time to
do a better job on the really important things, you'll have a good
chance of avoiding unproductive tasks. Remember, many people
who worry about offending others wind up living according to
other people's priorities.

Don't Procrastinate. Procrastination is usually a deeply   11
rooted habit. But we can change our habits provided we use the

right system. William James, the father of American psychology, discussed such a system in his famous *Principles of Psychology*, published in 1890. It works as follows:

1. Decide to start changing as soon as you finish reading this article, while you are motivated. Taking that first step promptly is important.
2. Don't try to do too much too quickly. Just force yourself right now to do one thing you have been putting off. Then, beginning tomorrow morning, start each day by doing the most unpleasant thing on your schedule. Often it will be a small matter: an overdue apology; a confrontation with a fellow worker; an annoying chore you know you should tackle. Whatever it is, do it before you begin your usual morning routine. This simple procedure can well set the tone for your day. You will get a feeling of exhilaration from knowing that although the day is only 15 minutes old, you have already accomplished the most unpleasant thing you have to do all day.

There is one caution: Do not permit any exceptions. William James compared it to rolling up a ball of string; a single slip can undo more than many turns can wind up. Be tough with yourself, for the first few minutes of each day, for the next two weeks, and I promise you a new habit of priceless value. 12

Apply Radical Surgery. Time-wasting activities are like cancers. They drain off vitality and have a tendency to grow. The only cure is radical surgery. If you are wasting your time in activities that bore you, divert you from your real goals, and sap your energy, cut them out, once and for all. 13

The principle applies to personal habits, routines, and activities as much as to ones associated with your work. Check your appointment calendar, your extracurricular activities, your reading list, your television viewing habits, and ax everything that doesn't give you a feeling of accomplishment or satisfaction. 14

Delegate. An early example of failure to delegate is found in the Bible. Moses, having led his people out of Egypt, was so impressed with his own knowledge and authority that he insisted on ruling personally on every controversy that arose in Israel. His wise father-in-law, Jethro, recognizing that this was poor use of a leader's time, recommended a two-phase approach: First, educate the people concerning the laws; second, select capable leaders and 15 give them full authority over routine matters, freeing Moses to concentrate on major decisions. The advice is still sound.

You don't have to be a national leader or a corporate executive 16
to delegate, either. Parents who don't delegate household chores are doing a disservice to themselves and their children. Running a Boy Scout troop can be as time-consuming as running General Motors if you try to do everything yourself. One caution: Giving subordinates jobs that neither you nor anyone else wants to do isn't delegating, it's assigning. Learn to delegate the challenging and rewarding tasks, along with sufficient authority to make necessary decisions. It can help to free your time.

Don't Be a "Workaholic." Most successful executives I 17
know work long hours, but they don't let work interfere with the really important things in life, such as friends, family, and fly fishing. This differentiates them from the workaholic who becomes addicted to work just as people become addicted to alcohol. Symptoms of work addiction include refusal to take a vacation, inability to put the office out of your mind on weekends, a bulging briefcase, and a spouse, son, or daughter who is practically a stranger.

Counseling can help people cope with such problems. But for 18
starters, do a bit of self-counseling. Ask yourself whether the midnight oil you are burning is adversely affecting your health. Ask where your family comes in your list of priorities, whether you are giving enough of yourself to your children and spouse, and whether you are deceiving yourself by pretending that the sacrifices you are making are really for them.

Above all else, good time management involves an awareness 19
that today is all we ever have to work with. The past is irretrievably gone; the future is only a concept. British art critic John Ruskin had the word "TODAY" carved into a small marble block that he kept on his desk as a constant reminder to "Do It Now." But my favorite quotation is by an anonymous philosopher:

> Yesterday is a canceled check.
> Tomorrow is a promissory note.
> Today is ready cash. Use it!

UNDERSTANDING DETAILS

1. What are the ten techniques for managing time that Bliss learned from observing successful members of Congress at work? Explain each in your own words.
2. According to Bliss, what is the difference between "delegating" and "assigning" chores (paragraph 16)?
3. What is a "workaholic" (paragraph 17)? What characteristics identify this type of person?
4. Explain Bliss's favorite quotation:

> Yesterday is a canceled check.
> Tomorrow is a promissory note.
> Today is ready cash. Use It!

What does this saying have to do with time management?

ANALYZING MEANING

1. Why is concentration such an important part of time management? Have you found this to be true in your own experience? Explain your answer.
2. Which of Bliss's guidelines for managing time could you benefit from most? How could it help you? Why do you have trouble in this area?
3. Why does Bliss advise us not to be workaholics? Does this advice conflict with the other guidelines Bliss lists in this essay? Why or why not?
4. In what parts of the essay does Bliss refer to our personal lives? According to the author, how can we balance our personal and professional lives? How realistic are these ideas?

DISCOVERING RHETORICAL STRATEGIES

1. Bliss introduces each new suggestion for managing time as a command and then fully explains each command. How effective is this approach? What effect would headings beginning with present participles have on the essay (e.g., planning, taking breaks, avoiding clutter)?
2. How does Bliss organize his techniques for managing time? Is this order successful? Explain your answer.

3. What is Bliss's general attitude toward time management? In your opinion, is this an efficient attitude toward the subject?
4. What other rhetorical modes does Bliss use to support this process analysis essay? Give examples of each of these modes.

MAKING CONNECTIONS

1. How would William Ouchi ("Japanese and American Workers: Two Casts of Mind") respond to Bliss's essay? Would he agree or disagree with the author's recommendations and conclusions? Do Bliss's suggestions about time management sound more "Japanese" or "American," according to Ouchi's definition of each society's business practices?
2. Bliss's essay analyzing the process of managing our time and Jessica Mitford's essay ("Behind the Formaldehyde Curtain") analyzing funeral customs both try to persuade us to adopt a certain opinion as they describe a process. Which essay is more convincing to you? Explain your answer in detail.
3. Pretend that you are Edwin Bliss giving advice to young Russell Baker ("The Saturday Evening Post"), who wants to become a good salesperson. Which of Bliss's suggestions should Baker follow most earnestly? Why? Which of these suggestions would be most helpful in your own life?

IDEAS FOR DISCUSSION/WRITING

Preparing to Write

Write freely about various aspects of time management: Do you manage time well from day to day? What benefits can you receive from managing your time better? Can you identify any disadvantages that could result from managing your time better? How can you avoid these problems? Are you a workaholic, or do you strike a good balance between the various aspects of your life? What is the relationship between time management and quality of life?

Choosing a Topic

1. You have been asked by the editor of your campus newspaper to adapt Bliss's suggestions to the life of a student. Write a

process analysis essay adjusting Bliss's ten guidelines to a college environment.

2. Interview someone in your class about his or her ability to use time wisely. Use Bliss's guidelines to establish whether the person manages time well. Then, direct a process analysis essay to this person, briefly evaluating his or her time-management skills and then offering suggestions for improvement.

3. At times, Bliss's approach to time management (do all you can in a day) seems to conflict with the fundamental tenets for leading a quality life (relax and enjoy yourself). Do you think these two aspects of life are incompatible, or are there ways to reconcile the two? Write an essay for your classmates detailing a solution to this dilemma.

Before beginning your essay, you might want to consult the checklists on pages 219–220.

JESSICA MITFORD　　(1917–1996)

Behind the Formaldehyde Curtain

Once called "Queen of the Muckrakers" in a *Time* magazine review, Jessica Mitford has written scathing exposés of the Famous
Writers' School, American funeral directors, television executives,
prisons, a "fat farm" for wealthy women, and many other venerable
social institutions. She was born in England into the gentry, immigrated to the United States, and later became a naturalized American citizen. After working at a series of jobs, she achieved literary
fame at age forty-six with the publication of *The American Way of
Death* (1963), which relentlessly shatters the image of funeral directors as "compassionate, reverent family-friends-in-need." Her
other major works include *Kind and Unusual Punishment: The Prison
Business* (1973); *Poison Penmanship: The Gentle Art of Muckraking*
(1979), an anthology of Mitford's articles in the *Atlantic, Harper's*,
and other periodicals covering a twenty-two-year time span; two
volumes of autobiography, *Daughters and Rebels* (1960) and *A Fine
Old Madness* (1977); *Faces of Philip: A Memoir of Philip Toynbee*
(1984); *Grace Had an English Heart: The Story of Grace Darling, Heroine and Victorian Superstar* (1988); and *The American Way of Birth*
(1992). Superbly skilled in the techniques of investigative reporting,
satire, and black humor, Mitford was described in a *Washington Post*
article as "an older, more even-tempered, better-read Jane Fonda
who has maintained her activism long past middle age."

Preparing to Read

The following essay, taken from *The American Way of Death*,
clearly illustrates the ruthless manner in which Mitford exposes the
greed and hypocrisy of the American mortuary business. As you prepare to read this article, think for a few minutes about funeral customs in our society: Have you attended a funeral service recently?
Which rituals seemed particularly vivid to you? What purpose did
these symbolic actions serve? What other interesting customs are you
aware of in American society? What purpose do these customs serve?
What public images do these customs have? Are these images accurate? Do you generally approve or disapprove of these customs?

T he drama begins to unfold with the arrival of the corpse at   1
the mortuary.

Alas, poor Yorick! How surprised he would be to see   2
how his counterpart of today is whisked off to a funeral parlor and
is in short order sprayed, sliced, pierced, pickled, trussed,
trimmed, creamed, waxed, painted, rouged, and neatly dressed—
transformed from a common corpse into a Beautiful Memory Picture. This process is known in the trade as embalming and
restorative art and is so universally employed in the United States
and Canada that the funeral director does it routinely, without
consulting corpse or kin. He regards as eccentric those few who
are hardy enough to suggest that it might be dispensed with. Yet
no law requires embalming, no religious doctrine commends it,
nor is it dictated by considerations of health, sanitation, or even of
personal daintiness. In no part of the world but in Northern
America is it widely used. The purpose of embalming is to make
the corpse presentable for viewing in a suitably costly container;
and here too the funeral director routinely, without first consulting the family, prepares the body for public display.

Is all this legal? The processes to which a dead body may be   3
subjected are after all to some extent circumscribed by law. In
most states, for instance, the signature of next of kin must be
obtained before an autopsy may be performed, before the
deceased may be cremated, before the body may be turned over
to a medical school for research purposes; or such provision must
be made in the decedent's will. In the case of embalming, no such
permission is required nor is it ever sought. A textbook, *The
Principles and Practices of Embalming*, comments on this: "There is
some question regarding the legality of much that is done within
the preparation room." The author points out that it would be
most unusual for a responsible member of a bereaved family to
instruct the mortician, in so many words, to "*embalm*" the body of
a deceased relative. The very term "embalming" is so seldom
used that the mortician must rely upon custom in the matter.
The author concludes that unless the family specifies otherwise,
the act of entrusting the body to the care of a funeral establishment carries with it an implied permission to go ahead and
embalm.

Embalming is indeed a most extraordinary procedure, and one   4
must wonder at the docility of Americans who each year pay

hundreds of millions of dollars for its perpetuation, blissfully ignorant of what it is all about, what is done, how it is done. Not one in ten thousand has any idea of what actually takes place. Books on the subject are extremely hard to come by. They are not to be found in most libraries or bookshops.

In an era when huge television audiences watch surgical operations in the comfort of their living rooms, when, thanks to the animated cartoon, the geography of the digestive system has become familiar territory even to the nursery school set, in a land where the satisfaction of curiosity about almost all matters is a national pastime, the secrecy surrounding embalming can, surely, hardly be attributed to the inherent gruesomeness of the subject. Custom in this regard has within this century suffered a complete reversal. In the early days of American embalming, when it was performed in the home of the deceased, it was almost mandatory for some relative to stay by the embalmer's side and witness the procedure. Today, family members who might wish to be in attendance would certainly be dissuaded by the funeral director. All others, except apprentices, are excluded by law from the preparation room.   5

A close look at what does actually take place may explain in large measure the undertaker's intractable reticence concerning a procedure that has become his major *raison d'être*. Is it possible he fears that public information about embalming might lead patrons to wonder if they really want this service? If the funeral men are loath to discuss the subject outside the trade, the reader may, understandably, be equally loath to go on reading at this point. For those who have the stomach for it, let us part the formaldehyde curtain. . . .   6

The body is first laid out in the undertaker's morgue—or rather, Mr. Jones is reposing in the preparation room—to be readied to bid the world farewell.   7

The preparation room in any of the better funeral establishments has the tiled and sterile look of a surgery, and indeed the embalmer-restorative artist who does his chores there is beginning to adopt the term "dermasurgeon" (appropriately corrupted by some mortician-writers as "demisurgeon") to describe his calling. His equipment, consisting of scalpels, scissors, augers, forceps, clamps, needles, pumps, tubes, bowls, and basins, is crudely imitative of the surgeon's, as is his technique, acquired in a nine- or   8 twelve-month post-high-school course in an embalming school. He is supplied by an advanced chemical industry with a bewildering array of fluids, sprays, pastes, oils, powders, creams, to fix or soften tissue, shrink or distend it as needed, dry it here, restore the moisture there. There are cosmetics, waxes and paints to fill and cover features, even plaster of Paris to replace entire limbs. There are ingenious aids to prop and stabilize the cadaver: A Vari-Pose Head Rest, the Edwards Arm and Hand Positioner, the Repose Block (to support the shoulders during the embalming), and the Throop Foot Positioner, which resembles an old-fashioned stocks.

Mr. John H. Eckels, president of the Eckels College of Mortuary Science, thus describes the first part of the embalming procedure: "In the hands of a skilled practitioner, this work may be done in a comparatively short time and without mutilating the body other than by slight incision—so slight that it scarcely would cause serious inconvenience if made upon a living person. It is necessary to remove the blood, and doing this not only helps in the disinfecting, but removes the principal cause of disfigurements due to discoloration."   9

Another textbook discusses the all-important time element: "The earlier this is done, the better, for every hour that elapses between death and embalming will add to the problems and complications encountered. . . . " Just how soon should one get going on the embalming? The author tells us, "On the basis of such scanty information made available to this profession through its rudimentary and haphazard system of technical research, we must conclude that the best results are to be obtained if the subject is embalmed before life is completely extinct—that is, before cellular death has occurred. In the average case, this would mean within an hour after somatic death." For those who feel that there is something a little rudimentary, not to say haphazard, about this advice, a comforting thought is offered by another writer. Speaking of fears entertained in early days of premature burial, he points out, "One of the effects of embalming by chemical injection, however, has been to dispel fears of live burial." How true; once the blood is removed, chances of live burial are indeed remote.   10

To return to Mr. Jones, the blood is drained out through the veins and replaced by embalming fluid pumped in through the ar-   11 teries. As noted in *The Principles and Practices of Embalming*, "every operator has a favorite injection and drainage point—a fact which becomes a handicap only if he fails or refuses to forsake his favorites when conditions demand it." Typical favorites are the carotid artery, femoral artery, jugular vein, subclavian vein. There are various choices of embalming fluid. If Flextone is used, it will produce a "mild, flexible rigidity. The skin retains a velvety softness, the tissues are rubbery and pliable. Ideal for women and children." It may be blended with B. and G. Products Company's Lyf-Lyk tint, which is guaranteed to reproduce "nature's own skin texture . . . the velvety appearance of living tissue." Suntone comes in three separate tints: Suntan; Special Cosmetic Tint, a pink shade "especially indicated for young female subjects"; and Regular Cosmetic Tint, moderately pink.

About three to six gallons of a dyed and perfumed solution of 12 formaldehyde, glycerin, borax, phenol, alcohol, and water is soon circulating through Mr. Jones, whose mouth has been sewn together with a "needle directed upward between the upper lip and gum and brought out through the left nostril," with the corners raised slightly "for a more pleasant expression." If he should be bucktoothed, his teeth are cleaned with Bon Ami and coated with colorless nail polish. His eyes, meanwhile, are closed with flesh-tinted eye caps and eye cement.

The next step is to have at Mr. Jones with a thing called a tro- 13 car. This is a long, hollow needle attached to a tube. It is jabbed into the abdomen, poked around the entrails and chest cavity, the contents of which are pumped out and replaced with "cavity fluid." This done, and the hole in the abdomen sewn up, Mr. Jones's face is heavily creamed (to protect the skin from burns which may be caused by leakage of the chemicals), and he is covered with a sheet and left unmolested for a while. But not for long—there is more, much more, in store for him. He has been embalmed, but not yet restored, and the best time to start the restorative work is eight to ten hours after embalming, when the tissues have become firm and dry.

The object of all this attention to the corpse, it must be re- 14 membered, is to make it presentable for viewing in an attitude of healthy repose. "Our customs require the presentation of our dead in the semblance of normality . . . unmarred by the ravages of illness, disease, or mutilation," says Mr. J. Sheridan Mayer in his *Restorative Art*. This is rather a large order since few people die in the full bloom of health, unravaged by illness and unmarked by some disfigurement. The funeral industry is equal to the challenge: "In some cases the gruesome appearance of a mutilated or disease-ridden subject may be quite discouraging. The task of restoration may seem impossible and shake the confidence of the embalmer. This is the time for intestinal fortitude and determination. Once the formative work is begun and affected tissues are cleaned or removed, all doubts of success vanish. It is surprising and gratifying to discover the results which may be obtained."

The embalmer, having allowed an appropriate interval to   15 elapse, returns to the attack, but now he brings into play the skill and equipment of sculptor and cosmetician. Is a hand missing? Casting one in plaster of Paris is a simple matter. "For replacement purposes, only a cast of the back of the hand is necessary; this is within the ability of the average operator and is quite adequate." If a lip or two, a nose or an ear should be missing, the embalmer has at hand a variety of restorative waxes with which to model replacements. Pores and skin texture are simulated by stippling with a little brush, and over this cosmetics are laid on. Head off? Decapitation cases are rather routinely handled. Ragged edges are trimmed, and head joined to torso with a series of splints, wires, and sutures. It is a good idea to have a little something at the neck—a scarf or a high collar—when time for viewing comes. Swollen mouth: Cut out tissue as needed from inside the lips. If too much is removed, the surface contour can easily be restored by padding with cotton. Swollen necks and cheeks are reduced by removing tissue through vertical incisions made down each side of the neck. "When the deceased is casketed, the pillow will hide the suture incisions. . . . As an extra precaution against leakage, the suture may be painted with liquid sealer."

The opposite condition is more likely to present itself—that of   16 emaciation. His hypodermic syringe now loaded with massage cream, the embalmer seeks out and fills the hollowed and sunken areas by injection. In this procedure the backs of the hands and fingers and the under-chin area should not be neglected.

Positioning the lips is a problem that recurrently challenges the   17 ingenuity of the embalmer. Closed too tightly, they tend to give a stern, even disapproving expression. Ideally, embalmers feel, the lips should give the impression of being ever so slightly parted, the upper lip protruding slightly for a more youthful appearance. This takes some engineering, however, as the lips tend to drift apart. Lip drift can sometimes be remedied by pushing one or two straight pins through the inner margin of the lower lip and then inserting them between the two front upper teeth. If Mr. Jones happens to have no teeth, the pins can just as easily be anchored in his Armstrong Face Former and Denture Replacer. Another method to maintain lip closure is to dislocate the lower jaw, which is then held in its new position by a wire run through holes which have been drilled through the upper and lower jaws at the midline. As the French are fond of saying, *il faut souffrir pour être belle.*

If Mr. Jones had died of jaundice, the embalming fluid will very likely turn him green. Does this deter the embalmer? Not if he has intestinal fortitude. Masking pastes and cosmetics are heavily laid on, burial garments and casket interiors are color-correlated with particular care, and Jones is displayed beneath rose-colored lights. Friends will say "How *well* he looks." Death by carbon monoxide, on the other hand, can be rather a good thing from the embalmer's viewpoint: "One advantage is the fact that this type of discoloration is an exaggerated form of a natural pink coloration." This is nice because the healthy glow is already present and needs but little attention.   18

The patching and filling completed, Mr. Jones is now shaved, washed, and dressed. Cream-based cosmetic, available in pink, flesh, suntan, brunette, and blond, is applied to his hands and face, his hair is shampooed and combed (and, in the case of Mrs. Jones, set), his hands manicured. For the horny-handed son of toil special care must be taken; cream should be applied to remove ingrained grime, and the nails cleaned. "If he were not in the habit of having them manicured in life, trimming and shaping is advised for appearance—never questioned by kin."   19

Jones is now ready for casketing (this is the present participle of the verb "to casket"). In this operation his right shoulder should be depressed slightly "to turn the body a bit to the right and soften the appearance of lying flat on the back." Positioning the hands is a matter of importance, and special rubber positioning blocks may be used. The hands should be cupped slightly for a more lifelike, relaxed appearance. Proper placement of the body   20 requires a delicate sense of balance. It should lie as high as possible in the casket, yet not so high that the lid, when lowered, will hit the nose. On the other hand, we are cautioned, placing the body too low "creates the impression that the body is in a box."

Jones is next wheeled into the appointed slumber room where a   21
few last touches may be added—his favorite pipe placed in his hand or, if he was a great reader, a book propped into position. (In the case of little Master Jones a Teddy bear may be clutched.) Here he will hold open house for a few days, visiting hours 10 A.M. to 9 P.M.

All now being in readiness, the funeral director calls a staff con-   22
ference to make sure that each assistant knows his precise duties. Mr. Wilber Kriege writes "This makes your staff feel that they are a part of the team, with a definite assignment that must be properly carried out if the whole plan is to succeed. You never heard of a football coach who failed to talk to his entire team before they go on the field. They have drilled on the plays they are to execute for hours and days, and yet the successful coach knows the importance of making even the bench-warming third-string substitute feel that he is important if the game is to be won." The winning of *this* game is predicated upon glass-smooth handling of the logistics. The funeral director has notified the pallbearers whose names were furnished by the family, has arranged for the presence of clergyman, organist, and soloist, has provided transportation for everybody, has organized and listed the flowers sent by friends. In *Psychology of Funeral Service*, Mr. Edward A. Martin points out: "He may not always do as much as the family thinks he is doing, but it is his helpful guidance that they appreciate in knowing they are proceeding as they should. . . . The important thing is how well his services can be used to make the family believe they are giving unlimited expression to their own sentiment."

The religious service may be held in a church or in the chapel   23
of the funeral home; the funeral director vastly prefers the latter arrangement, for not only is it more convenient for him but it affords him the opportunity to show off his beautiful facilities to the gathered mourners. After the clergyman has had his say, the mourners queue up to file past the casket for a last look at the deceased. The family is *never* asked whether they want an open-casket ceremony; in the absence of their instruction to the contrary, this is taken for granted. Consequently, well over 90

percent of all American funerals feature the open casket—a custom unknown in other parts of the world. Foreigners are astonished by it. An English woman living in San Francisco described her reaction in a letter to the writer:

> I myself have attended only one funeral here—that of an elderly fellow worker of mine. After the service I could not understand why everyone was walking towards the coffin (sorry, I mean casket), but thought I had better follow the crowd. It shook me rigid to get there and find the casket open and poor old Oscar lying there in his brown tweed suit, wearing a suntan makeup and just the wrong shade of lipstick. If I had not been extremely fond of the old boy, I have a horrible feeling that I might have giggled. Then and there I decided that I could never face another American funeral—even dead.

The casket (which has been resting throughout the service on a   24
Classic Beauty Ultra Metal Casket Bier) is now transferred by a hydraulically operated device called Porto-Lift to a balloon-tired, Glide Easy casket carriage which will wheel it to yet another conveyance, the Cadillac Funeral Coach. This may be lavender, cream, light green—anything but black. Interiors, of course, are color-correlated, "for the man who cannot stop short of perfection."

At graveside, the casket is lowered into the earth. This office,   25
once the prerogative of friends of the deceased, is now performed by a patented mechanical lowering device. A "Life-time Green" artificial grass mat is at the ready to conceal the sere earth, and overhead, to conceal the sky, is a portable Steril Chapel Tent ("resists the intense heat and humidity of summer and the terrific storms of winter . . . available in Silver Grey, Rose, or Evergreen"). Now is the time for the ritual scattering of earth over the coffin, as the solemn words "earth to earth, ashes to ashes, dust to dust" are pronounced by the officiating cleric. This can today be accomplished "with a mere flick of the wrist with the Gordon Leak-Proof Earth Dispenser. No grasping of a handful of dirt, no soiled fingers. Simple, dignified, beautiful, reverent! The modern way!" The Golden Earth Dispenser (at $5) is of nickel-plated brass construction. It is not only "attractive to the eye and long wearing"; it is also "one of the 'tools' for building better public relations" if presented as "an appropriate non-commercial gift" to the clergyman. It is shaped something like a saltshaker.

Untouched by human hand, the coffin and the earth are now   26
united.

It is in the function of directing the participants through the   27
maze of gadgetry that the funeral director has assigned to himself
his relatively new role of "grief therapist." He has relieved the
family of every detail, he has revamped the corpse to look like a
living doll, he has arranged for it to nap for a few days in a slumber room, he has put on a well-oiled performance in which the
concept of *death* has played no part whatsoever—unless it was in-
considerately mentioned by the clergyman who conducted the religious service. He has done everything in his power to make the
funeral a real pleasure for everybody concerned. He and his team
have given their all to score an upset victory over death.

UNDERSTANDING DETAILS

1. List the major steps of the embalming process that the author
   reveals in this essay.
2. Why, according to Mitford, do funeral directors not want to
   make public the details of embalming? To what extent do you
   think their desire for secrecy is warranted?
3. Why isn't the permission of a family member needed for embalming? From Mitford's perspective, what does this custom
   reveal about Americans?
4. In what ways has embalming become the undertaker's *raison
   d'être*? How do American funeral customs encourage this procedure?

ANALYZING MEANING

1. What is Mitford's primary purpose in this essay? Why do you
   think she has analyzed this particular process in such detail?
2. Explain the title of this essay.
3. Do you think the author knows how gruesome her essay is?
   How can you tell? What makes the essay so horrifying? How
   does such close attention to macabre detail help Mitford accomplish her purpose?
4. What does Mitford mean when she argues that the funeral director and his team "have given their all to score an upset victory over death" (paragraph 27)? Who or what is "the team"?

Why does Mitford believe death plays no part in American burial customs?

DISCOVERING RHETORICAL STRATEGIES

1. Why does Mitford begin her essay with a one-sentence paragraph? Is it effective? Why or why not?
2. A euphemism is the substitution of a deceptively pleasant term for a straightforward, less pleasant one. In what way is "Beautiful Memory Picture" (paragraph 2) a euphemism? How are we reminded of this phrase throughout the essay? What other euphemisms can you find in this selection?
3. What tone does Mitford establish in the essay? What is her reason for creating this particular tone? What is your reaction to it?
4. What other rhetorical strategies does Mitford use besides gruesome examples and illustrations to make her point? Give examples of each of these different strategies.

MAKING CONNECTIONS

1. Imagine that Stephen King ("Why We Crave Horror Movies") has just read Mitford's essay on funeral customs. According to King, what would be the source of our fascination with these macabre practices? Why do essays like Mitford's both intrigue and repulse us at the same time?
2. Compare and contrast Mitford's use of examples with those used by Harold Krents ("Darkness at Noon") or Paul Roberts ("How to Say Nothing in Five Hundred Words"). How often does each author use examples? What is the relationship between the frequency of examples in each essay and the extent to which you are convinced by the author's argument?
3. In this essay, Mitford lifts the curtain on certain bizarre funeral practices in much the same way that Judith Wallerstein and Sandra Blakeslee expose the trauma of divorce ("Second Chances for Children of Divorce"), Nancy Gibbs deconstructs the mythology of rape ("When Is It Rape?), and Barbara Ehrenreich lays bare "The Ecstasy of War." Which of these "exposés" seems most complete and devastating to you? Explain your answer.

IDEAS FOR DISCUSSION/WRITING

Preparing to Write

Write freely about a particularly interesting custom in America or in another country: Why does this custom exist? What role does it play in the society? What value does it have? What are the details of this custom? In what way is this custom a part of your life? Your family's life? What purpose does it serve for you? Is it worth continuing? Why or why not?

Choosing a Topic

1. In a process analysis essay directed to your classmates, explain a custom you do not approve of. Decide on your tone and purpose before you begin to write.
2. In a process analysis essay directed to your classmates, explain a custom you approve of. Select a specific tone and purpose before you begin to write.
3. You have been asked to address a group of students at a college of mortuary science. In this role, you have an opportunity to influence the opinion of these students concerning the practice of embalming. Write a well-reasoned lecture to this group arguing either for or against the process of embalming.

Before beginning your essay, you might want to consult the checklists on pages 219–220.

PAUL ROBERTS   (1917–1967)

How to Say Nothing in Five Hundred Words

Paul Roberts was an English professor specializing in structural linguistics who wrote a number of influential books and articles on language use. Born in San Luis Obispo, California, the author received his B.A. from San Jose State University and his M.A. and Ph.D. from the University of California at Berkeley. He taught English and linguistics for several years at San Jose State and at Cornell University, then became director of languages at the Center of American Studies in Rome, where he lived until his death in 1967. His principal books, familiar to a generation of college students, include *Understanding Grammar* (1954), *Patterns of English* (1956), *Understanding English* (1958), *English Sentences* (1962), and *English Syntax* (1964).

Preparing to Read

The following essay, from *Understanding English*, discusses ways to avoid several common problems faced by beginning college writers. As you prepare to read this article, pause for a moment to consider your own ability in writing: What are your strengths? What types of errors do you commonly make? What have you done in the past to remedy these flaws? Do you have any writing problems for which you have no solutions? What advice would you give to another student who wishes to improve his or her writing?

It's Friday afternoon, and you have almost survived another   1
week of classes. You are just looking forward dreamily to the
weekend when the English instructor says: "For Monday you
will turn in a five-hundred-word composition on college football."

Well, that puts a good big hole in the weekend. You don't   2
have any strong views on college football one way or the other.
You get rather excited during the season and go to all the home
games and find it rather more fun than not. On the other hand,
the class has been reading Robert Hutchins in the anthology and
perhaps Shaw's "Eighty-Yard Run," and from the class discus-

sion you have got the idea that the instructor thinks college football is for the birds. You are no fool. You can figure out what
side to take.

After dinner you get out the portable typewriter that you got   3
for high school graduation. You might as well get it over with
and enjoy Saturday and Sunday. Five hundred words is about two
double-spaced pages with normal margins. You put in a sheet of
paper, think up a title, and you're off:

> Why College Football Should Be Abolished
> College football should be abolished because it's bad for the school and
> also bad for the players. The players are so busy practicing that they don't
> have any time for their studies.

This, you feel, is a mighty good start. The only trouble is that   4
it's only thirty-two words. You still have four hundred and sixty-
eight to go, and you've pretty well exhausted the subject. It
comes to you that you do your best thinking in the morning, so
you put away the typewriter and go to the movies. But the next
morning you have to do your washing and some math problems,
and in the afternoon you go to the game. The English instructor
turns up too, and you wonder if you've taken the right side after
all. Saturday night you have a date, and Sunday morning you
have to go to church. (You can't let English assignments interfere
with your religion.) What with one thing and another, it's ten
o'clock Sunday night before you get out the typewriter again.
You make a pot of coffee and start to fill out your views on college football. Put a little meat on the bones.

> Why College Football Should Be Abolished
>
> In my opinion, it seems to me that college football should be abolished.   5
> The reason why I think this to be true is because I feel that football is bad for
> the colleges in nearly every aspect. As Robert Hutchins says in his article in
> our anthology in which he discusses college football, it would be better if the
> colleges had race horses and had races with one another, because then the
> horses would not have to attend classes. I firmly agree with Mr. Hutchins on
> this point, and I am sure that many other students would agree too.
>   One reason why it seems to me that college football is bad is that it has   6
> become too commercial. In the olden times when people played football just
> for the fun of it, maybe college football was all right, but they do not play
> football just for the fun of it now as they used to in the old days. Nowadays

college football is what you might call a big business. Maybe this is not true at all schools, and I don't think it is especially true here at State, but certainly this is the case at most colleges and universities in America nowadays, as Mr. Hutchins points out in his very interesting article. Actually the coaches and alumni go around to the high schools and offer the high school stars large salaries to come to their colleges and play football for them. There was one case where a high school star was offered a convertible if he would play football for a certain college.

Another reason for abolishing college football is that it is bad for the play- 7 ers. They do not have time to get a college education, because they are so busy playing football. A football player has to practice every afternoon from three to six and then he is so tired that he can't concentrate on his studies. He just feels like dropping off to sleep after dinner, and then the next day he goes to his classes without having studied and maybe he fails the test.

(Good ripe stuff so far, but you're still a hundred and fifty-one 8 words from home. One more push.)

Also I think college football is bad for the colleges and the universities because not very many students get to participate in it. Out of a college of ten thousand students only seventy-five or a hundred play football, if that many. Football is what you might call a spectator sport. That means that most people go to watch it but do not play it themselves.

(Four hundred and fifteen. Well, you still have the conclusion, 9 and when you retype it, you can make the margins a little wider.)

These are the reasons why I agree with Mr. Hutchins that college football should be abolished in American colleges and universities.

On Monday you turn it in, moderately hopeful, and on Friday 10 it comes back marked "weak in content" and sporting a big "D."

This essay is exaggerated a little, not much. The English in- 11 structor will recognize it as reasonably typical of what an assignment on college football will bring in. He knows that nearly half of the class will contrive in five hundred words to say that college football is too commercial and bad for the players. Most of the other half will inform him that college football builds character and prepares one for life and brings prestige to the school. As he reads paper after paper all saying the same thing in almost the same words, all bloodless, five hundred words dripping out of nothing, he wonders how he allowed himself to get trapped into teaching English when he might have had a happy and interesting life as an electrician or a confidence man.

Well, you may ask, what can you do about it? The subject is   12
one on which you have few convictions and little information. Can you be expected to make a dull subject interesting? As a matter of fact, this is precisely what you are expected to do. This is the writer's essential task. All subjects, except sex, are dull until somebody makes them interesting. The writer's job is to find the argument, the approach, the angle, the wording that will take the reader with him. This is seldom easy, and it is particularly hard in subjects that have been much discussed: College Football, Fraternities, Popular Music, Is Chivalry Dead?, and the like. You will feel that there is nothing you can do with such subjects except repeat the old bromides. But there are some things you can do which will make your papers, if not throbbingly alive, at least less insufferably tedious than they might otherwise be.

Avoid the Obvious Content

Say the assignment is college football. Say that you've decided   13
to be against it. Begin by putting down the arguments that come to your mind: It is too commercial, it takes the students' minds off their studies, it is hard on the players, it makes the university a kind of circus instead of an intellectual center, for most schools it is financially ruinous. Can you think of any more arguments, just off hand? All right. Now when you write your paper, *make sure that you don't use any of the material on this list.* If these are the points that leap to your mind they will leap to everyone else's too, and whether you get a "C" or a "D" may depend on whether the instructor reads your paper early when he is fresh and tolerant or late, when the sentence "In my opinion, college football has become too commercial," inexorably repeated, has brought him to the brink of lunacy.

Be against college football for some reason or reasons of your   14
own. If they are keen and perceptive ones, that's splendid. But even if they are trivial or foolish or indefensible, you are still ahead so long as they are not everybody else's reasons too. Be against it because the colleges don't spend enough money on it to make it worthwhile, because it is bad for the characters of the spectators, because the players are forced to attend classes, because the football stars hog all the beautiful women, because it competes

with baseball and is therefore un-American and possibly Communist inspired. There are lots of more or less unused reasons for being against college football.

Sometimes it is a good idea to sum up and dispose of the trite   15
and conventional points before going on to your own. This has the advantage of indicating to the reader that you are going to be neither trite nor conventional. Something like this:

> We are often told that college football should be abolished because it has become too commercial or because it is bad for the players. These arguments are no doubt very cogent, but they don't go to the heart of the matter.

Then you go to the heart of the matter.

Take the Less Usual Side

One rather simple way of getting into your paper is to take the   16
side of the argument that most of the citizens will want to avoid. If the assignment is an essay on dogs, you can, if you choose, explain that dogs are faithful and lovable companions, intelligent, useful as guardians of the house and protectors of children, indispensable in police work—in short, when all is said and done, man's best friends. Or you can suggest that those big brown eyes conceal, more often than not, a vacuity of mind and an inconstancy of purpose; that the dogs you have known most intimately have been mangy, ill-tempered brutes, incapable of instruction; and that only your nobility of mind and fear of arrest prevent you from kicking the flea-ridden animals when you pass them on the street.

Naturally personal convictions will sometimes dictate your ap-   17
proach. If the assigned subject is "Is Methodism Rewarding to the Individual?" and you are a pious Methodist, you have really no choice. But few assigned subjects, if any, will fall in this category. Most of them will lie in broad areas of discussion with much to be said on both sides. They are intellectual exercises, and it is legitimate to argue now one way and now another, as debaters do in similar circumstances. Always take the side that looks to you hardest, least defensible. It will almost always turn out to be easier to write interestingly on that side.

This general advice applies where you have a choice of sub-   18
jects. If you are to choose among "The Value of Fraternities" and "My Favorite High School Teacher" and "What I Think About Beetles," by all means plump for the beetles. By the time the in-

structor gets to your paper, he will be up to his ears in tedious tales about the French teacher at Bloombury High and assertions about how fraternities build character and prepare one for life. Your views on beetles, whatever they are, are bound to be a refreshing change.

Don't worry too much about figuring out what the instructor   19 thinks about the subject so that you can cuddle up with him. Chances are his views are no stronger than yours. If he does have convictions and you oppose him, his problem is to keep from grading you higher than you deserve in order to show he is not biased. This doesn't mean that you should always cantankerously dissent from what the instructor says; that gets tiresome too. And if the subject assigned is "My Pet Peeve," do not begin, "My pet peeve is the English instructor who assigns papers on 'my pet peeve.'" This was still funny during the War of 1812, but it has sort of lost its edge since then. It is in general good manners to avoid personalities.

Slip Out of Abstraction

If you will study the essay on college football [near the begin-   20 ning of this essay], you will perceive that one reason for its appalling dullness is that it never gets down to particulars. It is just a series of not very glittering generalities: "Football is bad for the colleges," "it has become too commercial," "football is a big business," "it is bad for the players," and so on. Such round phrases thudding against the reader's brain are unlikely to convince him, though they may well render him unconscious.

If you want the reader to believe that college football is bad for   21 the players, you have to do more than say so. You have to display the evil. Take your roommate, Alfred Simkins, the second-string center. Picture poor old Alfy coming home from football practice every evening, bruised and aching, agonizingly tired, scarcely able to shovel the mashed potatoes into his mouth. Let us see him staggering up to the room, getting out his econ textbook, peering desperately at it with his good eye, falling asleep and failing the test in the morning. Let us share his unbearable tension as Saturday draws near. Will he fail, be demoted, lose his monthly allowance, be forced to return to the coal mines? And if he succeeds, what will be his reward? Perhaps a slight ripple of applause when the third-string center replaces him, a moment of elation in the locker room if the team wins, of despair if it loses. What will he look back on when he graduates from college? Toil and torn ligaments. And what will be his future? He is not good enough for pro football, and he is too obscure and weak in econ to succeed in stocks and bonds. College football is tearing the heart from Alfy Simpkins and, when it finishes with him, will callously toss aside the shattered hulk.

This is no doubt a weak enough argument for the abolition 22 of college football, but it is a sight better than saying, in three or four variations, that college football (in your opinion) is bad for players.

Look at the work of any professional writer and notice how 23 constantly he is moving from the generality, the abstract statement, to the concrete example, the facts and figures, the illustration. If he is writing on juvenile delinquency, he does not just tell you that juveniles are (it seems to him) delinquent and that (in his opinion) something should be done about it. He shows you juveniles being delinquent, tearing up movie theatres in Buffalo, stabbing high school principals in Dallas, smoking marijuana in Palo Alto. And more than likely he is moving toward some specific remedy, not just a general wringing of the hands.

It is no doubt possible to be *too* concrete, too illustrative or 24 anecdotal, but few inexperienced writers err this way. For most the soundest advice is to be seeking always for the picture, to be always turning general remarks into seeable examples. Don't say, "Sororities teach girls the social graces." Say, "Sorority life teaches a girl how to carry on a conversation while pouring tea, without sloshing the tea into the saucer." Don't say, "I like certain kinds of popular music very much." Say, "Whenever I hear Gerber Sprinklittle play 'Mississippi Man' on the trombone, my socks creep up my ankles."

Get Rid of Obvious Padding

The student toiling away at his weekly English theme is too 25 often tormented by a figure: five hundred words. How, he asks himself, is he to achieve this staggering total? Obviously by never using one word when he can somehow work in ten.

He is therefore seldom content with a plain statement like 26 "Fast driving is dangerous." This has only four words in it. He takes thought, and the sentence becomes:

In my opinion, fast driving is dangerous.

Better, but he can do better still:

In my opinion, fast driving would seem to be rather dangerous.

If he is really adept, it may come out:

In my humble opinion, though I do not claim to be an expert on this complicated subject, fast driving, in most circumstances, would seem to be rather dangerous in many aspects, or at least so it would seem to me.

Thus four words have been turned into forty, and not an iota of content has been added.

Now this is a way to go about reaching five hundred words, 27 and if you are content with a "D" grade, it is as good a way as any. But if you aim higher, you must work differently. Instead of stuffing your sentences with straw, you must try steadily to get rid of the padding, to make your sentences lean and tough. If you are really working at it, your first draft will greatly exceed the required total, and then you will work it down, thus:

It is thought in some quarters that fraternities do not contribute as much as might be expected to campus life.

Some people think that fraternities contribute little to campus life.

The average doctor who practices in small towns or in the country must toil night and day to heal the sick.

Most country doctors work long hours.

When I was a little girl, I suffered from shyness and embarrassment in the presence of others.

I was a shy little girl.

It is absolutely necessary for the person employed as a marine fireman to give the matter of steam pressure his undivided attention at all times.

The fireman has to keep his eye on the steam gauge.

You may ask how you can arrive at five hundred words at this 28 rate. Simple. You dig up more real content. Instead of taking a couple of obvious points off the surface of the topic and then circling warily around them for six paragraphs, you work in and explore, figure out the details. You illustrate. You say that fast driving is dangerous, and then you prove it. How long does it take to stop a car at forty and at eighty? How far can you see at night? What happens when a tire blows? What happens in a head-on collision at fifty miles an hour? Pretty soon your paper will be full of broken glass and blood and headless torsos, and reaching five hundred words will not really be a problem.

Call a Fool a Fool

Some of the padding in freshman themes is to be blamed not   29 on anxiety about the word minimum but on excessive timidity. The student writes, "In my opinion, the principal of my high school acted in ways that I believe every unbiased person would have to call foolish." This isn't exactly what he means. What he means is, "My high school principal was a fool." If he was a fool, call him a fool. Hedging the thing about with "in-my-opinion's" and "it-seems-to-me's" and "as-I-see-it's" and "at-least-from-my-point-of-view's" gains you nothing. Delete these phrases whenever they creep into your paper.

The student's tendency to hedge stems from a modesty that in   30 other circumstances would be commendable. He is, he realizes, young and inexperienced, and he half suspects that he is dopey and fuzzy-minded beyond the average. Probably only too true. But it doesn't help to announce your incompetence six times in every paragraph. Decide what you want to say and say it as vigorously as possible, without apology and in plain words.

Linguistic diffidence can take various forms. One is what we   31 call *euphemism*. This is the tendency to call a spade "a certain garden implement" or women's underwear "unmentionables." It is stronger in some eras than others and in some people than others, but it always operates more or less in subjects that are touchy or taboo: death, sex, madness, and so on. Thus we shrink from saying "He died last night" but say instead "passed away," "left us," "joined his Maker," "went to his reward." Or we try to take off the tension with a lighter cliché: "kicked the bucket," "cashed in his chips," "handed in his dinner pail." We have found all sorts of ways to avoid saying *mad*: "mentally ill," "touched," "not quite right upstairs," "feeble-minded," "innocent," "simple," "off his trolley," "not in his right mind." Even such a now plain word as *insane* began as a euphemism with the meaning "not healthy."

Modern science, particularly psychology, contributes many   32 polysyllables in which we can wrap our thoughts and blunt their force. To many writers there is no such thing as a bad schoolboy. Schoolboys are maladjusted or unoriented or misunderstood or in the need of guidance or lacking in continued success toward satisfactory integration of the personality as a social unit, but they are never bad. Psychology no doubt makes us better men and women, more sympathetic and tolerant, but it doesn't make writing any easier. Had Shakespeare been confronted with psychology, "To be or not to be" might have come out, "To continue as a social unit or not to do so. That is the personality problem. Whether 'tis a better sign of integration at the conscious level to display a psychic tolerance toward the maladjustments and repressions induced by one's lack of orientation in one's environment or—" But Hamlet would never have finished the soliloquy.

Writing in the modern world, you cannot altogether avoid   33 modern jargon. Nor, in an effort to get away from euphemism, should you salt your paper with four-letter words. But you can do much if you will mount guard against those roundabout phrases, those echoing polysyllables that tend to slip into your writing to rob it of its crispness and force.

Beware of Pat Expressions

Other things being equal, avoid phrases like "other things   34 being equal." Those sentences that come to you whole, or in two or three doughy lumps, are sure to be bad sentences. They are no creation of yours but pieces of common thought floating in the community soup.

Pat expressions are hard, often impossible, to avoid, because   35 they come too easily to be noticed and seem too necessary to be dispensed with. No writer avoids them altogether, but good writers avoid them more often than poor writers.

By "pat expressions" we mean such tags as "to all practical in-   36 tents and purposes," "the pure and simple truth," "from where I sit," "the time of his life," "to the ends of the earth," "in the twinkling of an eye," "as sure as you're born," "over my dead body," "under cover of darkness," "took the easy way out," "when all is said and done," "told him time and time again," "parted the best of friends," "stand up and be counted," "gave him the best years of her life," "worked her fingers to the bone." Like other clichés, these expressions were once forceful. Now we should use them only when we can't possibly think of anything else.

Some pat expressions stand like a wall between the writer and thought. Such a one is "the American way of life." Many student writers feel that when they have said that something accords with the American way of life or does not they have exhausted the subject. Actually, they have stopped at the highest level of abstraction. The American way of life is the complicated set of bonds between a hundred and eighty million ways. All of us know this when we think about it, but the tag phrase too often keeps us from thinking about it.

So with many another phrase dear to the politician: "this great land of ours," "the man in the street," "our national heritage." These may prove our patriotism or give a clue to our political beliefs, but otherwise they add nothing to the paper except words.

Colorful Words

The writer builds with words, and no builder uses a raw material more slippery and elusive and treacherous. A writer's work is a constant struggle to get the right word in the right place, to find that particular word that will convey his meaning exactly, that will persuade the reader or soothe him or startle or amuse him. He never succeeds altogether—sometimes he feels that he scarcely succeeds at all—but such successes as he has are what make the thing worth doing.

There is no book of rules for this game. One progresses through everlasting experiment on the basis of ever-widening experience. There are few useful generalizations that one can make about words as words, but there are perhaps a few.

Some words are what we call "colorful." By this we mean that they are calculated to produce a picture or induce an emotion. They are dressy instead of plain, specific instead of general, loud instead of soft. Thus, in place of "Her heart beat," we may write, "Her heart *pounded, throbbed, fluttered, danced.*" Instead of "He sat in his chair," we may say, "He *lounged, sprawled, coiled.*" Instead of "It was hot," we may say, "It was *blistering, sultry, muggy, suffocating, steamy, wilting.*"

However, it should not be supposed that the fancy word is always better. Often it is as well to write "Her heart beat" or "It was hot" if that is all it did or all it was. Ages differ in how they like their prose. The nineteenth century liked it rich and smoky. The twentieth has usually preferred it lean and cool. The twentieth century writer, like all writers, is forever seeking the exact word, but he is wary of sounding feverish. He tends to pitch it low, to understate it, to throw it away. He knows that if he gets too colorful, the audience is likely to giggle.

See how this strikes you: "As the rich, golden glow of the sunset   43 died away along the eternal western hills, Angela's limpid blue eyes looked softly and trustingly into Montague's flashing brown ones, and her heart pounded like a drum in time with the joyous song surging in her soul." Some people like that sort of thing, but most modern readers would say, "Good grief," and turn on the television.

Colored Words

Some words we call not so much colorful as colored—that is,   44 loaded with associations, good or bad. All words—except perhaps structure words—have associations of some sort. We have said that the meaning of a word is the sum of the contexts in which it occurs. When we hear a word, we hear with it an echo of all the situations in which we have heard it before.

In some words, these echoes are obvious and discussable. The   45 word *mother*, for example, has for most people, agreeable associations. When you hear *mother* you probably think of home, safety, love, food, and various other pleasant things. If one writes, "She was like a mother to me," he gets an effect which he would not get in "She was like an aunt to me." The advertiser makes use of the associations of *mother* by working it in when he talks about his product. The politician works it in when he talks about himself.

So also with such words as *home, liberty, fireside, contentment, pa-   46 triot, tenderness, sacrifice, childlike, manly, bluff, limpid.* All of these words are loaded with associations that would be rather hard to indicate in a straightforward definition. There is more than a literal difference between "They sat around the fireside" and "They sat around the stove." They might have been equally warm and happy around the stove, but *fireside* suggests leisure, grace, quiet tradition, congenial company, and *stove* does not.

Conversely, some words have bad associations. *Mother* suggests   47 pleasant things, but *mother-in-law* does not. Many mothers-in-law are heroically lovable and some mothers drink gin all day and beat their children insensible, but these facts of life are beside the point. The point is that *mother* sounds good and *mother-in-law* does not.

Or consider the word *intellectual.* This would seem to be a   48
complimentary term, but in point of fact it is not, for it has picked up associations of impracticality and ineffectuality and general dopiness. So also such words as *liberal, reactionary, Communist, socialist, capitalist, radical, schoolteacher, truck driver, undertaker, operator, salesman, huckster, speculator.* These convey meaning on the literal level, but beyond that—sometimes, in some places—they convey contempt on the part of the speaker.

The question of whether to use loaded words or not depends   49
on what is being written. The scientist, the scholar, try to avoid them; for the poet, the advertising writer, the public speaker, they are standard equipment. But every writer should take care that they do not substitute for thought. If you write, "Anyone who thinks that is nothing but a Socialist (or Communist or capitalist)," you have said nothing except that you don't like people who think that, and such remarks are effective only with the most naive readers. It is always a bad mistake to think your readers more naive than they really are.

Colorless Words

But probably most student writers come to grief not with   50
words that are colorful or those that are colored but with those that have no color at all. A pet example is *nice,* a word we would find it hard to dispense with in casual conversation but which is no longer capable of adding much to a description. Colorless words are those of such general meaning that in a particular sentence they mean nothing. Slang adjectives like *cool* ("That's real cool") tend to explode all over the language. They are applied to everything, lose their original force, and quickly die.

Beware also of nouns of very general meaning, like *circum-*   51
stances, cases, instances, aspects, factors, relationships, attitudes, eventualities, etc. In most circumstances you will find that those cases of writing which contain too many instances of words like these will in this and other aspects have factors leading to unsatisfactory relationships with the reader resulting in unfavorable attitudes on his part and perhaps other eventualities, like a grade of "D." Notice

also what "etc." means. It means "I'd like to make this list longer, but I can't think of any more examples."

UNDERSTANDING DETAILS

1. According to Roberts, what is a writer's principal task? How does this task help introduce the rest of the essay?
2. List the nine guidelines Roberts suggests for good writing, and explain each briefly.
3. Can you give five examples of euphemisms now in current use (without repeating any of the ones Roberts uses)? Why is our society so dependent upon euphemisms? What social function do such words serve?
4. What are "colorful words," "colored words," and "colorless words," according to Roberts? Add five examples of your own to each of these lists in the essay.

ANALYZING MEANING

1. What is the principal purpose of this essay? Does it accomplish its purpose in your opinion? Explain your answer.
2. To what extent do you identify with the college student described by the author at the outset of this essay? In what important ways are you different?
3. According to Roberts, why do students have a tendency to "hedge"? In what ways does hedging detract from the overall effect of an essay? Give an example of hedging from one of your papers. How could you have made the statement more forceful?
4. Does Roberts follow his own suggestions for good writing in this essay? Why or why not? Give examples that illustrate how successfully the author follows his own advice.

DISCOVERING RHETORICAL STRATEGIES

1. How does Roberts organize the elements of his essay? Why does he choose this particular order? Is it effective in achieving his purpose? Why or why not?
2. Describe in some detail Roberts's intended audience. How did you come to this conclusion?

3. Analyze Roberts's use of humor throughout this essay (especially in his last paragraph). How does he raise our awareness regarding language as he makes us laugh at ourselves?
4. Roberts predominantly uses examples to show how to attack a writing task. What other rhetorical strategies does he use to make his point about good writing? Give an example of each of these strategies.

MAKING CONNECTIONS

1. Both Roberts and Garrison Keillor ("How the Crab Apple Grew") give advice about how to write a good essay, though each author delivers his suggestions differently. Compare and contrast how these authors provide advice to their readers. Which essay do you find most convincing? Explain your answer.
2. Read through Mary Roach's "Meet the Bickersons," and identify, according to Roberts's definition of the terms, ten "colorful," ten "colored," and ten "colorless" words in Roach's essay. Which category of words could you find most easily? Why? Which of these three types of words does Roberts use most often in his own essay?
3. Which essay in *The Prose Reader* does the best job of following Roberts's advice on how to write a good paper? Examine that essay in detail, explaining how it successfully fails to follow the guidelines set up in "How to Say Nothing in Five Hundred Words."

IDEAS FOR DISCUSSION/WRITING

Preparing to Write

Write freely about your own writing weaknesses: What problems do you have to watch out for in your own writing? Do these problems fluctuate with different kinds of assignments (essays, reports, research papers, or business writing)? How do you try to improve upon these weak areas when you find them?

Choosing a Topic

1. One of your friends who is still in high school has asked you for information about college-level English courses. Write to this friend, using process analysis to explain how to survive

freshman composition. Decide on a purpose and a point of view before you begin to write.

2. The student may not be the only one who needs improvement in this essay. The instructor's assignment of "a five-hundred-word composition on college football" does not promise to generate exciting prose. Devise a writing assignment on the topic of college sports that will get students more involved than the original assignment. Include purpose, audience, and the writer's role in your directions. Then, write a process analysis essay explaining how to create a well-crafted writing assignment.

3. Using the guidelines Roberts suggests in his article, write an essay analyzing one of your recent papers.

Before beginning your essay, you might want to consult the checklists on pages 219–220.

SHERWIN NULAND   (1930–   )

Accidents, Suicide, and Euthanasia

A native New Yorker and a product of the Bronx city schools, Dr. Sherwin Nuland earned his medical degree at Yale University, where he has been a Professor of Surgery since 1962. During his distinguished thirty-five-year career, he has cared for more than 10,000 patients, authored a number of clinical papers in the field of medical history, and contributed scientific essays to *The New Yorker*, *Discover*, *The New Republic*, *Time*, *The New York Review of Books*, and several other prominent popular journals. Nuland has also written *Doctors: The Biography of Medicine* (1988), a history of the medical profession told in the form of biographies of fourteen of its most influential contributors, and *The Wisdom of the Body* (1997), which joins together his interests in history, human biology, ethics, and the nature of humanity. His most influential book, however, is *How We Die: Reflections on Life's Final Chapter*, a study of the process of dying which has sold more than half a million copies, been translated into sixteen different languages, and won the 1994 National Book Award. His most recent book, *The Mysteries Within: A Surgeon Reflects on Medical Myths*, was published in 2000. A pioneer in the emerging field of biomedical ethics, the author has been a founding member of the Bioethics Committee at the Yale-New Haven Hospital since its inception in 1986. An avid tennis player and reader, Dr. Nuland advises students using *The Prose Reader* to "consider everything you write—even a note to your mother—a piece of literature."

Preparing to Read

Taken from *How We Die*, the following essay addresses the issue of terminal illness and the right to die. Before reading it, think for a few minutes about your beliefs about the quality of life: What do you believe is essential to make life worthwhile? Would suicide ever be appropriate? How strong is your will to live? Do you know anyone whose will to live is diminished? Explain the situation. Do you believe people should have the right to die? If so, what would be the circumstances?

Taking one's own life is almost always the wrong thing to
do. There are two circumstances, however, in which that
may not be so. Those two are the unendurable infirmities
of a crippling old age and the final devastations of terminal disease.
The nouns are not important in that last sentence—it is the adjectives that cry out for attention, for they are the very crux of the
issue and will tolerate no compromise or "well, almosts": *unendurable, crippling, final,* and *terminal.*

During his long lifetime, the great Roman orator Seneca gave   2
much thought to old age:

> I will not relinquish old age if it leaves my better part intact. But if it begins
> to shake my mind, if it destroys its faculties one by one, if it leaves me not life
> but breath, I will depart from the putrid or tottering edifice. I will not escape by
> death from disease so long as it may be healed, and leaves my mind unimpaired.
> I will not raise my hand against myself on account of pain, for so to die is to be
> conquered. But I know that if I must suffer without hope of relief, I will depart,
> not through fear of the pain itself, but because it prevents all for which I would
> live.

These words are so eminently sensible that few would disagree
that suicide would appear to be among the options that the frail
elderly should consider as the days grow more difficult, at least
those among them who are not barred from doing so by their
personal convictions. Perhaps the philosophy expressed by Seneca
explains the fact that elderly white males take their own lives at a
rate five times the national average. Is theirs not the "rational suicide" so strongly defended in journals of ethics and the op-ed
pages of our daily newspapers?

Hardly so. The flaw in Seneca's proposition is a striking example   3
of the error that permeates virtually every one of the publicized discussions of modern-day attitudes toward suicide—a very large proportion of the elderly men and women who kill themselves do it
because they suffer from quite remediable depression. With proper
medication and therapy, most of them would be relieved of the
cloud of oppressive despair that colors all reason gray, would then realize that the edifice topples not quite so much as thought, and that
hope of relief is less hopeless than it seemed. I have more than once
seen a suicidal old person emerge from depression and rediscovered
thereby a vibrant friend. When such men or women return to a less

despondent vision of reality, their loneliness seems to them less stark and their pain more bearable because life has become interesting again and they realize that there are people who need them. All of this is not to say that there are no situations in which   4 Seneca's words deserve heeding. But should this be so, the Roman's doctrine would then deserve consultation, counsel, and the leavening influence of a long period of mature thought. A decision to end life must be as defensible to those whose respect we seek as it is to ourselves. Only when that criterion has been satisfied should anyone consider the finality of death.

Against such a standard, the suicide of Percy Bridgman was   5 close to being irreproachable. Bridgman was a Harvard professor whose studies in high-pressure physics won him a Nobel Prize in 1946. At the age of seventy-nine and in the final stages of cancer, he continued to work until he could no longer do so. Living at his summer home in Randolph, New Hampshire, he completed the index to a seven-volume collection of his scientific works, sent it off to the Harvard University Press, and then shot himself on August 20, 1961, leaving a suicide note in which he summed up a controversy that has since embroiled an entire world of medical ethics: "It is not decent for Society to make a man do this to himself. Probably, this is the last day I will be able to do it myself.

When he died, Bridgman seemed absolutely clear in his mind   6 that he was making the right choice. He worked right up to the final day, tied up loose ends, and carried out his plan. I'm not certain how much consideration he gave to consulting others, but his decision had certainly not been kept a secret from friends and colleagues, because there is ample evidence of his having at least informed some of them in advance. He had become so sick that he felt it doubtful that he would much longer be capable of mustering up the strength to carry out his ironclad resolve.

In his final message, Bridgman deplored the necessity of per-   7 forming his deed unaided. A colleague reported a conversation in which Bridgman said, "I would like to take advantage of the situation in which I find myself to establish a general principle; namely, that when the ultimate end is as inevitable as it now appears to be, the individual has a right to ask his doctor to end it for him." If a single sentence were needed to epitomize the battle in which we are all now joined, you have just read it.

No contemporary discussion of suicide, at least not one written   8
by a physician, can skirt the issue of the doctor's role in assisting
patients toward their mortality. The crucial word in this sentence
is *patients*—not just people, but *patients,* specifically the patients of
the doctor who contemplates the assisting. The guild of Hippocrates should not develop a new specialty of accoucheurs to the
grave so that conscience-stricken oncologists, surgeons, and other
physicians may refer to others those who wish to exit the planet.
On the other hand, any degree of debate about physicians' participation should be welcomed if it will bring out into the open a
muted practice that has existed since Aesculapius was in swaddling
clothes.

Suicide, especially this newly debated form, has become fash-   9
ionable lately. In centuries long past, those who took their own
lives were at best considered to have committed a felony against
themselves; at worst, their crime was viewed as a mortal sin. Both
attitudes are implicit in the words of Immanuel Kant: "Suicide is
not abominable because God forbids it; God forbids it because it
is abominable."

But things are different today; we have a new wrinkle on sui-   10
cide, aided and perhaps encouraged by self-styled consultants on
the limits of human suffering. We read in our tabloids and glossy
magazines that the actions of the deceased are, under certain sanctioned circumstances, celebrated with tributes such as are usually
reserved for New Age heroes, which a few of them seem to have
become. As for the pop cultural icons, medical and otherwise,
who assist them—we are treated to the spectacle of those publicized peddlers of death willingly expounding their philosophies
on TV talk shows. They extol their own selflessness even as the
judicial system seeks to prosecute them.

In 1988, there appeared in the *Journal of the American Medical*   11
Association an account by a young gynecologist-in-training who,
in the wee hours of one night, murdered—*murder* is the only
word for it—a cancer-ridden twenty-year-old woman because it
pleased him to interpret her plea for relief as a plea for death that
only he could grant. His method was to inject a dose of intra-
venous morphine of at least twice the recommended strength and
then to stand by until her breathing "became irregular, then
ceased." The fact that the self-appointed deliverer had never seen
his victim before did not deter him from not only carrying out

but actually publishing the details of his misconceived mission of mercy, saturated with the implicit fulsome certainty of his wisdom. Hippocrates winced, and his living heirs wept in spirit.

Though American doctors quickly reached a condemning consensus about the behavior of the young gynecologist, they responded very differently three years later in a case of quite another sort. Writing in the *New England Journal of Medicine,* an internist from Rochester, New York, described a patient he identified only as Diane, whose suicide he knowingly facilitated by prescribing the barbiturates she requested. Diane, the mother of a college-age son, had been Dr. Timothy Quill's patient for a long time. Three and a half years earlier, he had diagnosed a particularly severe form of leukemia, and her disease had progressed to the point where "bone pain, weakness, fatigue, and fevers began to dominate her life." 12

Rather than agree to chemotherapy that stood little chance of arresting the lethal assault of her cancer, Diane early in her course had made it clear to Dr. Quill and his several consultants that she feared the debilitation of treatment and the loss of control of her body far more than she feared death. Slowly, patiently, with rare compassion and the help of his colleagues, Quill came to accept Diane's decision and the validity of her grounds for making it. The process by which he gradually recognized that he should help speed her death is exemplary of the humane bond that can exist and be enhanced between a doctor and a competent terminally ill patient who rationally chooses and with consultation confirms that it is the right way to make her quietus. For those whose worldview allows them this option, Dr. Quill's way of dealing with the thorny issue of assent (since then elaborated in a wise and outspoken book published in 1993) may prove to be a reference point on the compass of medical ethics. Physicians like the young gynecologist, and the inventors of suicide machines too, have a great deal to learn from the Dianes and the Timothy Quills. 13

Quill and the gynecologist represent the diametrically opposed approaches which dominate discussions of the physician's role in helping patients to die—they are the ideal and the feared. Debates have raged, and I hope will continue to rage, over the stance that should be taken by the medical community and others, and there are many shades of opinion. 14

In the Netherlands, euthanasia guidelines have been drawn up   15
by common consensus, allowing competent and fully informed
patients to have death administered in carefully regulated circumstances. The usual method is for the physician to induce deep
sleep with barbiturates and then to inject a muscle-paralyzing drug
to cause cessation of breathing. The Dutch Reformed Church has
adopted a policy, described in its publication *Euthanasie en Pas-*
toraat—"Euthanasia and the Ministry"—that does not obstruct the
voluntary ending of life when illness makes it intolerable. Their
very choice of words signifies the churchmen's sensitivity to the
difference between this and ordinary suicide, or *zelfmoord,* literally
"self-murder." A new term has been introduced to refer to death
under circumstances of euthanasia: *zelfdoding,* which might best be
translated as "self-deathing."

UNDERSTANDING DETAILS

1. According to Nuland, what are two instances in which suicide
   would be understandable?
2. What is a common, curable problem among terminally ill
   patients?
3. What are a patient's main responsibilities before choosing suicide?
4. What are the guidelines, according to Nuland, for performaing
   a "rational suicide" (paragraph 2)?

ANALYZING MEANING

1. What are some of the ethical issues that physician-assisted suicides trigger?
2. What are some of the legal issues concerning physician-assisted
   suicides?
3. Explain the notion of "rational suicide" through some examples from your own experience.
4. Do you agree with Nuland that suicide can be justified? Explain your answer.

DISCOVERING RHETORICAL STRATEGIES

1. How does Nuland's introduction prepare us for the information that follows? In your opinion, is this an effective beginning to this essay?

2. Who do you think is Nuland's primary audience? On what information do you base your answer?
3. What does the story of Percy Bridgman add to this process analysis essay? What other rhetorical strategies does Nuland use in this essay?
4. How does the author organize the specific guidelines for committing a justifiable suicide? Is this order effective? Why or why not?

MAKING CONNECTIONS

1. Nuland's essay is an *informative* process analysis: that is, it explains how and why suicides in the elderly and sick occur. Pick one of the other process analysis essays from this section of the book that illustrates a *directive* approach—how something is done. How are these two essays different from each other in terms of their organization and approach?
2. If Fred Pelka ("Hating the Sick: Health Chauvinism and Its Cure") had written an essay similar to Nuland's about how and when to die, how would it have been different from "Accidents, Suicide, and Euthanasia"? In your opinion, what different issues would Pelka be concerned with? What would be the principal reasons for these differences?
3. How do you think Malcolm Cowley ("The View from 80") and Michael Dorris ("The Broken Cord") would react to Nuland's main ideas in this essay? On what would they each base their reactions?

IDEAS FOR DISCUSSION/WRITING

Preparing to Write

Write freely about various encounters you have had with sick or depressed people: What was your connection with these people? How did they handle their illness? Did they consider suicide? Were you instrumental in helping these people in any way? Do you think suicide is a viable option in some cases? If so, in what circumstances? Have you yourself ever been depressed? How did you handle the situation?

Choosing a Topic

1. A popular magazine has asked you to explain the details of a particular health-care job (either paid or unpaid). This could

include taking care of a sick relative at home as well as working in a health-care facility. For the magazine, write a process analysis essay explaining this aspect of health care. The explanation should be aimed at people who are simply interested in health care in general. Gather any information you need before you begin to write.

2. The editors of this magazine have asked you to revise your essay for a group of people looking for work. This time, the editors want you to persuade their readers to work in the health-care field. In this case, present your process analysis essay as a sales pitch to the general public, explaining the benefits of this type of work along with your detailed directions for carrying out a specific job.

3. Depression is a widespread illness in contemporary American society, especially among college students. As a result, your college newspaper is running a special series of articles on school-related depression. Find out as much as you can about this disease, its causes, and its cures, and write an article for your campus newspaper on depression and how to avoid it.

Before beginning your essay, you might want to consult the checklists on pages 219–220.

MARK HANSEN   (1956–   )

E-mail: What You Should—
And Shouldn't—Say

Born in Port Arthur, Texas, Mark Hansen has a B.S. in psychology, an M.S. in industrial engineering, and over twenty years' experience as a licensed professional engineer specializing in the fields of safety and ergonomics. Currently the director of the Division of Quality, Health, Safety, and Environmental for Weatherford International, Inc., an oil field service company in Houston, Texas, he has also held supervisory positions at Union Texas Petroleum, Eagle Environmental Health, the Dixie Chemical Company, the Mission Research Corporation, and Loral Command and Control Systems. He has published over one hundred articles and book chapters in his field and received numerous awards for promoting safety in the workplace. His advice to students using *The Prose Reader* is "to read everything you can get your hands on. Reading books, trade publications, technical journals, and business magazines refreshes me and allows me to grow as a professional. I am always learning. Once you quit learning, you begin antiquating." In his spare time, Hansen enjoys playing golf, biking, and helping to raise his daughter.

Preparing to Read

The following essay, from a journal called *Professional Safety*, offers extremely helpful advice for people who use e-mail as a form of communication. As you prepare to read this essay, take a few minutes to think about communication in general: What form of communication works best for you? Do you often send and receive e-mail? Do you surf the Internet? How much time do you spend online per day? Do you enjoy the time you spend online? How has e-mail changed our society? What are the advantages of e-mail? The disadvantages?

Most e-mail users remember to check the spelling in the 1
messages they compose. But they often neglect to
check how their communication will come across to
their readers. Even well-meaning individuals write messages that
they would never say aloud. To ensure that your e-mail does not
short-circuit a business relationship, consider these 11 common-
sense guidelines.

1. Think about who may read your message. You should 2
consider not only the person the message is for, but others who
may read it. Consider the possibility that your message will take an
unexpected turn and appear in the wrong mailbox. Do you need
to comment about a third party in your message? Is what you
need to say negative or could it be construed as such? If so, consider using the phone or a face-to-face meeting.

2. Picture the recipient's reaction to your message. 3
Would you say the same thing you are writing to this person in a
face-to-face conversation? Have you inadvertently been sarcastic
or judgmental? Is the recipient someone who might put a negative spin on your message?

Remember: in a verbal conversation, you might try to temper 4
the bluntness in your message or the exasperation you feel by
using facial expression or tone. But this is difficult to achieve via
e-mail, even if you use a smile symbol. Why chance creating anxiety or distrust?

3. Avoid beginning with criticism. Don't start a message 5
with "Why didn't you answer me sooner?" Though some pro-
crastinators may deserve such a blunt reminder, you'll do more
for any relationship if you open with a positive statement.

Example: "I wasn't sure if my message got through yesterday, 6
so here it is again." Electronic messages that begin with "why
didn't you" can come across as even more directing and authori-
tarian than when speaking on the phone or in person.

4. Don't send a message that you would be embarrassed 7
to send to a family member. Why risk sending something
that has innuendoes or remarks that would offend someone?
Apply what I call the "Aunt Alma test." If my prim-and-proper
Aunt Alma would not find the remark amusing or appropriate, I
scrap it. Save funny remarks and jokes for a face-to-face conversation with an audience you know will be amused.

5. Make sure your message is not too cryptic. Have you   8
clearly stated all the reader needs to know? Or have you withheld
certain details so that you retain control and force the recipient to
"read between the lines," guess, or assume?

Keep this in mind: Information control is a communication   9
power-play that can easily backfire.

6. Check your messages for grammatical idiosyncrasies.   10
Do you often use ellipses instead of completing your thoughts?
Do you get carried away with particular punctuation—e-mail
symbols some use in place of words to indicate thoughts and feelings? Some symbols may confuse rather than communicate.

7. Read and reread messages before sending them.   11
Would you be offended by the tone? If your tone is harsh, the recipient may think that s/he has done something to offend you.

8. Make sure your message is concise. Do you consis-   12
tently write more than necessary? Are you swamping your readers
with too many details? Do you give so much information—important, unimportant, and in particular order—that your reader
cannot easily conclude what matters and what does not?

A poll published in *Oregon Business* found that 26 percent of re-   13
spondents spend an hour each day reading and replying to e-mail;
14 percent spent more than an hour. So, do everything possible to
compose messages that will help your reader save time. Some
guidelines:

- Limit messages to one screen so the reader will not have to
  scroll down

- Use numbers, bullets, etc., to highlight key points

9. Avoid cluttering others' electronic space with non-   14
urgent items that you could send via fax or regular mail.
Do you immediately broadcast every tidbit you come across?
Don't assume that those you communicate with are not up to
speed on the latest news and trends.

This also falls under the "know your audience" heading. Make   15
it your business to know what information sources they use. If
you know they subscribe to magazine X or only service Y, why
fire off a message about something you just read there?

10. Don't let e-mail become a substitute for in-person or   16
phone conversations. Guard against using e-mail to converse

with colleagues in the office next door. Unless the message must be in writing, try communicating the old-fashioned way: face to face. Walk down the hall to speak with colleagues. Invite them to lunch. Use the phone. Often, a phone conversation takes a fraction of the time needed to compose a message, send it, and wait for an answer.

11. Remember the human element in communication. 17 Readers will respond more willingly to the writer who does so. Do you add a personal line when you know the reader well? Do you say thank you? The e-mail medium may be cutting-edge, but it will never replace the old-fashioned "please" and "thank you."

Unless some clever person creates a courtesy checking pro- 18 gram, you'll benefit from your own courtesy check. That means you must recognize that the tone of what you write should reflect the type of message you yourself expect to find in your electronic in-box.

UNDERSTANDING DETAILS

1. What is the main purpose of this essay?
2. Name three of Hansen's categories that you will find most useful in writing and editing your own e-mail messages.
3. What does Hansen mean when he says, "Remember the human element in communication" (paragraph 17)?
4. What is a "courtesy check" (paragraph 18), according to Hansen?

ANALYZING MEANING

1. What role does the recipient play in Hansen's guidelines for writing e-mail messages?
2. What is the advantage of reading and rereading e-mail messages before sending them?
3. What does tone have to do with writing effective e-mail messages?
4. Why do you think Hansen cites the poll from *Oregon Business* (paragraph 13)? Are these statistics effective at this point in the essay?

DISCOVERING RHETORICAL STRATEGIES

1. How would you characterize the tone of this essay? What specific details bring you to this conclusion?
2. Who do you think is Hansen's primary audience in this essay? On what do you base your answer?
3. What is Hansen's method of organizing his advice in this essay?
4. Explain Hansen's title. What are some other possible titles for this essay?

MAKING CONNECTIONS

1. Compare and contrast Hansen's suggestions about editing and censoring our e-mails with the other forms of communication censorship advocated by Paul Roberts's "How to Say Nothing in Five Hundred Words," Judith Viorst's "The Truth about Lying," Mary Roach's "Meet the Bickersons," and Rita Mae Brown's "Writing as a Moral Act."
2. Examine the effect of e-mail on personal communication in light of Geoffrey Meredith's "The Demise of Writing" and Mitchell Stephens's "The Death of Reading."
3. How useful is Mark Hansen's business advice in comparison to that offered by the following authors: Edwin Bliss's "Managing Your Time" and William Ouchi's "Japanese and American Workers: Two Casts of Mind"?

IDEAS FOR DISCUSSION/WRITING

Preparing to Write

Write freely about your e-mail habits: How much time do you spend reading e-mail? Do you generally write quick or lengthy responses to your e-mail? Do you enjoy reading and writing e-mail messages? How is e-mail different from a phone conversation? From a letter? What unique guidelines do you follow in each medium?

CHOOSING A TOPIC

1. Using Hansen's advice, explain what characterizes successful communication in your opinion. Direct your essay to new college students.

2. In order to get a laugh, explain a funny example of miscommunication from your own experience. What did you learn from this "catastrophe"?
3. Prepare for your English class a two- to three-minute talk on one of the following topics:
   How TV Sells Products to Kids
   How the Newspaper Communicates
   The Role of Music Videos in Our Culture Today
   The Benefits of E-mail Messages
   The Benefits of Talking in Person
   The Future of Formal Written Letters

Before beginning your essay, you might want to consult the checklists on pages 219–220.

CHAPTER WRITING ASSIGNMENTS
Practicing Process Analysis

1. Make a list of some of the activities you do well. Choose one activity, and think about exactly what you must do to perform this skill. Write an essay that describes to another person the process of doing this activity well. Be as specific and clear in your directions as you can.

2. Identify a task or responsibility that seems impossible for you to do well. What keeps you from performing this task with skill or efficiency? Write an essay that describes how to fail at this activity. Describe this method for failure in a humorous or sarcastic manner.

3. What is your best method for solving major life problems? Think of times in your life when you have had to solve a problem or make an important decision. Write an essay that explains to a person looking for problem-solving ideas the method you rely on when faced with important problems that need to be solved.

Exploring Ideas

1. How do you think e-mail affects the way people communicate? Do you think e-mail has mostly positive or negative effects on people's writing? Use specific examples to support your opinion.

2. Find a recent advertisement on television, in the newspaper, on a billboard, or on the radio that you think is especially successful. Examine this ad, and write an essay explaining its success. What makes it good? Whom does it reach? How effectively does it address its target population?

3. Should we "force" students to stay in school until the age of sixteen, or should we allow students who do not choose to go to school the right to drop out before they finish high school? Respond to these questions in an organized essay.

5

DIVISION/CLASSIFICATION

Finding Categories

Both division and classification play important roles in our everyday lives: Bureau drawers separate one type of clothing from another; kitchen cabinets organize food, dishes, and utensils into proper groups; grocery stores shelve similar items together so shoppers can easily locate what they want to buy; school notebooks with tabs help students divide up their academic lives; newspapers classify local and national events in order to organize a great deal of daily information for the general public; and our own personal classification systems assist us in separating what we like from what we don't so that we can have access to our favorite foods, our favorite cars, our favorite entertainment, our favorite people. The two processes of division and classification are so natural to us, in fact, that we sometimes aren't even aware we are using them.

DEFINING DIVISION/CLASSIFICATION

Division and classification are actually mirror images of each other. Division is the basic feature of process analysis, which we studied in the last chapter: It moves from a general concept to subdivisions of that concept or from a single category to multiple subcategories. Classification works in the opposite direction, moving from specifics to a group with common traits or from multiple subgroups to a single, larger, and more inclusive category. These techniques work together in many ways: A college, for example, is *divided* into departments (single to multiple), whereas courses are *classified* by department (multiple to single); the medical field is *divided* into specialties, whereas doctors are *classified* by a single specialty; a cookbook is *divided* into chapters, whereas recipes are *classified* according to type; and athletics is *divided* into specific sports, whereas athletes are *classified* by the sport in which they participate. Division is the separation of an idea or an item into its basic parts, such as a home into rooms, a course into assignments, or a job into various duties or responsibilities; classification is the organization of items with similar features into a group or groups, such as identifying all green-eyed people in a large group, omitting all carbohydrates from your diet, or watching only the track and field events during the Olympics.

Classification is an organizational system for presenting a large amount of material to a reader or listener. This process helps us make sense of the complex world we live in by letting us work with smaller, more understandable units of that world. Classification must be governed by some clear, logical purpose (such as focusing on all lower-division course requirements), which will then dictate the system of categories to be used. The plan of organization that results should be as flexible as possible, and it should illustrate the specific relationship to each other of items in a group and of the groups themselves to one another.

As you already know, many different ways of classifying the same elements are possible. If you consider the examples at the outset of this chapter, you will realize that bureau drawers vary from house to house and even from person to person; that no one's kitchen is set up exactly the same way as someone else's; and that grocery stores have similar but not identical systems of classification. (Think, for instance, of the many different schemes for organizing dairy products, meats, foreign foods, etc.) In addition, your friends probably use a method different from yours to organize their school notebooks; different newspapers vary their presentation of the news; and two professors will probably teach the same course material in separate ways. We all have distinct and uniquely logical methods of classifying the elements in our own lives.

The following student paragraph about friends illustrates both division and classification. As you read it, notice how the student writer moves back and forth smoothly from general to specific and from multiple to single:

> The word friend can refer to many different types of relationships. Close friends are "friends" at their very best: people for whom we feel respect, esteem, and, quite possibly, even love. We regard these people and their well-being with kindness, interest, and goodwill; we trust them and will go out of our way to help them. Needless to say, we could all use at least one close friend. Next come "casual friends," people with whom we share a particular interest or activity. The investment of a great amount of time and energy in developing this type of friendship is usually not required, though casual friends often become close friends with the passage of time. The last division of "friend" is most general and is composed of all those individuals whose acquaintance we have made and who feel no hostility toward us. When one is counting friends, this group should certainly be included, since such friendships often develop into "casual" or "close" relationships. Knowing people in all three groups is necessary, however, because all types of friends undoubtedly help us live healthier, happier lives.

THINKING CRITICALLY BY USING DIVISION/CLASSIFICATION

The thinking strategies of division and classification are the flip sides of each other: Your textbook is *divided* into chapters (one item divided into many), but chapters are *classified* (grouped) into sections or units. Your brain performs these mental acrobatics constantly, but to be as proficient at this method of thinking as possible, you need to be aware of the cognitive activities you go through. Focusing on these two companion patterns of thought will develop your skill in dealing with these complex schemes as it simultaneously increases your overall mental capabilities.

You might think of division/classification as a driving pattern that goes forward and then doubles back on itself in reverse. Division is a movement from a single concept to multiple categories, while classification involves gathering multiple concepts into a single group. Dividing and/or classifying helps us make sense of our subject by using categories to highlight similarities and differences. In the case of division, you are trying to find what differences break the items into separate groups, while, with classification, you let the similarities among the items help you put the material into meaningful categories. Processing your material in this way helps your readers see your particular subject in a new way and often brings renewed insights to both reader and writer.

Experimenting with division and classification is important to your growth as a critical thinker. It will help you process complex information so you can understand more fully your options for dealing with material in all subject areas. Practicing division and classification separate from other rhetorical modes makes you concentrate on improving this particular pattern of thinking before adding it to your expanding arsenal of critical thinking skills.

1. Study the table of contents of a magazine that interests you. Into what sections is the magazine divided? What distinguishing features does each section have? Now study the various advertisements in the same magazine. What different categories would you use to classify these ads? List the ads in each category.
2. Make a chart classifying the English instructors at your school. Explain your classification system to the class.
3. List six to eight major concerns you have about American society. Which of these are most important? Which are least important? Now classify these concerns into two or three distinct categories.

READING AND WRITING DIVISION/ CLASSIFICATION ESSAYS

Though writers of division/classification essays will probably use both division and classification in their essays, they should decide if they are primarily going to break down a topic into many separate parts or group together similar items into one coherent category; a writer's purpose will, of course, guide him or her in this decision. Readers must likewise recognize and understand which of these two parallel operations an author is using to structure an essay. Another important identifying feature of division/ classification essays is an explanation (explicit or implicit) of the significance of a particular system of organization.

How to Read a Division/Classification Essay

Preparing to Read. As you approach the selections in this chapter, you should study all the material that precedes each essay so you can prepare yourself for your reading. First of all, what hints does the title give you about what you are going to read? To what extent does Judy Brady reveal her attitude toward women in her title? Who do you think Judith Wallerstein and Sandra Blakeslee's audience is in "Second Chances for Children of Divorce"? Does Judith Viorst's title give us any indication about her point of view in "The Truth About Lying"? Then, see what you can learn from scanning each essay and reading its synopsis in the Rhetorical Table of Contents.

Also important as you prepare to read the essays in this chapter is your knowledge about each author and the conditions under which each essay was written: What does the biographical material tell you about Phyllis Schneider's "Memory: Tips You'll Never Forget"? About Franklin Zimring's "Confessions of an Ex-Smoker"? Knowing where these essays were first published will give you even more information about each author's purpose and audience.

Finally, before you begin to read, answer the Preparing to Read questions, and then think freely for a few minutes about the general topic: What do you want to know about children of divorce from Wallerstein and Blakeslee? What are some different types of lies you have told (Viorst)?

Reading. As you read each essay for the first time, write down your initial reactions to the topic itself, to the preliminary material, to the mood the writer sets, or to a specific incident in the essay. Make associations between the essay and your own experiences.

In addition, create a context for each essay by drawing on the preliminary material you just read about the essay: What is Schneider implying about the relationship between remembering and forgetting, and why does she care about this relationship? What is significant about Zimring's point of view in "Confessions of an Ex-Smoker"? According to Viorst, why are some lies permissible?

Also in this first reading, notice when the writers divided (split up) or classified (gathered together) their material to make their point. Finally, read the questions after each essay, and let them guide your second reading of the selection.

Rereading. When you read these division/classification essays a second time, notice how the authors carefully match their dominant rhetorical approach (in this case, division or classification) to their purpose in a clear thesis. What, for example, is Brady's dominant rhetorical approach to her subject? How does this approach further her purpose? What other rhetorical strategies support her thesis? Then see how these writers logically present their division or classification systems to their readers, defining new categories as their essays progress. Finally, notice how each writer either implicitly or explicitly explains the significance or value of his or her division/classification system. How do Wallerstein and Blakeslee explain their system of organization? And how does Viorst give her organizing principle significance? Now answer the questions after each essay to check your understanding and to help you analyze your reading in preparation for the discussion/writing topics that follow.

For a more complete survey of reading guidelines, you may want to consult the checklist on pages 20–21 of the Introduction.

How to Write a Division/Classification Essay

Preparing to Write. You should approach a division/classification essay in the same way you have begun all your other writing assignments—with some kind of prewriting activity that will help you generate ideas, such as the Preparing to Write questions featured in this chapter. The prewriting techniques outlined in the Introduction on pages 21–27 can help you approach these questions imaginatively. Before you even consider the selection and arrangement of details, you need to explore your subject, choose a topic, and decide on a specific purpose and audience. The best way to explore your subject is to think about it, read about it, and then write about it. Look at it from all possible angles, and see what patterns and relationships emerge. To choose a specific topic, you might begin by listing any groups, patterns, or combinations you discover within your subject matter. Your purpose should take shape as you form your thesis, and your audience is probably dictated by the assignment. Making these decisions before you write will make the rest of your task much easier.

Writing. As you begin to write, certain guidelines will help you structure your ideas for a division/classification essay:

1. First, declare an overall purpose for your division/classification.
2. Then, divide the item or concept you are dealing with into categories.
3. Arrange these categories into a logical sequence.
4. Define each category, explaining the difference between one category and another and demonstrating that difference through examples.
5. Explain the significance of your classification system (Why is it worth reading? What will your audience learn from it?).

All discussion in such an essay should reinforce the purpose stated at the beginning of your paper. Other rhetorical modes—such as narration, example, and comparison/contrast—will naturally be used to supplement your classification.

To make your division/classification as workable as possible, take special care that your categories do not overlap and that all topics fall into their proper places. If, for example, you were dividing/classifying all the jobs performed by students in your writing class, the categories of (1) indoor work and (2) outdoor work would probably be inadequate because some jobs fit into both categories. At a pizza parlor, a florist, or a gift shop, for example, a delivery person's time would be split between indoor and outdoor work. So you would need to alter the classification system to avoid this problem. The categories of (1) indoor work, (2) outdoor work, and (3) a combination of indoor and outdoor work would be much more useful for this task. Making sure your categories don't overlap will help make your classification essays more readable and more accurate.

Rewriting. As you rewrite your division/classification essays, consider carefully the probable reactions of your readers to the form and content of your paper:

- Does your thesis communicate your purpose clearly?
- Have you divided your topic into separate and understandable categories?
- Are these categories arranged logically?

• Do you explain the significance of your particular classification system?

More guidelines for writing and rewriting are available on pages 32–34 of the Introduction.

STUDENT ESSAY: DIVISION/CLASSIFICATION AT WORK

The following student essay divides skiers into interesting categories based on their physical abilities. As you read it, notice how the student writer weaves the significance of his study into his opening statement of purpose. Also, pay particular attention to his logical method of organization and clear explanation of categories as he moves with ease from multiple to single and back to multiple again throughout the essay.

People on the Slopes

When I first learned to ski, I was amazed by the shapes who whizzed by me and slipped down trails marked only by a black diamond signifying "most difficult," while others careened awkwardly down the "bunny slopes." These skiers, I discovered, could be divided into distinct categories— for my own entertainment and for the purpose of finding appropriate skiing partners.

First are the "poetic skiers." They glide down the mountainside silently with what seems like no effort at all. They float from side to side on the intermediate slopes, their knees bent perfectly above parallel skis, while their sharp skills allow them to bypass slower skiers with safely executed turns at remarkable speeds.

The "crazy skiers" also get down the mountain quickly, but with a lot more noise attending their descent. At every hill, they yell a loud "Yahoo!" and slam their skis into the snow. These go-for-broke athletes always whiz by faster than everyone else, and they especially seem to love the

Margin annotations:

Subject

Thesis statement

Overall purpose

First category

Definition

Supporting details

Second category

Definition

Supporting details (with humor)

crowded runs where they can slide over the backs of other people's skis. I often find crazy skiers in mangled messes at the bottoms of steep hills, where they are yelling loudly, but not the famous "Yahoo!"

Transition

After being overwhelmed by the crazy skiers, I am always glad to find other skiers like myself: "the average ones." We are polite on the slopes, concentrate on improving our technique with every run, and ski the beginner slopes only at the beginning of the day to warm up. We go over the moguls (small hills) much more cautiously than the crazy or poetic skiers, but we still seek adventure with a little jump or two each day. We remain a silent majority on the mountain.

Third category

Definition

Supporting details (comparative)

Below us in talent, but much more evident on the mountainside, are what I call the "eternal beginners." These skiers stick to the same beginner slope almost every run of every day during their vacation. Should they venture onto an intermediate slope, they quickly assume the snowplow position (a pigeon-toed stance) and never leave it. Eternal beginners weave from one side of the run to the other and hardly ever fall, because they proceed so slowly; however, they do yell quite a bit at the crazies who like to run over the backs of their skis.

Transition

Fourth category

Definition

Supporting details

Having always enjoyed people-watching, I have fun each time I am on the slopes observing the myriad of skiers around me. I use these observations to pick out possible ski partners for myself and others. Since my mother is an eternal beginner, she has more fun skiing with someone who shares her interests than with my dad, who is a poetic skier with solitude on his mind. After taking care of Mom, I am free to find a partner I'll enjoy. My sister, the crazy skier of the

Transition

Significance of classification system

Concluding
remarks

family, just heads for the rowdiest group she can find! As the years go by and my talents grow, I am trusting my perceptions of skier types to help me find the right partner for life on and off the slopes. No doubt watching my fellow skiers will always remain an enjoyable pastime.

Student Writer's Comments

To begin this paper—the topic of which occurred to me as I flew over snow-capped mountains on a trip—I brainstormed. I jotted down the general groups of skiers I believed existed on the slopes and recorded characteristics of each group as they came to me. The ideas flowed quite freely at this point, and I enjoyed imagining the people I was describing. This prewriting stage brought back some great memories from the slopes that cluttered my thinking at times, but in most cases one useless memory triggered two or three other details or skiing stories that helped me make sense of my division/classification system.

I then felt ready to write a first draft but was having a lot of trouble coming up with a sensible order for my categories. So I just began to write. My categories were now clear to me, even though I wanted to work a little more on their labels. And the definitions of each category came quite naturally as I wrote. In fact, the ease with which they surfaced made me believe that I really had discovered some ultimate truth about types of skiers. I also had tons of details and anecdotes to work with from my brainstorming session. When I finished the body of my first draft (it had no introduction or conclusion yet), I realized that every paragraph worked nicely by itself—four separate category paragraphs. But these paragraphs didn't work together yet at all.

As I reworked the essay, I knew my major job was to reorganize my categories in some logical way and then smooth out the prose with transitions that would make the essay work as a unified whole. To accomplish this, I wrote more drafts of this single paper than I can remember writing for any other assignment. But I feel that the order and the transitions finally work now. The essay moves logically from type to type, and I think my transitions justify my arrangement along the way. My overall purpose came to me as I was reorganizing my categories, at which point I was able to write my introduction and conclusion. After I had put my purpose into words, the significance of my division/classification system became clear. I saved it, however, for the conclusion.

The most exciting part of this paper was realizing how often I had used these mental groupings in pairing my family and friends with other skiers. I had just never labeled, defined, or organized the categories I had created. Writing this paper helped me verbalize these categories and ended up being a lot of fun (especially when it was finished).

SOME FINAL THOUGHTS ON DIVISION/CLASSIFICATION

The essays collected in this chapter use division and/or classification as their primary organizing principle. All of these essays show both techniques at work to varying degrees. As you read these essays, you might also want to be aware of the other rhetorical modes that support these division/classification essays, such as description and definition. Finally, pay special attention to how these authors bring significance to their systems of classification and, as a result, to their essays themselves.

DIVISION/CLASSIFICATION IN REVIEW

Reading Division/Classification Essays

Preparing to Read

- ✓ What assumptions can you make from the essay's title?
- ✓ Can you guess what the general mood of the essay is?
- ✓ What is the essay's purpose and audience?
- ✓ What does the synopsis in the Rhetorical Table of Contents tell you about the essay?
- ✓ What can you learn from the author's biography?
- ✓ Can you guess what the author's point of view toward the subject is?
- ✓ What are your responses to the Preparing to Read questions?

Reading

- ✓ What do you think the "context" of the essay is?
- ✓ Did the author use division or classification most often?
- ✓ Did you preview the questions that follow the essay?

Rereading

- ✓ How does division or classification help the author accomplish his/her purpose?
- ✓ What other rhetorical strategies does the author use to support the essay's purpose?
- ✓ How does the writer explain the significance of his/her division/classification system?
- ✓ What are your responses to the questions after the essay?

Writing Division/Classification Essays

Preparing to Write

- ✓ What are your responses to the Preparing to Write questions?
- ✓ What is your purpose?
- ✓ Who is your audience?

Writing

- ✓ Do you declare an overall purpose for your essay?
- ✓ Do you divide the item or concept you are dealing with into categories?
- ✓ Do you arrange these categories into a logical sequence?
- ✓ Do you define each category, explaining the difference between one category and another and demonstrating that difference through examples?
- ✓ Do you explain the significance of your division/classification system?
- ✓ Are the categories in your essay distinct from one another so they don't overlap?
- ✓ What rhetorical strategies support your essay?

Rewriting

- ✓ Does your thesis communicate your purpose clearly?

✓ Have you divided your topic into separate and understand-able categories?

✓ Are these categories arranged logically?

✓ Do you explain the significance of your particular classifica-tion system?

PHYLLIS SCHNEIDER   (1947–   )

Memory: Tips You'll Never Forget

Born in Seattle, Washington, Phyllis Schneider received her B.A. in English at Pacific Lutheran University and her M.A. in Advanced Writing at the University of Washington. She has been articles editor at *Seventeen* magazine, editor in chief of *YM* magazine, and managing editor of *Weight Watchers* magazine. She currently works for Consumers Union, the publisher of *Consumer Reports*, for whom she writes a fundraising newsletter and various promotional materials. She has also published articles in *Working Woman*, *Redbook*, *Woman's Day*, *New Choices*, *Parents* magazine, and many other periodicals, and she writes health-care career supplements for the Greater New York Hospital Association and *The New York Times*. A lover of animals (she has a mixed-breed dog named "Jenny"), she also enjoys making jewelry in her spare time and serving as an associate at an Episcopal convent. Her advice to students using *The Prose Reader* is to "learn grammar." "Many young people have the enthusiasm to write well," she explains, "but not the proper skills."

Preparing to Read

The following essay, originally published in *New Choices*, offers us some important insights into the strengths and weaknesses of our memories in an attempt to classify some of the typical memory lapses we all experience on a daily basis. Prior to reading this essay, consider the strengths and weaknesses of your own memory. What information do you remember best? What do you have trouble remembering? Do you have any minor problems with your memory on a daily basis? Do your memory lapses fall into any particular categories? What are these categories?

When my husband, Ted, started "losing" our car, I 1 began to worry. In his 30s and 40s, he'd leave a store or a theater and head straight for our vehicle—no problem. But shortly after his 50th birthday, Ted walked into a mall parking garage and stopped short. Scratching his head, he asked, "Where did we park?"

In the ensuing months, there were times when Ted would for-   2
get where he put his glasses, his keys, his wallet. And walking by a
restaurant one day, he remarked, "Remember what a great dinner
we had there"? I'd never been in that restaurant and said so. But he
insisted: he'd ordered the sole, and I'd had the salmon; we had both
agreed it was one of the best restaurants we'd ever been to.

Though I found Ted's memory lapses troublesome, most experts   3
would say that such forgetfulness doesn't necessarily signal trouble.
"You needn't worry about these lapses unless you experience a noticeable and consistent decline in memory or you aren't able to
function at work," says psychologist Daniel L. Schacter of Harvard
University. At that point, of course, you should see a doctor.

For most people, such lapses are just a normal—if annoying—   4
part of life. Mild deficits in memory do begin in the 40s and 50s
and increase in later years, but stress, fatigue, and a mere lack of
attention all can trigger temporary memory glitches in people of
all ages.

Here are some common types and strategies for minimizing   5
difficulties.

"It's on the Tip of My Tongue."   You start to introduce an   6
old friend to someone, and suddenly you can't remember that
someone's name—even though you sense it just beyond the grasp
of your memory. Or you can't quite retrieve the name of a movie
you just saw. Such tip-of-the-tongue—or TOT—incidents happen to most everyone, notes Deborah Burke, a psychologist at
Pomona College in Claremont, Calif.

These lapses have nothing to do with remembering the mean-   7
ing of a word, but rather with its sound, "Often, the sound of a
word is arbitrary and senseless," says Burke. This sheer arbitrari-
ness sometimes can make word retrieval challenging.

The best way to prevent the problem is to use the name of a   8
person or object as frequently as possible. "I tell clients to do what
salespeople often do—repeat people's names several times just before you plan to see them," says psychologist Liz Zelinski of the
University of Southern California in Los Angeles.

A TOT experience can seem worse when a similar-sounding,   9
but incorrect, word pops into your head and stays there. Burke tells
the story of a student who was trying to remember the name of a
particular recreational vehicle. The student wanted the word *Win-*

nebago, but she could only come up with *rutabaga.* When this happens shift your focus to something else, suggests Burke. "If you stop fretting about it, the correct word eventually will come to you."

"Where Did I Put My Keys?" Most episodes of absent- 10
mindedness—forgetting where you left something or wondering why you just entered a room—are caused by a simple lack of attention, says Harvard's Schacter. "You're supposed to remember something, but you haven't encoded it deeply."

Encoding, Schacter explains, is a special way of paying atten- 11
tion to an event that has a major impact on recalling it later. Failure to encode properly can create annoying situations. If you put your cell phone in a pocket, for example, and don't pay attention to what you did because you're involved in a conversation, you'll probably forget that the phone is in the jacket now hanging in your closet. "Your memory per se isn't failing you," says Schacter. "Rather, you didn't give your memory system the information it needed."

Lack of interest can also lead to absent-mindedness. "A man 12
who can recite baseball scores from 30 years ago," says Zelinski, "may not remember to drop a letter in the mailbox." Women have slightly better memories than men, possibly because they pay more attention to their environment, and memory relies on just that.

Visual cues can help prevent absent-mindedness, says Schacter. 13
"But be sure the cue is clear and available," he cautions. If you want to remember to take a medication with lunch, put the pill bottle on the kitchen table—don't leave it in the medicine chest and write yourself a note that you tuck in a pocket.

Another common episode of absent-mindedness: walking into 14
a room and wondering why you're there. Most likely, you were thinking about something else. "Everyone does this from time to time," says Zelinski. The best thing to do is to return to where you were before entering the room, and you'll likely remember.

"That's Not the Way I Remember It." Most of us occa- 15
sionally experience a memory error called "misattribution." You correctly remember something that happened but attribute it to the wrong source. For example, you share a story with a friend and credit it to your mutual acquaintance Jim. Although the inci-

dent actually happened to John—from whom you heard of it in the first place—you remain convinced that it originated with Jim.

In a similar way, people often come up with ideas that were   16 someone else's to begin with—a phenomenon known as unintentional plagiarism. At dinner one night, a friend related "her" recent experience at a store: Seeing a mother carrying her baby in a backpack, she remarked on the cute toy clutched in the infant's fist. "Oh, no—that's not hers!" the mother exclaimed. "She must have grabbed it from a shelf."

Then my friend's daughter piped up: "Mom, that happened to   17 me. I told you about it last month."

False memory, another trick the mind can play, is closely re-   18 lated to misattribution. You may "remember" that you fell off the pier when your father took you fishing, though in reality you only witnessed such a scene in a movie many years ago.

As annoying as these kinds of memory lapses can be, there's a   19 positive side, says Schacter. If our brains did store all that we saw, heard, or read, we'd be overwhelmed. Our ability to splice together bits of necessary information and throw out the rest is essential for sound thinking.

I find this theory reassuring. Now when my husband forgets   20 where the car is, I tell myself that he's busy selecting and storing information that really important to him—like ordering tickets to a sporting event—instead of concentrating on trivial stuff. And when we pass the restaurant that he insists we dined at years ago, I just smile and let him savor his memory of a delectable—and obviously unforgettable—dinner.

UNDERSTANDING DETAILS

1. What exactly is Schneider classifying in this essay? Explain her three categories.
2. What is the positive side of memory lapses, according to Schneider?
3. Which of these memory problems have you experienced? How did you solve the problem?
4. What are some of the main causes of memory lapses?

ANALYZING MEANING

1. Are you surprised to know that experts agree that lapses in memory don't "necessarily signal trouble" (paragraph 3)? Explain your answer.
2. Which of Schneider's categories do you suppose is most common among students?
3. Why do you think Schneider cited so many experts in this essay? What do these authoritative voices add to her essay?
4. What do all the solutions Schneider proposes for each type of memory lapse have in common?

DISCOVERING RHETORICAL STRATEGIES

1. In what ways does Schneider use division and classification in this essay? How does she give significance or value to her system of organization? What other rhetorical techniques does she use to accomplish her purpose?
2. What types of memory lapses do you experience in a typical day? How would you classify these lapses?
3. What is Schneider's point of view toward forgetfulness in general?
4. Why do you think Schneider opened and closed her essay with references to her husband? Is her beginning and ending effective? Explain your answer.

MAKING CONNECTIONS

1. Examine the tricks memory plays on us by contrasting Schneider's essay with Malcolm Cowley's "The View from 80," Russell Baker's "The Saturday Evening Post," Robert Ramirez's "The Barrio," and Michael Dorris's "The Broken Cord."
2. Compare and contrast the way Schneider organizes her advice with the organizational techniques of Edwin Bliss's "Managing Your Time," Paul Roberts's "How to Say Nothing in Five Hundred Words," and Mark Hanson's "E-Mail: What You Should—and Shouldn't—Say."
3. Schneider defines "encoding" as "a special way of paying attention to an event that has a major impact on recalling it later." What advice do you think each of the following authors would give us about "encoding" important events in life: Ray Brad-

bury ("Summer Rituals"), Russell Baker ("The Saturday Evening Post"), Annie Dillard ("Living Like Weasels"), and Eudora Welty ("Listening")?

IDEAS FOR DISCUSSION/WRITING

Preparing to Write

Write freely about various memory lapses you have experienced. What activities do they involve? Are they easily classified? Do they occur frequently in your life? When do they happen?

Choosing a Topic

1. Your English teacher has asked about the accuracy of your memory. Respond to this question by classifying for this teacher all the different types of memory work you do in a typical day. Remember that each memory task you do should fit into a specific category. Decide on a point of view before you begin to write.

2. Speculate about the memory of a close friend or relative by analyzing that person's behavior and preferences. Remember that analysis is based on the process of division. Divide this person's behavior and preferences into logical parts; then study those parts so that you can better understand the person's reasoning techniques. Decide on a purpose and audience before you begin to write.

3. If the mental activities we perform say something important about us, analyze yourself by writing an essay that classifies the different mental activities you have carried out in the last week. Discuss your choices as you proceed.

Before beginning your essay, you might want to consult the checklists on pages 282–284.

JUDY BRADY   (1937–   )

Why I Want a Wife

Judy Brady is a freelance writer and political activist who was born in San Francisco. She earned a B.F.A. in painting from the University of Iowa, married, raised two daughters, and then returned to San Francisco, where she is now an "ex-wife" who works as a secretary: "I must spend my days working in the corporate world where image has become so much more important than reality. It's crazy-making. My relief comes from doing political work with other people who have found the courage to acknowledge what is really going on and then act accordingly." Strong commitment to the feminist movement has taken her to Cuba for several visits, which have prompted the publication of articles about such diverse topics as abortion, literacy, unions, and the role of women in society. The author now devotes much of her time to the politics of cancer. Her most recent publication is *One in Three: Women with Cancer Confront an Epidemic* (1991), an anthology of poems, stories, and essays that "make accessible through personal testimony the facts of the cancer epidemic in this country." Her advice to students using *The Prose Reader* is to be "brutally honest" in their written work. She insists that "glossy writing, devoid of emotional truth and honesty, is quite useless."

Preparing to Read

The following essay first appeared under the author's married name, Judy Syfers. It was originally published in the preview issue of *Ms.* magazine (Spring 1972) and was later reprinted in the periodical's December 1979 issue. In it, Brady presents a wry, satirical view of woman's conventional social role as a docile servant to her husband. As you prepare to read this article, take a few moments to think about the various roles you play in your life: How many distinct roles do you play? Do you act differently as a student? A friend? A lover? A member of your family? An employee? How does each role make you feel? What different expectations are placed on you in each of these roles? Who sets these expectations? How clearly are they stated? What happens when you do not fulfill each of these roles properly?

I belong to that classification of people known as wives. I am A   1
Wife. And, not altogether incidentally, I am a mother.

Not too long ago a male friend of mine appeared on the   2
scene fresh from a recent divorce. He had one child, who is, of
course, with his ex-wife. He is looking for another wife. As I
thought about him while I was ironing one evening, it suddenly
occurred to me that I, too, would like to have a wife. Why do I
want a wife?

I would like to go back to school so that I can become econom-   3
ically independent, support myself, and, if need be, support those
dependent upon me. I want a wife who will work and send me to
school. And while I am going to school, I want a wife to take care
of my children. I want a wife to keep track of the children's doctor
and dentist appointments. And to keep track of mine, too. I want a
wife to make sure my children eat properly and are kept clean. I
want a wife who will wash the children's clothes and keep them
mended. I want a wife who is a good nurturant attendant to my
children, who arranges for their schooling, makes sure that they
have an adequate social life with their peers, takes them to the park,
the zoo, etc. I want a wife who takes care of the children when
they are sick, a wife who arranges to be around when the children
need special care, because, of course, I cannot miss classes at school.
My wife must arrange to lose time at work and not lose the job. It
may mean a small cut in my wife's income from time to time, but I
guess I can tolerate that. Needless to say, my wife will arrange and
pay for the care of the children while my wife is working.

I want a wife who will take care of *my* physical needs. I want a   4
wife who will keep my house clean. A wife who will pick up
after my children, a wife who will pick up after me. I want a wife
who will keep my clothes clean, ironed, mended, replaced when
need be, and who will see to it that my personal things are kept in
their proper place so that I can find what I need the minute I
need it. I want a wife who cooks the meals, a wife who is a *good*
cook. I want a wife who will plan the menus, do the necessary
grocery shopping, prepare the meals, serve them pleasantly, and
then do the cleaning up while I do my studying. I want a wife
who will care for me when I am sick and sympathize with my
pain and loss of time from school. I want a wife to go along when
our family takes a vacation so that someone can continue to care
for me and my children when I need a rest and change of scene.

I want a wife who will not bother me with rambling com- 5
plaints about a wife's duties. But I want a wife who will listen to
me when I feel the need to explain a rather difficult point I have
come across in my course of studies. And I want a wife who will
type my papers for me when I have written them.

I want a wife who will take care of the details of my social life. 6
When my wife and I are invited out by my friends, I want a wife
who will take care of the babysitting arrangements. When I meet
people at school that I like and want to entertain, I want a wife
who will have the house clean, will prepare a special meal, serve it
to me and my friends, and not interrupt when I talk about things
that interest me and my friends. I want a wife who will have
arranged that the children are fed and ready for bed before my
guests arrive so that the children do not bother us. I want a wife
who takes care of the needs of my guests so that they feel comfortable, who makes sure that they have an ashtray, that they are
passed the hors d'oeuvres, that they are offered a second helping
of the food, that their wine glasses are replenished when necessary, that their coffee is served to them as they like it. And I want
a wife who knows that sometimes I need a night out by myself.

I want a wife who is sensitive to my sexual needs, a wife who 7
makes love passionately and eagerly when I feel like it, a wife
who makes sure that I am satisfied. And, of course, I want a wife
who will not demand sexual attention when I am not in the
mood for it. I want a wife who assumes the complete responsibility for birth control, because I do not want more children. I want
a wife who will remain sexually faithful to me so that I do not
have to clutter up my intellectual life with jealousies. And I want
a wife who understands that *my* sexual needs may entail more
than strict adherence to monogamy. I must, after all, be able to
relate to people as fully as possible.

If, by chance, I find another person more suitable as a wife than 8
the wife I already have, I want the liberty to replace my present
wife with another one. Naturally, I will expect a fresh, new life;
my wife will take the children and be solely responsible for them
so that I am left free.

When I am through with school and have a job, I want my 9
wife to quit working and remain at home so that my wife can
more fully and completely take care of a wife's duties.

My God, who *wouldn't* want a wife? 10

UNDERSTANDING DETAILS

1. How many categories of wifely duties does Brady refer to in this essay? How are they related?
2. How does the author define the term *wife*? Is her portrayal of wives realistic? According to this essay, how do husbands differ from wives?
3. Why does the author want a wife? Explain your answer in some detail.
4. What would be your answer to Brady's question at the end of her essay: "My God, who *wouldn't* want a wife?" (paragraph 10)?

ANALYZING MEANING

1. What is the overall purpose of Brady's essay? How do you know? What clues make this purpose clear?
2. What type of wife does Brady ask for in this essay? What motivates this wife? Where are this person's loyalties? What are this wife's convictions?
3. Is this essay as pertinent today as it was in 1972? From your perspective, how have sexual roles changed since 1972? How are wives' roles today different from your mother's role as a wife?
4. Do you want a "wife"? What qualities would this person have? Explain your answer in detail.

DISCOVERING RHETORICAL STRATEGIES

1. Where in this essay does the author use division? Where does she use classification? Give specific examples. What other rhetorical modes does Brady use in her essay?
2. List the topics of each paragraph in the body of the essay (paragraphs 3–9). What advantages does this order have over other possible arrangements of the same ideas? How would the effect have been altered if Brady had changed the order of these ideas?
3. This essay works principally through parallel structure, in which similar grammatical elements are repeated in a series of phrases or clauses. Look, for example, at the following sentence:

> I want *a wife who* is sensitive to my sexual needs,
> *a wife who* makes love passionately and eagerly when I feel like it,
> *a wife who* makes sure that I am satisfied (paragraph 7).

The repetitions in this example are italicized, whereas the parallel structures are lined up under each other. Find two other instances of this technique in the essay, and explain how each works. What effect does this rhetorical technique have on you as you read this essay?

4. What point of view does Brady take in her article? What tone results from this point of view? Look up the term *satire* in a literary dictionary, and explain what use Brady is making of this verbal technique.

MAKING CONNECTIONS

1. Imagine a conversation between Judy Brady, Germaine Greer ("A Child Is Born"), and Gloria Steinem ("The Politics of Muscle") in which each author attempts to define the proper role of women in our society. How would these writers differ in their definitions of "a woman's place in America"? What limitations, if any, would each place upon women in today's society? Do you think there should be any limits placed upon what women can do? If so, what should those limits be?

2. Brady and Bill Cosby ("The Baffling Question") both use effective irony (saying the opposite of what they really mean) in their essays. Write out a single sentence explaining each author's main point. What do these authors gain or lose by using irony to express their opinions? Does understanding such essays require more or less reader involvement than reading a non-ironic essay? Explain your answer.

3. To what extent would Jill Leslie Rosenbaum and Meda Chesney-Lind ("Appearance and Delinquency: A Research Note") argue that the gender inequities described by Brady are related to the sexism embedded in our culture? Would you agree with Rosenbaum and Chesney-Lind? Explain your answer.

IDEAS FOR DISCUSSION/WRITING

Preparing to Write

Write freely about your own various roles in life: What are some of the major roles you play (e.g., husband, wife, girlfriend, boyfriend, sister, brother, son, daughter, student, friend, employee)? What personal characteristics define the different roles you play? Which of these roles is most comfortable for you? Which is least comfortable? How does each of these roles make you feel about yourself?

Choosing a Topic

1. Use division to explain one of the roles you play in life. Break down the role into its basic parts, and then discuss those parts in an essay written to your English class. Make sure you decide on a purpose and a point of view before you begin to write.
2. Do you feel that husbands are ever categorized or exploited in much the same way as Brady's "wife"? Write an essay entitled "Why I Want a Husband" that presents the other side of the story.
3. Using Brady's ironic method, write an essay for your classmates in which you claim to need something that you could never have.

Before beginning your essay, you might want to consult the checklists on pages 282–284.

JUDITH WALLERSTEIN   (1921–   )
SANDRA BLAKESLEE   (1943–   )

Second Chances for Children of Divorce

Judith Wallerstein grew up in New York City, earned her Ph.D. at Lund University in Sweden, and now lives and works in Marin County, California, where she serves as director of the Center for the Family in Transition. Since 1965, she has taught psychology at the University of California at Berkeley, where she specializes in divorce and its effect on family members. Her first book, *Surviving the Breakup* (coauthored by Joan Kelly, 1980), analyzes the impact of divorce on young children in the family. Her next, *Second Chances: Men, Women, and Children a Decade After Divorce* (1989), is a study of the long-term effects of divorce on teenagers and young adults. Her most recent book, *The Unexpected Legacy of Divorce* (2000), is a study of the effects of divorce on children twenty-five years after their parents' breakup. Now hard at work on a study of happy marriages, Wallerstein is very concerned about what is happening to the American family. "There's a lot of anger in relationships between men and women today," she explains. "It's always easier to express anger than love." An avid reader, she collects ideas the way "other people collect recipes." She advises college students to read as much as possible: "The first prerequisite a writer must have is a love of reading." Her coauthor on *Second Chances*, Sandra Blakeslee, was born in Flushing, New York, and earned her B.S. degree at Berkeley, where her specialty was neurobiology. She is currently the West Coast science and medicine correspondent for the *New York Times*. A former Peace Corps volunteer in Borneo, she advises students using *The Prose Reader* to travel as much as possible: "You need a wide range of experiences to be a good writer." Blakeslee goes mountain biking and running in her spare time.

Preparing to Read

In the following essay from *Second Chances*, Wallerstein and Blakeslee classify the psychological tasks children who have suffered through the divorce of their parents must complete to free themselves from the past. As you prepare to read this article, take a few minutes to think about the effects of divorce on yourself or someone you know: How close have you been to a divorce experience? How were people directly associated with the experience affected? What differences did you notice in the way adults and children responded to the same situation? What feelings were most common among the adults? Among the children? Why do you think the divorce rate has been so high during the last fifty years? Do you think this trend will continue, or will it taper off in the next few years?

At each stage in the life cycle, children and adults face predictable and particular issues that represent the coming together of the demands of society and a biological and psychological timetable. Just as we physically learn to sit, crawl, walk, and run, we follow an equivalent progression in our psychological and social development. Each stage presents us with a sequence of tasks we must confront. We can succeed or fail in mastering them, to varying degrees, but everyone encounters the tasks. They begin at birth and end at death. 1

Children move upward along a common developmental ladder, although each goes it alone at his or her own pace. Gradually, as they pass through the various stages, children consolidate a sense of self. They develop coping skills, conscience, and the capacity to give and receive love. 2

Children take one step at a time, negotiating the rung they are on before they can move up to the next. They may—and often do—falter in this effort. The climb is not steady under the best of circumstances, and most children briefly stand still in their ascent. They may even at times move backward. Such regressions are not a cause for alarm; rather, they may represent an appropriate response to life's stresses. Children who fail one task are not stalled forever; they will go on to the next stage, although they may be weakened in their climb. Earlier failures will not necessarily imperil their capacity as adults to trust a relationship, make a commitment, hold an appropriate job, or be a parent—to make use of their second chances at each stage of development. 3

I propose that children who experience divorce face an additional set of tasks specific to divorce in addition to the normal developmental tasks of growing up. Growing up is inevitably harder 4 for children of divorce because they must deal with psychological issues that children from well-functioning intact families do not have to face.

The psychological tasks of children begin as difficulties, escalate 5 between the parents during the marriage, and continue through the separation and divorce and throughout the postdivorce years.

TASK: Understanding the Divorce

The first and most basic task at the time of separation is for the 6 children to understand realistically what the divorce means in their family and what its concrete consequences will be. Children, especially very young children, are thrown back on frightening and vivid fantasies of being abandoned, being placed in foster care, or never seeing a departed parent again, or macabre fantasies such as a mother being destroyed in an earthquake or a father being destroyed by a vengeful mother. All of these fantasies and the feelings that accompany them can be undone only as the children, with the parents' continuing help, begin to understand the reality and begin to adjust to the actual changes that the divorce brings.

The more mature task of understanding what led to the marital 7 failure awaits the perspective of the adolescent and young adult. Early on, most children regard divorce as a serious error, but by adolescence most feel that their parents never should have married. The task of understanding occurs in two stages. The first involves accurately perceiving the immediate changes that divorce brings and differentiating fantasy fears from reality. The second occurs later, when children are able at greater distance and with more mature understanding to evaluate their parents' actions and can draw useful lessons for their own lives.

TASK: Strategic Withdrawal

Children and adolescents need to get on with their own lives as 8 soon as possible after the divorce, to resume their normal activities at school and at play, to get back physically and emotionally to the normal tasks of growing up. Especially for adolescents who may have been beginning to spread their wings, the divorce pulls them back into the family orbit, where they may become consumed with care for siblings or a troubled parent. It also intrudes on their academic and social life, causing them to spend class time preoccupied with worry and to pass up social activities because of demands at home. This is not to say that children should ignore the divorce. Their task is to acknowledge their concern and to provide appropriate help to their parents and siblings, but they should strive to remove the divorce from the center of their own thoughts so that they can get back to their own interests, pleasures, problems, and peer relationships. To achieve this task, children need encouragement from their parents to *remain* children.

TASK: Dealing with Loss

In the years following divorce, children experience two profound losses. One is the loss of the intact family together with the symbolic and real protection it has provided. The second is the loss of the presence of one parent, usually the father, from their daily lives.   9

In dealing with these losses, children fall back on many fantasies to mask their unhappiness. As we have seen, they may idealize the father as representative of all that is lacking in their current lives, thinking that if only he were present, everything would be better.   10

The task of absorbing loss is perhaps the single most difficult task imposed by divorce. At its core, the task requires children to overcome the profound sense of rejection, humiliation, unlovability, and powerlessness they feel with the departure of one parent. When the parent leaves, children of all ages blame themselves. They say, "He left me because I was not lovable. I was not worthy." They conclude that had they been more lovable, worthy, or different, the parent would have stayed. In this way, the loss of the parent and lowered self-esteem become intertwined.   11

To stave off these intensely painful feelings of rejection, children continually try to undo the divorce scenario, to bring their parents back together, or to somehow win back the affection of the absent parent. The explanation "Had he loved me, he would not have left the family" turns into a new concern. "If he loved me, he would visit more often. He would spend more time with me." With this in mind, the children not only are pained at the outset but remain vulnerable, sometimes increasingly, over the years. Many reach out during adolescence to increase contact with the parent who left, again to undo the sad scenario and to rebuild their self-esteem as well.   12

This task is easier if parents and children have a good relation-   13
ship, within the framework of a good visiting or joint custody
arrangement.

Some children are able to use a good, close relationship with   14
the visiting parent to promote their growth within the divorced
family. Others are able to acknowledge and accept that the visiting parent could never become the kind of parent they need, and
they are able to turn away from blaming themselves. Still others
are able to reject, on their own, a rejecting parent or to reject a
role model that they see as flawed. In so doing, these youngsters
are able to effectively master the loss and get on with their lives.

TASK: *Dealing with Anger*

Divorce, unlike death, is always a voluntary decision for at least   15
one of the partners in a marriage. Everyone involved knows this.
The child understands that divorce is not a natural disaster like an
earthquake or tornado; it is caused by the decision of one or both
of the parents to separate. Its true cause lies in the parents' failure
to maintain the marriage, and someone is culpable.

Given this knowledge, children face a terrible dilemma. They   16
know that their unhappiness has been caused by the very people
charged with their protection and care—their parents are the
agents of their distress. Furthermore, the parents undertook this
role voluntarily. This realization puts children in a dreadful bind
because they know something that they dare not express—out of
fear, out of anxiety, out of a wish to protect their parents.

Children get angry at their parents, experiencing divorce as in-   17
difference to their needs and perceiving parents sometimes realistically as self-centered and uncaring, as preaching a corrupt
morality, and as weak and unable to deal with problems except by
running away.

At the same time, children are aware of their parents' needi-   18
ness, weaknesses, and anxiety about life's difficulties. Although
children have little understanding of divorce, except when the
fighting has been open and violent, they fully recognize how unhappy and disorganized their parents become, and this frightens
them very much. Caught in a combination of anger and love, the
children are frightened and guilty about their anger because they
love their parents and perceive them as unhappy people who are

trying to improve their lives in the face of severe obstacles. Their concern makes it difficult even to acknowledge their anger.

A major task, then, for children is to work through this anger, 19 to recognize their parents as human beings capable of making mistakes, and to respect them for their real efforts and their real courage.

Cooling of anger and the task of forgiveness go hand in hand 20 with children's growing emotional maturity and capacity to appreciate the various needs of the different family members. As anger diminishes, young people are better able to put the divorce behind them and experience relief. As children forgive their parents, they forgive themselves for feeling anger and guilt and for failing to restore the marriage. In this way, children can free themselves from identification with the angry or violent parent or with the victim.

TASK: Working Out Guilt

Young children often feel responsible for divorce, thinking that 21 their misbehavior may have caused one parent to leave. Or, in a more complicated way, they may feel that their fantasy wish to drive a wedge between their mother and father has been magically granted. Many guilty feelings arise at the time of divorce but dissipate naturally as children mature. Others persist, usually with roots in a profound continuing sense of having caused the unthinkable—getting rid of one parent so as to be closer to the other.

Other feelings of guilt are rooted in children's realization that 22 they were indeed a cause of marital difficulty. Many divorces occur after the birth of a child, and the child correctly comprehends that he or she really did drive a wedge between the adults.

We see another kind of guilt in girls who, in identifying with 23 their troubled mothers, become afraid to surpass their mothers. These young women have trouble separating from their mothers, whom they love and feel sorry for, and establishing their own successful relationships with suitable young men. The children of divorce need to separate from guilty ties that bind them too closely to a troubled parent and to go on with their lives with compassion and love.

TASK: *Accepting the Permanence of the Divorce*

At first, children feel a strong and understandable need to deny 24
the divorce. Such early denial may be a first step in the coping
process. Like a screen that is alternately lowered and raised, the
denial helps children confront the full reality of the divorce, bit by
bit. They cannot take it in all at once.

Nevertheless, we have learned that five and even ten years after 25
divorce, some children and adolescents refuse to accept the divorce as a permanent state of affairs. They continue to hope, consciously or unconsciously, that the marriage will be restored,
finding omens of reconciliation even in a harmless handshake or a
simple friendly nod.

In accepting permanence, the children of divorce face a more 26
difficult task than children of bereavement. Death cannot be undone, but divorce happens between living people who can change
their minds. A reconciliation fantasy taps deep into children's psy-
ches. Children need to feel that their parents will still be happy together. They may not overcome this fantasy of reconciliation until
they themselves finally separate from their parents and leave home.

TASK: *Taking a Chance on Love*

This is perhaps the most important task for growing children 27
and for society. Despite what life has dealt them, despite lingering
fears and anxieties, the children of divorce must grow, become
open to the possibility of success or failure, and take a chance on
love. They must hold on to a realistic vision that they can both
love and be loved.

This is the central task for youngsters during adolescence and at 28
entry into young adulthood. And as we have seen, it is the task on
which so many children tragically flounder. Children who lose a
parent through death must take a chance on loving with the
knowledge that all people eventually die and that death can take
away our loved ones at any time. Children who lose the intact family through divorce must also take a chance on love, knowing realistically that divorce is always possible but being willing nevertheless
to remain open to love, commitment, marriage, and fidelity.

More than the ideology of hoping to fall in love and find com- 29
mitment, this task involves being able to turn away from the

model of parents who could not stay committed to each other. While all the young people in our study were in search of romantic love, a large number of them lived with such a high degree of anxiety over fears of betrayal or of not finding love that they were entirely unable to take the kind of chances necessary for them to move emotionally into successful young adulthood.

This last task, taking a chance on love, involves being able to   30
venture, not just thinking about it, and not thinking one way and behaving another. It involves accepting a morality that truly guides behavior. This is the task that occupies children of divorce throughout their adolescence. It is what makes adolescence such a critical and difficult time for them. The resolution of life's tasks is a relative process that never ends, but this last task, which is built on successfully negotiating all the others, leads to psychological freedom from the past. This is the essence of second chances for children of divorce.

UNDERSTANDING DETAILS

1. Name the seven categories into which Wallerstein and Blakeslee divide the psychological growth of the children of divorce. How long will it take most children to perform these tasks?
2. Choose one of these tasks and explain it in your own words.
3. According to Wallerstein and Blakeslee, what is probably the most difficult task that results from divorce? Why do the authors believe this stage is so painful?
4. What did Wallerstein and Blakeslee find out about their subjects' ability to deal with love in their lives?

ANALYZING MEANING

1. In your opinion, which of the emotional tasks that Wallerstein and Blakeslee describe is likely to be most traumatic in a child's life after a divorce? On what do you base your conclusion?
2. What is the relationship suggested in this essay between the parents' divorce and a child's sense of rejection?
3. In what ways does dealing with all facets of their anger create a problem for children of divorce? Do you know anyone who has worked through such a problem? Explain your answer in detail.

4. How might an understanding of the seven tasks discussed in this essay help people deal more effectively with children affected by divorce?

DISCOVERING RHETORICAL STRATEGIES

1. How do Wallerstein and Blakeslee organize their categories in this essay? Why do they place these tasks in this particular order?
2. What is the authors' general attitude toward divorce? What references in the essay reveal this point of view?
3. Describe the authors' intended audience. What makes you think they are directing their comments to this group?
4. What other rhetorical modes do Wallerstein and Blakeslee use in this essay besides division and classification? How do these other modes support the authors' division/classification system?

MAKING CONNECTIONS

1. Compare and contrast the love and support needed by children of divorce with the love and support provided naturally by the non-Western families described in Germaine Greer's "A Child Is Born." Do children of divorce need anything, according to Wallerstein and Blakeslee, that would not be furnished by a typical non-Western family? If so, what would it be?
2. What are the principal differences between Wallerstein and Blakeslee's prescriptions for how a child can best cope with the death of his or her parents' relationship and the way in which funeral directors in Jessica Mitford's "Behind the Formaldehyde Curtain" help us endure the death of a friend or relative? Which coping mechanisms are the same? Which are different?
3. Wallerstein and Blakeslee divide their essay into seven "tasks" that must be accomplished by children of divorce. Find a division/classification essay in this section of *The Prose Reader* that has more subdivisions. Then, find one that has fewer. How does the number of subdivisions in a division/classification essay affect your ability to understand the author's entire argument? Which of these essays is the easiest to follow? Which is the most difficult? Why?

IDEAS FOR DISCUSSION/WRITING

Preparing to Write

Write freely about your thoughts on divorce and the effects of divorce on others: Do you know anyone who has gone through a divorce? How did the experience affect the couple getting divorced? How did it affect their friends, their relatives, and their children? How do you think the high divorce rate is affecting Americans in general? Why is America's national divorce rate so high? What changes could we make to lower the divorce rate?

Choosing a Topic

1. Assume that you are an expert on the variety and scope of college relationships. In an essay written for your classmates, divide your observations on different types of relationships into categories that will show students the full range of these associations in a college setting.

2. Because you have been involved with divorce in some way, you have been asked to submit to your college newspaper an editorial classifying the various ways in which different types of people react to divorce (husbands, wives, children, friends, and so on). You have been told to pay particular attention to the reactions of college students whose parents are going through or have gone through a divorce.

3. In an essay written for the general public, speculate about the reasons for the high national divorce rate. Use your own experience, interview others, or consult sources in the library to investigate the reasons for this trend. Suggest how we could solve this problem in America.

Before beginning your essay, you might want to consult the checklists on pages 282–284.

FRANKLIN ZIMRING   (1942–   )

Confessions of an Ex-Smoker

Born in Los Angeles, Franklin Zimring earned his B.A. at Wayne State University and his law degree at the University of Chicago and then served for ten years as the director of the Center for Studies in Criminal Justice at the University of Chicago before moving to his present post as director of the Earl Warren Legal Institute at the University of California at Berkeley. A specialist in legal policy, he has published a number of books on a wide variety of topics, many of which were coauthored with colleague Gordon Hawkins, including *The Citizen's Guide to Gun Control* (1987), *The Scale of Imprisonment* (1991), *The Search for Rational Drug Control* (1992), *Incapacitation: Penal Confinement and the Restraint of Crime* (1995), and *Crime is Not the Problem: Lethal Violence in America* (1997), *American Youth Violence* (1998), and *Punishment and Democracy: Three Strikes and You're Out* (2000). His advice to students using *The Prose Reader* is to "listen to your own internal prompter as you write." A great believer in E. M. Forster's famous question "How do I know what I think till I see what I say?," Zimring counsels students to "relax and decide what you really think about a topic, and then express it as clearly and concisely as possible." The author's own relaxation comes from the sport of swimming, to which he confesses a "religious devotion."

Preparing to Read

Originally published in *Newsweek* magazine (April 20, 1987), the following article is one in a series of "Mid-Life Memoranda" that Zimring has been writing since 1985. It offers a witty classification of ex-smokers into four distinct groups: zealots, evangelists, the elect, and the serene. As you prepare to read this essay, think for a few moments about your own addictions: Have you ever had any addictions? Were they good addictions or bad? Are any of these addictions still with you? Why are these addictions part of your life? Do you want to change the status of these addictions? Why or why not? What do you think causes people to be addicted to certain substances or behavior? How can we break away from addictions successfully?

Americans can be divided into three groups—smokers, 1 nonsmokers, and that expanding pack of us who have quit. Those who have never smoked don't know what they're missing, but former smokers, ex-smokers, reformed smokers can never forget. We are veterans of a personal war, linked by that watershed experience of ceasing to smoke and by the temptation to have just one more cigarette. For almost all of us ex-smokers, smoking continues to play an important part in our lives. And now that it is being restricted in restaurants around the country and will be banned in almost all indoor public places in New York State, it is vital that everyone understand the different emotional states cessation of smoking can cause. I have observed four of them; and in the interest of science I have classified them as those of the zealot, the evangelist, the elect, and the serene. Each day, each category gains new recruits.

Not all antitobacco zealots are former smokers, but a substantial 2 number of fire-and-brimstone opponents do come from the ranks of the reformed. Zealots believe that those who continue to smoke are degenerates who deserve scorn not pity and the penalties that will deter offensive behavior in public as well. Relations between these people and those who continue to smoke are strained.

One explanation for the zealot's fervor in seeking to outlaw to- 3 bacco consumption is his own tenuous hold on abstaining from smoking. But I think part of the emotional force arises from sheer envy as he watches and identifies with each lung-filling puff. By making smoking in public a crime, the zealot seeks reassurance that he will not revert to bad habits; give him strong social penalties, and he won't become a recidivist.

No systematic survey has been done yet, but anecdotal evi- 4 dence suggests that a disproportionate number of doctors who have quit smoking can be found among the fanatics. Just as the most enthusiastic revolutionary tends to make the most enthusiastic counterrevolutionary, many of today's vitriolic zealots include those who had been deeply committed to tobacco habits.

By contrast, the antismoking evangelist does not condemn 5 smokers. Unlike the zealot, he regards smoking as an easily curable condition, as a social disease, and not a sin. The evangelist spends an enormous amount of time seeking and preaching to the unconverted. He argues that kicking the habit is not *that* difficult. After all, *he* did it; moreover, as he describes it, the benefits of quitting are beyond measure and the disadvantages are nil.

The hallmark of the evangelist is his insistence that he never 6 misses tobacco. Though he is less hostile to smokers than the zealot, he is resented more. Friends and loved ones who have been the targets of his preachments frequently greet the resumption of smoking by the evangelist as an occasion for unmitigated glee.

Among former smokers, the distinctions between the evange- 7 list and the elect are much the same as the differences between proselytizing and nonproselytizing religious sects. While the evangelists preach the ease and desirability of abstinence, the elect do not attempt to convert their friends. They think that virtue is its own reward and subscribe to the Puritan theory of predestination. Since they have proved themselves capable of abstaining from tobacco, they are therefore different from friends and relatives who continue to smoke. They feel superior, secure that their salvation was foreordained. These ex-smokers rarely give personal testimony on their conversion. They rarely speak about their tobacco habits, while evangelists talk about little else. Of course, active smokers find such blue-nosed behavior far less offensive than that of the evangelist or the zealot, yet they resent the elect simply because they are smug. Their air of self-satisfaction rarely escapes the notice of those lighting up. For active smokers, life with a member of the ex-smoking elect is less stormy than with a zealot or evangelist, but it is subtly oppressive nonetheless.

I have labeled my final category of former smokers the serene. 8 This classification is meant to encourage those who find the other psychic styles of ex-smokers disagreeable. Serenity is quieter than zealotry and evangelism, and those who qualify are not as self-righteous as the elect. The serene ex-smoker accepts himself and also accepts those around him who continue to smoke. This kind of serenity does not come easily nor does it seem to be an immediate option for those who have stopped. Rather it is a goal, an end stage in a process of development during which some former smokers progress through one or more of the less-than-positive psychological points en route. For former smokers, serenity is thus a positive possibility that exists at the end of the rainbow. But all former smokers cannot reach that promised land.

What is it that permits some former smokers to become serene? 9
I think the key is self-acceptance and gratitude. The fully mature former smoker knows he has the soul of an addict and is grateful for the knowledge. He doesn't regret that he quit smoking, nor any of his previous adventures with tobacco. As a former smoker, he is grateful for the experience and memory of craving a cigarette.

Serenity comes from accepting the lessons of one's life. And ex-smokers who have reached this point in their world view have much to be grateful for. They have learned about the potential and limits of change. In becoming the right kind of former smoker, they developed a healthy sense of self. This former smoker, for one, believes that it is better to crave (one hopes only occasionally) and not to smoke than never to have craved at all. And by accepting that fact, the reformed smoker does not need to excoriate, envy, or disassociate himself from those who continue to smoke.

UNDERSTANDING DETAILS

1. What are the four categories of reformed smokers that Zimring has observed? What characterizes each type?
2. What is the difference between the "elect" and the "serene" ex-smokers according to the author?
3. What is the general purpose of this division/classification essay?
4. How are becoming "the right kind of former smoker" and "a healthy sense of self" (paragraph 10) related? How do they affect one another?

ANALYZING MEANING

1. How does Zimring portray smokers in this essay? What effect does this attitude have on the rest of the essay?
2. What type of ex-smoker do you think would be most difficult to live with and why?
3. Why do you think many doctors who stop smoking become zealots?

4. Do you agree with Zimring that the key to being a "serene" ex-smoker is "self-acceptance and gratitude" (paragraph 9)? Are these positive qualities in an ex-smoker? Explain your answer in detail.

DISCOVERING RHETORICAL STRATEGIES

1. Who do you think is Zimring's specific audience for this essay? Explain your answer.
2. What do you think is Zimring's purpose in writing this essay? How did you come to this conclusion?
3. Zimring discusses these types of reformed smokers in a specific order. Explain this progression and discuss whether it is effective in achieving Zimring's overall purpose.
4. What rhetorical modes support the author's division/classification? Give examples of each.

MAKING CONNECTIONS

1. Compare Zimring's description of the addictive nature of tobacco with Michael Dorris's account of alcohol addiction in "The Broken Cord." Which substance do you think is most addictive? Explain your answer.
2. Use Zimring's definition of a "zealot" to help analyze essays by Fred Pelka ("Hating the Sick: Health Chauvinism and Its Cure"), Mario Cuomo ("Freedom of the Press Must Be Unlimited"), and John Merrill ("Freedom of the Press Must Be Limited"). To what extent are these authors zealots in support of their cause? Which author is most passionate in his opinion? Which is the least? Are you zealous about any particular issue? If so, which one? What is your personal opinion about this issue?
3. Examine Jessica Mitford's "Behind the Formaldehyde Curtain," Judy Brady's "Why I Want a Wife," and Germaine Greer's "A Child Is Born" in order to determine whether any of these authors has reached Zimring's level of "serenity" in life? Which of these writers would you characterize as "zealots"? Which as "evangelists"? Which as "the elect"? What are the principal differences in the approaches of these three authors?

IDEAS FOR DISCUSSION/WRITING

Preparing to Write

Write freely about the role addiction plays in our lives in America: What do you know about addiction in general? What different substances and activities can people be addicted to? How can they break an addiction? What addictions are most dominant in American society? In what ways have you avoided addiction? In what ways are you addicted? What are your worst addictions? What are some of your friends' addictions? What do your addictions say about your personality? What do your friends' addictions say about them? What are some of America's major addictions? How could we alleviate these problems?

CHOOSING A TOPIC

1. Your high school graduating class has decided to put together a brochure about substance abuse and addiction brochure for students starting high school. You have been asked to explain addiction and its consequences to this audience. Make your essay as vivid as possible.

2. Pretend that your college newspaper is running a special issue distinguishing between different generations of students. In a coherent essay written for the readers of this newspaper, classify the students of your generation in some logical, interesting fashion. Remember that classification is a rhetorical movement from "many" to "one." Group the members of your generation by some meaningful guidelines or general characteristics that you establish. Be sure to decide on a purpose and a point of view before you begin to write.

3. You have had many different types of friends over the years. Discuss one type of friend by dividing into logical categories the actual behavior of that type of person. Discuss each part of your division, giving examples as frequently as possible. Decide on a purpose and a point of view before you begin to write.

Before beginning your essay, you might want to consult the checklists on pages 282–284.

JUDITH VIORST   (1931–   )

The Truth About Lying

A poet, journalist, writer of children's books, and contributing editor of *Redbook* magazine, Judith Viorst reached the top of *The New York Times* best-seller list with *Necessary Losses* (1986), a detailed examination of "the loves, illusions, dependencies, and impossible expectations that all of us have to give up in order to grow." She earned her B.A. at Rutgers University in 1952 and began writing poetry. These early efforts, she claims, were "terrible poems about dead dogs, mostly . . . the meaning of life, death, pain, lust, and suicide." Her first complete book of poetry, however, entitled *The Village Square* (1965), was quite successful, as were such subsequent volumes as *People and Other Aggravations* (1971), *How Did I Get to Be Forty and Other Atrocities* (1976), *Love and Guilt and the Meaning of Life* (1984), and *Forever Fifty and Other Negotiations* (1989). Additional publications include *The Washington, D.C. Underground Gourmet* (1970), *Yes, Married: A Saga of Love and Complaint* (1972), *Love and Guilt and the Meaning of Life, Etc.* (1979), *The Good-bye Book* (1988), *Earrings!* (1990), *Murdering Mr. Monti: A Merry Tale of Sex and Violence* (1994), *Imperfect Control* (2000), and several books for children. The author lives in Washington with her husband, Milton Viorst (a syndicated political columnist).

Preparing to Read

"The Truth About Lying," originally published in the March 1981 issue of *Redbook* magazine, classifies and describes the different categories of lies we all experience at some point in our lives. As you prepare to read this essay, take a few moments to consider various lies you have told: Under what conditions are you tempted to lie? When have you actually lied? Why did you do so? Can you generalize about the types of lies you habitually tell? Are you irritated when people lie to you? Why or why not? In what circumstances might lying be acceptable? Why?

I've been wanting to write on a subject that intrigues and chal-   1
lenges me: the subject of lying. I've found it very difficult to
do. Everyone I've talked to has a quite intense and personal
but often rather intolerant point of view about what we can—and
can never *never*—tell lies about. I've finally reached the conclusion
that I can't present any ultimate conclusions, for too many people
would promptly disagree. Instead, I'd like to present a series of
moral puzzles, all concerned with lying. I'll tell you what I think
about them. Do you agree?

Social Lies

Most of the people I've talked with say that they find social   2
lying acceptable and necessary. They think it's the civilized way
for folks to behave. Without these little white lies, they say, our
relationships would be short and brutish and nasty. It's arrogant,
they say, to insist on being so incorruptible and so brave that you
cause other people unnecessary embarrassment or pain by com-
pulsively assailing them with your honesty. I basically agree.
What about you?

Will you say to people, when it simply isn't true, "I like your   3
new hairdo," "You're looking much better," "It's so nice to see
you," "I had a wonderful time"?

Will you praise hideous presents and homely kids?   4

Will you decline invitations with "We're busy that night—so   5
sorry we can't come," when the truth is you'd rather stay home
than dine with the So-and-sos?

And even though, as I do, you may prefer the polite evasion of   6
"You really cooked up a storm" instead of "The soup"—which
tastes like warmed-over coffee—"is wonderful," will you, if you
must, proclaim it wonderful?

There's one man I know who absolutely refuses to tell social   7
lies. "I can't play that game," he says; "I'm simply not made that
way." And his answer to the argument that saying nice things to
someone doesn't cost anything is, "Yes, it does—it destroys your
credibility." Now, he won't, unsolicited, offer his views on the
painting you just bought, but you don't ask his frank opinion unless you want *frank*, and his silence at those moments when the
rest of us liars are muttering, "Isn't it lovely?" is, for the most part,
eloquent enough. My friend does not indulge in what he calls

"flattery, false praise, and mellifluous comments." When others tell fibs, he will not go along. He says that social lying is lying, that little white lies are still lies. And he feels that telling lies is morally wrong. What about you?

Peace-Keeping Lies

Many people tell peace-keeping lies; lies designed to avoid irri- 8 tation or argument; lies designed to shelter the liar from possible blame or pain; lies (or so it is rationalized) designed to keep trouble at bay without hurting anyone.

I tell these lies at times, and yet I always feel they're wrong. I 9 understand why we tell them, but still they feel wrong. And whenever I lie so that someone won't disapprove of me or think less of me or holler at me, I feel I'm a bit of a coward, I feel I'm dodging responsibility, I feel . . . guilty. What about you?

Do you, when you're late for a date because you overslept, say 10 that you're late because you got caught in a traffic jam?

Do you, when you forget to call a friend, say that you called 11 several times but the line was busy?

Do you, when you didn't remember that it was your father's 12 birthday, say that his present must be delayed in the mail?

And when you're planning a weekend in New York City and 13 you're not in the mood to visit your mother, who lives there, do you conceal—with a lie, if you must—the fact that you'll be in New York? Or do you have the courage—or is it the cruelty?—to say, "I'll be in New York, but sorry—I don't plan on seeing you"?

(Dave and his wife Elaine have two quite different points of 14 view on this very subject. He calls her a coward. She says she's being wise. He says she must assert her right to visit New York sometimes and not see her mother. To which she always patiently replies: "Why should we have useless fights? My mother's too old to change. We get along much better when I lie to her.")

Finally, do you keep the peace by telling your husband lies on the 15 subject of money? Do you reduce what you really paid for your shoes? And in general do you find yourself ready, willing, and able to lie to him when you make absurd mistakes or lose or break things?

"I used to have a romantic idea that part of intimacy was con- 16 fessing every dumb thing that you did to your husband. But after a couple of years of that," says Laura, "have I changed my mind!"

And having changed her mind, she finds herself telling peace-   17
keeping lies. And yes, I tell them too. What about you?

Protective Lies

Protective lies are lies folks tell—often quite serious lies—be-   18
cause they're convinced that the truth would be too damaging.
They lie because they feel there are certain human values that su-
persede the wrong of having lied. They lie, not for personal gain,
but because they believe it's for the good of the person they're
lying to. They lie to those they love, to those who trust them
most of all, on the grounds that breaking this trust is justified.

They may lie to their children on money or marital matters.   19

They may lie to the dying about the state of their health.   20

They may lie about adultery, and not—or so they insist—to   21
save their own hide, but to save the heart and the pride of the
men they are married to.

They may lie to their closest friend because the truth about her   22
talents or son or psyche would be—or so they insist—utterly devastating.

I sometimes tell such lies, but I'm aware that it's quite pre-   23
sumptuous to claim I know what's best for others to know.
That's called playing God. That's called manipulation and control.
And we never can be sure, once we start to juggle lies, just where
they'll land, exactly where they'll roll.

And furthermore, we may find ourselves lying in order to back   24
up the lies that are backing up the lie we initially told.

And furthermore—let's be honest—if conditions were re-   25
versed, we certainly wouldn't want anyone lying to us.

Yet, having said all that, I still believe that there are times when   26
protective lies must nonetheless be told. What about you?

If your Dad had a very bad heart and you had to tell him some   27
bad family news, which would you choose: to tell him the truth
or lie?

If your former husband failed to send his monthly child-   28
support check and in other ways behaved like a total rat, would
you allow your children—who believed he was simply wonderful—to continue to believe that he was wonderful?

If your dearly beloved brother selected a wife whom you deeply   29
disliked, would you reveal your feelings or would you fake it?

And if you were asked, after making love, "And how was that 30
for you?" would you reply, if it wasn't too good, "Not too
good"?

Now, some would call a sex lie unimportant, little more than 31
social lying, a simple act of courtesy that makes all human intercourse run smoothly. And some would say all sex lies are bad
news and unacceptably protective. Because, says Ruth, "a man
with an ego that fragile doesn't need your lies—he needs a psy-
chiatrist." Still others feel that sex lies are indeed protective lies,
more serious than simple social lying, and yet at times they tell
them on the grounds that when it comes to matters sexual, everybody's ego is somewhat fragile.

"If most of the time things go well in sex," says Sue, "I think 32
you're allowed to dissemble when they don't. I can't believe it's
good to say, 'Last night was four stars, darling, but tonight's performance rates only a half.'"

I'm inclined to agree with Sue. What about you? 33

Trust-Keeping Lies

Another group of lies are trust-keeping lies, lies that involve 34
triangulation, with *A* (that's you) telling lies to *B* on behalf of *C*
(whose trust you'd promised to keep). Most people concede that
once you've agreed not to betray a friend's confidence, you can't
betray it, even if you must lie. But I've talked with people who
don't want you telling them anything that they might be called
on to lie about.

"I don't tell lies for myself," says Fran, "and I don't want to 35
have to tell them for other people." Which means, she agrees,
that if her best friend is having an affair, she absolutely doesn't
want to know about it.

"Are you saying," her best friend asks, "that if I went off with a 36
lover and I asked you to tell my husband I'd been with you, that
you wouldn't lie for me, that you'd betray me?"

Fran is very pained but very adamant. "I wouldn't want to be- 37
tray you, so . . . don't ask me."

Fran's best friend is shocked. What about you? 38

Do you believe you can have close friends if you're not pre- 39
pared to receive their deepest secrets?

Do you believe you must always lie for your friends? 40

Do you believe, if your friend tells a secret that turns out to be   41
quite immoral or illegal, that once you've promised to keep it,
you must keep it?

And what if your friend were your boss—if you were perhaps   42
one of the President's men—would you betray or lie for him
over, say, Watergate?

As you can see, these issues get terribly sticky.   43

It's my belief that once we've promised to keep a trust, we   44
must tell lies to keep it. I also believe that we can't tell Watergate
lies. And if these two statements strike you as quite contradictory,
you're right—they're quite contradictory. But for now they're
the best I can do. What about you?

Some say that truth will out and thus you might as well tell the   45
truth. Some say you can't regain the trust that lies lose. Some say
that even though the truth may never be revealed, our lies pervert
and damage our relationships. Some say . . . well, here's what
some of them have to say.

"I'm a coward," says Grace, "about telling close people impor-   46
tant, difficult truths. I find that I'm unable to carry it off. And so if
something is bothering me, it keeps building up inside till I end
up just not seeing them any more."

"I lie to my husband on sexual things, but I'm furious," says   47
Joyce, "that he's too insensitive to know I'm lying."

"I suffer most from the misconception that children can't take   48
the truth," says Emily. "But I'm starting to see that what's harder
and more damaging for them is being told lies, is *not* being told
the truth."

"I'm afraid," says Joan, "that we often wind up feeling a bit of   49
contempt for the people we lie to."

And then there are those who have no talent for lying.   50

"Over the years, I tried to lie," a friend of mine explained,   51
"but I always got found out and I always got punished. I guess I
gave myself away because I feel guilty about any kind of lying. It
looks as if I'm stuck with telling the truth."

For those of us, however, who are good at telling lies, for those   52
of us who lie and don't get caught, the question of whether or
not to lie can be a hard and serious moral problem. I liked the remark of a friend of mine who said, "I'm willing to lie. But just as
a last resort—the truth's always better."

"Because," he explained, "though others may completely ac-   53
cept the lie I'm telling, I don't."

I tend to feel that way too.   54

What about you?   55

UNDERSTANDING DETAILS

1. Viorst discusses four types of lies in this essay. Explain each in your own words.
2. What types of lies are most serious? What does the author mean by "serious"?
3. What does Viorst mean by "Watergate lies" in paragraph 44? What is your feeling about this level of trust-keeping lies?
4. According to Viorst, what is the relationship between lying and her self-image?

ANALYZING MEANING

1. In what ways is lying a moral problem?
2. Why do people respond in so many different ways to the issue of lying?
3. In your opinion or experience, what are the principal consequences of lying? Do the negative consequences outweigh the positive, or is the reverse true? Explain your answer in as much detail as possible.
4. How do you feel about lying? Does your opinion vary according to the type of lie you tell? Why? Explain your answer in detail.

DISCOVERING RHETORICAL STRATEGIES

1. In this essay, Viorst works with both division and classification as she arranges lies into several distinct categories. Write down the main subdivisions of her classification system; then, list under each category the examples she cites. How has she organized these categories? Do all her examples support the appropriate classification? How does she give significance or value to this system of classification?
2. Who do you think is Viorst's intended audience? What specific verbal clues in the essay help you reach this conclusion?

3. Notice that the author repeats the question "What about you?" several times. What effect does this repetition have on your response to the essay?

4. What other rhetorical modes besides division/classification does Viorst use to make her point in the essay? Give specific examples to support your answers.

MAKING CONNECTIONS

1. Judith Viorst categorizes several different types of lies as "a series of moral puzzles" (paragraph 1). To what extent do Sherwin Nuland ("Accidents, Suicide, and Euthanasia"), Shelby Steele ("Affirmative Action: The Price of Preference"), and Barbara Ehrenreich ("The Ecstasy of War") all deal with "moral puzzles" in their essays? Which of these "puzzles" is most easily solved? Which is most difficult? Why?

2. In "Behind the Formaldehyde Curtain," Jessica Mitford exposes the "lies" surrounding funeral homes. Would Viorst agree with Mitford that funeral directors lie to us? If so, why do they do so?

3. How separate and exclusive are Viorst's categories of lies? Could some lies fit within two categories at the same time? Examine Phyllis Schneider's "Memory: Tips You'll Never Forget" and/or Franklin Zimring's "Confessions of an Ex-Smoker" to determine if these authors' categories overlap in the same way that Viorst's do. Do division/classification essays work better if there is little or no overlap between categories? If so, why?

IDEAS FOR DISCUSSION/WRITING

Preparing to Write

Write freely about various lies you have told in the past: When did you lie? When did you consider lying but told the truth? In what types of situations do you most often resort to lying? Why do you lie in these circumstances? How does lying make you feel? How does telling the truth make you feel? Do you have a general philosophy about lying that you try to follow? If so, what is it?

Choosing a Topic

1. At some time in our lives, we all tell or receive lies as Viorst defines them. Choose a particularly memorable lie (one you either told or received), and classify all your feelings connected with the experience. What did you learn from the situation?

2. You have decided that your future roommate/spouse deserves an honest profile of your personality before you begin living together. Analyze for him or her some fundamental truths about your character by classifying your reactions to the information in one of the categories in Viorst's essay.

3. Being in school presents a number of potential opportunities for lying. Answers to such questions as "Why is your homework late?" "Why can't you go out this weekend?" and "Why did you miss class yesterday?" can get people *into* or *out of* all sorts of trouble. For a friend of yours still in high school, write an essay offering advice on handling situations such as these. Devise a useful classification system for these school-related dilemmas; then, explain what your experiences have taught you in each case about lying.

Before beginning your essay, you might want to consult the checklists on pages 282–284.

CHAPTER WRITING ASSIGNMENTS

Practicing Division/Classification

1. Do you think public schools should teach students ethics and personal values? If so, which values should schools teach in order to produce "good citizens"? Classify these values in an essay, and explain how these categories would have fit into your high school curriculum.

2. What problems are most destructive to a healthy relationship? Choose a specific type of relationship (friend, spouse, parent-child), and write an essay discussing various categories of problems that can cause the most trouble in this type of relationship. Explain why the qualities you identify would be destructive in the kind of relationship you describe.

3. Think about the ideal _____ (fill in the blank with one of the many roles we play every day [for example, wife, husband, teacher, student, friend, or cousin]). List the qualities that person needs. What categories do these qualities fall into? Why are these characteristics ideal? Write an essay explaining the categories you have developed for the role you chose to discuss.

Exploring Ideas

1. We all have bad habits, but few people know how to break them. What advice do you have for people who want to change their behavior in some important way or break a bad habit? How do you know your method works?

2. Explain a cultural tradition we are in danger of losing in society today. Discuss the value of the tradition itself and the ways this tradition is changing, along with the value and effects of this change. Make sure you discuss this topic in an unbiased way.

3. How do a person's cultural views and beliefs affect the educational process? In what ways does our current system of education acknowledge, hinder, or ignore our diverse cultural backgrounds? In a well-developed essay, discuss how our educational system successfully or unsuccessfully deals with our various cultural differences.

6

COMPARISON/CONTRAST
Discovering Similarities and Differences

Making comparisons is such a natural and necessary part of our everyday lives that we often do so without conscious effort. When we were children, we compared our toys with those of our friends, we contrasted our height and physical development to other children's, and we constantly evaluated our happiness in comparison with that evidenced by our parents and childhood companions. As we grew older, we habitually compared our dates, teachers, parents, friends, cars, and physical attributes. In college, we learn about anthropology by writing essays on the similarities and differences between two African tribes, about political science by contrasting the Republican and Democratic platforms, about business by comparing annual production rates, and about literature by comparing Shakespeare with Marlowe or Browning with Tennyson. Comparing and contrasting various elements in our lives helps us make decisions, such as which course to take or which house to buy, and it justifies preferences that we already hold, such as liking one city more than another or loving one person more than the next. In these ways and in many others, the skillful use of comparison and contrast is clearly essential to our social and professional lives.

DEFINING COMPARISON/CONTRAST

Comparison and contrast allow us to understand one subject by putting it next to another. Comparing involves discovering likenesses or similarities, whereas contrasting is based on finding differences. Like division and classification, comparison and contrast are generally considered part of the same process, because we usually have no reason for comparing unless some contrast is also involved. Each technique implies the existence of the other. For this reason, the word *compare* is often used to mean both techniques.

Comparison and contrast are most profitably applied to two items that have something in common, such as cats and dogs or cars and motorcycles. A discussion of cats and motorcycles, for example, would probably not be very rewarding or stimulating, because they do not have much in common. If more than two items are compared in an essay, they are still most profitably discussed in pairs: for instance, motorcycles and cars, cars and bicycles, or bicycles and motorcycles.

An analogy is an extended, sustained comparison. Often used to explain unfamiliar, abstract, or complicated thoughts, this rhetorical technique adds energy and vividness to a wide variety of college-level writing. The process of analogy differs slightly from comparison/contrast in three important ways: Comparison/contrast begins with subjects from the same class and places equal weight on both of them. In addition, it addresses both the similarities and the differences of these subjects. Analogy, conversely, seldom explores subjects from the same class and focuses principally on one familiar subject in an attempt to explain another, more complex one. Furthermore, it deals only with similarities, not with contrasts. A comparison/contrast essay, for example, might study two veterans' ways of coping with the trauma of the Gulf War by pointing out the differences in their methods as well as the similarities. An analogy essay might use the familiar notion of a fireworks display to reveal the chilling horror of the lonely hours after dark during this war: "Nights in the Persian Gulf were similar to a loud, unending fireworks display. We had no idea when the next blast was coming, how loud it would be, or how close. We cringed in terror after dark, hoping the next surprise would not be our own death." In this example, rather than simply hearing about an event, we participate in it through this highly refined form of comparison.

The following student paragraph compares and contrasts married and single life. As you read it, notice how the author compares similar social states and, in the process, justifies her current lifestyle:

> *Recently I saw a bumper sticker that read, "It used to be wine, women, and song, and now it's beer, the old lady, and TV." Much truth may be found in this comparison of single and married lifestyles. When my husband and I used to date, for example, we'd go out for dinner and drinks and then maybe see a play or concert. Our discussions were intelligent, often ranging over global politics, science, literature, and other lofty topics. He would open doors for me, buy me flowers, and make sure I was comfortable and happy. Now, three years later, after marriage and a child, the baby bottle has replaced the wine bottle, the smell of diapers wipes out the scent of roses, and our nights on the town are infrequent, cherished events. But that's all right. A little bit of the excitement and mystery may be gone, but these intangible qualities have given way to a sturdy, dependable trust in each other and a quiet confidence about our future together.*

THINKING CRITICALLY BY USING COMPARISON/CONTRAST

Comparison and contrast are basic to a number of different thought processes. We compare and contrast quite naturally on a daily basis, but all of us would benefit greatly from being more aware of these companion strategies in our own writing. They help us not only in perceiving our environment but also in understanding and organizing large amounts of information.

The basic skill of finding similarities and differences will enhance your ability to create accurate descriptions, to cite appropriate examples, to present a full process analysis, and, of course, to classify and label subjects. It is a pattern of thought that is essential to more complex thinking strategies, so perfecting the ability to use it is an important step in your efforts to improve your critical thinking.

Once again, we are going to practice this strategy in isolation to get a strong sense of its mechanics before we combine it with other rhetorical modes. Isolating this mode will make your reading and writing even stronger than they are now, because the individual parts of the thinking process will be more vigorous and effective, thus making your academic performance more powerful than ever.

1. Find magazine ads that use comparison/contrast to make a point or sell a product. What is the basis of each comparison? How effective or ineffective is each comparison?
2. Compare or contrast the experience of spending time with a special person to another type of experience (e.g., a roller-coaster ride, drowning, sleeping, or a trip across the United States). Be as specific as possible in your comparison.
3. Have you ever been to the same place twice? Think for a moment about how the first and second visits to this place differed. How were they similar? What were the primary reasons for the similarities and differences in your perceptions of these visits?

READING AND WRITING COMPARISON/ CONTRAST ESSAYS

Many established guidelines regulate the development of a comparison/contrast essay and should be taken into account from both the reading and the writing perspectives. All good comparative studies serve a specific purpose. They attempt either to examine their subjects separately or to demonstrate the superiority of one over the other. In evaluating two different types of cars, for example, a writer might point out the amazing gas mileage of one model and the smooth handling qualities of the other or the superiority of one car's gas mileage over that of another. Whatever the intent, comparison/contrast essays need to be clear and logical and to have a precise purpose.

How To Read A Comparison/Contrast Essay

Preparing to Read.   As you begin reading this chapter, pull together as much preliminary material as possible for each essay so you can focus your attention and have the benefit of prior knowledge before you start to read. In particular, you should try to discover what is being compared or contrasted and why. From the title of his essay, can you tell what Bruce Catton is comparing in "Grant and Lee: A Study in Contrasts"? What does William

Ouchi's title ("Japanese and American Workers: Two Casts of Mind") suggest to you? From glancing at the essay itself and reading the synopsis in the Rhetorical Table of Contents, what do you think Annie Dillard's essay will try to accomplish?

Also, before you begin to read these essays, try to discover information about the author and about the conditions under which each essay was written. What is Germaine Greer's stand on childbirth customs in the Middle East? To what extent do you expect her opinions on this topic to color her comparison of these customs in the Middle East and America? Why is Ouchi qualified to write about Japanese and American workers? Does he reveal his background in his essay?

Finally, just before you begin to read, answer the Preparing to Read questions, and then make some free associations with the general topic of each essay: For example, what do you think are some of the similarities and differences in childbirth customs between Third World countries and the Western world (Germaine Greer)? What is your general view on women's bodybuilding (Gloria Steinem)?

Reading.   As you read each comparison/contrast essay for the first time, be sure to record your own feelings and opinions. Some of the issues presented in this chapter are highly controversial. You will often have strong reactions to them, which you should try to write down as soon as possible.

In addition, you may want to comment on the relationship between the preliminary essay material, the author's stance in the essay, and the content of the essay itself. For example, what motivated Steinem to write "The Politics of Muscle"? Who is her primary audience? What is Dillard's tone in "Living Like Weasels," and how does it further her purpose? Answers to questions such as these will provide you with a context for your first reading of these essays and will assist you in preparing to analyze the essays in more depth on your second reading.

At this point in the chapter, you should make certain you understand each author's thesis and then take a close look at his or her principal method of organization: Is the essay arranged (1) point by point, (2) subject by subject, (3) as a combination of these two, or (4) as separate discussions of similarities and differences between two subjects? (See the chart on page 330 for an illustration of these options.) Last, preview the questions that follow the essay before you read it again.

Rereading. When you read these essays a second time, you should look at the comparison or contrast much more closely than you have up to now. First, look in detail at the writer's method of organization (see the chart on page 330). How effective is it in advancing the writer's thesis?

Next, you should consider whether each essay is fully developed and balanced: Does Catton compare similar items? Does Greer discuss the same qualities of her subjects? Does Ouchi deal with all aspects of the comparison between Japanese and American workers? Is Steinem's treatment of her subjects well balanced? And does Dillard give her audience enough specific details to clarify the extent of her comparison? Do all the writers in this chapter use well-chosen transitions so you can move smoothly from one point to the next? Also, what other rhetorical modes support each comparison/contrast in this chapter?

Finally, the answers to the questions after each selection will let you evaluate your understanding of the essay and help you analyze its contents in preparation for the discussion/writing topics that follow.

For a more thorough inventory of the reading process, you should turn to pages 20–21 in the Introduction.

How to Write a Comparison/Contrast Essay

Preparing to write. As you consider various topics for a comparison/contrast essay, you should answer the Preparing to Write questions that precede the assignments and then use the prewriting techniques explained in the Introduction (pp. 21–27) to generate even more ideas on these topics.

As you focus your attention on a particular topic, keep the following suggestions in mind:

1. Always compare/contrast items in the same category (e.g., compare two professors, but not a professor and a swimming pool).
2. Have a specific purpose or reason for writing your essay.
3. Discuss the same qualities of each subject (if you evaluate the teaching techniques of one professor, do so for the other professor as well).
4. Use as many pertinent details as possible to expand your comparison/contrast and to accomplish your stated purpose.
5. Deal with all aspects of the comparison that are relevant to the purpose.

6. Balance the treatment of the different subjects of your comparison (i.e., don't spend more time on one than on another).
7. Determine your audience's background and knowledge so that you will know how much of your comparison should be explained in detail and how much can be skimmed over.

Next, in preparation for a comparison/contrast project, you might list all the elements of both subjects that you want to compare. This list can then help you give your essay structure as well as substance. At this stage in the writing process, the task may seem similar to pure description, but a discussion of two subjects in relation to one another rapidly changes the assignment from description to comparison.

Writing. The introduction of your comparison/contrast essay should (1) clearly identify your subjects, (2) explain the basis of your comparison/contrast, and (3) state your purpose and the overall limits of your particular study. Identifying your subject is, of course, a necessary and important task in any essay. Similarly, justifying the elements you will be comparing and contrasting creates interest and gives your audience some specifics to look for in the essay. Finally, your statement of purpose or thesis (for example, to prove that one professor is superior to another) should include the boundaries of your discussion. You cannot cover all the reasons for your preference in one short essay, so you must limit your consideration to three or four basic categories (perhaps teaching techniques, the clarity of the assignments given, classroom attitude, and grading standards). The introduction is the place to make all these limits known.

You can organize the body of your paper in one of four ways: (1) a point-by-point, or alternating, comparison; (2) a subject-by-subject, or divided, comparison; (3) a combination of these two methods; or (4) a division between the similarities and differences. (See the chart on page 330.)

The point-by-point comparison evaluates both subjects in terms of each category. If the issue, for example, is which of two cars to buy, you might discuss both models' gasoline mileage first; then, their horsepower; next, their ease in handling; and, finally, their standard equipment. Following the second method of organization, subject by subject, you would discuss the gasoline mileage, horsepower, ease in handling, and standard equipment of car A first and then follow the same format for car B. The third option would allow you to introduce, say, the standard equipment of each car point by point (or car by car) and then to explain the other features in your comparison (miles per gallon, horsepower, and ease in handling) subject by subject. To use the last method of organization, you might discuss the similarities between the two models first and the differences second (or vice

Methods of Organization

Point by Point*

MPG, car A
MPG, car B

Horsepower, car A
Horspower, car B

Handling, car A
Handling, car B

Equipment, car A
Equipment, car B

---

*Emphasizes individual points. Is best for long essays. Helpful hint: Use transitions to avoid lists.

Subject by Subject+

MPG, car A
Horsepower, car A
Handling, car A
Equipment, car A

MPG, car B
Horsepower car B
Handling, car B
Equipment, car B

+Emphasizes each subject. Is best for short essays. Helpful hint: Use transitions to avoid two separate essays.

Combination

Equipment, car A
Equipment, car B

———

MPG, car A
Horsepower, car A
Handling, car A

MPG, car B
Horsepower, car B
Handling, car B

Similarities/Differences

Similarities:
    MPG, cars A & B

Differences:
    Horsepower, cars A & B
    Handling, cars A & B
    Equipment, cars A & B

versa). If the cars you are comparing have similar miles-per-gallon (MPG) ratings but completely different horsepower, steering systems, and optional equipment, you could discuss the gasoline mileage and then emphasize the differences by mentioning them later in the essay. If, instead, you are trying to emphasize the fact that the MPG ratings of these models remain consistent despite their differences, then reverse the order of your essay.

When confronted with the task of choosing a method of organization for a comparison/contrast essay, you need to find the pattern that best suits your purpose. If you want single items to stand out in a discussion, for instance, the best choice will be the point-by-point system; it is especially appropriate for long essays but has a tendency to turn into an exercise in listing if you don't pay careful attention to your transitions. If, however, the subjects themselves (rather than the itemized points) are the most interesting feature of your essay, you should use the subject-by-subject comparison; this system is particularly good for short essays in which the readers can retain what was said about one subject while they read about a second subject. Through this second system of organization, each subject becomes a unified whole, an approach to an essay that is generally effective unless the theme becomes awkwardly divided into two separate parts. You must also remember, if you choose this second method of organization, that the second (or last) subject is in the most emphatic position because that is what your readers will have seen most recently. The final two options for organizing a comparison/contrast essay give you some built-in flexibility so that you can create emphasis and attempt to manipulate reader opinion simply by the structure of your essay.

Using logical transitions in your comparison/contrast essays will establish clear relationships between the items in your comparisons and will also move your readers smoothly from one topic to the next. If you wish to indicate comparisons, use such words as *like, as, also, in like manner, similarly,* and *in addition;* to signal contrasts, try *but, in contrast to, unlike, whereas,* and *on the one hand/on the other hand.*

The conclusion of a comparison/contrast essay summarizes the main points and states the deductions drawn from those points. As you choose your method of organization, remember not to get locked into a formulaic approach to your subjects, which will adversely affect the readability of your essay. To avoid making your reader feel like a spectator at a verbal table tennis match, be straightforward, honest, and patient as you discover and recount the details of your comparison.

Rewriting.   When you review the draft of your comparison/contrast essay, you need once again to make sure that you communicate your purpose as effectively as possible to your intended audience. Two guidelines previously mentioned should help you accomplish this goal:

- Do you identify your subjects clearly?
- Does your thesis clearly state the purpose and overall limits of your particular study?

You will also need to pay close attention to the development of your essay:

- Are you attempting to compare/contrast items from the same general category?
- Do you discuss the same qualities of each subject?
- Do you balance the treatment of the different subjects of your essay?
- Do you organize your topic as effectively as possible?
- Does your conclusion contain a summary and analysis of your main points?

For further information on writing and revising your comparison/contrast essays, consult the checklists on pages 32–34 of the Introduction.

STUDENT ESSAY: COMPARISON/ CONTRAST AT WORK

The following student essay compares the advantages and disadvantages of macaroni and cheese versus tacos in the life of a harried college freshman. As you read it, notice that the writer states his intention in the first paragraph and then expands his discussion with appropriate details to produce a balanced essay. Also, try to determine what effect he creates by using two methods of organization: first subject by subject, then point by point.

Dormitory Chef

To this day, I will not eat either maca- Topics
roni and cheese or tacos. No, it's not
because of any allergy; it's because during
my freshman year at college, I prepared
one or the other of these scrumptious
dishes more times than I care to remember.
However, my choice of which culinary
delight to cook on any given night was
not as simple a decision as one might
imagine.

Basis of comparison (margin, left)

Thesis statement: Purpose and limits of comparison (margin, right)

Macaroni and cheese has numerous advantages for the dormitory chef. First of all,
it is inexpensive. No matter how poor one
may be, there's probably enough change
under the couch cushion to buy a box at
the market. All that starch for only $2.29.
What a bargain! Second, it can be prepared
in just one pan. This is especially important
given the meager resources of the average
dorm kitchen. Third, and perhaps most important, macaroni and cheese is odorless. By
odorless, I mean that no one else can smell
it. It is a well-known fact that dorm residents hate to cook and that they love nothing better than to wander dejectedly around
the kitchen with big, sad eyes after someone else has been cooking. But with macaroni and cheese, no enticing aromas are
going to find their way into the nose of any
would-be mooch.

Paragraph on Subject A: Macaroni and cheese (margin, left)

Point 1 (Price) (margin, right)

Point 2 (Preparation) (margin, right)

Point 3 (Odor) (margin, left)

Tacos, on the other hand, are a different
matter altogether. For the dorm cook, the
most significant difference is obviously the
price. To enjoy tacos for dinner, the adventurous dorm gourmet must purchase no
fewer than five ingredients from the market: corn tortillas, beef, lettuce, tomatoes,
and cheese. Needless to say, this is a major

Paragraph on Subject B: Tacos (margin, left)

Transition (margin, right)

Point 1 (Price) (margin, right)

Point 2 (Prepara-tion) expenditure. Second, the chef must adroitly shuffle these ingredients back and forth among his or her very limited supply of pans and bowls. And finally, tacos smell **Point 3 (Odor)** great. That wouldn't be a problem if the tacos didn't also smell great to about twenty of the cook's newest—if not closest—friends, who appear with those same pathetic, starving eyes mentioned earlier. When this happens, the cook will be lucky to get more than two of his own creations.

Subject B Tacos, then, wouldn't stand much of a **Transition** chance if they didn't outdo macaroni and **Subject A** **Paragraph on Point 4:Taste** cheese in one area: taste. Taste is almost—but not quite—an optional requirement in the opinion of a frugal dormitory hash-slinger. Taste is just important enough so that tacos are occasionally prepared, despite their disadvantages.

Transition But tacos have other advantages besides **Subject B** **Paragraph on Point 5: Color** their taste. With their enticing, colorful ingredients, they even look good. The only thing that can be said about the color of macaroni and cheese is that it's a color not **Subject A** found in nature.

Transition On the other hand, macaroni and cheese **Subject A** is quick. It can be prepared in about ten **Paragraph on Point 6: Time** minutes, while tacos take more than twice **Subject B** as long. And there are occasions—such as final exam week—when time is a scarce and precious resource.

Transition As you can see, quite a bit of thinking went into my choice of food in my **Summary** younger years. These two dishes essentially **Analysis** got me through my freshman year and indirectly taught me how to make important decisions (like what to eat). But I still feel a **Concluding statement** certain revulsion when I hear their names today.

Student Writer's Comments

I compare and contrast so many times during a typical day that I took this rhetorical technique for granted. In fact, I had overlooked it completely. The most difficult part of writing this essay was finding two appropriate subjects to compare. Ideally, I knew they should be united by a similarity. So I brainstormed to come up with some possible topics. Then, working from this list of potential subjects, I began to freewrite to see if I could come up with two topics in the same category on which I could write a balanced comparison. Out of my freewriting came this reasoning: Macaroni and cheese and tacos, in reality, are two very different kinds of food from the same category. Proving this fact is easy and might even result in an interesting essay. Their similar property of being popular dorm foods unites the two despite their differences and also gives me two important reasons for writing the comparison: to discover why they are both popular dorm delicacies and to determine which one has more advantages for my particular purposes. In proportion to writing and revising, I spent most of my time choosing my topic, brainstorming, freewriting, and rebrainstorming to make sure I could develop every aspect of my comparison adequately. Most of my prewriting work took the form of two columns, in which I recorded my opinions on the choice between macaroni and cheese versus tacos.

Sitting down to mold my lists into an essay posed an entirely new set of problems. From the copious notes I had taken, I easily wrote the introductory paragraph, identifying my topics, explaining the basis of my comparison/contrast, and stating the purpose and limits of my study (my thesis statement). But now that I faced the body of the essay, I needed to find the best way to organize my opinions on these two dorm foods: point by point, subject by subject, a combination of these two, or a discussion of similarities and differences?

I wrote my first draft discussing my topics point by point. Even with an occasional joke and a few snide comments interjected, the essay reminded me of a boring game of table tennis with only a few attempts at changing the pace. I started over completely with my second draft and worked through my topics subject by subject. I felt this approach was better, but not quite right for my particular purpose and audience. I set out to do some heavy-handed revising.

Discussing my first three points (price, preparation, and odor) subject by subject seemed to work quite well. I was actually satisfied with the first half of my discussion of these two subjects. But the essay really started to get sluggish when I brought up the fourth point: taste. So I broke off my discussion there and rewrote the second half of my essay point by point, dealing with taste, color, and time each in its own paragraph. This change gave my essay the new direction it needed to keep the readers' attention and also offered me some new insights into my comparison. Then, I returned to the beginning of my essay and revised it for readability, adding transitions and making sure the paper now moved smoothly from one point or subject to the next. Finally, I added my final paragraph, including a brief summary of my main points and an explanation of the deductions I had made. My concluding remark ("But I still feel a certain revulsion when I hear their names today.") came to me as I was putting the final touches on this draft.

What I learned from writing this particular essay is that comparison/contrast thinking, more than thinking in other rhetorical modes, is much like a puzzle. I really had to spend an enormous amount of time thinking through, mapping out, and rethinking my comparison before I could start to put my thoughts in essay form. The results are rewarding, but I sure wore out a piece of linoleum on the den floor on the way to my final draft.

SOME FINAL THOUGHTS ON COMPARISON/CONTRAST

The essays in this section demonstrate various methods of organization as well as a number of distinct stylistic approaches to writing a comparison/contrast essay. As you read these selections, pay particular attention to the clear, well-focused introductions; the different logical methods of organization; and the smooth transitions between sentences and paragraphs.

COMPARISON/CONTRAST IN REVIEW

Reading Comparison/Contrast Essays

Preparing to Read

✓ What assumptions can you make from the essay's title?

✓ Can you guess what the general mood of the essay is?

✓ What is the essay's purpose and audience?

✓ What does the synopsis in the Rhetorical Table of Contents tell you about the essay?

✓ What can you learn from the author's biography?

✓ Can you guess what the author's point of view toward the subject is?

✓ What are your responses to the Preparing to Read questions?

Reading

✓ What is the author's thesis?

✓ How is the essay organized: point by point? subject by subject? as a combination of the two? as separate discussions of similarities and differences between two subjects?

✓ Did you preview the questions that follow the essay?

Rereading

✓ Is the writer's method of organization effective for advancing the essay's thesis?

✓ Is the essay fully developed?

✓ What other rhetorical strategies does the author use to support the essay's purpose?

✓ What are your responses to the questions after the essay?

Writing Comparison/Contrast Essays

Preparing to Write

✓ What are your responses to the Preparing to Write questions?

✓ What is your purpose?

✓ Are you comparing/contrasting items in the same category (e.g., two professors, but not a professor and a swimming pool)?

✓ Do you have a specific purpose or reason for writing your essay?

✓ Are you going to discuss the same qualities of each subject?

✓ Have you generated as many pertinent details as possible to expand your comparison/contrast and to accomplish your stated purpose?

Writing

✓ Does your introduction (1) clearly identify your subjects, (2) explain the basis of your comparison/contrast, and (3) state your purpose and the overall limits of your particular study?

✓ Does your thesis include the boundaries of your discussion?

✓ Have you limited your discussion to three or four basic categories?

✓ Is your paper organized in one of the following ways: point by point, subject by subject, as a combination of the two, or as separate discussions of similarities and differences between two subjects?

✓ Does your conclusion summarize your main points and state the deductions you made from those points?

Rewriting

✓ Do you identify your subjects clearly?

✓ Does your thesis clearly state the purpose and overall limits of your particular study?

✓ Are you attempting to compare/contrast items from the same general category?

✓ Do you discuss the same qualities of each subject?

✓ Do you balance the treatment of the different subjects of your essay?

✓ Did you organize your topic as effectively as possible?

✓ Does your conclusion contain a summary and analysis of your main points?

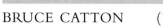

BRUCE CATTON   (1899–1978)

Grant and Lee: A Study in Contrasts

Bruce Catton was a much-loved and respected historian of the U.S. Civil War, whose many books and articles have brought an "eyewitness" vividness to this crucial period in American development. Believing that history "ought to be a good yarn," Catton saw himself as more of a reporter than a historian, stripping away the romantic glamour of war to reveal with vigor and clarity the reality of this important historical era. A native of Benzonia, Michigan, the author was fascinated during his childhood by stories told by the many Civil War veterans who had returned to his small town. Catton attended Oberlin College, worked for a time as a newspaper reporter, and then turned his attention principally to researching and writing about the Civil War. His most popular and influential book was *A Stillness at Appomattox* (the third part of his *Army of the Potomac* trilogy), which won both the Pulitzer Prize and the National Book Award for history in 1954. Among his many other books are *This Hallowed Ground* (1956), *The Coming Fury* (1961), *Terrible Swift Sword* (1963), *Grant Takes Command* (1969), and *Michigan: A Bicentennial History* (1976). For the last twenty-four years of his life, Catton was also editor of *American Heritage* magazine.

Preparing to Read

The following essay is taken from *The American Story* (1956), a collection of essays by distinguished historians; it examines the similarities and differences between Generals Grant and Lee at the conclusion of the Civil War. As you prepare to read this article, take a few moments to consider heroes in your life: What special qualities turn people into heroic figures? Why do you think some heroes are admired more than others? What historical events bring forth heroes? How does American society act in general toward these people? Why do most of us seem to need heroic figures in our lives?

When Ulysses S. Grant and Robert E. Lee met in the 1
parlor of a modest house at Appomattox Court House,
Virginia, on April 9, 1865, to work out the terms for
the surrender of Lee's Army of Northern Virginia, a great chapter
in American life came to a close, and a great new chapter began.

These men were bringing the Civil War to its virtual finish. To 2
be sure, other armies had yet to surrender, and for a few days the
fugitive Confederate government would struggle desperately and
vainly, trying to find some way to go on living now that its chief
support was gone. But in effect it was all over when Grant and
Lee signed the papers. And the little room where they wrote out
the terms was the scene of one of the poignant, dramatic contrasts
in American history.

They were two strong men, these oddly different generals, and 3
they represented the strengths of two conflicting currents that,
through them, had come into final collision.

Back of Robert E. Lee was the notion that the old aristocratic con- 4
cept might somehow survive and be dominant in American life.

Lee was tidewater Virginia, and in his background were family, 5
culture, and tradition . . . the age of chivalry transplanted to a New
World which was making its own legends and its own myths. He embodied a way of life that had come down through the age of knighthood and the English country squire. America was a land that was
beginning all over again, dedicated to nothing much more complicated than the rather hazy belief that all men had equal rights and
should have an equal chance in the world. In such a land Lee stood for
the feeling that it was somehow of advantage to human society to
have a pronounced inequality in the social structure. There should be
a leisure class, backed by ownership of land; in turn, society itself
should be keyed to the land as the chief source of wealth and influence. It would bring forth (according to this ideal) a class of men with
a strong sense of obligation to the community; men who lived not to
gain advantage for themselves, but to meet the solemn obligations
which had been laid on them by the very fact that they were privileged. From them the country would get its leadership; to them it
could look for the higher values—of thought, of conduct, of personal
deportment—to give it strength and virtue.

Lee embodied the noblest elements of this aristocratic ideal. 6
Through him, the landed nobility justified itself. For four years,
the Southern states had fought a desperate war to uphold the

ideals for which Lee stood. In the end, it almost seemed as if the Confederacy fought for Lee; as if he himself was the Confederacy . . . the best thing that the way of life for which the Confederacy stood could ever have to offer. He had passed into legend before Appomattox. Thousands of tired, underfed, poorly clothed Confederate soldiers, long since past the simple enthusiasm of the early days of the struggle, somehow considered Lee the symbol of everything for which they had been willing to die. But they could not quite put this feeling into words. If the Lost Cause, sanctified by so much heroism and so many deaths, had a living justification, its justification was General Lee.

Grant, the son of a tanner on the Western frontier, was every- 7 thing Lee was not. He had come up the hard way and embodied nothing in particular except the eternal toughness and sinewy fiber of the men who grew up beyond the mountains. He was one of a body of men who owed reverence and obeisance to no one, who were self-reliant to a fault, who cared hardly anything for the past but who had a sharp eye for the future.

These frontier men were the precise opposites of the tidewater 8 aristocrats. Back of them, in the great surge that had taken people over the Alleghenies and into the opening Western country, there was a deep, implicit dissatisfaction with a past that had settled into grooves. They stood for democracy, not from any reasoned conclusion about the proper ordering of human society, but simply because they had grown up in the middle of democracy and knew how it worked. Their society might have privileges, but they would be privileges each man had won for himself. Forms and patterns meant nothing. No man was born to anything, except perhaps to a chance to show how far he could rise. Life was competition.

Yet along with this feeling had come a deep sense of belonging 9 to a national community. The Westerner who developed a farm, opened a shop, or set up in business as a trader could hope to prosper only as his own community prospered—and his community ran from the Atlantic to the Pacific and from Canada down to Mexico. If the land was settled, with towns and highways and accessible markets, he could better himself. He saw his fate in terms of the nation's own destiny. As its horizons expanded, so did his. He had, in other words, an acute dollars-and-cents stake in the continued growth and development of his country.

And that, perhaps, is where the contrast between Grant and   10
Lee becomes most striking. The Virginia aristocrat, inevitably,
saw himself in relation to his own region. He lived in a static society which could endure almost anything except change. Instinctively, his first loyalty would go to the locality in which that
society existed. He would fight to the limit of endurance to defend it, because in defending it he was defending everything that
gave his own life its deepest meaning.

The Westerner, on the other hand, would fight with an equal   11
tenacity for the broader concept of society. He fought so because
everything he lived by was tied to growth, expansion, and a constantly widening horizon. What he lived by would survive or fall
with the nation itself. He could not possibly stand by unmoved in
the face of an attempt to destroy the Union. He would combat it
with everything he had, because he could only see it as an effort
to cut the ground out from under his feet.

So Grant and Lee were in complete contrast, representing two   12
diametrically opposed elements in American life. Grant was the
modern man emerging; beyond him, ready to come on the stage,
was the great age of steel and machinery, of crowded cities and a
restless burgeoning vitality. Lee might have ridden down from the
old age of chivalry, lance in hand, silken banner fluttering over his
head. Each man was the perfect champion of his cause, drawing
both his strengths and his weaknesses from the people he led.

Yet it was not all contrast, after all. Different as they were—in   13
background, in personality, in underlying aspiration—these two
great soldiers had much in common. Under everything else, they
were marvelous fighters. Furthermore, their fighting qualities
were really very much alike.

Each man had, to begin with, the great virtue of utter tenacity   14
and fidelity. Grant fought his way down the Mississippi Valley in
spite of acute personal discouragement and profound military
handicaps. Lee hung on in the trenches at Petersburg after hope
itself had died. In each man there was an indomitable quality. . . .
the born fighter's refusal to give up as long as he can still remain
on his feet and lift his two fists.

Daring and resourcefulness they had, too; the ability to think   15
faster and move faster than the enemy. These were the qualities
which gave Lee the dazzling campaigns of Second Manassas and
Chancellorsville and won Vicksburg for Grant.

Lastly, and perhaps greatest of all, there was the ability, at the   16
end, to turn quickly from war to peace once the fighting was
over. Out of the way these two men behaved at Appomattox
came the possibility of a peace of reconciliation. It was a possibility not wholly realized, in the years to come, but which did, in
the end, help the two sections to become one nation again . . .
after a war whose bitterness might have seemed to make such a
reunion wholly impossible. No part of either man's life became
him more than the part he played in this brief meeting in the
McLean house at Appomattox. Their behavior there put all succeeding generations of Americans in their debt. Two great Americans, Grant and Lee—very different, yet under everything very
much alike. Their encounter at Appomattox was one of the great
moments of American history.

UNDERSTANDING DETAILS

1. What two conflicting views of American life does the author
   believe these two generals represented?
2. What special qualities of Grant and Lee does Catton contrast to
   achieve his purpose? What qualities does he compare?
3. How did both Grant and Lee respond to progress and change
   in general? Explain your answer in detail.
4. What does Catton imply about the behavior of these two generals at Appomattox Court House? According to this essay,
   why was the encounter of Grant and Lee at Appomattox "one
   of the great moments of American history" (paragraph 16)?

ANALYZING MEANING

1. What is Catton's purpose in this essay? What truths, according
   to the author, needed to be made clear about these two great
   Civil War generals? Why did Catton study similarities as well
   as differences in these two men?
2. What does Catton mean when he says, "Life was competition"
   (paragraph 8) in Grant's philosophy? What aspects of this philosophy do you see in today's society?
3. In what ways were Lee and Grant emblems of the past and the
   future, respectively?
4. About the actions of these men at Appomattox, Catton says,
   "Their behavior there put all succeeding generations of Ameri-

cans in their debt" (paragraph 16). What does he mean by this statement? What influences of these two men can we still see in our culture today?

DISCOVERING RHETORICAL STRATEGIES

1. Which of the four main methods of organizing a comparison/contrast essay does Catton use? How many paragraphs does the author spend on each part of his comparison? Why do you think he spends this amount of time on each?
2. What transitional words or phrases does the author use to move from one part of this essay to the next? Give at least three specific examples. Do these devices hold the essay together effectively? Explain your answer.
3. In what ways does the last paragraph of this essay echo the first paragraph? Why is this echoing technique an effective way to end the essay?
4. What other rhetorical strategies besides comparison and contrast does Catton use to achieve his purpose in this essay? Give examples of each strategy.

MAKING CONNECTIONS

1. Like Bruce Catton, Alice Walker ("Beauty: When the Other Dancer Is the Self") describes one particular moment in time when life was changed forever. What similarities can you find between the two important events described by each of these authors?
2. First, Catton contrasts Grant and Lee, and then he compares them. How is this structural approach different from the comparison/contrast essays written by Germaine Greer ("A Child Is Born") and William Ouchi ("Japanese and American Workers: Two Casts of Mind")? Which organizational technique do you find most effective? Explain your answer.
3. According to Catton, Grant and Lee each represented "the strengths of two conflicting currents that, through them, had come into final collision" (paragraph 3). Along the same lines, how does an "unfamiliar country" symbolize old age for Malcolm Cowley in "The View from 80"? In other words, how do both authors use symbols to give significance to everyday events?

IDEAS FOR DISCUSSION/WRITING

Preparing To Write

Write freely about heroes and heroines in American society: Name some public figures you respect. Why do you admire them? What qualifies someone as a heroic figure in your opinion? What do most of the heroes and heroines you admire have in common? How are they different? How are history and heroic figures related in your mind?

Choosing a Topic

1. In an essay written for your classmates, compare and/or contrast two famous people in history. As Catton did, try to explain what forces in society these figures represent. Decide on a clear focus and point of view before you begin.
2. Choose two people who have had a significant influence on your life. Then, compare and/or contrast how they have affected you.
3. America has had many new beginnings throughout its history. The time at the end of the Civil War, discussed in this essay, was one of them. Explain to your classmates another new beginning for America. What were the details of this new start? Who were the heroes? Where, when, how, and why did it take place?

Before beginning your essay, you might want to consult the checklists on pages 337–338.

A Child Is Born

Germaine Greer is one of the world's best-known and most controversial feminist authors. Australian by birth, she earned degrees at the universities of Melbourne and Sydney, then won a scholarship to Cambridge University in England, where she received a doctorate in Shakespeare. Early jobs as a teacher and a television actress gave way to a career as a writer and a political activist. Her first book, *The Female Eunuch* (1970), is a sharply written indictment of women for allowing themselves to be passively stereotyped, subjugated, and symbolically castrated by society. *The Obstacle Race* (1979) followed, a survey of the trials and triumphs of women painters throughout history. *Sex and Destiny: The Politics of Human Fertility* (1984) is a well-researched, thorough investigation into the global politics of human reproduction. More recent publications include *Shakespeare* (1985), *The Madwoman's Underclothes* (1986), *Kissing the Rod: An Anthology of Seventeenth-Century Women's Verse* (1988), *Daddy, We Hardly Knew You* (1989), *The Change: Women, Aging and the Menopause* (1991), and *The Whole Woman* (1999). Through her books, numerous articles, and television appearances, Greer continues to project a spirited, stimulating, and intelligent defense of women's rights. She lectures occasionally at the University of Warwick near her home in Coventry, England, and describes herself as an "anarchist," an "atheist," and a "supergroupie" with great affection for jazz and rock music.

Preparing to Read

In the following essay, excerpted from *Sex and Destiny*, Greer compares the role of children in traditional agricultural societies with that of children in Western industrialized countries. As you prepare to read this essay, take a few moments to think about your own family structure and that of other people you know: What has happened to the Western family unit over the last fifty to a hundred years? Does it play a more important or less important role in our society? What are the advantages of our society's concept of the "family"? The disadvantages? How do you think our family life differs from that of Eastern cultures? What are the advantages and disadvantages of these two approaches to the family unit? What do you think will be the future role of the family in the Western world?

In many societies women still go forth from their mother's 1 house at marriage to live with a mother-in-law and the wives of their husband's brothers. It is a truism of anthropology that such women do not become members of their new family until they have borne a child. If we consider that in such societies the marriage was quite likely to have been arranged, it is understandable that the bride, too, longs for the child who will stand in the same intimate relationship to her as she with her own mother. The Western interpretation of such mores is that they are backward, cruel and wrong; it is assumed that the sexual relations between the spouses are perfunctory and exploitative and that all mothers-in-law are unjust and vindictive. At a conference to mark International Women's Day at the U.N. Secretariat in Vienna in 1981, two members of an organization called Amnesty for Women provided the assembled women with a description of typical Muslim marriage which was no more than a coarse ethnocentric libel. The one Muslim woman on the panel, who may have been virtually the only Muslim present, looked up in astonishment to hear the domestic life of her people described in terms of the utmost squalor, but, less willing to divide the consensus than were the speakers, she decided to hold her tongue. One of the greatest difficulties in the way of feminists who are not chauvinistic and want to learn from women who still live within a female society is the tendency of those women to withdraw into silent opposition when participating in international forums conducted in languages which they cannot speak with fluency; women officials of the Sudanese government told me that they had given up going to international conferences, even though the trips were a tremendous treat, because they were tired of being told about their own lives instead of being consulted.

Thus in the West we would regard it as outrageous that a 2 woman could lose her own name and become known as the mother of her firstborn, once she has borne it—although of course most of us do not protest against the sinking of the woman's lineage under her husband's name at marriage. In many traditional societies the relationship between mother and child is more important than the relationship between husband and wife: In some, indeed, the child's relationship with the rest of his family is as important as or even more important than either. Among the fierce Rajputs, a bridegroom leaving to collect his bride "sucks his mother's breast to signify that the highest duty of a Rajput is to uphold the dignity of his mother's milk."

The woman who satisfies the longings of her peers by produc- 3 ing the child they are all anxious to see finds her achievement celebrated in ways that dramatize her success. Among the few first-person accounts of how this works in practice is this one from a young Sylheti woman:

> If a girl is lucky, and her parents are alive, she goes to her mother's house for the last few months of her pregnancy and about the first three months of the baby's life. There she gets a lot of love and care. She is asked, "What would you like to eat? What do you fancy?" All the time she is looked after. The whole matter of pregnancy is one of celebration. When the baby is born it is an occasion of joy for the whole family. The naming ceremony is lovely. It is held when the baby is seven days old. A new dress is bought for it and a new sari for the mother. There is feasting and singing until late at night. The women and girls gather and sing songs. Garlands of tumeric and garlic are worn to ward off evil spirits. That's when the name is chosen. . . . The cere- mony is held for the birth of a boy or a girl. Of course it is considered better to have a boy, but the birth of a girl is celebrated with the same joy by the women in the family. We sit together eating *pan* and singing. Some of us might be young unmarried girls, others aged ladies of forty or fifty. There are so many jokes, so much laughter. People look so funny eating *pan* and singing. The men don't take much part. They may come and have a look at the baby, but the singing, the gathering together at night—it is all women. The songs are simple songs which are rarely written down. They are about the lives of women in Bengal.

Among the rewards of pregnancy in this case, as in many oth- 4 ers, is that the woman gets to go home to visit her mother and sis- ters; the nostalgic tone of the description, which is clearly tinged with rose, may be the product of the contrast that this young woman finds in England. Another of the Asian women who found a voice in Amrit Wilson's book gives a similarly rosy pic- ture of rearing a child in Bangladesh:

> In Bangladesh children under the age of five or six are looked after by the whole family. All the children of the joint family are looked after together.

They are taken to the pond for a bath perhaps by one daughter-in-law, and she bathes them all. Then they all come in and sit down to eat. Perhaps the youngest daughter-in-law has cooked the meal. Another woman feeds them. As for playing, the children play out of doors with natural objects. Here people say that Asian children don't play with toys. In Bangladesh they don't need toys. They make their own simple things. . . . In the afternoon they love to hear Rupthoka [fairy tales]. Maybe there is a favorite aunt; she tells them these stories. But at night when they get sleepy they always go to their mother and sleep in her embrace. But other women do help a lot; in fact they have such strong relationships with the child that it is not uncommon for them to be called Big Mother or Small Mother.

The system does not always work as well as it does in this ac-   5
count by Hashmat Ara Begum, but it is the ideal that lies behind the common sight of children carrying children in the subcontinent. In the tone of her explanation of the fact that Asian children do not have toys, the strain of confrontation with the industrialized lifestyle can be sensed; deprived of the real Bangladeshi world, Asian children have yet to develop a taste for the expensive surrogate objects with which we placate our children for their lack of human contact. The Asian lifestyle seems austere to consumerist society; to the immigrants, the British lifestyle seems inhuman. Transplanted from their villages to the decaying inner suburbs of dull industrial towns, these women suffer greatly, despite the fact that they have a better chance of bearing healthy children than they had at home. Their misery is not simply explained by their ignorance of the language or the thinly disguised racist hostility that they encounter. Their entire support system has vanished; from never being alone they have moved into a situation of utter solitude, for which their relative affluence cannot compensate. The crisis of childbirth, faced, as it is for all women in the West, without psychological support and involving severe outrage to Muslim modesty, frequently precipitates them into depressed states. (The attitude of medical personnel to these women, based as it is on utter incomprehension of their terror and despair, is a contributory factor.) Amrit Wilson went to visit one such woman, forced into emotional dependence upon a husband who was working long hours to give the family the good life they had come to England to find. "Late, late at night my husband comes home. He loves the babies. He is a good husband, but what can he do? And what can I do? How can I live, sister, how can I live?"

Children in the West, then, are a far greater burden than they   6
are in the countries that these women came from; not only are
women more likely to be dealing with the children alone, but the
children themselves are more demanding than they are in a non-
consumer society. In the Egyptian village, for example, "there are
invariably at least two grown-up women attending to the rearing
of the child. As the newborn baby, or even any child, has no special cradle, cot or bed, it always sleeps by its mother or sits on her
lap."

The Egyptian baby is not trained in consumer behavior any   7
more than the Bangladeshi baby. In the last hundred years the
consumerism of Western babies has gone ahead by leaps and
bounds. The baby carriage, a relatively modern invention, is the
most expensive item, and, significantly, the one that is paraded
before the public; to it are added the baby's layette, crib, cot, diapers, and the like, all clearly designed for baby's use and therefore
instantly obsolescent. Some of the impedimenta, such as bootees
and talcum powder, are completely useless, but most are designed
to keep baby dry, tidy and out of contact, hemmed in from the
real world by bassinet walls or perambulator covers or, most
bizarre of all, the bars of the playpen. The child who has no pram,
no crib, and certainly no room of its own cannot be escaped, especially if it cannot be put down on the floor, either because precious water cannot be spared to wash it very often or because it is
made of dirt. Children who are constantly attached to adults obviously cannot be segregated; they must come into the work place
and into the sleeping place and the patterns of both must be mod-
ified to receive them. Often drudgery separates adults from children, if they are working on road gangs or construction sites, for
example, but the separation is seen as another of the trials of
poverty.

The child's socialization will be carried out in the midst of his   8
kin group; it is not easy to drive the wedge of professional care
into traditional families. There is no need of a play group, because
the play group is right there, nor for that matter of the nursery
school. The noise of children is a constant accompaniment to
daily life, and probably a good deal less fraying to the nerves than
the cacophony of consumer society. Mothers are not so vulnerable
to infantile ill temper because they do not have to take sole responsibility for it. Reward and punishment are doled out accord-

ing to family practice; mothers don't have to rush to Dr. Spock to find out how to deal with some particularly antisocial manifestation. The family ethos prevails as it has prevailed for generations, without anxious soul-searching, which is not to say that it is always humane or just, but simply that it is not a cause of internalized tension. The extended family is in many ways a boring and oppressive environment, but it does offer a sense and a context to mothering which two-bedroom ranch houses in the suburbs do not. The children may be grubby, they may be less well-nourished than Western children, but they have a clear sense of the group they belong to and their own role within it. They will not be found screaming for all the goods displayed in the supermarket (and to make them so scream is the point of the display), until their frantic mothers lose control and bash them and then compound the injury by poking sweets into their mouths.

The closeness of adults and children in traditional societies is partly a result of the exclusion of women from the public sphere and their generally low levels of literacy, but these disabilities are in part compensated for by the centrality of the household in daily life. There is little in the way of public or commercial amusement; entertainments and celebrations take place in the household and children are included. Men may go to the coffeehouse or the mudhif for their entertainment, but their freedom to do so is not regarded with envy, for women and children are capable of having riotous good fun on their own. Perhaps the most important difference between mothering in traditional societies and mothering in our own is that the traditional mother's role increases in complexity and importance as she grows older. If she is skillful and fortunate enough to keep her sons and her sons' wives as members of her household, she will enjoy their service and companionship as she grows older. She will have time to play with her grandchildren; her flagging pace will match their unsteady steps. As she sinks into feebleness, her sons' wives will assume her responsibilities and care for her until the last. The ideal situation is not inevitable—dispossessed old women can be found begging and dying on the streets of India—but success is possible. The role of matriarch is a positive one which can be worked towards by an intelligent and determined woman. Mistreating daughters-in-law is unlikely to further her aims, because discontented wives are a principal cause of the fissioning of the extended family. Because the household is an essential unit in the production of goods and services, her role as manager of it is a challenging one, beside which the role of the Western housewife seems downright impoverished. Even her absent daughters, whose departure for their husbands' dwelling places caused her such grief, keep close to her in feeling. One of the most remarkable aspects of Elizabeth Warnock Fernea's life as the veiled wife of an American anthropologist in an Iraqi village was the utter certainty of the Iraqi women that she must have been as attached to her mother as they were:

> "Where is your mother?" Kulthum asked. I told her she was in America far away. . . . The women clucked in sympathy.
> "Poor girl," they said, "poor child. . . ."
> "When you have children, you will not feel so alone without your mother," prophesied Kulthum.

When she announced her impending return to America, the women saw only one reason for their going: 10

> "Ask Mr. Bob to bring your mother, and then you'll never have to leave us and go back to America."

Mrs. Fernea did not volunteer to reveal the truth about the status of mothers in Western society. Eventually the Iraqi women confronted her with it: 11

> "And is it true," asked Basima, "that in America they put all the old women in houses by themselves, away from their families?"
> I admitted that this was sometimes true and tried to explain, but my words were drowned in the general murmur of disapproval.
> "What a terrible place that must be!"
> "How awful!"
> "And their children let them go?"
> . . . . It had never occurred to me before, but the idea of old people's homes must have been particularly reprehensible to these women whose world lay within the family unit and whose lives of toil and childbearing were rewarded in old age, when they enjoyed repose and respect as members of their children's households.

This discussion of the difference in the role of mothers in highly industrialized bureaucratic communities and in traditional agricultural communities is not meant as a panegyric of the disappearing world, but simply to indicate something of the context in which the birthrate in the developed world has fallen. There is   12 little point in feeling sorry for Western mothers, who are most often as anxious to be freed of their children as their children are to be freed of them. The inhabitants of old people's homes and retirement villages do not sit sobbing and railing against destiny, although they do compete with each other in displaying the rather exiguous proofs of their children's affection. As the recession bites deeper and unemployment rises, more and more adult children are having to remain dependent on their parents, who are lamenting loudly and wondering more vociferously than usual why they let themselves in for such a thankless task as parenting. The point of the contrast is simply to caution the people of the highly industrialized countries which wield such massive economic and cultural sway over the developing world against assuming that one of the things they must rescue the rest of the world from is parenting. Because motherhood is virtually meaningless in our society is no ground for supposing that the fact that women are still defined by their mothering function in other societies is simply an index of their oppression. We have at least to consider the possibility that a successful matriarch might well pity Western feminists for having been duped into futile competition with men in exchange for the companionship and love of children and other women.

UNDERSTANDING DETAILS

1. How do traditional and Western childbearing methods vary? How does Greer account for these differences?
2. What are the main differences and similarities between the roles of mothers in traditional and Western societies? Explain your answer in detail.
3. What is the relationship between consumerism and child rearing in Greer's comparison? What behavior results from this relationship?
4. According to the author, what is the precise difference between the extended family and the nuclear family?

ANALYZING MEANING

1. Of all the examples the author cites in her essay, which one convinces you most effectively that raising children in tradi-

tional countries is a more meaningful activity than it is in Western society? Why?

2. Why do you think the extended family has become relatively obsolete in the Western world? In your opinion, what is its future fate in Western society? Explain your reasoning.

3. This essay ends on a fairly negative note. Explain in your own words Greer's last sentence (paragraph 12), and discuss its implications about Western society. In your opinion, is this an effective ending? Why or why not?

4. How are children socialized in traditional societies? What aspects of this process would not be appropriate in a "consumer society"? Explain your answer in detail.

DISCOVERING RHETORICAL STRATEGIES

1. How does the author organize her comparison? Which of the four main types of organization best describes Greer's essay? Is this format a good choice for accomplishing her purpose? Why or why not?

2. Does the author omit or downplay any of the distinctions between Western and traditional child care that might be detrimental to her argument? If so, what are these distinctions?

3. What opinions of her own does Greer reveal about methods of child rearing in the two communities? What references betray these opinions?

4. Why do you think Greer has chosen comparison/contrast to prove her point in this essay? How effective is this technique? What other rhetorical modes does the author use to state her case?

MAKING CONNECTIONS

1. Imagine that Germaine Greer, Bill Cosby ("The Baffling Question"), and Michael Dorris ("The Broken Cord") are having a conversation about the "rewards" of pregnancy. Compare and contrast Cosby's and Dorris's opinions about the trials and tribulations of being pregnant and delivering a baby in the United States with Greer's more optimistic version of what goes on in non-Western societies. Which of these authors would you agree with most? Explain your answer.

2. Based on the information contained in Judy Brady's "Why I Want a Wife" and Greer's article, what do you think the main differences are between the treatment of women in Western and non-Western societies. In which of these societies are women valued more highly? Explain your answer.

3. Just as Greer's article reveals a great deal about American child-raising customs through her comparison with non-Western methods, so does William Ouchi's "Japanese and American Workers: Two Casts of Mind" illustrate a number of problems in the corporate United States by contrasting our work ethic with that of the Japanese. Do Greer and Ouchi identify any of the same flaws in American society? If so, what are they?

IDEAS FOR DISCUSSION/WRITING

Preparing to Write

Write freely about the Western family: What generally constitutes a "family" in the industrialized West? How has its makeup changed over the years? Is the family unit a significant part of our society, or is the individual more important? What facts and observations support your opinion? In what ways do you think the American family will change in the next fifty to a hundred years? In your opinion, will these be positive or negative changes?

Choosing a Topic

1. For your college sociology class, compare the extended family with the nuclear family by discussing the principal advantages and disadvantages of each.

2. As objectively as possible, describe to a friend some of your family's cherished traditions. When possible, compare and/or contrast your family's traditions with those of your friend's family. Give someone you like more insight into yourself by helping the person understand which traditions your family values.

3. You have been asked to make a prediction about the future of the American family for *The Sociological Quarterly*. The readers of this journal are especially interested in whether the family as a group or the family as individuals will become more prominent after the year 2000. Offer your prediction and explain

your reasoning in a comparison/contrast essay to be published in this periodical.

Before beginning your essay, you might want to consult the checklists on pages 337–338.

WILLIAM OUCHI   (1943–   )

Japanese and American Workers: Two Casts of Mind

Born in Honolulu, Hawaii, William Ouchi is an internationally known expert on business management—particularly on the relationship between American and Japanese corporations. Ouchi was educated at Williams College, Stanford University, and the University of Chicago; since then, he has taught in business programs at several major American universities, most recently at the Anderson Graduate School of Management at UCLA, where he is vice dean and faculty director of the Executive Education Program. The author has also served as associate study director for the National Opinion Research Center and as a business consultant for many of America's most successful companies. He has written three books on organization and management: *Theory Z: How American Business Can Meet the Japanese Challenge* (1981) is a thorough analysis of the differences between American and Japanese industrial productivity; *The M-Form Society: How American Teamwork Can Recapture the Competitive Edge* (1984) is the result of a three-year study by a team of sixteen researchers led by Ouchi; and *Organizational Economics* (1986) is a textbook coedited with Jay Barney. He advises students using *The Prose Reader* to spend plenty of time revising their material. "No one writes a good first draft," he explains. "You must continue to revise your work till you understand exactly what you want to say and you have constructed a group of sentences that say it clearly." Ouchi lives with his wife and three children in Santa Monica, California, where he enjoys playing golf as frequently as his busy schedule allows.

Preparing to Read

The following essay, excerpted from *Theory Z*, compares and contrasts Japan's collective work ethic with the American spirit of individualism. As you prepare to read this essay, think about your own work ethic: When you study, for example, do you prefer working alone or with a group of people? What kinds of jobs have you held during your life? Did they stress individual or collective behavior? Were you often rewarded for individual achievement, or did you work mostly within a homogeneous group? In what sort of work environment are you most productive? Most satisfied?

Perhaps the most difficult aspect of the Japanese for Western- 1 ers to comprehend is the strong orientation to collective values, particularly a collective sense of responsibility. Let me illustrate with an anecdote about a visit to a new factory in Japan owned and operated by an American electronics company. The American company, a particularly creative firm, frequently attracts attention within the business community for its novel approaches to planning, organizational design, and management systems. As a consequence of this corporate style, the parent company determined to make a thorough study of Japanese workers and to design a plant that would combine the best of East and West. In their study they discovered that Japanese firms almost never make use of individual work incentives, such as piecework or even individual performance appraisal tied to salary increases. They concluded that rewarding individual achievement and individual ability is always a good thing.

In the final assembly area of their new plant long lines of young 2 Japanese women wired together electronic products on a piece-rate system: The more you wired, the more you got paid. About two months after opening, the head foreladies approached the plant manager. "Honorable plant manager," they said humbly as they bowed, "we are embarrassed to be so forward, but we must speak to you because all of the girls have threatened to quit work this Friday." (To have this happen, of course, would be a great disaster for all concerned.) "Why," they wanted to know, "can't our plant have the same compensation system as other Japanese companies? When you hire a new girl, her starting wage should be fixed by her age. An eighteen-year-old should be paid more than a sixteen-year-old. Every year on her birthday, she should receive an automatic increase in pay. The idea that any one of us can be more productive than another must be wrong, because none of us in final assembly could make a thing unless all of the other people in the plant had done their jobs right first. To single one person out as being more productive is wrong and is also personally humiliating to us." The company changed its compensation system to the Japanese model.

Another American company in Japan had installed a suggestion   3
system much as we have in the United States. Individual workers were encouraged to place suggestions to improve productivity into special boxes. For an accepted idea the individual received a bonus amounting to some fraction of the productivity savings realized from his or her suggestion. After a period of six months, not a single suggestion had been submitted. The American managers were puzzled. They had heard many stories of the inventiveness, the commitment, and the loyalty of Japanese workers, yet not one suggestion to improve productivity had appeared.

The managers approached some of the workers and asked why   4
the suggestion system had not been used. The answer: "No one can come up with a work improvement idea alone. We work together, and any ideas that one of us may have are actually developed by watching others and talking to others. If one of us was singled out for being responsible for such an idea, it would embarrass all of us." The company changed to a group suggestion system, in which workers collectively submitted suggestions. Bonuses were paid to groups which would save bonus money until the end of the year for a party at a restaurant or, if there was enough money, for family vacations together. The suggestions and productivity improvements rained down on the plant.

One can interpret these examples in two quite different ways.   5
Perhaps the Japanese commitment to collective values is an anachronism that does not fit with modern industrialism but brings economic success despite that collectivism. Collectivism seems to be inimical to the kind of maverick creativity exemplified in Benjamin Franklin, Thomas Edison, and John D. Rockefeller. Collectivism does not seem to provide the individual incentive to excel which has made a great success of American enterprise. Entirely apart from its economic effects, collectivism implies a loss of individuality, a loss of the freedom to be different, to hold fundamentally different values from others.

The second interpretation of the examples is that the Japanese   6
collectivism is economically efficient. It causes people to work well together and to encourage one another to better efforts. Industrial

life requires interdependence of one person on another. But a less obvious but far-reaching implication of the Japanese collectivism for economic performance has to do with accountability.

In the Japanese mind, collectivism is neither a corporate or in- 7 dividual goal to strive for nor a slogan to pursue. Rather, the nature of things operates so that nothing of consequence occurs as a result of individual effort. Everything important in life happens as a result of teamwork or collective effort. Therefore, to attempt to assign individual credit or blame to results is unfounded. A Japanese professor of accounting, a brilliant scholar trained at Carnegie-Mellon University who teaches now in Tokyo, remarked that the status of accounting systems in Japanese industry is primitive compared to those in the United States. Profit centers, transfer prices, and computerized information systems are barely known even in the largest Japanese companies, whereas they are commonplace in even small United States organizations. Though not at all surprised at the difference in accounting systems, I was not at all sure that the Japanese were primitive. In fact, I thought their system a good deal more efficient than ours.

Most American companies have basically two accounting sys- 8 tems. One system summarizes the overall financial state to inform stockholders, bankers, and other outsiders. That system is not of interest here. The other system, called the managerial or cost accounting system, exists for an entirely different reason. It measures in detail all of the particulars of transactions between departments, divisions, and key individuals in the organization, for the purpose of untangling the interdependencies between people. When, for example, two departments share one truck for deliveries, the cost accounting system charges each department for part of the cost of maintaining the truck and driver, so that at the end of the year, the performance of each department can be individually assessed, and the better department's manager can receive a larger raise. Of course, all of this information processing costs money, and furthermore may lead to arguments between the departments over whether the costs charged to each are fair.

In a Japanese company a short-run assessment of individual per- 9 formance is not wanted, so the company can save the considerable expense of collecting and processing all of that information. Companies still keep track of which department uses a truck how often and for what purposes, but like-minded people can interpret some simple numbers for themselves and adjust their behavior accordingly. Those insisting upon clear and precise measurement for the purpose of advancing individual interests must have an elaborate information system. Industrial life, however, is essentially integrated and interdependent. No one builds an automobile alone, no one carries through a banking transaction alone. In a sense the Japanese value of collectivism fits naturally into an industrial setting, whereas the Western individualism provides constant conflicts. The image that comes to mind is of Chaplin's silent film "Modern Times" in which the apparently insignificant hero played by Chaplin successfully fights against the unfeeling machinery of industry. Modern industrial life can be aggravating, even hostile, or natural: All depends on the fit between our culture and our technology.

The *shinkansen* or "bullet train" speeds across the rural areas of   10
Japan giving a quick view of cluster after cluster of farmhouses surrounded by rice paddies. This particular pattern did not develop purely by chance, but as a consequence of the technology peculiar to the growing of rice, the staple of the Japanese diet. The growing of rice requires construction and maintenance of an irrigation system, something that takes many hands to build. More importantly, the planting and the harvesting of rice can only be done efficiently with the cooperation of twenty or more people. The "bottom line" is that a single family working alone cannot produce enough rice to survive, but a dozen families working together can produce a surplus. Thus the Japanese have had to develop the capacity to work together in harmony, no matter what the forces of disagreement or social disintegration, in order to survive.

Japan is a nation built entirely on the tips of giant, suboceanic   11
volcanoes. Little of the land is flat and suitable for agriculture. Terraced hillsides make use of every available square foot of arable land. Small homes built very close together further conserve the land. Japan also suffers from natural disasters such as earthquakes and hurricanes. Traditionally homes are made of light construction materials, so a house falling down during a disaster will not crush its occupants and also could be quickly and inexpensively rebuilt. During the feudal period until the Meiji restoration of 1868, each feudal lord sought to restrain his subjects from moving from one village to the next for fear that a neighboring lord might

amass enough peasants with which to produce a large agricultural surplus, hire an army, and pose a threat. Apparently bridges were not commonly built across rivers and streams until the late nineteenth century, since bridges increased mobility between villages.

Taken all together, this characteristic style of living paints the picture of a nation of people who are homogeneous with respect to race, history, language, religion, and culture. For centuries and generations these people have lived in the same village next door to the same neighbors. Living in close proximity and in dwellings which gave very little privacy, the Japanese survived through their capacity to work together in harmony. In this situation, it was inevitable that the one most central social value which emerged, the one value without which the society could not continue, was that an individual does not matter.   12

To the Western soul this is a chilling picture of society. Subordinating individual tastes to the harmony of the group and knowing that individual needs can never take precedence over the interests of all is repellent to the Western citizen. But a frequent theme of Western philosophers and sociologists is that individual freedom exists only when people willingly subordinate their self-interests to the social interest. A society composed entirely of self-interested individuals is a society in which each person is at war with the other, a society which has no freedom. This issue, constantly at the heart of understanding society, comes up in every century, and in every society, whether the writer be Plato, Hobbes, or B. F. Skinner. The question of understanding which contemporary institutions lie at the heart of the conflict between automatism and totalitarianism remains. In some ages, the kinship group, the central social institution, mediated between these opposing forces to preserve the balance in which freedom was realized; in other times the church or the government was most critical. Perhaps our present age puts the work organization as the central institution.   13

In order to complete the comparison of Japanese and American living situations, consider a flight over the United States. Looking out of the window high over the state of Kansas, we see a pattern of a single farmhouse surrounded by fields, followed by another single homestead surrounded by fields. In the early 1800s in the state of Kansas there were no automobiles. Your nearest neighbor was perhaps two miles distant; the winters were long, and the   14 snow was deep. Inevitably, the central social values were self-reliance and independence. Those were the realities of that place and age that children had to learn to value.

The key to the industrial revolution was discovering that   15
non-human forms of energy substituted for human forms could increase the wealth of a nation beyond anyone's wildest dreams. But there was a catch. To realize this great wealth, non-human energy needed huge complexes called factories with hundreds, even thousands of workers collected into one factory. Moreover, several factories in one central place made the generation of energy more efficient. Almost overnight, the Western world was transformed from a rural and agricultural country to an urban and industrial state. Our technological advance seems to no longer fit our social structure: In a sense, the Japanese can better cope with modern industrialism. While Americans still busily protect our rather extreme form of individualism, the Japanese hold their individualism in check and emphasize co-operation.

UNDERSTANDING DETAILS

1. Describe in your own words the two different philosophies Ouchi is comparing in this essay.
2. What is Ouchi's main point in this essay? Where does he introduce his purpose?
3. According to the author, what is the most difficult aspect of the Japanese business ethic for Westerners to understand?
4. Why does "collectivism" work better for the Japanese than for the Americans? What is its history in Japan? How is it different from Western "individualism"?

ANALYZING MEANING

1. What is Ouchi's personal opinion of the two value systems he is comparing? At what points does he reveal his preference?
2. Why does the author introduce the origins of American and Japanese living conditions?
3. Which set of business values do you prefer after reading Ouchi's comparison? Explain the reasons for your preference.

4. In what ways is the "work organization" the middle ground between automatism and totalitarianism today? Give examples of this observation from your own experience.

DISCOVERING RHETORICAL STRATEGIES

1. How does Ouchi organize this essay? Outline the main points he covers for each subject.
2. Why do you think the author introduces the two anecdotes at the outset of this essay? How do these stories help Ouchi achieve his purpose?
3. Who do you think is the author's intended audience? How much knowledge about these two subjects does he assume they have? What evidence can you give to support your answer?
4. What other rhetorical strategies besides comparison and contrast does Ouchi use to achieve his purpose in this essay? Give examples of each strategy.

MAKING CONNECTIONS

1. Ouchi argues persuasively that geography has played a major role in Japan's orientation toward "collective" values. Scarcity of land and crowded conditions have forced Japanese citizens to work together harmoniously in ways that seem alien to our concept of self-reliance and independence born on the wide-open American frontier. In what similar ways does geography play a part in the essays by John McPhee ("The Pines"), Susan Austin ("Land and Bones"), Bruce Catton ("Grant and Lee: A Study in Contrasts"), and Annie Dillard ("Living Like Weasels")?
2. Imagine that Ouchi, Germaine Greer ("A Child Is Born"), and Robert Ramirez ("The Barrio") are having a conversation about the importance of cooperation among people who live close together. What would these authors say are the principal difficulties of achieving such necessary cooperation? What would they say are the main rewards? How "cooperative" is the neighborhood in which you live? Do you wish it were more so? Why or why not?
3. Compare the suggestions made by Ouchi and Edwin Bliss ("Managing Your Time") concerning how American busi-

nesses could work more effectively and efficiently. What ideas would you like to share with our business leaders to help make American industry more productive?

IDEAS FOR DISCUSSION/WRITING

Preparing to Write

Write freely about the work ethic that characterizes your immediate environment—at school, at home, or on the job: How do the people in each of these environments feel about one another? How do you feel about them? When are you most productive in these environments? What are the circumstances? Do you work better individually or collectively? Why?

Choosing a Topic

1. Would you prefer to live your social life individually or collectively (as Ouchi defines the two methods)? Explain your preference to a friend, comparing the advantages and disadvantages of both situations. What implications does your preference have? Be sure to make your purpose as clear as possible.
2. Would you rather work in a factory that follows the Japanese or the American method of organization outlined by Ouchi? Explain your preference to your best friend or your immediate supervisor at work. Compare the advantages and disadvantages of both situations. What implications does your preference have? Be sure to make your purpose as clear as possible.
3. *Leisure* magazine has asked you to compare work and leisure from a college student's point of view. Consider the advantages and disadvantages of each. Be sure to decide on a purpose before you begin to write your comparison.

Before beginning your essay, you might want to consult the checklists on pages 337–338.

The Politics of Muscle

Once described as a writer with "unpretentious clarity and force-ful expression," Gloria Steinem is one of the foremost organizers and champions of the modern women's movement. She was born in Toledo, Ohio, earned a B.A. at Smith College, and pursued graduate work in political science at the universities of Delhi and Calcutta in India before returning to America to begin a free-lance career in journalism. One of her earliest and best-known ar-ticles, "I Was a Playboy Bunny," was a witty exposé of the entire Playboy operation written in 1963 after she had worked under-cover for two weeks in the New York City Playboy Club. In 1968 she and Clay Felker founded *New York* magazine; then, in 1972, they started *Ms.* magazine, which sold out its entire 300,000-copy run in eight days. Steinem's subsequent publica-tions have included *Outrageous Acts and Everyday Rebellions* (1983), *Marilyn: Norma Jean* (1986), *Bedside Book of Self-Esteem* (1989), and *Moving Beyond Words* (1994). She has also written several televi-sion scripts and is a frequent contributor to such periodicals as *Es-quire, Vogue, Cosmopolitan, Seventeen,* and *Life.* An articulate and passionate spokesperson for feminist causes, Steinem has been honored nine times by the *World Almanac* as one of the twenty-five most influential women in America.

Preparing to Read

Taken from the author's newest book, *Moving Beyond Words,* "The Politics of Muscle" is actually an introduction to a longer essay entitled "The Strongest Woman in the World," which cele-brates the virtues of women's bodybuilding champion Bev Fran-cis. In this introductory essay, Steinem examines the sexual politics of women's weightlifting and the extent to which a "new beauty standard" has begun to evolve because of pioneers in the sport like Francis. As you prepare to read this essay, examine for a few minutes your own thoughts about the associations Americans make with weakness and strength in both men and women: Which sex do you think of as stronger? In America, what does strength have to do with accomplishment? With failure? Do these associations vary for men and women? What does weakness suggest in American culture? Do these suggestions vary for men and women? What are the positive values Americans associate with muscles and strength? With helplessness and weakness? What are the negative values Americans associate with muscles and strength? With helplessness and weakness? What connections have you made from your experience between physical strength and gender roles?

I come from a generation of women who didn't do sports. 1 Being a cheerleader or a drum majorette was as far as our imaginations or role models could take us. Oh yes, there was also being a strutter—one of a group of girls (and we were girls then) who marched and danced and turned cartwheels in front of the high school band at football games. Did you know that big football universities actually gave strutting scholarships? That shouldn't sound any more bizarre than football scholarships, yet somehow it does. Gender politics strikes again.

But even winning one of those rare positions, the stuff that 2 dreams were made of, was more about body display than about the considerable skill they required. You could forget about trying out for them if you didn't have the right face and figure, and my high school was full of girls who had learned to do back flips and twirl flaming batons, all to no avail. Winning wasn't about being the best in an objective competition or achieving a personal best, or even about becoming healthy or fit. It was about *being chosen*.

That's one of many reasons why I and other women of my 3 generation grew up believing—as many girls still do—that the most important thing about a female body is not what it does but how it looks. The power lies not within us but in the gaze of the observer. In retrospect, I feel sorry for the protofeminist gym teachers who tried so hard to interest us in half-court basketball and other team sports thought suitable for girls in my high school, while we worried about the hairdo we'd slept on rollers all night to achieve. Gym was just a stupid requirement you tried to get out of, with ugly gym suits whose very freedom felt odd on bodies accustomed to being constricted for viewing. My blue-collar neighborhood didn't help much either, for it convinced me that sports like tennis or golf were as remote as the country clubs where they were played—mostly by men anyway. That left tap dancing and ballet as my only exercise, and though my dancing school farmed us out to supermarket openings and local nightclubs, where we danced our hearts out in homemade costumes, those events were about display too, about smiling and pleasing and, even during the rigors of ballet, about looking ethereal and hiding any muscles or strength.

My sports avoidance continued into college, where I went   4 through shock about class and wrongly assumed athletics were only for well-to-do prep school girls like those who brought their own lacrosse sticks and riding horses to school. With no sports training to carry over from childhood—and no place to become childlike, as we must when we belatedly learn basic skills—I clung to my familiar limits. Even at the casual softball games where *Ms.* played the staffs of other magazines, I confined myself to cheering. As the *Ms.* No Stars, we prided ourselves on keeping the same lineup, win or lose, and otherwise disobeying the rules of the jockocracy, so I contented myself with upsetting the men on the opposing team by cheering for their female team members. It's amazing how upset those accustomed to conventional divisions can become when others refuse to be divided by them.

In my case, an interest in the politics of strength had come not   5 from my own experience but from observing the mysterious changes in many women around me. Several of my unathletic friends had deserted me by joining gyms, becoming joggers, or discovering the pleasure of learning to yell and kick in self-defense class. Others who had young daughters described the unexpected thrill of seeing them learn to throw a ball or run with a freedom that hadn't been part of our lives in conscious memory. On campuses, I listened to formerly anorexic young women who said their obsession with dieting had diminished when they discovered strength as a third alternative to the usual fat-versus-thin dichotomy. Suddenly, a skinny, androgynous, "boyish" body was no longer the only way to escape the soft, female, "victim" bodies they associated with their mothers' fates. Added together, these examples of before-and-after-strength changes were so dramatic that the only male analogues I could find were Vietnam amputees whose confidence was bolstered when they entered marathons in wheelchairs or on artificial legs, or paralyzed accident survivors whose sense of themselves was changed when they learned to play wheelchair basketball. Compared to their handicapped female counterparts, however, even those men seemed to be less transformed. Within each category, women had been less encouraged to develop whatever muscle and skills we had.

Since my old habits of ignoring my body and living inside my   6
head weren't that easy to break, it was difficult to change my nonathletic ways. Instead, I continued to learn secondhand from watching my friends, from reading about female strength in other cultures, and from asking questions wherever I traveled.

Though cultural differences were many, there were political   7
similarities in the way women's bodies were treated that went as deep as patriarchy itself. Whether achieved through law and social policy, as in this and other industrialized countries, or by way of tribal practice and religious ritual, as in older cultures, an individual woman's body was far more subject to other people's rules than was that of her male counterpart. Women always seemed to be owned to some degree as the means of reproduction. And as possessions, women's bodies then became symbols of men's status, with a value that was often determined by what was rare. Thus, rich cultures valued thin women, and poor cultures valued fat women. Yet all patriarchal cultures valued weakness in women. How else could male dominance survive? In my own country, for example, women who "belong" to rich white men are often thinner (as in "You can never be too rich or too thin") than those who "belong" to poor men of color; yet those very different groups of males tend to come together in their belief that women are supposed to be weaker than men; that muscles and strength aren't "feminine."

If I had any doubts about the psychological importance of cul-   8
tural emphasis on male/female strength difference, listening to arguments about equality put them to rest. Sooner or later, even the most intellectual discussion came down to men's supposedly superior strength as a justification for inequality, whether the person arguing regretted or celebrated it. What no one seemed to explore, however, was the inadequacy of physical strength as a way of explaining oppression in other cases. Men of European origin hadn't ruled in South Africa because they were stronger than African men, and blacks hadn't been kept in slavery or bad jobs in the United States because whites had more muscles. On the contrary, males of the "wrong" class or color were often confined to

laboring positions precisely because of their supposedly greater strength, just as the lower pay females received was often rationalized by their supposedly lesser strength. Oppression has no logic—just a self-fulfilling prophecy, justified by a self-perpetuating system.

The more I learned, the more I realized that belief in great   9 strength differences between women and men was itself part of the gender mind-game. In fact, we can't really know what those differences might be, because they are so enshrined, perpetuated, and exaggerated by culture. They seem to be greatest during the childbearing years (when men as a group have more speed and upper-body strength, and women have better balance, endurance, and flexibility) but only marginal during early childhood and old age (when females and males seem to have about the same degree of physical strength). Even during those middle years, the range of difference *among* men and *among* women is far greater than the generalized difference *between* males and females as groups. In multiracial societies like ours, where males of some races are smaller than females of others, judgments based on sex make even less sense. Yet we go right on assuming and praising female weakness and male strength.

But there is a problem about keeping women weak, even in a   10 patriarchy. Women are workers, as well as the means of reproduction. Lower-class women are especially likely to do hard physical labor. So the problem becomes: How to make sure female strength is used for work but not for rebellion? The answer is: Make women ashamed of it. Though hard work requires lower-class women to be stronger than their upper-class sisters, for example, those strong women are made to envy and imitate the weakness of women who "belong" to, and are the means of reproduction for, upper-class men—and so must be kept even *more* physically restricted if the lines of race and inheritance are to be kept "pure." That's why restrictive dress, from the chadors, or full-body veils, of the Middle East to metal ankle and neck rings in Africa, from nineteenth-century hoop skirts in Europe to corsets and high heels here, started among upper-class women and then sifted downward as poor women were encouraged to envy or imitate them. So did such bodily restrictions as bound feet in China, or clitoridectomies and infibulations in much of the Middle East and Africa, both of which practices began with women whose bodies were the means of reproduction for the powerful, and gradually became generalized symbols of feminity. In this country, the self-starvation known as anorexia nervosa is mostly a white, upper-middle-class, young-female phenomenon, but all women are encouraged to envy a white and impossibly thin ideal.

Sexual politics are also reflected through differing emphases on   11 the reproductive parts of women's bodies. Whenever a patriarchy wants females to populate a new territory or replenish an old one, big breasts and hips become admirable. Think of the bosomy ideal of this country's frontier days, or the *zaftig*, Marilyn Monroe–type figure that became popular after the population losses of World War II. As soon as increased population wasn't desirable or necessary, hips and breasts were deemphasized. Think of the Twiggy look that arrived in the 1960s.

But whether bosomy or flat, *zaftig* or thin, the female ideal re-   12 mains weak, and it stays that way unless women ourselves organize to change it. Suffragists shed the unhealthy corsets that produced such a tiny-waisted, big-breasted look that fainting and smelling salts became routine. Instead, they brought in bloomers and bicycling. Feminists of today are struggling against social pressures that exalt siliconed breasts but otherwise stick-thin silhouettes. Introducing health and fitness has already led to a fashion industry effort to reintroduce weakness with the waif look, but at least it's being protested. The point is: Only when women rebel against patriarchal standards does female muscle become more accepted.

For these very political reasons, I've gradually come to believe   13 that society's acceptance of muscular women may be one of the most intimate, visceral measures of change. Yes, we need progress everywhere, but an increase in our physical strength could have more impact on the everyday lives of most women than the occasional role model in the boardroom or in the White House.

UNDERSTANDING DETAILS

1. According to Steinem, what is "gender politics" (paragraph 1)?
2. In what ways does Steinem equate "winning" with "being chosen" (paragraph 2)? Why is this an important premise for her essay?
3. What does Steinem mean when she says, "Oppression has no logic" (paragraph 8)? Explain your answer in detail.

4. In what ways does "power" lie with the observer rather than within the female?

ANALYZING MEANING

1. Why does Steinem call the female body a "victim" body (paragraph 5)? What did girls' mothers have to do with this association?
2. Do you agree with the author that a woman's body is "far more subject to other people's rules than [is] that of her male counterpart" (paragraph 7)? Explain your answer giving examples from your own experience.
3. What is Steinem implying about the political overtones connected with female weakness and male strength? According to Steinem, why are these judgments so ingrained in American social and cultural mores?
4. What are Steinem's reasons for saying that "society's acceptance of muscular women may be one of the most intimate, visceral measures of change" (paragraph 13)? Do you agree with this statement or not? Explain your reaction in detail.

DISCOVERING RHETORICAL STRATEGIES

1. Who do you think is Steinem's intended audience for this essay? On what do you base your answer.
2. In your opinion, what is Steinem's primary purpose in this essay? Explain your answer in detail.
3. How appropriate is the title of this essay? What would be some possible alternate titles?
4. What rhetorical modes support the author's comparison/contrast? Give examples of each.

MAKING CONNECTIONS

1. To what extent would Judy Brady ("Why I Want a Wife") agree with Gloria Steinem's assertion that "the most important thing about a female body is not what it does but how it looks" (paragraph 3)? Do you agree or disagree with this assertion? Give at least three reasons for your opinion.
2. If Steinem is correct that American women have not traditionally found power in their muscles, where have they found it? If

you were able to ask Germaine Greer ("A Child Is Born") or Bronwyn Jones ("Arming Myself with a Gun Is Not the Answer") this same question, what do you think their responses would be? With whom would you agree most? Explain your answer.

3. How would Nancy Gibbs ("When Is It Rape?") feel about the revolution Steinem describes in women's bodybuilding that is bringing renewed power and strength to women of all ages. To what extent might Gibbs see this trend as an antidote to the epidemic of sex crimes against women?

IDEAS FOR DISCUSSION/WRITING

Preparing to Write

Write freely about the definition and role of strength and weakness in American society: What does strength generally mean in American society? What does weakness mean? What associations do you have with both modes of behavior? Where do these associations come from? What are the political implications of these associations? The social implications? In what ways are strength and weakness basic to the value system in American culture?

Choosing a Topic

1. Compare two different approaches to the process of succeeding in a specific job or activity. Develop your own guidelines for making the comparison; then, write an essay for your fellow students about the similarities and differences you have observed between these two different approaches. Be sure to decide on a purpose and a point of view before you begin to write.

2. Interview your mother and your father about their views on physical strength in their separate family backgrounds. If you have grandparents or stepparents, interview them as well. Then compare and contrast these various influences in your life. Which of them are alike? Which are different? How have you personally dealt with these similarities and differences? Be sure to decide on a purpose and a point of view before you begin to write.

3. In her essay, Steinem argues that "an increase in our [women's] physical strength could have more impact on the everyday lives

of most women than the occasional role model in the board-room or in the White House" (paragraph 13). Do you agree with the author? Write an essay to be published in your home-town newspaper explaining your views on this issue.

Before beginning your essay, you might want to consult the checklists on pages 337–338.

ANNIE DILLARD   (1945–   )

Living Like Weasels

Born in Pittsburgh, Pennsylvania, Annie Dillard earned her B.A. and M.A. degrees at Hollins College before embarking on a splendid career as a poet, essayist, and literary critic. After early jobs as a columnist for *The Living Wilderness* and an editor at *Harper's Magazine*, Dillard was a Scholar in Residence at Western Washington University and then a Distinguished Professor and Writer in Residence at Wesleyan University, where she currently lives and works. The success of her first book of poems entitled *Tickets for a Prayer Wheel* (1974) was soon eclipsed by the publication of her most important and influential work, *Pilgrim at Tinker Creek* (1974), for which she won a Pulitzer Prize for general non-fiction in 1975. Typical of her early writing, the book chronicles her scientific, philosophical, and spiritual observations while living on Tinker Creek in Virginia's scenic Roanoke Valley. These two books were followed by a number of other popular publications, including *Holy the Firm* (1978), *Living by Fiction* (1982), *Teaching a Stone to Talk: Expeditions and Encounters* (1982), *Encounters With Chinese Writers* (1984), *Inventing the Truth* (1987), *The Writing Life* (1990), *The Living* (1992), *Mornings Like This* (1995), and *For the Time Being* (2000). Often likened to American novelist Henry David Thoreau for her ability to transform anecdotes of animal behavior into transcendental symbols, Dillard lives in Middletown, Connecticut, with her husband, Robert Richardson, and their children Cody Rose, Carin, and Shelly.

Preparing to Read

The following essay, taken from *Teaching the Stone to Talk*, gives us insight into what we can learn from the animal kingdom about living in general. It compares the way a weasel lives out of necessity to the way we live by choice. As you prepare to read this essay, examine for a few minutes your own ideas on the ideal life: What would be the major features of this life? Why would you choose this lifestyle? Do you have any models for this ideal? Is this ideal close to the way you live now? What would you most like to change about your current life?

A weasel is wild. Who knows what he thinks? He sleeps in his underground den, his tail draped over his nose. Sometimes he lives in his den for two days without leaving. Outside, he stalks rabbits, mice, muskrats, and birds, killing more bodies than he can eat warm, and often dragging the carcasses home. Obedient to instinct, he bites his prey at the neck, either splitting the jugular vein at the throat or crunching the brain at the base of the skull, and he does not let go. One naturalist refused to kill a weasel who was socketed into his hand deeply as a rattlesnake. The man could in no way pry the tiny weasel off, and he had to walk half a mile to water, the weasel dangling from his palm, and soak him off like a stubborn label.

And once, says Ernest Thompson Seton—once, a man shot an eagle out of the sky. He examined the eagle and found the dry skull of a weasel fixed by the jaws to his throat. The supposition is that the eagle had pounced on the weasel and the weasel swiveled and bit as instinct taught him, tooth to neck, and nearly won. I would like to have seen that eagle from the air a few weeks or months before he was shot: was the whole weasel still attached to his feathered throat, a fur pendant? Or did the eagle eat what he could reach, gutting the living weasel with his talons before his breast, bending his beak, cleaning the beautiful airborne bones?

I have been reading about weasels because I saw one last week. I startled a weasel who startled me, and we exchanged a long glance.

Twenty minutes from my house, through the woods by the quarry and across the highway, is Hollins Pond, a remarkable piece of shallowness, where I like to go at sunset and sit on a tree trunk. Rollins Pond is also called Murray's Pond; it covers two acres of bottomland near Tinker Creek with six inches of water and six thousand lily pads. In winter, brown-and-white steers stand in the middle of it, merely dampening their hooves; from the distant shore they look like miracle itself, complete with miracle's nonchalance. Now, in summer, the steers are gone. The water lilies have blossomed and spread to a green horizontal plane that is terra firma to plodding blackbirds, and tremulous ceiling to black leeches, crayfish, and carp.

This is, mind you, suburbia. It is a five-minute walk in three directions to rows of houses, though none is visible here. There's a 55 mph highway at one end of the pond, and a nesting pair of wood ducks at the other. Under every bush is a muskrat hole or a beer can. The far end is an alternating series of fields and woods, fields and woods, threaded everywhere with motorcycle tracks— in whose bare clay wild turtles lay eggs.

So. I had crossed the highway, stepped over two low barbed- 6 wire fences, and traced the motorcycle path in all gratitude through the wild rose and poison ivy of the pond's shoreline up into high grassy fields. Then I cut down through the woods to the mossy fallen tree where I sit. This tree is excellent. It makes a dry, upholstered bench at the upper, marshy end of the pond, a plush jetty raised from the thorny shore between a shallow blue body of water and a deep blue body of sky.

The sun had just set. I was relaxed on the tree trunk, en- 7 sconced in the lap of lichen, watching the lily pads at my feet tremble and part dreamily over the thrusting path of a carp. A yellow bird appeared to my right and flew behind me. It caught my eye; I swiveled around—and the next instant, inexplicably, I was looking down at a weasel, who was looking up at me.

Weasel! I'd never seen one wild before. He was ten inches 8 long, thin as a curve, a muscled ribbon, brown as fruitwood, soft-furred, alert. His face was fierce, small and pointed as a lizard's; he would have made a good arrowhead. There was just a dot of chin, maybe two brown hairs' worth, and then the pure white fur began that spread down his underside. He had two black eyes I didn't see, any more than you see a window.

The weasel was stunned into stillness as he was emerging from 9 beneath an enormous shaggy wild rose bush four feet away. I was stunned into stillness twisted backward on the tree trunk. Our eyes locked, and someone threw away the key.

Our look was as if two lovers, or deadly enemies, met unex- 10 pectedly on an overgrown path when each had been thinking of something else: a clearing blow to the gut. It was also a bright blow to the brain, or a sudden beating of brain, with all the charge and intimate grate of rubbed balloons. It emptied our lungs. It felled the forest, moved the fields, and drained the pond; the world dismantled and tumbled into that black hole of eyes. If you and I looked at each other that way, our skulls would split and drop to our shoulders. But we don't. We keep our skulls. So.

He disappeared. This was only last week, and already I don't 11 remember what shattered the enchantment. I think I blinked, I think I retrieved my brain from the weasel's brain and tried to memorize what I was seeing, and the weasel felt the yank of separation, the careening splashdown into real life and the urgent current of instinct. He vanished under the wild rose. I waited motionless, my mind suddenly full of data and my spirit with pleadings, but he didn't return.

Please do not tell me about "approach-avoidance conflicts." I 12 tell you I've been in that weasel's brain for sixty seconds, and he was in mine. Brains are private places, muttering through unique and secret tapes—but the weasel and I both plugged into another tape simultaneously, for a sweet and shocking time. Can I help it if it was a blank?

What goes on in his brain the rest of the time? What does a 13 weasel think about? He won't say. His journal is tracks in clay, a spray of feathers, mouse blood and bone: uncollected, unconnected, loose-leaf, and blown.

I would like to learn, or remember, how to live. I come to 14 Hollins Pond not so much to learn how to live as, frankly, to forget about it. That is, I don't think I can learn from a wild animal how to live in particular—shall I suck warm blood, hold my tail high, walk with my footprints precisely over the prints of my hands?—but I might learn something of mindlessness, something of the purity of living in the physical senses and the dignity of living without bias or motive. The weasel lives in necessity and we live in choice, hating necessity and dying at the last ignobly in its talons. I would like to live as I should, as the weasel lives as he should. And I suspect that for me the way is like the weasel's: open to time and death painlessly, noticing everything, remembering nothing, choosing the given with a fierce and pointed will.

I missed my chance. I should have gone for the throat. I should have lunged for that streak of white under the weasel's chin and held on held on through mud and into the wild rose, held on for a dearer life. We could live under the wild rose wild as weasels, mute and uncomprehending. I could very calmly go wild. I could live two days in the den, curled, leaning on mouse fur, sniffing bird bones, blinking, licking, breathing musk, my hair tangled in the roots of grasses. Down is a good place to go, where the mind is single. Down is out, out of your ever-loving mind and back to your careless senses. I remember muteness as a prolonged and giddy fast, where every moment is a feast of utterance received.

Time and events are merely poured, unremarked, and ingested directly, like blood pulsed into my gut through a jugular vein. Could two live that way? Could two live under the wild rose, and explore by the pond, so that the smooth mind of each is as everywhere present to the other, and as received and as unchallenged, as falling snow?

We could, you know. We can live any way we want. People take vows of poverty, chastity, and obedience—even of silence—by choice.

The thing is to stalk your calling in a certain skilled and supple way, to locate the most tender and live spot and plug into that pulse. This is yielding, not fighting. A weasel doesn't "attack" anything; a weasel lives as he's meant to, yielding at every moment to the perfect freedom of single necessity.

I think it would be well, and proper, and obedient, and pure, to grasp your one necessity and not let it go, to dangle from it limp wherever it takes you. Then even death, where you're going no matter how you live, cannot you part. Seize it and let it seize you up aloft even, till your eyes burn out and drop; let your musky flesh fall off in shreds, and let your very bones unhinge and scatter, loosened over fields, over fields and woods, lightly, thoughtless, from any height at all, from as high as eagles.

UNDERSTANDING DETAILS

1. What is Dillard comparing in this essay? What does suburban life have to do with her comparison?
2. What does Dillard learn from weasels about the process of living?
3. What do you think Dillard means when she says, "The weasel lives in necessity and we live in choice" (paragraph 14)?
4. What about living like a weasel is appealing to Dillard?

ANALYZING MEANING

1. What is important to Dillard about her time at Hollins Creek?
2. Describe in your own words the intense, sixty-second connection between the author and the weasel.
3. What do freedom and mindlessness have to do with each other in this essay?

4. What is Dillard referring to when she tells you "to grasp your own necessity and not let it go, to dangle from it limp wherever it takes you? (paragraph 17)?

DISCOVERING RHETORICAL STRATEGIES

1. In what way does the information Dillard tells us about weasels at the beginning of the essay set up the entire essay? Explain your answer.
2. Who do you think is Dillard's intended audience? On what evidence do you base your answer?
3. What is the author's attitude toward her subject in this essay? What details in the essay reveal this point of view?
4. Which rhetorical modes does Dillard use to support her analogy? How effective are these choices in fulfilling her purpose?

MAKING CONNECTIONS

1. Compare and contrast Annie Dillard's conclusions about the brutish instincts of beasts with Barbara Ehrenreich's similar discoveries about men in battle in "The Ecstasy of War."
2. When Dillard suggests we can learn from weasels how to live our lives, she is using metaphor to clarify a particular topic (in this case, living). In the same fashion, Malcolm Cowley ("The View from 80") and Rita Mae Brown ("Writing as a Moral Act") both use metaphors to help make their prose more vivid and understandable for their readers. Which author uses metaphors most effectively? Why do you feel this way?
3. Compare and contrast Dillard's views on nature with those of Ray Bradbury ("Summer Rituals") and John McPhee ("The Pines"). What role does nature play in each of their lives?

IDEAS FOR DISCUSSION/WRITING

Preparing to Write

Write freely about your ideal existence: What are the main characteristics of this existence? Why are these characteristics important to you? What is "ideal" about them? How would you rank them from most to least important to you? Is your life close to this ideal? What would you like to change in your life to make it more ideal?

Choosing a Topic

1. In an essay written for your peers, explain your ideal existence. Is your ideal based on anyone's life in particular? In what way is he or she a role model for you? Does this person play an active part in helping you reach your ideal existence?
2. Write a comparison essay explaining your attraction to your favorite animal. Why do you like this animal? What do your feelings about this animal tell other people about you?
3. For people unfamiliar with a part of nature you like, compare it to something they know well. Explain as many parallels between the two as you can so that the part of nature becomes more clearly defined as your essay progresses.

Before beginning your essay, you might want to consult the checklists on pages 337–338.

CHAPTER WRITING ASSIGNMENTS

Practicing Comparison/Contrast

1. Compare one feature of your culture to the same aspect of someone else's culture. Make sure you are not making random or biased judgments, but are exploring similarities, differences, and their significance.
2. Compare the styles of two different writers in *The Prose Reader*. First, identify the major features of each writer's style. Then narrow your ideas to a few points of comparison. For example, perhaps one writer is serious and another funny; one writer may write long, complex sentences, while another writes mostly simple sentences. Discuss the differences in the effect each essay has on the reader based on these specific differences in style.
3. Discuss the major differences between two views on a political issue or between two political candidates. Identify the main sources of the differences, and then defend the point of view you believe is most reasonable.

Exploring a Theme

1. What does being "an individual" mean? How important is individualism to you personally? When might being an individual clash with the needs of society? Identify and discuss a situation in which individualism and the needs of society might conflict. If such a conflict occurs, which needs should prevail and why?
2. Identify a disturbing trend that you see in American society. Describe this trend in an essay, providing examples from your observations and experiences.
3. Think about a business or organization that is not what it appears to be. Then write an essay explaining the differences between the image this business or organization projects and the way it actually functions. Include specific examples to illustrate the differences between its image and the reality experienced by its customers or clients.

7

DEFINITION

Limiting the Frame of Reference

Definitions help us function smoothly in a complex world. All effective communication, in fact, is continuously dependent on our unique human ability to understand and employ accurate definitions of a wide range of words, phrases, and abstract ideas. If we did not work from a set of shared definitions, we would not be able to carry on coherent conversations, write comprehensible letters, or respond to even the simplest radio and television programs. Definitions help us understand basic concrete terms (such as automobiles, laser beams, and the gross domestic product), discuss various events in our lives (such as snowboarding, legal proceedings, and a Cinco de Mayo celebration), and grasp difficult abstract ideas (such as democracy, ambition, and resentment). The ability to comprehend definitions and use them effectively helps us keep our oral and written level of communication accurate and accessible to a wide variety of people.

DEFINING DEFINITION

Definition is the process of explaining a word, object, or idea in such a way that the reader (or listener) knows as precisely as possible what we mean. A good definition sets up intellectual boundaries by focusing on the special qualities of a word or phrase that set it apart from other similar words or phrases. Clear definitions always give the writer and the reader a mutual starting point on the sometimes bumpy road to successful communication.

Definitions vary from short, dictionary-length summaries to longer, "extended" accounts that determine the form of an entire essay. Words or ideas that require expanded definitions are usually abstract, complex, or unavoidably controversial; they generally bear many related meanings or many shades of meaning. Definitions can be *objective* (technically precise and generally dry) or *subjective* (colored with personal opinion), and they can be used to instruct, to entertain, or to accomplish a combination of these two fundamental rhetorical goals.

In the following excerpt, a student defines "childhood" by putting it into perspective with other important stages of life. Though mostly entertaining, the paragraph is also instructive as the student objectively captures the essence of this phase of human development:

Childhood is a stage of growth somewhere between infancy and adolescence. Just as each developmental period in our lives brings new changes and concerns, childhood serves as the threshold to puberty—the time we learn to discriminate between good and bad, right and wrong, love and lust. Childhood is neither a time of irresponsible infancy nor responsible adulthood. Rather, it is marked by duties that we don't really want, challenges that excite us, feelings that puzzle and frighten us, and limitless opportunities that help us explore the world around us. Childhood is a time when we solidify our personalities in spite of pressures to be someone else.

THINKING CRITICALLY BY USING DEFINITION

Definitions are building blocks in communication that help us make certain we are functioning from the same understanding of terms and ideas. They give us a foundation to work from in both reading and writing. Definitions force us to think about meanings and word associations that make other logical strategies stronger and easier to work with.

The process of thinking through our definitions forces us to come to some understanding about a particular term or concept we are mentally wrestling with. Articulating that definition helps us move to other modes of thought and higher levels of understanding. Practicing definitions in isolation to get a feel for them is much like separating the skill of peddling from the process of riding a bike. The better you get at peddling, the more natural the rest of the cycling process becomes. The following exercises ask you to practice definitions in a number of different ways. Being more conscious of what definition entails will make it more useful to you in both your reading and your writing.

1. Define one of the concrete words and one of the abstract words listed here in one or two sentences. What were some of the differences between the process you went through to explain the concrete word and the abstract word? What can you conclude from this brief exercise about the differences in defining abstract and concrete words? Concrete: *cattle, book, ranch, water, gum.* Abstract: *freedom, progress, equality, fairness, boredom.*
2. Define the word *grammar.* Consult a dictionary, several handbooks, and maybe even some friends to get their views on the subject. Then, write a humorous definition of grammar that consolidates all these views into a single definition.
3. In what ways can you "define" yourself? What qualities or characteristics are crucial to an understanding of you as a person?

READING AND WRITING DEFINITION ESSAYS

Extended definitions, which usually range from two or three paragraphs to an entire essay, seldom follow a set pattern of development or organization. Instead, as you will see from the examples in this chapter, they draw on a number of different techniques to help explain a word, object, term, concept, or phenomenon.

How to Read a Definition Essay

Preparing to Read.   As you begin to read each of the definition essays in this chapter, take some time to consider the author's title and the synopsis of the essay in the Rhetorical Table of Contents: How much can you learn about Nancy Gibbs's topic from her title "When Is It Rape?" What do you sense is the general mood of Mary Pipher's "Beliefs About Families"? What do you think Lois Smith Brady's attitude toward love is in "How to Find True Love: Or Rather, How It Finds You"?

Equally important as you prepare to read is scanning an essay and finding information from its prefatory material about the author and the circumstances surrounding the composition of the essay. What do you think is Robert Ramirez's purpose in his definition of the barrio? And what can you learn about Ellen Goodman and the role of work in our lives?

Last, as you prepare to read these essays, answer the prereading questions before each essay, and then spend a few minutes thinking freely about the general subject of the essay at hand: What do you want to know from Pipher about families? What role does romantic love play in your life (Brady)? What interests you about communities (Goodman)?

Reading.   As you read a definition essay, as with all essays, be sure to record your initial reactions to your reading material. What are some of your thoughts or associations in relation to each essay?

As you get more involved in the essay, reconsider the preliminary material so you can create a context within which to analyze what the writer is saying: What is Gibbs's purpose in writing "When Is It Rape?" Does her tone effectively support that purpose? Who do you think is Ramirez's primary audience? Do you think his essay will effectively reach that group of people? In what ways is Brady qualified to write about true love?

Also, determine at this point whether the author's treatment of his or her subject is predominantly objective or subjective. Then, make sure you understand the main points of the essay on the literal, interpretive, and analytical levels by reading the questions that follow.

Rereading.   When you read these definition essays for a second time, check to see how each writer actually sets forth his or her definition: Does the writer put each item in a specific category with clear boundaries? Do you understand how the item being defined is different from other items in the same category? Did the author name the various components of the item, explain its etymology (linguistic origin and history), discuss what it is not, or perform a combination of these tasks?

To evaluate the effectiveness of a definition essay, you need to reconsider the essay's primary purpose and audience. If Gibbs is trying to get the general reader to understand the seriousness of

date rape, how effective is she? In like manner, is Pipher successful in communicating to the same audience the value of the family unit?

Especially applicable is the question of what other rhetorical
strategies help the author communicate this purpose. What other
modes does Ramirez use to help him define the barrio? Through
what other modes does Goodman define a working community?

For an inventory of the reading process, you can review the
guidelines on pages 20–21 of the Introduction.

How to Write a Definition Essay

Preparing to Write.   As with other essays, you should begin
the task of writing a definition essay by answering the prewriting
questions featured in this text and then by exploring your subject
and generating other ideas. (See the explanation of various prewriting techniques on pages 21–27 of the Introduction.) Be sure
you know what you are going to define and how you will approach your definition. You should then focus on a specific audience and purpose as you approach your writing assignment.

Writing.   The next step toward developing a definition essay
is usually to describe the general category to which the word belongs and then to contrast the word with all other words in that
group. To define *exposition,* for example, you might say that it is a
type of writing. Then, to differentiate it from other types of writing, you could go on to say that its main purpose is to "expose,"
or present information, as opposed to rhetorical modes such as description and narration, which describe and tell stories. In addition, you might want to cite some expository methods, such as
example, process analysis, division/classification, and compari-
son/contrast.

Yet another way to begin a definition essay is to provide a
term's etymology. Tracing a word's origin often illuminates its
current meaning and usage as well. *Exposition,* for example, comes
from the Latin *exponere,* meaning "to put forth, set forth, display,
declare, or publish" (*ex* = out; *ponere* = to put or place). This information can generally be found in any good dictionary or in a
good encyclopedia.

Another approach to defining a term is to explain what it does
not mean. For example, *exposition* is not creative writing. By limit-

ing the readers' frame of reference in these various ways, you are helping to establish a working definition for the term under consideration.

Finally, rhetorical methods that we have already studied, such as description, narration, example, process analysis, division/classification, and comparison/ contrast, are particularly useful to writers in expanding their definitions. To clarify the term *exposition,* you might **describe** the details of an expository theme, **narrate** a story about the wide use of the term in today's classroom, or **give examples** of assignments that would produce good expository writing. In other situations, you could **analyze** various writing assignments and discuss the **process** of producing an expository essay, **classify** exposition apart from creative writing and then **divide** it into categories similar to the headings of this book, or **compare** and **contrast** it with creative writing. Writers also use definition quite often to support other rhetorical modes.

Rewriting.   Reviewing and revising a definition essay is a relatively straightforward task:

- Have you chosen an effective beginning for your paper?
- Did you create a reasonable context for your definition?
- Have you used appropriate rhetorical strategies to develop your ideas?
- Have you achieved your overall purpose as effectively as possible?

Other guidelines to direct your writing and revising appear on pages 32–34 of the Introduction.

STUDENT ESSAY: DEFINITION AT WORK

In the following essay, a student defines "the perfect yuppie." Notice how the writer puts this term in a category and then explains the limits of that category and the uniqueness of this term within the category. To further inform her audience of the features of "yuppiedom," the student calls on the word's etymology, its dictionary definition, an itemization of the term's basic characteristics, a number of examples that explain those characteristics, and, finally, a general discussion of causes and effects that regulate a yuppie's behavior.

The Perfect Yuppie

Etymology/
dictionary
definition

Many people already know that the letters YUP stand for "young urban professional." *Young* in this context is understood to mean fortyish; *urban* often means suburban; and *professional* means most definitely college-educated. Double the *P* and add an *I* and an *E* at the end, and you get *yuppie*— that 1980s bourgeois, the marketers' darling, and the 1960s' inheritance. But let's not generalize. Not every forty-year-old suburban college graduate qualifies as a yuppie. Nor is every yuppie in his or her forties. True yuppiness involves much more than the words that make up the acronym. Being the little sister of a couple of yups, I am in an especially good position to define the perfect yuppie. I watched two develop.

General category of word being defined

Subject

Limitations set

Why the dictionary definition is inadequate

Writer's credibility

The essence of yuppiness is generally new money. In the yuppie's defense, I will admit that most yuppies have worked hard for their money and social status. Moreover, the baby boom of which they are a part has caused a glut of job seekers in their age bracket, forcing them to be competitive if they want all the nice things retailers have designed for them. But with new money comes an interesting combination of wealth, naiveté, and pretentiousness.

General characteristic

Cause/ Effect

General characteristic

For example, most yuppies worthy of the title have long ago traded in their fringed suede jackets for fancy fur coats. Although they were animal rights activists in the 1960s, they will not notice the irony of this change. In fact, they may be shameless enough to parade in their fur coats—fashion-show style— for friends and family. Because of their "innocence," yuppies generally will not see the vulgarity of their actions.

Specific example

Cause/ Effect

Specific example

General characteristic

Because they are often quite wealthy, yuppies tend to have a lot of "things." They are simply overwhelmed by the responsibility of spending all that money. For example, one yup I know has fourteen pairs of sunglasses and seven watches. She, her husband, and their three children own at least twenty collections of everything from comic books to Civil War memorabilia. Most yuppies have so much money that I often wonder why the word "yuppie" does not have a dollar sign in it somewhere.

Specific example

Specific example

General characteristic

Perhaps in an effort to rid themselves of this financial burden, all good yuppies go to Europe as soon as possible. Not Germany or France or Portugal, mind you, but Europe. They do not know what they are doing there and thus generally spend much more money than they need to—but, after all, no yuppie ever claimed to be frugal. Most important, they bring home slides of Europe and show them to everyone they know. A really good yuppie will forget and show you his or her slides more than once. Incidentally, when everyone has seen the slides of Europe twice, the yuppie's next stop is Australia.

Cause/ Effect

Cause/ Effect

General characteristic

General characteristic

A favorite pastime of yuppies is having wine-tasting parties for their yuppie friends. At these parties, they must make a great to-do about tasting the wine, cupping their faces over the glass with their palms (as if they were having a facial), and even sniffing the cork, for goodness sake. I once knew a yuppie who did not understand that a bottle of wine could not be rejected simply because he found he "did not like that kind." Another enjoyed making a show of having his wife choose and taste the wine occasionally, which they both thought was adorable.

Specific example

Specific example

Specific example

What it is not

Some yuppie wanna-be's drive red or black BMWs, but don't let them fool you. A genuine, hard-core yuppie will usually own a gold or silver Volvo station wagon. In this yuppie-mobile, the yuppie wife will chauffeur her young yupettes to and from their modeling classes, track meets, ballet, the manicurist, and boy scouts, for the young yuppie is generally as competitive and socially active as his or her parents. On the same topic, one particularly annoying trait of yuppie parents is bragging about their yupettes. You will know yuppies by the fact that they have the smartest, most talented children in the world. They will show you their kids' report cards, making sure you notice any improvements from last quarter.

General characteristic

Specific examples

Cause/ Effect

General characteristic

Specific example

Division/ Classification

Perhaps I have been harsh in my portrayal of the perfect yuppie, and, certainly, I will be accused by some of stereotyping. But consider this: I never classify people as yuppies who do not so classify themselves. The ultimate criterion for being yuppies is that they will always proudly label themselves as such.

General characteristic and concluding statement

Student Writer's Comments

The most difficult part about writing this definition essay was choosing a topic. I knew it had to be a word or phrase with different shades of meaning, but it also had to be either something I knew more about than the average person or something I had an unusual perspective on. I figured *yuppie* was a good word, not only because it has different meanings for different people, but also because it is an acronym, and acronyms tend to be greater than the sum of their parts.

I started by looking the word up in the dictionary and writing down its etymology (which I later referred to in my opening sentence). I then used freewriting to record the various meanings and natural associations I have with the word *yuppie*, which helped me discover relationships between these meanings and associations. I felt my mind wandering freely over all aspects of this word as I filled up pages and pages of freewriting. I then felt as if I had enough material to work with, so I began to write a draft of my essay.

I started writing the essay from the beginning, a process that was a real novelty for me. After citing the etymology of my word and placing it in a general category, I explained why the dictionary definition was inadequate. Then, I let the general characteristics I associate with the word take me step by step through the essay. As I wrote, I found myself mentally reorganizing my prewriting notes so that I could stay slightly ahead of my actual writing. I kept looping back and forth into my notes, looking for the next best characters to introduce, then writing, then going back to my notes again. I generated my entire first draft this way and revised the order only slightly in my final draft.

As I reworked my essay before handing it in, I added some humor from my own experience with my older sisters and looked closely at other rhetorical modes I had used to support my definition. Naturally, I had scattered examples throughout my essay and had discussed causes and effects quite openly. I revised my paper to make some of the connections I had had in mind clearer by either adding transitions or explaining the relationships in other words. I found that this process lengthened my essay quite a bit as I revised. I also worked on the essay at this point to bring out a secondary point I had had in mind, which is that some yuppies have lost the 1960s values they once had but often don't even realize it.

I spent the remainder of my time on my conclusion, which I rewrote from scratch four times. I finally ended up directly addressing the classification of yuppies, at which point I stumbled on the ultimate criterion for being a yuppy: "They will always proudly label themselves as such." When I reached this insight, I knew my paper was finished, and I was content with the results. I also realized that rewriting the conclusion so many times had given me a headache, but the pain was worth it.

SOME FINAL THOUGHTS ON DEFINITION

The following selections feature extended definitions whose main purpose is to explain a specific term or idea to their readers. Each essay in its own way helps its audience identify with various parts of the definitions, and each successfully communicates the unique qualities of the term or idea in question. Notice what approaches to definition each writer takes and how these approaches limit the readers' frame of reference in the process of effective communication.

DEFINITION IN REVIEW

Reading Definition Essays

Preparing to Read

- ✓ What assumptions can you make from the essay's title?
- ✓ Can you guess what the general mood of the essay is?
- ✓ What is the essay's purpose and audience?
- ✓ What does the synopsis in the Rhetorical Table of Contents tell you about the essay?
- ✓ What can you learn from the author's biography?
- ✓ Can you guess what the author's point of view toward the subject is?
- ✓ What are your responses to the Preparing to Read questions?

Reading

- ✓ Have you recorded your reactions to the essay?
- ✓ Is the author's treatment of the subject predominantly subjective or objective?
- ✓ Did you preview the questions that follow the essay?

Rereading

- ✓ How does the author lay out the definition?
- ✓ What is the essay's main purpose and audience?
- ✓ What other rhetorical strategies does the author use to support the essay's purpose?
- ✓ What are your responses to the questions after the essay?

Writing Definition Essays

Preparing to Write

- ✓ What are your responses to the Preparing to Write questions?

✓ Do you know what you are going to define and how you will approach your topic?

✓ Who is your audience?

Writing

✓ Does the beginning of your essay suit your purpose?

✓ Do you use effective strategies to define your word or concept effectively?

✓ What rhetorical strategies do you use to expand your definition essay?

Rewriting

✓ Have you chosen an effective beginning for your paper?

✓ Did you create a reasonable context for your definition?

✓ Have you used appropriate rhetorical strategies to develop your ideas?

✓ Have you achieved your overall purpose as effectively as possible?

NANCY GIBBS   (1960–   )

When Is It Rape?

Nancy Gibbs, a New York City native, graduated summa cum laude from Yale with a degree in history; she also attended Oxford University, where she studied politics and philosophy while on a prestigious Marshall Scholarship. In 1985, she began working for *Time* magazine, where she was originally assigned to the international section. Two years later, she transferred to business and the economy just in time to help cover the stock market crash of 1987. The following year she became a feature writer, covering such topics as child labor laws, racism on campus, the elderly in America, emergency care, the right to die, homelessness, and the changing doctor–patient relationship. She is currently a senior editor of *Time*, where she writes many of the magazine's cover stories. Her book *Children of Light* (1985) details the history of Quaker education in the state of New York. A frequent guest on radio and television talk shows, Gibbs is also an active member of the Fifth Avenue Presbyterian Church, where she serves as head of the board of deacons. In her spare time, she enjoys sailing and dancing. Her advice to students using *The Prose Reader* is to "keep writing." "The more you do it," she explains, "the better you get." She also urges student writers to seek out criticism from someone they respect: "Find a writing mentor, and pay attention to what that person tells you."

Preparing to Read

The following essay, originally published in *Time* (June 3, 1991), examines the social, legal, and moral aspects of rape—particularly "date rape"—and its effects on the men and women involved. As you prepare to read Gibbs's definition of date rape, pause a few moments to think about any associations you make with the word *rape*: What is your definition of *rape*? Why might different people have developed different definitions for this word? Why has this topic been so hotly debated on college campuses? What biases do people have in connection with rape? Why do so few rape victims ever report the crime? How successful has our legal system been in dealing with this problem in the past?

Be careful of strangers and hurry home, says a mother to her daughter, knowing that the world is a frightful place but not wishing to swaddle a child in fear. Girls grow up scarred by caution and enter adulthood eager to shake free of their parents' worst nightmares. They still know to be wary of strangers. What they don't know is whether they have more to fear from their friends.

Most women who get raped are raped by people they already know—like the boy in biology class, or the guy in the office down the hall, or their friend's brother. The familiarity is enough to make them let down their guard, sometimes even enough to make them wonder afterward whether they were "really raped." What people think of as "real rape"—the assault by a monstrous stranger lurking in the shadows—accounts for only 1 out of 5 attacks.

So the phrase "acquaintance rape" was coined to describe the rest, all the cases of forced sex between people who already knew each other, however casually. But that was too clinical for headline writers, and so the popular term is the narrower "date rape," which suggests an ugly ending to a raucous night on the town.

These are not idle distinctions. Behind the search for labels is the central mythology about rape: that rapists are always strangers, and victims are women who ask for it. The mythology is hard to dispel because the crime is so rarely exposed. The experts guess— that's all they can do under the circumstances—that while 1 in 4 women will be raped in her lifetime, less than 10% will report the assault, and less than 5% of the rapists will go to jail.

When a story of the crime lodges in the headlines, the myths have a way of cluttering the search for the truth. The tale of Good Friday in Palm Beach landed in the news because it involved a Kennedy. William Kennedy Smith met a woman at a bar, invited her back home late at night, and apparently had sex with her on the lawn. She says it was rape, and the police believed her story enough to charge him with the crime. Perhaps it was the bruises on her leg; or the instincts of the investigators who found her, panicked and shaking, curled up in the fetal position on a couch; or the lie-detector tests she passed.

On the other side, Smith adamantly protested that he was a man falsely accused. His friends and family testified to his gentle nature and moral fiber and insisted that he could not possibly have committed such a crime. The case shoved the debate over date rape into the minds of average men and women. Plant the topic in a conversation, and chances are it will ripen into a bitter argument or a jittery sequence of pale jokes.

Women charge that date rape is the hidden crime; men complain   7
it is hard to prevent a crime they can't define. Women say it isn't taken seriously; men say it is a concept invented by women who like to tease but not take the consequences. Women say the date-rape debate is the first time the nation has talked frankly about sex; men say it is women's unconscious reaction to the excesses of the sexual revolution. Meanwhile, men and women argue among themselves about the "gray area" that surrounds the whole murky arena of sexual relations, and there is no consensus in sight.

In court, on campus, in conversation, the issue turns on the   8
elasticity of the word *rape*, one of the few words in the language with the power to summon a shared image of a horrible crime.

At one extreme are those who argue that for the word to retain   9
its impact, it must be strictly defined as forced sexual intercourse: a gang of thugs jumping a jogger in Central Park, a psychopath preying on old women in a housing complex, a man with an ice pick in a side street. To stretch the definition of the word risks stripping away its power. In this view, if it happened on a date, it wasn't rape. A romantic encounter is a context in which sex *could* occur, and so what omniscient judge will decide whether there was genuine mutual consent?

Others are willing to concede that date rape sometimes occurs,   10
that sometimes a man goes too far on a date without a woman's consent. But this infraction, they say, is not as ghastly a crime as street rape, and it should not be taken as seriously. The *New York Post*, alarmed by the Willy Smith case, wrote in an editorial, "If the sexual encounter, *forced or not*, has been preceded by a series of consensual activities—drinking, a trip to the man's home, a walk on a deserted beach at 3 in the morning—the charge that's leveled against the alleged offender should, it seems to us, be different than the one filed against, say, the youths who raped and beat the jogger."

This attitude sparks rage among women who carry scars received at the hands of men they knew. It makes no difference if   11
the victim shared a drink or a moonlit walk or even a passionate kiss, they protest, if the encounter ended with her being thrown to the ground and forcibly violated. Date rape is not about a misunderstanding, they say. It is not a communications problem. It is

not about a woman's having regrets in the morning for a decision she made the night before. It is not about a "decision" at all. Rape is rape, and any form of forced sex—even between neighbors, co-workers, classmates, and casual friends—is a crime.

A more extreme form of that view comes from activists who   12
see rape as a metaphor, its definition swelling to cover any kind of oppression of women. Rape, seen in this light, can occur not only on a date but also in a marriage, not only by violent assault but also by psychological pressure. A Swarthmore College training pamphlet once explained that acquaintance rape "spans a spectrum of incidents and behaviors, ranging from crimes legally defined as rape to verbal harassment and inappropriate innuendo."

No wonder, then, that the battles become so heated. When in-   13
nuendo qualifies as rape, the definitions have become so slippery that the entire subject sinks into a political swamp. The only way to capture the hard reality is to tell the story.

A 32-year-old woman was on business in Tampa last year for   14
the Florida supreme court. Stranded at the courthouse, she accepted a lift from a lawyer involved in her project. As they chatted on the ride home, she recalls, "he was saying all the right things, so I started to trust him." She agreed to have dinner, and afterward, at her hotel door, he convinced her to let him come in to talk. "I went through the whole thing about being old-fashioned," she says. "I was a virgin until I was 21. So I told him talk was all we were going to do."

But as they sat on the couch, she found herself falling asleep.   15
"By now, I'm comfortable with him, and I put my head on his shoulder. He's not tried anything all evening, after all." Which is when the rape came. "I woke up to find him on top of me, forcing himself on me. I didn't scream or run. All I could think about was my business contacts and what if they saw me run out of my room screaming rape.

"I thought it was my fault. I felt so filthy, I washed myself over   16
and over in hot water. Did he rape me?, I kept asking myself. I didn't consent. But who's gonna believe me? I had a man in my hotel room after midnight." More than a year later, she still can't tell the story without a visible struggle to maintain her composure. Police referred the case to the state attorney's office in Tampa, but without more evidence it decided not to prosecute. Although her attacker has admitted that he heard her say no, maintains the

woman, "he says he didn't know that I meant no. He didn't feel he'd raped me, and he even wanted to see me again."

Her story is typical in many ways. The victim herself may not   17
be sure right away that she has been raped, that she had said no and been physically forced into having sex anyway. And the rapist commonly hears but does not heed the protest. "A date rapist will follow through no matter what the woman wants because his agenda is to get laid," says Claire Walsh, a Florida-based consultant on sexual assaults. "First comes the dinner, then a dance, then a drink, then the coercion begins." Gentle persuasion gives way to physical intimidation, with alcohol as the ubiquitous lubricant. "When that fails, force is used," she says. "Real men don't take no for an answer."

The Palm Beach case serves to remind women that if they go   18
ahead and press charges, they can expect to go on trial along with their attacker, if not in a courtroom then in the court of public opinion. The *New York Times* caused an uproar on its own staff not only for publishing the victim's name but also for laying out in de-tail her background, her high school grades, her driving record, along with an unattributed quote from a school official about her "little wild streak." A freshman at Carleton College in Minnesota, who says she was repeatedly raped for four hours by a fellow stu-dent, claims that she was asked at an administrative hearing if she performed oral sex on dates. In 1989 a man charged with raping at knife-point a woman he knew was acquitted in Florida because his victim had been wearing lace shorts and no underwear.

From a purely legal point of view, if she wants to put her at-   19
tacker in jail, the survivor had better be beaten as well as raped, since bruises become a badge of credibility. She had better have reported the crime right away, before taking the hours-long shower that she craves, before burning her clothes, before curling up with the blinds down. And she would do well to be a woman of shining character. Otherwise the strict constructionist defini-tions of rape will prevail in court. "Juries don't have a great deal of sympathy for the victim if she's a willing participant up to the nonconsensual sexual intercourse," says Norman Kinne, a prose-cutor in Dallas. "They feel that many times the victim has placed herself in the situation." Absent eyewitnesses or broken bones, a case comes down to her word against his, and the mythology of rape rarely lends her the benefit of the doubt.

She should also hope for an all-male jury, preferably composed   20
of fathers with daughters. Prosecutors have found that women
tend to be harsh judges of one another—perhaps because to find a
defendant guilty is to entertain two grim realities: that anyone
might be a rapist, and that every woman could find herself a victim. It may be easier to believe, the experts muse, that at some
level the victim asked for it. "But just because a woman makes a
bad judgment, does that give the guy a moral right to rape her?"
asks Dean Kilpatrick, director of the Crime Victim Research and
Treatment Center at the Medical University of South Carolina.
"The bottom line is, Why does a woman's having a drink give a
man the right to rape her?"

Last week the Supreme Court waded into the debate with a   21
7-to-2 ruling that protects victims from being harassed on the
witness stand with questions about their sexual history. The Jus-
tices, in their first decision on "rape shield laws," said an accused
rapist could not present evidence about a previous sexual relationship with the victim unless he notified the court ahead of time. In
her decision, Justice Sandra Day O'Connor wrote that "rape victims deserve heightened protection against surprise, harassment,
and unnecessary invasions of privacy."

That was welcome news to prosecutors who understand the   22
reluctance of victims to come forward. But there are other impediments to justice as well. An internal investigation of the Oak-
land police department found that officers ignored a quarter of all
reports of sexual assaults or attempts, though 90% actually warranted investigation. Departments are getting better at educating
officers in handling rape cases, but the courts remain behind. A
New York City task force on women in the courts charged that
judges and lawyers were routinely less inclined to believe a
woman's testimony than a man's.

The present debate over degrees of rape is nothing new: All   23
through history, rapes have been divided between those that mat-
tered and those that did not. For the first few thousand years, the
only rape that was punished was the defiling of a virgin, and that
was viewed as a property crime. A girl's virtue was a marketable
asset, and so a rapist was often ordered to pay the victim's father
the equivalent of her price on the marriage market. In early Baby-
lonian and Hebrew societies, a married woman who was raped
suffered the same fate as an adulteress—death by stoning or

drowning. Under William the Conqueror, the penalty for raping a virgin was castration and loss of both eyes—unless the violated woman agreed to marry her attacker, as she was often pressured to do. "Stealing an heiress" became a perfectly conventional means of taking—literally—a wife.

It may be easier to prove a rape case now, but not much. Until   24 the 1960s it was virtually impossible without an eyewitness; judges were often required to instruct jurors that "rape is a charge easily made and hard to defend against; so examine the testimony of this witness with caution." But sometimes a rape was taken very seriously, particularly if it involved a black man attacking a white woman—a crime for which black men were often executed or lynched.

Susan Estrich, author of *Real Rape*, considers herself a lucky   25 victim. This is not just because she survived an attack 17 years ago by a stranger with an ice pick, one day before her graduation from Wellesley. It's because police, and her friends, believed her. "The first thing the Boston police asked was whether it was a black guy," recalls Estrich, now a University of Southern California law professor. When she said yes and gave the details of the attack, their reaction was, "So, you were really raped." It was an instructive lesson, she says, in understanding how racism and sexism are factored into perceptions of the crime.

A new twist in society's perception came in 1975, when Susan   26 Brownmiller published her book *Against Our Will: Men, Women and Rape*. In it she attacked the concept that rape was a sex crime, arguing instead that is was a crime of violence and power over women. Throughout history, she wrote, rape has played a critical function. "It is nothing more or less than a conscious process of intimidation, by which *all men* keep *all women* in a state of fear."

Out of this contention was born a set of arguments that have   27 become politically correct wisdom on campus and in academic circles. This view holds that rape is a symbol of women's vulnerability to male institutions and attitudes. "It's sociopolitical," insists Gina Rayfield, a New Jersey psychologist. "In our culture men hold the power, politically, economically. They're socialized not to see women as equals."

This line of reasoning has led some women, especially radical-   28 ized victims, to justify flinging around the term rape as a political weapon, referring to everything from violent sexual assaults to inappropriate innuendos. Ginny, a college senior who was really raped when she was 16, suggests that false accusations of rape can serve a useful purpose. "Penetration is not the only form of violation," she explains. In her view, rape is a subjective term, one that women must use to draw attention to other, nonviolent, even nonsexual forms of oppression. "If a woman did falsely accuse a man of rape, she may have had reasons to," Ginny says. "Maybe she wasn't raped, but he clearly violated her in some way."

Catherine Comins, assistant dean of student life at Vassar, also   29
sees some value in this loose use of "rape." She says angry victims of various forms of sexual intimidation cry rape to regain their sense of power. "To use the word carefully would be to be careful for the sake of the violator, and the survivors don't care a hoot about him." Comins argues that men who are unjustly accused can sometimes gain from the experience. "They have a lot of pain, but it is not a pain that I would necessarily have spared them. I think it ideally initiates a process of self-exploration. 'How do I see women?' 'If I didn't violate her, could I have?' 'Do I have the potential to do to her what they say I did?' Those are good questions."

Taken to extremes, there is an ugly element of vengeance at work   30
here. Rape is an abuse of power. But so are false accusations of rape, and to suggest that men whose reputations are destroyed might benefit because it will make them more sensitive is an attitude that is sure to backfire on women who are seeking justice for all victims. On campuses where the issue is most inflamed, male students are outraged that their names can be scrawled on a bathroom-wall list of rapists and they have no chance to tell their side of the story.

"Rape is what you read about in the *New York Post* about 17   31
little boys raping a jogger in Central Park," says a male freshman at a liberal-arts college, who learned that he had been branded a rapist after a one-night stand with a friend. He acknowledges that they were both very drunk when she started kissing him at a party and ended up back in his room. Even through his haze, he had some qualms about sleeping with her: "I'm fighting against my hormonal instincts, and my moral instincts are saying, 'This is my friend and if I were sober, I wouldn't be doing this,'" But he went ahead anyway. "When you're drunk, and there are all sorts of ambiguity, and the woman says 'Please, please' and then she says no sometime later, even in the middle of the act, there still may very well be some kind of violation, but it's not the same

thing. It's not rape. If you don't hear her say no, if she doesn't say it, if she's playing around with you—oh, I could get squashed for saying it—there is an element of say no, mean yes."

The morning after their encounter, he recalls, both students 32 woke up hung over and eager to put the memory behind them. Only months later did he learn that she had told a friend that he had torn her clothing and raped her. At this point in the story, the accused man starts using the language of rape. "I felt violated," he says. "I felt like she was taking advantage of me when she was very drunk. I never heard her say 'No!,' 'Stop!,' anything." He is angry and hurt at the charges, worried that they will get around, shatter his reputation and force him to leave the small campus.

So here, of course, is the heart of the debate. If rape is sex 33 without consent, how exactly should consent be defined and communicated, when and by whom? Those who view rape through a political lens tend to place all responsibility on men to make sure that their partners are consenting at every point of a sexual encounter. At the extreme, sexual relations come to resemble major surgery, requiring a signed consent form. Clinical psychologist Mary P. Koss of the University of Arizona in Tucson, who is a leading scholar on the issue, puts it rather bluntly: "It's the man's penis that is doing the raping, and ultimately he's responsible for where he puts it."

Historically, of course, this has never been the case, and there are 34 some who argue that it shouldn't be—that women too must take responsibility for their behavior, and that the whole realm of intimate encounters defies regulation from on high. Anthropologist Lionel Tiger has little patience for trendy sexual politics that make no reference to biology. Since the dawn of time, he argues, men and women have always gone to bed with different goals. In the effort to keep one's genes in the gene pool, "it is to the male advantage to fertilize as many females as possible, as quickly as possible and as efficiently as possible." For the female, however, who looks at the large investment she will have to make in the offspring, the opposite is true. Her concern is to "select" who "will provide the best set up for their offspring." So, in general, "the pressure is on the male to be aggressive and on the female to be coy."

No one defends the use of physical force, but when the coer- 35 cion involved is purely psychological, it becomes hard to assign blame after the fact. Journalist Stephanie Gutmann is an ardent foe of what she calls the date-rape dogmatists. "How can you make sex completely politically correct and completely safe?" she asks. "What a horribly bland, unerotic thing that would be! Sex is, by nature, a risky endeavor, emotionally. And desire is a violent emotion. These people in the date-rape movement have erected so many rules and regulations that I don't know how people can have erotic or desire-driven sex."

Nonsense, retorts Cornell professor Andrea Parrot, co-author   36 of *Acquaintance Rape: The Hidden Crime*. Seduction should not be about lies, manipulation, game playing or coercion of any kind, she says. "Too bad that people think that the only way you can have passion and excitement and sex is if there are miscommunications and one person is forced to do something he or she doesn't want to do." The very pleasures of sexual encounters should lie in the fact of mutual comfort and consent: "You can hang from the ceiling, you can use fruit, you can go crazy and have really wonderful sensual erotic sex, if both parties are consenting."

It would be easy to accuse feminists of being too quick to clas-   37 sify sex as rape, but feminists are to be found on all sides of the debate, and many protest the idea that all the onus is on the man. It demeans women to suggest that they are so vulnerable to coercion or emotional manipulation that they must always be escorted by the strong arm of the law. "You can't solve society's ills by making everything a crime," says Albuquerque attorney Nancy Hollander. "That comes out of the sense of overprotection of women, and in the long run that is going to be harmful to us."

What is lost in the ideological debate over date rape is the fact   38 that men and women, especially when they are young, and drunk, and aroused, are not very good at communicating. "In many cases," says Estrich, "the man thought it was sex, and the woman thought it was rape, and they are both telling the truth." The man may envision a celluloid seduction, in which he is being commanding, she is being coy. A woman may experience the same event as a degrading violation of her will. That some men do not believe a woman's protests is scarcely surprising in a society so drenched with messages that women have rape fantasies and a desire to be overpowered.

By the time they reach college, men and women are loaded with   39 cultural baggage, drawn from movies, television, music videos, and "bodice ripper" romance novels. Over the years they have watched

Rhett sweep Scarlett up the stairs in *Gone With the Wind*; or Errol Flynn, who was charged twice with statutory rape, overpower a protesting heroine who then melts in his arms; or Stanley rape his sister-in-law Blanche du Bois while his wife is in the hospital giving birth to a child in *A Streetcar Named Desire*. Higher up the cultural food chain, young people can read of date rape in Homer or Jane Austen, watch it in *Don Giovanni* or *Rigoletto*.

The messages come early and often, and nothing in the femi-   40
nist revolution has been able to counter them. A recent survey of sixth- to ninth-graders in Rhode Island found that a fourth of the boys and a sixth of the girls said it was acceptable for a man to force a woman to kiss him or have sex if he has spent money on her. A third of the children said it would not be wrong for a man to rape a woman who had had previous sexual experiences.

Certainly cases like Palm Beach, movies like *The Accused,* and   41
novels like Avery Corman's *Prized Possessions* may force young people to re-examine assumptions they have inherited. The use of new terms, like acquaintance rape and date rape, while controversial, has given men and women the vocabulary they need to express their experiences with both force and precision. This dialogue would be useful if it helps strip away some of the dogmas, old and new, surrounding the issue. Those who hope to raise society's sensitivity to the problem of date rape would do well to concede that it is not precisely the same sort of crime as street rape, that there may be very murky issues of intent and degree involved.

On the other hand, those who downplay the problem should   42
come to realize that date rape is a crime of uniquely intimate cruelty. While the body is violated, the spirit is maimed. How long will it take, once the wounds have healed, before it is possible to share a walk on a beach, a drive home from work, or an evening's conversation without always listening for a quiet alarm to start ringing deep in the back of the memory of a terrible crime?

UNDERSTANDING DETAILS

1. Define the term *date rape* in your own words.
2. What is the central mythology in the American culture about rapists and their victims? Explain it in detail.
3. What are the main differences of opinion between men and women on the issue of date rape?
4. According to most women, when does sex become a crime?

ANALYZING MEANING

1. Explain three of the many ambiguous issues associated with the word *rape*.
2. After Gibbs wrote this essay, William Kennedy Smith was acquitted of the charge of rape in a dramatic case televised for the American public. In what ways does this verdict help us understand "date rape" more clearly? What role did the media play in this understanding?
3. Why is Gibbs not surprised that some men don't believe women's protests? What lessons have these men learned from the media as they were growing up?
4. Exactly what is Gibbs asking when she says, "How long will it take, once the wounds have healed, before it is possible to share a walk on a beach, a drive home from work, or an evening's conversation without always listening for a quiet alarm to start ringing deep in the back of the memory of a terrible crime?" (paragraph 42)?

DISCOVERING RHETORICAL STRATEGIES

1. What rhetorical techniques explained at the beginning of this chapter does Gibbs use in her definition?
2. Choose from this essay a difference of opinion between men and women, and explain the reasoning at work on each side.
3. Gibbs has to choose her words very carefully in an essay on a subject charged with so many emotional and political ramifications. Choose one paragraph from this essay, and explain how different words would send different messages and associations. Would these changes be for the better or worse, considering Gibbs's intended audience?
4. What rhetorical strategies, besides definition, does Gibbs use in this essay? Give examples of each strategy.

MAKING CONNECTIONS

1. If Nancy Gibbs, Judy Brady ("Why I Want a Wife"), and Germaine Greer ("A Child Is Born") were interviewed, how do you think each author would complete the following sentence: "Women are exploited when _____." How would you complete the same sentence? Have you ever been exploited? What were the circumstances? How did you respond?

2. Gibbs strips away the mythology surrounding rape in the same way that Jessica Mitford ("Behind the Formaldehyde Curtain") reveals the morbid reality behind American funeral customs. In what way have these misleading myths kept us from changing public attitudes toward these two controversial issues?

3. Imagine a conversation between Gibbs and Jill Leslie Rosenbaum and Meda Chesney-Lind ("Appearance and Delinquency: A Research Note") in which all three authors claim that the high incidence of rape in America is understandable, perhaps even predictable, in a culture that devalues women. What is your reaction to this assertion?

IDEAS FOR DISCUSSION/WRITING

Preparing to Write

Write freely about your reactions to crimes in general: What makes an action a crime? What are the most common crimes in America today? Has your definition of rape changed since you read this article? Is there a distinction in your mind between "street rape" and "date or acquaintance rape"? If so, what is the difference? Why do you think rape has become such a frequently committed crime? Why is the issue of rape receiving so much attention on college campuses? What other crimes are common occurrences on college campuses?

Choosing a Topic

1. In a coherent essay written for your classmates, define a serious injustice or crime (other than rape) that frequently takes place on college campuses. What type of people usually commit these injustices or crimes? Why do they do so? Why are such activities "unjust" or "criminal"? Before you begin to write, decide on a purpose and point of view.

2. Do you think rape is a sex crime or a "crime of violence and power over women" (paragraph 26), as Susan Brownmiller argues in her book? Discuss this issue in a well-developed essay, and draw your own conclusions from your discussion.

3. Choose one of the definitional techniques explained in the introduction to this chapter, and define the word *crime* in a well-developed, logically organized essay written for the general public. Introduce your main topic at the beginning of your

essay; then explain and illustrate it clearly as your essay progresses. You may use other definition techniques in addition to
the controlling one.

*Before beginning your essay, you might want to consult the checklists on
pages 393–394.*

ROBERT RAMIREZ   (1949–   )

The Barrio

Robert Ramirez was born and raised in Edinburg, a southern Texas town near the Mexican border in an area that has been home to his family for almost two hundred years. After graduating from the University of Texas–Pan American, he taught freshman composition and worked for a while as a photographer. For the next several years, he was a salesman, reporter, and announcer/anchor for the CBS affiliate station KGBT-TV in Harlingen, Texas. His current job has brought him full circle, back to the University of Texas–Pan American, where he serves as a development officer responsible for alumni fund-raising. He loves baseball and once considered a professional career, but he now contents himself with bike riding, swimming, and playing tennis. A conversion to the Baha'i faith in the 1970s has brought him much spiritual happiness. When asked to give advice to students using *The Prose Reader*, Ramirez responded, "The best writing, like anything else of value, requires a great deal of effort. Rewriting is 90 percent of the process. Sometimes, if you are fortunate, your work can take on a life of its own, and you end up writing something important that astounds and humbles you. This is what happened with 'The Barrio,' which is much better than the essay I originally intended. There's an element of the divine in it, as there is in all good writing."

Preparing to Read

First titled "The Woolen Sarape," Ramirez's essay was written while he was a student at the University of Texas–Pan American. His professor, Edward Simmens, published it in an anthology entitled *Pain and Promise: The Chicano Today* (1972). In it, the author defines the exciting, colorful, and close-knit atmosphere typical of many Hispanic barrios or communities. As you prepare to read this essay, take a few moments to think about a place that is very special to you: What are its physical characteristics? What memories are connected to this place for you? What kinds of people live there? What is the relationship of these people to each other? To people in other places? Why is this place so special to you? Is it special to anyone else?

The train, its metal wheels squealing as they spin along the 1
silvery tracks, rolls slower now. Through the gaps between the cars blinks a streetlamp, and this pulsing light
on a barrio street corner beats slower, like a weary heartbeat, until
the train shudders to a halt, the light goes out, and the barrio is
deep asleep.

Throughout Aztlán (the Nahuatl term meaning "land to the 2
north"), trains grumble along the edges of a sleeping people.
From Lower California, through the blistering Southwest, down
the Rio Grande to the muddy Gulf, the darkness and mystery of
dreams engulf communities fenced off by railroads, canals, and ex-
pressways. Paradoxical communities, isolated from the rest of the
town by concrete columned monuments of progress, and yet
stranded in the past. They are surrounded by change. It eludes
their reach, in their own backyards, and the people, unable and
unwilling to see the future, or even touch the present, perpetuate
the past.

Leaning from the expressway or jolting across the tracks, one 3
enters a different physical world permeated by a different attitude.
The physical dimensions are impressive. It is a large section of
town which extends for fifteen blocks north and south along the
tracks, and then advances eastward, thinning into nothingness beyond the city limits. Within the invisible (yet sensible) walls of the
barrio are many, many people living in too few houses. The
homes, however, are much more numerous than on the outside.

Members of the barrio describe the entire area as their home. It 4
is a home, but it is more than this. The barrio is a refuge from the
harshness and the coldness of the Anglo world. It is a forced
refuge. The leprous people are isolated from the rest of the community and contained in their section of town. The stoical pariahs
of the barrio accept their fate, and from the angry seeds of rejection grow the flowers of closeness between outcasts, not the
thorns of bitterness and the mad desire to flee. There is no want
to escape, for the feeling of the barrio is known only to its inhabitants, and the material needs of life can also be found here.

The *tortillería* fires up its machinery three times a day, produc- 5
ing steaming, round, flat slices of barrio bread. In the winter, the
warmth of the tortilla factory is a wool sarape in the chilly morning hours, but in the summer, it unbearably toasts every noontime
customer.

The *panadería* sends its sweet messenger aroma down the dimly   6
lit street, announcing the arrival of fresh, hot, sugary *pan dulce.*

The small corner grocery serves the meal-to-meal needs of cus-   7
tomers, and the owner, a part of the neighborhood, willingly
gives credit to people unable to pay cash for foodstuffs.

The barbershop is a living room with hydraulic chairs, radio,   8
and television, where old friends meet and speak of life as their
salted hair falls aimlessly about them.

The pool hall is a junior level country club where *'chucos,* strangers   9
in their own land, get together to shoot pool and rap, while veterans,
unaware of the cracking, popping balls on the green felt, complacently
play dominoes beneath rudely hung *Playboy* foldouts.

The *cantina* is the night spot of the barrio. It is the country club   10
and the den where the rites of puberty are enacted. Here the
young become men. It is in the taverns that a young dude shows
his *machismo* through the quantity of beer he can hold, the stories
of *rucas* he has had, and his willingness and ability to defend his
image against hardened and scarred old lions.

No, there is no frantic wish to flee. It would be absurd to leave   11
the familiar and nervously step into the strange and cold Anglo
community when the needs of the Chicano can be met in the
barrio.

The barrio is closeness. From the family living unit, familial re-   12
lationships stretch out to immediate neighbors, down the block,
around the corner, and to all parts of the barrio. The feeling of
family, a rare and treasurable sentiment, pervades and accounts for
the inability of the people to leave. The barrio is this attitude
manifested on the countenances of the people, on the faces of
their homes, and in the gaiety of their gardens.

The color-splashed homes arrest your eyes, arouse your curios-   13
ity, and make you wonder what life scenes are being played out in
them. The flimsy, brightly colored, wood-frame houses ignore no
neon-brilliant color. Houses trimmed in orange, chartreuse, lime
green, yellow, and mixtures of these and other hues beckon the
beholder to reflect on the peculiarity of each home. Passing
through this land is refreshing like Brubeck, not narcoticizing like
revolting rows of similar houses, which neither offend nor please.

In the evenings, the porches and front yards are occupied with   14
men calmly talking over the noise of children playing baseball in
the unpaved extension of the living room, while the women cook

supper or gossip with female neighbors as they water the *jardines*. The gardens mutely echo the expressive verses of the colorful houses. The denseness of multicolored plants and trees gives the house the appearance of an oasis or a tropical isand hideaway, sheltered from the rest of the world.

Fences are common in the barrio, but they are fences and not   15
the walls of the Anglo community. On the western side of town, the high wooden fences between houses are thick, impenetrable walls, built to keep the neighbors at bay. In the barrio, the fences may be rusty, wire contraptions or thick green shrubs. In either case you can see through them and feel no sense of intrusion when you cross them.

Many lower-income families of the barrio manage to maintain   16
a comfortable standard of living through the communal action of family members who contribute their wages to the head of the family. Economic need creates interdependence and closeness. Small barefooted boys sell papers on cool, dark Sunday mornings, deny themselves pleasantries, and give their earnings to *mamá*. The older the child, the greater the responsibility to help the head of the household provide for the rest of the family.

There are those, too, who for a number of reasons have not   17
achieved a relative sense of financial security. Perhaps it results from too many children too soon, but it is the homes of these people and their situation that numbs rather than charms. Their houses, aged and bent, oozing children, are fissures in the horn of plenty. Their wooden homes may have brick-pattern asbestos tile on the outer walls, but the tile is not convincing.

Unable to pay city taxes or incapable of influencing the city to   18
live up to its duty to serve all the citizens, the poorer barrio families remain trapped in the nineteenth century and survive as best they can. The backyards have well-worn paths to the outhouses, which sit near the alley. Running water is considered a luxury in some parts of the barrio. Decent drainage is usually unknown, and when it rains, the water stands for days, an incubator of health hazards and an avoidable nuisance. Streets, costly to pave, remain rough, rocky trails. Tires do not last long, and the constant rattling and shaking grind away a car's life and spread dust through screen windows.

The houses and their *jardines*, the jollity of the people in an ad-   19
verse world, the brightly feathered alarm clock pecking away at

supper and cautiously eyeing the children playing nearby, produce a mystifying sensation at finding the noble savage alive in the twentieth century. It is easy to look at the positive qualities of life in the barrio and look at them with a distantly envious feeling. One wishes to experience the feelings of the barrio and not the hardships. Remembering the illness, the hunger, the feeling of time running out on you, the walls, both real and imagined, reflecting on living in the past, one finds his envy becoming more elusive, until it has vanished altogether.

Back now beyond the tracks, the train creaks and groans, the 20 cars jostle each other down the track, and as the light begins its pulsing, the barrio, with all its meanings, greets a new dawn with yawns and restless stretchings.

UNDERSTANDING DETAILS

1. Define the barrio in your own words.
2. What is the difference between fences in the barrio and in the Anglo community?
3. In Ramirez's view, what creates "interdependence and closeness" (paragraph 16)? How does this phenomenon work in the barrio?
4. According to Ramirez, why are the houses in the barrio so colorful? What do you think is the relationship between color and happiness in the barrio?

ANALYZING MEANING

1. Why does Ramirez call the people in the barrio "leprous" (paragraph 4)?
2. What does the author mean when he says, "The barrio is closeness" (paragraph 12)? How does this statement compare with the way you feel about your neighborhood? Why can't people leave the barrio?
3. Why might people look at the barrio with "a distantly envious feeling" (paragraph 19)? What other feelings may alter or even erase this sense of envy?
4. In what ways does the barrio resemble the communal living of various social groups in the 1960s?

DISCOVERING RHETORICAL STRATEGIES

1. How does Ramirez use the train to help him define the barrio? In what ways would the essay be different without the references to the train?

2. Ramirez uses metaphors masterfully throughout this essay to help us understand the internal workings of the barrio. He relies on this technique especially in paragraphs 4 through 10. For example, a metaphor that explains how relationships develop in the barrio is "The stoical pariahs of the barrio accept their fate, and from the angry seeds of rejection grow the flowers of closeness between outcasts, not the thorns of bitterness and the mad desire to flee" (paragraph 4). In this garden metaphor, "rejection" is likened to "angry seeds," "closeness between outcasts" to "flowers," and "bitterness" to "thorns." Find four other metaphors in these paragraphs, and explain how the comparisons work. What are the familiar and less familiar items in each comparison?

3. What tone does Ramirez establish in this essay? How does he create this tone?

4. The dominant method the author uses to organize his essay is definition. What other rhetorical strategies does Ramirez use to support his definition?

MAKING CONNECTIONS

1. Compare and contrast the "feeling of family" described by Ramirez with that depicted by Germaine Greer in "A Child Is Born" and Mary Pipher in "Beliefs About Families."

2. Ramirez does a wonderful job of creating a sensual experience in his essay as he chronicles the vivid sights, sounds, smells, tastes, and textures of life in the barrio. In the same way, Susan Austin ("Land and Bones") and John McPhee ("The Pines") appeal to our senses in their descriptions of two remote wilderness areas. Which author's prose style do you find most sensual? Explain your answer.

3. While Ramirez defines the "barrio" through description, Nancy Gibbs ("When Is It Rape?") and Ellen Goodman ("A Working Community") define their principal topics differently. How do the three authors differ in constructing their definitions? Which technique do you find most persuasive? Explain your answer.

IDEAS FOR DISCUSSION/WRITING

Preparing to Write

Write freely about a place that is special to you: Describe this place from your perspective. Is this place special to anyone else? Describe this place from someone else's perspective. How do these descriptions differ? What characteristics differentiate this place from other places? What makes this place special to you? Use some metaphors to relay to your readers your feelings about certain features of this place. Do you think this place will always be special to you? Why or why not?

Choosing a Topic

1. Ramirez's definition of the barrio demonstrates a difference between an insider's view and an outsider's view of the same location. In an essay for your classmates, define your special place from both the inside and the outside. Then discuss the similarities and differences between these two points of view.

2. In essay form, define the relationships among the people who are your extended family. These could be people from your neighborhood, your school, your job, or a combination of places. How did these relationships come about? Why are you close to these people? Why are these people close to you? To each other?

3. What primary cultural or social traditions have made you what you are today? In an essay written to a close friend, define the two or three most important traditions you practiced as a child, and explain what effects they had on you.

Before beginning your essay, you might want to consult the checklists on pages 393–394.

MARY PIPHER   (1947–   )

Beliefs About Families

The oldest of seven children, Mary Pipher was born in Springfield, Missouri. She earned her B.A. in cultural anthropology at the University of California, Berkeley, and her Ph.D. in clinical psychology at the University of Nebraska. Currently a professor in the graduate clinical training program at the University of Nebraska, Lincoln, she became a writer only after her children had been raised, declaring that "Writing has been the great gift of my middle years. It is my reason to wake up in the morning." Her first book, *Hunger Pains: The Modern Woman's Tragic Quest for Thinness* (1987), was followed by *Reviving Ophelia: Saving the Selves of Adolescent Girls* (1994), an enormously influential study of the world of teenage girls. Her most recent books are *The Shelter of Each Other: Rebuilding Our Families* (1996), which examines family relationships in America today, and *Another Country: Navigating the Emotional Terrain of Our Elders* (1999), an analysis of how the United States isolates and misunderstands its senior citizens. An avid outdoorswoman who loves hiking, backpacking, and watching sunsets, Pipher has the following advice for students using *The Prose Reader*: "What all writers have in common is a yearning to communicate. That yearning is what makes it impossible not to write. The important thing for all writers is to care enough about the quality of the writing to keep working."

Preparing to Read

The following essay from *The Shelter of Each Other: Rebuilding Our Families* attempts to define the notion of "family" in contemporary society. As you prepare to read this essay, take a few moments to think about the role family plays in your life: Are you close to your biological family? Are you a part of any other groups that function like a family? How do they work? Are you aware of your roles in these various groups? What is the relationship betwen your role in your immediate family and your personal goals? Does your family provide support for you and what you want to accomplish?

When I speak of families, I usually mean biological families. There is a power in blood ties that cannot be denied. But in our fragmented, chaotic culture, many people don't have biological families nearby. For many people, friends become family. Family is a collection of people who pool resources and help each other over the long haul. Families love one another even when that requires sacrifice. Family means that if you disagree, you still stay together.

Families are the people for whom it matters if you have a cold, are feuding with your mate or training a new puppy. Family members use magnets to fasten the newspaper clippings about your bowling team on the refrigerator door. They save your drawings and homemade pottery. They like to hear stories about when you were young. They'll help you can tomatoes or change the oil in your car. They're the people who will come visit you in the hospital, will talk to you when you call with "a dark night of the soul" and will loan you money to pay the rent if you lose your job. Whether or not they are biologically related to each other, the people who do these things are family.

If you are very lucky, family is the group you were born into. But some are not that lucky. When Janet was in college, her parents were killed in a car wreck. In her early twenties she married, but three years later she lost her husband to leukemia. She has one sister, who calls mainly when she's suicidal or needs money. Janet is a congresswoman in a western state, a hard worker and an idealist. Her family consists of the men, women, and children she's grown to depend on in the twenty-five years she's lived in her community. Except for her beloved dog, nobody lives with her. But she brings the cinnamon rolls to one family's Thanksgiving dinner and has a Mexican fiesta for families at her house on New Year's Eve. She attends Bar Mitzvahs, weddings, school concerts, and soccer matches. She told me with great pride, "When I sprained my ankle skiing last year, three families brought me meals."

I think of Morgan, a jazz musician who long ago left his small town and rigid, judgmental family. He had many memories of his father whipping him with a belt or making him sleep in the cold. Once he said to me, "I was eighteen years old before anyone ever told me I had something to offer." Indeed he does. He plays the violin beautifully. He teaches improvisation and jazz violin and

organizes jazz events for his town. His family is the family of musicians and music lovers that he has built around him over the years.

If you are very unlucky, you come from a nuclear family that   5
didn't care for you. Curtis, who as a boy was regularly beaten by
his father, lied about his age so that he could join the Navy at sixteen. Years later he wrote his parents and asked if he could return
home for Christmas. They didn't answer his letter. When I saw
him in therapy, I encouraged him to look for a new family,
among his cousins and friends from the Navy. Sometimes cutoffs,
tragic as they are, are unavoidable.

I think of Anita, who never knew her father and whose   6
mother abandoned her when she was seven. Anita was raised by
an aunt and uncle, whom she loved very much. As an adult she
tracked down her mother and tried to establish a relationship, but
her mother wasn't interested. At least Anita was able to find other
family members to love her. She had a family in her aunt and
uncle.

Family need not be traditional or biological. But what family   7
offers is not easily replicated. Let me share a Sioux word, *tiospaye,*
which means the people with whom one lives. The *tiospaye* is
probably closer to a kibbutz than to any other Western institution. The *tiospaye* gives children multiple parents, aunts, uncles
and grandparents. It offers children a corrective factor for problems in their nuclear families. If parents are difficult, there are
other adults around to soften and diffuse the situation. Until the
1930s, when the *tiospaye* began to fall apart with sale of land, mi-
gration and alcoholism, there was not much mental illness among
the Sioux. When all adults were responsible for all children, people grew up healthy.

What *tiospaye* offers and what biological family offers is a place   8
that all members can belong to regardless of merit. Everyone is included regardless of health, likability or prestige. What's most
valuable about such institutions is that people are in by virtue of
being born into the group. People are in even if they've committed a crime, been a difficult person, become physically or mentally
disabled or are unemployed and broke. That ascribed status was
what Robert Frost valued when he wrote that home "was something you somehow hadn't to deserve."

Many people do not have access to either a supportive biologi-   9
cal family or a *tiospaye.* They make do with a "formed family."

Others simply prefer a community of friends to their biological families. The problem with formed families is they often have less staying power. They might not take you in, give you money if you lose a job or visit you in a rest home if you are paralyzed in a car crash. My father had a stroke and lost most of his sight and speech. Family members were the people who invited him to visit and helped him through the long tough years after his stroke. Of course, there are formed families who do this. With the AIDS crisis, many gays have supported their friends through terrible times. Often immigrants will help each other in this new country. And there are families who don't stick together in crisis. But generally blood is thicker than water. Families come through when they must.

Another problem with formed families is that not everyone has   10
the skills to be included in that kind of family. Friendship isn't a product that can be obtained for cash. People need friends today more than ever, but friends are harder to make in a world where people are busy, moving, and isolated. Some people don't have the skills. They are shy, abrasive, or dull. Crack babies have a hard time making friends, as do people with Alzheimer's. Formed families can leave many people out.

From my point of view the issue isn't biology. Rather the is-   11
sues are commitment and inclusiveness. I don't think for most of us it has to be either/or. A person can have both a strong network of friends and a strong family. It is important to define family broadly so that all kinds of families, such as single-parent families, multigenerational families, foster families and the families of gays are included. But I agree with David Blankenberg's conclusion in his book *Rebuilding the Nest*: "Even with all the problems of nuclear families, I will support it as an institution until something better comes along."

Americans hold two parallel versions of the family—the ideal-   12
ized version and the dysfunctional version. The idealized version portrays families as wellsprings of love and happiness, loyal, wholesome, and true. This is the version we see in *Leave It to Beaver* or *Father Knows Best*. The dysfunctional version depicts families as disturbed and disturbing, and suggests that salvation lies in extricating oneself from all the ties that bind. Both versions have had their eras. In the 1950s the idealized version was at its zenith. Extolling family was in response to the Depression and war, which

separated families. People who had been wrenched away from home missed their families and thought of them with great longing. They idealized how close and warm they had been.

In the 1990s the dysfunctional version of family seems the most   13 influential. This belief system goes along with the culture of narcissism, which sells people the idea that families get in the way of individual fulfillment. Currently, many Americans are deeply mistrustful of their own and other people's families. Pop psychology presents families as pathology-producing. Talk shows make families look like hotbeds of sin and sickness. Day after day people testify about the diverse forms of emotional abuse that they suffered in their families. Movies and television often portray families as useless impediments.

In our culture, after a certain age, children no longer have per-   14 mission to love their parents. We define adulthood as breaking away, disagreeing and making up new rules. Just when teenagers most need their parents, they are encouraged to distance themselves from them. A friend told me of walking with her son in a shopping mall. They passed some of his friends, and she noticed that suddenly he was ten feet behind, trying hard not to be seen with her. She said, "I felt like I was drooling and wearing purple plaid polyester." Later her son told her that he enjoyed being with her, but that his friends all hated their parents and he would be teased if anyone knew he loved her. He said, "I'm confused about this. Am I supposed to hate you?"

This socialized antipathy toward families is unusual. Most cul-   15 tures revere and respect family. In Vietnam, for example, the tender word for lover is "sibling." In the Kuma tribe of Papua New Guinea, family members are valued above all others. Siblings are seen as alter egos, essential parts of the self. The Kuma believe that mates can be replaced, but not family members. Many Native American tribes regard family members as connected to the self. To be without family is to be dead.

From the Greeks, to Descartes, to Freud and Ayn Rand, West-   16 erners have valued the independent ego. But Americans are the most extreme. Our founders were rebels who couldn't tolerate oppression. When they formed a new government they emphasized rights and freedoms. Laws protected private property and individual rights. Responsibility for the common good was not mandated.

American values concerning independence may have worked   17
better when we lived in small communities surrounded by endless
space. But we have run out of space and our outlaws live among
us. At one time the outlaw mentality was mitigated by a strong
sense of community. Now the values of community have been
superseded by other values.

We have pushed the concept of individual rights to the limits.   18
Our laws let adults sell children harmful products. But laws are not
our main problem. People have always been governed more by
community values than by laws. Ethics, rather than laws, determine
most of our behavior. Unwritten rules of civility—for taking turns,
not cutting in lines, holding doors open for others and lowering
our voices in theaters—organize civic life. Unfortunately, those
rules of civility seem to be crumbling in America. We are becoming a nation of people who get angry when anyone gets in our way.

Rudeness is everywhere in our culture. Howard Stern, G.   19
Gordon Liddy, and Newt Gingrich are rude. It's not surprising
our children copy them. Phil Donahue and Jay Leno interrupt,
and children learn to interrupt. A young man I know was recently
injured on a volleyball court. The player who hurt him didn't
apologize or offer to help him get to an emergency room. An official told him to get off the floor because he was messing it up
with his blood and holding up the game. I recently saw an old
man hesitate at a busy intersection. Behind him drivers swore and
honked. He looked scared and confused as he turned into traffic
and almost wrecked his car. At a festival a man stood in front of
the stage, refusing to sit down when people yelled out that they
couldn't see. Finally another man wrestled him to the ground. All
around were the omnipresent calls of "Fuck You." Over coffee a
local politician told me she would no longer attend town meetings. She said, "People get out of control and insult me and each
other. There's no dialogue, it's all insults and accusations."

We have a crisis in meaning in our culture. The crisis comes   20
from our isolation from each other, from the values we learn in a
culture of consumption and from the fuzzy, self-help message that
the only commitment is to the self and the only important question is—Am I happy? We learn that we are number one and that
our own immediate needs are the most important ones. The crisis
comes from the message that products satisfy and that happiness
can be purchased.

We live in a money-driven culture. But the bottom line is not   21
the only line, or even the best line for us to hold. A culture organized around profits instead of people is not user friendly to families. We all suffer from existential flu, as we search for meaning in
a culture that values money, not meaning. Everyone I know
wants to do good work. But right now we have an enormous gap
between doing what's meaningful and doing what is reimbursed.

UNDERSTANDING DETAILS

1. How does Pipher define *families*? What particular activities
   characterize a "family" member?
2. What do "commitment and inclusiveness" (paragraph 11) have
   to do with being in a family?
3. According to Pipher, what are the two parallel versions of the
   family and when were they dominant?
4. According to Pipher, what poses the biggest problem to the
   integrity of the family as a unit?

ANALYZING MEANING

1. In what way does the Sioux word *tiospaye* (paragraph 7) describe the traits of a family?
2. According to Pipher, why do "people need friends today more
   than ever" (paragraph 10)?
3. What is difficult about "formed families" (paragraph 10)?
4. Do you agree with Pipher that we have "a crisis of meaning in
   our culture" (paragraph 20). Explain your answer in detail.

DISCOVERING RHETORICAL STRATEGIES

1. Why does the author introduce the stories of Janet, Morgan,
   Curtis, and Anita?
2. What do you think Pipher's purpose is in this essay?
3. Pipher approaches her definition from many different angles
   before suggesting that the American culture is facing a crisis in
   understanding and agreeing upon what a family is. How do
   her various definitions support her statement about a crisis?
   Explain your answer.
4. What rhetorical modes support the author's definition? Give
   examples of each.

MAKING CONNECTIONS

1. Which parts of Mary Pipher's definition of "family" would Judith Wallerstein and Sandra Blakeslee ("Second Chances for Children of Divorce"), Germaine Greer ("A Child Is Born"), and Robert Ramirez ("The Barrio") most agree with? Why?
2. Imagine that Russell Baker ("The Saturday Evening Post"), Germaine Greer ("A Child Is Born"), and Mary Pipher are discussing the extent to which people within a family have to compromise. Which author would you probably agree with and why?
3. Compare and contrast the ways in which Nancy Gibbs ("When Is It Rape?"), Robert Ramirez ("The Barrio"), and Mary Pipher begin their definition essays.

IDEAS FOR DISCUSSION/WRITING

Preparing to Write

Write freely about the qualities that constitute a good family member: How do you recognize a good family member? What characterizes him or her? Do you personally appreciate your biological family? Are you a part of other families? If so, what are the characteristics of these families? Why is some type of family important to our well-being? What role does the notion of family play in your self-definition?

Choosing a Topic

1. Write an essay for your classmates defining "a family" that you belong to.
2. In a well-organized essay, use examples to define the dysfunctional family as it exists today. Be as specific as possible.
3. The relationship between family and individual has changed since your parents were in school. Explain to them the current relationship between you and your family. What are the connections between your personal goals and your role in your immediate family?

Before beginning your essay, you might want to consult the checklists on pages 393–394.

LOIS SMITH BRADY   (1944–   )

How to Find True Love: Or Rather, How It Finds You

Lois Smith Brady was born in Philadelphia and educated at the Putney School, a farm boarding school in Vermont. She later earned a B.A. in English from the University of Pennsylvania and an M.F.A. in creative writing from Stanford. After an early job as an editorial assistant at *Esquire* magazine, she began writing the "VOWS" column for the *New York Times* "Styles" section, which is a weekly report on a newly married couple emphasizing their love story rather than the details of their wedding. She has written two books: *Love Lessons* (1999) and *VOWS: Weddings of the Nineties from the New York Times* (2000). She and her husband and their two young sons live in an old farmhouse in Bridgehampton, Long Island, from which she e-mails her column every week to the *Times*. She enjoys doing yoga in her spare time, which she describes as "wonderful for writing—it strengthens your back and your imagination at the same time." She advises students using *The Prose Reader* "to start writing, writing, writing. It doesn't matter what you write at first. Write a letter to your mother, to your old boyfriend, anything to get going. Develop the habit of writing every day, day after day. Write on Christmas day, write on every holiday. If you're traveling, write in a journal. You'll write terrible stuff, perhaps, but you'll also create some real gems along the way, and that's only the beginning. Just one beautiful sentence can start your career."

Preparing to Read

The following essay, taken from a collection of essays called *Love Lessons*, attempts to define the abstract notion of love. As you prepare to read Lois Brady's essay, take a few moments to think about your own experience with love: How often have you been in love? How do you know you are in love? In what ways do you express your love? What do you expect from your partner? What are some of the main characteristics he or she has to have? Where do you look for love if you want to find it?

I began to learn about love in dancing school, at age 12. I re- 1
member thinking on the first day I was going to fall madly in
love with one of the boys and spend the next years of my life
kissing and waltzing.

During class, however, I sat among the girls, waiting for a boy 2
to ask me to dance. To my complete shock, I was consistently
one of the last to be asked. At first I thought the boys had made a
terrible mistake. I was so funny and pretty, and I could beat
everyone I knew at tennis and climb trees faster than a cat. Why
didn't they dash toward me?

Yet class after class, I watched boys dressed in blue blazers and 3
gray pants head toward girls in flowered shifts whose perfect
ponytails swung back and forth like metronomes. They fell easily
into step with one another in a way that was completely mysterious to me. I came to believe that love belonged only to those
who glided, who never shimmied up trees or even really touched
the ground.

By the time I was 13, I knew how to subtly tilt my head and 4
make my tears fall back into my eyes, instead of down my cheeks,
when no one asked me to dance. I also discovered the "powder
room," which became my softly lit, reliable retreat. Whenever I
started to cry, I'd excuse myself and run in there.

I finally stopped crying when I met Matt, who was quiet and 5
hung out on the edges of the room. When we danced for the first
time, he wouldn't even look me in the eyes. But he was cute, and
he told great stories. We became good buddies, dancing every
dance together until the end of school.

I learned from him my most important early lesson about ro- 6
mance: that the potential for love exists in corners, in the most
unlikely as well as the most obvious places.

For years my love life continued to be one long tragicomic 7
novel. In college I fell in love with a tall English major who rode
a motorcycle. He stood me up on our sixth date—an afternoon of
sky diving. I jumped out of the plane alone and landed in a parking lot.

In my mid-20s I moved to New York City where love is as hard 8
to find as a legal parking spot. My first Valentine's Day there, I went
on a date to a crowded bar on the Upper West Side. Halfway
through dinner my date excused himself and never returned.

At the time, I lived with a beautiful roommate. Flowers piled 9 up at our door like snowdrifts, and the light on the answering machine always blinked in a panicky way, overloaded with messages from her admirers. Limousines purred outside, with dates waiting for her behind tinted windows.

In my mind, love was something behind a tinted window, part 10 apparition, part shadow, definitely unreachable. Whenever I spotted happy-looking couples, I'd wonder where they found love and want to follow them home for the answer.

After a few years in the city, I got my dream job—writing 11 about weddings for a magazine called *7 Days.* I had to find interesting engaged couples and write up their love stories. I got to ask total strangers the things I'd always wanted to know.

I found at least one sure answer to the question "How do you 12 know it's love?" You know when the everyday things surrounding you—the leaves, the shade of light in the sky, a bowl of strawberries—suddenly shimmer with a kind of unreality.

You know when the tiny details about another person, ones 13 that are insignificant to most people, seem fascinating and incredible to you. One groom told me he loved everything about his future wife, from her handwriting to the way she scratched on their apartment door like a cat when she came home. One bride said she fell in love with her fiancé because "one night, a moth was flying around a light bulb, and he caught it and let it out the window. I said, 'That's it. He's the guy.'"

You also know it's love when you can't stop talking to each 14 other. Almost every couple I've ever interviewed said that on their first or second date, they talked for hours and hours. For some, falling in love is like walking into a soundproof confessional booth, a place where you can tell all.

Finding love can be like discovering a gilded ballroom on the 15 other side of your dingy apartment, and at the same time like finding a pair of great old blue jeans that are exactly your size and seem as if you've worn them forever. I can't tell you how many women have told me they knew they were in love because they forgot to wear makeup around their boyfriend. Or because they felt at ease hanging around him in flannel pajamas. There's some modern truth to Cinderella's tale—it's love when you're incredibly comfortable, when the shoe fits perfectly.

Finally, I think you're in love if you can make each other laugh   16
at the very worst times—when the IRS is auditing you or when
you're driving a convertible in a rainstorm or when your hair is
turning gray. As someone once told me, 90 percent of being in
love is making each other's lives funnier and easier, all the way to
the deathbed.

Seven years ago I started writing about love and weddings for   17
The New York Times in a column called "Vows." And now that
I have been on this beat for so long, a strange thing has happened: I'm considered an expert on love. The truth is, love is
still mostly a mystery to me. The only thing I can confidently
say is this: Love is as plentiful as oxygen. You don't have to be
thin, naturally blonde, super-successful, socially connected,
knowledgeable about politics, or even particularly charming to
find it.

I've interviewed many people who were down on their luck in   18
every way—a ballerina with chronic back problems, a physicist
who had been on 112 (he counted) disastrous blind dates, a clarinet
player who was a single dad and could barely pay the rent. But
love, when they found it, brought humor, candlelight, home-
cooked meals, fun, adventure, poetry, and long conversations into
their lives.

When people ask me where to find love, I tell a story about   19
one of my first job interviews. It was with an editor at a famous
literary magazine. I had no experience or skills, and he didn't for
one second consider hiring me. But he gave me some advice I
will never forget. He said, "Go out into the world. Work hard
and concentrate on what you love to do, writing. If you become
good, we will find you."

That's why I always tell people looking for love to wait for that   20
"I won the lottery" feeling—wait, wait, wait! Don't read articles
about how to trap, seduce, or hypnotize a mate. Don't worry
about your lipstick or your height, because it's not going to matter. Just live your life well, take care of yourself, and don't mope
too much. Love will find you.

Eventually it even found me. At 28, I met my husband in a sta-   21
tionery store. I was buying a typewriter ribbon, and he was looking at Filofaxes. I remember that his eyes perfectly matched his
faded jeans. He remembers that my sneakers were full of sand. He

still talks about those sneakers and how they evoked his child-hood—bonfires by the ocean, driving on the sand in an old Jeep—all those things that he cherished.

How did I know that it was true love? Our first real date lasted   22
for nine hours; we just couldn't stop talking. I had never been able to dance in my life, but I could dance with him, perfectly in step. I have learned that it's love when you finally stop tripping over your toes.

A year after we met, we married.   23

I have come to cherish writing the "Vows" column. With each   24
story I hear, I have proof that love, optimism, guts, grace, perfect partners, and good luck do, in fact, exist. Love, in my opinion, is not a fantasy, not the stuff of romance novels or fairy tales. It's as gritty and real as the subway, it comes around just as regularly, and as long as you can stick it out on the platform, you won't miss it.

UNDERSTANDING DETAILS

1. How did Brady learn that "the potential for love exists in cor-ners, in the most unlikely as well as the most obvious places" (paragraph 6)?
2. What was Brady's "dream job" (paragraph 11)? Why did she like it so much?
3. In what ways was Brady's love life similar to a "tragicomic novel" (paragraph 7)?
4. What does Brady mean when she says "Love will find you" (paragraph 20)?

ANALYZING MEANING

1. Why was Brady preoccupied with the question "How do you know it's love?"?
2. According to Brady, what are three of the main symptoms of being in love? Explain each in your own words.
3. Why is Brady considered an expert on love at this point in her life? What did she do to earn this honor?
4. What does Brady mean by that "'I won the lottery'" feeling" (paragraph 20)? Why should people wait for this feeling?

DISCOVERING RHETORICAL STRATEGIES

1. In your opinion, what is Brady's primary purpose in this essay? Explain your answer in detail.
2. Who do you think is Brady's intended audience for this essay? On what do you base your answer?
3. Brady skillfully uses several similes (a comparison of two unlike items, using "like" or "as") to make her definition clearer and more vivid. Her reference to the girls' ponytails that "swung back and forth like metronomes" (paragraph 3) compares the ponytails to metronomes (small pendulums used by musicians) and gives us a very clear image of these "perfect ponytails." Find two more similes, and explain what they add to Brady's essay.
4. What rhetorical strategies support the author's definition? Give examples of each.

MAKING CONNECTIONS

1. Contrast Brady's view of love with that expressed in Lewis Sawaquat's "For My Indian Daughter," Garrison Keillor's "How the Crab Apple Grew," Judy Brady's "Why I Want a Wife," and Germaine Greer's "A Child Is Born."
2. According to Brady, "You also know it's love when you can't stop talking to each other." Analyze the importance of communication within families by examining the following essays: Amy Tan's "Mother Tongue," Judith Viorst's "The Truth About Lying," Mary Pipher's "Beliefs About Families," and Mary Roach's "Meet the Bickersons."
3. Compare and contrast Brady's description of "true love" of another person with the love of smoking in Franklin Zimring's "Confessions of an Ex-Smoker," the love of bodybuilding in Gloria Steinem's "The Politics of Muscle," the love of horror movies in Stephen King's "Why We Crave Horror Movies," and the love of alcohol in Michael Dorris's "The Broken Cord."

IDEAS FOR DISCUSSION/WRITING

Preparing to Write

Write freely about your views on love: Is romantic love currently a positive force in your life? Do you like being in love? How do you find the perfect mate? If you don't have a partner now, when and where do you expect to find one? What characteristics must this person have? What characteristics do you want to share with someone? What do you want out of a relationship?

Choosing a Topic

1. You have been asked to speak at freshman orientation at your college. Your assigned topic is "The Role of Love in a College Student's Life." Using Brady's article as a resource, define love from a student's perspective. (Remember to cite your source whenever necessary.) Supplement your definition with examples from your own experience and observations.

2. For a group of people your own age, define your dream job. What are the essential features of this job? Why do you want this job? What will this job do for you? What will you do for society with this job?

3. Write a letter to one of your past loves explaining why the relationship didn't work. This could focus on his or her inadequacies as a partner or perhaps on the reasons the two of you weren't good together. Give examples to support your main points.

Before beginning your essay, you might want to consult the checklists on pages 393-394.

ELLEN GOODMAN   (1941–   )

A Working Community

Ellen Goodman is a nationally syndicated columnist and associate editor of the *Boston Globe*, who frequently pens newspaper columns on such topics as feminism, child rearing, divorce, alternative lifestyles, and gardening. Although Goodman once appealed principally to women, her essays now interest readers of both sexes who are, in the words of *New York Times* critic John Leonard, "full of gratitude for having been introduced to a witty and civilized human being in a vulgar and self-pitying decade." Born in Newton, Massachusetts, and educated at Radcliffe College, Goodman began her career in journalism as a researcher and reporter at *Newsweek* magazine, then moved to the *Detroit Free Press* as a feature writer. In 1967, she was hired as a feature writer and "At Large" columnist by the *Boston Globe*. Her first book was *Turning Points* (1979), which examines how men and women have reacted to the changes brought on by the feminist movement. Other publications include five collections of her best newspaper columns: *Close to Home* (1979), *At Large* (1981), *Keeping in Touch* (1985), *Making Sense* (1989), and *Value Judgments* (1993). She is also co-author with Patricia O'Brien of *I Know Just What You Mean: The Power of Friendship in Women's Lives* (2000). In 1980, Goodman's reputation as a first-rate journalist was confirmed when she was awarded the Pulitzer Prize for distinguished commentary. Syndicated now in more than 300 newspapers throughout the country, Goodman lives in Brookline, Massachusetts.

Preparing to Read

The following essay, originally written for the *Washington Post*, proposes a new definition of "community." Before you read this essay, take a few moments to consider your views on the concept of community: What does "community" mean to you? Are different communities a part of your life? What roles do you play in these communities? Why do you play these roles? How do these different communities contribute to who you are? Which communities are your favorites? Which are your least favorite? Explain your answer.

I have a friend who is a member of the medical comunity. It does not say that, of course, on the stationery that bears her home address. This membership comes from her hospital work. 1

I have another friend who is a member of the computer com- munity. This is a fairly new subdivision of our economy, and yet he finds his sense of place in it. 2

Other friends and acquaintances of mine are members of the academic community, or the business community, or the journal- istic community. 3

Though you cannot find these on any map, we know where we belong. 4

None of us, mind you, was born into these communities. Nor did we move into them, U-Hauling our possessions along with us. None has papers to prove we are card-carrying members of one such group or another. Yet it seems that more and more of us are identified by work these days, rater than by street. 5

In the past, most Amerians lived in neighborhoods. We were members of precincts or parishes or school districts. My dictionary still defines community, first of all in geographic terms, as "a body of people who live in one place." 6

But today fewer of us do our living in that one place; more of us just use it for sleeping. Now we call our towns "bedroom sub- urbs," and many of us, without small children as icebreakers, would have trouble naming all the people on our street. 7

It's not that we are more isolated today. It's that many of us have transferred a chunk of our friendships, a major portion of our every- day social lives, from home to office. As more of our neighbors work away from home, the workplace becomes our neighborhood. 8

The kaffeeklatsch of the fifties is the coffee break of the eight- ies. The water cooler, the hall, the elevator, and the parking lot are the back fences of these neighborhoods. The people we have lunch with day after day are those who know the running saga of our mother's operations, our child's math grades, our frozen pipes, and faulty transmissions. 9

We may be strangers at the supermarket that replaced the cor- ner grocer, but we are known at the coffee shop in the lobby. We share with each other a cast of characters from the boss in the cor- ner office to the crazy lady in Shipping, to the lovers in Market- ing. It's not surprising that when researchers ask Americans what they like best about work, they say it is "the shmoose factor." 10

When they ask young mothers at home what they miss most about work, it is the people.

Not all the neighborhoods are empty, nor is every workplace a 11 friendly playground. Most of us have had mixed experiences in these environments. Yet as one woman told me recently, she knows more about the people she passes on the way to her desk than on her way around the block. Our new sense of community hasn't just moved from house to office building. The labels that we wear connect us with members from distant companies, cities, and states. We assume that we have something "in common" with other teachers, nurses, city planners.

It's not unlike the experience of our immigrant grandparents. 12 Many who came to this country still identified themselves as members of the Italian community, the Irish community, the Polish community. They sought out and assumed connections with people from the old country. Many of us have updated that experience. We have replaced ethnic identity with professional identity, the way we replaced neighborhoods with the workplace.

This whole realignment of community is surely most obvious 13 among the mobile professions. People who move from city to city seem to put roots down into their professions. In an age of specialists, they may have to search harder to find people who speak the same language.

I don't think that there is anything massively disruptive about 14 this shifting sense of community. The continuing search for connection and shared enterprise is very human. But I do feel uncomfortable with our shifting identity. The balance has tipped, and we seem increasingly dependent on work for our sense of self.

If our offices are our new neighborhoods, if our professional ti- 15 tles are our new ethnic tags, then how do we separate our selves from our jobs? Self-worth isn't just something to measure in the marketplace. But in these new communities, it becomes harder to tell who we are without saying what we do.

UNDERSTANDING DETAILS

1. What does Goodman mean when she says, "The kaffeklatsch of the fifties is the coffee break of the nineties" (paragraph 9)?
2. According to Goodman, how has our sense of community changed during the past few years?

3. How is a sense of community related to a sense of belonging?
4. Explain Goodman's statement about self-worth at the end of her essay: "Self-worth isn't just something to measure in the marketplace" (paragraph 15).

ANALYZING MEANING

1. Why are our towns called "bedroom suburbs" (paragraph 7)?
2. Why do you think Americans generally say they like "the shmoose factor" (paragraph 10) best about work?
3. Do you feel you have something in common with students around the world? Explain your answer.
4. According to Goodman, in what way is our identity as humans changing? Explain your answer.

DISCOVERING RHETORICAL STRATEGIES

1. Goodman starts her essay off with four very short paragraphs. What effect does this technique have on the essay as a whole?
2. Goodman's essay is made up to a large extent of items in a series and independent clauses that present her ideas as equivalent and balanced with one another. Find two examples of each of these techniques, and explain how they help Goodman make her point.
3. Goodman asks only one question in this essay. What is that question? Where does it appear in the essay? And what effect does it have on the essay as a whole?
4. What other rhetorical strategies, besides definition, does Goodman use in this essay? Give examples of each.

MAKING CONNECTIONS

1. Imagine that Goodman, William Ouchi ("Japanese and American Workers: Two Casts of Mind"), and Robert Ramirez ("The Barrio") were discussing the relationships between "identity" and "community." How would each explain this relationship? Who would you most likely agree with? Explain your answer.
2. Compare and contrast the ways in which Goodman, Peter Salins ("Take a Ticket"), and Barbara Ehrenreich ("The Ecstasy of War") describe the relative difficulty levels of join-

ing various "communities." Which community mentioned by these authors would be most difficult to belong to? Which would be least difficult? Why?

3. To what extent would Goodman and Mary Pipher ("Beliefs About Families") agree that a family is a "community"? Compare and contrast the way each of these authors defines her central term ("communities" and "families"). Which definition seems most complete and convincing to you? Why?

IDEAS FOR DISCUSSION/WRITING

Preparing to Write

Write freely about your current response to the idea of "community": What role does our sense of community play in American society today? In what ways are communities important to a society? What communities do you belong to? What role do communities play in your life? Why do you belong to these communities? What do you have in common with other "members" of these communities? Has your sense of community changed as you grew older? In what ways?

Choosing a Topic

1. Choose a "community" to which you belong and define your role in that group.
2. For your college newspaper, define the term "students" or "faculty" as communities in the academic world. Determine an audience and focus before you begin to write.
3. Write an essay in which you agree or disagree with the last line of Goodman's essay: "But in these new communities, it becomes harder and harder to tell who we are without saying what we do" (paragraph 15). Make sure you support your opinion with enough evidence.

Before beginning your essay, you might want to consult the checklists on pages 393–394.

CHAPTER WRITING ASSIGNMENTS

Practicing Definition

1. Identify a term people use to describe you (for example, *trustworthy*, *sloppy*, or *athletic*). In a well-developed essay, define this term as clearly as you can, and discuss whether or not it accurately represents you. Support your claim with carefully chosen details.

2. In what ways do our families define us? How do our families shape who we are and who we have become? In an essay, define the concept of family by explaining how your family members relate to each other.

3. Think of an object you value greatly. For example, a ring might represent a special relationship. Then, in essay form, explain what this object says about you. Why is it your favorite? What does it mean to you?

Exploring Ideas

1. Have you ever felt jealous? What do you think are the most common sources of jealousy? Do you think that jealousy is mostly a productive or unproductive emotion? Write an essay discussing the main qualities of jealousy. What do most people need to know about this feeling?

2. Think of all the "communities" to which you belong (for example, school, church, neighborhood, friends). Choose one that is really important to you, and, in an essay, identify the major features of this community. What makes this community so important in your life?

3. In essay form, describe an ugly part of your campus or city, and explore some important ways this place could be improved or changed. What effects do you think these changes might have on your community or campus? How did you come to this conclusion?

8

CAUSE/EFFECT

Tracing Reasons and Results

Wanting to know why things happen is one of our earliest, most basic instincts: Why can't I go out, Mommy? Why are you laughing? Why won't the dog stop barking? Why can't I swim faster than my big brother? These questions, and many more like them, reflect the innately inquisitive nature that dwells within each of us. Closely related to this desire to understand *why* is our corresponding interest in *what* will happen in the future as a result of some particular action: What will I feel like tomorrow if I stay up late tonight? How will I perform in the track meet Saturday if I practice all week? What will be the result if I mix together these two potent chemicals? What will happen if I turn in my next English assignment two days early?

A daily awareness of this intimate relationship between causes and effects allows us to begin to understand the complex and interrelated series of events that make up our lives and the lives of others. For example, trying to understand the various causes of the conflict in the Persian Gulf teaches us about international relations; knowing our biological reactions to certain foods helps us make decisions about what to eat; understanding the interrelated reasons for the outbreak of World War II offers us insight into historical trends and human nature; knowing the effects of sun-shine on various parts of our bodies helps us make decisions about how much ultraviolet exposure we can tolerate and what suntan lotion to use; and understanding the causes of America's most recent recession will help us respond appropriately to the next economic crisis we encounter. More than anything else, tracing causes and effects teaches us how to think clearly and react intelligently to our multifaceted environment.

In college, you will often be asked to use this natural interest in causes and effects to analyze particular situations and to discern general principles. For example, you might be asked some of the following questions on essay exams in different courses:

Anthropology: Why did the Mayan culture disintegrate?

Psychology: Why do humans respond to fear in different ways?

Biology: How do lab rats react to caffeine?

History: What were the positive effects of the Spanish–American War?

Business: Why did so many computer manufacturing companies go bankrupt in the early 1980s?

Your ability to answer such questions will depend in large part on your skill at understanding cause/effect relationships.

DEFINING CAUSE/EFFECT

Cause/effect analysis requires the ability to look for connections between different elements and to analyze the reasons for those connections. As the name implies, this rhetorical mode has two separate components: cause and effect. A particular essay might concentrate on cause (Why do you live in a dorm?), on effect (What are the resulting advantages and disadvantages of living in a dorm?), or on some combination of the two. In working with causes, we are searching for any circumstances from the past that may have caused a single event; in looking for effects, we seek occurrences that took place after a particular event and resulted from that event. Like process analysis, cause/effect makes use of our intellectual ability to analyze. Process analysis addresses *how* something happens, whereas causal analysis discusses *why* it happened and *what* the result was. A process analysis paper, for example, might explain how to advertise more effectively to increase sales, whereas a cause/effect study would discover that three specific elements contributed to an increase in sales: effective advertising, personal service, and selective discounts. The study of causes and effects, therefore, provides many different and helpful ways for humans to make sense of and clarify their views of the world.

Looking for causes and effects requires an advanced form of thinking. It is more complex than most rhetorical strategies we have studied because it can exist on a number of different and progressively more difficult levels. The most accurate and effective causal analysis accrues from digging for the real or ultimate causes or effects, as opposed to those that are merely superficial or immediate. Actress Angela Lansbury would have been out of work on an episode of the television show *Murder, She Wrote*, for example, if her character had stopped her investigation at the immediate cause of death (slipping in the bathtub) rather than searching diligently for the *real* cause (an overdose of cocaine administered by an angry companion, which resulted in the slip in the tub). Similarly, voters would be easy to manipulate if they considered only the immediate effects of a tax increase (a slightly higher tax bill) rather than the ultimate benefits that would result (the many years of improved education that our children would receive because of the specialized programs created by such an increase). Only the discovery of the actual reasons for an event or an idea will lead to the logical and accurate analysis of causes and effects important to a basic understanding of various aspects of our lives.

Faulty reasoning assigns causes to a sequence of actions without adequate justification. One such logical fallacy is called *post hoc, ergo propter hoc* ("after this, therefore because of this"): The fact that someone lost a job after walking under a ladder does not mean that the two events are causally related; by the same token, if we get up every morning at 5:30 A.M., just before the sun rises, we cannot therefore conclude that the sun rises *because* we get up (no matter how self-centered we are!). Faulty reasoning also occurs when we oversimplify a particular situation. Most events are connected to a multitude of causes and effects. Sometimes one effect has many causes: A student may fail a history exam because she's been working two part-time jobs, she was sick, she didn't study hard enough, and she found the instructor very boring. One cause may also have many effects. If a house burns down, the people who lived in it will be out of a home. If we look at such a tragic scene more closely, however, we may also note that the fire traumatized a child who lived there, helped the family learn what good friends they had, encouraged the family to double their future fire insurance, and provided the happy stimulus that they needed to make a long-dreamed-of move to another city. One event has thus resulted in many interrelated effects. Building an argument on insecure foundations or oversimplifying the causes or effects connected with an event will seriously hinder the construction of a rational essay. No matter what the nature of the cause/effect analysis, it must always be based on clear observation, accurate facts, and rigorous logic.

In the following paragraph, a student writer analyzes some of the causes and effects connected with the controversial issue of euthanasia. Notice how he makes connections and then analyzes those connections as he consistently explores the immediate and ultimate effects of being able to stretch life beyond its normal limits through new medical technology:

> *Along with the many recent startling advancements in medical technology have come a number of complex moral, ethical, and spiritual questions that beg to be answered. We now have the ability to prolong the life of the human body for a very long time. But what rights do patients and their families have to curtail cruel and unusual medical treatment that stretches life beyond its normal limits? This dilemma has produced a ripple effect in society. Is the extension of life an unquestionable goal in itself, regardless of the quality of that life? Modern scientific technology has forced doctors to reevaluate the exact meaning and purpose of their profession. For example, many medical schools and undergraduate university programs now routinely offer classes on medical ethics—an esoteric and infrequently taught subject only a few years ago. Doctors and scholars alike are realizing that medical personnel alone cannot be expected to decide on the exact parameters of life. In like manner, the judicial process must now evaluate the legal complexities of mercy killings and the rights of patients to die with dignity and without unnecessary medical intervention. The insurance business, too, wrestles with the catastrophic effects of new technology on the costs of today's hospital care. In short, medical progress entails more than microscopes, chemicals, and high-tech instruments. If we are to develop as a thoughtful, just, and merciful society, we must consider not only the*

physical well-being of our nation's patients, but their emotional, spiritual, and financial status as well.

THINKING CRITICALLY BY USING CAUSE/EFFECT

Thinking about causes and effects is one of the most advanced mental activities that we perform. It involves complex operations that we must think through carefully, making sure all connections are reasonable and accurate. Unlike other rhetorical patterns, cause/effect thinking requires us to see specific relationships between two or more items. To practice this strategy, we need to look for items or events that are causally related—that is, one that has caused the other. Then, we can focus on either the causes (the initial stimulus), the effects (the results), or a combination of the two.

Searching for causes and effects requires a great deal of digging that is not necessary for most of the other modes. Cause/effect necessitates the ultimate in investigative work. The mental exertion associated with this thinking strategy is sometimes exhausting, but it is always worth going through when you discover relationships that you never saw before or when you uncover links in your reasoning that were previously unknown or obscure to you.

If you've ever had the secret desire to be a private eye or an investigator of any sort, practicing cause/effect reasoning can be lots of fun. It forces you to see relationships among multiple items and then to make sense of those connections. Completing exercises in this skill by itself will once again help you perfect the logistics of cause/effect thinking before you mix and match it with other thinking strategies.

1. Choose a major problem you see in our society, and list what you think are the main causes of this problem on one side of a piece of paper and the effects on the other side. Compare the two lists to see how they differ. Then, compare and contrast your list with those written by other students.

2. What "caused" you to become a student? What influences led you to this choice at this point in your life? How has being a student affected your life? List several overall effects.

3. List the effects of one of the following: getting a speeding ticket, winning the U.S. Open tennis tournament, graduating from college, or watching TV till the wee hours of the morning.

READING AND WRITING CAUSE/EFFECT ESSAYS

Causal analysis is usually employed for one of three main purposes: (1) to prove a specific point (such as the necessity for stricter gun control), in which case the writer generally deals totally with facts and with conclusions drawn from those facts; (2) to argue against a widely accepted belief (for example, the assertion that cocaine is addictive), in which case the writer relies principally on facts, with perhaps some pertinent opinions; or (3) to speculate on a theory (for instance, why the crime rate is higher in most major cities than it is in rural areas), in which case the writer probably presents hypotheses and opinions along with facts. This section will explore these purposes in cause/effect essays from the standpoint of both reading and writing.

How to Read a Cause/Effect Essay

Preparing to Read.   As you set out to read the essays in this chapter, begin by focusing your attention on the title and the synopsis of the essay you are about to read and by scanning the essay itself: What do you think Stephen King is going to talk about in "Why We Crave Horror Movies"? What does the synopsis in the Rhetorical Table of Contents tell you about Michael Dorris's "The Broken Cord" or about Richard Rodriguez's "The Fear of Losing a Culture"?

Also, at this stage in the reading process, you should try to learn as much as you can about the author of the essay and the reasons he or she wrote it. Ask yourself questions like the following: What is King's intention in "Why We Crave Horror Movies"? Who is Mary Roach's intended audience in "Meet the Bickersons"? And what is Alice Walker's point of view in "Beauty: When the Other Dancer Is the Self"?

Finally, before you begin to read, answer the prereading questions for each essay and then consider the proposed essay topic from a variety of perspectives: For example, concerning Rodriguez's topic, how important to you is your ethnic or national background? Which segments of American society are most aware of cultural differences? Which the least? Do you have a desire to understand relationships better? What do you want to know from Roach about people and arguing?

Reading. As you read each essay in this chapter for the first time, record your spontaneous reactions to it, drawing as often as possible on the preliminary material you already know: What do you think of horror movies (King)? What is Dorris suggesting about fetal alcohol babies? Have you experienced an addiction of any kind? Why did Roach choose the title she did?

Whenever you can, try to create a context for your reading: What is the tone of Rodriguez's comments about culture? How does this tone help him communicate with his audience? What do you think Walker's purpose is in her essay concerning her childhood accident? How clearly does she get this purpose across to you?

Also, during this reading, note the essay's thesis and check to see if the writer thoroughly explores all possibilities before settling on the primary causes and/or effects of a particular situation; in addition, determine whether the writer clearly states the assertions that naturally evolve from a discussion of the topic. Finally, read the questions following each essay to get a sense of the main issues and strategies in the selection.

Rereading. When you reread these essays, you should focus mainly on the writer's craft. Notice how the authors narrow and focus their material, how they make clear and logical connections between ideas in their essays, how they support their conclusions with concrete examples, how they use other rhetorical modes to accomplish their cause/effect analysis, and how they employ logical transitions to move us smoothly from one point to another. Most important, however, ask yourself if the writer actually discusses the real causes and/or effects of a particular circumstance: What does King say are the primary reasons people crave horror movies? According to Roach, why do many couples have trouble in their marriages? What are the primary causes and effects of Walker's childhood injury?

For a thorough outline of the reading process, consult the checklist on pages 20-21 of the Introduction.

How to Write a Cause/Effect Essay

Preparing to Write. Beginning a cause/effect essay requires— as does any other essay—exploring and limiting your subject, specifying a purpose, and identifying an audience. The Preparing

444   CHAPTER 8 ~ Cause/Effect

to Write questions before the essay assignments, coupled with the prewriting techniques outlined in the Introduction (pp. 21–27), encourage you to consider specific issues related to your reading. The assignments themselves will then help you limit your topic and determine a particular purpose and audience for your message. For cause/effect essays, determining a purpose is even more important than usual, because your readers can get hopelessly lost unless your analysis is clearly focused.

Writing. For all its conceptual complexity, a cause/effect essay can be organized quite simply. The introduction generally presents the subject(s) and states the purpose of the analysis in a clear thesis. The body of the paper then explores all relevant causes and/or effects, typically progressing either from least to most influential or from most to least influential. Finally, the concluding section summarizes the various cause–effect relationships established in the body of the paper and clearly states the conclusions that can be drawn from those relationships.

The following additional guidelines should assist you in producing an effective cause/effect essay in all academic disciplines:

1. Narrow and focus your material as much as possible.
2. Consider all possibilities before assigning real or ultimate causes or effects.
3. Show connections between ideas by using transitions and key words—such as *because, reasons, results, effects*, and *consequences*—to guide your readers smoothly through your essay.
4. Support all inferences with concrete evidence.
5. Be as objective as possible in your analysis so that you don't distort logic with personal biases.
6. Understand your audience's opinions and convictions, so that you know what to emphasize in your essay.
7. Qualify your assertions to avoid overstatement and oversimplification.

These suggestions apply to both cause/effect essay assignments and exam questions.

Rewriting. As you revise your cause/effect essays, ask yourself the following important questions:

• Is your thesis stated clearly at the outset of your paper?

- Does it include your subject and your purpose?

- Do you accomplish your purpose as effectively as possible for your particular audience?

- Do you use logical reasoning throughout the essay?

- Do you carefully explore all relevant causes and/or effects, searching for the real (as opposed to the immediate) reasons in each case?

- Do you state clearly the conclusions that can be drawn from your paper?

More specific guidelines for writing and revising your essays appear on pages 32–34 of the Introduction.

STUDENT ESSAY: CAUSE/EFFECT AT WORK

In the following essay, the student writer analyzes the effects of contemporary TV soap operas on young people: Notice that she states her subject and purpose at the beginning of the essay and then presents a combination of facts and opinions in her exploration of the topic. Notice also that, in her analysis, the writer is careful to draw clear connections between her perceptions of the issue and various objective details in an attempt to trace the effects of this medium in our society today. At the end of her essay, look at her summary of the logical relationships she establishes in the body of the essay and her statements about the conclusions she draws from these relationships.

Distortions of Reality

Background   Television's contributions to society, positive and negative, have been debated continually since this piece of technology invaded the average American household in the 1950s. Television has brought an unlimited influx of new information, ideas, and cultures into our homes. However, based on my observations of my thirteen-year-old cousin, Katie, and her friends, I think we need to take a closer look at the effects of soap operas on adolescents today. The distortions of reality portrayed on these programs are frighteningly misleading and, in my opinion, can be very confusing to young people.

Transition   During the early 1990s, the lifestyle of the typical soap opera "family" has been radically transformed from comfortable pretentiousness to blatant and unrealistic decadence. The characters neither live nor dress like the majority of their viewers, who are generally middle-class Americans. These television families live in large, majestic homes that are flawlessly decorated. The ac-

Concrete examples   tors are often adorned in beautiful designer clothing, fur coats, and expensive jewelry, and this opulent lifestyle is sustained by people with no visible means of income. Very few of the characters seem to "work" for a living. When they do, upward mobility—without the benefit of the proper education or suitable training—and a well-planned marriage come quickly.

Transition   From this constant barrage of conspicuous consumption, my cousin and her friends seem to have a distorted view of everyday economic realities. I see Katie and her group becoming obsessed with the appearance of their clothes and possessions. I frequently

Concrete examples   hear them berate their parents' jobs and modest homes. With noticeable arrogance, these young adolescents seem to view their parents' lives as "failures" when compared to the effortless, luxurious lifestyles portrayed in the soaps.

Transition   One of the most alluring features of this genre is its masterful use of deception. Conflicts between characters in soap operas are based on secrecy and misinformation. Fail-

Concrete examples   ure to tell the truth and to perform honorable deeds further complicates the entangled

Thesis statement

First distortion of reality

First effect

lives and love affairs of the participants. But when the truth finally comes out and all mistakes and misdeeds become public, the culprits and offenders hardly ever suffer for their actions. In fact, they appear to leave the scene of the crime guilt-free.

Second distortion of reality

Transition

Regrettably, Katie and her friends consistently express alarming indifference to this lack of moral integrity. In their daily viewing, they shrug off underhanded scenes of scheming and conniving, and they marvel at how the characters manipulate each other into positions of powerlessness or grapple in distasteful love scenes. I can only conclude that continued exposure to this amoral behavior is eroding the fundamental values of truth and fidelity in these kids.

Concrete examples

Second effect

Transition

Also in the soaps, the powers-that-be conveniently disregard any sense of responsibility for wrongdoing. Characters serve jail terms quickly and in relative comfort. Drug or alcohol abuse does not mar anyone's physical appearance or behavior, and poverty is virtually nonexistent. Usually, the wrongdoer's position, wealth, and prestige are quickly restored—with little pain and suffering.

Third distortion of reality

Concrete examples

Adolescents are clearly learning that people can act without regard for the harmful effects of their actions on themselves and others when they see this type of behavior go unpunished. Again, I notice the result of this delusion in my cousin. Recently, when a businessman in our community was convicted of embezzling large sums of money from his clients, Katie was outraged because he was sentenced to five years in prison, unlike her daytime TV "heartthrob," who had been given a suspended sentence for a

Third effect

Concrete examples

similar crime. With righteous indignation, Katie claimed that the victims, many of whom had lost their entire savings, should have realized that any business investment involves risk and the threat of loss. Logic and common sense evaded Katie's reasoning as she insisted on comparing television justice with real-life scruples.

The writers and producers of soap operas argue that the shows are designed to entertain viewers and are not meant to be reflections of reality. Theoretically, this may be true, but I can actually see how these soap operas are affecting my cousin and her crowd. Although my personal observations are limited, I cannot believe they are unique or unusual. Too many young people think that they can amass wealth and material possessions without an education, hard work, or careful financial planning; that material goods are the sole measure of a person's success in life; and that honesty and integrity are not necessarily admirable qualities.

Ultimate effect

Proposed solution   Soap operas should demonstrate a realistic lifestyle and a responsible sense of behavior. The many hours adolescents spend in front of the television can obviously influence their view of the world. As a society, we cannot afford the consequences resulting from the distortions of reality portrayed every day in these shows.

Student Writer's Comments

In general, writing this essay was not as easy as I had anticipated during my prewriting phase. Although I was interested in and familiar with my topic, I had trouble fitting all the pieces together: matching causes with effects, examples with main points, and problems with solutions.

My prewriting activities were a combination of lists and journal entries that gave me loads of ideas and phrasing to work with in my drafts. From this initial thinking exercise, I made an informal outline of the points I wanted to make. I played with the order of these topics for a while and then began to write.

Because I had spent so much time thinking through various causal relationships before I began to write, I generated the first draft with minimal pain. But I was not happy with it. The examples that I had chosen to support various points I wanted to make did not fit as well as they could, and the whole essay was unfocused and scattered. Although all writing requires support and focus, I realized that a cause/effect essay demands special attention to the relationship between specific examples and their ultimate causes and/or effects. As a result, I had to begin again to revise my sprawling first draft.

I spent my first revising session on the very sloppy introduction and conclusion. I felt that if I could tighten up these parts of the essay, I would have a clearer notion of my purpose and focus. I am convinced now that the time I spent on the beginning and ending of my essay really paid off. I rewrote my thesis several times until I finally arrived at the statement in the draft printed here. This final thesis statement gave me a clear sense of direction for revising the rest of my paper.

I then worked through my essay paragraph by paragraph, making sure that the examples and illustrations I cited supported as effectively as possible the point I was making. I made sure that the causes and effects were accurately paired, and I reorganized sections of the essay that didn't yet read smoothly. I put the final touches on my conclusion and handed in my paper—with visions of causes, effects, and soap opera characters still dancing around in my head.

SOME FINAL THOUGHTS ON CAUSE/EFFECT

The essays in this chapter deal with both causes and effects in a variety of ways. As you read each essay, try to discover its primary purpose and the ultimate causes and/or effects of the issue under discussion. Note also the clear causal relationships that each author sets forth on solid foundations supported by logical reasoning. Although the subjects of these essays vary dramatically, each essay exhibits the basic elements of effective causal analysis.

CAUSE/EFFECT IN REVIEW

Reading Cause/Effect Essays

Preparing to Read

- ✓ What assumptions can you make from the essay's title?
- ✓ Can you guess what the general mood of the essay is?
- ✓ What is the essay's purpose and audience?
- ✓ What does the synopsis in the Rhetorical Table of Contents tell you about the essay?
- ✓ What can you learn from the author's biography?
- ✓ Can you guess what the author's point of view toward the subject is?
- ✓ What are your responses to the Preparing to Read questions?

Reading

- ✓ What is the author's thesis?
- ✓ What are the primary causes and/or effects in the essay?
- ✓ Did you preview the questions that follow the essay?

Rereading

- ✓ How does the writer narrow and focus the essay?
- ✓ Does the writer make clear and logical connections between the ideas in the essay?
- ✓ What concrete examples support the author's conclusions?
- ✓ Does the writer discuss the real causes and effects?
- ✓ What are your responses to the questions after the essay?

Writing Cause/Effect Essays

Preparing to Write

- ✓ What are your responses to the Preparing to Write questions?
- ✓ What is your purpose?
- ✓ Who is your audience?

Writing

✓ Do you narrow and focus your material as much as possible?

✓ Do you consider all possibilities before assigning real or ultimate causes or effects?

✓ Do you show connections between ideas by using transitions and key words?

✓ Do you support all inferences with concrete evidence?

✓ Are you as objective as possible in your analysis so that you don't distort logic with personal biases?

✓ Do you understand your audience's opinions and convictions, so that you know what to emphasize in your essay?

✓ Do you qualify your assertions to avoid overstatement and oversimplification?

Rewriting

✓ Is your thesis stated clearly at the outset of your paper?

✓ Does it include your subject and your purpose?

✓ Do you accomplish your purpose as effectively as possible for your particular audience?

✓ Do you use logical reasoning throughout the essay?

✓ Do you carefully explore all relevant causes and/or effects, searching for the real (as opposed to the immediate) reasons in each case?

✓ Do you state clearly the conclusions that can be drawn from your paper?

STEPHEN KING   (1947–   )

Why We Crave Horror Movies

"People's appetites for terror seem insatiable," Stephen King once remarked, an insight that may help justify his phenomenal success as a writer of horror fiction since the mid-1970s. His books have sold over one hundred million copies, and the movies made from them have generated more income than the gross domestic product of several small countries. After early jobs as a janitor, a laundry worker, and a high school English teacher in Portland, Maine, King turned to writing full time following the spectacular sales of his first novel, *Carrie* (1974), which focuses on a shy, socially ostracized young girl who takes revenge on her cruel classmates through newly developed telekinetic powers. King's subsequent books have included *The Shining* (1976), *Firestarter* (1980), *Cujo* (1981), *The Dark Tower* (1982), *Christine* (1983), *Pet Sematary* (1983), *Misery* (1987), *The Stand* (1990), *Four Past Midnight* (1990), *The Waste Lands* (1992), *Delores Claiborne* (1993), *Desperation* (1996), *Bag of Bones* (1999), and *On Writing: A Memoir of the Craft* (2000). Asked to explain why readers and moviegoers are so attracted to his tales of horror, King recently explained that most people's lives "are full of fears—that their marriage isn't working, that they aren't going to make it on the job, that society is crumbling all around them. But we're really not supposed to talk about things like that, and so they don't have any outlets for all those scary feelings. But the horror writer can give them a place to put their fears, and it's OK to be afraid then, because nothing is real, and you can blow it all away when it's over." A cheerful though somewhat superstitious person, King, who now lives in Bangor, Maine, admits to doing most of his best writing during the morning hours. "You think I want to write this stuff at night?" he once asked a reviewer.

Preparing to Read

As you prepare to read this article, consider your thoughts on America's emotional condition: How emotionally healthy are Americans? Were they more emotionally healthy twenty years ago? A century ago? What makes a society emotionally healthy?

Emotionally unhealthy? How can a society maintain good health? What is the relationship between emotional health and a civilized society?

I think that we're all mentally ill; those of us outside the asy- 1
lums only hide it a little better—and maybe not all that much
better, after all. We've all known people who talk to themselves, people who sometimes squinch their faces into horrible
grimaces when they believe no one is watching, people who have
some hysterical fear—of snakes, the dark, the tight place, the long
drop . . . and, of course, those final worms and grubs that are
waiting so patiently underground.

When we pay our four or five bucks and seat ourselves at 2
tenth-row center in a theater showing a horror movie, we are
daring the nightmare.

Why? Some of the reasons are simple and obvious. To show 3
that we can, that we are not afraid, that we can ride this roller
coaster. Which is not to say that a really good horror movie may
not surprise a scream out of us at some point, the way we may
scream when the roller coaster twists through a complete 360 or
plows through a lake at the bottom of the drop. And horror
movies, like roller coasters, have always been the special province
of the young; by the time one turns 40 or 50, one's appetite for
double twists or 360-degree loops may be considerably depleted.

We also go to reestablish our feelings of essential normality; the 4
horror movie is innately conservative, even reactionary. Freda
Jackson as the horrible melting woman in *Die, Monster, Die!* confirms for us that no matter how far we may be removed from the
beauty of a Robert Redford or a Diana Ross, we are still light-
years from true ugliness.

And we go to have fun. 5

Ah, but this is where the ground starts to slope away, isn't it? 6
Because this is a very peculiar sort of fun, indeed. The fun comes
from seeing others menaced—sometimes killed. One critic has
suggested that if pro football has become the voyeur's version of
combat, then the horror film has become the modern version of
the public lynching.

It is true that the mythic, "fairy-tale" horror film intends to 7
take away the shades of gray. . . . It urges us to put away our more

civilized and adult penchant for analysis and to become children again, seeing things in pure blacks and whites. It may be that horror movies provide psychic relief on this level because this invitation to lapse into simplicity, irrationality, and even outright madness is extended so rarely. We are told we may allow our emotions a free rein . . . or no rein at all.

If we are all insane, then sanity becomes a matter of degree. If   8
your insanity leads you to carve up women, like Jack the Ripper or the Cleveland Torso Murderer, we clap you away in the funny farm (but neither of those two amateur-night surgeons was ever caught, heh-heh-heh); if, on the other hand, your insanity leads you only to talk to yourself when you're under stress or to pick your nose on your morning bus, then you are left alone to go about your business . . . though it is doubtful that you will ever be invited to the best parties.

The potential lyncher is in almost all of us (excluding saints,   9
past and present; but then, most saints have been crazy in their own ways), and every now and then, he has to be let loose to scream and roll around in the grass. Our emotions and our fears form their own body, and we recognize that it demands its own exercise to maintain proper muscle tone. Certain of these emotional muscles are accepted—even exalted—in civilized society; they are, of course, the emotions that tend to maintain the status quo of civilization itself. Love, friendship, loyalty, kindness— these are all the emotions that we applaud, emotions that have been immortalized in the couplets of Hallmark cards and in the verses (I don't dare call it poetry) of Leonard Nimoy.

When we exhibit these emotions, society showers us with posi-   10
tive reinforcement; we learn this even before we get out of diapers. When, as children, we hug our rotten little puke of a sister and give her a kiss, all the aunts and uncles smile and twit and cry, "Isn't he the sweetest little thing?" Such coveted treats as chocolate-covered graham crackers often follow. But if we deliberately slam the rotten little puke of a sister's fingers in the door, sanctions follow— angry remonstrance from parents, aunts, and uncles; instead of a chocolate-covered graham cracker, a spanking.

But anticivilization emotions don't go away, and they demand   11
periodic exercise. We have such "sick" jokes as, "What's the difference between a truckload of bowling balls and a truckload of dead babies?" (You can't unload a truckload of bowling balls with

a pitchfork . . . a joke, by the way, that I heard originally from a ten-year-old.) Such a joke may surprise a laugh or a grin out of us even as we recoil, a possibility that confirms the thesis: If we share a brotherhood of man, then we also share an insanity of man. None of which is intended as a defense of either the sick joke or insanity but merely as an explanation of why the best horror films, like the best fairy tales, manage to be reactionary, anarchistic, and revolutionary all at the same time.

The mythic horror movie, like the sick joke, has a dirty job to   12
do. It deliberately appeals to all that is worst in us. It is morbidity unchained, our most base instincts let free, our nastiest fantasies realized . . . , and it all happens, fittingly enough, in the dark. For those reasons, good liberals often shy away from horror films. For myself, I like to see the most aggressive of them—*Dawn of the Dead*, for instance—as lifting a trap door in the civilized forebrain and throwing a basket of raw meat to the hungry alligators swimming around in that subterranean river beneath.

Why bother? Because it keeps them from getting out, man. It   13
keeps them down there and me up here. It was Lennon and Mc-Cartney who said that all you need is love, and I would agree with that.

As long as you keep the gators fed.   14

UNDERSTANDING DETAILS

1. Why, in King's opinion, do civilized people enjoy horror movies?
2. According to King, in what ways are horror movies like roller coasters?
3. According to King, how are horror films like public lynchings?
4. What is the difference between "emotions that tend to maintain the status quo of civilization" (paragraph 9) and "anticivilization emotions" (paragraph 11)?

ANALYZING MEANING

1. How can horror movies "reestablish our feelings of essential normality" (paragraph 4)?
2. What is "reactionary, anarchistic, and revolutionary" (paragraph 11) about fairy tales? About horror films?

3. Why does the author think we need to exercise our anticivilization emotions? What are some other ways we might confront these emotions?
4. Explain the last line of King's essay: "As long as you keep the gators fed" (paragraph 14).

DISCOVERING RHETORICAL STRATEGIES

1. What is the cause/effect relationship King notes in society between horror movies and sanity?
2. Why does King begin his essay with such a dramatic statement as "I think that we're all mentally ill" (paragraph 1)?
3. Who do you think is the author's intended audience for this essay? Describe them in detail. How did you come to this conclusion?
4. What different rhetorical strategies does King use to support his cause/effect analysis? Give examples of each.

MAKING CONNECTIONS

1. Apply Stephen King's definition of "horror" to such horrific experiences as the preparation of a dead body for its funeral (Jessica Mitford, "Behind the Formaldehyde Curtain"), rape (Nancy Gibbs, "When Is It Rape?"), and/or caring for a fetal alcohol syndrome child (Michael Dorris, "The Broken Cord"). In what way is each of these events "horrible"? What are the principal differences between watching a horror movie and living through a real-life horror like a rape?
2. In this essay, King gives us important insights into his own writing process, especially into how horror novels and movies affect their audiences. Compare and contrast his revelation of the techniques of his trade with those advanced by Paul Roberts ("How to Say Nothing in Five Hundred Words"), Natalie Goldberg ("The Rules of Writing Practice"), or Kurt Vonnegut ("How to Write with Style"), all of whom are discussing the writing process. Whose advice is most helpful to you? Explain your answer.
3. Compare King's comments about "fear" with similar insights into fear by such other authors as Fred Pelka ("Hating the Sick: Health Chauvinism and Its Cure"), Richard Rodriguez ("The

Fear of Losing a Culture"), and Alice Walker ("Beauty: When the Other Dancer Is the Self"). How would each of these writers define the term differently? With which author's definition would you most likely agree? Explain your answer.

IDEAS FOR DISCUSSION/WRITING

Preparing to Write

Write freely about how most people maintain a healthy emotional attitude: How would you define emotional well-being? When are people most emotionally healthy? Most emotionally unhealthy? What do your friends and relatives do to maintain a healthy emotional life? What do you do to maintain emotional health? What is the connection between our individual emotional health and the extent to which our society is civilized?

Choosing a Topic

1. Think of a release other than horror films for our most violent emotions. Is it an acceptable release? Write an essay for the general public explaining the relationship between this particular release and our "civilized" society.

2. If you accept King's analysis of horror movies, what role in society do you think other types of movies play (e.g., love stories, science-fiction movies, and comedies)? Choose one type, and explain its role to your college composition class.

3. Your psychology instructor has asked you to explain your opinions on the degree of sanity or insanity in America at present. In what ways are we sane? In what ways are we insane? Write an essay for your psychology instructor explaining in detail your observations along these lines.

Before beginning your essay, you might want to consult the checklists on pages 450–451.

MICHAEL DORRIS   (1945–1997)

The Broken Cord

Michael Dorris, a descendant of Modoc American Indians and Irish and French settlers, grew up in Kentucky and Montana. He earned his B.A. at Georgetown University and his Master of Arts degree at Yale and was for many years a professor of anthropology and Native-American Studies at Dartmouth, where he was also head of the Native-American Studies program. His training was quite eclectic. "I came to cultural anthropology," he has explained, "by way of an undergraduate program in English and classics and a Master's Degree in history of the theater." He was also a Guggenheim Fellow (1978), a Rockefeller Fellow (1985), a member of the Smithsonian Institution Council, a National Endowment for the Humanities consultant, a National Public Radio commentator, and a member of the editorial board of the *American Indian Culture and Research Journal* during his distinguished academic career. His many publications included *Native Americans: Five Hundred Years After* (1975); a bestselling novel, *A Yellow Raft in Blue Water* (1987); *The Broken Cord* (1989), a work of nonfiction that won the Heartland Prize, the Christopher Medal, and the National Book Critics Circle Award; *Morning Girl* (1992), a book of short stories; and two more novels, *Working Men* (1993) and *Rooms in the House of Stone* (1993). Dorris also coauthored several books with his wife, Louise Erdrich, including *Route Two and Back* (1991), a collection of travel essays. Prior to his recent death, he advised students using *The Prose Reader* to "work at as many kinds of jobs as possible while they are young and to keep daily journals of their experiences and impressions."

Preparing to Read

The following excerpt from *The Broken Cord* details some of Dorris's frustrations in raising his adopted son, Adam, who suffered from fetal alcohol syndrome until his death in 1991. As you prepare to read this article, take a few moments to think about your own physical and mental growth: What do you know about your birth? How did you develop as a child? Are you reaching your physical and mental potential? How do you know? Are there any barriers

between you and this potential? What are they? How can you sur-
mount them? How will you maintain your potential?

Adam's birthdays are, I think, the hardest anniversaries, 1
even though as an adoptive father I was not present to
hear Adam's first cry, to feel the aspirated warmth of his
body meeting air for the first time. I was not present to count his
fingers, to exclaim at the surprise of gender, to be comforted by
the hope at the heart of his new existence.

From what I've learned, from the sum of gathered profiles di- 2
vided by the tragedy of each case, the delivery of my premature
son was unlikely to have been a joyous occasion. Most fetal alcohol babies emerge not in a tide, the facsimile of saline, primordial,
life-granting sea, but instead enter this world tainted with stale
wine. Their amniotic fluid literally reeks of Thunderbird or Ripple, and the whole operating theater stinks like the scene of a
three-day party. Delivery room staff who have been witness time
and again tell of undernourished babies thrown into delirium
tremens when the cord that brought sustenance and poison is sev-
ered. Nurses close their eyes at the memory. An infant with the
shakes, as cold turkey as a raving derelict deprived of the next fix,
is hard to forget.

Compared to the ideal, Adam started far in the hole, differ- 3
ently from the child who began a march through the years without the scars of fetters on his ankles, with eyes and ears that
worked, with nothing to carry except what he or she collected
along the path.

Adam's birthdays are reminders for me. For each celebration 4
commemorating that he was born, there is the pang, the rage, that
he was not born whole. I grieve for what he might have, what he
should have been. I magnify and sustain those looks of understanding or compassion or curiosity that fleet across his face, fast as
a breeze, unexpected as the voice of God—the time he said to me
in the car, the words arising from no context I could see, "Kansas
is between Oklahoma and Texas." But when I turned in amaze-
ment, agreeing loudly, still ready after all these years to discover a
buried talent or passion for geography, for anything, that possible
person had disappeared.

"What made you say that?" I asked. 5

"Say what?" he answered. "I didn't say anything."   6

The sixteenth birthday, the eighteenth. The milestones.   7
The driver's license, voting, the adult boundary-marker birthdays. The days I envisioned while watching the mail for the response to my first adoption application, the days that set forth like distant skyscrapers as I projected ahead through my years of fatherhood. I had given little specific consideration to what might come between, but of those outstanding days I had been sure. They were the pillars I followed, the oases of certainty. Alone in the cabin in Alaska or in the basement apartment near Franconia while I waited for the definition of the rest of my life to commence, I planned the elaborate cake decorations for those big birthdays, the significant presents I would save to buy. Odd as it may seem, the anticipation of the acts of letting Adam go began before I even knew his name. I looked forward to the proud days on which the world would recognize my son as progressively more his own man. Those were among the strongest hooks that bonded me to him in my imagination.

As each of these anniversaries finally came and went, nothing   8
like I expected them to be, I doubly mourned. First, selfishly, for me, and second for Adam, because he didn't know what he was missing, what he had already missed, what he would miss. I wanted to burst through those birthdays like a speeding train blasts a weak gate, to get past them and back into the anonymous years for which I had made no models, where there were no obvious measurements, no cakes with candles that would never be lit.

It was a coincidence that Adam turned twenty-one as this book   9
neared completion, but it seemed appropriate. On the morning of his birthday, I rose early and baked him a lemon cake, his favorite, and left the layers to cool while I drove to Hanover to pick him up. His gifts were wrapped and on the kitchen table—an electric shaver, clothes, a Garfield calendar. For his special dinner he had requested tacos, and as always I had reserved a magic candle—the kind that keeps reigniting no matter how often it is blown out—for the center of his cake.

I was greeted at Adam's house by the news that he had just had   10
a seizure, a small one this time, but it had left him groggy. I helped him on with his coat, bent to tie his shoelace, all the while talking about the fun we would have during the day. He looked

out the window. Only the week before he had been laid off from his dishwashing job. December had been a bad month for seizures, some due to his body's adjustment to a change in dosage and some occurring because Adam had skipped taking medicine altogether. The bowling alley's insurance carrier was concerned and that, combined with an after-Christmas slump in business, decided the issue. Now he was back at Hartford for a few weeks while Ken Krambert and his associates sought a new work placement. I thought perhaps Adam was depressed about this turn of events, so I tried to cheer him up as we drove south on the familiar road to Cornish.

"So, Adam," I said, making conversation, summoning the conventional words, "do you feel any older? What's good about being twenty-one?"   11

He turned to me and grinned. There *was* something good.   12

"Well," he answered, "now the guys at work say I'm old enough to drink."   13

His unexpected words kicked me in the stomach. They crowded every thought from my brain.   14

"Adam, you can't," I protested. "I've told you about your birth-mother, about your other father. Do you remember what happened to them?" I knew he did. I had told him the story several times, and we had gone over it together as he read, or I read to him, parts of this book.   15

Adam thought for a moment. "They were sick?" he offered finally. "That's why I have seizures?"   16

"No, they weren't sick. They died, Adam. They died from drinking. If you drank, it could happen to you." My memory played back all the statistics about sons of alcoholic fathers and their particular susceptibility to substance abuse. "It would not mix well with your medicine."   17

Adam sniffed, turned away, but not before I recognized the amused disbelief in his expression. He did not take death seriously, never had. It was an abstract concept out of his reach and therefore of no interest to him. Death was less real than Santa Claus—after all, Adam had in his album a photograph of himself seated on Santa Claus's lap. Death was no threat, no good reason to refuse his first drink.   18

My son will forever travel through a moonless night with only the roar of wind for company. Don't talk to him of mountains, of   19 tropical beaches. Don't ask him to swoon at sunrises or marvel at the filter of light through leaves. He's never had time for such things, and he does not believe in them. He may pass by them close enough to touch on either side, but his hands are stretched forward, grasping for balance instead of pleasure. He doesn't wonder where he came from, where he's going. He doesn't ask who he is, or why. Questions are a luxury, the province of those at a distance from the periodic shock of rain. Gravity presses Adam so hard against reality that he doesn't feel the points at which he touches it. A drowning man is not separated from the lust for air by a bridge of thought—he is one with it—and my son, conceived and grown in an ethanol bath, lives each day in the act of drowning. For him there is no shore.

UNDERSTANDING DETAILS

1. Why are Adam's birthdays difficult for Dorris?
2. What are some of the problems Adam was born with?
3. Why will Adam never reach his full potential?
4. In what ways did Dorris feel Adam's birthdays would be "oases of certainty" (paragraph 7)? How did the actual celebrations differ from these expectations?

ANALYZING MEANING

1. Why does Dorris "doubly" mourn (paragraph 8) his son's birthdays? Explain your answer.
2. In what way was "the definition of the rest of [Dorris's] life" (paragraph 7) connected with his son's birthdays?
3. In what way is death like Santa Claus for Adam? Explain your answer.
4. What does Dorris mean when he says "Questions are a luxury" for his son (paragraph 19)?

DISCOVERING RHETORICAL STRATEGIES

1. At what points in this essay does Dorris either directly or indirectly analyze the causes of Adam's behavior? When does he study its effects (on either himself or his son)? Divide a piece of paper in half. List the causes of Adam's behavior on one side and the effects on the other. Record the paragraph references

in each case. Then, discuss the pattern that emerges from your two lists. Does Dorris give more attention to the causes or the effects of Adam's behavior? Why do you think the author develops his essay around this particular emphasis?

2. Dorris uses several comparisons to help his readers understand what raising a fetal alcohol child is like. Look, for example, at paragraph 19, in which he compares Adam's life to "a moonless night" and to "the act of drowning." Find two other vivid comparisons in this essay. What do all these comparisons add to the essay? What effect do they have on the essay as a whole?

3. What tone does Dorris establish in his essay? Describe it in three or four well-chosen words. How does he create this tone? What effect does this particular tone have on you as a reader?

4. What rhetorical strategies does Dorris use to support his cause/effect analysis? Give examples of each.

MAKING CONNECTIONS

1. Contrast Dorris's definition of "addiction" with the definitions in the following essays that discuss other addictive topics: Kimberly Wozencraft's "Notes from the Country Club," Franklin Zimring's "Confessions of an Ex-Smoker," and/or Stephen King's "Why We Crave Horror Movies." What substance is addictive in these essays? Which addiction do you think would be most difficult to recover from? Explain your answer.

2. Love and concern for a child is the principal topic of Dorris's essay, as it is in Lewis Sawaquat's "For My Indian Daughter," Russell Baker's "The Saturday Evening Post," Bill Cosby's "The Baffling Question," Judith Wallerstein and Sandra Blakeslee's "Second Chances for Children of Divorce," and Germaine Greer's "A Child Is Born." If we were able to get all these authors together in a roundtable discussion about parent–child relationships, do you think they would agree on any of the issues? If so, what would these areas of agreement be?

3. Birthdays are milestones in Dorris's essay, just as they are for Malcolm Cowley in "The View from 80." What are the principal differences in the ways each author celebrates these birthdays? Why do these differences exist?

IDEAS FOR DISCUSSION/WRITING

Preparing to Write

Write freely about the process of growing up and reaching your potential: What special problems did you experience while growing up? How did you deal with these problems? How did your parents deal with these problems? Do you feel you are heading toward your full potential, or have you already reached it? How do you plan to reach or maintain your potential? What experiences or people have disappointed you mainly because they were not what you expected? What were their shortcomings? Can these shortcomings be remedied? What effects do such shortcomings have on society as a whole?

Choosing a Topic

1. In a conversation with your mother, father, or another close relative, explain what problems you found most difficult as you were growing up, and speculate about the causes of those problems. In dialogue form, record the conversation as accurately as possible. Add an introduction, a conclusion, and an explanation of your discussion in order to mold the conversation into an essay.

2. In the last paragraph of his essay, Dorris implies that his son is slowly drowning in his birth-mother's alcohol abuse. This essay is Dorris's process of grieving about "what [his son] was missing, what he had already missed, what he would miss" (paragraph 8). In an essay of your own, explain something (a process, a person, an event, a relationship, or an activity) that disappointed you mainly because your expectations weren't met. What were the principal reasons for your disappointment? What were the effects of your disappointment? What could have changed the situation?

3. Many forms of addiction and abuse plague our society at present. In an essay written for your composition class, choose one of these problems and speculate on its primary causes and effects in society today. As often as possible, give specific examples to support your observations.

Before beginning your essay, you might want to consult the checklists on pages 450–451.

RICHARD RODRIGUEZ   (1944–   )

The Fear of Losing a Culture

Richard Rodriguez was raised in Sacramento, California, the son of industrious working-class Mexican immigrant parents. He attended parochial schools there and later continued his education at Stanford University, Columbia University, London's Warburg Institute, and, finally, the University of California at Berkeley, where he earned a Ph.D. in English Renaissance literature. A writer and journalist, he is now associate editor of the Pacific News Service in San Francisco. In 1982, he received wide critical acclaim for the publication of his autobiography, *Hunger of Memory: The Education of Richard Rodriguez*, which detailed his struggle to succeed in a totally alien culture. A regular contributor to the *Los Angeles Times*, he has also published essays in *New Republic, Time, Harper's, American Scholar, Columbia Forum,* and *College English*. His most recent book is *Days of Obligation: An Argument with My Mexican Father* (1992), an autobiographical study of Mexican immigrants in America. Asked to provide advice for students using *The Prose Reader*, Rodriguez explained that "there is no 'secret' to becoming a writer. Writing takes time—and patience, more than anything else. If you are willing to rewrite and rewrite and rewrite, you will become a good writer."

Preparing to Read

The following essay, originally published in *Time* magazine (July 11, 1988), discusses the causes and effects of cultural pride. As you prepare to read this essay, take a few moments to think about culture and assimilation: How would you describe America's culture? Does it have a central core of its own? What are the main features of this American culture? To what extent are Americans threatened by the intrusion of other cultures? What can be gained through assimilation with another culture? What can be lost?

What is culture?   1

The immigrant shrugs. Latin American immigrants   2
come to the United States with only the things they

need in mind—not abstractions like culture. Money. They need dollars. They need food. Maybe they need to get out of the way of bullets.

Most of us who concern ourselves with the Hispanic-American   3
culture, as painters, musicians, writers—or as sons and daughters—are the children of immigrants. We have grown up on this side of the border, in the land of Elvis Presley and Thomas Edison; our lives are prescribed by the mall, by the DMV and the Chinese restaurant. Our imaginations yet vascillate between an Edenic Latin America (the blue door)—and the repellent plate glass of a real American city—which has been good to us.

Hispanic-American culture is where the past meets the future.   4
Hispanic-American culture is not an Hispanic milestone only, not simply a celebration at the crossroads. America transforms into pleasure what America cannot avoid. Is it any coincidence that at a time when Americans are troubled by the encroachment of the Mexican desert, Americans discover a chic in cactus, in the decorator colors of the Southwest? In sand?

Hispanic-American culture of the sort that is now showing (the   5
teen movie, the rock song) may exist in an hourglass, may in fact be irrelevant to the epic. The US Border Patrol works through the night to arrest the flow of illegal immigrants over the border, even as Americans wait in line to get into *La Bamba*. Even as Americans vote to declare, once and for all, that English shall be the official language of the United States, Madonna starts recording in Spanish.

But then so is Bill Cosby's show irrelevant to the 10 o'clock   6
news, where families huddle together in fear on porches, pointing at the body of the slain boy bagged in tarpauline—which is not to say that Bill Cosby or Michael Jackson are irrelevant to the future or without neo-Platonic influence. Like players within the play, they prefigure, they resolve. They make black and white audiences aware of a bond that may not yet exist.

Before a national TV audience, Rita Moreno tells Geraldo   7
Rivera that her dream as an actress is to play a character rather like herself: "I speak English perfectly well . . . I'm not dying from poverty . . . I want to play *that* kind of Hispanic woman, which is to say, an American citizen." This is an actress talking, these are show-biz pieties. But Moreno expresses as well the general Hispanic-American predicament. Hispanics want to belong to America without betraying the past.

Hispanics fear losing ground in any negotiation with the 8
American city. We come from an expansive, an intimate culture
that has been judged second-rate by the United States of America.
For reasons of pride, therefore, as much as of affection, we are reluctant to give up our past. Hispanics often express a fear of "losing" culture. Our fame in the United States has been our
resistance to assimilation.

The symbol of Hispanic culture has been the tongue of 9
flame—Spanish. But the remarkable legacy Hispanics carry from
Latin America is not language—an inflatable skin—but breath itself, capacity of soul, an inclination to live. The genius of Latin
America is the habit of synthesis.

We assimilate. Just over the border there is the example of 10
Mexico, the country from which the majority of U.S. Hispanics
come. Mexico is mestizo—Indian and Spanish. Within a single
family, Mexicans are light-skinned and dark. It is impossible for
the Mexican to say, in the scheme of things, where the Indian begins and the Spaniard surrenders.

In culture as in blood, Latin America was formed by a rape that 11
became a marriage. Due to the absorbing generosity of the Indian,
European culture took on new soil. What Latin America knows is
that people create one another as they marry. In the music of
Latin America you will hear the litany of bloodlines—the African
drum, the German accordian, the cry from the minaret.

The United States stands as the opposing New World expe- 12
riment. In North America the Indian and the European
stood apace. Whereas Latin America was formed by a medieval
Catholic dream of one world—of meltdown conversion—the
United States was built up from Protestant individualism. The
American melting pot washes away only embarrassment; it is the
necessary initiation into public life. The American faith is that our
national strength derives from separateness, from "diversity." The
glamour of the United States is a carnival promise: You can lose
weight, get rich as Rockefeller, touch up your roots, get a
divorce.

Immigrants still come for the promise. But the United States 13
wavers in its faith. As long as there was space enough, sky
enough, as long as economic success validated individualism,
loneliness was not too high a price to pay (the cabin on the prairie
or the Sony Walkman).

At the beginning of the century, two alternative cultures   14
beckon the American imagination—both highly communal cultures—the Asian and the Latin American. The United States is a
literal culture. Americans devour what we might otherwise fear to
become. Sushi will make us corporate warriors. Combination
Plate #3, smothered in mestizo gravy, will burn a hole in our
hearts.

Latin America offers passion. Latin America has a life—I mean   15
life—big clouds, unambiguous themes, death, birth, faith, that the
United States, for all its quality of life, seems without now. Latin
America offers communal riches: an undistressed leisure, a kitchen
table, even a full sorrow. Such is the solitude of America; such is
the urgency of American need; Americans reach right past a
fledgling, homegrown Hispanic-American culture for the real
thing—the darker bottle of Mexican beer, the denser novel of a
Latin American master.

For a long time, Hispanics in the United States withheld from   16
the United States our Latin American gift. We denied the value of
assimilation. But as our presence is judged less foreign in America,
we will produce a more generous art, less timid, less parochial.
Carlos Santana, Luis Valdez, Linda Ronstadt—Hispanic Americans do not have a "pure" Latin American art to offer. Expect
bastard themes, expect ironies, comic conclusions. For we live on
the side of the border, where Kraft manufactures bricks of "Mexican style" Velveeta and where Jack in the Box serves "Fajita
Pita."

The flame-red Chevy floats a song down the Pan American Highway: 17
From a rolled-down window, the grizzled voice of Willie Nelson rises in
disembodied harmony with the voice of Julio Iglesias. Gabby Hayes and
Cisco are thus resolved.

Expect marriage. We will change America even as we will   18
be changed. We will disappear with you into a new miscegena-
tion.

Along the border, real conflicts remain. But the ancient tear   19
separating Europe from itself—the Catholic Mediterranean from
the Protestant north—may yet heal itself in the New World. For
generations, Latin America has been the place—the bed—of a
confluence of so many races and cultures that Protestant North
America shuddered to imagine it.

Imagine it.   20

UNDERSTANDING DETAILS

1. In what way is "culture" an abstraction? Explain your answer.
2. What does Rodriguez mean when he says "Hispanic-American culture is where the past meets the future" (paragraph 4)?
3. In what ways are Asian and Latin American cultures "communal" whereas America's is "literal" (paragraph 14)?
4. What does Rodriguez claim is the source of the hostility Hispanics have traditionally felt from other Americans?

ANALYZING MEANING

1. To what extent do you think Hispanics can belong to America "without betraying the past" (paragraph 7)? How might they accomplish this?
2. What is the main difference in philosophy between North America and Latin America? Why is assimilation so difficult under these circumstances?
3. What does Rodriguez mean when he says that "people create one another when they meet" (paragraph 11)? Explain your answer in detail.
4. What do North America and Latin America have to offer each other? What can they learn from each other?

DISCOVERING RHETORICAL STRATEGIES

1. According to Rodriguez, the fact that Hispanics sometimes don't easily assimilate into American culture causes some consequences and is the result of others. List the causes of this action in one column and the effects in another. In what way does the question of assimilation become a focal point for the essay?
2. Why does Rodriguez introduce the Asian culture into this essay? How does this reference help strengthen his argument?
3. Rodriguez ends his essay with a one-sentence paragraph. What effect does this ending have on you? Explain your answer.
4. What other rhetorical strategies besides cause and effect does Rodriguez use to support his essay about Hispanic-American assimilation? Give examples of each.

MAKING CONNECTIONS

1. Rodriguez, Robert Ramirez ("The Barrio"), and Peter Salins ("Take a Ticket") all discuss the complex topic of how immigrants can assimilate into a new culture without "betraying their past." Compare and contrast their opinions on this controversial subject; then give your own views on the issue.
2. Rodriguez's image of an "Edenic" former Latin culture is similar to the pleasant memories John McPhee provides of an unspoiled wilderness area before the intrusions of civilization ("The Pines") and Bruce Catton's depiction of Robert E. Lee's tidewater Virginia aristocratic heritage ("Grant and Lee: A Study in Contrasts"). To what extent do you think each of these memories has been warped and changed by the passage of time? How accurate are your own recollections of pleasant events and places from the past?
3. How many different causes does Rodriguez suggest to explain why some Hispanic-Americans resist assimilation into American culture? Contrast the number of causes Rodriguez mentions with the number introduced by Stephen King ("Why We Crave Horror Movies") and Michael Dorris ("The Broken Cord"). How does the number of causes in a cause/effect essay influence your ability to follow the author's argument?

IDEAS FOR DISCUSSION/WRITING

Preparing to Write

Write freely about culture and assimilation: What makes up a culture? In what ways do merging cultures threaten one another? What does assimilation consist of? Why is assimilation between cultures such an emotional issue? What are the ground rules in the process of assimilation? What major cultural changes is our country experiencing at present? In what way are these changes affecting you personally?

Choosing a Topic

1. We all confront assimilation every day in different situations. We may choose to assimilate into a club we want to join but may refuse to make the necessary changes to fit into a fast-moving party scene. For an article in your campus newspaper

demonstrating the constant role of assimilation in our lives, explain the causes and/or effects of one time you chose or refused to assimilate. What were the circumstances leading up to your decision? What were the consequences of your decision?

2. America is currently undergoing some dramatic cultural changes. We are rapidly becoming a multiracial, multicultural society. In an essay written for your local newspaper, analyze the causes and effects of some of these changes, and explain how they are affecting you personally.

3. As a foreign-exchange student, you have just arrived in another country to attend college for one year. Naturally, you realize that you must adapt to many new customs and attitudes; however, you will still cling to many of your country's ways. In an essay, explain which of your national traditions you would find most difficult to give up and why. Do you think assimilating into a new culture and still holding on to your beliefs and customs is possible? Explain your reasoning.

Before beginning your essay, you might want to consult the checklists on pages 450–451.

MARY ROACH   (1959–   )

Meet the Bickersons

A native of Hanover, New Hampshire, Mary Roach received her
B.A. in psychology from Wesleyan University, then worked as a
copy editor and a public relations consultant for the San Francisco
Zoo. Following five years in the business world, she began her career as a freelance writer after deciding that "it was a lot easier to
write the stuff in the first place than to clean it up after someone
else had written it." She has been a contributor for many years to
the "Diversions" section of the *San Francisco Examiner Sunday
Magazine*, focusing on such quirky, interesting topics as drive-in
movies and old black-and-white photo booths. She is currently a
contributing editor for such well-known periodicals as *Health,
Discover, Wired, Muse* (the Smithsonian Museum's children's magazine), and *SALON.com* (an on-line journal). Asked to give advice to students using *The Prose Reader*, she confides that "people
think writing is harder than it is. They tie themselves up in knots
over it. Good writing is really just talking on paper. If it were difficult to do, I would not be that successful at it." Roach now lives
in San Francisco, where her hobbies include bird watching, reading, and traveling.

Preparing to Read

The following humorous essay on arguing, originally published
in *Health* magazine, explains different strategies for arguing among
couples. Before you read this essay, think for a moment about
how important arguing fairly is to you: Do you argue fairly? Do
you expect your partner to argue fairly? What are the qualities of
a fair argument? Do you argue with other people? Are you able to
control your temper? Do you feel better after you argue? Why or
why not? When is arguing most worthwhile? When is it never
worthwhile? Do you have any special ground rules for arguing
with the people you love?

Psychologists have long said it's possible to predict whether a couple will stay happily married simply by looking at how they fight. This did not bode well for yours truly, who got married not too long ago. Pretty much all I'd learned about spousal arguing came from *The Newlywed Game,* which taught us 1) that the proper form of conflict resolution is to hit your partner over the head with a large piece of poster board and 2) that most problems can be resolved with the acquisition of a brand-new washer and dryer or a gift pack of Turtle Wax. 1

I've been told I'm defensive—"like a cornered mongoose" were the exact words. I've also been criticized for being sarcastic, overreacting, and crying too easily. I don't deny these things (though if you were to accuse me of them in the heat of battle, you can be sure I would—vehemently, and with pointy little teeth bared). 2

I had a boyfriend who tried to change me. He asked me to use a therapy technique called "active listening," a mainstay of many modern marriage counselors. It's supposed to make you a more fair, less combative arguer. I (and here's something you couldn't see coming) objected to this, stating that I was already an active listener. My ex countered that deep sighs, nostril flares, pacing, and storming from the room did not qualify. Active listening means focusing carefully on what your partner is saying, as though there were going to be a test, because, in fact, there is. You are required to paraphrase your beloved's misguided rantings—sorry, feelings—beginning with the phrase "What I hear you saying is . . ." 3

I agreed to try it. He went first. Minutes passed. Fortunately, we were on the phone at the time, which allowed me to scribble notes. He finished and fell silent. 4

"What I hear you saying," I began, "is that you think I'm defensive, and I don't allow you to feel what you're feeling and that makes you incredibly . . . truncated, wait, flat-footed?" 5

"Frustrated." 6

"Of course." 7

"You're cheating," he said. "You're writing things down." 8

"Am not." 9

Nothing—not counseling, not even Turtle Wax—was going to save that relationship. 10

With Ed, I was determined to do things right and asked a   11
friend with a degree in counseling for advice. She encouraged me
to use "I" statements because "you" statements put people on the
defensive. For instance, one does not say to one's beloved, "You
never do the dishes, you self-centered pea brain." One says, "I
feel angry and taken advantage of when the people I love leave
their dishes for me, especially when it was those people who dirt-
ied them in the first place and ate the leftovers they knew darn
well I was planning to have for lunch."

Another suggested technique was validation, in which each   12
partner makes an effort to endorse the other's feelings: "I can see
why you'd be upset with my failing to wash one small dish and
eating an eighth of a taco. I would be, too, if I were an oversensi-
tive, petty person who only focuses on the negative."

A while back I put all these techniques to work. We were   13
driving, and I had failed to notice a stop sign, which even the
most vigilant driver will do from time to time, am I right? Ed did
not fail to notice the stop sign, as was evinced by his slamming of
the imaginary brakes on his side of the car. "When you constantly
remark upon my driving irregularities," I began, "I feel scruti-
nized and inadequate, and by the way, who was it that nearly got
us killed by turning into traffic outside Costco?"

Ed was unperturbed by the Costco barb. What got him was the   14
I-feel-blah-dee-blah business. "Why don't you just get mad and
call me a back-seat driver, and that'd be that?"

Later that evening I tried to explain what I'd learned about   15
"you" statements and active listening and validating feelings. Ed
listened carefully. Then he took my hand in his. "When you talk
about things like this, I feel, let me see, like throwing up. How
was that?"

Shortly after, Ed left a newspaper clipping on my desk. It de-   16
scribed a university study in which 130 newlywed pairs were
videotaped arguing and then tracked for six years. It turns out the
couples who stayed married had seldom used techniques like active listening and validation. The researcher was "shocked" to
find that the happy couples fought like normal people—getting
angry, clearing the air, and making up. (Their spats, however,
were tinged with soothing and humor.)

This was one instance in which I was glad to be proved wrong. So 17
thrilled was I at the prospect of never again having to begin a sentence with "What I hear you saying is" that I made a vow on the spot
that the next time Ed got mad at me, I would not get defensive.

It happened on a Saturday afternoon. I had thrown away a set 18
of circa-1970 stereo speakers that Ed had wanted to keep because
they might come in handy for taking up space in the basement for
the next ten years. It didn't go quite the way I'd envisioned. I
heard myself lambasting Ed for having gone through the garbage,
checking up on what I'd junked. "You're scrutinizing me!"

Ed looked flabbergasted. "You toss things without even asking!" 19

The bell rang, and we withdrew to our corners. Around din- 20
nertime I appeared in the kitchen with the speakers, dusted and
polished. Ed, in turn, promised not to supervise my spring cleaning. He asked me to let him know when I caught him checking
over something I'd done. "I'm not even aware of it. So please tell
me." He smiled sweetly. "And then I'll deny it."

UNDERSTANDING DETAILS

1. What is "active listening" (paragraph 3)? What verbal technique did Roach learn as an active listener?
2. Explain the technique of "validation" in your own words.
3. Does Roach think she is too defensive? What animal did
   someone compare her defensiveness to?
4. What did a university study learn about the argumentative
   habits of 130 newlywed couples? How did Roach feel about
   the findings of this study?

ANALYZING MEANING

1. According to psychologists, how does the way couples fight affect the survival of their marriages?
2. Why was Roach trying different strategies for getting along
   with her partner?
3. Who is Ed? Why was Roach trying so hard to make her relationship with Ed work?
4. What does Roach mean when she says about the first
   boyfriend, "Nothing—not counseling, not even Turtle Wax—
   was going to save that relationship" (paragraph 10)?

DISCOVERING RHETORICAL STRATEGIES

1. List the causes and effects that this essay studies.
2. What is the general mood of Roach's essay?
3. Roach begins her essay with some references to the *Newlywed Game*. What do the poster board, a washer and dryer, and Turtle Wax have to do with that game? Do you think this is an effective way to start her essay? Explain your answer.
4. What other rhetorical strategies support this cause/effect essay? Give examples of each.

MAKING CONNECTIONS

1. Compare and contrast Roach's conclusions about successful communications within a relationship with similar advice provided in Judy Brady's "Why I Want a Wife," Wallerstein and Blakeslee's "Second Chances for Children of Divorce," Judith Viorst's "The Truth About Lying," and Mary Pipher's "Beliefs About Families."
2. Analyze Roach's prescription for dealing with anger in light of the following essays: Brent Staples's "A Brother's Murder," Sherwin Nuland's "Accidents, Suicide, and Euthanasia," and Michael Dorris's "The Broken Cord."
3. Compare Roach's use of humor in her essay to similar uses of humor in Russell Baker's "The Saturday Evening Post," Garrison Keillor's "How the Crab Apple Grew," and Bill Cosby's "The Baffling Question."

IDEAS FOR DISCUSSION/WRITING

Preparing to Write

Write freely about your views on arguing: Do you know how to argue? Have you ever been sorry for anything you said while you were arguing? Do you argue with your parents differently than you argue with your friends? With your boyfriends/girlfriends/spouses? Why do you argue? What do you try to accomplish when you argue? Does arguing usually make you feel better or worse? Is it difficult to make up after you argue? How do you make up?

Choosing a Topic

1. Your college newspaper is accepting essays on your interests in life. Write an essay for the newspaper explaining in detail your most passionate interest. Cover both the causes and effects of this interest. (This interest does not have to be related to school matters.)
2. Your college counselor/advisor wants to know if you consider yourself emotionally healthy. In a detailed essay written for this counselor, who is writing a letter of recommendation for you, explain why you are or are not in good emotional health. What events/attitudes/activities have played a part in developing your mental health?
3. Americans seem to be obsessed with their health these days. Why do you think this is so? How did this obsession start?

Before beginning your essay, you might want to consult the checklists on pages 450–451.

Beauty: When the Other Dancer Is the Self

Born in Eatonton, Georgia, and educated at Spelman College and Sarah Lawrence College, Alice Walker is best known for her Pulitzer Prize-winning novel *The Color Purple* (1983), which was later made into an immensely popular movie of the same title. The book details a young African-American woman's search for self-identity within a world contaminated by racial prejudice and family crisis. Although many critics have argued that the work "transcends culture and gender," Walker's focus on the racial and ethnic climate of the Deep South is crucial to the novel's success and importance. The author has explained that "the Black woman is one of America's greatest heroes," though she has been denied credit for her accomplishments and "oppressed beyond recognition." Most of Walker's other novels and collections of short stories echo the same theme, and most share the "sense of affirmation" featured in *The Color Purple* that overcomes the anger and social indignity suffered by so many of her characters. The author's many other publications include *In Love and Trouble: Stories of Black Women* (1973), *Meridian* (1976), *You Can't Keep a Good Woman Down* (1981), *In Search of Our Mothers' Gardens* (1983), *Living by the Word* (1988), *To Hell with Dying* (1988), *The Temple of My Familiar* (1989), *Possessing the Secret of Joy* (1992), *Everyday Use* (1994), *Alice Walker Banned* (1996), and *By the Light of My Father's Smile* (1998). Walker has been a professor and writer-in-residence at Wellesley College, the University of Massachusetts, the University of California at Berkeley, and Brandeis University. She is also a member of the board of trustees of Sarah Lawrence College. Walker currently lives in Mendocino, California.

Preparing to Read

The following essay, from *In Search of Our Mothers' Gardens*, focuses on young Alice Walker's reaction to being blinded in one eye as a result of an accident with a BB gun. As you begin to read this essay, take a few minutes to consider the role of physical appearance in our lives: Do you find that you often judge people based on their physical appearance? Do you feel that people judge

you based on your appearance? What other characteristics play a
part in your judgment of others? How important are good looks to
you? Why do they carry this importance for you? What specific
people affect the way you feel about yourself? Do you want more
control over your own self-esteem? How can you gain this control?

It is a bright summer day in 1947. My father, a fat, funny man   1
with beautiful eyes and a subversive wit, is trying to decide
which of his eight children he will take with him to the
county fair. My mother, of course, will not go. She is knocked
out from getting most of us ready: I hold my neck stiff against the
pressure of her knuckles as she hastily completes the braiding and
then beribboning of my hair.

My father is the driver for the rich old white lady up the road.   2
Her name is Miss Mey. She owns all the land for miles around, as
well as the house in which we live. All I remember about her is
that she once offered to pay my mother thirty-five cents for cleaning her house, raking up piles of her magnolia leaves, and washing
her family's clothes, and that my mother—she of no money, eight
children, and a chronic earache—refused it. But I do not think of
this in 1947. I am two and a half years old. I want to go everywhere my daddy goes. I am excited at the prospect of riding in a
car. Someone has told me fairs are fun. That there is room in the
car for only three of us doesn't faze me at all. Whirling happily in
my starchy frock, showing off my biscuit-polished patent-leather
shoes and lavender socks, tossing my head in a way that makes my
ribbons bounce, I stand, hands on hips, before my father. "Take
me, Daddy," I say with assurance; "I'm the prettiest!"

Later, it does not surprise me to find myself in Miss Mey's shiny   3
black car, sharing the back seat with the other lucky ones. Does not
surprise me that I thoroughly enjoy the fair. At home that night I
tell the unlucky ones all I can remember about the merry-go-
round, the man who eats live chickens, and the teddy bears, until
they say: that's enough, baby Alice. Shut up now, and go to sleep.

It is Easter Sunday, 1950. I am dressed in a green, flocked, scal-   4
loped-hem dress (handmade by my adoring sister, Ruth) that has
its own smooth satin petticoat and tiny hot-pink roses tucked into
each scallop. My shoes, new T-strap patent leather, again highly
biscuit-polished. I am six years old and have learned one of the

longest Easter speeches to be heard that day, totally unlike the speech I said when I was two: "Easter lilies / pure and white / blossom in / the morning light." When I rise to give my speech I do so on a great wave of love and pride and expectation. People in the church stop rustling their new crinolines. They seem to hold their breath. I can tell they admire my dress, but it is my spirit, bordering on sassiness (womanishness), they secretly applaud.

"That girl's a little *mess*," they whisper to each other, pleased.   5

Naturally I say my speech without stammer or pause, unlike   6 those who stutter, stammer, or, worst of all, forget. This is before the word "beautiful" exists in people's vocabulary, but "Oh, isn't she the *cutest* thing!" frequently floats my way. "And got so much sense!" they gratefully add . . . for which thoughtful addition I thank them to this day.

It was great fun being cute. But then, one day, it ended.   7

I am eight years old and a tomboy. I have a cowboy hat, cowboy   8 boots, checkered shirt and pants, all red. My playmates are my brothers, two and four years older than I. Their colors are black and green, the only difference in the way we are dressed. On Saturday nights we all go to the picture show, even my mother; Westerns are her favorite kind of movie. Back home, "on the ranch," we pretend we are Tom Mix, Hopalong Cassidy, Lash LaRue (we've even named one of our dogs Lash LaRue); we chase each other for hours rustling cattle, being outlaws, delivering damsels from distress. Then my parents decide to buy my brothers guns. These are not "real" guns. They shoot "BBs," copper pellets my brothers say will kill birds. Because I am a girl, I do not get a gun. Instantly I am relegated to the position of Indian. Now there appears a great distance between us. They shoot and shoot at everything with their new guns. I try to keep up with my bow and arrows.

One day while I am standing on top of our makeshift   9 "garage"—pieces of tin nailed across some poles—holding my bow and arrow and looking out toward the fields, I feel an incredible blow in my right eye. I look down just in time to see my brother lower his gun.

Both brothers rush to my side. My eye stings, and I cover it   10 with my hand. "If you tell," they say, "we will get a whipping. You don't want that to happen, do you?" I do not. "Here is a piece of wire," says the older brother, picking it up from the roof; "say you stepped on one end of it and the other flew up and hit you." The pain is beginning to start. "Yes," I say. "Yes, I will say that is what happened." If I do not say this is what happened, I know my brothers will find ways to make me wish I had. But now I will say anything that gets me to my mother.

Confronted by our parents we stick to the lie agreed upon. 11 They place me on a bench on the porch, and I close my left eye while they examine the right. There is a tree growing from underneath the porch that climbs past the railing to the roof. It is the last thing my right eye sees. I watch as its trunk, its branches, and then its leaves are blotted out by the rising blood.

I am in shock. First there is intense fever, which my father tries 12 to break using lily leaves bound around my head. Then there are chills: my mother tries to get me to eat soup. Eventually, I do not know how, my parents learn what has happened. A week after the "accident" they take me to see a doctor. "Why did you wait so long to come?" he asks, looking into my eye and shaking his head. "Eyes are sympathetic," he says. "If one is blind, the other will likely become blind too."

This comment of the doctor's terrifies me. But it is really how 13 I look that bothers me most. Where the BB pellet struck there is a glob of whitish scar tissue, a hideous cataract, on my eye. Now when I stare at people—a favorite pastime, up to now—they will stare back. Not at the "cute" little girl, but at her scar. For six years I do not stare at anyone, because I do not raise my head.

Years later, in the throes of a mid-life crisis, I ask my mother 14 and sister whether I changed after the "accident." "No," they say, puzzled. "What do you mean?"

What do I mean? 15

I am eight, and, for the first time, doing poorly in school, where 16 I have been something of a whiz since I was four. We have just moved to the place where the "accident" occurred. We do not know any of the people around us because this is a different county. The only time I see the friends I knew is when we go back to our old church. The new school is the former state penitentiary. It is a large stone building, cold and drafty, crammed to overflowing with boisterous, ill-disciplined children. On the third floor there is a huge circular imprint of some partition that has been torn out.

"What used to be here?" I ask a sullen girl next to me on our   17
way past it to lunch.

"The electric chair," says she.   18

At night I have nightmares about the electric chair and about   19
all the people reputedly "fried" in it. I am afraid of the school,
where all the students seem to be budding criminals.

"What's the matter with your eye?" they ask, critically.   20

When I don't answer (I cannot decide whether it was an "acci-   21
dent" or not), they shove me, insist on a fight.

My brother, the one who created the story about the wire,   22
comes to my rescue. But then brags so much about "protecting"
me, I become sick.

After months of torture at the school, my parents decide to   23
send me back to our old community, to my old school. I live
with my grandparents and the teacher they board. But there is
no room for Phoebe, my cat. By the time my grandparents decide there *is* room, and I ask for my cat, she cannot be found.
Miss Yarborough, the boarding teacher, takes me under her
wing and begins to teach me to play the piano. But soon she
marries an African—a "prince," she says—and is whisked away
to his continent.

At my old school there is at least one teacher who loves me.   24
She is the teacher who "knew me before I was born" and bought
my first baby clothes. It is she who makes life bearable. It is her
presence that finally helps me turn on the one child at the school
who continually calls me "one-eyed bitch." One day I simply
grab him by his coat and beat him until I am satisfied. It is my
teacher who tells me my mother is ill.

My mother is lying in bed in the middle of the day, something   25
I have never seen. She is in too much pain to speak. She has an
abscess in her ear. I stand looking down on her, knowing that if
she dies, I cannot live. She is being treated with warm oils and hot
bricks held against her cheek. Finally a doctor comes. But I must
go back to my grandparents' house. The weeks pass but I am
hardly aware of it. All I know is that my mother might die, my
father is not so jolly, my brothers still have their guns, and I am
the one sent away from home.

"You did not change," they say.   26

Did I imagine the anguish of never looking up?   27

I am twelve. When relatives come to visit I hide in my room.   28
My cousin Brenda, just my age, whose father works in the post
office and whose mother is a nurse, comes to find me. "Hello,"
she says. And then she asks, looking at my recent school picture,
which I did not want taken, and on which the "glob," as I think
of it, is clearly visible, "You still can't see out of that eye?"

"No," I say, and flop back on the bed over my book.   29
That night, as I do almost every night, I abuse my eye. I rant   30
and rave at it, in front of the mirror. I plead with it to clear up be-
fore morning. I tell it I hate and despise it. I do not pray for sight.
I pray for beauty.
"You did not change," they say.   31

I am fourteen and baby-sitting for my brother Bill, who lives in   32
Boston. He is my favorite brother, and there is a strong bond
between us. Understanding my feelings of shame and ugliness he
and his wife take me to a local hospital, where the "glob" is
removed by a doctor named O. Henry. There is still a small
bluish crater where the scar tissue was, but the ugly white stuff is
gone. Almost immediately I become a different person from the
girl who does not raise her head. Or so I think. Now that
I've raised my head I win the boyfriend of my dreams. Now that
I've raised my head I have plenty of friends. Now that I've raised
my head classwork comes from my lips as faultlessly as Easter
speeches did, and I leave high school as valedictorian, most popular student, and *queen*, hardly believing my luck. Ironically, the
girl who was voted most beautiful in our class (and was) was later
shot twice through the chest by a male companion, using a "real"
gun, while she was pregnant. But that's another story in itself. Or
is it?
"You did not change," they say.   33

It is now thirty years since the "accident." A beautiful journal-   34
ist comes to visit and to interview me. She is going to write a
cover story for her magazine that focuses on my latest book. "Decide how you want to look on the cover," she says. "Glamorous,
or whatever."
Never mind "glamorous," it is the "whatever" that I hear.   35
Suddenly all I can think of is whether I will get enough sleep the

night before the photography session: if I don't, my eye will be tired and wander, as blind eyes will.

At night in bed with my lover I think up reasons why I should   36
not appear on the cover of a magazine. "My meanest critics will say I've sold out," I say. "My family will now realize I write scandalous books."

"But what's the real reason you don't want to do this?" he asks.   37

"Because in all probability," I say in a rush, "my eye won't be   38
straight."

"It will be straight enough," he says. Then, "Besides, I thought   39
you'd made your peace with that."

And I suddenly remember that I have.   40

I remember:

I am talking to my brother Jimmy, asking if he remembers   41
anything unusual about the day I was shot. He does not know I consider that day the last time my father, with his sweet home remedy of cool lily leaves, chose me, and that I suffered and raged inside because of this. "Well," he says, "all I remember is standing by the side of the highway with Daddy, trying to flag down a car. A white man stopped, but when Daddy said he needed somebody to take his little girl to the doctor, he drove off."

I remember:

I am in the desert for the first time. I fall totally in love with it.   42
I am so overwhelmed by its beauty, I confront for the first time, consciously, the meaning of the doctor's words years ago: "Eyes are sympathetic. If one is blind, the other will likely become blind too." I realize I have dashed about the world madly, looking at this, looking at that, storing up images against the fading of the light. *But I might have missed seeing the desert!* The shock of that possibility—and gratitude for over twenty-five years of sight—sends me literally to my knees. Poem after poem comes—which is perhaps how poets pray.

ON SIGHT

I am so thankful I have seen
The Desert
And the creatures in the desert
And the desert Itself.

The desert has its own moon
Which I have seen
With my own eye.
There is no flag on it.

Trees of the desert have arms
All of which are always up
That is because the moon is up
The sun is up
Also the sky
The stars
Clouds
None with flags.

If there were flags, I doubt
the trees would point.
Would you?

But mostly, I remember this:

I am twenty-seven, and my baby daughter is almost three.   43
Since her birth I have worried about her discovery that her
mother's eyes are different from other people's. Will she be embarrassed? I think. What will she say? Every day she watches a
television program called *Big Blue Marble*. It begins with a picture
of the earth as it appears from the moon. It is bluish, a little
battered-looking, but full of light, with whitish clouds swirling
around it. Every time I see it I weep with love, as if it is a picture
of Grandma's house. One day when I am putting Rebecca down
for her nap, she suddenly focuses on my eye. Something inside
me cringes, gets ready to try to protect myself. All children are
cruel about physical differences, I know from experience, and that
they don't always mean to be is another matter. I assume Rebecca
will be the same.

But no-o-o-o. She studies my face intently as we stand, her in-   44
side and me outside her crib. She even holds my face maternally
between her dimpled little hands. Then, looking every bit as serious and lawyerlike as her father, she says, as if it may just possibly
have slipped my attention: "Mommy, there's a *world* in your eye."
(As in, "Don't be alarmed, or do anything crazy.") And then,
gently, but with great interest: "Mommy, where did you *get* that
world in your eye?"

For the most part, the pain left then. (So what, if my brothers   45
grew up to buy even more powerful pellet guns for their sons and
to carry real guns themselves. So what, if a young "Morehouse
man" once nearly fell off the steps of Trevor Arnett Library because he thought my eyes were blue.) Crying and laughing I ran
to the bathroom, while Rebecca mumbled and sang herself off to
sleep. Yes indeed, I realized, looking into the mirror. There *was* a
world in my eye. And I saw that it was possible to love it: that in
fact, for all it had taught me of shame and anger and inner vision,
I *did* love it. Even to see it drifting out of orbit in boredom, or
rolling up out of fatigue, not to mention floating back at attention
in excitement (bearing witness, a friend has called it), deeply suitable to my personality, and even characteristic of me.

That night I dream I am dancing to Stevie Wonder's song "Al-   46
ways" (the name of the song is really "As," but I hear it as "Always"). As I dance, whirling and joyous, happier than I've ever
been in my life, another bright-faced dancer joins me. We dance
and kiss each other and hold each other through the night. The
other dancer has obviously come through all right, as I have done.
She is beautiful, whole and free. And she is also me.

UNDERSTANDING DETAILS

1. What time frame in the author's life does this essay cover?
2. What is the focal point of the essay? What activities lead up to
   this "accident"? What are the long-term effects of this "accident"?
3. In what ways does Walker think her life changed after she was
   shot in the eye?
4. Describe the author's relationship with her brothers—before
   and after the accident.

ANALYZING MEANING

1. Why is Walker devastated by the scar tissue in her eye? Which
   bothers her more—the scar tissue or the blindness? Explain
   your answer.
2. Which of the people introduced in the essay (other than her
   family members) mean the most to her? List them in order of
   importance. Then explain why each is important in this cause/
   effect essay.

3. List the changes that Walker mentions in her actions and personality. Then analyze these changes by discussing their causes and effects.

4. Why is Rebecca's declaration "Mommy, there's a *world* in your eye" (paragraph 44) so important to the author? What changes in Walker result from this particular encounter with her daughter?

DISCOVERING RHETORICAL STRATEGIES

1. Why do you think Walker wrote this essay? What was she trying to accomplish by writing it?
2. How does Walker use blank spaces between her paragraphs? In what ways does this spacing contribute to her essay?
3. Why does Walker put the sentences "It was fun being cute. But then, one day, it ended" (paragraph 7) by themselves in italics?
4. Explain the emotional ups and downs in the essay. How does Walker's language change in each case?

MAKING CONNECTIONS

1. Walker's essay centers on a single momentous event, the blinding of her right eye, that affected her life from the instant it happened. In the following essays, similarly significant events shape the lives of the principal characters: Ray Bradbury's "Summer Rituals," Sandra Cisneros's "Only daughter," and Michael Dorris's "The Broken Cord." Compare and contrast the extent to which any of these events influences the characters involved.

2. One of Walker's primary themes involves the eventual acceptance of who we are in life. Locate the same theme in Malcolm Cowley's "The View from 80," Lewis Sawaquat's "For My Indian Daughter," or Richard Rodriguez's "The Fear of Losing a Culture"; then decide which of these authors seems most content with his or her own self-image. How did you come to this conclusion?

3. The relationship between Walker's original injury and the shyness and insecurity that result from it imply a negative cause/effect connection. Find an essay in this section of the book that implies a positive connection between a cause and its effect. How are the two essays different? How are they the same?

IDEAS FOR DISCUSSION/WRITING

Preparing to Write

Write freely about your self-esteem and the role of self-esteem in the life of college students: How important is self-esteem to you personally? To your academic performance? What affects your self-esteem most? Why do these events affect you? Do they help or hinder your self-esteem? What elements affect the self-esteem of other students you know? Of friends of yours? Of relatives? What effects have you observed in college students that result from low self-esteem? In friends? In relatives? How do you control your self-esteem? Do you recommend this method to others?

Choosing a Topic

1. Low self-esteem can cause a number of serious problems in different aspects of college students' lives. Conduct a study of the causes and effects of low self-esteem in the lives of several students at your school. Write an essay for the college community explaining these causes and effects.

2. Your campus newspaper is printing a special issue highlighting the psychological health of different generations of college students. Interview some people who represent a generation other than your own. Then characterize the students in this generation for the newspaper. In essay form, introduce the features you have discovered, and then discuss their causes and effects.

3. Some people believe self-esteem is a result of peer groups; others say that it is a result of one's family environment. What do you think? *Time* magazine is soliciting student reactions on this issue and has asked for your opinion. Where do you stand on this question? Give specific examples that support your opinion. Respond in essay form.

CHAPTER WRITING ASSIGNMENTS
Practicing Cause/Effect

1. Think about a time in your life when you had definite, clear expectations of an event or experience. Where did these expectations come from? Were they high or low? Were they fulfilled or not? If not, what went wrong? Explain the situation surrounding this experience in a coherent essay.

2. Brainstorm about some challenges or difficult times you have faced. Then describe the most important challenge you have overcome. Explain why this experience was so difficult and what helped you face and conquer it.

3. What do you believe are the major causes of violence in American society? Write an essay that explains why the causes you cite are real or valid. Can you propose any possible solutions to the predicament you describe?

Exploring Ideas

1. How does our reading help us perceive the world? Do you think short stories, plays, and poems help us understand people's behavior and feelings? Write an essay responding to these questions.

2. Compare your memory of a particular childhood experience with that of another family member. How accurately do you both seem to remember this same event? What do you think accounts for the differences in what we remember about various events? What do these differences say about us? Write an essay exploring these questions, using the event from your childhood to support your discussion.

3. Television has been blamed for causing violent behavior, shortening attention spans, and exposing young people to sexually explicit images. Should we as a society monitor what appears on television more closely, or should parents be responsible for censoring what their children watch? Write an essay that takes a stand on this issue.

9

ARGUMENT
AND PERSUASION

Inciting People to Thought or Action

A lmost everything we do or say is an attempt to persuade. Whether we dress up to impress a potential employer or argue openly with a friend about an upcoming election, we are trying to convince various people to see the world our way. However, some aspects of life are particularly dependent upon persuasion. Think, for example, of all the television, magazine, and billboard ads we see urging us to buy certain products or of the many impassioned appeals we read and hear on such controversial issues as school prayer, abortion, gun control, and nuclear energy. Religious leaders devote their professional lives to convincing people to live a certain way and believe in certain religious truths, whereas scientists and mathematicians use rigorous logic and natural law to convince us of various hypotheses. Politicians make their living persuading voters to elect them and then support them throughout their terms of office. In fact, anyone who wants something from another person or agency, ranging from federal money for a research project to a new bicycle for Christmas, must use some form of persuasion to get what he or she desires. The success or failure of this type of communication is easily determined: If the people being addressed change their actions or attitudes in favor of the writer or speaker, the attempt at persuasion has been successful.

DEFINING ARGUMENT AND PERSUASION

The terms *argument* and *persuasion* are often used interchangeably, but one is actually a subdivision of the other. Persuasion names a purpose for writing. To persuade your readers is to convince them to think, act, or feel a certain way. Much of the writing you have been doing in this book has persuasion as one of its goals: A description of an African tribe might have a "dominant impression" you want your readers to accept; in an essay comparing various ways of celebrating Thanksgiving, you might try to convince your readers to believe that these similarities and differences actually exist; and in writing an essay exam on the causes of the Vietnam War, you are trying to convince your instructor that your reasoning is clear and your conclusions sound. In a sense, some degree of persuasion propels all writing.

More specifically, however, the process of persuasion involves appealing to one or more of the following: to reason, to emotion, or to a sense of ethics. An *argument* is an appeal predominantly to your readers' reason and intellect. You are working in the realm of argument when you deal with complex issues that are debatable; opposing views (either explicit or implicit) are a basic requirement of argumentation. But argument and persuasion are taught together because good writers are constantly blending these three appeals and adjusting them to the purpose and audience of a particular writing task. Although reason and logic are the focus of this chapter, you need to learn to use all three methods of persuasion as skillfully as possible to write effective essays.

An appeal to reason relies upon logic and intellect and is usually most effective when you are expecting your readers to disagree with you in some way. This type of appeal can help you change your readers' opinions or influence their future actions through the sheer strength of logical validity. If you want to argue, for example, that pregnant women should refrain from smoking cigarettes, you could cite abundant statistical evidence that babies born to mothers who smoke have lower birth weights, more respiratory problems, and a higher incidence of sudden infant death syndrome than the children of nonsmoking mothers. Because smoking clearly endangers the health of the unborn child, reason dictates that mothers who wish to give birth to the healthiest possible babies should avoid smoking during pregnancy.

Emotional appeals, however, attempt to arouse your readers' feelings, instincts, senses, and biases. Used most profitably when your readers already agree with you, this type of essay generally validates, reinforces, and/or incites in an effort to get your readers to share your feelings or ideas. In order to urge our lawmakers to impose stricter jail sentences for alcohol abuse, you might describe a recent tragic accident involving a local twelve-year-old girl who was killed by a drunk driver as she rode her bicycle to school one morning. By focusing on such poignant visual details as the condition of her mangled bike, the bright red blood stains on her white dress, and the anguish on the faces of parents and friends, you could build a powerfully persuasive essay that would be much more effective than a dull recitation of impersonal facts and nationwide statistics.

An appeal to ethics, the third technique writers often use to encourage readers to agree with them, involves cultivating a sincere, honest tone that will establish your reputation as a reliable, qualified, experienced, well-informed, and knowledgeable person whose opinions on the topic under discussion are believable because they are ethically sound. Such an approach is often used in conjunction with logical or emotional appeals to foster a verbal environment that will result in minimal resistance from its readers. Michael Jordan, former Chicago Bulls basketball star, is an absolute master at creating this ethical, trustworthy persona as he, along with Tweety Bird, coaxes his television viewers to purchase the latest long-distance calling plan. In fact, the old gag question "Would you buy a used car from this man?" is our instinctive response to all forms of attempted persuasion, whether the salesperson is trying to sell us Puppy Chow or gun control, hair spray or school prayer. The more believable we are as human beings, the better chance we will have of convincing our audience.

The following student paragraph is directed primarily toward the audience's logical reasoning ability. Notice that the writer states her assertion and then gives reasons to convince her readers to change their ways. The student writer also brings both emotion and ethics into the argument by choosing her words and examples with great precision.

Have you ever watched a pair of chunky thighs, a jiggling posterior, and an extra-large sweatshirt straining to cover a beer belly and thought, "Thank God I don't look like that! I'm in pretty good shape...for someone my age." Well, before you become too smug and self-righteous, consider what kind of shape you're really in. Just because you don't look like Shamu the Whale doesn't mean you're in good condition. What's missing, you ask? Exercise. You can diet all day, wear the latest slim-cut designer jeans, and still be in worse shape than someone twice your age if you don't get a strong physical workout at least three times a week. Exercise is not only good for you, but it can also be fun—especially if you find a sport that makes you happy while you sweat. Your activity need not be expensive: Jogging, walking, basketball, tennis, and handball are not costly, unless you're seduced by the glossy sheen of the latest sporting fashions and accessories. Most of all, however, regular exercise is important for your health. You can just as easily drop dead from a sudden heart attack in the middle of a restaurant when you're slim and trim as when you're a slob. Your heart and lungs need regular workouts to stay healthy. So do yourself a favor and add some form of exercise to your schedule. You'll feel better and live longer, and your looks will improve, too!

THINKING CRITICALLY BY USING ARGUMENT AND PERSUASION

Argument and persuasion require you to present your views on an issue through logic, emotion, and good character in such a way that you convince an audience of your point of view. This rhetorical mode comes at the end of this book because it is an extremely complex and sophisticated method of reasoning. The more proficient you become in this strategy of thinking and presenting your views, the more you will get what you want out of life (and out of school). Winning arguments means getting the pay raises you need, the refund you deserve, and the grades you've worked so hard for.

In a successful argument, your logic must be flawless. Your conclusions should be based on clear evidence, which must be organized in such a way that it builds to an effective, convincing conclusion. You should constantly have your purpose and audience in mind as you build your case; at the same time, issues of emotion and good character should support the flow of your logic.

Exercising your best logical skills is extremely important to all phases of your daily survival—in and out of the classroom. Following a logical argument in your reading and presenting a logical response to your course work are the hallmarks of a good student. Right now, put your best logic forward and work on your reasoning and persuasive abilities in the series of exercises below. Isolate argument and persuasion from the other rhetorical strategies so that you can practice it and strengthen your ability to argue by itself before you combine it with other methods.

1. Bring to class two magazine ads—one ad that tries to sell a product and another that tries to convince the reader that a particular action or product is wrong or bad (unhealthy, misinterpreted, politically incorrect, etc.). How does each ad appeal to the reader's logic? How does the advertiser use emotion and character in his or her appeal?
2. Think of a recent book you have read. How could you persuade a friend either to read or not to read this book?
3. Fill in the following blanks: The best way to _____ is to _____. (For example, "The best way to <u>lose weight</u> is to <u>exercise</u>.") Then list ways you might use to persuade a reader to see your point of view in this statement.

READING AND WRITING PERSUASIVE ESSAYS

Although persuasive writing can be approached essentially in three different ways—logically, emotionally, and/or ethically— our stress in this chapter is on logic and reason, because they are at the heart of most college writing. As a reader, you will see how various forms of reasoning and different methods of organization affect your reaction to an essay. Your stand on a particular issue will control the way you process information in argument and persuasion essays. As you read the essays in this chapter, you will also learn to recognize emotional and ethical appeals and the different effects they create. In your role as a writer, you need to be fully aware of the options available to you as you compose. Although the basis of your writing will be logical argument, you will see that you can learn to control your readers' responses to your essays by choosing your evidence carefully, organizing it wisely, and seasoning it with the right amount of emotion and ethics—depending on your purpose and audience.

How to Read Persuasive Essays

Preparing to Read. As you prepare to read the essays in this chapter, spend a few minutes browsing through the preliminary material for each selection: What does Bronwyn Jones's title, "Arming Myself with a Gun Is Not the Answer," prepare you for? What can you learn from scanning Shelby Steele's essay, "Affirmative Action: The Price of Preference," and reading its synopsis in the Rhetorical Table of Contents?

Also, you should bring to your reading as much information as you can from the authors' biographies: Why do you think Shelby Steele writes about affirmative action? Does he have the proper qualifications to teach us about "The Price of Preference"? What is the source of Peter Salins's interest in immigration ("Take a Ticket")? For the essays in this chapter that present two sides of an argument (on technology vs. books and freedom of the press), what biographical details prepare us for each writer's stand on the issue? Who were the original audiences for these pro and con arguments?

Last, before you read these essays, try to generate some ideas on each topic so that you can take the role of an active reader. In this text, the Preparing to Read questions will help you get ready for this task. Then, you should speculate further on the general subject of the essay: What are the main arguments related to gun control? What side do you think Jones is on? Where do you stand on the subject? How do you think affirmative action is working nationally? What would you change about America's approach to this controversial topic? What would you continue?

Reading. Be sure to record your spontaneous reactions to the persuasive essays in this chapter as you read them for the first time: What are your opinions on each subject? Why do you hold these opinions? Be especially aware of your responses to the essays representing opposing viewpoints at the end of the chapter; know where you stand in relation to each side of the issues here.

Use the preliminary material before an essay to help you create a framework for your responses to it: Who was Jones's primary audience when her essay was first published? In what ways is the tone of her essay appropriate for that audience? Why is Steele so interested in affirmative action? What motivated Salins to publish his arguments on immigration? Which argument on technology versus books do you find most convincing? On freedom of the press?

Your main job at this stage of reading is to determine each author's primary assertion or proposition (thesis statement) and to create an inquisitive environment for thinking critically about the essay's ideas. In addition, take a look at the questions after each selection to make sure you are picking up the major points of the essay.

Rereading. As you reread these persuasive essays, notice how the writers integrate their appeals to logic, to emotion, and to ethics. Also, pay attention to the emphasis the writers place on one or more appeals at certain strategic points in the essays: How does Steele integrate these three appeals in "Affirmative Action: The Price of Preference"? Which of these appeals does he rely on to help bring his essay to a close? How persuasive is his final appeal? What combination of appeals does Peter Salins use in "Take a Ticket"? In what way does the tone of his writing support what he is saying? How does he establish this tone?

Also, determine what other rhetorical strategies help these writers make their primary points. How do these strategies enable each writer to establish a unified essay with a beginning, a middle, and an end?

Then answer the questions after each reading selection to make certain you understand the essay on the literal, interpretive, and analytical levels in preparation for the discussion/writing assignments that follow.

For a list of guidelines for the entire reading process, see the checklists on pages 20–21 of the Introduction.

How to Write Persuasive Essays

Preparing to Write. The first stage of writing an essay of this sort involves, as usual, exploring and then limiting your topic. As you prepare to write your persuasive paper, first try to generate as many ideas as possible—regardless of whether they appeal to logic, emotion, or ethics. To do this, review the prewriting techniques in the Introduction and answer the Preparing to Write questions. Then choose a topic. Next, focus on a purpose and a specific audience before you begin to write.

Writing. Most persuasive essays should begin with an assertion or a proposition stating what you believe about a certain issue. This thesis should generally be phrased as a debatable statement, such as, "If individual states reinstituted the death penalty, Americans would notice an immediate drop in violent crimes." At this point in your essay, you should also justify the significance of the issue you will be discussing: "Such a decline in the crime rate would affect all our lives and make this country a safer place in which to live."

The essay should then support your thesis in a variety of ways. This support may take the form of facts, figures, examples, opinions by recognized authorities, case histories, narratives/anecdotes, comparisons, contrasts, or cause/effect studies. This evidence is most effectively organized from least to most important when you are confronted with a hostile audience (so that you can lead your readers through your reasoning step by step) and from most to least important when you are facing a supportive audience (so that you can build on their loyalty and enthusiasm as you advance your thesis). In fact, you will be able to engineer your best support if you know your audience's opinions, feelings, and background before you write your essay, so that your intended "target" is as clear as possible. The body of your essay will undoubtedly consist of a combination of logical, emotional, and ethical appeals—all leading to some final summation or recommendation.

The concluding paragraph of a persuasive essay should restate your main assertion (in terms slightly different from your original statement) and should offer some constructive recommendations about the problem you have been discussing (if you haven't already done so). This section of your paper should clearly bring your argument to a close in one final attempt to move your audience to accept or act on the viewpoint you present. Let's look more closely now at each of the three types of appeals used in such essays: logical, emotional, and ethical.

To construct a *logical* argument, you have two principal patterns available to you: inductive reasoning or deductive reasoning. The first encourages an audience to make what is called an "inductive leap" from several particular examples to a single, useful generalization. In the case of the death penalty, for instance, you might cite a number of examples, figures, facts, and case studies illustrating the effectiveness of capital punishment in various states, thereby leading up to your firm belief that the death penalty should be reinstituted. Used most often by detectives, scientists, and lawyers, the process of inductive reasoning addresses the audience's ability to think logi-cally by moving them systematically from an assortment of selected evidence to a rational and ordered conclusion.

In contrast, deductive reasoning moves its audience from a broad, general statement to particular examples supporting that statement. In writing such an essay, you would present your thesis statement about capital punishment first and then offer clear, or-derly evidence to support that belief. Although the mental process we go through in creating a deductive argument is quite sophisti-cated, it is based on a three-step form of reasoning called the *syllo-gism*, which most logicians believe is the foundation of logical thinking. The traditional syllogism has

A major premise: All humans fear death.

A minor premise: Criminals are humans.

A conclusion: Therefore, criminals fear death.

As you might suspect, this type of reasoning is only as accurate as its original premises, so you need to be sure your premises are true so your argument is valid.

In constructing a logical argument, you should take great care to avoid the two types of fallacies in reasoning found most fre-quently in lower-division college papers: giving too few examples to support an assertion and citing examples that do not represent the assertion fairly. If you build your argument on true statements and abundant, accurate evidence, your essay will be effective.

Persuading through *emotion* necessitates controlling your read-ers' instinctive reactions to what you are saying. You can accom-plish this goal in two different ways: (1) by choosing your words with even greater care than usual and (2) by using figurative language whenever appropriate. In the first case, you must be es-pecially conscious of using words that have the same general de-notative (or dictionary) meaning but bear decidedly favorable or unfavorable connotative (or implicit) meanings. For example, notice the difference between *slender* and *scrawny, patriotic* and *chauvinistic,* or *compliment* and *flattery.* Your careful attention to the choice of such words can help readers form visual images with certain positive or negative associations that subtly encourage them to follow your argument and adopt your opinions. Second, the effective use of figurative language—especially similes and metaphors—makes your writing more vivid, thus triggering your readers' senses and encouraging them to accept your views. Both of these techniques will help you manipulate your readers into the position of agreeing with your ideas.

Ethical appeals, which establish you as a reliable, well-informed person, are accomplished through (1) the tone of your essay and (2) the number and type of examples you cite. Tone is created through deliberate word choice: Careful attention to the mood implied in the words you use can convince your readers that you are serious, friendly, authoritative, jovial, or methodical—depending on your intended purpose. In like manner, the examples you supply to support your assertions can encourage readers to see you as experienced, insightful, relaxed, or intense. In both of these cases, winning favor for yourself will usually also gain approval for your opinions.

Rewriting.   To rework your persuasive essays, you should play the role of your readers and impartially evaluate the different appeals you have used to accomplish your purpose:

- Is your thesis statement clear?
- Is the main thrust of your essay argumentative (an appeal to reason)?
- Do the other appeals you use effectively accomplish your purpose with your intended audience?
- Does your conclusion restate your argument, make a recommendation, and bring your essay to a close?

You should also look closely at the way your appeals work together in your essay:

- When you use logic, is that section of your paper arranged through either inductive or deductive reasoning?
- Is that the most effective order to achieve your purpose?
- In appealing to the emotions, have you chosen your words with proper attention to their denotative and connotative effects?
- Have you chosen examples carefully to support your thesis statement?
- Are these examples suitable for your purpose and audience?

Any additional guidance you may need as you write and revise your persuasive essays is furnished on pages 32–34 of the Introduction.

STUDENT ESSAY: ARGUMENT AND PERSUASION AT WORK

The following student essay uses all three appeals to make its point about the power of language in shaping our view of the world. First, the writer sets forth her character references (ethical appeal) in the first paragraph, after which she presents her thesis and its significance in paragraph 2. The support for her thesis is a combination of logical and emotional appeals, heavy on the logical, as the writer moves her paragraphs from general to particular in an effort to convince her readers to adopt her point of view and adjust their language use accordingly.

The Language of Equal Rights

Ethical appeal

Up front, I admit it. I've been a card-carrying feminist since junior high school. I want to see an Equal Rights Amendment to the U.S. Constitution, equal pay for equal—and comparable—work, and I go dutch on dates. Furthermore, I am quite prickly on the subject of language. I'm one of those women who bristles at terms like *lady doctor* (you know they don't mean a gynecologist), *female policeman* (a paradox), and *mankind* instead of *humanity* (are they really talking about me?).

Emotional appeal

Many people ask "How important are mere words, anyway? You know what we really mean." A question like this ignores the symbolic and psychological importance of language. What words "mean" can go beyond what a speaker or writer consciously intends, reflecting personal and cultural biases that run so deep that most of the time we aren't even aware they exist. "Mere words" are incredibly important:

Assertion or thesis statement

Significance of assertion	They are our framework for seeing and understanding the world.
Logical appeal	*Man*, we are told, means woman as well as man, just as *mankind* supposedly stands for all of humanity. In the introduction of a sociology textbook I recently read, the author was anxious to demonstrate his awareness of the controversy over sexist language and to assure his female readers that, despite his use of noninclusive terms, he was not forgetting the existence or importance of women in society. He was making a conscious decision to continue to use *man* and *mankind* instead of *people, humanity*, etc., for ease of expression and aesthetic reasons. "Man" simply sounds better, he explained. I flipped through the table of contents and found "Man and Society," "Man and Nature," "Man and Technology," and, near the end, "Man and Woman." At what point did *Man* quit meaning *people* and start meaning men again? The writer was obviously unaware of the answer to this question, because it is one he would never think to ask. Having consciously addressed the issue only to dismiss it, he reverted to form.
Logical appeal	The very ambiguity of *man* as the generic word for our species ought to be enough to combat any arguments that we keep it because we all "know what it means" or because it is both traditional and sounds better. And does it really sound all that much better, or are we just more used to it, more comfortable? Our own national history proves that we can be comfortable with a host of words and attitudes that strike us as unjust and ugly today. A lot of white folks probably thought that Negroes were getting pretty stuffy and picky when

Examples organized deductively

Emotional appeal

Examples organized deductively

they began to insist on being called *blacks*. After all, weren't there more important things to worry about, like civil rights? But black activists recognized the emotional and symbolic significance of having a name that was parallel to the name that the dominant race used for itself—a name equal in dignity, lacking that vaguely alien, anthropological sound. After all, whites were called *Caucasians* only in police reports, textbooks, and autopsies. *Negro* may have sounded better to people in the bad old days of blatant racial bigotry, but we adjusted to the word *black* and have now moved on to African American, and more and more people of each race are adjusting to the wider implications and demands of practical, as well as verbal, labels.

Emotional appeal

In a world where *man* and *human* are offered as synonymous terms, I don't think it is a coincidence that women are still vastly underrepresented in positions of money, power, and respect. Children grow up learning a language that makes maleness the norm for anything that isn't explicitly designated as female, giving little girls a very limited corner of the universe to picture themselves in. Indeed, the language that nonfeminists today claim to be inclusive was never intended to cover women in the first place. "One man, one vote" and "All men are created equal" meant just that. Women had to fight for decades to be included even as an afterthought; it took constitutional amendments to convince the government and the courts that women are human too.

Logical appeal

Examples organized deductively

The message is clear. We have to start speaking about people, not men, if we are going to start thinking in terms of both

Conclusion/restatement

> women and men. A "female man" will
> never be the equal of her brother.

Student Writer's Comments

The hardest task for me in writing this essay was coming up with a topic! The second hardest job was trying to be effective without getting preachy, strident, or wordy. I wanted to persuade an audience that would no doubt include the bored, the hostile, and the indifferent, and I was worried about losing their attention.

I chose my topic after several prewriting sessions that generated numerous options for me to write about. I stumbled on the idea of sexist language in one of these sessions and then went on to generate new material on this particular topic. Eventually satisfied that I had enough ideas to stay with this topic, I doubled back and labeled them according to each type of appeal.

Even before I had written my thesis, I had a good idea of what I wanted to say in this essay. I began working from an assertion that essentially remained the same as I wrote and revised my essay. It's more polished now, but its basic intention never changed.

To create my first draft, I worked from my notes, labeled by type of appeal. I let the logical arguments guide my writing, strategically introducing emotional and ethical appeals as I sensed they would be effective. I appealed to ethics in the beginning of the essay to establish my credibility, and I appealed to the readers' emotions occasionally to vary my pace and help my argument gain momentum. I was fully aware of what I was doing when I moved from one appeal to another. I wrote from a passionate desire to change people's thinking about language and its ability to control our perceptions of the world.

Next, I revised my entire essay several times, playing the role of different readers with dissimilar biases in each case. Every time I worked through the essay, I made major changes in the introduction and the conclusion as well. At this point, I paid special attention to the denotation, connotation, and tone of my words (especially highly charged language) and to the examples I had chosen to support each point I decided to keep in my argument. Though I moved a lot of examples around and thought of better ones in some cases, I was eventually happy with the final product. I am especially pleased with the balance of appeals in the final draft.

SOME FINAL THOUGHTS ON ARGUMENT AND PERSUASION

As you can tell from the selections that follow, the three different types of persuasive appeals usually complement one another in practice. Most good persuasive essays use a combination of these methods to achieve their purposes. Good persuasive essays also rely on various rhetorical modes we have already studied—such as example, process analysis, division/classification, comparison/contrast, definition, and cause/effect—to advance their arguments. In the following essays, you will see a combination of appeals and a number of different rhetorical modes at work.

ARGUMENT AND PERSUASION IN REVIEW

Reading Argument and Persuasion Essays

Preparing to Read

- ✓ What assumptions can you make from the essay's title?
- ✓ Can you guess what the general mood of the essay is?
- ✓ What is the essay's purpose and audience?
- ✓ What does the synopsis in the Rhetorical Table of Contents tell you about the essay?
- ✓ What can you learn from the author's biography?
- ✓ Can you guess what the author's point of view toward the subject is?
- ✓ What are your responses to the Preparing to Read questions?

Reading

- ✓ What is the author's main assertion or thesis?
- ✓ What are the primary appeals at work in the essay?
- ✓ Did you preview the questions that follow the essay?

Rereading

- ✓ How does the writer integrate the appeals in the essay?
- ✓ What is the tone of the essay? How does the author establish this tone?

✓ What other rhetorical strategies does the author use to support the essay's purpose?

✓ What are your responses to the questions after the essay?

Writing Argument and Persuasion Essays

Preparing to Write

✓ What are your responses to the Preparing to Write questions?

✓ Do you narrow and focus your material as much as possible?

✓ What is your purpose?

✓ Who is your audience?

Writing

✓ Is your thesis a debatable question?

✓ Do you justify the organization of your essay?

✓ Is your essay organized effectively for what you are trying to accomplish?

✓ Does the body of your essay directly support your thesis?

✓ Do you understand your audience's opinions, convictions, and backgrounds so that you know what to emphasize in your essay?

✓ Does your conclusion restate your main assertion and offer some constructive recommendations?

Rewriting

✓ Is your thesis statement clear?

✓ Is the main thrust of your essay argumentative (an appeal to reason)?

✓ Will the balance of these appeals effectively accomplish your purpose with your intended audience?

✓ Does your conclusion restate your argument, make a recommendation, and bring your essay to a close?

✓ When you use logic, is that section of your paper arranged through either inductive or deductive reasoning? Is that the most effective order to achieve your purpose?

✓ In appealing to the emotions, have you chosen your words with proper attention to their denotative and connotative effects?

✓ Have you used figurative language whenever appropriate?

✓ Have you chosen examples carefully to support your thesis statement?

BRONWYN JONES   (1956–   )

Arming Myself with a Gun Is Not the Answer

Born in Leonia, New Jersey, Bronwyn Jones was educated at the Manhattan School of Music and worked for a while as a professional harpist. She later received her B.A. in French and English Literature from Columbia University and her M.A. in English from Hunter College. Currently an English professor at Northwestern Michigan College in Traverse City, she specializes in teaching freshman composition, introduction to literature, and women in literature courses. In addition, she devotes a great deal of time to working with local arts and environmental organizations and to freelance writing about the problems of violence and mental illness. In her spare time, she appears with a group of English teachers called the "Beach Bards," who specialize in "by heart" poetry recitation and storytelling, "radio theatre" productions accompanied by music, and creative writing workshops. She also enjoys reading, cross-country skiing, swimming, and kayaking. She advises students using *The Prose Reader* "to write about what you feel passionately about in as much detail as possible."

Preparing to Read

In the following essay, originally published in *Newsweek* (May 2000), Bronwyn Jones logically and persuasively presents her opinions on various issues connected with guns and mental illness in contemporary society. As you prepare to read her essay, take a few moments to focus your own thoughts on the relationship between violent crimes and mental health: In your opinion, how are mental illness and violent crimes related? Why do you think people resort to violent crimes? Do you think people should have guns to protect themselves? Why or why not? Do you think more guns in private hands would increase or decrease the violence in the United States?

When my father died 15 years ago, my brother and I in-   1
herited the old Midwestern farmhouse our grandparents had purchased in the 1930s. I was the one who

decided to give up my harried existence as a teacher in New York City and make a life in this idyllic village, population 350, in northern Michigan.

A full-time job in the English department of a nearby college 2 quickly followed. I settled into small-town life, charmed by a community where your neighbors are also your friends and no one worries about locking a door. Eventually I forgot about the big-city stress of crowds, noise, and crime.

I felt safe enough to keep my phone number listed so col- 3 leagues and students could reach me after hours. I was totally unprepared when I returned home one evening to an answering machine filled with incoherent and horribly threatening messages. I could identify the voice—it belonged to a former student of mine. Shocked and frightened, I called 911, and an officer arrived in time to pick up the phone and hear the man threaten to rape and kill me. The cop recognized the caller as the stalker in a similar incident that had been reported a few years before, and immediately rushed me out of the house. I soon learned that my would-be assailant had been arrested, according to police, drunk, armed with a 19-inch double-edged knife and just minutes from my door.

It was revealed in court testimony that my stalker was a schizo- 4 phrenic who had fallen through the cracks of the mental-health system. In spite of my 10-year personal-protection order, I live with the fear that he will return unsupervised to my community. Time and again, colleagues and friends have urged me to get a gun to protect myself.

And why shouldn't I? This part of rural Michigan is home to 5 an avid gun culture. Nov. 15, the opening of deer-hunting season, is all but an official holiday. It is not uncommon to see the bumper sticker CHARLTON HESTON IS MY PRESIDENT displayed, along with a gun rack, on the back of local pickup trucks.

A good friend recommended several different handguns. The 6 assistant prosecutor on the case told me that I'd have no problem getting a concealed-weapons permit. A female deputy offered to teach me how to shoot.

But I haven't gotten a gun, and I'm not going to. When I 7 questioned them, my friends and colleagues had to admit that they've used guns only for recreational purposes, never for self-defense. The assistant prosecutor said that he would never carry a concealed weapon himself. And an ex-cop told me that no matter how much you train, the greatest danger is of hurting yourself.

The truth is when you keep a gun for self-protection, you live   8
with constant paranoia. For me, owning a gun and practicing at a target range would be allowing my sense of victimization to corrupt my deepest values.

Contrary to all the pro-gun arguments, I don't believe guns are   9
innocent objects. If they were, "gunnies" wouldn't display them as badges of security and freedom. When someone waves a gun around, he or she is advertising the power to snuff out life. But guns are no deterrent. Like nuclear weapons, they only ensure greater devastation when conflict breaks out or the inevitable human error occurs.

I never needed a weapon in the years prior to my terrifying ex-   10
perience. And while I learned not to flinch at the sight of men and women in fluorescent orange carrying rifles into the woods at the start of deer season, owning a gun for play or protection didn't occur to me. But I've learned firsthand that even small, close-knit communities are subject to the kind of social problems— like disintegrating families and substance abuse—that can propel a troubled person toward violence. So I now carry pepper spray and my cell phone at all times.

In Michigan—and elsewhere—as federal funding for state   11
mental-health care continues to shrink and state psychiatric hospitals are forced to close, the numbers of untreated, incarcerated, and homeless mentally ill are rising. People with serious mental illness and violent tendencies need 24-hour care. It costs less to house them in group homes with trained counselors than it does to keep them in prisons or hospitals. But until states fund more of this kind of care, people like my stalker will continue to return unsupervised to our communities.

And people like me will be forced to consider getting guns to   12
protect ourselves. I am lucky. I survived, though not unchanged. I know my fear cannot be managed with a gun. The only reasonable response is to do what I can to help fix the mental-health system. Awareness, education, and proper funding will save more lives and relieve more fear than all the guns we can buy.

UNDERSTANDING DETAILS

1. Why did Jones consider getting a gun to protect herself?
2. What does Jones mean when she says, "It costs less to house them in group homes with trained counselors than it does to keep them in prisons or hospitals" (paragraph 11)?
3. What is Jones implying when she says, "I survived, though not unchanged" (paragraph 12)?
4. State Jones's main point in a complete sentence of your own.

ANALYZING MEANING

1. What does Jones mean when she says, "For me, owning a gun and practicing at a target range would be allowing my sense of victimization to corrupt my deepest values" (paragraph 8)?
2. Why does Jones still live in fear?
3. Do you agree with Jones when she says, "Awareness, education, and proper funding will save more lives and relieve more fear than all the guns we can buy" (paragraph 12)? Explain your answer in detail.
4. According to Jones, how are paranoia and having a gun for self-protection connected?

DISCOVERING RHETORICAL STRATEGIES

1. Do you think Jones's story about her grandparents' old Midwestern farmhouse is an effective beginning for her essay? Why or why not?
2. Why does Jones refer to Charlton Heston in this essay? What does he have to do with gun control?
3. Are you convinced by this essay that improving the mental health system will reduce violent acts and fear in American society? What details or examples are most persuasive to you?
4. What additional rhetorical strategies does Jones use to develop her argument? Give examples of each.

MAKING CONNECTIONS

1. Compare and contrast Jones's view of violence in America with that expressed in Brent Staples's "A Brother's Murder,"

Nancy Gibbs's "When Is It Rape?," Stephen King's "Why We Crave Horror Movies," and Rosenbaum and Chesney-Lind's "Appearance and Delinquency: A Research Note."
2. How does Jones's opinion about the safety of her community compare with the same theme in Ray Bradbury's "Summer Rituals," Germaine Greer's "A Child Is Born," Robert Ramirez's "The Barrio," and Ellen Goodman's "A Working Community"?
3. Contrast Jones's response to her need for personal safety with Gloria Steinem's description of women's body-building in "The Politics of Muscle" and Nancy Gibbs's discussion of the mythology of sexual violence in "When Is It Rape?"

IDEAS FOR DISCUSSION/WRITING

Preparing to Write

Write freely about your view of mental illness in American society today: Why is mental illness increasing today? What can we do about this increase? Do you think mental illness is related in any way to violent crimes? In what ways? Do you have any constructive suggestions for controlling or treating mental illness? What would be some of the advantages of controlling mental illness in the United States? Would more guns for self-protection help or hinder the crime rate? Why should we care?

Choosing a Topic

1. Your old high school has asked you to talk to its senior class about the use of guns for self-protection. What is your opinion on this subject? Write a well-developed statement on this issue to be presented to the current senior class.
2. Your parents are interested in personal safety on your college campus. Interview several students and some key people involved in the campus security office. Then write up your findings in letter form.
3. Jones says she doesn't believe "guns are innocent objects" (paragraph 9). Write a well-developed essay arguing for or against this contention.

Before beginning your essay, you might want to consult the checklists on pages 504–505.

SHELBY STEELE   (1946–   )

Affirmative Action: The Price of Preference

Born in Chicago, Shelby Steele earned his B.A. at Coe College in Iowa, his M.A. at Southern Illinois University, and his Ph.D. at the University of Utah. An early succession of articles in *Harper's*, the *American Scholar*, the *Washington Post*, the *New Republic*, and the *New York Times Book Review* earned him a National Magazine Award in 1989. One of his essays on race relations was selected for inclusion in *The Best American Essays of 1989*. His most well-known publication, however, is *The Content of Our Character: A New Vision of Race in America*, a controversial best-seller that won the National Book Critics Circle Award in 1991. In it, the author examines his own life as a middle-class African-American in a world where both blacks and whites have become trapped into seeing "color before character." He argues that social policies designed to lessen racial differences have instead made these diversities much greater and that the posture of "victimization" adopted by many members of his own race has detracted from rather than enhanced the movement toward cultural equality. His advice to students using *The Prose Reader* is concise and helpful: "Use simple, concrete, Anglo-Saxon words; avoid jargon, colloquialisms, and the passive voice. Try to give clarity and immediacy to your work by writing about emotions and events you know from your own experience." Steele is currently a research fellow at the Hoover Institution where he wrote his most recent book, *A Dream Deferred: The Second Betrayal of Black Freedom in America* (1999). In his infrequent spare time, he enjoys swimming, jogging, and reading.

Preparing to Read

In the following chapter from *The Content of Our Character*, Steele argues that affirmative action programs, however well intentioned and fairly administered, demoralize and stigmatize blacks as "inferior" to their white counterparts in society. The net result is a culture of "victimization" that seeks to exploit rather than overcome past racial injustices. As you prepare to read this essay, take a few moments to think about your own views on affirmative action: Exactly how does this concept work? How effective is it in your community? In your job? In your school? In what ways has affirmative action affected you directly? From your perspective, what are the principal advantages of affirmative action? The disadvantages? How much longer do you think it will be necessary in America?

In a few short years, when my two children will be applying to college, the affirmative action policies by which most universities offer black students some form of preferential treatment will present me with a dilemma. I am a middle-class black, a college professor, far from wealthy, but also well-removed from the kind of deprivation that would qualify my children for the label "disadvantaged." Both of them have endured racial insensitivity from whites. They have been called names, have suffered slights, and have experienced firsthand the peculiar malevolence that racism brings out in people. Yet, they have never experienced racial discrimination, have never been stopped by their race on any path they have chosen to follow. Still, their society now tells them that if they will only designate themselves as black on their college applications, they will likely do better in the college lottery than if they conceal this fact. I think there is something of a Faustian bargain in this.

Of course, many blacks and a considerable number of whites would say that I was sanctimoniously making affirmative action into a test of character. They would say that this small preference is the meagerest recompense for centuries of unrelieved oppression. And to these arguments other very obvious facts must be added. In America, many marginally competent or flatly incompetent whites are hired every day—some because their white skin suits the conscious or unconscious racial preference of their employer. The white children of alumni are often grandfathered into elite universities in what can only be seen as a residual benefit of historic white privilege. Worse, white incompetence is always an individual matter, while for blacks it is often confirmation of ugly stereotypes. The Peter Principle was not conceived with only blacks in mind. Given that unfairness cuts both ways, doesn't it only balance the scales of history that my children now receive a slight preference over whites? Doesn't this repay, in a small way, the systematic denial under which their grandfather lived out his days?

So, in theory, affirmative action certainly has all the moral sym-   3
metry that fairness requires—the injustice of historical and even contemporary white advantage is offset with black advantage; preference replaces prejudice, inclusion answers exclusion. It is reformist and corrective, even repentant and redemptive. And I would never sneer at these good intentions. Born in the late forties in Chicago, I started my education (a charitable term in this case) in a segregated school and suffered all the indignities that come to blacks in a segregated society. My father, born in the South, only made it to the third grade before the white man's fields took permanent priority over his formal education. And though he educated himself into an advanced reader with an al-·most professorial authority, he could only drive a truck for a living and never earned more than ninety dollars a week in his entire life. So yes, it is crucial to my sense of citizenship, to my ability to identify with the spirit and the interests of America, to know that this country, however imperfectly, recognizes its past sins and wishes to correct them.

Yet good intentions, because of the opportunity for innocence   4
they offer us, are very seductive and can blind us to the effects they generate when implemented. In our society, affirmative action is, among other things, a testament to white goodwill and to black power, and in the midst of these heavy investments, its effects can be hard to see. But after twenty years of implementation, I think affirmative action has shown itself to be more bad than good and that blacks—whom I will focus on in this essay—now stand to lose more from it than they gain.

In talking with affirmative action administrators and with   5
blacks and whites in general, it is clear that supporters of affirmative action focus on its good intentions while detractors emphasize its negative effects. Proponents talk about "diversity" and "pluralism"; opponents speak of "reverse discrimination," the unfairness of quotas and set-asides. It was virtually impossible to find people outside either camp. The closest I came was a white male manager at a large computer company who said, "I think it amounts to reverse discrimination, but I'll put up with a little of that for a little more diversity." I'll live with a little of the effect to gain a little of the intention, he seemed to be saying. But this only

makes him a halfhearted supporter of affirmative action. I think many people who don't really like affirmative action support it to one degree or another anyway.

I believe they do this because of what happened to white and   6 black Americans in the crucible of the sixties when whites were confronted with their racial guilt and blacks tasted their first real power. In this stormy time white absolution and black power coalesced into virtual mandates for society. Affirmative action became a meeting ground for these mandates in the law, and in the late sixties and early seventies it underwent a remarkable escalation of its mission from simple antidiscrimination enforcement to social engineering by means of quotas, goals, timetables, setasides, and other forms of preferential treatment.

· Legally, this was achieved through a series of executive orders   7 and EEOC [Equal Employment Opportunity Commission] guidelines that allowed racial imbalances in the workplace to stand as proof of racial discrimination. Once it could be assumed that discrimination explained racial imbalances, it became easy to justify group remedies to presumed discrimination, rather than the normal case-by-case redress for proven discrimination. Preferential treatment through quotas, goals, and so on is designed to correct imbalances based on the assumption that they always indicate discrimination. This expansion of what constitutes discrimination allowed affirmative action to escalate into the business of social engineering in the name of anti-discrimination, to push society toward statistically proportionate racial representation, without any obligation of proving actual discrimination.

What accounted for this shift, I believe, was the white mandate   8 to achieve a new racial innocence and the black mandate to gain power. Even though blacks had made great advances during the sixties without quotas, these mandates, which came to a head in the very late sixties, could no longer be satisfied by anything less than racial preferences. I don't think these mandates in themselves were wrong, since whites clearly needed to do better by blacks and blacks needed more real power in society. But, as they came together in affirmative action, their effect was to distort our understanding of racial discrimination in a way that allowed us to offer the remediation of preference on the basis of mere color rather than actual injury. By making black the color of preference, these mandates have reburdened society with the very marriage of color and preference (in reverse) that we set out to eradicate. The old sin is reaffirmed in a new guise.

But the essential problem with this form of affirmative action is   9
the way it leaps over the hard business of developing a formerly oppressed people to the point where they can achieve proportionate representation on their own (given equal opportunity) and goes straight for the proportionate representation. This may satisfy some whites of their innocence and some blacks of their power, but it does very little to truly uplift blacks.

A white female affirmative action officer at an Ivy League uni-   10
versity told me what many supporters of affirmative action now say: "We're after diversity. We ideally want a student body where racial and ethnic groups are represented according to their proportion in society." When affirmative action escalated into social engineering, diversity became a golden word. It grants whites an egalitarian fairness (innocence) and blacks an entitlement to proportionate representation (power). *Diversity* is a term that applies democratic principles to races and cultures rather than to citizens, despite the fact that there is nothing to indicate that real diversity is the same thing as proportionate representation. Too often the result of this on campuses (for example) has been a democracy of colors rather than of people, an artificial diversity that gives the appearance of an educational parity between black and white students that has not yet been achieved in reality. Here again, racial preferences allow society to leapfrog over the difficult problem of developing blacks to parity with whites and into a cosmetic diversity that covers the blemish of disparity—a full six years after admission, only about 26 percent of black students graduate from college.

Racial representation is not the same thing as racial develop-   11
ment, yet affirmative action fosters a confusion of these very different needs. Representation can be manufactured; development is always hard-earned. However, it is the music of innocence and power that we hear in affirmative action that causes us to cling to it and to its distracting emphasis on representation. The fact is that after twenty years of racial preferences, the gap between white and black median income is greater than it was in the seventies. None of this is to say that blacks don't need policies that ensure our right to equal opportunity, but what we need more is the development that will let us take advantage of society's efforts to include us.

I think that one of the most troubling effects of racial prefer-   12
ences for blacks is a kind of demoralization, or put another way,
an enlargement of self-doubt. Under affirmative action the quality
that earns us preferential treatment is an implied inferiority. However this inferiority is explained—and it is easily enough explained
by the myriad deprivations that grew out of our oppression—it is
still inferiority. There are explanations, and then there is the fact.
And the fact must be borne by the individual as a condition apart
from the explanation, apart even from the fact that others like
himself also bear this condition. In integrated situations where
blacks must compete with whites who may be better prepared,
these explanations may quickly wear thin and expose the individual to racial as well as personal self-doubt.

All of this is compounded by the cultural myth of black inferi-   13
ority that blacks have always lived with. What this means in practical terms is that when blacks deliver themselves into integrated
situations, they encounter a nasty little reflex in whites, a mind-
less, atavistic reflex that responds to the color black with alarm.
Attributions may follow this alarm if the white cares to indulge
them, and if they do, they will most likely be negative—one such
attribution is intellectual ineptness. I think this reflex and the attributions that may follow it embarrass most whites today; therefore,
it is usually quickly repressed. Nevertheless, on an equally atavistic
level, the black will be aware of the reflex his color triggers and
will feel a stab of horror at seeing himself reflected in this way.
He, too, will do a quick repression, but a lifetime of such stab-
bings is what constitutes his inner realm of racial doubt.

The effects of this may be a subject for another essay. The   14
point here is that the implication of inferiority that racial preferences engender in both the white and black mind expands rather
than contracts this doubt. Even when the black sees no implication of inferiority in racial preferences, he knows that whites do,
so that—consciously or unconsciously—the result is virtually the
same. The effect of preferential treatment—the lowering of normal standards to increase black representation—puts blacks at war
with an expanded realm of debilitating doubt, so that the doubt itself becomes an unrecognized preoccupation that undermines their
ability to perform, especially in integrated situations. On largely
white campuses, blacks are five times more likely to drop out than
whites. Preferential treatment, no matter how it is justified in the

light of day, subjects blacks to a midnight of self-doubt and so often transforms their advantage into a revolving door.

Another liability of affirmative action comes from the fact that   15
it indirectly encourages blacks to exploit their own past victimization as a source of power and privilege. Victimization, like implied inferiority, is what justifies preference, so that to receive the benefits of preferential treatment one must, to some extent, become invested in the view of one's self as a victim. In this way, affirmative action nurtures a victim-focused identity in blacks. The obvious irony here is that we become inadvertently invested in the very condition we are trying to overcome. Racial preferences send us the message that there is more power in our past suffering than our present achievements—none of which could bring us a *preference* over others.

When power itself grows out of suffering, then blacks are en-   16
couraged to expand the boundaries of what qualifies as racial oppression, a situation that can lead us to paint our victimization in vivid colors, even as we receive the benefits of preference. The same corporations and institutions that give us preference are also seen as our oppressors. At Stanford University minority students—some of whom enjoy as much as $15,000 a year in financial aid—recently took over the president's office demanding, among other things, more financial aid. The power to be found in victimization, like any power, is intoxicating and can lend itself to the creation of a new class of super-victims who can feel the pea of victimization under twenty mattresses. Preferential treatment rewards us for being underdogs rather than for moving beyond that status—a misplacement of incentives that, along with its deepening of our doubt, is more a yoke than a spur.

But, I think, one of the worst prices that blacks pay for prefer-   17
ence has to do with an illusion. I saw this illusion at work recently in the mother of a middle-class black student who was going off to his first semester of college. "They owe us this, so don't think for a minute that you don't belong there." This is the logic by which many blacks, and some whites, justify affirmative action— it is something "owed," a form of reparation. But this logic overlooks a much harder and less digestible reality, that it is impossible to repay blacks living today for the historic suffering of the race. If all blacks were given a million dollars tomorrow morning it would not amount to a dime on the dollar of three centuries of

oppression, nor would it obviate the residues of that oppression that we still carry today. The concept of historic reparation grows out of man's need to impose a degree of justice on the world that simply does not exist. Suffering can be endured and overcome; it cannot be repaid. Blacks cannot be repaid for the injustice done to the race, but we can be corrupted by society's guilty gestures of repayment.

Affirmative action is such a gesture. It tells us that racial prefer-   18
ences can do for us what we cannot do for ourselves. The corruption here is in the hidden incentive *not* to do what we believe preferences will do. This is an incentive to be reliant on others just as we are struggling for self-reliance. And it keeps alive the illusion that we can find some deliverance in repayment. The hardest thing for any sufferer to accept is that his suffering excuses him from very little and never has enough currency to restore him. To think otherwise is to prolong the suffering.

Several blacks I spoke with said they were still in favor of affir-   19
mative action because of the "subtle" discrimination blacks were subject to once on the job. One photojournalist said, "They have ways of ignoring you." A black female television producer said, "You can't file a lawsuit when your boss doesn't invite you to the insider meetings without ruining your career. So we still need affirmative action." Others mentioned the infamous "glass ceiling" through which blacks can see the top positions of authority but never reach them. But I don't think racial preferences are a protection against this subtle discrimination; I think they contribute to it.

In any workplace, racial preferences will always create two-tiered   20
populations composed of preferreds and unpreferreds. This division makes automatic a perception of enhanced competence for the unpreferreds and of questionable competence for the preferreds—the former earned his way, even though others were given preference, while the latter made it by color as much as by competence. Racial preferences implicitly mark whites with an exaggerated superiority just as they mark blacks with an exaggerated inferiority. They not only reinforce America's oldest racial myth, but, for blacks, they have the effect of stigmatizing the already stigmatized.

I think that much of the "subtle" discrimination that blacks talk   21
about is often (not always) discrimination against the stigma of questionable competence that affirmative action delivers to blacks. In this sense, preferences scapegoat the very people they seek to

help. And it may be that at a certain level employers impose a glass ceiling, but this may not be against the race so much as against the race's reputation for having advanced by color as much as by competence. Affirmative action makes a glass ceiling virtually necessary as a protection against the corruptions of preferential treatment. This ceiling is the point at which corporations shift the emphasis from color to competency and stop playing the affirmative action game. Here preference backfires for blacks and becomes a taint that holds them back. Of course, one could argue that this taint, which is, after all, in the minds of whites, becomes nothing more than an excuse to discriminate against blacks. And certainly the result is the same in either case—blacks don't get past the glass ceiling. But this argument does not get around the fact that racial preferences now taint this color with a new theme of suspicion that makes it even more vulnerable to the impulse in others to discriminate. In this crucial yet gray area of perceived competence, preferences make whites look better than they are and blacks worse, while doing nothing whatever to stop the very real discrimination that blacks may encounter. I don't wish to justify the glass ceiling here, but only to suggest the very subtle ways that affirmative action revives rather than extinguishes the old rationalizations for racial discrimination.

In education, a revolving door; in employment, a glass ceiling.   22

I believe affirmative action is problematic in our society because it tries to function like a social program. Rather than ask it to ensure equal opportunity we have demanded that it create parity between the races. But preferential treatment does not teach skills, or educate, or instill motivation. It only passes out entitlement by color, a situation that in my profession has created an unrealistically high demand for black professors. The social engineer's assumption is that this high demand will inspire more blacks to earn Ph.D.'s and join the profession. In fact, the number of blacks earning Ph.D.'s has declined in recent years. A Ph.D. must be developed from preschool on. He requires family and community support. He must acquire an entire system of values that enables him to work hard while delaying gratification. There are social programs, I believe, that can (and should) help blacks *develop* in all these areas, but entitlement by color is not a social program; it is a dubious reward for being black.   23

It now seems clear that the Supreme Court, in a series of recent   24
decisions, is moving away from racial preferences. It has disal-
lowed preferences except in instances of "identified discrimination," eroded the precedent that statistical racial imbalances are
prima facie evidence of discrimination, and in effect granted white
males the right to challenge consent decrees that use preference to
achieve racial balances in the workplace. One civil rights leader
said, "Night has fallen on civil rights." But I am not so sure. The
effect of these decisions is to protect the constitutional rights of
everyone rather than take rights away from blacks. What they do
take away from blacks is the special entitlement to more rights
than others that preferences always grant. Night has fallen on
racial preferences, not on the fundamental rights of black Americans. The reason for this shift, I believe, is that the white mandate
for absolution from past racial sins has weakened considerably
during the eighties. Whites are now less willing to endure unfairness to themselves in order to grant special entitlements to blacks,
even when these entitlements are justified in the name of past suffering. Yet the black mandate for more power in society has remained unchanged. And I think part of the anxiety that many
blacks feel over these decisions has to do with the loss of black
power they may signal. We had won a certain specialness, and
now we are losing it.

But the power we've lost by these decisions is really only the   25
power that grows out of our victimization—the power to claim
special entitlements under the law because of past oppression.
This is not a very substantial or reliable power, and it is important
that we know this so we can focus more exclusively on the kind
of development that will bring enduring power. There is talk
now that Congress will pass new legislation to compensate for
these new limits on affirmative action. If this happens, I hope that
their focus will be on development and anti-discrimination rather
than entitlement, on achieving racial parity rather than jerry-
building racial diversity.

I would also like to see affirmative action go back to its original   26
purpose of enforcing equal opportunity—a purpose that in itself
disallows racial preferences. We cannot be sure that the dis-
criminatory impulse in America has yet been shamed into extinc-
tion, and I believe affirmative action can make its greatest

contribution by providing a rigorous vigilance in this area. It can guard constitutional rather than racial rights and help institutions evolve standards of merit and selection that are appropriate to the institution's needs yet as free of racial bias as possible (again, with the understanding that racial imbalances are not always an indication of racial bias). One of the most important things affirmative action can do is to define exactly what racial discrimination is and how it might manifest itself within a specific institution. The impulse to discriminate *is* subtle and cannot be ferreted out unless its many guises are made clear to people. Along with this there should be monitoring of institutions and heavy sanctions brought to bear when actual discrimination is found. This is the sort of affirmative action that America owes to blacks and to itself. It goes after the evil of discrimination itself, while preferences only sidestep the evil and grant entitlement to its *presumed* victims.

But if not preferences, then what? I think we need social policies that are committed to two goals: the educational and economic development of disadvantaged people, regardless of race, and the eradication from our society—through close monitoring and severe sanctions—of racial, ethnic, or gender discrimination. Preferences will not deliver us to either of these goals, since they tend to benefit those who are not disadvantaged—middle-class white women and middle-class blacks—and attack one form of discrimination with another. Preferences are inexpensive and carry the glamour of good intentions—change the numbers and the good deed is done. To be against them is to be unkind. But I think the unkindest cut is to bestow on children like my own an undeserved advantage while neglecting the development of those disadvantaged children on the East Side of my city who will likely never be in a position to benefit from a preference. Give my children fairness; give disadvantaged children a better shot at development—better elementary and secondary schools, job training, safer neighborhoods, better financial assistance for college, and so on. Fewer blacks go to college today than ten years ago; more black males of college age are in prison or under the control of the criminal justice system than in college. This despite racial preferences.

The mandates of black power and white absolution out of which preferences emerged were not wrong in themselves. What was wrong was that both races focused more on the goals of these

27

28

mandates than on the means to the goals. Blacks can have no real power without taking responsibility for their own educational and economic development. Whites can have no racial innocence without earning it by eradicating discrimination and helping the disadvantaged to develop. Because we ignored the means, the goals have not been reached, and the real work remains to be done.

UNDERSTANDING DETAILS

1. Why does specifying his children's race on their college applications present a problem for Steele?
2. According to Steele, what is fair about affirmative action?
3. Why does Steele think affirmative action is "more bad than good" (paragraph 4)?
4. According to Steele, what are the principal negative consequences of affirmative action? Explain each in your own words.

ANALYZING MEANING

1. What does Steele mean when he says, "*Diversity* is a term that applies democratic principles to races and cultures rather than to citizens" (paragraph 10)?
2. In Steele's opinion, what is the difference between "racial representation" and "racial development" (paragraph 11)? Why is affirmative action not closing this gap?
3. How do racial preferences "mark whites with an exaggerated superiority just as they mark blacks with an exaggerated inferiority" (paragraph 20)? What is the relationship in Steele's mind between the "implied inferiority" of affirmative action and "personal self-doubt" (paragraph 12) in the African-American community?
4. Steele argues that preferential treatment based on race perpetuates the revolving door in education and the glass ceiling in employment. Give examples from your own experience to support or refute this claim.

DISCOVERING RHETORICAL STRATEGIES

1. In paragraph 22, Steele uses the metaphors of "a revolving door" and "a glass ceiling" to help illustrate the problems of preferential treatment. Explain these two images in as much

detail as you can. How effective are they in making Steele's points?

2. What is the dominant type of appeal (see pages 491–492 of the chapter introduction) that Steele uses in this essay? What parts of Steele's argument are most persuasive to you? Why do you think they are persuasive?

3. Who do you think is Steele's intended audience? Describe them in detail.

4. Which different rhetorical strategies does Steele use to develop his argument? Give examples of each.

MAKING CONNECTIONS

1. Steele, Fred Pelka ("Hating the Sick: Health Chauvinism and Its Cure"), and Harold Krentz ("Darkness at Noon") all discuss various types of social prejudice. Who or what would each of these authors say is responsible for these different prejudices? Which of these prejudices would they say is most injurious to American society and why?

2. Discuss the relative balance of the logical, emotional, and ethical appeals in the essays by Steele and Peter Salins ("Take a Ticket"). Which author uses logic most? Who relies most heavily on emotion? Whose ethical appeal is the strongest? What do the dominance of these appeals have to do with the subject matter of each essay?

3. In his essay, Steele refers to affirmative action as "social engineering." Explain what you feel the author means by this phrase, and then locate and examine the same concept in essays by Richard Rodriguez ("The Fear of Losing a Culture"), Peter Salins ("Take a Ticket"), and/or Rita Mae Brown ("Writing as a Moral Act").

IDEAS FOR DISCUSSION/WRITING

Preparing to Write

Write freely about your thoughts on affirmative action: In what areas does affirmative action work most effectively? In what areas does it work less well? What are the main social consequences of affirmative action? Are you directly affected by affirmative action in any way? Have you witnessed or experienced any discrimination in hiring? What solutions do you propose to solve the problem of discrimination in the job market? How might these solutions be implemented?

Choosing a Topic

1. In paragraph 16 of this essay, Steele claims, "Preferential treatment rewards us for being underdogs rather than for moving beyond that status." Direct an essay to your classmates in which you agree or disagree with this statement. Be sure to explain your reasoning carefully.

2. In your opinion, how serious is racial or sexual discrimination at your school or at your job? How is it manifested? Who suffers most from this discrimination? In a coherent essay, persuade your friends that discrimination is or is not a serious social evil at your school or your workplace.

3. In an essay written for a group of employers, present a proposal other than affirmative action for controlling discrimination in the workplace. Explain the details of its implementation and its projected long-term effects.

Before beginning your essay, you might want to consult the checklists on pages 504–505.

PETER SALINS   (1938–   )

Take a Ticket

Peter Salins is currently provost and vice chancellor for the State University of New York system and a senior fellow at the Manhattan Institute for Public Policy, a conservative "think tank" in New York City. The educational experience that prepared him for these prestigious positions was varied and eclectic: a B.A. in architecture, an M.A. in regional planning, and a Ph.D. in social science and planning, all of which were earned at Syracuse University. This combined background in architecture and social science gave him an "architectural sensitivity" that informs his writing and helps him move "in an orderly way from one space to another" in his essays. "The written word," he advises students using *The Prose Reader,* "should work together with other words like the foundation, frame, mortar, and bricks of a building. Essays should solve intellectual problems in the same way that buildings solve architectural ones." In addition, students should "make certain their essays have a central argument." They should "keep their writing simple and to the point and try to develop their concepts in interesting ways." Among Salins's many publications are *The Ecology of Housing Destruction* (1980), *Housing America's Poor* (1987), *New York Unbound* (1988), *Scarcity by Design* (1992), and *Assimilation, American Style* (1997).

Preparing to Read

The following essay, originally published in the *New Republic* on December 27, 1993, contains a well-researched, carefully reasoned analysis of the current immigration situation in America. Before you read this essay, think about your views on immigration: Are you pleased with the past U.S. immigration policies? What changes would you make in these practices? What other ideas do you have about immigration? Do you think families should be reunited through immigration? What general limitations or restrictions should be put on immigration to the United States? What are your greatest fears about immigration? Your greatest hopes for immigration?

The trouble with the immigration debate of the past year or 1 so is that much of it is simply unreal. Intellectuals have been arguing over abstractions, while the insecurities of ordinary Americans have been inflamed by prejudice and misinformation. Those both for and against immigration behave as if it were politically conceivable that the United States might drastically cut immigration again, as we did in the 1920s, and as if our borders could be effectively sealed if we chose to do so. In spite of resurgent nativism, any proposal to sharply curtail legal immigration would meet massive resistance across the political spectrum—from liberals who see open immigration as a basic ingredient of the universalist American idea to conservatives attached to free markets and open international borders. If it came to a vote in Congress, a bipartisan proimmigration alliance would emerge even stronger than the one behind NAFTA [North American Free Trade Agreement], using the same arguments (the long-term economic benefits of immigration outweighing its short-term stresses, the politics of fear versus the politics of hope, etc.). Buttressing the argument would be our proven inability to stem illegal immigration, because any reduction in the quota of legal immigrants almost certainly would be offset by an increase in illegal immigration—an unsettling prospect for most Americans, but especially for the nativists.

So rather than contesting the volume of immigrants, we might 2 re-examine how we actually allocate immigration in a world where the number of potential immigrants vastly exceeds the most generous quota we could tolerate, and how we treat immigrants once they get here. But first, a few facts to reassure ourselves about the benign nature of immigration. To begin with, America is not being inundated with immigrants. While the volume has risen steadily since the national origins quota system was scrapped in 1965, the rate of immigration relative to the nation's base population is far below historic levels. Due in large part to the amnesty of 1.5 million illegal aliens as part of the Immigration Reform and Control Act of 1986 (Simpson-Rodino), the average rate of legal immigration in the 1981 to 1990 period reached a post-Depression high of 3.1 percent per 1,000 U.S. residents. This rate is below that of every decade from 1830 to 1930, and is about the same as the long-term immigration rate since American independence. Moreover, the percentage of foreign-born in the U.S. population has fallen from 8.8 percent in 1940 to 6.8 percent today.

As important as the volume of immigration is its geography. 3
Most immigrants remain near America's gateways at the perimeter
of the country. The greatest number, nearly 40 percent of the
total since 1987, live in Southern California, with other large
cohorts in New York City, south Florida, Texas, and Chicago.
Most of the rest can be found in a handful of urban areas on the
east and west coasts. Most Americans do not live near immigrants.
This suggests either that the new nativism is confined to the pe-
ripheral immigrant bastions or that some nativists don't need to
meet immigrants to dislike them.

Another critical fact: immigrants have been moving to—and 4
staying in—America's cities, filling a vacuum left by native urban
households that have been fleeing to the suburbs for more than
forty years. Until a new surge of immigration into New York in
the 1980s, the city had been losing population—nearly a million
from 1970 to 1980. Since 1980 New York is the only city east of
the Mississippi to gain population. Wherever they have settled,
immigrants have reclaimed inner-city neighborhoods that had
fallen into a state of advanced decay. True, poor blacks and other
native minorities moved to these zones of white abandonment
first, but at unviably low densities, and with households whose
poverty and pathology only exacerbated their devastation.

In spite of their growing presence in American cities, immi- 5
grants have not displaced the native minority poor in the labor
force. Hypothetically, the low-wage, low-skill work done by the
least skilled immigrants in these ethnic enclaves might otherwise
have employed native blacks or Puerto Ricans. But most of these
jobs didn't exist before the immigrants came, and most native
workers would have spurned them even if they had. As a matter
of fact, recent studies show that the unemployment rates of blacks
living in or near immigrant enclaves actually fell, following the
immigrant influx. Immigrant labor also does not appreciably
lower native workers' wages very much. A study by LaLonde and
Topel estimates that when immigrant participation in a local labor
market doubles, the wages of young blacks in general may fall by
4 percent or less, and those of other minorities are unaffected.

How about the indirect economic impact of immigration, on 6
state and local government budgets, that California's Governor
Pete Wilson is so concerned about? All these immigrant children
require an education, and, at $5,000 per child—thousands more

than their parents' local tax contribution—they have filled up the inner-city schools. Here, too, the burden looks greater in the abstract than in reality. Frankly, these inner-city school systems—in New York, Chicago, Miami, and L.A.—were dying before the immigrants came. With declining populations, the districts still absorbed a large amount of public funds, without much to show for them. Just as with the cities' dying neighborhoods, the immigrants rescued the schools, not only from bankruptcy, but also irrelevance.

What about that most frightening of the nightmare scenarios promoted by the immigration alarmists: that America will become—God help us—a *nonwhite nation*. Of course, the proper response to this hobgoblin should be: So what? But even those who secretly harbor misgivings about a radical change in the country's racial profile can relax, because the vanishing white majority scare is vastly overblown. The two largest immigrant groups are Hispanic and Asian. Now, Hispanic is not a racial category at all; it's a linguistic one. Even the newer label for this group—Latino—is not racial, it's geographic. Whatever the label, the Latino cohort is very racially mixed, from as white as any Northern European to darker than most native blacks. The vast majority, however, including most Mexicans, have a mixed racial background, and—not that it matters—don't look very different from Americans of Southern European descent, and classify themselves as white in surveys. The same is increasingly the case for Asians. 7

The truth is the immigration scare does not reflect a genuine problem; it reflects a genuine panic. The panic is brought on by economic dislocation, which is all too easily laid at the door of immigrants. That is not to say there should not be an immigration debate. On the contrary, it is long overdue. The debate should be not about how many, but rather who, and how, they should be let into the country. Categorical preferences built into the current immigration policy exacerbate both the geographic and ethnic concentration of immigrants, adding to the burden of their assimilation, and pouring fuel on the nativist fires. It's time it was overhauled. 8

The liberalization of immigration legislated in 1965 was supposed to end the Northern European bias of the nativist-inspired national origins quota system of 1925. The reforms certainly succeeded in that respect, redirecting immigration from Northern Europe to Latin America and Asia. But, at the same time, the pref- 9 erence categories of the current law have perpetuated the root bias of a national origins system, only with a new set of favored nationalities. The largest preference categories under present immigration policy promote "family reunification." This means that once a nationality gains a significant demographic foothold in the United States, it has a vested claim on the immigration quota roughly in proportion to its share of the foreign-born population: exactly the concept that animated the old national origins system. Indeed, the family preferences were written into the 1965 law primarily to reassure the nativists that the national origins idea was not being scrapped entirely. Since the new law's inception, around 70 percent of all legal immigrants have been admitted under one or another family reunification preference category. And with the amnesty provision of the Simpson-Rodino law, the preference has been effectively extended to millions of illegal immigrants as well.

The primary beneficiaries of immigration's family reunification   10
tilt have been Mexicans. Since 1981 more than 30 percent of all legal immigrants to the United States have come from Mexico. The fact that Mexicans account for only 18 percent of all legal immigration since 1965 proves that the national origins bias of family reunification increases over time. Family preferences have also ensured that what remains of the pool of legal entrants is dominated by other Latin Americans and Asians from just a few countries: the Philippines, China, Korea, and India. The Simpson-Rodino amnesty of 2.5 million illegals, the vast majority of them Mexicans, has further intensified the nationality biases of family reunification, and has been a major factor in provoking a nativist backlash.

The question we failed to ask in these matters is: Why family?   11
The truth is, the family preference violates the underlying rationale of immigration. The United States has historically welcomed immigrants, to a much greater extent than any other modern society, for a number of reasons. Cynics say it did so because some of its most powerful industries needed cheap labor. Sure, but this need could have been filled by merely admitting "guest workers" as the Europeans do. There has been a deeply idealistic aspect to most Americans' acceptance of immigrants. Americans believe in starting over and giving people with ambition and determination, at home and abroad, the opportunity to do so. Americans also realize, intuitively, that immigrants have the ability to recharge the national batteries, supplying new skills, new perspectives, new

cultural attributes, that can make the country a more successful and cosmopolitan nation. It was because the national origins immigration quotas violated these basic precepts that the old system was scrapped in 1965. Well, the current system is coming to violate them even more, with nationality biases greater than those of the old system, and mostly because of the family bias.

The other favored set of foreigners are those admitted under   12 refugee and asylum preferences, who account for 15 percent of all immigrants during the last decade. Refugee and asylum preferences have a solid justification, given all the repressive regimes in the world, but they have been seriously compromised by our foreign policy biases. When both Nicaragua and El Salvador were in turmoil during the 1980s, Nicaraguans fleeing a Communist dictatorship were accepted as refugees, while Salvadorans fleeing right-wing death squads were not. Likewise, Cubans were admitted as refugees from the time Castro took power, while no dictator is bloody enough for Haitians to be welcomed. And since most Third World autocracies are also poor, every refugee/asylum case involves a judgment call as to whether its motivation is economic or political.

So there are good reasons to change the preference system.   13 How to do it? There are some who would replace the family-based preferences with ones favoring high levels of skill or education, like Canada does. But such a "designer immigration" bias is not only unfair—vesting the privilege of American immigration in precisely those who have been the most privileged in their native lands—it is not even especially helpful to the economy. Our real labor needs—notwithstanding popular perceptions and high unemployment rates among unskilled natives—are at the bottom of the labor market, mainly in services. And the labor market's demand for skilled professionals is amply met by the large number of foreign students who stay and work here after their graduation and by immigrants admitted on other than skill preferences.

Why not, instead of unfair family rules and unnecessary skills   14 rules, adopt a policy that effectively makes admission to the United States a matter of "first-come, first-served." Of the roughly 700,000 legal (nonamnesty) immigration slots we make available in a typical year, perhaps 150,000 could be reserved for the spouses or minor children of U.S. residents—a much reduced preference for the reunification of nuclear families, and perhaps 75,000 could be set aside for refugees. The other 475,000 could be available for applicants from any nation on earth. How might such a system work? Subject to an annual global cap, applications for immigration would be reviewed and approved in the order they were received at designated centers in each country. To avoid having the immigrant pool swamped by applicants from the most populous countries (with 40 percent of the world's population, China and India might dominate such a system) perhaps no country's annual quota should exceed some percentage of the total. However it were fleshed out, the objective of such a first-come, first-served concept would be to offer immigration to the most highly motivated candidates, from a maximally diverse set of backgrounds, selected by the fairest and most objective of procedures.

The United States has not made a mistake by admitting millions of immigrants since the law was changed in 1965. Indeed, America's liberal immigration policy is one of our proudest public accomplishments. But America's liberal immigration policy is more likely to find continued acceptance among most Americans and keep the nativists at bay if the immigration preference system is changed to assure a fairer and more nationally diverse pool of immigrants. So let's not turn our backs on one of the most successful American ideas. Let's get it right.

15

UNDERSTANDING DETAILS

1. What is the focus of this essay? Where does Salins state this focus?
2. What approach does Salins think the United States should take toward immigration?
3. What do the nativists fear about unchecked immigration?
4. What does Salins mean by "the politics of fear" and "the politics of hope" (paragraph 1)? In what ways are they opposed to one another?

ANALYZING MEANING

1. Explain the distinction that Salins makes between the "abstract" and the "real."
2. Why do most Americans believe in and continue to support the concept of immigration? How does immigration reflect their own beginnings in the United States?

3. Do you see the family reunification issue as a problem within the larger issue of immigration? Explain your answer in detail.

4. Why is an increase in illegal immigration "an unsettling prospect for most Americans" (paragraph 1)? Why does Salins add "but especially for the nativists" (paragraph 1)?

DISCOVERING RHETORICAL STRATEGIES

1. Why do you think Salins begins his essay with statistics about the rate of immigration? Is this an effective opening? Explain your answer.

2. Salins explains in paragraph 2 that he is going to present some facts to prove "the benign nature of immigration." How does he group these facts? In what order does he present his categories? Are you convinced by his discussion? Explain your answer.

3. Who do you think is Salins's intended audience? On what do you base this conclusion?

4. Describe the tone of this essay. Is it well chosen for its audience? Explain your answer.

MAKING CONNECTIONS

1. Both Salins and Richard Rodriguez ("The Fear of Losing a Culture") argue for the concept of immigration, though each gives different reasons for his opinion. Compare and contrast why the two authors believe so strongly in the privilege of immigration to America.

2. What kind of balance does Salins achieve in his essay between logical, emotional, and ethical appeals? Contrast this balance with that reached by Mitchell Stephens in "The Death of Reading." Which author relies more on logic? Who uses emotion more? Whose essay has the strongest ethical appeal? What is the relationship between the balance of appeals in each essay and the author's topic?

3. Imagine that Salins, Sandra Cisneros ("Only daughter"), Robert Ramirez ("The Barrio"), and Richard Rodriguez ("The Fear of Losing a Culture") were discussing the greatest benefits immigrants bring to America. Which benefits would each author cite as most valuable to our country? Which do you think are most important? Why?

IDEAS FOR DISCUSSION/WRITING

Preparing to Write

Write freely about your feelings on immigration in general: Is immigration a positive or negative force? When is it positive? When is it negative? What causes immigration to be positive or negative? What are your views on immigration to the United States? Why is it such a controversial topic at this point in American history? What can the United States do to solve its immigration problems? Does a solution seem likely to you?

Choosing a Topic

1. As a movie reviewer, you have been commissioned to evaluate a movie that deals with immigration in some way. What is the movie saying about immigration? In what ways does this message represent the opinions of American society as a whole?
2. In an essay written for *Time* magazine, you have been asked to respond directly to Salins's article. Do you think Salins's approach to immigration is reasonable? Give specific examples to support your argument.
3. Research and describe the immigration practices of another country. Explain how the country's views on immigration are carried out in specific practice. Give as many examples as possible to support your explanation.

Before beginning your essay, you might want to consult the checklists on pages 504–505.

Computers and Books

The next two essays debate the role of writing and books as we know them today. The first essay, by Geoffrey Meredith, claims that "in 100 years, few people will want to read at all, and fewer still will know how to write." Born in Pittsburgh, Pennsylvania, Geoffrey Meredith earned his B.A. at Princeton and his M.B.A. at Stanford, then spent twenty years working for Ogilvy and Mather, an advertising agency in New York and San Francisco. He is currently founder and principal partner of Lifestage Matrix Marketing, a consulting firm in Lafayette, California, that addresses the challenges of rapid technological and demographic change in business markets, particularly with respect to "the graying of America." A specialist in the field of "cohort marketing," which he pioneered, Meredith has divided the United States into seven separate "cohorts" or demographic groups, which are defined by specific events such as the depression or the rise of electronic communication. He is currently co-authoring a book with Charles Schewe entitled *Cohort Analysis and Marketing,* which will detail his work with such corporate giants as Coca-Cola, Levi's, Kellogg's, and Nestlé. An avid tennis, squash, and chess player, he also enjoys fly fishing in his spare time. Asked to give advice to students using *The Prose Reader,* Meredith encouraged them to "edit and re-edit." He admits to being "slightly discouraged" with the writing abilities of today's students, which he blames on a move away from "text-based" education.

Kevin Kelly argues that books and writing will always be part of our culture even if they go through a slight evolution in the future. Kevin Kelly has had a fascinating career as an author, editor, publisher, and photojournalist specializing in such trend-setting topics as virtual reality, ecological restoration, the global teenager, artificial life, and the Internet culture. In the late 1980s, he conceived and oversaw the publication of four versions of the *Whole Earth Catalog,* a compendium of all the best "tools" available for self-education. From 1984 to 1990, Kelly was publisher and editor of *The Whole Earth Review,* a journal of unorthodox technical news. In 1993 he helped launch *Wired* magazine and served as its executive editor until 1999, when he became an editor-at-large. Among his many publications are *Out of Control: The New Biology of Machines, Economic and Social Systems* (1994) and *New Rules for the New Economy* (1998), a U.S. best-seller that has already been translated into German, Spanish, Italian, Greek, Chinese, Japanese, Korean, Dutch, Swedish, and Estonian. Kelly lives in Pacifica, California, a small coastal town just south of San Francisco, where he keeps one honey beehive. His advice to students using *The Prose Reader* is to learn to write well through cyberspace: "When you e-mail a person, you are first concerned about communicating and only secondly concerned about style—the bugaboo that trips up most beginning writers. Send and post; then listen to the responses to what you write."

Preparing to Read

The following essays were first published in *The Futurist* and *Time* respectively. Before you begin to read these essays, think about technology and its effect on American society: How do you think technology will change over the next 10 years? Over the next 50 years? Over the next 100 years? How will these changes affect you? How will they affect American society? How do you think these changes will affect our literacy level? How do you think they will affect our individual thinking? Our reading skills? Our writing skills?

GEOFFREY MEREDITH   (1943–   )

The Demise of Writing

It may seem curious at a time when Amazon.com has a market 1
value approximately that of New Zealand, but books as we
know them are a dying breed. Indeed, there are unmistakable
signs that text will atrophy by the end of the next century; it will
be used mainly for instructional purposes and be accessible only to
the technological elite.

It may seem inconceivable that text will have mostly disap- 2
peared within the lifetime of anyone alive today, but remember,
the rate of change is accelerating. If the World Wide Web can go
from an obscure geekish curiosity to the driving economic force
of the developed world in about five years, what will 50 or 70 or
100 years bring?

We're not seeing profound changes yet; what can be seen 3
today, if you know where to look, are indications around the
edges of our experience. The pattern they form points clearly in
one direction: the end of text.

Moveable type is already gone, replaced by the digital font. Ink 4
on paper will be next, replaced by the electronic tablet. Already,
commercial versions of the digital book are available: thin LCD
panels with text stored in RAM. The Rocket eBook has a 4½"
by 3" screen, weighs about a pound and a half, and can store
4,000 pages of text and graphics. Today's typical novel can be
downloaded in about three minutes from a transportable medium
(like CD-ROM) or downloaded from a computer or the Internet. The "textport" will beome the checkout desk of the virtual
library of 2010.

Currently, the technology is clunky (bulky batteries that last 5
only four to nine hours), inelegant (the text is hard to read unless conditions are perfect), and expensive (about $500 for the
eBook, plus $20 per book). However, all that will change very
soon. By 2005, the bookpad will cost about $20, weigh no more
than six ounces, reproduce text with greater clarity than ink-on-
paper, and be able to store an encyclopedia (or 500 novels) on a
single chip. Of particular appeal to an aging population, the type
size will be variable—you'll make it as large as your eyesight
requires.

But that's the short-term, mechanical aspect. Over the longer 6
term, the printed word will vanish as a medium of expression. By
2070, the only people using text as literature (as opposed to information transmission) will be an elite and mostly very elderly
priesthood, for whom it will be an arcane art form—sort of like
the sonnet or haiku today. The demise of text for literature will
result from several developments.

Increasing Illiteracy

Even in the United States, at a time when technological 7
"progress" makes reading a survival skill, one-fifth of the population
is functionally illiterate. A small percentage of these are older people
with little formal education. A much larger percentage are youths—
high-school and even *college* graduates, who, despite their degrees,
can't fill out a simple employment form. And this is *functional* illiteracy. The percentage who can fill out the employment form but not
understand Tom Wolfe (let alone Shakespeare) is vastly larger.

From our current perspective this seems strange. Yet we are 8
fooled by thinking that our time represents the way things always
were and always will be. When it comes to reading, today's 80%
literacy rate is an anomaly, the result of dramatically higher education levels. Remember, the baby-boomer cohort is not only the
best educated cohort in history—it's likely the best educated that
ever will be.

This is why the most recent version of Microsoft's *Word* pro- 9
gram includes not just spelling checkers but subroutines that suggest and correct syntax, grammar, and even paragraph structure.
And clearly these functions are needed.

Increasing Use of Pictures and Sound

Today, expressive and instructional communications are in- 10
creasingly transmitted either orally or visually. An example is the
so-called "graphic novel," a fusion of comic-book illustration and
serious prose. The cartoon strip that preceded it was an attempt to
circumvent illiteracy during the first half of this century, and it
became firmly established in the United States during the low-
education days of the Depression.

Comic strips became so popular with those who otherwise had 11
great difficulty reading newspapers that a weeks' worth were bundled into one place, and the comic book was born. Its current

transmogrification into the graphic novel (for example, *Maus* by Art Spiegelman or *Tantrum* by Jules Feiffer) further diminishes text.

If the graphic novel works as ink-on-paper, imagine how   12
much better it will work on an eBook. The images, which are cartoonlike stills now, will be digital photo images and moving 3-D holograms by 2010. And machine gun fire won't be written out as "Braaaaaakkk!" on paper, we'll hear it from a sound chip and built-in speakers.

The proliferation of aural and visual expression will continue to   13
be driven by technological advances, specifically voice-recognition capability and the removal of bandwidth limitations on full-motion video.

Voice Recognition

Microprocessors' ability to understand and respond to verbal in-   14
structions and communicate via voice output is poised on the edge of a great leap forward, one that will finally fulfill the promise of the microchip as an indispensable tool and helpmate of the masses. Voice chips are going to change our world sooner than we expect. No longer will we interact with devices via text and keyboard; we'll talk to them, perhaps even giving them names:

"Sven," we'll say to our computer, "make reservations for me   15
to fly to Denver today. I want to arrive about 7 P.M. and stay at the Brown Palace. Charge it to my business Visa."

"VCR, record the World Cup satellite feed from Brazil this af-   16
ternoon and the Pavarotti concert tomorrow night, and remind me about them when I get home from Denver."

"Toaster, a little bit darker on the next piece, please."   17

And even as Microsoft gets into the business of telling us how   18
to write, it's hedging its bet by preparing to bring the Audible, Inc., audiobook technology to Windows CE devices. Dick I. Brass, Microsoft vice president for technology development, says in *Forbes*, "You're going to be able to play a book on every platform Microsoft makes."

Realistic Video

"A picture is worth a thousand words" isn't just a saying. The   19
cerebral cortex can process 1,000 times as much information, 1,000 times faster visually than verbally. The reason is that the

optic nerve has a bandwidth—or data-transmission rate—a trillion times larger than a standard telephone line, so sending moving images over phone lines is insufferably slow.

Why? Because the slowest speed that even approximates full- 20 motion video is 20 frames per second. Movies operate at 24. TV flickers at 30. Traditionally, every pixel—or picture element— must be repainted every frame. So a standard 720 by 480 pixel television screen has to be repainted a minimum of 20 times a second. That's 720 by 480 multiplied 20 times each second, multiplied by 60 for one minute of motion, which is a lot of pixels per minute and a lot of information whether you transmit it in digital or analog form. A coaxial cable can handle this amount of data, but not a phone line. That's why picturephones have never worked: Compression algorithms can cut the transmission flow somewhat, but not enough for anything better than a freeze-frame image every 10 seconds or so.

But the bandwidth barrier is about to be broken. The nature of 21 the technology that will ultimately do it doesn't matter—it could be satellite transmission or fiber or something totally new. Bandwidth limitations are too critical not to be overcome, and, as soon as they are, text will take another giant leap backwards. Why spend a lot of time typing in a memo when you can simply speak it and send it? You'll be able to communicate 1,000 times more information visually and verbally than with text alone.

For the receiver, the information will be much easier to assimi- 22 late and the impact many times greater. Already we see how hard it is to use traditional methods to teach kids who have been raised in the fast-paced, visual world of MTV—lecturing doesn't begin to cut it, let alone a textbook.

And as for the sender, after a decade or two with this vastly en- 23 hanced visual capability, who will bother to learn how to *write* well? We write to communicate linear thinking, which does extraordinarily well in part because it *causes* linear thinking—the way we *express* thought impacts the way we think. And as we increasingly communicate with multilayered, asynchronous images, our thinking will become increasingly nonlinear as well.

Baseball versus football provides a simple but instructive exam- 24 ple. Baseball—linear and sequential, ordered, one-thing-at-a-time—was our national pastime until the advent of television. Television is images, multilayered, where instant replay can even (momentarily) reverse the arrow of time. This is a medium made for football, where many things happen at once—and it's a medium that helps *make* football the new national pastime, as the 30-frame-per-second image begins to transform our past mode of linear, sequential one-batter-at-a-time thinking.

The implications of this are profound. As the image replaces   25
text as the main form of communication, our collective thought processes will move from being linear and single and sequential to simultaneous and multilayered and holistic. Society will become less "left-brained" and analytical and more "right-brained" and intuitive. The more we think nonlinearly the less we will communicate with text, which will cause even more nonlinear thinking, which will lead to less text, and so forth in a continuously self-reinforcing cycle.

When you put all these trends together, you may begin to see   26
how 50 years from now books, newspapers, and magazines will be but quaint relics of the past. In 100 years, few people will want to read at all, and fewer still will know how to write. Text will be outmoded, except for instruction booklets and the aptly named textbooks containing technical information.

In Gen-X speak, "Text is toast." Communication, both factual   27
and expressive, will be through sound and pictures. We will have returned to the troubadour, the cave painter, the oral tradition, come full circle back to the age of Homer.

KEVIN KELLY   (1952–   )

Will We Still Turn Pages?

Washington and Wall Street are bedeviled by a specter—
the specter of dot-com start-ups and the rise of the
nerd class. The fantastic wealth of the new economy
and the renegade attitude of its Netizens are deeply upsetting to
the old order. The result is a cultural battle illustrated most dramatically by the Microsoft case. Surprisingly, the outcome of this
conflict has a lot to say about whether we will still turn pages as
we read.

On one side of this clash we have People of the Book. These
are the good people who make newspapers, magazines, the doc-
trines of law, the offices of regulation, and the rules of finance.
They live by the book, by the authority derived from authors,
and are centered at the power points of New York City and
Washington. The foundation of this culture is ultimately housed
in texts. They are all on the same page, so to speak.

On the other side (and on an axis that runs through Hollywood and Redmond, Wash.) we have the People of the Screen.
The People of the Screen tend to ignore the classic logic of
books; they prefer the dynamic flux of the screen: Movie screens,
TV screens, computer screens, Game Boy screens, telephone
screens, pager screens, and Day-Glo megapixel screens we can
only imagine today, plastered on every surface.

Screen culture is a world of constant flux, of endless sound
bites, quick cuts and half-baked ideas. It is a flow of gossip tidbits,
news headlines, and floating first impressions. Notions don't stand
alone but are massively interlinked to everything else; truth is not
delivered by authors and authorities but is assembled by the audience. Screen culture is fast, like a 30-sec. movie trailer, and as liquid and open-ended as a website.

In this world, code—as in computer code—is more important
than law, which is fixed in texts. Code displayed on a screen is
endlessly tweakable by users, while law is not. Yet code can shape
behavior as much as, if not more than, law.

On a screen, words move, meld into pictures, change color
and perhaps even meaning. Sometimes there are no words at all,

only pictures or diagrams or glyphs that may be deciphered into multiple meanings. This is terribly unnerving to any civilization based on text logic.

The People of the Book fear that the page (and reading and 7 writing) will die. Who will adhere to the linear rationality found in books, new and old? Who will obey rules if books of laws are diminished or replaced by lines of code? Who will turn nicely bound pages when everything is available (almost free) on flickering screens? Perhaps only the rich will read books on paper. Perhaps only a few will pay attention to the wisdom on their pages.

They need not fear. The People of the Screen (working at 8 places like E Ink and Xerox) are creating thin films of paper and plastic that hold digital ink. A piece of paper then becomes a paper screen: one minute it has a poem on it, the next it has the weather. Bind a hundred of these digital pages between covers, and you have a book that can change its content yet still be read like a book. You turn the pages (a way to navigate through text that is hard to improve), and when you are finished, you slap it into a holster to fill it with another text. The ordinary reader might have a collection of several dozen leatherbound and different-size book containers, ones that mold themselves to the reader's hands and habits over many readings. "This story is formatted to be viewed on an oversize L book," it says on the first screen, and so you pick your favorite oversize Moroccan book shell and sit to read in luxurious ease.

Or digital ink can be printed together with the circuits for 9 wireless transmission onto a generously sized tabloid sheet tough as Tyvek. The tabloid sits on the table all day, as news articles come and go. All the typographic conventions of a newspaper or magazine are obeyed, but the paper doesn't come and go. It stays.

The page will not die. It is too handy and highly evolved. The 10 same flat sheet of enhanced paper is so nimble, in fact, that there is no reason why a movie could not be played on it as well. Drama, music videos, great epics in full color all dance across this new page. The eternal sheaf becomes both book and TV screen. Indeed the resolution will be fine enough to read words floating in, around, and through cinematic images. We see the beginnings of that already on some websites where image and text intermingle. Is this a movie or an essay? We don't know.

In the end we will have TV that we read and books that we   11
watch. The People of the Book will keep turning their pages, and
the People of the Screen will keep clicking their screens. All on
the same piece of paper. Long live the page!

UNDERSTANDING DETAILS

1. What are Meredith ("The Demise of Writing") and Kelly
   ("Will We Still Turn Pages?") each saying about the written
   word in these two essays?
2. What arguments can you think of to add to both of their essays?
3. Why is Meredith convinced that books, as we know them
   today, will disappear? According to Meredith, what will replace these books?
4. According to Kelly, what are the main characteristics of the
   People of the Book and the People of the Screen? Do they
   share any common traits?

ANALYZING MEANING

1. Which stand on this particular argument is most convincing to
   you? Which examples or statistics persuade you most effectively? Explain your reaction to these two positions.
2. According to Meredith, how will our thought processes change
   over the next 50 years? What will cause these changes in our
   thinking? How will these changes affect our use of language?
3. What characterizes the "new page" that Kelly describes? How
   can it become "both book and TV screen" (paragraph 10)?
4. How might the opinions in these two essays be reconciled?
   Can you make a compromise prediction that combines both
   views of the computer world?

DISCOVERING RHETORICAL STRATEGIES

1. Who do you think is the intended audience for each of these
   essays? Are there any important differences between these audiences in your opinion?
2. These two authors make their points with completely different
   writing voices. Describe the tone or mood of each essay, and
   explain whether you think that particular voice is most effective for the author's purpose.

3. How does the organization of the two essays differ? What is the general organizing principle in each case?
4. What other rhetorical strategies does each essay use to make its point? Give examples of each strategy.

MAKING CONNECTIONS

1. If Russell Baker ("The Saturday Evening Post"), Mitchell Stephens ("The Death of Reading"), and Rita Mae Brown ("Writing as a Moral Act") read the essays by Meredith and Kelly, which side of the argument would each of these authors take and why?
2. Compare and contrast the joy that Donald Hall finds in reading with Geoffrey Meredith's assertion that books are "a dying breed." According to Hall, what will we lose in our society when "text is toast"?
3. Compare the ritual of turning the pages of a book with other repetitive symbolic actions in Ray Bradbury's "Summer Rituals," Germaine Greer's " A Child Is Born," and Richard Rodriguez's "The Fear of Losing a Culture."

IDEAS FOR DISCUSSION/WRITING

Preparing to Write

Write freely about your views on technology: Where do you think we are headed technologically? How do you think growth in technology will affect the reading and writing skills of students? Do you prefer working with words on a computer screen or on paper? What changes in technology would help your reading skills? Your writing? Are these realistic changes? How is technology related to our speaking? To our thinking?

Choosing a Topic

1. In his essay, Geoffrey Meredith states, "In 100 years, few people will want to read at all, and fewer still will know how to write" (paragraph 26). Do you agree with this statement? Present your own argument on this topic, supporting your opinion with clear examples and facts.
2. Having access to pornography through computers has been an issue on college campuses since we have been able to browse

the Internet. What role should colleges play in controlling students' access to pornography? Is this a form of censorship? What about our constitutional right to freedom of speech? In an essay written for your college administration, argue for or against putting limits on pornography accessed from college computers.

3. Your local library is sponsoring a writing contest with a first-place prize of $1000. All contestants must write a 500-word essay on the following topic: "How does the process of reading printed books help make us better human beings?" Write an essay on this topic that will win the first-place award.

Before beginning your essay, you might want to consult the checklists on pages 504–505.

Freedom of the Press

The following two essays debate the limits of freedom of the press in America. The first, by former New York governor Mario Cuomo, argues that this freedom must be unlimited because the press plays an important role in watching our government and keeping our citizens well informed so that they can function effectively in our democratic society. Before he became governor of New York (1983–1994), Cuomo went to St. John's University, where he earned his B.A. in Latin American studies and his law degree. Later, he worked as an attorney in a law firm and as a professor at St. John's Law School and then became secretary of state and later lieutenant governor of the State of New York. He is currently in private legal practice in New York City. His publications include *Diaries of Mario M. Cuomo: The Campaign for Governor* (1984), *Lincoln on Democracy* (1990), and *The Forest Hills Controversy* (1992).

John Merrill, who argues that freedom of the press needs some limits to protect us from the excesses of unethical journalists, has a B.A. in history and English from Delta State University, an M.A. in journalism from Louisiana State University, an M.A. in philosophy from the University of Missouri, and a Ph.D. in mass communications from the University of Iowa. Currently a professor emeritus of journalism at the University of Missouri, he has published twenty-two books, among them *The Imperative of Freedom* (1974), *Existential Journalism* (1977), and *The Legacy of Wisdom* (1995). His advice to students using *The Prose Reader* is that "writing is a lonely activity, but it can be very rewarding when you see the results of your hard work." He admits that he often has to reread one of his many books to find out what he thinks about a particular topic.

Preparing to Read

Cuomo's essay originally appeared as "Preserving Freedom of the Press" in *USA Today Magazine* (January 1988), while Merrill's article was first published under the title "Needed: An Ethical Press" in *The World and I* (February 1988). Before you begin to read these essays, think for a minute about your opinion of the media: Do you believe the press does an accurate job of reporting information to the public? How could it do a better job? What are its main flaws? Do you think the press should have total freedom? Do you think it should be limited in any way? In what ways? Do you think the press is always as ethical as it should be? How do you interpret the reference to "freedom...of the press" in the First Amendment of the Constitution?

MARIO CUOMO   (1932–   )

Freedom of the Press Must Be Unlimited

The more I learn about government and especially about 1
democracy, the more deeply convinced I become that one
of our greatest strengths as a people is our right to full and
free expression. No people have benefited more from the gift of
free speech and a free press. Never before in history has the gift
been so generously given or so fully used. From the very launching of our nation, these freedoms were regarded as essential pro-
tections against official repression.

When the geniuses who designed this wonderful ship of state 2
came to draw the blueprints, they remembered Britain and other
lands which had discouraged criticism of government and public
officials, declaring it defamatory and seditious. The Founding Fathers considered that to be one of the worst parts of British
tyranny. They were convinced that much of the struggle for
American freedom would be the struggle over a free press. So,
they were careful to provide that the right of free expression,
through a free press, would be preserved in their new nation, especially insofar as the press dealt with government and public officials. They declared that right of free expression in the First
Amendment to the Constitution and wrote it in the simplest, least
ambiguous language they could fashion: "Congress shall make no
law respecting an establishment of religion, or prohibiting the free
exercise thereof, or abridging the freedom of speech or of the
press. . . ."

Having provided for the right of free speech for the whole citi- 3
zenry, they went further and provided separately for "freedom
of . . . the press"; as broadly as possible, not tentatively, not em-
broidered with nuances, not shrouded and bound up in conditions, but plainly and purely.

Gambling on Liberty

The Founding Fathers knew precisely what they were dealing 4
with. The press of their time was not only guilty of bad taste and
inaccuracy, it was partisan, reckless, sometimes vicious, and, in-

deed, the Founding Fathers were themselves often at the point end of the press sword.

In view of that experience, they might have written amendments that never mentioned freedom of the press, or they might have tried to protect against an imperfect press like the one they dealt with—with conditions, qualifications, requirements, and penalties—but they did not. They knew the dangers. They knew that broad freedoms inevitably would be accompanied by some abuse and even harm to innocent people. Knowing all the odds, they chose to gamble on liberty.

The gamble has made us all rich. Over all, the press has been a force for good—educating our people, guarding our freedom, watching our government—challenging it, goading it, revealing it, forcing it into the open. Teapot Dome, the Pentagon Papers, Watergate, the revelations of corruption in New York City—these are all examples of disclosures that might never have occurred were it not for our free press. The press' insistence on forcing the White House to begin to tell the truth about the Iranian arms transaction is a dramatic reminder of how the press works incessantly to assure our liberty by guaranteeing our awareness. Less dramatically, the work of revelation by the press goes on day after day at all levels of government, all over the nation.

Surely, the preservation of this extraordinary strength is worth our eternal vigilance. That is why I believe it is appropriate to consider the matter of freedom of the press now, at this moment. It appears to me—and to others as well—that we are approaching a time when shifts in our law seriously may dilute the protection of the press and thereby weaken the fabric of this society.

Our Constitution is not self-executing; it must be interpreted and applied by the Supreme Court. In effect, no matter how plain the language of the great document may appear to the rest of us, the Constitution will say what the Supreme Court says it says. The dimensions of the right to a free press are therefore in the care and at the mercy of the Supreme Court.

In recent decades, the Court has dealt often with the First Amendment and most of the time has expanded its reach, culminating in the landmark protection of the press in the case of *New York Times v. Sullivan* in 1964. *Sullivan* said that, notwithstanding the fact that the press was inaccurate, even negligent, and the inaccuracy substantially damaged a public figure, there would be no liability on the part of the press. Only if the press were guilty of actual malice—that is, a deliberate falsification or conduct that evinced a reckless disregard—could there be a recovery.

This protection obviously was designed to free the press from 10 the chilling—maybe paralyzing—effect of huge damage awards as a consequence of inaccuracy in trying to report the truth. Some believed this was too much protection; they called it a license to defame, an invitation to dangerous, harmful carelessness. However, some—I among them—thought it was good and necessary policy, good and necessary law; that gamble the Founders took was still a good one.

Changing Interpretations

Supreme Court law, however, is not static or permanent; it 11 changes. In 1985, Justice Byron R. White, who joined the majority in *Sullivan*, announced that he had become convinced the Court had struck "an improvident balance" in 1964. He urged that a better approach would be to return to much less protective common-law standards of liability. In a 1986 case, Justice William H. Rehnquist indicated that he too would like to revisit *Sullivan* with an eye to the possibility of overruling it. . . .

Conservatives generally seem to sense this is a good time to 12 strike. Some recently have proposed making simple "negligence" the standard for responsibility for injurious inaccuracy. What would it do to a small newspaper, magazine, or station to be subjected to a multi-million-dollar verdict, because a jury discovered its reporter did not make what the jury considered to be a reasonable search, perhaps in the library, perhaps through clips, perhaps seeking out witnesses; perhaps checking their stories, checking out their references, going to experts?

There is considerable other evidence to suggest that the courts 13 are moving gradually, but consistently, away from *Sullivan* and toward less protection for the press. Floyd Abrams, a noted attorney and expert on the First Amendment, says the *Sullivan* principles are now under "sustained attack."

One more point about the Supreme Court: putting aside its 14 somewhat esoteric legal jurisdiction, the truth is that the Court is a living institution. Its nine members are subject to the same public events that affect and instruct you and me. Their decisions to some extent reflect changing circumstances in the world around them or changing ideas about what is reasonable or wise.

This means that, when trying to predict a change in First   15 Amendment rulings, the quality of the press as perceived by the public is a relevant factor. In the *Federalist Papers*, Alexander Hamilton asked: "What is the liberty of the press? . . . Its security, whatever fine declarations may be inserted in any constitution respecting it, must altogether depend on public opinion and on the general spirit of the people and the government."

This is still true today. A press regarded by the public as reck-   16 less invites the attention of the Supreme Court and tempts it to perform corrective judicial surgery. That is what Mr. Dooley meant when he said, "Th' Supreme Coort follows th' iliction returns."

This raises a number of questions: What is the public percep-   17 tion of the press today? Is it regarded as less than perfect? If so, how specifically?

Official Criticism

It might be worth noting here that, in earlier times, many of   18 our leading public officials were among the press' harshest critics. Today, the press is apt to refer to a public official who criticizes the media as "Nixonian." If, however, presidential labels are appropriate, the media might just as fairly call its critics "Washingtonian," "Jeffersonian," "Lincolnian," "Taftian," "Wilsonian," "Rooseveltian," "Kennedyesque," or "Johnsonian."

For example, George Washington called the press "infamous   19 scribblers." Thomas Jefferson wrote: "Even the least informed of the people have learnt that nothing in a newspaper is to be believed."

Theodore Roosevelt added action to his vitriol. He had Joseph   20 Pulitzer and his *New York World* indicted for criminal libel after the newspaper charged corruption in connection with the digging of the Panama Canal.

William Howard Taft found one paper so bad as to be "intolera-   21 ble." He told his assistant not to show him *The New York Times*. "I don't think reading the *Times* will do me any good and would only be provocative in me of . . . anger and contemptuous feeling."

Woodrow Wilson lost his conciliatory disposition in dealing   22 with the press. He said, "The real trouble is that the newspapers get the real facts but do not find them to their taste and do not use them as given them, and in some of the newspaper offices, news is deliberately invented."

The Best Evidence

The truth is that criticism of the press by its natural targets—   23 public officials, governors, presidents—however illustrious, is not necessarily good evidence of the press' imperfection. Indeed, it can be argued that it is the best evidence of the press' effectiveness.

The press' job is to find the whole truth, especially that part of   24 it which is forgotten, ignored, deliberately concealed, or distorted by public officials. The better the press does its job, the more likely future generations will be reading colorful condemnations of reporters and commentators by today's politicians, and the more likely that the historical record will be truthful and accurate.

I think I understand this as a public official myself. Although I   25 believe I have been treated very well by the press overall, from time to time I have had occasion to make my own criticisms of some members of the press and their coverage in particular cases. The response has revealed that politicians are not the only ones who are sensitive.

Of much more concern to the press than criticism from me   26 and other public officials should be the criticism that comes from candid, thoughtful members of the press itself. Recently, it has been harsh indeed. What is worse is that the public at large appears to agree.

Harper's Magazine observed in 1985 that, when the *Westmoreland*   27 case hit the headlines, a "flood" of commentary from the press ensued. Editorial writers noted that the press was "widely maligned, criticized, abused, and worst of all, 'distrusted.'" They pointed to numerous polls and "the public's conspicuous failure to be outraged when reporters were barred from Grenada." *Harper's* continued, "Though Americans ritually intone their devotion to the 'freedom of the press,' they delight in repeating another prized national dictum: 'Don't believe what you read in the papers.'"

The press itself attributes much of this public disfavor to its   28 own curable defects. Thus, "pack journalism" is a frequently heard complaint, citing the press' dependence on one another, forging a uniform point of view so as to avoid embarrassing differences, written as though every statement previously made by any reporter is indisputable, and the clannish locking of arms against critics from the outside. As Hodding Carter said in 1985, "We are very, very good at pitching and very, very bad at catching. . . . The press appears to be paranoid when facing criticism itself."

Tom Wicker adds a larger and more substantive complaint. He 29 feels the media generally is too prone to promote what it believes is easiest for people to accept and in the process fails to cover significant issues adequately.

The criticism that is set out here easily could be offset with 30 generous accolades from sources equally credible. That is not the point. No one is more eager than I to proclaim how successfully the press has done its job over the last couple of hundred years, or how much better government might do its job. Still, we must recognize the fact that this nation currently is debating—in the place where we make the rules, the Court—whether or not to limit the freedom of the press despite its good record of 200 years.

The possibility of limitation is a real one. I believe it requires 31 that we admit the media's confessions of imperfection and what appears to be a disconcertingly serious loss of public favor that could encourage restrictions of First Amendment rights.

The first thing we must do is sound the alert and make it clear 32 that we are facing a real threat of restriction of the constitutional freedom of the press. That is not easy. The drift of the Supreme Court does not get reported in the morning headlines. It is an elusive subject to which we must direct attention. Then, we must hope—and we cannot be sure it will work—that the reaction will affect, for the better, both the press and the courts. . . .

Freedom and Responsibility

Let me offer you what I believe is an opportunity for all the 33 media to make a contribution to the forming of public policy in this nation: Cover the public issues more thoroughly. Cover campaigns even more extensively. Cover state and local government more deeply, not just press events created by candidates or public officials. . . .

The press is about finding the truth and telling it to the people. 34 In pursuit of that, I am making a case for the broadest possible freedom of the press. However, with that great gift comes great responsibility. The press—print and electronic—has the power to inform, but that implies the power to distort. The press can lead our society toward a more mature and discriminating understanding of the process by which we choose our leaders, make our rules, and construct our values, or it can encourage people to despise our systems and avoid participating in them. The press can teach our children a taste for violence, encourage a fascination with perversity and inflicted pain, or it can show them a beauty they have not known. The press can make us wiser, fuller, surer, and sweeter than we are.

One of the miracles of this democracy is that all of us—both   35
the press and the public—are free to make the choices. We must work to keep it that way, to keep the miracle alive.

JOHN MERRILL   (1924–   )

Freedom of the Press Must Be Limited

Journalists in the United States who enjoy bashing everything   1
and everybody in sight are beginning to get growing amounts
of their own medicine. The spotlight of criticism is being
focused on them and the media they serve.

As the media grow in power and as they cling to their self-   2
designation as a "watchdog on government" and other self-
enhancing labels, they increasingly indulge in what many people
consider irresponsible or unethical practices. In their mad rush to
meet deadlines and what they see as their prime responsibility "to
let the people know," American journalists have been pushing
ethics out of the picture and enthroning expediency and self-
interest. Many critics would contend that "ethical journalism" in
today's world is really oxymoronic.

Whether ethics and journalism are contradictory terms or not,   3
it must be said that a considerable degree of unethical activity exists in the press. And often this activity is poorly reported, if at all,
because of the press's natural self-interest and its capacity for controlling the news and having the last word.

Certainly the American media must be commended for their   4
alertness to governmental and social immorality and questionable
activities. Such media attention does, no doubt, help to keep society "honest" and "careful"—at least to a certain degree. But the
media also need to look to their own houses; they themselves must
have a greater resolve to be ethical—if for no other reason than to
improve their negative image among a skeptical public. . . .

The Press as "Watchdog"

The "adversarial relationship" between press and government   5
is an important consideration for the press. It may well be a myth,
as some say, but it is a very important one to journalists. It is a responsibility, in the press's own journalistic dogma, that forces the
news establishment of the country to act as a watchdog on government. Many of the ethical problems of the press spring from
the assumption that the press must be a check on government, be

a critic of government, keep the government honest, and so on. This prompts the press to dig and probe, snipe and snoop; it causes the press to speculate and to deal in innuendo in its attempt to unearth corruption in high places and to explain the misdeeds of others.

This concept is responsible for the press's accentuating the neg-   6 ative in government matters, seldom revealing positive activities or trends. Of course, the press could stress the positive, defend government positions, and have a partnership relationship with the government; it has no constitutional mandate to do otherwise. Only its own self-assigned duty has generated this adversarial relationship to government.

Many of the press's modern critics see such a self-assigned duty   7 as another instance of press arrogance that often pushes the journalists into unethical areas where damage is done to the whole social fabric and where many good potential public servants are dissuaded from participation in the governmental arena due to the persistent and prying minions of the press.

This "watchdog" attitude of the press fosters—or creates—   8 the idea that government is necessarily and inherently evil and must be checked. And, in this game, the press has set itself up as the institution that must keep the government honest. Today, as an increasing number of voices are asking who checks the checker, the press falls back on its constitutional freedom guarantee, and when all the rhetoric is done, the answer from the press is essentially this: *Nobody checks the checker.* The press is free and autonomous.

Such a perspective is filled with danger, especially when signifi-   9 cant numbers of journalists are unconcerned with ethics. And there is no real evidence to show that journalists are any less evil and need less careful scrutiny than government employees. But, say the journalists, the press is "free," and this is paramount in the United States.

Confusion over Freedom

One reason the press is confused about ethics is that it is con-   10 fused about its freedom, which it sees as endangered if it puts too much emphasis on its "responsibilities." Talk of responsibility leads to obligations and duties, say the press people, and therefore tends to restrict press freedom. So the journalists always get back to stressing *press freedom* and deemphasizing *press responsibility*. The result is that this deep antipathy to the concept of "social responsibility" keeps journalists from giving much continuing and serious thought to ethics.

What journalists should do is recognize that the concept of   11 "press freedom" can just as easily include the freedom to be positive as negative, and that it can include the freedom of the press to be an ally or apologist for government as well as an adversary. In fact, when the press convinces itself that it is an adversary or watchdog vis-à-vis government, it thereby restricts its own freedom by accepting a very limited role. This "adversary dogma," interestingly, is not even consistent with libertarian theory, and it would seem that journalists who talk about "press freedom" would cease being tied to this "adversary role."

A Know-It-All Press

Press people say that their negative approach to news is natural   12 and that the people want such news. Anyway, how can the people put their house in order if they do not know that it is out of order? The fact is that journalists, by and large, see themselves as a kind of permanent, relentless opposition to government. They must watch government carefully; they must protect the people from government crimes and excesses. But does every grin and every act of every politician contribute anything important to the public understanding? What about news balance? It means little if the journalist is mainly concerned about pouring out every scrap of information. Where is the balanced overview that tries to correct distortions resulting from all these bits and pieces of disjointed "news"? It is not to be found, for the press is dedicated to its specious formula of accentuating the negative and watchdogging ("hounding"?) the government. . . .

Never, however, does it seem that the press asks itself this basic   13 question: Where does the press get this directive? The answer, of course, is that it has no such mandate, except that which it constantly whispers in its own ears. Maybe the press should remember that, after all, the people at least elect government officials (or some of them); the people never elect an editor, an anchorperson, a news director, a publisher, or a reporter.

The People's "Right to Know"

The other journalistic shibboleth that impinges on press ethics   14
and seems so dear to the heart of media people is "the people's
right to know." In any discussion about press ethics or press responsibility, this sacred tenet is dragged out to support almost any
journalistic tactic. After all, the story goes, the people have a right
to know this or that and we, the journalists, must see to it that
they do. This "right to know" concept is fraught with semantic
and logical implications, and is one that causes many anxious moments for journalists (and government officials, too) who think seriously about ethics.

Do Journalists Represent the Public?

Many media people, obviously not comfortable with the right   15
granted them in the First Amendment, feel they must justify their
activities vis-à-vis government by appealing to a people's right to
know. This justification goes something like this: We're not really
getting this information for ourselves; we're getting it for the
people who have a right to know it. Therefore, you people in
government are obligated to give it to us because we are representatives of the people. (Isn't this rather strange? Many of us
thought that government officials were the representatives of the
people, and the journalists were private-sector, profit-making employees of capitalistic enterprises and not representatives of anybody except publishers and other media owners and managers.)

Perhaps more fundamental is this question: Where do the peo-   16
ple get this "right to know"? Much has been written on this subject, but little has been resolved. Perhaps one can infer such a
"right" from the free-press clause of the Bill of Rights. It would
certainly have to be inferred, for nowhere is such a right specified.
Some persons, admitting the lack of a constitutional right to
know, insist that it is a "natural" right. At any rate, if there is such
a right to know, then the press needs to rethink its own position,
for it is abridging this "right" every single day. And it is abridging
it in the name of editorial self-determination or "press freedom."

Journalists constantly decide what they will and will not publish;   17
they arbitrarily determine what the public will or will not know.
They call this reporting and editing, of course. Certainly they do
not call it news management—they reserve that term for govern-

mental activities. But it really is news management; in fact, news management is what journalism is all about. Journalists know this, of course, but talk about and advocate a "people's right to know."

Such concepts as the "watchdog function" of the press (adversar- 18 ial role) and the "people's right to know," well entrenched in the traditional dogma of American journalism, evidence a considerable confusion in the minds of journalists about the nature of press freedom. And this leads to difficulty in developing any kind of consistent journalistic ethics. Little wonder there is so much ethical confusion—in fact, a kind of ethical vacuum—in American journalism. The basic philosophical foundation stones are not very solid, and the mortar holding them together is rapidly turning to powder.

The press looks at ethics from a vested-interest and relativistic 19 perspective, shying away from any absolutes and relegating ethics to particular times, circumstances, and problems. Journalists, by and large, conceive of ethics as prudential actions in certain circumstances that will achieve some preconceived plan of theirs— such as getting information from a source. What they often do is to engage in trying to attain their ends and then justifying or rationalizing the means they use. The philosopher Immanuel Kant would not have considered this ethics at all. Journalism conferences show that, almost without exception, participants shy away from absolutes and the Kantian emphasis on "duty to principle," preferring instead to embrace relativistic and personal morality where any option they choose can be justified as the ethical one.

There seems to be no will today for the press to break through 20 self-serving platitudes and gain any real insight into the ethical issues that beg to be dealt with. No common standards exist for normative press ethics. Absolutes are shunned, and everything beyond a strictly personal or individualized ethics is seen as endangering diversity and, by extension, journalistic freedom.

A Competitive Profession

Ethical decisions confront the journalist at every turn. Most 21 often the journalist looks on his decision making as "professional" or institutional and deals with it as such—rather than approaching it from a truly ethical perspective. "It's newsworthy; so we'll print it." This is an example of considering journalism from a pragmatic or professional perspective instead of going to the ethical level. "If we don't print it, some other medium will," journalists often say.

"It's the policy of our newspaper to do it, so we do it," the standard excuse goes. Competition, not ethics, too often determines editorial decisions.

This journalistic reflex action is understandable for several reasons. Beyond the fact that American journalists are highly institutionalized, routinized creatures of habit, they are part of a highly competitive, capitalistic enterprise; as such they are largely concerned with doing what "works" best. Secondly, they are suspicious of "social ethics" or any group-imposed rules or system of restraints that might cause them to lose their sense of identity and freedom. And lastly, and probably most important of all, journalists know very little and appear uninterested in learning about philosophical ethics. In other words, they appear not to have what Kant would call the "will to be ethical." Journalistic pragmatism has taken precedence over journalistic ethics. Too often journalists, engulfed as they are in the daily routine of habit, tradition and pragmatism, leave the business of morality—personal and social— to theologians and academics.

The press, for its part, is so protective of its traditional idea of individualism and pluralism that it resists anything that might result in standardization or conformity—even codes of ethics and news councils are often suspect. Such a situation is probably still basically in place, but evidence exists that things are changing, that journalists are becoming more serious about ethics and are merging their concern for pragmatism with a recognition that such a concern is not contradictory to ethics. Perhaps this long-time dedication to pragmatism is the very machine that will move the press toward a higher morality. Now they may be seeing that "ethics is the best policy" for long-term success. . . .

Across the country people are beginning to talk about the use of anonymous sources, inaccurate quotes, unbalanced stories, biased and false statements in news stories, shocking and even gruesome photographs, gossip masquerading as news, political bias in the news, and a large number of other questionable practices. Press people themselves are becoming more conscious of ethical problems: Do we print the name of the rape victim? What about the name of the accused rapist? Do we really believe in full-disclosure reporting—in the people's right to know? Or do we place ethics above such full-disclosure reporting? What really are our responsibilities, and to whom are they owed? Do the ends

22

23

24

(such as getting the story) really justify the means? Any means, which means? Such questions, and many others, are presently being taken seriously by journalists.

Doing the Right Thing

It may be that the time has not yet come for a journalistic revolution in ethics. The day of the Kantian "will to be ethical" may still be over the horizon, but there are indications that ethical consciousness is rising in the press and considerable soul-searching about the right thing to do is now mingling with concern about such traditional shibboleths as the people's right to know and the press as a watchdog on government.   25

Many journalists are recognizing at long last that their calling is a public trust as well as a business and that the press is a powerful ethical force in society, relegating to them an important responsibility. The thought has finally struck home that maybe, just maybe, the people have just as much a right not to know as to know certain things, and that the press can point out positive and helpful facts about government as well as negative and harmful ones.   26

UNDERSTANDING DETAILS

1. What are the main arguments of Cuomo ("Freedom of the Press Must Be Unlimited") and Merrill ("Freedom of the Press Must Be Limited")? Explain the principal disagreement between these two points of view.
2. What arguments can you think of to add to both sides of this essay?
3. What are the main reasons Cuomo insists that the press needs its freedom?
4. What are the main problems that Merrill identifies concerning freedom of the press?

ANALYZING MEANING

1. Which side of this particular argument is most convincing to you? Which examples or statistics persuade you most effectively?
2. Do you agree with Cuomo or Merrill about the freedom of the press? Explain your answer.

3. Do you agree with Cuomo that freedom and responsibility are intricately related? Explain your answer.
4. How might the views in these two essays be reconciled? Can you recommend a compromise between the two?

DISCOVERING RHETORICAL STRATEGIES

1. Who do you think is the intended audience for each of these essays? Are there any important differences between these audiences in your opinion?
2. Describe the tone or mood of each essay and explain whether you think that particular voice was the most effective for the author's purpose.
3. How does the organization of the two essays differ? What is the general organizing principle in each case?
4. What other rhetorical strategies does each essay use to make its point? Give examples of each strategy.

MAKING CONNECTIONS

1. Imagine that Mario Cuomo, John Merrill, Russell Baker ("The Saturday Evening Post"), Judith Viorst ("The Truth About Lying"), Nancy Gibbs ("When Is It Rape?"), and Rita Mae Brown ("Writing as a Moral Act") were having a round-table discussion about the topic of freedom of the press. Which authors would be most strongly in favor of total freedom? Who would probably agree with Merrill that some limits should be placed on journalistic freedom? Which side would you agree with? Explain your answer.
2. Examine the balance between logical, emotional, and ethical appeals in both the Cuomo and Merrill essays. Which author relies most heavily on logic? Which on emotion? Whose ethical appeal is strongest? Which essay is most convincing to you? Why? Does your tendency to agree with this essay have anything to do with its balance among the three appeals? Explain your answer.
3. Cuomo and Merrill discuss law as a remedy to social problems in the same way that the following other authors do: Shelby Steele ("Affirmative Action: The Price of Preference"), Peter

Salins ("Take a Ticket"), and Jill Rosenbaum and Meda Chesney-Lind ("Appearance and Delinquency: A Research Note"). In which of these essays is the law portrayed as a device for solving problems? In which has the law itself become a problem? Pick one of these essays, and explain your own feelings on whether the law has been a help or a hindrance concerning the issue discussed.

IDEAS FOR DISCUSSION/WRITING

Preparing to Write

Write freely about your opinion of the media: What do you think of the media in general? In your opinion, is any one form of media more accurate, reliable, or interesting than another? On what do you base this judgment? What do you think are the main motives of the press in reporting information to the public? What guidelines do you think it follows in reporting the news? What form of media do you rely on most for the news? Why do you rely on this form? What does ethics have to do with freedom of the press?

Choosing a Topic

1. Your school newspaper has been charged with unethical reporting, and the school administration is considering whether to limit its freedom. The president of the college is soliciting opinions, and you decide to send your suggestions in essay form to the president. Justify your opinions as thoroughly as possible.
2. The media are a vital part of our lives today. In what ways do they affect the morals and values of our society? Of us individually? How much freedom should the media be allowed to have? In an essay written for your peers, write a set of guidelines for keeping the media ethical. Explain the details of these guidelines.
3. Choose an important national or international event from the recent past, and analyze the media's coverage of that event. Consider newspapers, TV newscasts, *Time, Newsweek,* and so on as sources of information. How did the coverage of these media vary? Now that the event has passed, are you aware that any of these sources were more accurate than others? More

interesting? More ethical? Present a summary of your findings and your conclusions in an essay addressed to your classmates.

Before beginning your essay, you might want to consult the checklists on pages 504–505.

CHAPTER WRITING ASSIGNMENTS
Practicing Argument/Persuasion

1. What is the best method for disciplining a child? What kinds of "discipline" constitute child abuse? What rights should parents have in deciding how to discipline their children? Write an essay explaining what disciplinary actions you believe are acceptable and arguing why others are unacceptable.

2. Do you think limits should be put on free speech? If so, what should these limits be? If not, why not? What is the reasoning behind your opinion? Write an essay, supporting your position with examples.

3. Many people argue that terminally ill patients should be able to use extreme measures to find comfort and peace in the final stages of their lives. What rights do you think terminally ill patients should have? Should they be able to use drugs that have not been approved by the Food and Drug Administration? Should they be allowed to use illegal drugs, such as marijuana, to relieve their suffering? Should patients be able to receive assistance in speeding up the process of their own death? Or should terminally ill patients have exactly the same rights as other patients? Write an essay in which you argue for the rights you think terminally ill patients should receive. Support your position with concrete details.

Exploring Ideas

1. Do you think people are prone to violence because of inborn qualities or because of learned behavior? Why are some people violent while others are passive or restrained? Where does this difference come from in your opinion—nature or nurture?

2. Look up the term *affirmative action* in the dictionary. Ask a variety of people about their positive and negative experiences with affirmative action, as well as their definition of this term. Write an essay in which you explain your position on affirmative action, using your interviews as background and support.

3. American society often argues about whether or not voting materials and other government documents should be printed in multiple languages. Does this practice work against the notion of speaking only one language in America? Write an essay that explains your opinion on this issue. Be sure to include specific examples to support your argument.

10

DOCUMENTED ESSAYS
Reading and Writing from Sources

We use sources every day in both informal and formal situations. We explain the source of a phone message, for example, or we refer to an instructor's comments in class. We use someone else's opinion in an essay, or we quote an expert to prove a point. We cite sources both in speaking and in writing through summary, paraphrase, and direct quotation. Most of your college instructors will ask you to write papers using sources so they can see how well you understand the course material. The use of sources in academic papers requires you to understand what you have read and to integrate this reading material with your own opinions and observations—a process that requires a high level of skill in thinking, reading, and writing.

DEFINING DOCUMENTED ESSAYS

Documented essays provide you with the opportunity to perform sophisticated and exciting exercises in critical thinking; they draw on the thinking, reading, and writing abilities you have built up over the course of your academic career, and they often require you to put all the rhetorical modes to work at their most analytical level. Documented essays demonstrate the process of analytical thinking at its best in different disciplines.

In the academic world, documented essays are also called *research papers, library papers,* and *term papers.* Documented essays are generally written for one of three reasons: (1) to **report,** (2) to **interpret,** or (3) to **analyze.**

The most straightforward, uncomplicated type of documented essay **reports** information, as in a survey of problems that children have in preschool. The second type of documented essay both presents and **interprets** its findings. It examines a number of different views on a specific issue and weighs these views as it draws its own conclusions. A topic that falls into this category would be whether children who have attended preschool are more sociable than those who have not. After considering evidence on both sides, the writer would draw his or her own conclusions on this topic. A documented essay that **analyzes** a subject presents a hypothesis, tests the hypothesis, and analyzes or evaluates its conclusions. This type of essay calls for the most advanced form of critical thinking. It might look, for example, at the reasons preschool children are more or less socially flexible than nonpreschool children. At its most proficient, this type of writing requires a sophisticated degree of evaluation that forces you to judge your reading, evaluate your sources, and ultimately scrutinize your own reasoning ability as the essay takes shape.

Each of these types of documented essays calls for a higher level of thinking, and each evolves from the previous category. In other words, interpreting requires some reporting, and analyzing draws on both reporting and interpreting.

In the following paragraph, a student reports, interprets, analyzes, and uses sources to document the problem of solid waste in America. Notice how the student writer draws her readers into the essay with a commonly used phrase about America and then questions the validity of its meaning. The student's opinions give shape to the paragraph, while her use of sources helps identify the problem and support her contentions.

> *"America the Beautiful"* is a phrase used to describe the many wonders of nature found throughout our country. America's natural beauty will fade, however, if solutions to our solid waste problems are

not discovered soon. America is a rich nation socially, economically, and politically. But these very elements may be the cause of Americans' wastefulness. Americans now generate approximately 160 million tons of solid waste a year—3 1/2 pounds per person per day. We live in a consumer society where convenience, ready-to-use, and throwaway are words that spark the consumer's attention (Cook 60). However, many of the products associated with these words create a large part of our problem with solid waste (Grossman 39). We are running out of space for our garbage. The people of America are beginning to produce responses to this problem. Are we too late? A joint effort between individuals, businesses, government industries, and local, state, and federal governments is necessary to establish policies and procedures to combat this war on waste. The problem requires not one solution, but a combination of solutions involving technologies and people working together to provide a safe and healthy environment for themselves and future generations.

READING AND WRITING DOCUMENTED ESSAYS

Reading and writing documented essays involves the skillful integration of two complex operations: research and writing. Reading documented essays critically means understanding the material and evaluating the sources as you proceed. Writing documented essays includes reading and understanding sources on the topic you have chosen and then combining this reading with your own conclusions. The two skills are, essentially, mirror images of one another.

How to Read Documented Essays

Preparing to Read.   You should approach a documented essay in much the same way that you approach any essay. First, take a few minutes to look at the preliminary material for each selection: What can you learn from scanning Ehrenreich's essay ("The Ecstasy of War") and Chesney-Lind's essay ("Appearance and Delinquency: A Research Note") or from reading their synopses in the Rhetorical Table of Contents? What does Barbara Ehrenreich's title, "The Ecstasy of War," prepare you to read? And what questions do you have about "appearance and delinquency" before you read Rosenbaum and Chesney-Lind's essay?

Also, you should learn as much as you can from the authors' biographies: What is Ehrenreich's interest in war? What biographical details prepare us for her approach to this topic? What are Rosenbaum's and Chesney-Lind's backgrounds? Do they have the proper qualifications to write about "appearance and delinquency"?

Another important part of preparing to read a documented essay is surveying the sources cited. Turn to the end of the essay and look at the sources. What publications does Ehrenreich draw from? Are these books and magazines well respected? Do you recognize any of the authorities Rosenbaum and Chesney-Lind quote?

Last, before you read these essays, try to generate some ideas on each topic so you can participate as fully as possible in your reading. The Preparing to Read questions will get you ready for this task. Then, try to speculate further on the topic of each essay: What is the connection for Ehrenreich between war and ecstasy? What does this relationship tell us about human nature in general? Why has the relationship between female appearance and delinquency gained so much momentum in the United States? Where will this momentum take us in the future?

Reading.   As you react to the material in this chapter, you should respond to both the research and the writing. Record your responses as you read the essay for the first time: What are your reactions to the information you are reading? Are the sources appropriate? How well do they support the author's main points?

Use the preliminary material before each essay to help you create a framework for your responses to it: What motivated Ehrenreich to publish her essay on war? Do you find it convincing? Who was Rosenbaum and Chesney-Lind's primary audience when their essay was first published? In what ways is the tone of their essay appropriate for that audience?

Your main job at this stage is to determine each essay's primary assertion (thesis statement), note the sources that support this thesis, and begin to ask yourself questions about the essay so you can respond critically to your reading. In addition, take a look at the questions after each selection to make sure you are comprehending the major ideas of the essay.

Rereading.   As you reread these documented essays, take some time to become aware of the difference between fact and opinion, to weigh and evaluate the evidence brought to bear on the arguments, to consider the sources the writers use, to judge the interpretation of the facts cited, to determine what the writers omitted, and to confirm your own views on the issues at hand. All these skills demand the use of critical thinking strategies at their most sophisticated level.

You need to approach this type of argument with an inquiring mind, asking questions and looking for answers as you read the essays. Be especially conscious of the appeals (logical, emotional, and ethical) at work in each essay (see Chapter 9 Introduction), and take note of other rhetorical strategies that support each author's main argument.

Also, be aware of your own thought processes as you sort facts from opinions. Know where you stand personally in relation to each side of the issues here.

For a list of guidelines for the entire reading process, see the checklists on pages 20–21 of the Introduction.

How to Write Documented Essays

Preparing to Write. Just as with any writing assignment, you should begin the task of writing a documented essay by exploring and limiting your topic. In this case, however, you draw on other sources to help you with this process. You should seek out both primary and secondary sources related to your topic. **Primary sources** are works of literature, historical documents, letters, diaries, speeches, eyewitness accounts, and your own experiments, observations, and conclusions; **secondary sources** explain and analyze information from other sources. Any librarian can help you search for both types of sources related to your topic.

After you have found a few sources on your general topic, you should scan and evaluate what you have discovered so you can limit your topic further. Depending on the required length of your essay, you will want to find a topic broad enough to be researched, established enough to let you discover ample sources on it in the library, and significant enough to demonstrate your abilities to grapple with important ideas and draw meaningful conclusions. The Preparing to Write questions can help you generate and focus your ideas.

Once you have established these limitations, you might try writing a tentative thesis. At this point, asking a question and attempting to find an answer are productive. But you should keep in mind that your thesis is likely to be revised several times as the range of your knowledge changes and your paper takes different turns while you research and write. Then decide on a purpose and audience for your essay.

Once your tentative thesis is formed, you should read your sources for ideas and take detailed notes on your reading. These notes will probably fall into one of four categories: (1) *summary*—a condensed statement of someone else's thoughts or observations; (2) *paraphrase*—a restatement in your own words of someone else's ideas or observations; (3) *direct quotations from sources*; or (4) *a combination of these forms*. Be sure to make a distinction in your notes between actual quotes and paraphrases or summaries. Also, record the sources of all your notes—especially of quoted, summarized, and paraphrased material—which you may need to cite in your essay.

As you gather information, you should consider keeping a "research journal" where you can record your own opinions, interpretations, and analyses in response to your reading. This journal should be separate from your notes on sources and is the place where you can make your own discoveries in relation to your topic by jotting down thoughts and relationships among ideas you are exposed to, by keeping a record of sources you read and others you want to look at, by tracking and developing your own ideas and theories, and by clarifying your thinking on an issue.

Finally, before you write your first draft, you might want to write an informal working outline for your own information. Such an exercise can help you check the range of your coverage and the order and development of your ideas. With an outline, you can readily see where you need more information, less information, or more solid sources. Try to be flexible, however. This outline may change dramatically as your essay develops.

Writing.   Writing the first draft of a documented essay is your chance to discover new insights and to find important connections between ideas that you may not be aware of yet. This draft is your opportunity to demonstrate that you understand the issue at hand and your sources on three increasingly difficult levels—literal, interpretive, and analytical; that you can organize your material effectively; that you can integrate your sources (in the form of summaries, paraphrases, or quotations) with your opinions; and that you can document (that is, cite) your sources.

To begin this process, look again at your thesis statement and your working outline, and adjust them to represent any new discoveries you have made as you read your sources and wrote in your research journal. Then, organize your research notes and information in some logical fashion.

When you begin to draft your paper, write the sections of the essay that you feel most comfortable about first. Throughout the essay, feature your own point of view and integrate summaries, paraphrases, and quotations from other sources into your own analysis. Each point you make should be a section of your paper consisting of your own conclusion and your support for that conclusion (in the form of facts, examples, summaries, paraphrases, and quotations). Remember that the primary reason for doing such an assignment is to let you demonstrate your ability to synthesize material, draw your own conclusions, and analyze your sources and your own reasoning.

A documented paper usually blends three types of material:

1. *Common knowledge, such as the places and dates of events (even if you have to look them up).*
   EXAMPLE: Neil Armstrong and Edwin Aldrin first walked on the moon on July 20, 1969.
2. *Your own thoughts and observations.*
   EXAMPLE: Armstrong and Aldrin's brief walk on the moon's surface was the beginning of a new era in the U.S. space program.
3. *Someone else's thoughts and observations.*
   EXAMPLE: President Richard Nixon reacted to the moonwalk in a telephone call to the astronauts: "For one priceless moment in the history of man all the people on this earth are truly one—one in their pride in what you have done and one in our prayers that you will return safely to earth."

Of these three types of information, you must document or cite your exact source only for the third type. Negligence in citing your sources, whether purposeful or accidental, is called *plagiarism*, which comes from a Latin word meaning "kidnapper." Among student writers, plagiarism usually takes one of three forms: (1) using words from another source without quotation marks; (2) using someone else's ideas in the form of a summary or paraphrase without citing your source; and (3) using someone else's term paper as your own.

Avoiding plagiarism is quite simple: You just need to remember to acknowledge the sources of ideas or wording that you are using to support your own contentions. Acknowledging your sources also gives you credit for the reading you have done and for the ability you have developed to use sources to support your observations and conclusions.

Documentation styles vary from discipline to discipline. Ask your instructor about the particular documentation style he or she wants you to follow. The most common styles are the Modern Language Association (MLA) style, used in humanities courses, and the American Psychological Association (APA) style, used in behavioral sciences and science courses. (See any writing handbook for more details on documentation formats.)

The World Wide Web is an exciting new source of information for your research papers. Electronic sources include on-line journals and magazines, CD-ROMs, software programs, newsletters, discussion groups, bulletin boards, gopher sites, and e-mail. But not all electronic sources are equally accurate and reliable. Based on your topic, you need to exercise your best judgment and get your instructor's help in assessing the most useful on-line sites for your purposes. If you use electronic sources in any of your papers, remember that you have two goals in any citation: (1) to acknowledge the author and (2) to help the reader locate the material. Then you should check the MLA or APA Home Pages for their current guidelines for on-line documentation: The URL for the Modern Language Association is http://www.mla.org and for the American Psychological Association, http://www.apa.org.

Even though documentation styles vary somewhat from one discipline to another, the basic concept behind documentation is the same in all disciplines: You must give proper credit to other writers by acknowledging the sources of the summaries, paraphrases, and quotations that you use to support your ideas in your documented paper. Once you grasp this basic concept and accept it, you will have no trouble avoiding plagiarism.

Rewriting.   To rewrite your documented essay, you should play the role of your readers and impartially evaluate your argument and the sources you have used as evidence in that argument.

To begin with, revise your thesis to represent all the discoveries you made as you wrote your first draft. Then, look for problems in logic throughout the essay; you might even develop an outline at this point to help evaluate your reasoning:

- Are the essay's assertions clear?
- Are they adequately supported?
- Are other points of view recognized and examined?
- Does the organization of your paper further your assertions/argument?
- Have you removed irrelevant material?

Next, check your documentation style:

- Is your source material (either summarized, paraphrased, or quoted) presented fairly and accurately?
- Have you rechecked the citations for all the sources in your paper?
- Do you introduce the sources in your paper when appropriate?
- Are your sources in the proper format according to your instructor's guidelines (MLA, APA, or another)?

Then, proofread carefully. Finally, prepare your paper to be submitted to your instructor:

- Have you followed your instructor's guidelines for your title page, margins, page numbers, tables, and abstracts?
- Have you prepared an alphabetical list of your sources for the end of your paper?

Any additional guidance you may need as you write and revise your documented essays is furnished on pages 32–34 of the Introduction.

STUDENT ESSAY: DOCUMENTATION AT WORK

The following student essay uses documented sources to support its conclusions and observations about our eating habits today. First, the writer creates a profile of carnivorous species in contrast to human beings. She then goes on to discuss the harsh realities connected with eating meat. After recognizing and refuting some opposing views, this student writer ends her paper with her own evaluation of the situation and a list of some famous vegetarians. Throughout the essay, the student writer carefully supports her principal points with summaries, paraphrases, and quotations from other sources. Notice that she uses the MLA documentation style and closes the paper with an alphabetical list of "Works Cited."

Food for Thought

The next time you sit down to a nice steak dinner, pause for a moment to consider whether you are biologically pro-

Background information grammed to eat meat. Unlike carnivores, such as lions and tigers, with claws and sharp front teeth allowing them to tear and eat raw flesh, humans are omnivores, with fingers that can pluck fruits and grains and flat teeth that can grind these vegetable foods. To digest their meals, carnivores *Common knowledge* have an acidic saliva and a very strong hydrochloric acid digestive fluid. In contrast, we humans have an alkaline saliva, and our digestive fluids are only one-tenth as potent as those of carnivores. Moreover, carnivores

Common knowledge have an intestinal tract barely three times their body length, which allows for faster elimination of rotting flesh; humans have an intestinal tract eight to twelve times our body length, better enabling us to digest plant nutrients. What happens, then, when we eat flesh? The effects of a meat-based *Thesis* diet are far-reaching: massive suffering of the animals killed and eaten, a myriad of diseases in humans, and a devastating effect on world ecology.

Student's first conclusion The atrocities committed daily to provide meat should be enough to make a meat-based diet completely unconscionable. Ac- *Summary of secondary source* cording to Peter Singer, of People for the Ethical Treatment of Animals (PETA),

Citation (MLA form)

every year several hundred million cattle, pigs, and sheep and 3 billion chickens are slaughtered to provide food for humans (Singer 92). That is equal to 6,278 animals every minute of every day—and those are just the ones that make it to the slaughterhouse. Over 500,000 animals die in transit each year (150).

Support for conclusion #1

Paraphrase of secondary source (fact)

A slaughterhouse is not a pretty sight. Anywhere from 50 to 90 percent of the cattle are slaughtered in a "kosher" manner. "Kosher" sounds innocent enough, but what it actually means is that the animal must be "healthy and moving" at the time of death. This requires the animals to be fully conscious as "a heavy chain is clamped around one of their rear legs; then they are jerked off their feet and hang upside down" for anywhere from two to five minutes, usually twisting in agony with a broken leg, while they are moved down the conveyer belt to be slaughtered (Robbins 140–41).

Summary of secondary source

While we would like to assume the animals we eat are healthy at the time of butchering, this is often not the case. Most veal calves, for example, are near death from anemia when sent to the butcher (Diamond and Diamond 238). Inspections have revealed leukosis (cancer) in 90 percent of the chickens (Robbins 67), pneumonia rates of 80 percent and stomach ulcers of 53 percent in pigs (94). Salmonellosis is found in 90 percent of the chickens dressed and ready to be purchased (303).

Student's opinion

Examples from secondary sources

Student's second conclusion

Even if we, like the industry leaders, could turn a cold heart to the plight of our fellow creatures, we would still find many reasons to warrant a vegetarian diet, beginning with our own health. Recapping just a few of the hundreds of studies that link diet to disease, we might consider the following:

—A study of nearly 90,000 American women published in the *New England Journal of Medicine* reports that daily pork, lamb, or beef eaters have a 250 percent greater likelihood of developing colon cancer than people who consume these foods once a month or less ("Red Meat Alert").

—Heart specialist Dr. Dean Ornish states, "It's no surprise that half of all Americans develop heart disease because the typical U.S. diet puts everyone at risk" (Marcus 3).

—The *Journal of the American Medical Association* stated that a vegetarian diet could prevent 97 percent of coronary occlusions (Robbins 247).

—Even though officials in Great Britain and other countries deny any connection between BIV, a bovine disease very closely related to the human HIV virus, and HIV, many companies are refusing to handle any meat or dairy products from BIV-infected herds (Clayton 585)

The effects of meat diets go beyond causing human disease and death. <u>Perhaps the most frightening legacy being left by America's dietary ritual is just now being realized, and that is the profound ecological impact factory farming is having on our planet</u>. Every five seconds, one acre of forest is cleared in America, and one estimate is that 87 percent is cleared for either livestock grazing or growing livestock feed (Robbins 361). Approximately six square yards of jungle must be cleared for every single hamburger made of imported beef. By the late 1970s, nearly two-thirds of all agricultural land was used as pastureland for

Marginal notes:

Paraphrase of secondary sources (facts)

Support for second conclusion

Quotation from secondary source

Student's third conclusion

Support for third conclusion

Paraphrase of secondary sources (facts)

animals while countless people living just outside of those same pasturelands were starving to death (Rifkin 99). Says Alan Durning, senior researcher at the World-watch Institute in Washington, D.C., "Producing the red meat and poultry eaten each year by a typical American takes energy equal to 50 gallons of gasoline. Supplying vegetarians with nourishment requires one-third less energy on the farm" (4).

Quotation from secondary source

Student's opinion

Forests are not all that we are sacrificing. Local governments are constantly calling for water conservation, yet over 50 percent of all water used in America goes into grain production for livestock. According to one study, the water required to feed a meat eater for one day is 4,000 gallons, but it is only 1,200 gallons for a lacto-ovo (dairy and egg eating) vegetarian and 300 gallons for a vegan (one who consumes no animal-derived products) (Robbins 367). Not only is the vast amount of water wasted through a meat-based diet outrageous, but the added cost of controlling animal waste must also be taken into account. One cow produces sixteen times as much waste as one human, and cattle waste produces ten times the water pollution that human waste does (372–373).

Paraphrase of secondary sources (facts)

Student's opinion

A third loss is even more serious than the losses of forests and water. This year, 60 million people will die of starvation, yet in America, we feed 80 percent of our corn and 95 percent of our oats to farm animals. The feed given to cattle alone, excluding pigs and chickens, would feed double the population of humans worldwide. Three and one-quarter acres of farmland are needed to provide meat for one person per year. A lacto-ovo vegetarian can be fed from just one-half of an acre per year; a vegan needs only one-sixth of an acre. This means twenty vegans can eat a healthy diet for the same acreage needed to feed just one meat eater. Cutting our meat habit by only 10 percent would provide enough food for all of the 60 million people worldwide who will starve this year (352–353).

Paraphrase of secondary sources (facts)

Student's final remarks

With all the devastation the average American diet is creating, we must begin to take responsibility for the consequences of our actions. Let us follow in the footsteps of such famous vegetarians as Charles Darwin, Leonardo da Vinci, Albert Einstein, Sir Isaac Newton, Plato, Pythagoras, Socrates, and Tolstoy (Parham 185). Every time we sit down to eat, we can choose either to contribute to or to help put an end to this suffering and destruction. Only one move matters, and that is the one we make with our forks.

Notes

[1]For more information on meat and its effects on our health and the environment, see <http://www.envirolink.org/arrs/essays/BB9. html>.

Works Cited

Alphabetical list of sources

Clayton, Julie. "Spectre of AIDS haunts reports of sick cows." *Nature* 367 (1994): 585.

Diamond, Harvey, and Marilyn Diamond. *Fit for Life II, Living Health.* New York: Warner, 1987.

Durning, Alan B. "Fat of the Land." *World Watch Magazine.* July 1992 <http://envirolink.org/arrs/essays/fat.html>.

Marcus, Erik. *Vegan: The New Ethics of Eating.* Ithaca, NY: McBooks Press, 1998.

Modern Language Association format

Parham, Barbara. *What's Wrong with Eating Meat?* Denver: Ananda Marga, 1981.

"Red Meat Alert." *New Scientist* 22/29 Dec. 1990: 9.

Rifkin, Jeremy. "Beyond beef: The cattle industry threatens the environment, human health, and the world food supply." *Utne Reader* 50 (1992): 96-109.

Robbins, John. *Diet for a New America.* Walpole: Stillpoint, 1987.

Singer, Peter. *Animal Liberation: A New Ethics for Our Treatment of Animals.* New York: Hearst, 1975.

Student Writer's Comments

From the moment this essay was assigned, I knew my topic would be vegetarianism, because I felt the key to a convincing argument was to select a topic I was passionate about. Since I was undertaking the task of speaking out against the time-honored American tradition of eating meat, I knew I needed to approach the topic in as nonthreatening a manner as possible. I wanted to be graphic as I appealed to the emotions, concerns, and ethics of my audience, so that my message would not easily be forgotten, but I had to strike a careful balance, so that I would not alienate my readers by appearing preachy, accusatory, or unduly crude.

I began the process of writing this paper by going to the library every chance I had (between classes, during lunch, and at night before I went home) and collecting information on the horror stories connected with eating meat. (I had been a loyal vegetarian for years and actually wanted some concrete information on some of the choices I had made in my own eating habits.) I found plenty of horror stories, but I also uncovered some counterarguments that I hadn't been aware of. I was fascinated by the information—both facts and opinions—that I was discovering. But the material wasn't taking any shape at all yet; the only common denominator was the general topic and my interest level.

I was taking notes on notecards, so I had filled quite a stack of cards when I stopped to reread all my material to see if I could put it into any coherent categories. Happily, my notes fell quite naturally into three divisions: (1) the overwhelming cruelty to the animals that we kill and eat, (2) the diseases resulting from eating animals, and (3) the effect of this type of slaughter on world ecology. After this exercise, I could see right away that I had enough material on the suffering of the animals killed for human consumption, and my material in this area was from well-known, reputable sources. My notes on world ecology would also be sufficient with a few more library sessions, but I had to do some serious investigation on the topic of human diseases in reference to meat eaters or else drop the topic altogether. I had some stray notes that didn't fit any of these categories, but I decided to worry about those later. I tried my hand at a thesis statement, which I think had been floating around in my head for days. Then I wrote the paper topic by topic over a period of several days. I didn't attempt the introduction and the conclusion until I began to rewrite. As I composed the essay, I was especially aware of the types of material I had to support each of my topics. I had a good distribution of summaries, paraphrases, and quotations and had remembered to keep careful notes on my sources, so I put my source and page numbers into my first draft. I also had several examples for each of my topics and a good blend of facts and opinions.

When I rewrote, I kept in mind that I would be successful in arguing my case only if my words caused the readers to make a change, however small, in their own behavior. I reworked my research paper several times as I played different readers with various biases, during which time I paid special attention to word choice and sentence structure.

Overall, writing this paper gave me a great deal of pleasure. I feel even stronger in my determination to be a vegetarian, and now I have some concrete reasons (and their sources!) for my natural instincts.

SOME FINAL THOUGHTS ON DOCUMENTED ESSAYS

The two essays that follow offer vigorous exercises in critical thinking. They also use a combination of the three different types of persuasive appeals we studied in Chapter 9 (logical, emotional, and ethical) and draw on a wealth of rhetorical modes that we have studied throughout the book. In the first essay, Barbara Ehrenreich illustrates the Modern Language Association documentation style as she uses sources to support her thesis that people do not have a natural instinct to kill. The second essay, by Jill Leslie Rosenbaum and Meda Chesney-Lind, explains the connection between female appearance and judgments in criminal cases; its use of sources illustrates the American Psychological Association documentation style. As you read these essays, be aware of the combination of appeals at work, the various rhetorical modes each author uses to further her argument, and the way each author uses sources to support the topics within each essay.

DOCUMENTED ESSAYS IN REVIEW

Reading Documented Essays

Preparing to Read

✓ What assumptions can you make from the essay's title?

✓ Can you guess what the general mood of the essay is?

✓ What is the essay's purpose and audience?

✓ What does the synopsis in the Rhetorical Table of Contents tell you about the essay?

✓ What can you learn from the author's biography?

✓ Can you guess what the author's point of view toward the subject is?

✓ What are your responses to the Preparing to Read questions?

Reading

✓ What are your initial reactions to the essay?

✓ What is the author's main assertion or thesis?

✓ What sources does the author cite to support the thesis?

✓ What questions do you have about this topic?

✓ Did you preview the questions that follow the essay?

Rereading

✓ How does the author use facts and opinions in the essay?

✓ Are the sources the writer cites valid and reliable?

✓ Are the sources cited in the essay respected in the field?

✓ Does the author interpret facts accurately?

✓ Has the author omitted any necessary information?

Writing Documented Essays

Preparing to Write

✓ What are your responses to the Preparing to Write questions?

✓ What is your purpose?

✓ Who is your audience?

Writing

✓ Do you have a thesis statement?

✓ Do you use both primary and secondary sources in your essay?

✓ Have you organized your material?

✓ Have you avoided plagiarism and cited your sources correctly?

✓ Do you use the appropriate documentation style?

Rewriting

✓ Are the essay's assertions clear? Are they adequately supported?

✓ Are other points of view recognized and examined?

✓ Does the organization of your paper further your assertions/argument?

✓ Have you removed irrelevant material?

✓ Is your source material (either summarized, paraphrased, or quoted) presented fairly and accurately?

✓ Have you rechecked the citations for all the sources in your paper?

✓ Do you introduce the sources in your paper when appropriate?

✓ Are your sources in the proper format according to your instructor's guidelines (MLA, APA, or another)?

✓ Have you followed your instructor's guidelines for your title page, margins, page numbers, tables, and abstracts?

✓ Have you prepared an alphabetical list of your sources for the end of your paper?

BARBARA EHRENREICH   (1941–)

The Ecstasy of War

Barbara Ehrenreich is a respected author, lecturer, and social commentator with opinions on a wide range of topics. After earning a B.A. from Reed College in chemistry and physics and a Ph.D. from Rockefeller University in cell biology, she turned almost immediately to freelance writing, producing a succession of books and pamphlets on a dazzling array of subjects. Early publications examined student uprisings, health care in America, nurses and midwives, poverty, welfare, economic justice for women, and the sexual politics of disease. Her most recent books include *The Hearts of Men: American Dreams and the Flight from Commitment* (1983), *Fear of Falling: The Inner Life of the Middle Class* (1989), *The Worst Years of Our Lives: Irreverent Notes from a Decade of Greed* (1990), *Blood Rites: Origins and History of the Passions of War* (1997), and *Nickel and Dimed* (2001). Ehrenreich is also well known as a frequent guest on television and radio programs, including *The Today Show, Good Morning America, Nightline, Crossfire,* and *The Phil Donohue Show.* Her many articles and reviews have appeared in the *New York Times Magazine, Esquire,* the *Atlantic Monthly,* the *New Republic, Vogue, Harper's,* and the *Wall Street Journal.* She has been an essayist for *Time* since 1990. Ehrenreich, whose favorite hobby is "voracious reading," lives in Syosset, New York.

Preparing to Read

Taken from *Blood Rites: Origins and History of the Passions of War* (1997), the following essay analyzes the psychology of war. Its citations and bibliography illustrate proper MLA (Modern Language Association) documentation form. As you prepare to read this article, take a few minutes to think about aggression in society today: Do you think aggression plays a significant role in American society? In other societies? What do you think is the origin of aggression? In your opinion, what role does aggression play in war? In everyday life? How do you react to aggressive behavior? How do people you associate with react to aggressive behavior?

"So elemental is the human need to endow the shedding of blood
with some great and even sublime significance that it renders the
intellect almost entirely helpless" (Van Creveld 166).

D ifferent wars have led to different theories of why men   1
fight them. The Napoleonic Wars, which bore along
with them the rationalist spirit of the French Revolution,
inspired the Prussian officer Carl von Clausewitz to propose that
war itself is an entirely rational undertaking, unsullied by human
emotion. War, in his famous aphorism, is merely a "continuation
of policy . . . by other means," with policy itself supposedly resulting from the same kind of clearheaded deliberation one might
apply to a game of chess. Nation-states were the leading actors on
the stage of history, and war was simply one of the many ways
they advanced their interests against those of other nation-states. If
you could accept the existence of this new super-person, the nation, a battle was no more disturbing and irrational than, say, a
difficult trade negotiation—except perhaps to those who lay dying
on the battlefield.

World War I, coming a century after Napoleon's sweep   2
through Europe and northern Africa, led to an opposite assessment of the human impulse to war. World War I was hard to
construe as in any way "rational," especially to that generation of
European intellectuals, including Sigmund Freud, who survived
to ponder the unprecedented harvest of dead bodies. History textbooks tell us that the "Great War" grew out of the conflict
between "competing imperialist states," but this Clausewitzian interpretation has little to do with the actual series of accidents,
blunders, and miscommunications that impelled the nations of
Europe to war in the summer of 1914.[1] At first swept up in the
excitement of the war, unable for weeks to work or think of anything else, Freud was eventually led to conclude that there is some
dark flaw in the human psyche, a perverse desire to destroy,
countering Eros and the will to live (Stromberg 82).

So these are, in crude summary, the theories of war which   3
modern wars have left us with: That war is a means, however
risky, by which men seek to advance their collective interests and
improve their lives. Or, alternatively, that war stems from subra-
tional drives not unlike those that lead individuals to commit vio-

lent crimes. In our own time, most people seem to hold both views at once, avowing that war is a gainful enterprise, intended to meet the material needs of the groups engaged in it, and, at the same time, that it fulfills deep and "irrational" psychological needs. There is no question about the first part of this proposition—that wars are designed, at least ostensibly, to secure necessaries like land or oil or "geopolitical advantage." The mystery lies in the peculiar psychological grip war exerts on us.

In the 1960s and '70s, the debate on the psychology of war   4 centered on the notion of an "aggressive instinct," peculiar to all humans or only to human males. This is not the place to summarize that debate, with its endless examples of animal behavior and clashes over their applicability to human affairs. Here I would simply point out that, whether or not there is an aggressive instinct, there are reasons to reject it as the major wellspring of war.

Although it is true that aggressive impulses, up to and including   5 murderous rage, can easily take over in the heat of actual battle, even this statement must be qualified to take account of different weaponry and modes of fighting. Hand-to-hand combat may indeed call forth and even require the emotions of rage and aggression, if only to mobilize the body for bursts of muscular activity. In the case of action-at-a-distance weapons, however, like guns and bows and arrows, emotionality of any sort can be a distinct disadvantage. Coolness, and the ability to keep aiming and firing steadfastly in the face of enemy fire, prevails. Hence, according to the distinguished American military historian Robert L. O'Connell, the change in the ideal warrior personality wrought by the advent of guns in the fifteenth and sixteenth centuries, from "ferocious aggressiveness" to "passive disdain" (O'Connell 119). So there is no personality type—"hot-tempered," "macho," or whatever—consistently and universally associated with warfare.

Furthermore, fighting itself is only one component of the   6 enterprise we know as war. Wars are not barroom brawls writ large, or domestic violence that has been somehow extended to strangers. In war, fighting takes place within battles—along with much anxious waiting, of course—but wars do not begin with battles and are often not decided by them either. Most of war consists of *preparation* for battle—training, the organization of supplies, marching and other forms of transport—activities which are hard to account for by innate promptings of any kind. There is no plausible instinct, for example, that impels a man to leave his home, cut his hair short, and drill for hours in tight formation. As anthropologists Clifton B. Kroeber and Bernard L. Fontana point out, "It is a large step from what may be biologically innate leanings toward individual aggression to ritualized, socially sanctioned, institutionalized group warfare" (Kroeber and Fontana 166).

War, in other words, is too complex and collective an activity to be accounted for by a single warlike instinct lurking within the individual psyche. Instinct may, or may not, inspire a man to bayonet the first enemy he encounters in battle. But instinct does not mobilize supply lines, manufacture rifles, issue uniforms, or move an army of thousands from point A on the map to B. These are "complicated, orchestrated, highly organized" activities, as social theorist Robin Fox writes, undertaken not by individuals but by entities on the scale of nations and dynasties (Fox 15). "The hypothesis of a killer instinct," according to a commentator summarizing a recent conference on the anthropology of war, is "not so much wrong as irrelevant" (McCauley, Clark in Haas 2).   7

In fact, throughout history, individual men have gone to near-suicidal lengths to avoid participating in wars—a fact that proponents of a warlike instinct tend to slight. Men have fled their homelands, served lengthy prison terms, hacked off limbs, shot off feet or index fingers, feigned illness or insanity, or, if they could afford to, paid surrogates to fight in their stead. "Some draw their teeth, some blind themselves, and others maim themselves, on their way to us" (Mitchell 42), the governor of Egypt complained of his peasant recruits in the early nineteenth century. So unreliable was the rank and file of the eighteenth-century Prussian army that military manuals forbade camping near a woods or forest: The troops would simply melt away into the trees (Delbrück 303).   8

Proponents of a warlike instinct must also reckon with the fact that even when men have been assembled, willingly or unwillingly, for the purpose of war, fighting is not something that seems to come "naturally" to them. In fact, surprisingly, even in the thick of battle, few men can bring themselves to shoot directly at individual enemies.[2] The difference between an ordinary man or boy and a reliable killer, as any drill sergeant could attest, is profound. A transformation is required: The man or boy leaves his former self behind and becomes something entirely different, per-   9 haps even taking a new name. In small-scale, traditional societies, the change was usually accomplished through ritual drumming, dancing, fasting, and sexual abstinence—all of which serve to lift a man out of his mundane existence and into a new, warriorlike mode of being, denoted by special body paint, masks, and head-dresses.

As if to emphasize the discontinuity between the warrior and   10 the ordinary human being, many cultures require the would-be fighting man to leave his humanness behind and assume a new form as an animal.[3] The young Scandinavian had to become a bear before he could become an elite warrior, going "berserk" (the word means "dressed in a bear hide"), biting and chasing people. The Irish hero Cuchulain transformed himself into a monster in preparation for battle: "He became horrible, many-shaped, strange, and unrecognizable," with one eye sucked into his skull and the other popping out of the side of the face (Davidson 84). Apparently this transformation was a familiar and meaningful one, because similarly distorted faces turn up frequently in Celtic art.

Often the transformation is helped along with drugs or social   11 pressure of various kinds. Tahitian warriors were browbeaten into fighting by functionaries called Rauti, or "exhorters," who ran around the battlefield urging their comrades to mimic "the devouring wild dog" (Keeley 146). The ancient Greek hoplites drank enough wine, apparently, to be quite tipsy when they went into battle (Hanson 126); Aztecs drank pulque; Chinese troops at the time of Sun Tzu got into the mood by drinking wine and watching "gyrating sword dancers" perform (Griffith, Samuel in Sun Tzu 37). Almost any drug or intoxicant has served, in one setting or another, to facilitate the transformation of man into warrior. Yanomamo Indians of the Amazon ingest a hallucinogen before battle; the ancient Scythians smoked hemp, while a neigh-boring tribe drank something called "hauma," which is believed to have induced a frenzy of aggression (Rolle 94–95). So if there is a destructive instinct that impels men to war, it is a weak one and often requires a great deal of help.

In seventeenth-century Europe, the transformation of man into   12 soldier took on a new form, more concerted and disciplined, and far less pleasant, than wine. New recruits and even seasoned vet-erans were endlessly drilled, hour after hour, until each man began to feel himself part of a single, giant fighting machine. The drill was only partially inspired by the technology of firearms. It's easy enough to teach a man to shoot a gun; the problem is to make him willing to get into situations where guns are being shot and to remain there long enough to do some shooting of his own. So modern military training aims at a transformation parallel to that achieved by "primitives" with war drums and paint: In the fanatical routines of boot camp, a man leaves behind his former identity and is reborn as a creature of the military—an automaton and also, ideally, a willing killer of other men.

This is not to suggest that killing is foreign to human nature or, more narrowly, to the male personality. Men (and women) have again and again proved themselves capable of killing impulsively and with gusto. But there is a huge difference between a war and an ordinary fight. War not only departs from the normal; it inverts all that is moral and right: In war one *should* kill, *should* steal, *should* burn cities and farms, *should* perhaps even rape matrons and little girls. Whether or not such activities are "natural" or at some level instinctual, most men undertake them only by entering what appears to be an "altered state"—induced by drugs or lengthy drilling, and denoted by face paint or khakis.

The point of such transformative rituals is not only to put men "in the mood." Returning warriors may go through equally challenging rituals before they can celebrate victory or reenter the community—covering their heads in apparent shame, for example; vomiting repeatedly; abstaining from sex (Keeley 144). Among the Maori, returning warriors could not participate in the victory celebration until they had gone through a whaka-hoa ritual, designed to make them "common" again: The hearts of slain enemies were roasted, after which offerings were made to the war god Tu, and the rest was eaten by priests, who shouted spells to remove "the blood curse" and enable warriors to reenter their ordinary lives (Sagan 18). Among the Taulipang Indians of South America, victorious warriors "sat on ants, flogged one another with whips, and passed a cord covered with poisonous ants, through their mouth and nose" (Métraux 397). Such painful and shocking postwar rites impress on the warrior that war is much more than a "continuation of policy . . . by other means." In war men enter an alternative realm of human experience, as far removed from daily life as those things which we call "sacred."

Notes

1. See, for example, Stoessinger, *Why Nations Go to War*, 14–20.
2. See Grossman, *On Killing*.
3. In the mythologies of the Indo-European tradition, Dumézil relates, thanks "either to a gift of metamorphosisl, or to a monstrous heredity, the eminent warrior possesses a veritable animal nature" (Dumézil 140).

Works Cited

Davidson, Hilda Ellis. *Myths and Symbols in Pagan Europe: Early Scandinavian and Celtic Religions*. Syracuse, NY: Syracuse University Press, 1988.

Delbrück, Hans. *History of the Art of War,* vol. 4. *The Dawn of Modern Warfare*. Lincoln: University of Nebraska Press, 1985.

Dumézil, Georges. *Destiny of the Warrior*. Chicago: University of Chicago Press, 1969.

Fox, Robin. "Fatal Attraction: War and Human Nature." *The National Interest* (Winter 1992/93): 11–20.

Grossman, Lt. Col. Dave. *On Killing: The Psychological Cost of Learning to Kill in War and Society*. Boston: Little, Brown, 1995.

Haas, Jonathan, ed. *The Anthropology of War*. Cambridge: Cambridge University Press, 1900.

Hanson, Victor Davis. *The Western Way of War: Infantry Battle in Classical Greece*. New York: Alfred A. Knopf, 1989.

Keeley, Lawrence H. *War Before Civilization: The Myth of the Peaceful Savage*. New York: Oxford University Press, 1996.

Kroeber, Clifton B. and Bernard L. Fontana. *Massacre on the Gila: An Account of the Last Major Battle Between American Indians, with Reflections on the Origin of War*. Tucson: University of Arizona Press, 1986.

Métraux, Alfred. "Warfare, Cannibalism, and Human Trophies." In *Handbook of South American Indians,* vol. 5, edited by Julian H. Steward. New York: Cooper Square Publishers, 1963.

Mitchell, Timothy. *Colonizing Egypt*. Berkeley: University of California Press, 1991.

O'Connell, Robert L. *Of Arms and Men: A History of War, Weapons, and Aggression*. New York: Oxford University Press, 1989.

Rolle, Renate. *The World of the Scythians*. Berkeley: University of California Press, 1989.

Sagan, Eli. *Cannibalism: Human Aggression and Cultural Form*. New York: Harper and Row, 1974.

Stoessinger, John G. *Why Nations Go to War*. New York: St. Martin's Press, 1993.

Stromberg, Roland. *Redemption by War: The Intellectuals and 1914*. Lawrence: University of Kansas Press, 1982.

Sun Tzu. *The Art of War*. Translated and with an introduction by Samuel B. Griffith. London: Oxford University Press, 1971.

Van Creveld, Martin. *The Transformation of War*. New York: Free Press, 1991.

UNDERSTANDING DETAILS

1. What do you think Ehrenreich's main purpose is in this essay?
2. According to Ehrenreich, what is the difference between hand-to-hand combat and fighting at a distance?
3. What does Ehrenreich say are the various components of what we call "war"?
4. In what ways do some cultures ritualize the transformation from regular citizen to warrior? Give three examples.

ANALYZING MEANING

1. Do you believe war can ever be emotionless and rational, like "a difficult trade negotiation" (paragraph 1)?
2. What do Clifton B. Kroeber and Bernard L. Fontana mean when they say, "It is a large step from what may be biologically innate learnings toward individual aggression to ritualized, socially sanctioned, institutionalized group warfare" (paragraph 6)?
3. Why is "the hypothesis of a killer instinct" "not so much wrong as irrelevant" to the "anthropology of war" (paragraph 7)?
4. Are you convinced by this essay that "in war men enter an alternative realm of human experience, as far removed from daily life as those things which we call 'sacred'" (paragraph 14)?

DISCOVERING RHETORICAL STRATEGIES

1. Who do you think is Ehrenreich's main audience? How did you come to this conclusion?
2. The author begins her discussion of war with different "theories of why men fight them [wars]" (paragraph 1). Is this an effective beginning for what Ehrenreich is trying to accomplish? Explain your answer.
3. What information in this essay is most persuasive to you? What is least persuasive?
4. What tone does the author establish by citing frequent statistics and referring to other sources in her essay?

MAKING CONNECTIONS

1. Compare and contrast Ehrenreich's insights on the psychology of war with Stephen King's theories on "Why We Crave Horror Movies." How do their ideas support one another? How do they contradict each other?
2. Compare Ehrenreich's use of examples with those of Rosenbaum and Chesney-Lind ("Appearance and Delinquency: A Research Note").
3. In a conversation between Ehrenreich and Nancy Gibbs ("When Is It Rape?") about the "aggressive instinct" in people, on what points would they agree and disagree? Give examples.

IDEAS FOR DISCUSSION/WRITING

Preparing to Write

Write freely about aggression in general: Why do people fight? Why do countries go to war? What are some ways in which people take out their aggression? Have you ever noticed people fighting just for the sake of fighting? When is aggression acceptable? When is it unacceptable?

Choosing a Topic

1. Ehrenreich claims that "even when men have been assembled, willingly or unwillingly, for the purpose of war, fighting is not something that seems to come 'naturally' to them" (para-

graph 8). Do you agree or disagree with this statement? Explain your reaction in a clearly reasoned argumentative essay. Cite Ehrenreich's selection whenever necessary.

2. In the last paragraph of her essay, Ehrenreich suggests that warriors often have to go through rituals to return to their civilizations. Use Ehrenreich's article as one of your sources; then, read further on such transformations. Next write a clear, well-documented argument expressing your opinion on a specific transformation. Organize your paper clearly, and present your suggestions logically, using proper documentation (citations and bibliography) to support your position.

3. Use additional sources to study the circumstances of a war you are familiar with. Then, referring to Ehrenreich's explanation of "the anthropology of war" (paragraph 7), write a well-documented argument explaining the causes and effects of the war by discussing or analyzing in depth the consequences you have discovered.

Before beginning your essay, you might want to consult the checklists on pages 582–583.

JILL LESLIE ROSENBAUM   (1955–   )
AND MEDA CHESNEY-LIND   (1947–   )

Appearance and Delinquency:
A Research Note

Jill Leslie Rosenbaum, a criminologist specializing in female crime, earned her B.A. in sociology at the University of Michigan, her M.S. in Addiction Studies at the University of Arizona, and her Ph.D. in criminal justice at State University of New York, Albany. She is currently a professor of criminal justice at California State University, Fullerton, where she has published recent articles in *Crime and Delinquency, Justice Quarterly*, and *Youth and Society*. In her spare time, she enjoys working out at a local gym, reading good novels, and participating in children's theatre. She has also done extensive work with the California Office of Criminal Justic Planning on the topic of sexual assault. Her advice to students using *The Prose Reader* is to "spend lots of time writing. Write and rewrite your work until it is perfect!" Her co-author, Meda Chesney-Lind, earned her B.A. at Whitman College and her M.A. and Ph.D. at the University of Hawaii. She is currently a professor of Women's Studies at the University of Hawaii at Manoa, where she has published three books on women and crime—*Girls, Delinquency, and Juvenile Justice* (1992, with Randall Shelden), *The Female Offender* (1997), and *Female Gangs in America* (1999, with John Hagedorn)—plus over fifty articles on related topics. Her recreational activities include walking and haunting thrift shops. She advises student writers "to practice, practice, practice," explaining that "you have to trust your instincts in order to become a better writer, which also requires patience, discipline, and a healthy sense of humor."

Preparing to Read

Taken from a journal entitled *Crime and Delinquency* (April 1994), the following essay explains that perceived attractiveness of female offenders in particular plays an important part in the criminal justice system. Its citations and bibliography illustrate proper APA (American Psychological Association) documentation form. As you prepare to read this article, take a few minutes to think about the influence appearance has on your view of the world: Do you consciously think about appearance? Do someone's looks influence your professional judgment of that person? Would a defendant's appearance affect your view of his or her guilt? Does appearance play any part in how well you listen to someone or whether or not you agree with a person? How does appearance affect your opinion of a stranger?

Women are judged by culturally derived standards of attractiveness. These culturally created standards affect women in all walks of life, including, it appears, the way they are treated by the criminal justice system. Research has shown that perception of physical appearance can have a significant impact on an individual's success in a variety of endeavors. These endeavors include dating opportunities (Crause and Mehrabian, 1977; Stretch and Figley, 1980; Walster, Aronson, Abrahams, and Rottman, 1966), the initiation of relationships (Murstein and Christy, 1976; Price and Vandenberg, 1979; White, 1980), teachers' evaluations of students (Clifford and Walster, 1973; Dion, 1973), and corporate success (Heilman and Stopeck, 1985; Heilman and Sarawatari, 1979).

The role of appearance in judgments of criminal reponsibility and the punishment of such behavior have also been the focus of a variety of psychological studies (Efran, 1974; Sigall and Ostrove, 1975; Stewart, 1980). These studies consistently indicate that physical attractiveness influences judgments of wrongdoing. Dion (1973) found that adult judgments of children's transgressions were affected by the attractiveness of the child. Transgressions, both mild and severe, were perceived to be less undesirable when committed by an attractive child than an unattractive child. Furthermore, subjects were less likely to attribute chronic antisocial behavior to attractive than to unattractive children.

The work of Sigall and Ostrove (1975) suggest that the sentences given to offenders are often conditioned by the appearance of the offender. Attractive female offenders, whose offense was not appearance-related (burglary), received greater leniency than unattractive offenders. However, when the offense was attractiveness-related (swindle), attractive offenders received harsher sentences than their unattractive counterparts. These findings are consistent with those of Efran (1974), whose work has shown that attractive defendants are much less likely to be found guilty than unattractive defendants. This becomes especially pronounced when males are judging the culpability of females. Sigall and Ostrove (1975) and Efran (1974) also indicate that when a female offender is seen as using her attractiveness to assist in the commission of a crime, attractive defendants were more likely to be found guilty.

Studies of appearance also demonstrate that society has higher   4
expectations for attractive individuals; some of these expectations pertain exclusively to women. For instance, attractive women are assumed to be more feminine and have a more socially desirable personality, and as a result, they are assumed to have greater overall happiness in their personal, social and professional lives (Dion, Berscheid, and Walster, 1973). It is also assumed that they are less likely to remain single, more likely to marry earlier, be better spouses, and be better sexual partners as well.

Although the lives of attractive women are assumed to be far   5
superior to those of less attractive women, some believe that attractive women have less integrity, and thus managerial opportunities for them may be hindered. In fact, Heilman and Sarawatari (1979) concluded that women with more masculine characteristics are believed to have greater ability than women with feminine characteristics. Thus, although attractive women are thought to be more feminine, they are also thought to be less well-suited for nontraditional female roles.

Finally, Emerson (1969) noted that judges and other juvenile   6
court personnel often expressed considerable interest in the appearance of girls appearing before the court he observed. He noted a judge's interest in whether runaway girls were "clean" after having been away from home for more than a day or two; the assumption was that if they were clean and/or heavily made up, they might be engaging in prostitution (1969, p. 112).

Since the establishment of the first juvenile court, there has   7
been ongoing interest by judges and other court workers in the sexual activity of girls. In the early days of the court (1899–1920), there was a clear bias against girls deemed sexually active and a harsh official response to their misbehavior. Virtually all of the girls who appeared before the first juvenile courts were charged with immorality or waywardness (Chesney-Lind, 1971; Schloss-

man and Wallach, 1978; Shelden, 1981; Rafter 1990), and the response of the courts to this noncriminal behavior frequently was incarceration.

In Honolulu during 1929–1930, over half of the girls referred 8
to court were charged with immorality, which meant evidence (or inferences drawn) of sexual intercourse. In addition, another 30% were charged with waywardness. Evidence of immorality was vigorously pursued both by arresting officers and social workers through lengthy questioning of the girl and, if possible, males with whom she was suspected of having sex. Other evidence of exposure was provided by gynecological examinations, which were routinely ordered. Doctors, who understood the purpose of such examinations, would routinely note the condition of the hymen: "admits intercourse-hymen ruptured," "no laceration," and "hymen ruptured" were typical of their notations. Girls during this period were also twice as likely as boys to be detained, and they remained in detention five times as long on the average as their male counterparts. They were also nearly three times more likely to be sentenced to training schools (Chesney-Lind, 1971) where well into the 1950s they continued to be half of those committed in Honolulu (Chesney-Lind, 1973).

National statistics reflect the official enthusiasm for the incar- 9
ceration of girls during the early part of this century; their share of the population of juvenile correctional facilities increased from 1880 (when girls were 19% of the population) to 1923 (when girls were 28%). By 1950, girls had climbed to 34% of the total, and in 1960 they were still 27% of those in correctional facilities. By 1980, this pattern appeared to be reversed, and girls were again 19% of those in correctional facilities (Calahan, 1986, p. 130), and in 1989, girls accounted for 11.9% of those held in public detention centers and training schools (Allen-Hagen, 1991, p. 4).

The decline in incarceration of juvenile females in public facili- 10
ties run by the juvenile justice system is directly linked to an intense debate on the issue of the institutionalization of young people, especially youth charged with noncriminal status offenses (e.g., running away from home, being incorrigible, truant, or in danger of leading a lewd and lascivious lifestyle). In particular, the Juvenile Justice and Delinquency Prevention Act (JJDPA) of 1974 stressed the need to divert and deinstitutionalize youth charged

with status offenses and provided states with a number of incentives to achieve this goal.

Critical to any understanding of the dynamics of gender bias in   11
the juvenile justice system, then, is an appreciation of the gendered
nature of delinquency, and particularly status offenses. It should be
understood that status offenses have also served as "buffer charges"
for the court's historic, but now implicit, interest in monitoring
girls' sexual activities and their obedience to parental authority
(Gold, 1971, p. 571). In essence, modern status offense charges
mask the court's historic interest in girls' propriety and obedience
to parental authority (Chesney-Lind and Shelden, 1992).

Because of the recent but eroding success of the JJDPA of   12
1974, it is perhaps essential to review the dynamics of sexism
within the juvenile justice system immediately prior to the passage
of this act. The study reported here, although relatively modest,
documents one aspect of the sexism that girls encountered as they
entered institutions in the 1960s: the interest of criminal justice
professionals in the physical appearance of girls.

Data and Methods   This analysis is based on the records of   13
159 women who, as juveniles, were committed to the California
Youth Authority (CYA) during the 1960s. Records were requested on all 240 of the girls who were sentenced to the CYA
between 1961 and 1965 from San Francisco and the Sacramento
Valley. There were 59 cases unavailable because the juvenile
records had been purged and another 22 cases could not be located. For the 159 cases where data was available, the records included the complete CYA files containing all comments/reports
regarding the ward and the case by the CYA intake workers,
counselors, teachers, living unit personnel, chaplains, social workers, and psychologists (for more information regarding data collection, see Warren and Rosenbaum, 1986).

The racial composition of these 159 cases was 51% Caucasian,   14
30% African-American, 9% Latino, and the remaining 10% were
Asian or Native American. Two-thirds of the girls had been committed to the CYA for status offenses, and more specifically, 49%
were charged with running away from home, 28% for being "beyond control," 12% for "being in danger of a lewd and lascivious
lifestyle," 7% for truancy, and 4% for curfew. To say that these
girls were committed for status offenses actually understates the

role of status offenses in their delinquency records; this group of girls committed 698 offenses prior to their commitment to the CYA. The average number of arrests was six, and over 90% of these were status offenses. There were no racial differences observed in the distribution of these offenses.

Each file was examined by two independent coders who coded   15
data on the type of offenses committed prior to CYA commitment, the gender of the social worker who did the evaluation of the ward, whether mention was made of the ward's appearance, and if so, the description given of the girl's appearance.[1] Reliability among the coders was over 96%. Because all of the girls in the sample were part of an experimental program and were randomly assigned to treatment programs, the length of their incarceration was not coded.

Findings   Female case workers did intake evaluations on 29%   16
(46) of the 159 cases, whereas males were responsible for 71% (113) of them. When female CYA personnel conducted the intake evaluation, there was no mention of physical appearance in any of the 46 cases for which they were responsible. This was not the case when males performed the evaluation; appearance was mentioned in 63% (75) of the cases.

A variety of physical descriptions was recorded for the 75   17
wards whose appearance was mentioned in the files. These show male staff concern with the physical maturity of the girls, as well as some evidence of racial stereotyping; indeed, of those where evaluative judgments about appearance were made, 60% were made about minority group females. Moreover, those viewing these young women of color adhered to "representations of race" (hooks, 1992) that negate any beauty that does not conform to White standards of appearance, while celebrating those images that mimic White appearance.

From the descriptions of the girls' appearance, four general cat-   18
egories emerged: attractive, unattractive, plain/wholesome, and "well-built."[2] Of the wards whose appearance was mentioned, 26% (19) were described as attractive (e.g., "The ward is an attractive, physically mature 13-year-old"), whereas 38% (27) were described as unattractive (e.g., "Her appearance is rather uninteresting and unattractive"); 19% as plain or wholesome; and 17% (14) were described as well-built.

Differences emerged when the relationship between the type   19
of offense and the mention of appearance in the intake evaluations
was examined. About 50% (56) of the girls who had been evaluated by a male had at least one immorality charge against them.
When females who had been charged with immorality offenses
(being in danger of leading a lewd and lascivious life and prostitution) were compared with those who had no such charge,
differences in the mention of appearance became especially pronounced. For instance, for those charged with one or more
counts of immorality, a physical description was present in 93%
(55) of the cases. However, when no immorality charges were
present, a physical description was included in only 37% (20) of
the cases (see Table 1). Looking at the data from another perspective, in cases where no description of the girl's appearance was
present, 89% (34) had no charges of immorality. As indicated in
Table 1, a significant relationship ($\chi^2 = 37.5$) was found between
having at least one immorality charge and having mention made
of the girl's appearance in her file.

Differences also existed with respect to the type of offenses   20
present and the description given. All of the girls who were described as attractive and all of the girls who were described as
well-built had been charged with at least one immorality offense.
However, only 26% of the girls described as plain/wholesome and
34% of those described as unattractive had similar charges against
them. Although these numbers are small, the magnitude of the
difference is clearly significant.

More Recent Data   To assess whether or not appearance re-   21
mains an issue today, more recent data from the CYA was examined. In the process of collecting data from the CYA files of all
girls who were wards of the CYA in 1990, close attention was

TABLE 1: Appearance by Presence of Immorality Charges

	Appearance Described	No Description Included	
Immorality charges	93 (55)	7 (4)	100 (59)
No immorality charges	37 (20)	63 (34)	100 (54)

$\chi^2 = 37.4$, 1 *df*, significance = .000.

paid to any mention of the girl's appearance. Similar attention was paid in a separate examination of the case files of all boys and girls who were confined in the Hawaii Youth Correctional Facility in 1989.

Although there were 214 girls who were wards of the CYA in 22 1990, comments regarding appearance were found in only eight files. All, except one who was described as slovenly and unattractive, were simply described as attractive. Five of the eight had arrests for violent crime; the other three had long records for property and drug offenses. Although the vast majority of the girls' arrests during the 1960s were for status offenses, only 4% of their 1990 counterparts' arrests were for status offenses.

Comments found in girls' files in Hawaii concerned when and 23 where they had been arrested for curfew violations. This same research effort noted that no such comments appeared in boys' files and that a third of the girls held in training schools were being held solely for "probation violation," which is a mechanism for continuing to incarcerate status offenders (Saiki, 1990, p. 23). The Hawaii study found that roughly half of the girls incarcerated during spring 1990 were "bootstrapped" status offenders (Costello and Worthington, 1991) and even for those girls who had committed criminal offenses, their offenses were far less serious than the boys and "the bulk of their juvenile offenses consisted of status offenses" (Saiki, 1990, p. 48).

Discussion The emphasis on physical appearance found in 24 this small study and the link between this interest in girls' appearance and their noncriminal delinquent behavior is more important than it might first seem. In essence, these observations provide a window into the worldview of the keepers of young women during the years prior to the passage of the JJDPA of 1974; sadly, they may also reflect a bias that remains in the states that have been resistant to the deinstitutionalization efforts signaled by the passage of that act. Like earlier studies, which found a large number of girls in institutions subjected to physical examinations to determine if they were virgins (see Chesney-Lind and Shelden, 1992), interest in the physical appearance of girls, and particularly their physical maturity, indicates substantial interest in the sexual behavior of girls and illuminates another important dimension of the sexual policing of girls (Cain, 1989)

Particularly troubling are the comments which indicate a pre-   25
sumed association between "beauty," specifically male Caucasian
standards of beauty, and sexual behavior. Certainly the fact that
these girls were incarcerated for noncriminal offenses indicates the
seriousness with which the criminal justice system viewed their
transgressions. In short, these data provide some support for the notion, suggested by Sigall and Ostrove (1975), as well as that by
Efran (1974), that judges, social workers, and other criminal justice
professionals (particularly if they are male) may look upon attractive
girls who engage in sexual "immorality" more harshly. They may
also overlook some of the same behaviors in less attractive girls.

Such a fascination with appearance is also at odds with the liter-   26
ature on street prostitutes. These studies indicate that the pace and
pressure of this life does not produce "attractive" young women,
but instead tends to take a physical toll on the girls engaged in the
behavior (Weisberg, 1985, p. 116). Indeed, some descriptions of
prostitutes describe them as unattractive, overweight, with poor
complexions and bad teeth (Winick and Kinsie, 1972, p. 35).

The remarks found in the files which were made by male in-   27
take workers suggest a fascination with the appearance of the
girls who were charged with immorality. Clearly there was considerable concern with their physical maturity and physical attraction. The comments regarding the girls' appearance suggest
that status offenses may have functioned as buffer charges for
suspected sexual behavior. Although it appears that at least in
California, where girls are no longer incarcerated for noncriminal offenses, this no longer seems to be a problem, national data
suggest that in some states, like Hawaii, the detention and incarceration of girls for noncriminal status offenses persists; thus the
concerns raised by this article may, sadly, not be of simply historic interest.

References

Allen-Hagen, B. (1991). *Children in custody 1989*. Washington,
    DC: Bureau of Justice Statistics.
Cain, M. (1989). *Growing up good: Policing the behavior of girls in
    Europe*. London: Sage.
Calahan, M. W. (1986). *Historical corrections statistics in the United
    States 1950–1984*. Washington, DC: U.S. Department of Jus-
    tice.

Chesney-Lind, M. (1971). *Female juvenile delinquency in Hawaii.* Master's thesis, University of Hawaii at Manoa.

———. (1973). Judicial enforcement of the female sex role. *Issues in Criminology 8,* 51–70.

Chesney-Lind, M., & Shelden, R. (1992). *Girls, delinquency, and the juvenile justice system.* Pacific Grove, CA: Brooks/Cole.

Clifford, M., & Walster, E. (1973). The effect of physical attractiveness on teacher expectations. *Sociology of Education 46,* 248–258.

Costello, J. C., & Worthington, N. L. (1991). Incarcerating status offenders: Attempts to circumvent the Juvenile Justice and Delinquency Prevention Act. *Harvard Civil Rights-Civil Liberties Law Review 16,* 41–81

Crause, B. B., & Mehrabian, A. (1977). Affiliation of opposite-sexed strangers. *Journal of Research in Personality 11,* 38–47.

Dion, K. (1973). Physical attractiveness and evaluation of children's transgressions. *Journal of Personality and Social Psychology 24,* 207–218.

Dion, K., Berscheid, E., & Walster, E. (1973) What is beautiful is good. *Journal of Personality and Social Psychology 24,* 285–290.

Efran, M. (1974). The effect of physical appearance on the judgment of guilt, interpersonal attraction, and severity of recommended punishment. *Journal of Experimental Research in Personality 8,* 45–54.

Emerson, R. (1969). *Judging delinquents.* Chicago: Aldine.

Flanagan, T. J., & McGarrell, E. F., eds. (1986). *Sourcebook of criminal justice statistics—1985.* Washington, DC: U.S. Department of Justice.

Gold, S. (1971). Equal protection for girls in need of supervision in New York State. *New York Law Forum 17,* 570–591.

Heilman, M., & Sarawatari, L. (1979). When beauty is beastly: The effects of appearance and sex on evaluations of job applicants for managerial and nonmanagerial jobs. *Organizational Behavior and Human Performance 23,* 360–372.

Heilman, M., & Stopeck, M. (1985). Attractiveness and corporate success: Different casual attributions for males and females. *Journal of Applied Psychology 70,* 379–388.

hooks, b. (1992). *Black looks.* Boston: South End Press.

Jamieson, K. M., & Flanagan, T., eds. (1987). *Sourcebook of criminal justice statistics—1986.* Washington, DC: U.S. Department of Justice, Bureau of Justice Statistics.

Murstein, B., & Christy, P. (1976). Physical attractiveness and marriage adjustment in middle aged couples. *Journal of Personality and Social Psychology 34*, 537–542.

Price, R., & Vandenberg, S. (1979). Matching for physical attractiveness in married couples. *Personality and Social Psychology Bulletin 5*, 398–399.

Rafter, N. (1990). *Partial justice: Women, prisons and social control.* New Brunswick, NJ: Transaction Books.

Saiki, S. (1990). Girls, double standards and status offenses in Hawaii's juvenile court. Unpublished paper. William Richardson School of Law, University of Hawaii.

Schlossman, S., & Wallach, S. (1978). The crime of precocious sexuality: Female delinquency in the progressive era. *Harvard Educational Review 48*, 65–94.

Shelden, R. (1981). Sex discrimination in the juvenile justice system: Memphis, Tennessee, 1900–1971. In *Comparing male and female offenders*, edited by M. Q. Warren. Beverly Hills, CA: Sage.

Sigall, H., & Ostrove, N. (1975). Beautiful but dangerous: Effects of offender attractiveness and nature of crime on juridic judgment. *Journal of Personality and Social Psychology 31*, 410–414.

Stewart, J. (1980). Defendant's attraction as a factor in the outcome of criminal trials: An observational study. *Journal of Applied Social Psychology 10*, 348–361.

Stretch, R., & Figley, C. (1980). Beauty and the beast: Predictions of interpersonal attraction in a dating experiment. *Psychology, a Quarterly Journal of Human Behavior 17*, 34–43.

Walster, E., Aronson, E., Abrahams, D., & Rottman, L. (1966). Importance of physical attractiveness in dating behavior. *Journal of Personality and Social Psychology 4*, 508–516.

Warren, M. Q., & Rosenbaum, J. (1986). Criminal careers of female offenders. *Criminal Justice and Behavior 13*, 393–418.

Weisberg, D. K. (1985). *Children of the night: A study of adolescent prostitution.* Lexington, MA: Lexington Books.

White, G. (1980). Physical attractiveness and courtship progress. *Journal of Personality and Social Psychology 39*, 660–668.

Winick, C., & Kinsie, P. M. (1972). *The lively commerce.* New York: Signet.

Notes

1. Nowhere on any of the CYA forms was there any particular place for a physical description of the ward. Comments were found throughout the narratives by the CYA personnel who became involved with the case. As far as we can tell, the issue of appearance was never discussed with regard to policy. It seemed to be merely an issue for the intake personnel.
2. These categories are broad and somewhat evasive; however, they were the factors that emerged during this analysis. It is important to remember that attractiveness is in the eye of the beholder and we, as researchers, are merely reporting the subjective assessments that we found.

UNDERSTANDING DETAILS

1. What do Rosenbaum and Chesney-Lind mean when they argue that "women are judged by culturally derived standards of attractiveness" (paragraph 1)?
2. How does being attractive usually affect judgments in the criminal justice system?
3. What expectations does society have of attractive people? Which sources do Rosenbaum and Chesney-Lind cite to verify these expectations?
4. What are "status acts"? In what ways did the Juvenile Justice and Delinquency Prevention Act (JJDPA) of 1974 affect the court's reaction to status acts?

ANALYZING MEANING

1. Can you explain the relationship the researchers found between appearance and immorality charges in California Youth Authority (CYA) females? Why do you think this relationship existed?
2. What effect do the recent data show the Juvenile Justice and Delinquency Prevention Act had on immorality charges since 1990? Can you explain this change?
3. Are males ever unfairly treated because of their appearance? If so, in what situations? Explain your answer in detail.

4. Can you speculate about the future of status and immorality offenses? Do you think they will continue to be connected to descriptions of appearance in female criminal records?

DISCOVERING RHETORICAL STRATEGIES

1. Who do you think is Rosenbaum and Chesney-Lind's main audience? How did you come to this conclusion?
2. The authors begin their essay by citing various professional sources that verify the connections in American society between appearance and success in various aspects of life. Is this an effective beginning for what Rosenbaum and Chesney-Lind are trying to accomplish? Explain your answer.
3. What information in this essay is most persuasive to you? Least persuasive?
4. What tone do the authors establish by citing statistics and referring to other sources in their essay?

MAKING CONNECTIONS

1. If Rosenbaum and Chesney-Lind were having a conversation about sexism with Judy Brady ("Why I Want a Wife"), what issues would the three writers agree on? What would they disagree on?
2. Compare and contrast the way Rosenbaum and Chesney-Lind use statistics and documentation in their argument with the use of this technique by Barbara Ehrenreich ("The Ecstasy of War"). Which author provides such information most skillfully? Explain your answer.
3. Examine the balance in Rosenbaum and Chesney-Lind's essay among logical, emotional, and ethical appeals. Then compare and contrast it with the balance in essays by Shelby Steele ("Affirmative Action: The Price of Preference") and Mitchell Stephens ("The Death of Reading"). Which author uses the most logic? Who uses emotion most? And whose ethical appeal is strongest? Which author do you find most convincing? Explain your answer.

IDEAS FOR DISCUSSION/WRITING

Preparing to Write

Write freely about your views on the relationship between appearance and delinquency: What role does the notion of appearance play in the justice system? Should it be a part of the system? When would it be appropriate? When would it be inappropriate? Do you find that you have certain biases regarding people's appearances? What are they? Do you know others who hold biases about attractiveness? Do the biases verge on sexism? Do they involve both males and females? What do these biases say about our society in general?

Choosing a Topic

1. Design a constructive solution to the problem of sexist criminal reports. Then, using Rosenbaum and Chesney-Lind's essay as your main source, write an argumentative essay presenting the problem as you understand it and offering a detailed solution to it. Cite Rosenbaum and Chesney-Lind's essay whenever necessary.

2. What do you think the role of appearance and behavior should be in America's judicial system? Use Rosenbaum and Chesney-Lind's article as one of your sources; then, read further on the subject. Finally, write a clear, well-documented argument on what part appearance and behavior should play in the court's judgment of criminals. Organize your paper carefully, and present your suggestions logically, using proper documentation (citations and bibliography) to support your position.

3. Choose another problem related to the American system of justice, and research it further. Then, write a well-documented argument explaining the problem and offering a solution based on the information you have discovered.

Before beginning your essay, you might want to consult the checklists on pages 582–583.

CHAPTER WRITING ASSIGNMENTS

Practicing Pro/Con

1. In what ways can the Internet benefit college students? How could the Internet pose problems for students? Research this topic. Then, in an essay, explore the advantages and disadvantages of the Internet for students. Provide examples to illustrate your points.

2. How well do you think national news broadcasts inform the public? Do they focus too much on negative rather than positive events in life? Investigate the role of television news over the last ten years. Then write an essay in which you review its history and discuss the role it should play in American society today.

3. What are the primary advantages and disadvantages of pursuing an online education or degree? After studying this option, write an essay discussing the reasons this type of education may benefit or hinder students and whether it is a worthwhile educational option.

Exploring Ideas

1. While voters often approve measures for funding more prisons, they are just as likely to vote against measures proposing to build new schools. As a society, should we work harder to fund new prisons, to build new schools, or to fund each equally? Research these options, and explain your view in a well-reasoned essay.

2. Most experts agree that young children learn languages easily, while older teens and adults often struggle to learn a new language. Should children be taught more than one language in elementary school so that they can become bilingual early in life? Or does a single language give the students an advantage in the school system? Investigate these options, and write an essay that explains why bilingual education for all children would or would not benefit their education.

3. In what ways is violence natural or unnatural to society? How does society promote or prohibit violence? Look into this issue. Then write an essay presenting your view about the ways violence may or may not be inherent in society.

11

Essays on Thinking, Reading, and Writing

In each of the preceding chapters, we have examined a single rhetorical mode in order to focus attention on how writers use that pattern to organize their thoughts. In this final chapter, ten essays on the topics of thinking, reading, and writing demonstrate a combination of rhetorical modes at work in each selection.

Our primary purpose in this text has been to show how thinking, reading, and writing work together as fine machinery to help all of us function as intelligent and productive human beings. Our introduction discusses the relationship of thinking, reading, and writing; the text itself illustrates the crucial interdependence of these skills; and this last chapter concludes the book by presenting essays by some of America's best writers on such related topics as listening, reading fiction, understanding the writing process, writing "with style," and the impact of technology on thinking, reading, and writing.

These essays are intended for you to read and enjoy, letting your mind run freely through the material as you recall in a leisurely way what you have learned in this text. They bring together the theoretical framework of this text as they illustrate how thinking, reading, and writing inform each other and work interdependently to make meaning. And they integrate the rhetorical patterns in such a way that each essay is a complex blend of the various rhetorical modes discussed in the preceding chapters— a perfect summary of the topics and strategies you have been working with throughout this text.

ROGER ROSENBLATT   (1940–)

"I Am Writing Blindly"

Besides the newsworthy revelation of Lieut. Captain Dimitri   1
Kolesnikov's dying message to his wife recovered from the
husk of the sunken submarine *Kursk*—that 23 of the 118
crewmen had survived in an isolated chamber for a while, in contradiction to claims by Russian officials that all had perished within
minutes of the accident—there was the matter of writing the message in the first place.

In the first place, in the last place, that is what we people do—   2
write messages to one another. We are a narrative species. We
exist by storytelling—by relating our situations—and the test of
our evolution may lie in getting the story right.

What Kolesnikov did in deciding to describe his position and   3
entrapment, others have also done—in states of repose or terror.
When a JAL airliner went down in 1985, passengers used the long
minutes of its terrible, spiraling descent to write letters to loved
ones. When the last occupants of the Warsaw Ghetto had finally
seen their families and companions die of disease or starvation, or
be carried off in trucks to extermination camps, and there could be
no doubt of their own fate, still they took scraps of paper on which
they wrote poems, thoughts, fragments of lives, rolled them into
tight scrolls, and slipped them into the crevices of the ghetto walls.

Why did they bother? With no countervailing news from the   4
outside world, they assumed the Nazis had inherited the earth; that
if anyone discovered their writings, it would be their killers, who
would snicker and toss them away. They wrote because, like
Kolesnikov, they had to. The impulse was in them, like a biological fact.

So enduring is this storytelling need that it shapes nearly every   5
human endeavor. Businesses depend on the stories told of past
failures and successes and on the myth of the mission of the company. In medicine, doctors increasingly rely on a patient's narrative of the progress of an ailment, which is inevitably more
nuanced and useful than the data of machines. In law, the same
thing. Every court case is a competition of tales told by the prosecutor and defense attorney; the jury picks the one it likes best.

All these activities derive from essential places in us. Psy- 6
chologist Jerome Bruner says children acquire language in order to
tell the stories that are already in them. We do our learning
through storytelling processes. The man who arrives at our door is
thought to be a salesman because his predecessor was a salesman.
When the patternmaking faculties fail, the brain breaks down.
Schizophrenics suffer from a loss of story.

The deep proof of our need to spill, and keep on spilling, lies 7
in reflex, often in desperate circumstances. A number of years ago,
Jean-Dominique Bauby, the editor of *Elle* magazine in Paris, was
felled by a stroke so destructive that the only part of his body that
could move was his left eyelid. Flicking that eyelid, he managed to
signal the letters of the alphabet, and proceeded to write his autobiography, *The Diving Bell and the Butterfly,* with the last grand gesture of his life.

All this is of acute and consoling interest to writers, whose odd 8
existences are ordinarily strung between asking why we do it and
doing it incessantly. The explanation I've been able to come up
with has to do with freedom. You write a sentence, the basic unit
of storytelling, and you are never sure where it will lead. The
readers will not know where it leads either. Your adventure becomes theirs, eternally recapitulated in tandem—one wild ride together. Even when you come to the end of the sentence, that dot,
it is still strangely inconclusive. I sometimes think one writes to
find God in every sentence. But God (the ironist) always lives in
the next sentence.

It is this freedom of the message sender and receiver that con- 9
nects them—sailor to wife, the dying to the living. Writing has
been so important in America, I think, because communication is
the soul and engine of democracy. To write is to live according to
one's terms. If you ask me to be serious, I will be frivolous.
Magnanimous? Petty. Cynical? I will be a brazen believer in all
things. Whatever you demand I will not give you—unless it is
with the misty hope that what I give you is not what you ask for
but what you want.

We use this freedom to break the silence, even of death, even 10
when—in the depths of our darkest loneliness—we have no clear
idea of why we reach out to one another with these frail, perish-
able chains of words. In the black chamber of the submarine,
Kolesnikov noted, "I am writing blindly." Like everyone else.

EUDORA WELTY (1909–)

Listening

I learned from the age of two or three that any room in our house, at any time of day, was there to read in, or to be read to. My mother read to me. She'd read to me in the big bedroom in the mornings, when we were in her rocker together, which ticked in rhythm as we rocked, as though we had a cricket accompanying the story. She'd read to me in the diningroom on winter afternoons in front of the coal fire, with our cuckoo clock ending the story with "Cuckoo," and at night when I'd got in my own bed. I must have given her no peace. Sometimes she read to me in the kitchen while she sat churning, and the churning sobbed along with *any* story. It was my ambition to have her read to me while *I* churned; once she granted my wish, but she read off my story before I brought her butter. She was an expressive reader. When she was reading "Puss in Boots," for instance, it was impossible not to know that she distrusted *all* cats.

It had been startling and disappointing to me to find out that story books had been written by *people*, that books were not natural wonders, coming up of themselves like grass. Yet regardless of where they came from, I cannot remember a time when I was not in love with them—with the books themselves, cover and binding and the paper they were printed on, with their smell and their weight and with their possession in my arms, captured and carried off to myself. Still illiterate, I was ready for them, committed to all the reading I could give them.

Neither of my parents had come from homes that could afford to buy many books, but though it must have been something of a strain on his salary, as the youngest officer in a young insurance company, my father was all the while carefully selecting and ordering away for what he and Mother thought we children should grow up with. They bought first for the future.

Besides the bookcase in the living room, which was always called "the library," there were the encyclopedia tables and dictionary stand under windows in our diningroom. Here to help us grow up arguing around the diningroom table were the *Unabridged Webster,* the *Columbia Encyclopedia, Compton's Pictured*

Encyclopedia, the *Lincoln Library of Information,* and later the *Book of Knowledge.* And the year we moved into our new house, there was room to celebrate it with the new 1925 edition of the *Britannica,* which my father, his face always deliberately turned toward the future, was of course disposed to think better than any previous edition.

In "the library," inside the mission-style bookcase with its three   5
diamond-latticed glass doors, with my father's Morris chair and the glass-shaded lamp on its table beside it, were books I could soon begin on—and I did, reading them all alike and as they came, straight down their rows, top shelf to bottom. There was the set of *Stoddard's Lectures,* in all its late nineteenth-century vocabulary and vignettes of peasant life and quaint beliefs and customs, with matching halftone illustrations: Vesuvius erupting, Venice by moonlight, gypsies glimpsed by their campfires. I didn't know then the clue they were to my father's longing to see the rest of the world. I read straight through his other love-from-afar: the *Victrola Book of the Opera,* with opera after opera in synopsis, with portraits in costume of Melba, Caruso, Galli-Curci, and Geraldine Farrar, some of whose voices we could listen to on our Red Seal records.

My mother read secondarily for information; she sank as a he-   6
donist into novels. She read Dickens in the spirit in which she would have eloped with him. The novels of her girlhood that had stayed on in her imagination, besides those of Dickens and Scott and Robert Louis Stevenson, were *Jane Eyre, Trilby, The Woman in White, Green Mansions, King Solomon's Mines.* Marie Corelli's name would crop up but I understood she had gone out of favor with my mother, who had only kept *Ardath* out of loyalty. In time she absorbed herself in Galsworthy, Edith Wharton, above all in Thomas Mann of the *Joseph* volumes.

St. Elmo was not in our house; I saw it often in other houses.   7
This wildly popular Southern novel is where all the Edna Earles in our population started coming from. They're all named for the heroine, who succeeded in bringing a dissolute, sinning roué and atheist of a lover (St. Elmo) to his knees. My mother was able to forgo it. But she remembered the classic advice given to rose growers on how to water their bushes long enough: "Take a chair and *St. Elmo.*"

To both my parents I owe my early acquaintance with a 8
beloved Mark Twain. There was a full set of Mark Twain and a
short set of Ring Lardner in our bookcase, and those were the volumes that in time united us all, parents and children.

Reading everything that stood before me was how I came upon 9
a worn old book without a back that had belonged to my father as
a child. It was called *Sanford and Merton*. Is there anyone left who
recognizes it, I wonder? It is the famous moral tale written by
Thomas Day in the 1780s, but of him no mention is made on the
title page of *this* book; here it is *Sanford and Merton in Words of One
Syllable* by Mary Godolphin. Here are the rich boy and the poor boy
and Mr. Barlow, their teacher and interlocutor, in long discourses
alternating with dramatic scenes—danger and rescue allotted to the
rich and the poor respectively. It may have only words of one syllable, but one of them is "quoth." It ends with not one but two
morals, both engraved on rings: "Do what you ought, come what
may," and "If we would be great, we must first learn to be good."

This book was lacking its front cover, the back held on by strips 10
of pasted paper, now turned golden, in several layers, and the
pages stained, flecked, and tattered around the edges; its garish illustrations had come unattached but were preserved, laid in. I had
the feeling even in my heedless childhood that this was the only
book my father as a little boy had had of his own. He had held
onto it and might have gone to sleep on its coverless face: He had
lost his mother when he was seven. My father had never made any
mention to his own children of the book, but he had brought it
along with him from Ohio to our house and shelved it in our
bookcase.

My mother had brought from West Virginia that set of 11
Dickens; those books looked sad, too—they had been through fire
and water before I was born, she told me, and there they were,
lined up—as I later realized, waiting for *me*.

I was presented, from as early as I can remember, with books of 12
my own, which appeared on my birthday and Christmas morning.
Indeed, my parents could not give me books enough. They must
have sacrificed to give me on my sixth or seventh birthday—it was
after I became a reader for myself—the ten-volume set of *Our
Wonder World*. These were beautifully made, heavy books I would
lie down with on the floor in front of the diningroom hearth, and

more often than the rest volume 5, *Every Child's Story Book*, was under my eyes. There were the fairy tales—Grimm, Andersen, the English, the French, "Ali Baba and the Forty Thieves"; and there was Aesop and Reynard the Fox; there were the myths and legends, Robin Hood, King Arthur, and St. George and the Dragon, even the history of Joan of Arc; a whack of *Pilgrim's Progress* and a long piece of *Gulliver*. They all carried their classic illustrations. I located myself in these pages and could go straight to the stories and pictures I loved; very often "The Yellow Dwarf" was first choice, with Walter Crane's Yellow Dwarf in full color making his terrifying appearance flanked by turkeys. Now that volume is as worn and backless and hanging apart as my father's poor *Sanford and Merton*. The precious page with Edward Lear's "Jumblies" on it has been in danger of slipping out for all these years. One measure of my love for *Our Wonder World* was that for a long time I wondered if I would go through fire and water for it as my mother had done for Charles Dickens; and the only comfort was to think I could ask my mother to do it for me.

I believe I'm the only child I know of who grew up with this   13 treasure in the house. I used to ask others, "Did you have *Our Wonder World*?" I'd have to tell them *The Book of Knowledge* could not hold a candle to it.

I live in gratitude to my parents for initiating me—and as early   14 as I begged for it, without keeping me waiting—into knowledge of the word, into reading and spelling, by way of the alphabet. They taught it to me at home in time for me to begin to read before starting to school. I believe the alphabet is no longer considered an essential piece of equipment for traveling through life. In my day it was the keystone to knowledge. You learned the alphabet as you learned to count to ten, as you learned "Now I lay me" and the Lord's Prayer and your father's and mother's name and address and telephone number, all in case you were lost.

My love for the alphabet, which endures, grew out of reciting   15 it but, before that, out of seeing the letters on the page. In my own story books, before I could read them for myself, I fell in love with various winding, enchanted-looking initials drawn by Walter Crane at the heads of fairy tales. In "Once upon a time," an "O" had a rabbit running it as a treadmill, his feet upon flowers.

When the day came, years later, for me to see the *Book of Kells*, all the wizardry of letter, initial, and word swept over me a thousand times over, and the illumination, the gold, seemed a part of the word's beauty and holiness that had been there from the start.

DIANE RUSSO CODY   (1948–   )

Good Reasons to Hone Your Writing Skills: Tips for Getting Along and Working Better

A memo appears on your desk. It was written by someone 1
you consider to be bright and knowledgeable. But you
don't quite get the point of the memo. It seems to ramble,
isn't organized, and doesn't come to any conclusion or make any
recommendations. You don't understand why. This person is extremely articulate over the phone or in meetings. Now you're
wondering just how capable this person really is.

Many a career has ground to a halt because of poor writing 2
skills. Improving your ability to communicate on paper can improve your chances of advancing. There are other reasons why
you should learn to write well. Here are some of them:

1. **Your writing precedes you and may gain you entry into** 3
   places you've never been. For example, when you write
   your résumé or job inquiry letters, your skills and intelligence
   are judged before you're seen. And the reports and memos
   you write may reach your company president's office—even
   if you've never been there. He or she may call you in to explain a point or perhaps to compliment you on a job well
   done.
2. **Writing thoughts down helps you organize them.** Some- 4
   times there's no better way to spot a flaw in a plan than by
   putting it down on paper. That's why costly and far-reaching
   business plans are always put in writing.
3. **Your powers of concentration increase.** Writing channels 5
   your thinking. You're forced to concentrate on the problem
   or task at hand. It keeps your mind from straying, and if you
   do stray, you need only read what you've written to get back
   on track.
4. **Good writing gets you noticed.** If you can compose a hard- 6
   hitting letter or memo, word will spread. Your boss will rely on
   you and your talents. He or she may recommend you when
   someone is needed for important projects that require a skilled
   communicator. You'll become known for your ability.

5. **You'll build a backlog of favors.** Good writers are often 7
sought out by members of other departments. As you help others, you'll build a network—people you can go to when you
need assistance on projects or tasks they do well. You can trade
favors.

These are just some of the reasons you should take the time to 8
hone your ability to write. Seize every opportunity to show off
your skills—because the more you write, the better you get.

DONALD HALL   (1928–   )

To Read Fiction

When we learn to read fiction, we acquire a pleasure and   1
a resource we never lose. Although literary study is im-
practical in one sense—few people make their living
reading books—in another sense it is almost as practical as breathing. Literature records and embodies centuries of human thought
and feeling, preserving for us the minds of people who lived before us, who were like us and unlike us, against whom we can
measure our common humanity and our historical difference. And
when we read the stories of our contemporaries, they illuminate
the world all of us share.

When we read great literature, something changes in us that   2
stays changed. Literature remembered becomes material to think
with. No one who has read *The Death of Ivan Ilych* well is quite the
same again. Reading adds tools by which we observe, measure,
and judge the people and the properties of our universe, we understand the actions and motives of others and of ourselves.

In the fable of the ant and the grasshopper, the wise ant builds   3
his storehouse against winter and prospers; the foolish grasshopper
saves nothing and perishes. Anyone who dismisses the study of literature on the ground that it will not be useful—to a chemist or
an engineer, to a foreman or an x-ray technician—imitates the
grasshopper. When we shut from our lives everything except food
and shelter, part of us starves to death. Food for this hunger is
music, painting, film, plays, poems, stories, and novels. Much
writing in newspapers, magazines, and popular novels is not literature, if we reserve that word for work of high quality. This reading gives us as little nourishment as most television and most fast
food. For the long winters and energetic summers of our lives, we
require the sustenance of literature.

Reading fiction old and new—taking into ourselves the work   4
of nineteenth-century Russian, contemporary English, Irish, and
especially American storytellers—we build a storehouse of knowledge and we entertain ourselves as well. But to take pleasure and
understanding from fiction we have to learn how to read it. No
one expects to walk up to a computer and be able to program it
without first learning something about computers. For some reason—perhaps because we are familiar with words from childhood

and take them for granted—we tend to think that a quick glance at the written word should reward us and that if we do not take instant satisfaction the work is beyond us, or not worth it, or irrelevant or boring. But all our lives, in other skills, we have needed instruction and practice—to be able to ride a bicycle, drive a car, play guitar, shoot baskets, typewrite, dance.

The knowledge we derive from literature can seem confusing.   5 Equally great works may contradict each other in the generalizations we derive from them. One work may recommend solitude, another society. One may advise us to seize the moment, another to live a life of contemplation. Or, two good readers may disagree about the implication of a work and each argue convincingly, with detailed references to the writing, in support of contrary interpretations. A complex work of fiction cannot be reduced to a simple, correct meaning. In an elementary arithmetic text, the answers may be printed in the back of the book. There are no answers to be printed in the back of . . . any collection of literature.

Such nebulousness, or ambiguity, disturbs some students. After   6 an hour's class discussion of a short story, with varying interpretations offered, they want to know "But what *does* it mean?" We must admit that literature is inexact, and its truth is not easily verifiable. Probably the story means several things at once, and not one thing at all. This is not to say, however, that it means anything that anybody finds in it. Although differing, equally defensible opinions are common, error is even more common.

When we speak of truth in the modern world, we usually mean   7 something scientific or tautological. Arithmetic contains the truth of tautology; two and two make four because our definitions of *two* and *four* say so. In laboratories we encounter the truth of statistics and the truth of observation. If we smoke cigarettes heavily, it is true that we have one chance in four to develop lung cancer. When we heat copper wire over a Bunsen burner, the flame turns blue.

But there is an older sense of truth, in which statements apparently opposite can be valid. In this older tradition, truth is dependent on context and circumstance, on the agreement of sensible men and women—like the "Guilty" or "Not guilty" verdict of a jury. Because this literary (or philosophical, or legal, or historical) truth is inexact, changeable, and subject to argument, literature can seem nebulous to minds accustomed to arithmetical certainty.

Let me argue this: If literature is nebulous or inexact; if it is im-   9
possible to determine, with scientific precision, the value or the
meaning of a work of art, *this inexactness is the price literature pays for
representing whole human beings.* Human beings themselves, in their
feelings and thoughts, in the wandering of their short lives, are
ambiguous and ambivalent, shifting mixtures of permanence and
change, direction and disorder. Because literature is true to life,
true to the complexities of human feeling, different people will
read the same work with different responses. And the storyteller's
art will sometimes affirm that opposite things are both true *because
they are.* Such a condition is not tidy; it is perhaps regrettable—but
it is human nature.

What's Good, What's Bad

The claims I make for fiction are large: that it alters and enlarges   10
our minds, our connections with each other past and present, our
understanding of our own feelings. These claims apply to excellent
literature only. This . . . suggests that some fiction is better than
other fiction, and that some narratives are not literature at all. Even
if judgments are always subject to reversal, even if there is no way
we can be certain of being correct, evaluation lives at the center
of literary study.

When I was nineteen, I liked to read everything: science fic-   11
tion, Russian novels, mystery stories, great poems, adventure magazines. Then for six months after an accident, sentenced to a hospital bed and a body cast, I set myself a reading list, all serious
books I had been thinking about getting to. Of course there was a
background to this choice: I had been taught by a good teacher
who had directed and encouraged and stimulated my reading. I
read through Shakespeare, the Bible in the King James version,
novels by Henry James and Ernest Hemingway and William
Faulkner. Toward the end of six months, taking physical therapy,
I hurried to finish the books I had assigned myself; I looked forward to taking a vacation among private detectives and adventur-
ers of the twenty-fourth century. I thought I would take a holiday
of light reading.

When I tried to read the light things, I experienced one of those   12
"turning points in life" we are asked to describe in freshman composition. I remember the dismay, the abject melancholy that crept
over me as I realized—restless, turning from book to book in

search of entertainment—that these books bored me; that I was ruined for life, that I would never again lose myself to stick-figure characters and artificial suspense. Literature ruined me for light reading. . . .

I don't mean to say that I was able to give reasons why Fyodor   13 Dostoyevsky's novel about a murder was better than Agatha Christie's or why Aldous Huxley's view of the future, though less exciting, was more satisfying than *Astounding Science Fiction*'s. But I began a lifetime of trying to figure out why. What *is* it that makes Chekhov so valuable to us? The struggle to name reasons for value—to evaluate works of art—is lifelong, and although we may never arrive at satisfactory explanations, the struggle makes the mind more sensitive, more receptive to the next work of literature it encounters. And as the mind becomes more sensitive and receptive to literature, it may become more sensitive and receptive to all sorts of things.

VINTON CERF   (1943–)

What Will Replace the Internet?

The Internet seems to have just arrived, so how can we possibly imagine what will replace it? In truth, early versions of the Net have been around since the 1960s and '70s, but only after the mid-1990s did it begin to have a serious public impact. Since 1994, the population of users has grown from about 13 million to more than 300 million around the world. About half are in North America, and most—despite significant progress in rolling out high-speed access—still reach the Internet by way of the public telephone network.

What will the Internet be like 20 years from now? Like the rest of infrastructure, the Internet will eventually seem to disappear by becoming ubiquitous. Most access will probably be via high-speed, low-power radio links. Most handheld, fixed, and mobile appliances will be Internet enabled. This trend is already discernible in the form of Internet-enabled cell phones and personal digital assistants. Like the servants of centuries past, our household helpers will chatter with one another and with the outside help.

At some point, the armada of devices we strap to our bodies like tools on Batman's belt will coalesce into a smaller number of multifunction devices. Equipped with radio links, a PDA can serve as an appliance-control remote, a digital wallet, a cell phone, an identity badge, an e-mail station, a digital book, a pager, and perhaps even a digital camera. There is sure to be a catchy name for this all-purpose Internet-enabled thingy, perhaps Wireless Internet Digital Gadget for Electronic Transactions, or WIDGET.

So many appliances, vehicles, and buildings will be online by 2020 that it seems likely there will be more things on the Internet than people. Internet-enabled cars and airplanes are coming online, and smart houses are being built every day. Eventually, programmable devices will become so cheap that we will embed them in the cardboard boxes into which we put other things for storage or shipping. These passive "computers" will be activated as they pass sensors and will be able to both emit and absorb information. Such innovations will facilitate increasingly automatic manufacturing, inventory control, shipping, and distribution. Checkout at the grocery store will be fully automatic, as will payment via your digital wallet.

The advent of programmable, nanoscale machines will extend 5 the Internet to things the size of molecules that can be injected under the skin, leading to Internet-enabled people. Such devices, together with Internet-enabled sensors embedded in clothing, will avoid a hospital stay for medical patients who would otherwise be there only for observation. The speech processor used today in cochlear implants for the hearing impaired could easily be connected to the Internet; listening to Internet radio could soon be a direct computer-to-brain experience!

The Internet will undergo substantial alteration as optical tech- 6 nologies allow the transmission of many trillions of bits per second on each strand of the Internet's fiber-optic backbone network. The core of the network will remain optical, and the edges will use a mix of access technologies, ranging from radio and infrared to optical fiber and the old twisted-pair copper telephone lines. By then, the Internet will have been extended, by means of an interplanetary Internet backbone, to operate in outer space.

How will this pervasive Internet access affect our daily lives? 7 More and more of the world's information will be accessible instantly and from virtually anywhere. In an emergency, our health records will be available for remote medical consultation with specialists and perhaps even remote surgery. More and more devices will have access to the global positioning system, increasing the value of geographically indexed databases. Using GPS with speech-understanding software that is emerging today, we will be able to get directions from our WIDGETS as easily as we once got them at a filling station. One can imagine driving in the car, asking our WIDGET for the name of the nearest Thai restaurant, getting an answer, asking for reservations and then for directions. Indeed, the car may be smart enough to handle the entire transaction and drive us there itself.

Is there any downside to a society suffused with information 8 and the tools to process it? Privacy will come at a premium. Enormous quantities of data about our daily affairs will flow across the Internet, working to make our lives easier. Despite our penchant for giving up privacy in exchange for convenience, our experiences online may make us yearn for the anonymity of the past. Who should have access to our medical records and our financial information, and how will that access be controlled? Will we be able to search and use the vast information stored online without leaving trails of personal cookie crumbs scattered across the Net? How will business transactions be taxed, and in what jurisdictions will disputed electronic transactions be resolved? How will intellectual property be protected? How will we prove that contracts were signed on a certain date, or that their terms and conditions have not been electronically altered? There are technical answers for many of these questions, but some require international agreements before they can be resolved.

Perhaps even more daunting, in the face of Internet-wide virus   9
attacks, is the realization that we will depend in larger and larger measure on the network's functioning reliably. Making this system of millions of networks sufficiently robust and resilient is a challenge for the present generation of Internet engineers. Failure could portend an increasingly fragile future. But I am an optimist. I believe we are going to live in a world abundant with information and with the tools needed to use it wisely.

NATALIE GOLDBERG

Rules of Writing Practice

For fifteen years now, at the beginning of every writing work- 1
shop, I have repeated the rules for writing practice. So, I will
repeat them again here. And I want to say why I repeat them:
Because they are the bottom line, the beginning of all writing, the
foundation of learning to trust your own mind. Trusting your own
mind is essential for writing. Words come out of the mind.

And I believe in these rules. Perhaps I'm a little fanatical about 2
them.

A friend, teasing me, said, "You act as if they are the rules to 3
live by, as though they apply to everything."

I smiled. "Okay, let's try it. Do they apply to sex?" 4

I stuck up my thumb for rule number one. "Keep your hand 5
moving." I nodded yes.

Index finger, rule number two. "Be specific." I let out a yelp of 6
glee. It was working.

Finger number three. "Lose control." It was clear that sex and 7
writing were the same thing.

Then, number four. "Don't think," I said. Yes, for sex, too, I 8
nodded.

I proved my point. My friend and I laughed. 9

Go ahead, try these rules for tennis, hang gliding, driving a car, 10
making a grilled cheese sandwich, disciplining a dog or a snake.
Okay. They might not always work. They work for writing. Try
them.

1. *Keep your hand moving.* When you sit down to write, whether 11
   it's for ten minutes or an hour, once you begin, don't stop. If
   an atom bomb drops at your feet eight minutes after you have
   begun and you were going to write for ten minutes, don't
   budge. You'll go out writing.

   What is the purpose of this? Most of the time when we 12
   write, we mix up the editor and creator. Imagine your writing
   hand as the creator and the other hand as the editor. Now bring
   your two hands together and lock your fingers. This is what
   happens when we write. The writing hand wants to write

about what she did Saturday night: "I drank whiskey straight all night and stared at a man's back across the bar. He was wearing a red T-shirt. I imagined him to have the face of Harry Belafonte. At three A.M., he finally turned my way, and I spit into the ashtray when I saw him. He had the face of a wet mongrel who had lost his teeth." The writing hand is three words into writing this first sentence—"I drank whiskey . . ."— when the other hand clenches her fingers tighter and the writing hand can't budge. The editor says to the creator, "Now, that's not nice, the whiskey and stuff. Don't let people know that. I have a better idea: 'Last night, I had a nice cup of warmed milk and then went to bed at nine o'clock.' Write that. Go ahead. I'll loosen my grip so you can."

If you keep your creator hand moving, the editor can't catch   13
up with it and lock it. It gets to write out what it wants. "Keep your hand moving" strengthens the creator and gives little space for the editor to jump in.

Keep your hand moving is the main structure for writing   14
practice.

2. *Lose control.* Say what you want to say. Don't worry if it's correct,   15
polite, appropriate. Just let it rip. Allen Ginsberg was getting a master's degree from Columbia University. Back then, they were doing rhymed verse. He had a lot of practice in formal meter, and so forth. One night, he went home and said to himself that he was going to write whatever he wanted and forget about formalities. The result was "Howl." We shouldn't forget how much practice in writing he had prior to this, but it is remarkable how I can tell students, "Okay, say what you want, go for it," and their writing takes a substantial turn toward authenticity.

3. *Be specific.* Not car, but Cadillac. Not fruit, but apple. Not bird,   16
but wren. Not codependent, neurotic man, but Harry, who runs to open the refrigerator for his wife, thinking she wants an apple, when she is headed for the gas stove to light her cigarette. Be careful of those pop-psychology labels. Get below the label and be specific to the person.

But don't chastise yourself as you are writing, "I'm an idiot;   17
Natalie said to be specific, and like a fool I wrote 'tree.'" Just gently note that you wrote "tree," drop to a deeper level, and next to "tree" write "sycamore." Be gentle with yourself. Don't give room for the hard grip of the editor.

4. *Don't think.* We usually live in the realm of second or third   18
   thoughts, thoughts on thoughts, rather than in the realm of first
   thoughts, the real way we flash on something. Stay with the
   first flash. Writing practice will help you contact first thoughts.
   Just practice and forget everything else.

   Now here are some rules that don't necessarily apply to sex,   19
   though you can try to apply them to sex if you like.

5. *Don't worry about punctuation, spelling, grammar.*   20
6. *You are free to write the worst junk in America.* You can be more   21
   specific, if you like: the worst junk in Santa Fe; New York;
   Kalamazoo, Michigan; your city block; your pasture; your
   neighborhood restaurant; your family. Or you can get more
   cosmic: free to write the worst junk in the universe, galaxy,
   world, hemisphere, Sahara Desert.
7. *Go for the jugular.* If something scary comes up, go for it. That's   22
   where the energy is. Otherwise, you'll spend all your time
   writing around whatever makes you nervous. It will probably
   be abstract, bland writing because you're avoiding the truth.
   Hemingway said, "Write hard and clear about what hurts."
   Don't avoid it. It has all the energy. Don't worry, no one ever
   died of it. You might cry or laugh, but not die.

I am often asked, "Well isn't there a time when we need to   23
stop our hand moving? You know, to figure out what we want
to say?"

It's better to figure out what you want to say in the actual act   24
of writing. For a long time, I was very strict with myself about
writing practice. I kept that hand moving no matter what. I
wanted to learn to cut through to first thoughts. Sure, you can stop
for a few moments, but it is a tricky business. It's good to stop if
you want, look up and get a better picture of what you're writing
about, but often I don't stay there. If I give myself a little gap, I'm
off for an hour daydreaming. You have to learn your own rhythm,
but make sure you do some focused, disciplined "keeping the
hand moving" to learn about cutting through resistance.

If you learn writing practice well, it is a good foundation for all   25
other writing.

When I was young, I played tennis. My arm wasn't very strong,   26
and I was impatient. I was so eager to play, I held the racquet up
higher on the grip than I was supposed to in order to compensate.

Unfortunately, I got used to using the racquet this way. I was a fine tennis player, but no matter how much I played, there was just so far I could improve, because I never mastered one of the important basics: the proper grip on the racquet.

I use this as an example for writing practice. Grow comfortable   27
with it in its basic form before you begin to veer off into your own manner and style. Trust it. It is as basic as drinking water.

Sometimes an interviewer asks me, "So writing practice is old   28
hat? Have you developed something new?"

And I say, "It would be like a Zen master teaching you medi-   29
tation one year and the next year saying, 'Forget compassion. Standing on our head is what's in.'"

The old essentials are still necessary. Stay with them under all   30
circumstances. It will make you stable—something unusual for a writer.

KURT VONNEGUT   (1922–   )

How to Write with Style

Newspaper reporters and technical writers are trained to reveal almost nothing about themselves in their writings. This makes them freaks in the world of writers, since almost all of the other ink-stained wretches in that world reveal a lot about themselves to readers. We call these revelations, accidental and intentional, elements of literary style.   1

These revelations are fascinating to us as readers. They tell us what sort of person it is with whom we are spending time. Does the writer sound ignorant or informed, crazy or sane, stupid or bright, crooked or honest, humorless or playful—? And on and on.   2

When you yourself put words on paper, remember that the most damning revelation you can make about yourself is that you do not know what is interesting and what is not. Don't you yourself like or dislike writers mainly for what they choose to show you or make you think about? Did you ever admire an empty-headed writer for his or her mastery of the language? No.   3

So your own winning literary style must begin with interesting ideas in your head. Find a subject you care about and which you in your heart feel others should care about. It is this genuine caring, and not your games with language, which will be the most compelling and seductive element in your style.   4

I am not urging you to write a novel, by the way—although I would not be sorry if you wrote one, provided you genuinely cared about something. A petition to the mayor about a pothole in front of your house or a love letter to the girl next door will do.   5

Do not ramble, though.   6

As for your use of language: Remember that two great masters of our language, William Shakespeare and James Joyce, wrote sentences which were almost childlike when their subjects were most profound. "To be or not to be?" asks Shakespeare's Hamlet. The longest word is three letters long. Joyce, when he was frisky, could put together a sentence as intricate and glittering as a necklace for Cleopatra, but my favorite sentence in his short story "Eveline" is this one: "She was tired." At that point in the story, no other words could break the heart of a reader as those words do.   7

Simplicity of language is not only reputable, but perhaps even   8
sacred. The Bible opens with a sentence well within the writing
skills of a lively fourteen-year-old: "In the beginning God created
the heavens and the earth."

It may be that you, too, are capable of making necklaces for   9
Cleopatra, so to speak. But your eloquence should be the servant
of the ideas in your head. Your rule might be this: If a sentence,
no matter how excellent, does not illuminate my subject in some
new and useful way, scratch it out. Here is the same rule paraphrased to apply to storytelling, to fiction: Never include a sentence which does not either remark on character or advance the
action.

The writing style which is most natural for you is bound to   10
echo speech you heard when a child. English was the novelist
Joseph Conrad's third language, and much that seems piquant in
his use of English was no doubt colored by his first language,
which was Polish. And lucky indeed is the writer who has grown
up in Ireland, for the English spoken there is so amusing and mu-
sical. I myself grew up in Indianapolis, Indiana, where common
speech sounds like a band saw cutting galvanized tin and employs
a vocabulary as unornamental as a monkey wrench.

In some of the more remote hollows of Appalachia, children   11
still grow up hearing songs and locutions of Elizabethan times.
Yes, and many Americans grow up hearing a language other than
English, or an English dialect a majority of Americans cannot understand.

All these varieties of speech are beautiful, just as the varieties of   12
butterflies are beautiful. No matter what your first language, you
should treasure it all your life. If it happens not to be standard
English, and if it shows itself when you write standard English, the
result is usually delightful, like a very pretty girl with one eye that
is green and one that is blue.

I myself find that I trust my own writing most, and others seem   13
to trust it most, too, when I sound most like a person from
Indianapolis, which is what I am. What alternatives do I have? The
one most vehemently recommended by teachers has no doubt
been pressed on you, as well: that I write like cultivated
Englishmen of a century or more ago.

I used to be exasperated by such teachers, but am no more. I   14
understand now that all those antique essays and stories with

which I was to compare my own work were not magnificent for their datedness or foreignness, but for saying precisely what their authors meant them to say. My teachers wished me to write accurately, always selecting the most effective words, and relating the words to one another unambiguously, rigidly, like parts of a machine. The teachers did not want to turn me into an Englishman after all. They hoped that I would become understandable—and therefore understood.

And there went my dream of doing with words what Pablo   15
Picasso did with paint or what any number of jazz idols did with music. If I broke all the rules of punctuation, had words mean whatever I wanted them to mean, and strung them together higgledy-piggledy, I would simply not be understood. So you, too, had better avoid Picasso-style or jazz-style writing, if you have something worth saying and wish to be understood.

If it were only teachers who insisted that modern writers stay   16
close to literary styles of the past, we might reasonably ignore them. But readers insist on the very same thing. They want our pages to look very much like pages they have seen before.

Why? It is because they themselves have a tough job to do, and   17
they need all the help they can get from us. They have to identify thousands of little marks on paper, and make sense of them immediately. They have to *read*, an art so difficult that most people do not really master it even after having studied it all through grade school and high school—for twelve long years.

So this discussion, like all discussions of literary styles, must fi-   18
nally acknowledge that our stylistic options as writers are neither numerous nor glamorous, since our readers are bound to be such imperfect artists. Our audience requires us to be sympathetic and patient teachers, ever willing to simplify and clarify—whereas we would rather soar high above the crowd, singing like nightingales.

That is the bad news. The good news is that we Americans are   19
governed under a unique Constitution, which allows us to write whatever we please without fear of punishment. So the most meaningful aspect of our styles, which is what we choose to write about, is unlimited.

Also: We are members of an egalitarian society, so there is no   20
reason for us to write, in case we are not classically educated aristocrats, as though we were classically educated aristocrats.

For a discussion of literary style in a narrower sense, in a more   21
technical sense, I commend to your attention *The Elements of Style*
by William Strunk, Jr., and E. B. White (Macmillan, 1979). It
contains such rules as this: "A participial phrase at the beginning of
a sentence must refer to the grammatical subject," and so on. E. B.
White is, of course, one of the most admirable literary stylists this
country has so far produced.

You should realize, too, that no one would care how well or   22
badly Mr. White expressed himself, if he did not have perfectly
enchanting things to say.

The Death of Reading

What's missing from these pictures?   1

- Three people sit in a doctor's waiting room. One stares at the television that rests on an end table; the second fiddles with a hand-held video game; the head of the third is wrapped in earphones.

- A couple of kids, waiting for bedtime, lie on the floor of a brightly painted room, busy manipulating the controls of a video game.

- Two hundred people sit in an airplane. Some have brought their own tapes, some doze, most stare up at a small movie screen.

What is missing from these pictures, and increasingly from our   2
lives, is the activity through which most of us learned much of what we know of the wider world. What's missing is the force that, according to a growing consensus of historians, established our patterns of thought and, in an important sense, made our civilization. What's missing is the venerable, increasingly dated activity that you—what's the matter? bored with all your CDs and videotapes?—are engaged in right now.

Ironically, but not coincidentally, reading has begun fading   3
from our culture at the very moment that its importance to that culture is finally being established. Its decline, many theorists believe, is as profound as, say, the fall of communism, and some have taken to prophesying that the downturn in reading could result in the modern world's cultural and political decline.

"A mode of thinking is being lost," laments Neil Postman,   4
whose book, *Amusing Ourselves to Death,* is a warning about the consequences of a falloff in reading. "We are losing a sort of psychic habit, a logic, a sense of complexity, an ability to spot contradictions and even falsity." Postman, a professor of communication arts at New York University, believes this loss is now being

felt in our cultural activities and in our politics, as well as in our children's SAT scores, and that it could get worse. But of course such prophecies are delivered in print, so no one pays much heed.

The anecdotal evidence that reading is in decline is copious and   5 compelling. "When I go out socially in Washington," confides Daniel Boorstin, a historian and former librarian of Congress, "I'm careful not to embarrass my dinner companions by asking what they have read lately. Instead I say, 'I suppose you don't have much time to read books nowadays.'"

That is a courtesy, alas, for which most of us would be grateful.   6 The fact is that few of us, and few of our friends and few of our children, have the time to read as much as we would like. We're too busy working or working out or playing or—OK, let's admit it—watching TV.

Our homes barely make room for reading. Those old islands of   7 quiet—libraries, studies, and dens—long ago were invaded by flat screens and Nintendos. Now they are called "family rooms" or, more accurately, "television rooms." And our architects seem to have given up providing us with bookshelves; instead they busy themselves designing "entertainment centers."

So we haven't quite gotten around to Stephen M. Hawking's *A*   8 *Brief History of Time* yet. We're saving Amy Tan's latest novel for vacation, maybe. And that pile of unread *New Yorker*s or *Rolling Stone*s or *Los Angeles Times Magazine*s keeps growing, each unread issue an additional piece of anecdotal evidence.

Those whose livelihoods depend on our reading suggest, opti-   9 mistically, that the widespread notion that it is in decline is an oversimplification. "I believe that people who used to read a lot of books read less now," concedes Alberto Vitale, chairman of Random House, the nation's largest publisher of trade (nontext) books. "But in my opinion, there are many *more* people reading books."

The optimists do have some statistics on their side. Books, the   10 oldest form of print, seem to be doing reasonably well. Publishers, in fact, are churning out more and more of them: 133,196 new ti-tles listed in *Books in Print* in the past year. That is about 16 times the number of titles printed 40 years ago (one of the reasons "keeping up" may seem so much harder for us than it did for our parents and grandparents). And publishers are selling more, too: about 2 billion books in 1990, an 11% increase over 1985. Reports of the death of the book seem greatly exaggerated.

Ah, but are these books actually being read? Not, in many cases, 11
from cover-to-cover. A recent Gallup Poll found many more people in 1990 than in 1957 who say they are currently reading a book or novel, but many fewer now than in 1975 who say they have completed a book in the past week. In a society where professional success now requires acquaintance with masses of esoteric information, books are often purchased to be consulted, not read. About 15% of the new titles in *Books in Print* are scientific or technical books.

Fiction and general-interest nonfiction works would seem to be 12
designed to be read, but lately these books also serve other functions. Their authors often employ them as routes to movie contracts or to tenure or to the intellectual renown that apparently comes with having catalogued definitively, in two or three dense volumes, how George Bernard Shaw, say, spent each of his evenings. Their publishers increasingly see these books not as collections of sentences and paragraphs that might be clarified and sharpened but as product that must be publicized and marketed so the balance sheets of the large conglomerates they now work for might tilt in the right direction.

Given the pace of modern life, the readers of these books, 13
too, may have other purposes in mind—a quick, conversation-enhancing skim perhaps. "People tend to read too rapidly," moans Russell Jacoby, author of *The Last Intellectual*. "They tend to read while commuting, watching a game on TV, or playing Nintendo." Jacoby, who recently taught history at UC Riverside, keeps threatening to open "slow-reading centers."

And books increasingly have another function for those who 14
purchase them. They have begun replacing the bottle of Scotch or the tie as gifts—giving them about the same chance of being opened as those ties had of being worn. The number of bookstores in the United States has been growing in recent decades, at a rate second only to that of fast-food restaurants, but according to statistics supplied by the American Booksellers Assn., more than one quarter of all their sales are in November and December—for the holidays.

In 1985, Michael Kinsley of the *New Republic* conducted an ex- 15
periment. Notes offering a $5 reward to anyone who saw them and called the magazine were hidden about three quarters of the

way through 70 copies of the hottest nonfiction books in Washington, D.C., bookstores. These were the books that all of Washington seemed to be talking about. "Washington" was apparently basing its comments on the reviews and maybe a quick skim. No one called.

"Fortunately for booksellers," Kinsley wrote, "their prosperity   16
depends on people buying books, not on people actually reading the bulky things." (Kinsley's advice to authors who would like their words actually to be read: "Cut out the middleman, and just write the review.")

Those of us with less disposable income, or less inclination to   17
dispose of it in bookstores, can still get our books from libraries. "You can't say people take books out of the library just to put them on the coffee table," says Simon Michael Bessie, chairman of the Center for the Book at the Library of Congress.

And library use is up. Public-library circulation in the United   18
States has grown from 4.7 "units" per capita per year in 1980 to 6.1 in 1989, according to a study by the Library Research Center at the University of Illinois. However, the "units" we are checking out of the library now include not only lots of school and business readings but also cassettes, CDs and videotapes.

Here is perhaps the most frightening of the statistics on books: 19
According to the Gallup Poll, the number of Americans who admitted to having read *no* books during the past year—and this is not an easy thing to admit to a pollster—doubled from 1978 to 1990, from 8% to 16%. "I cannot live without books," Thomas Jefferson, whose collection helped start the Library of Congress, told John Adams. More and more of us apparently can.

Magazines would appear to be better suited to our hectic lives,   20
if for no other reason than that they require much less of a time commitment than do books. Gathering evidence to confirm or deny this surmise, however, is not easy. There are too many different kinds of magazines and too many individual variations in their popularity. We do know that the magazine business has been in dire straits lately, but this has been caused by a falloff in advertising, not necessarily in circulation.

The best indicator of whether we are spending more or less   21
time with magazines may be "time-use" studies such as those compiled at the University of Maryland. These show that the proportion of the population that reads a magazine on a typical day

dropped from 38% in 1946 to 28% in 1985. Magazine publishers, however, can take some encouragement from the fact that most of that drop had occurred by the 1950s.

The statistics on newspaper readership are much less ambiguous   22
and much grimmer. According to the University of Maryland time-use studies, the share of the adult population that "read a newspaper yesterday" has declined from 85% in 1946 to 73% in 1965 to 55% in 1985. The numbers on per capita newspaper circulation and the percentage of American homes that receive a daily newspaper form similar graphs—graphs you could ski down.

"What has changed is the strength of the habit of reading a   23
newspaper," notes Al Gollin of the Newspaper Advertising Bureau. "It used to be one of those things that almost everybody did." No more. Americans on average now read newspapers much less frequently than they did 30 years ago, 20 years ago, even 10 years ago.

And young people have been losing the newspaper habit even   24
faster than their parents. "We are developing a generation that has no interest in reading except insofar as it is assigned in school," concludes Daniel Kevles, professor of humanities at Caltech. "They don't read newspapers or magazines. I sense a general lack of interest in public affairs among my students." A recent *Times Mirror* survey found that only 30% of Americans under the age of 35 said they had read a newspaper the previous day, compared to 67% in 1965.

The Gulf War provided further evidence of how far the news-   25
paper has fallen. According to a survey by Birch/Scarborough, a grand total of 8.9% of us said we kept up with war news primarily through newspapers. The days when we found most of our news set in type on a page are long gone.

Those time-use studies actually discovered a slight increase from   26
1965 to 1985 in the amount of time people said they spend reading books and magazines: from 1.7 to 1.9 hours a week. But if you throw in newspapers, the total time people spent with reading as their primary activity has dropped more than 30% in those years, from 4.2 hours a week to 2.8.

And this drop has occurred at the same time that the amount of   27
education Americans obtain has been rising dramatically. The percentage of Americans who have completed four years of high school has more than tripled since 1940, according to the Bureau

of the Census Current Population Survey, and the percentage of Americans completing four years of college has more than quadrupled.

If education still stimulated the desire to read, all the statistics on   28
reading would be shooting up. That they are not may say something about the quality of our educational system and about the interests of the students it now attracts. It certainly says something about reading and its future. If dramatically increased exposure to an educational system based on the printed word cannot get us to read, what will?

Reading's troubles are not difficult to explain. A hundred years   29
ago, on days when no circus was in town, people looking for entertainment had three alternatives: fulfilling biological needs, talking, or reading. Those looking for information were restricted to the latter two. Many of our ancestors, to be sure, were unable to read, but those who could relied upon it, as Thomas Jefferson did, with a desperation that is difficult for us to imagine.

Books, in those days, had a unique power to transport. "There   30
is no Frigate like a Book," wrote 19th-Century poet Emily Dickinson, "To take us Lands away." Now, of course, there are many easier ways of getting there.

"Our society is particularly ingenious at thinking up alternatives   31
to the book," notes Boorstin. Indeed, we have thought up an entire communications revolution, and there have not been many of those in human history. The first such revolution was the development of language hundreds of thousands of years ago; the second, the development of reading and writing in the Middle East about 5,000 years ago; the third, the invention of the printing press 500 years ago.

The fourth communications revolution—ours—began, per-   32
haps, with the experiments of Samuel Morse, Guglielmo Marconi, and Thomas Edison in the 19th Century, and it has been picking up steam ever since. Movies, recordings, radio, telephones, computers, photocopiers, and fax machines are all part of it. But, of course, the most powerful product of this revolution, so far, and the one that has posed the largest threat to reading, has been television.

Some print lovers have taken heart from the recent troubles of   33
the TV networks or from the fact that the amount of time the average American family keeps the TV on each day, as measured by

Nielsen, finally leveled off in the mid 1980s—at about seven hours a day. But, of course, we have since supplemented broadcast and even cable TV with other equally diverting forms of programming.

The first television wave washed over us in the 1950s and '60s. But then, while we were still getting used to having this perky new friend in our bedrooms, a second wave hit. In 1982, only 5.5% of American homes had videocassette recorders. Now 72.5% of them do, and, according to Nielsen, videotapes keep the set on an average of an extra half-hour each day in those homes. Add still more minutes for video games. So much for that leveling-off. 34

Russell Jacoby and his wife have found a sure way to protect themselves and their two children from the siren songs of the tube: When their set was stolen a number of years ago, they simply didn't replace it. But most of the rest of us now share our homes with one or more TV sets, which we turn on more than we would like to admit. "Everyone lies about how much time they and their families spend watching TV," Jacoby asserts. It is a wonder that we manage to find the time to read even as much as we do. 35

"There are only so many hours in the day," says Alberto Vitale of Random House, wistfully. 36

As a youth, Abraham Lincoln is reported to have spent so many hours buried in his books that the neighbors labeled him lazy. When Lincoln arrived in Congress, his fellow congressmen, by one account, dismissed him as a "bookworm." That insult is not heard much nowadays, nor are readers disparaged as lazy. 37

Instead, the more dedicated parents among us feel guilty if we don't manage to read to our children each evening, hoping the kids will pick up the habit we parents are rapidly losing. The First Lady campaigns for literacy. We end TV shows with pleas to read books. And, according to the Gallup Poll, 61% of us proclaim reading "more rewarding" than watching television; 73% lament that we read too few books; 92% attest that reading is a "good use" of our time. And 45% of the poll's respondents believe, against all the evidence, that they will be "reading more in the months and years ahead." 38

Reading certainly is well loved now that it is in decline. Yet it is no longer something that we ache to do. How many kids today surreptitiously finish books by flashlight under the covers? Instead, 39 reading, like eating broccoli, has now become something that we feel we *should* do (always a bad sign).

Some teenagers and—says Michael Silverblatt, host of KCRW's   40 "Bookworm" show—some Southern Californians actually find it hip to pretend to read less than they really do, but the vast majority of us sincerely, vigorously, and guiltily genuflect in front of the printed page. Never in human history has reading been more respected.

This is not surprising. One of the characteristics of any techno-   41 logical revolution is nostalgia for the old order. Socrates, who lived a few hundred years after the invention of the Greek alphabet, when writing was transforming Greek culture, strenuously argued the superiority of the oral culture it was replacing. According to Plato's (written) account, Socrates predicted that the use of writing would weaken memories and deprive "learners" of the chance to question what they were being taught.

Such nostalgia for the methods of oral tradition—memoriza-   42 tion, rhetoric, recital—kept them alive in the schools well into this century. Now similar calls are going out to defend the schools against the incursions of the new information technologies so that our educational institutions can serve as repositories of another fading tradition—reading.

We did not realize that we were living in the age of print until   43 it began to end. Only then did we gain the perspective to see the effects of reading on our thoughts. Those effects are profound, as anthropological studies of societies without reading have begun to show.

For example, the following statements were presented to mem-   44 bers of a mostly preliterate tribe in a remote area of the Soviet Union: "In the far north, where there is snow, all bears are white. Novaya Zembla is in the far north, and there is always snow there." Then these people were asked what color the bears are in Novaya Zemble. A typical response, as reported by Father Walter Ong in his book *Orality and Literacy:* "I don't know. I've seen a black bear. I've never seen any others. Each locality has its own animals." These people could not solve this simplest of logical puzzles.

It is not that such preliterate people are less intelligent than we   45 are. They simply think differently—"situationally." When words are written down, not just enunciated, they are freed from the subjective situations and experiences ("I've seen a black bear") in which they were imbedded. Written words can be played with, analyzed, rearranged, and organized into categories (black bears, white bears, places where there is always snow). The correspondences, connections, or contradictions among various statements can be carefully examined. As investigators such as Ong and anthropologist Jack Goody have explained, our system of logic—our ability to find principles that apply independently of situations—is a product of literacy. This logic, which goes back to the Egyptians, Hebrews, and Greeks, led to mathematics and philosophy and history. Among its accomplishments is our culture.

And when written words are set in print, they gain additional   46
powers. Our sentences grow even less connected to our persons as they are spelled out in the interchangeable letters of movable type. Our thoughts grow more abstract, more removed from the situations in which we happen to find ourselves. Superstitions, biases, and legendary characters like dragons and kings have difficulty fitting into these straight precise lines of type. Charts, maps, and columns of figures can be duplicated exactly for the first time. According to seminal media theorist Marshall McLuhan and historian Elizabeth Eisenstein, the scientific revolution and the Enlightenment were both products of the printing press.

"Reading is central to our culture," states Ong, a professor of   47
humanities at Saint Louis University. "It is connected to virtually all the forces that shaped our culture." Among those who ponder such matters, there is no longer much controversy about that. The question, as we leave the age of print for the uncharted waters of this new electronic age, is whether we risk losing much of what reading enabled us to gain.

Neil Postman, for one, fears that the answer is yes. "New com-   48
munications technologies giveth," he proclaims, "and they taketh away." On the debit side Postman would place recent developments in art, education, religion, journalism, and politics—all of which, in his view, are losing the seriousness and intellectual content print gave them as they are transformed into "show business" to meet the needs of electronic media.

Reading demands that we sit still, be quiet, and concentrate   49
hard enough to decode a system of symbols and follow extended arguments. This is an injunction that increasingly is falling on earphoned-plugged ears. Television and its electronic brethren are much less strict. We can be cleaning, daydreaming, or half-dozing;

they don't seem to care. All television demands is our gaze. Dazzling collages of imagery and rhythm are assembled just to get us to open our eyelids a bit wider.

Kings used to turn thumbs down on spectacles that bored them; 50 we simply press thumb to remote control, zapping any scene, exposition, or argument that takes much more than a fraction of a minute to unfold, "Thinking," Postman writes, "does not play well on TV."

Our entertainers, pundits, professors, ministers, and leaders, 51 therefore, are judged not so much on their ability to reason but on their ability to project a diverting image. Amuse us or we'll change the channel. Whether or not the points being made are valid is of less importance. Somehow this does not seem what Jefferson and the other founders had in mind when they entrusted us with governing a country.

Pessimists like Postman do not have much difficulty convincing 52 us that life on a late-20th-Century couch can be frivolous and vegetable-like. We already feel guilty that we are watching "the boob tube" rather than reading. However, making the case that life in that supposed golden age of reading was really much more noble than life today is more difficult.

As his example of political discourse before TV, Postman 53 chooses those astoundingly literate, three-hour-long debates between Lincoln and Stephen A. Douglas in 1858. But 18th- and 19th-Century American politics was not all conducted on this level. The slogans with which William Henry Harrison made his case for the presidency in 1840, for example—"Log Cabin and Hard Cider," "Tippecanoe and Tyler, too"—are as vacuous as anything concocted by Ronald Reagan's media wizards.

The arguments against TV are based on a certain amount of 54 such false nostalgia. People then did not read quite so much, and their reading material was not quite so exemplary as those pining for a lost golden age suggest. "We have no figures on how much or how well books were read in the past," Ong notes. "All we have are the comments of bibliophiles. There is no evidence, for example, that all the copies of the books printed in the 16th and 17th centuries were read. There is plenty of evidence that a lot of them were not read." Nevertheless, the doomsayers do have some harder evidence on their side.

There is, to begin with, the decline in writing skills, much fret-   55
ted over by educators in recent years. Written language demands
stricter rules of syntax and grammar than spoken language, and
these are the rules, first codified in printed dictionaries and grammar books, that we learn (or now fail to learn) in school. The sentences of the electronic age, because they are supplemented by images, can get away with playing by looser rules. Try, sometime, to
diagram the sentences of a TV-football "analyst."

It is not surprising, therefore, that students who watch and lis-   56
ten more and read less are losing command of their writing. As
anyone who has seen that rare thing, a letter written by a student,
knows, young people today often have considerable difficulty filling a page with clear, exact sentences. Their performance on recent SATs raises the question of whether they also have difficulty
producing clear, exact thought.

The average score on the SAT verbal test, taken by a large   57
number of college-bound high school students, was 466 (on a scale
of 200 to 800) in 1968. Then, as the first TV generation began
taking the test, scores began tumbling. The average score leveled
off from 1978 to 1987, but now, with the arrival of the MTV kids,
it has begun skidding again—down to 422 this year.

The College Boards do not test a representative sample of   58
American teenagers. More—and perhaps less qualified—students
are now going to college and therefore taking the test, which may
be driving scores down. Still, the correspondence between verbal
scores and the two waves of TV's assault upon reading is hard to
overlook.

"The decline in SAT scores has a lot to do with not reading,"   59
asserts College Board President Donald M. Stewart. Why? "The
ability to read is linked to the ability to process, analyze, and comprehend information," Stewart explains. "I guess that's called
thinking."

Michael Silverblatt of "Bookworm" uses an analogy that young   60
people might find more persuasive: "Just as people who don't
work out can't do certain things with their bodies, people who
don't read can't do certain things with their minds."

Boorstin puts the problem even more bluntly. He calls people   61
who do not read "self-handicapped" and says, "A person who
doesn't read books is only half-alive." And if the members of a society stop reading? "Then you have a half-alive society."

From the perspective of enthusiasts of the new culture of 62
videos, videotapes, video games, and CDs, all this must sound like
the whining of a ragged, nearly defeated old order. Not everyone
is convinced that all that is deep and serious in our society is in fact
under siege. "I know a number of extremely intelligent adults who
don't read more than a book or two a year but still remain healthy,
active contributors to society," says Wendy Lesser, editor of *Three
Penny Review,* a respected Berkeley literary publication. "I think if
you can get people to learn to discriminate between good and bad
TV programs, you've done more for them than you would by
simply forcing them to read a book, however trashy."

And even those who believe that the decline in reading does 63
herald some profound cultural changes are not convinced those
changes will necessarily be for the worse. Perhaps, they might
argue, the logic inculcated by writing and print is not the only way
of processing information about the world. Perhaps an immersion
in electronic forms of communication might lead to different but
equally valid ways of being smart—forms of intelligence that go
unrecognized by SAT tests. "I'm listening to that argument with
more and more sympathy," concedes Stewart of the College
Boards.

It is possible, moreover, that electronic forms of communica- 64
tion have more potential than is currently being expressed in either the vapid fantasies of Madonna videos or the static talk shows
and costume dramas of public television. These media might be
capable, given time, of creating a culture as profound and deep as
that of reading. These technologies might, in other words, have
more to "giveth" than we can yet imagine.

It took 2,000 years of writing before an alphabet was devel- 65
oped. It took a century and a half of printing before someone
thought to print a novel or a newspaper. New communications
technologies do not arrive upon the scene fully grown; they need
time to develop the methods and forms that best exploit their potential.

Our communications revolution, from this perspective, is still 66
quite young. TV has been around for only half a century. Most of
its programming is still recycled theater—mini-dramas and comedies; its more stylistically adventurous forms—commercials and
music videos—are little more than demonstrations of the visual capabilities of the medium.

Television's technicians have mastered the art of mating laugh   67
track to quip; they can make everything from cats to toothbrushes
dance. But TV still may not have stumbled upon the grammar and
syntax of video—the patterns and relations of images and sounds
that will enable us to communicate complex ideas with clarity and
exactness. Television may not yet have discovered the forms that
will do for that medium what the novel and the newspaper did for
print.

TV today grapples with difficult subjects only by getting slow   68
and boring. It is possible to imagine a television program that
would be difficult for the opposite reason: because it is too fast, too
busy, too full of information. Perhaps such super-dense television
would be able to plumb depths quickly enough to fit the video
generation's short attention spans, or perhaps this TV would be
stimulating enough to stretch those attention spans.

Does television really have such potential? Does a whole cul-   69
ture's worth of new perspectives, new ideas, new creations in fact
lie slumbering in our television sets, just waiting for programming
capable of awakening them? "Possibly," Daniel Kevles comments
with some skepticism, "but I think any more intelligent programming will still have to coexist with MTV and action dramas."

Still, if the electronic media can, even intermittently, transform   70
themselves into vehicles for ideas with the reach and capacity of
print it would be good news for our society. The Postmans of the
world could rest easy; we would not go giggling off into decadence and dictatorship. But such a development would represent
still more bad news for reading.

Is reading likely to survive the electronic age? Of course, Daniel   71
Boorstin says. He scoffs at the notion that books, magazines, or
newspapers are going to disappear any time soon. Boorstin calls
this the "displacement fallacy" and points out that radio survived
and prospered after the introduction of TV, despite many gloomy
predictions to the contrary. "New technologies tend to discover
unique opportunities for the old," Boorstin maintains.

Not every outdated communication technology succeeds in   72
finding such an opportunity. Consider smoke signals, for example,
or town criers or the telegram. Nevertheless, Boorstin has a point.

Books already have found some new functions for themselves—   73
as reference manuals for example. Magazines have survived in part
by discovering audiences too small and specialized for TV to

reach. And newspapers? Well, maybe *USA Today,* with its brief, snappy stories, is responding to a new opportunity presented by the TV generation's shortened attention spans. Or maybe newspapers are still searching for their niche in the electronic age.

Print and electronics also collaborate more than is generally rec-   74 ognized. According to the preliminary results of a study by Robert Kubey, communications professor at Rutgers University, words appear in about 20% of the images in a sample of 30 channels available on cable. And the alphabet has recently found a new life for itself on the keyboards of computers.

"I'm using about 20 times as much paper since I started using a   75 computer," Ong adds. "A new technology does not wipe out what went before; it transforms and enhances it. When people started writing, they didn't quit talking." Indeed, they probably spoke more logically.

However, the introduction of writing undoubtedly did cause   76 people to spend less time talking—because of the old not-enough-hours-in-the-day problem. And it probably did cause them to rely less on speech for communicating important information. So, whatever new forms print may assume in response to electronics, it is unlikely that print will regain its position as our major source of information or entertainment.

Reading still plays and, for the foreseeable future, will continue   77 to play, a crucial role in our society. Nevertheless, there is no getting around the fact that reading's role has diminished and likely will continue to shrink.

This does not mean we should begin turning first-grade classes   78 over to video lessons. Until the new technologies grow up a bit, it would not hurt any of us to read more to our children or take a book with us the next time we must sit and wait. And perhaps it was not a bad idea that you chose, instead of watching the Rams game or renting *Dances With Wolves,* to make it through this article.

Instantly Growing Up

Bing-Bong-Bong-Bing! It began with countless computer 1
kids tapping out chiming instant messages to their pals.
Now, in a classic case of adults playing techno-catch-up,
America's workforce is fast discovering the benefits of instant messaging too. An estimated 20 million employees, representing half
of all big U.S. companies, routinely fire off pop-up missives in lieu
of cumbersome conference calls or e-mail—which now seems as
plodding as a telegram. "This is no longer about teenagers and
chat," says John Patrick, vice president for Internet technology at
IBM, whose Lotus Development unit produces Sametime, the
leading instant-messaging program for business use. "If I were to
check right now," Patrick says, "there are probably 100 [instant-
message] meetings going on all over IBM."

Yet proprietary software like Sametime is just one reason why 2
IM chimes are suddenly ringing throughout the workplace. Far
more messages probably come from employees who have downloaded such programs as America Online's Instant Messenger
(AIM) or the rival Yahoo Messenger, both of which are available
free on the Internet. Workers aren't even waiting for information-
technology departments to install a corporate system. "This is all
spreading by word of mouth," says Neil MacDonald, a vice president of the Gartner Group research firm. "Companies weren't
planning on instant messaging, but it's become a critical part of
business today." Gartner predicts that by 2003 at least some employees at fully 90% of big U.S. companies will be swapping
instant messages. Although given the speed with which IM is
spreading, that date seems conservative.

Workers love IM for the same reason that kids do: it lets them 3
hold virtual meetings anytime and anyplace. No more playing
telephone tag or pulling down an e-mail screen. Instead, IM users
can spot who is online at a glance and start chatting right away.
And they can do so across time zones, oceans, and continents. At
the stroke of midnight on New Year's Eve in 1999, 80 IBM experts from around the world huddled online to monitor the company's defenses against the Y2K bug. "If there had been a crisis,"

Patrick says, "all the knowledgeable people would have instantly shared their expertise."

Such seamless communication is fast winning over everyone   4
from toy retailer FAO Schwarz—which has put a downloadable IM link to customer service on its website—to the U.S. Navy, which uses the Sametime system to connect a 16-ship battle group in the Atlantic Fleet. Closer to home, long-distance provider Sprint uses software designed by Bantu Inc. to enable employees to chat while watching online PowerPoint displays. Messages can also be sent and received by a variety of wireless devices, including cellular phones.

But for all its popularity, the IM world remains frustratingly   5
balkanized. At least a dozen systems are in service in the U.S. alone, many of them incompatible. This confusion adds to the pressure on AOL—which popularized instant messaging and commands a 90% share of the market—to allow rivals like Yahoo and Microsoft access to its IM systems. These cover some 80 million users under the AOL brand and a similar number under ICQ, an Israeli company that AOL bought two years ago. Says MacDonald: "AOL's installed base is the crown jewels of instant messaging."

In fact, AOL has licensed its IM protocols to more than a dozen   6
companies, including Lotus, Apple Computer, and the search-engine Lycos. But it has consistently blocked access to Microsoft and others that have tapped into its systems without authorization. AOL argues that such intrusions violate the security and privacy of AOL users and burden the servers that AOL has built and must pay to maintain. "Basically, anyone who has asked them politely has gotten in," says Joyce Graff, a research director at Gartner. "But when they have not been asked and suddenly another 2.5 million users start beating up on their server, they say, 'Excuse me, buddy, but you're not welcome here.'"

The licensing arrangement suits companies such as Lotus,   7
whose Sametime system encrypts messages and allows users to operate behind a fire wall designed to keep out intruders. Employees can then plug in to the AOL user base to chat with family, friends, or workers at other companies.

Access to AOL's IM users has become a hot issue for regulators   8
who are scrutinizing the company's proposed mega-merger with Time Warner. The Federal Trade Commission may demand some

form of open access as a condition for approving the deal, as has been hinted, or it could agree to allow instant messaging to remain unregulated. With the stakes so high as the review winds down, the atmosphere among regulators has become testy. Sources tell *Time* that the FTC, stung by leaks about the deliberations, has launched a probe to uncover any unauthorized tongue wagging within the agency.

On one issue all sides appear to agree: the industry would ben-   9
efit from a single standard that lets all IM systems communicate freely with one another. "It just makes no sense to keep them separate," says Laney Baker, a Salomon Smith Barney analyst. But striking a deal on a single standard is another matter. Just last week an industry group that had been struggling for months to create a unified protocol opted instead for as many as three separate standards that can interconnect. "The big players—AOL, Microsoft, and Yahoo—tried to dominate the field by saying, 'My solution is best,'" says Navi Radjou, who followed the talks for the Forrester Research firm. That left the standards group no choice but to recommend several protocols. The problem is that when new features like voice recognition are added to systems on one protocol, they may not connect well with the others.

Some critics doubt that AOL really has much interest in a com-   10
mon IM standard that would provide access to its enormous customer trove. "It comes down to this," says Blair Levin, a former FCC chief of staff who represents AOL opponents. "Everyone agrees there should be interoperability and that it should happen as quickly as possible. AOL says, 'Trust us to get this done.' We say, 'Look at the record.'"

Yet even as all sides bicker, instant messaging is becoming in-   11
dispensable to business users. At IBM, which runs 2 million instant messages a day, the technology is just getting started, says Patrick. IBM and Lotus engineers, he says, are currently assembling an IM system that combines voice recognition, language translation, and text-speech conversion. Its use? "I could ask a question to a customer-service representative in Spain, who could bring in the most knowledgeable person, who might happen to be Chinese. So you could begin to think of this as a real-time multilingual intercom." Now if only competing IM systems could blend together as smoothly.

RITA MAE BROWN   (1944–)

Writing as a Moral Act

L anguage is decanted and shared. If only one person is left 1
alive speaking a language—the case with some American
Indian languages—the language is dead. Language takes two
and their multiples.

Speaking is a social contract. You and I agree to exchange 2
sounds whose organized noises represent agreed-upon symbols.
Cat means the same thing to you as it does to me. It doesn't mean
a thing to a Portuguese person. You might think of a sleek tiger
cat, and I might be thinking of a long-haired red cat, but we are
in sync about the species. If you want to get fancy you could say
feline (Latin again) but we're in the same ballpark.

Up to this point we are in agreement. We are cooperating as 3
two individuals conceding to civilization. Literacy, or even simple
speech, is the starting point of civilization. The unspoken truth is
that we are unequal; we are different. If you and I were exactly the
same, a pair of identical strangers, we wouldn't need to speak to
one another or to write. You'd know what I was thinking and
vice versa. All communication rests upon inequality. That's the
sheer excitement of it. I don't know what you think. I can't wait
to find out. Language is the common thread by which we explore
our differences and, if we are both lucky and mature, the thread
that will bring us to a form of agreement or at least understanding.

Therefore it is imperative that people write and speak the truth. 4
There can be no community if a person is not as good as her/his
word. How easy to write that and how hard to put it in practice.
You, my reader, whoever you are, know things that will disturb
others. You must tell. Camus said, "It is immoral not to tell."

Again we can split hairs. A dear friend of mine has put on ten 5
pounds. Do I say, "Gee, Frank, you're fat as a toad" (the truth) or
"Frank, you look wonderful." It may be wonderful to see him, but
he still looks fat. I'll choose to make my friend feel better.

If Frank, involved in a sordid affair with the wife of another 6
friend of mine, asks my opinion, I'll tell him the truth. "Either she
leaves him and goes to you, or you leave her. Don't mess with
married people."

Telling the truth should be simple. Writing the truth should be   7
even easier because you don't have to look your listener/reader in
the eye. Writing the truth is far more treacherous. The act of
putting words down on paper gives them a glamour and permanence not associated with speech. Writing, to most everyone, is a
more serious act than speaking.

Every generation produces those people—writers, composers,   8
plastic artists, and even the re-creative artists—who shatter social
convention and tell the truth. They aren't saying "Here I am."
They are saying "Here you are." The "you" is both individual and
plural. In the case of *Oedipus Rex* or *Crime and Punishment*, this
recognition can be horrifying. In the case of *The Birds* or *School for
Scandal* it can be deliciously funny.

If this is prevented from happening (as in Stalin's Soviet Union,   9
Hitler's Germany, Botha's South Africa) the civilization begins to
die from the inside out. There may be a plethora of books in such
nations but they aren't upsetting. They merely entertain. Art must
both entertain and provoke.

If people refrain from telling what they know, how long before   10
they actively lie? Is there not a subtle and corrosive connection between withholding the truth and lying? You are as sick as you are
secret.

If you don't believe that words will be followed by deeds, how   11
can you trust anyone? How can you form a community? When
language no longer corresponds to reality, any form of betrayal and
misconduct are to be expected.

Writers are the moral purifiers of the culture. We may not be   12
pure ourselves, but we must tell the truth, which is a purifying act.
Therefore it is impossible for a real fiction writer to be the mouth-
piece for a political cause. A writer should, as should any citizen,
cherish his or her political beliefs but that's not the same as being
a propagandist.

By political beliefs I am not talking about the American two-   13
party system. The Republican party is a study in unlimited van-
dalism, and the Democratic party presides over the cadaver of lib-
eralism. The difference between Republicans and Democrats is
the difference between syphilis and gonorrhea. Political beliefs are
stronger than that. The separation of church and state is a political
belief. Affirming or repudiating capital punishment is a political

belief. The desire for a state-controlled economy is not only a political belief, in some nations it's a religion. You get the difference.
Our political parties skate over the political fashions that are current. Opportunism wears many masks.

Since politicians seek to conceal the truth in order to dupe the   14
public, every writer alive is critical of whatever political system
s/he lives in. Not everyone in politics is bad and politics is a necessary evil, *but* politics is never ever about the truth. Politics seeks
to conceal; Art, to reveal.

The severest blasts in Russia or in our own country are directed at   15
people the state considers expendable. First, writers get it because
they are potentially dangerous. Scientists run into walls only if they
become critical of the uses of science by the government. If they shut
up and continue as the hired help, they're okay. In our country, we
are too sophisticated to put writers in jail. It looks bad. Also, we are
very fortunate in that most of our elected officials are semi-illiterate,
and therefore they don't even know what we're writing. Should a
writer happen to become disturbing and powerful enough to come
to the attention of our civic worthies, then the fur flies. A politician
will cite the offending author and make a stink. His acolytes will press
to have the subversive texts banned from the libraries. (Actually, the
acolytes control the politician. S/he usually responds to their pressure.) Loathsome as it is, such talk does get into the newspapers, and
once publicity attaches itself to a book, the sales shoot upward. Bless
the narrow-minded! You can survive that. You'll know when
you're really in Dutch when the IRS hounds you. You think a
highly placed government official wouldn't stoop that low? You
think the IRS is not a punitive instrument of whatever administration is current? You also believe in the tooth fairy, don't you?

Communist and fascist nations recognize the power of writers.   16
They imprison them or drive them out of their homeland. The
United States of America, no matter how absurd and contradictory
our various administrations, has drawn the line here. When push
comes to shove, we defend the First Amendment. By defending
the First Amendment we are defending writers. Buried in the mar-
row of our collective bones is the recognition that we must know
the truth about ourselves. Even the most bigoted American hates
a liar. Despite our economic struggle, far better to be a writer here
than elsewhere.

Morality is involved in issues other than lying or withholding   17
information. What happens when the word is substituted for the
deed? Some act of faith is always involved in the connection between
theory and action. To write and talk and not produce the action is
to destroy faith. Once again, community becomes impossible.

The best example I can think of for this phenomenon involves
the protest movements of the late 1960s and early 1970s. While
the Nazis committed unspeakable acts (I mean unspeakable—they
had no word for what they were doing), the New Left and the
Women's Movement spoke incessantly but committed few acts.
This seems to be a hallmark of leftist politics: the substitution of
the word for the deed. Yes, some things got accomplished, but
compare it to the dedicated raising of money by the New Right
and the intelligent daily application of those funds, and you
quickly grasp the difference.

The New Right has few writers. The New Left was top-heavy   18
with them. From the New Left true fiction writers emerged, leaving behind the restrictions of ideology and moving toward a wider
embrace of human experience but, I hope, imbued with a belief
in justice, equality, and innovation. To date, not one decent fiction writer has emerged from the New Right.

I was one of those people to emerge from the New Left. I re-   19
call the early days of the movement. The blind were leading the
blind with great excitement into walls, into ravines, into the waiting rifles at Jackson and Kent State. These anguished memories are
then supplanted with pride; we did help to end a war which was
ill-conceived. We wrested a few changes from the system for the
nonwhite, and we created the conditions for the removal of a
President who may have committed criminal acts. From this
haunted terrain sprang a generation of scribblers. Perhaps the New
Right will fool me yet and bring forth fiction writers capable of
making us see ourselves as we really are. One thing is certain: That
writer or those writers will get clobbered by their former associates. The Right suffers little dissent.

Some writers maintain that they are apolitical. A worm is apolit-   20
ical; a human being is not. If you live in a political system and do not
seek to make it better, you are still a product of that system. Your
lack of involvement is a political statement. All Art rests on a political foundation but it need not concern itself with politics.

Go back to *The Iliad*. Achilles has plopped his butt in his tent   21
and won't fight. Agamemnon took a damsel awarded to Achilles
for his battle prowess. Briseis was her name, and Achilles, although
in love with Patroclus, a man, wanted the girl. Why not eat your
cake and have it too? The Greeks were not as ravaged by sexual
definitions as we are. Agamemnon, as head of the armed forces
(think of him as Eisenhower during World War II), could take this
woman. He had the power but he didn't have the right. Achilles,
by our standards, should set aside personal ego and fight for his
people. Achilles, by Greek standards, is absolutely right. His first
allegiance is to his honor. This conflict between the need of the
individual to be sovereign and the need of the community to tri-
umph/survive provides the context for the unfolding drama. *The
Iliad* has a political basis but you can read it without giving politics
a thought.

Even *Alice's Adventures in Wonderland* rests on a political foun-   22
dation. It can be read as a glorious fantasy, or it can be read as a
comment on the powerlessness of a child, of children in society.
You don't have to choose—you can read it on many levels, including reading it as a drug trip.

Both *The Iliad* and *Alice in Wonderland* ring true. People read   23
them today with as much pleasure as people derived from them
when they were first written. A work lives like that if it is morally
true.

You bring to a book your past, your system of beliefs. First, you   24
read a book and answer that book with those beliefs. If you are a
student of literature, you will study the environment of the writer,
and then you'll read the book again, setting aside your values.
When you've finished the second reading you can engage the
writer's beliefs with your own. Reading is an active moral and intellectual exchange. If you aren't reading books that challenge
you, you're reading the wrong books.

If you aren't writing books that challenge you, keep writing. It   25
takes years to get there. I know the book I wanted to write, the
challenging, lyrical work I dreamed about. You know only the
book I wrote. I am acutely aware of the gap between desire and
performance. Lash me though you might, you'll never hit me as
hard as I hit myself, for only I know the full extent of my failure.

Morality shifts. Infanticide was acceptable to the Greeks. It isn't   26
acceptable to us. Your work will reflect your implied faiths and

fears. Without your being necessarily conscious of it, your work reflects your society. Here's an example. Since *The Iliad*, Western writers have treated common experience as comic relief. This attitude depends on a clear class structure in which the superior classes, aristocrats, are assumed better than the inferior classes. When the middle classes began to assert themselves, this shifted. Chaucer in *The Canterbury Tales* presents sympathetic middle-class characters. Some are comic, and some are not, but none of them is heroic. A great revolution took place on the page. This accelerated over time. Shakespeare used all the classes, to his and our great profit.

27   Eventually, middle-class people developed the leisure in which to write, and what did they do? They wrote about themselves. As the Industrial Revolution wears on, their literature takes over. The middle-class character is not a king or a landed aristocrat but a lawyer or a doctor perhaps. Chekhov comes to my mind instantly. The tendency to present ordinary people (an assumption in itself— are there ordinary people?) as vaguely comic still exists but it isn't as strict a literary convention as it was for a good two thousand years.

28   When you reject inferiority at the lowest level, you topple the whole structure of dominance. The shift in literature, beginning with Chaucer, reflected real life and, in turn, had an impact upon real life. No longer were kings and queens so important. They were replaced with parliaments or by revolutions. They were replaced on the page. Morally, there's nothing wrong with having a king for your form of government or for your literary hero, but as an American I bet you don't write about one.

29   This struggle for literary representation bubbles over the decades. Today, the lower classes, thanks to programs to get them into colleges, are producing literature. The class in control of the arts, the middle class, finds itself besieged from below. Not only are the lower classes becoming literate, nonwhite and non-Christians have acquired the skills to create English literature. Stick around—the show is just beginning!

30   As Shakespeare arrived at a creative imbalance between the passing medieval world and the coming modern world (Bacon, Newton, Descartes), so we are at a similar overlap between the nation–state and global interdependence, between men and women, between whites and nonwhites, between the Christian world and

science, the Christian world and the non-Christian world, between spiritual concerns and material ones. Like Shakespeare we
find ourselves in a time where the future, so thrilling to the non-
rigid, terrifies the rigid. Every action has an equal and opposite reaction. Every cultural/social push forward is followed by people
organizing to hold back the hands of time. Those men who were
willing to kill you if you thought the earth revolved around the
sun instead of believing Ptolemy are still here. Those people, like
Elizabeth I, who killed their political enemies are here too. Like
Shakespeare, you've got to try to make sense of it. You don't have
to explain it. He didn't. You need to use it, use every bit of it.
This overlap and straining of divergent world views is a gift. Don't
ask to live in tranquil times. Literature doesn't grow there.

CHAPTER WRITING ASSIGNMENTS

Practicing Thinking, Reading, and Writing

1. Read Mitchell Stephens's essay "The Death of Reading." Then evaluate the evidence he offers to illustrate that the popularity of reading is on the decline. Write an essay that supports or argues one of Stephens's major points, and offer additional evidence to support or refute his point.

2. Read Donald Hall's essay "To Read Fiction," and discuss in an essay the differences between reading fictional works, such as short stories and novels, and reading non-fiction works, such as you might find in your college textbooks. How is each kind of reading important for a college student? What can we learn from each genre?

3. Read Kurt Vonnegut's essay "How to Write with Style" and Paul Roberts's essay "How to Say Nothing in 500 Words," and write a humorous essay that describes the process of writing with no style. Make recommendations to help other college-level writers identify the qualities that lead to bad writing.

Exploring Ideas

1. In what ways do you believe television, video games, movies, computers, and other technology have affected reading? In an essay written to other college students, identify the ways technology has improved and/or decreased the reading skills of a particular group of people (for example, college students, children, people on the job).

2. If thought is at least partly language-based, how does our ability to use language influence our ability to think? Can we have a thought that we have no language to express? Write an essay that explores the effect language skills have on our ability to think.

3. Choose a word that has changed over a period of time. Think about what it meant originally and the connotations or meanings it has acquired over time. How do changes in our words reflect changes in our thinking? Write an essay that explores the way changes in language reflect changes in thought, using the initial word you chose as an example.

GLOSSARY OF USEFUL TERMS

Numbers in parentheses indicate pages in the text where the term is defined and/or examples are given. Italicized terms within definitions are also defined in this glossary.

Abstract (155–156, 246–247) nouns, such as *truth* or *beauty,* are words that are neither specific nor definite in meaning; they refer to general concepts, qualities, and conditions that summarize an entire category of experience. Conversely, *concrete* terms, such as *apple, crabgrass, computer,* and *French horn,* make precise appeals to our senses. The word *abstract* refers to the logical process of abstraction, through which our minds are able to group together and describe similar objects, ideas, or attitudes. Most good writers use *abstract* terms sparingly in their *essays,* preferring instead the vividness and clarity of *concrete* words and phrases.

Allusion is a reference to a well-known person, place, or event from life or literature. In "Summer Rituals," for example, Ray Bradbury alludes to Herman Melville's great novel *Moby Dick* when he describes an old man who walks on his front porch "like Ahab surveying the mild mild day."

Analogy (324) is an extended *comparison* of two dissimilar objects or ideas.

Analysis (2–3, 16, 17, 208–209, 567) is examining and evaluating a topic by separating it into its basic parts and elements and studying it systematically.

Anecdote (102) is a brief account of a single incident.

Argumentation (490–505) is an appeal predominantly to *logic* and reason. It deals with complex issues that can be debated.

Attitude (105–106, 108) describes the narrator's personal feelings about a particular subject. In "Hating the Sick," Fred Pelka expresses disappointment and anger at the manner in which people who are sick are discriminated against by society. *Attitude* is one component of *point of view.*

Audience (27, 39, 44–45, 214, 494–495, 496–499) refers to the person or group of people for whom an *essay* is written.

Cause and effect (437–451) is a form of *analysis* that examines the causes and consequences of events and ideas.

Characterization (109) is the creation of imaginary yet realistic persons in fiction, drama, and *narrative* poetry.

Chronological order (27, 108, 161, 214) is a sequence of events arranged in the order in which they occurred. Brent Staples follows this natural time sequence in his *example* essay entitled "A Brother's Murder."

Classification (272–284) is the analytical process of grouping together similar subjects into a single category or class; *division* works in the opposite fashion, breaking down a subject into many different subgroups. In "The Truth About Lying," Judith Viorst classifies lies into several distinct categories.

Clichés (250–251) are words or expressions that have lost their freshness and originality through continual use. For example, "busy as a bee," "pretty as a picture," and "hotter than hell" have become trite and dull because of overuse. Good writers avoid clichés through vivid and original phrasing.

Climactic order (161) refers to the *organization* of ideas from one extreme to another—for example, from least important to most important, from most destructive to least destructive, or from least promising to most promising.

Cognitive skills (2–4) are mental abilities that help us send and receive verbal messages.

Coherence (161) is the manner in which an essay "holds together" its main ideas. A coherent *theme* will demonstrate such a clear relationship between its *thesis* and its logical structure that readers can easily follow the argument.

Colloquial expressions (253) are informal words, phrases, and sentences that are more appropriate for spoken conversations than for written essays.

Comparison (323–339) is an *expository* writing technique that examines the similarities between objects or ideas, whereas *contrast* focuses on differences.

Conclusions (33, 497) bring *essays* to a natural close by summarizing the argument, restating the *thesis,* calling for some specific action, or explaining the significance of the topic just discussed. If the *introduction* states your thesis in the form of a question to be answered or a problem to be solved, then your *conclusion* will be the final "answer" or "solution" provided in your paper. The *conclusion* should be approximately the same length as your *introduction* and should leave your reader satisfied that you have actually "concluded" your discussion rather than simply run out of ideas to discuss.

Concrete: See *abstract.*

Conflict is the struggle resulting from the opposition of two strong forces in the plot of a play, novel, or short story.

Connotation and Denotation (252–254, 498–499) are two principal methods of describing the meanings of words. *Connotation* refers to the wide array of positive and negative associations that most words naturally carry with them, whereas *denotation* is the precise, literal *definition* of a word that might be found in a dictionary. See, for example, Amy Tan's description of the terms "broken" or "fractured" English in "Mother Tongue."

Content and Form (31–33) are the two main components of an *essay.* *Content* refers to the subject matter of an *essay,* whereas its *form* consists of the graphic symbols that communicate the subject matter (word choice, spelling, punctuation, paragraphing, etc.).

Contrast: See *comparison.*

Deduction (498) is a form of logical reasoning that begins with a *general* assertion and then presents specific details and *examples* in support of that *generalization. Induction* works in reverse by offering a number of *examples* and then concluding with a *general* truth or principle.

Definition (383–394) is a process whereby the meaning of a term is explained. Formal *definitions* require two distinct operations: (1) finding the *general* class to which the object belongs and (2) isolating the object within that class by describing how it differs from other elements in the same category. Nancy Gibbs ("When Is It Rape?"), for example, defines rape as a crime (general class) and then differentiates it from other crimes (isolation) by explaining ways in which it is unique.

Denotation: See *connotation.*

Description (38–53) is a mode of writing or speaking that relates the sights, sounds, tastes, smells, or feelings of a particular experience to its readers or listeners. Good descriptive writers, such as those featured in Chapter 1, are particularly adept at receiving, selecting, and expressing sensory details from the world around them. Along with *persuasion, exposition,* and *narration, description* is one of the four dominant types of writing.

Development (27–30) concerns the manner in which a *paragraph* of an essay expands on its topic.

Dialect is a speech pattern typical of a certain regional location, race, or social group that exhibits itself through unique word choice, pronunciation, and/or grammatical *usage.* See John McPhee's "The Pines," in which Fred and Bill, two residents of a wilderness area in southern New Jersey, speak in a discernible *dialect.*

Dialogue is a conversation between two or more people, particularly within a novel, play, poem, short story, or other literary work.

Diction (27, 251–253, 498–499) is word choice. If a vocabulary is a list of words available for use, then good *diction* is the careful selection of those words to communicate a particular subject to a specific *audience.* Different types of *diction* include *formal* (scholarly books and articles), *informal* (essays in popular magazines), *colloquial* (conversations between friends, including newly coined words and expressions), *slang* (language shared by certain social groups), *dialect* (language typical of a certain region, race, or social group), *technical* (words that make up the basic vocabulary of a specific area of study, such as medicine or law), and *obsolete* (words no longer in use).

Division: See *classification.*

Documented essay (566–583) is a research or library paper that integrates *paraphrases, summaries,* and *quotations* from secondary sources with the writer's own insights and conclusions. Such *essays* normally include bibliographic references within the paper and, at the end, a list of the books and articles cited.

Dominant impression (41–42, 43, 44, 45) in *descriptive* writing is the principal effect the author wishes to create for the *audience.*

Editing (31–32, 33) is an important part of the *rewriting* process of an *essay* that requires writers to make certain their work observes the conventions of standard written English.

Effect: See *cause and effect.*

Emphasis (103, 496) is the stress given to certain words, phrases, sentences, and/or *paragraphs* within an *essay* by such methods as repeating important ideas; positioning thesis and *topic sentences* effectively; supplying additional details or *examples;* allocating more space to certain sections of an *essay;* choosing words carefully; selecting and arranging details judiciously; and using certain mechanical devices, such as italics, underlining, capitalization, and different colors of ink.

Essay is a relatively short prose composition on a limited topic. Most *essays* are five hundred to one thousand words long and focus on a clearly definable question to be answered or problem to be solved. *Formal essays,* such as Germaine Greer's "A Child Is Born," are generally characterized by seriousness of *purpose,* logical organization, and dignity of language; *informal essays,* such as Garrison Keillor's "How the Crab Apple Grew," are generally brief, humorous, and more loosely structured. *Essays* in this textbook have been divided into nine traditional *rhetorical* types, each of which is discussed at length in its chapter introduction.

Etymology (387) is the study of the origin and development of words.

Evidence (491, 494, 497, 567) is any material used to help support an *argument,* including details, facts, *examples,* opinions, and expert testimony. Just as a lawyer's case is won or lost in a court of law because of the strength of the *evidence* presented, so, too, does the effectiveness of a writer's essay depend on the evidence offered in support of its *thesis statement.*

Example (155–167) is an illustration of a *general* principle or *thesis statement.* Harold Krents's "Darkness at Noon," for instance, gives several different examples of prejudice against handicapped people.

Exposition is one of the four main *rhetorical* categories of writing (the others are *persuasion, narration,* and *description*). The principal purpose of expository prose is to "expose" ideas to your readers, to explain, define, and interpret information through one or more of the following modes of exposition: *example, process analysis, division/classification, comparison/contrast, definition,* and *cause/effect.*

Figurative language (45–46, 499) is writing or speaking that purposefully departs from the literal meanings of words to achieve a particularly vivid, expressive, and/or imaginative image. When, for example, Annie Dillard refers to "living like weasels," she is using *figurative language.* Other principal figures of speech include *metaphor, simile, hyperbole, allusion,* and *personification.*

Flashback (108) is a technique used mainly in *narrative* writing that enables the author to present scenes or conversations that took place prior to the beginning of the story.

Focus (25–29) is the concentration of a *topic* on one central point or issue.

Form: See *content.*

Formal essay: See *essay.*

Free association (22–23) is a process of generating ideas for writing through which one thought leads randomly to another.

General (155–156, 246–247) words are those that employ expansive categories, such as *animals, sports, occupations,* and *clothing; specific* words are more limiting and restrictive, such as *koala, lacrosse, computer programmer,* and *bow tie.* Whether a word is *general* or *specific* depends at least somewhat on its context: *Bow tie* is more specific than *clothing,* yet less *specific* than "the pink and green striped bow tie Aunt Martha gave me last Christmas." See also *abstract.*

Generalization (155–156, 158, 498) is a broad statement or belief based on a limited number of facts, *examples,* or statistics. A product of inductive reasoning, generalizations should be used carefully and sparingly in *essays.*

Hyperbole, the opposite of *understatement,* is a type of *figurative language* that uses deliberate exaggeration for the sake of emphasis or comic effect (e.g., "hungry enough to eat 20 chocolate eclairs").

Hypothesis (442, 567) is a tentative theory that can be proved or disproved through further investigation and analysis.

Idiom refers to a grammatical construction unique to a certain people, region, or class that cannot be translated literally into another language.

Illustration (155–156) is the use of *examples* to support an idea or *generalization.*

Imagery (44–45) is *description* that appeals to one or more of our five senses. See, for example, Malcolm Cowley's description in "The View from 80" of one of the pleasures of old age: "simply sitting still, like a snake on a sun-warmed stone, with a delicious feeling of indolence that was seldom attained in earlier years." Imagery is used to help bring clarity and vividness to descriptive writing.

Induction: See *deduction.*

Inference (498) is a *deduction* or *conclusion* derived from *specific* information.

Informal essay: See *essay.*

Introduction (33) refers to the beginning of an *essay.* It should identify the subject to be discussed, set the limits of that discussion, and clearly state the *thesis* or general *purpose* of the paper. In a brief (five-*paragraph*) *essay,* your *introduction* should be only one *paragraph;* for longer papers, you may want to provide longer introductory sections. A good *introduction* will generally catch the audience's attention by beginning with a quotation, a provocative statement, a personal *anecdote,* or a stimulating question that somehow involves its readers in the topic under consideration. See also *conclusion.*

Irony (171) is a figure of speech in which the literal, *denotative* meaning is the opposite of what is stated. Judy Brady's "Why I Want a Wife" is heavily ironic: What she really wants is for women to be treated as equals to men.

Jargon (249–250) is the special language of a certain group or profession, such as psychological *jargon,* legal *jargon,* or medical *jargon.* When jargon is excerpted from its proper subject area, it generally becomes confusing or humorous, as in "I have a latency problem with my backhand" or "I hope we can interface tomorrow night after the dance."

Levels of thought (1–2) is a phrase that describes the three sequential stages at which people think, read, and write: literal, interpretive, and analytical.

Logic (491, 498) is the science of correct reasoning. Based principally on *inductive* or *deductive* processes, *logic* establishes a method by which we can examine *premises* and *conclusions,* construct *syllogisms,* and avoid faulty reasoning.

Logical fallacy (438–440) is an incorrect conclusion derived from faulty reasoning. See also *post hoc, ergo propter hoc,* and *non sequitur.*

Metaphor (45–46, 498–499) is an implied *comparison* that brings together two dissimilar objects, persons, or ideas. Unlike a *simile,* which uses the words *like* or *as,* a *metaphor* directly identifies an obscure or difficult subject with another that is easier to understand. For example, when Susan Austin claims that she has taken the North Dakota landscape into her bones ("Land and Bones"), she is using a metaphor to describe the way in which she has internalized and learned to love this austere environment.

Mood (108, 498–499) refers to the atmosphere or *tone* created in a piece of writing. The mood of Jill Leslie Rosenbaum and Meda Chesney-Lind's "Appearance and Delinquency: A Research Note" is serious and scholarly; of Jessica Mitford's "Behind the Formaldehyde Curtain," sarcastic and derisive; and of Mary Roach's "Meet the Bickersons," good-humored and sensible.

Narration (102–116) is storytelling: the recounting of a series of events, arranged in a particular order and delivered by a narrator to a specific *audience* with a clear *purpose* in mind. Along with *persuasion, exposition,* and *description,* it is one of the four principal types of writing.

Non sequitur (497–498), from a Latin phrase meaning "it does not follow," refers to a *conclusion* that does not logically derive from its *premises.*

Objective (39, 43) writing is detached, impersonal, and factual; *subjective* writing reveals the author's personal feelings and attitudes. Judith Wallerstein and Sandra Blakeslee's "Second Chances for Children of Divorce" is an *example* of *objective* prose, whereas Amy Tan's "Mother Tongue" is essentially *subjective* in nature. Most good college-level *essays* are a careful mix of both approaches, with lab reports and technical writing toward the *objective* end of the scale and personal *essays* in composition courses at the *subjective* end.

Organization (27, 30–31, 102, 108, 160–161, 213–214, 496–499) refers to the order in which a writer chooses to present his or her ideas to the reader. Five main types of *organization* may be used to develop *paragraphs* or *essays:* (1) *deductive* (moving from general to specific), (2) *inductive* (from specific to general), (3) *chronological* (according to time sequence), (4) *spatial* (according to physical relationship in space), and (5) *climactic* (from one extreme to another, such as least important to most important).

Paradox is a seemingly self-contradictory statement that contains an element of truth. In "The View from 80," Malcolm Cowley paradoxically declares that the Ojibwa Indians were "kind to their old people" by killing them when they became decrepit.

Paragraphs are groups of interrelated sentences that develop a central topic. Generally governed by a *topic sentence,* a *paragraph* has its own *unity* and *coherence* and is an integral part of the logical *development* of an *essay.*

Parallelism (294–295) is a structural arrangement within sentences, *paragraphs,* or entire *essays* through which two or more separate elements are similarly phrased and developed. Look, for example, at Judy Brady's "Why I Want a Wife": "I want a wife who will plan the menus, do the necessary grocery shopping, prepare the meals, serve them pleasantly, and then do the cleaning up while I do my studying."

Paraphrase (570–571) is a restatement in your own words of someone else's ideas or observations.

Parody is making fun of a person, an event, or a work of literature through exaggerated imitation.

Person (46, 108) is a grammatical distinction identifying the speaker or writer in a particular context: first person (I or we), second person (you), and third person (he, she, it, or they). The *person* of an *essay* refers to the voice of the narrator. See also *point of view.*

Personification is *figurative language* that ascribes human characteristics to an abstraction, animal, idea, or inanimate object. Consider, for example, Robert Ramirez's description in "The Barrio" of the bakery that "sends its sweet messenger aroma down the dimly lit street, announcing the arrival of fresh, hot, sugary *pan dulce.*"

Persuasion (490–503) is one of the four chief forms of *rhetoric.* Its main purpose is to convince a reader (or listener) to think, act, or feel a certain way. It involves appealing to reason, to emotion, and/or to a sense of ethics. The other three main *rhetorical* categories are *exposition, narration,* and *description.*

Point of view (46, 108) is the perspective from which a writer tells a story, including *person, vantage point,* and *attitude.* Principal *narrative* voices are first-person, in which the writer relates the story from his or her own vantage point ("I began to learn about love in dancing school, at age 12," from "How to Find True Love: Or Rather, How It Finds You" by Lois Smith Brady); omniscient, a third-person technique in which the narrator knows everything and can even see into the minds of the various characters; and concealed, a third-person method in which the narrator can see and hear events but cannot look into the minds of the other characters.

Post hoc, ergo propter hoc (438–439), a Latin phrase meaning "after this, therefore because of this," is a *logical fallacy* confusing *cause and effect* with *chronology.* Just because Irving wakes up every morning before the sun rises doesn't mean that the sun rises *because* Irving wakes up.

Premise (496–499) is a proposition or statement that forms the foundation of an *argument* and helps support a *conclusion.* See also *logic* and *syllogism.*

Prereading (5–8, 20) is thoughtful concentration on a topic before reading an *essay.* Just as athletes warm up their physical muscles before competition, so, too, should students activate their "mental muscles" before reading or writing *essays.*

Prewriting (21–28, 30–32), which is similar to *prereading,* is the initial stage in the composing process during which writers consider their topics, generate ideas, narrow and refine their *thesis statements,* organize their ideas, pursue any necessary research, and identify their *audiences.* Although prewriting occurs principally, as the name suggests, "before" an essay is started, writers usually return to this "invention" stage again and again during the course of the writing process.

Process analysis (208–220), one of the seven primary modes of *exposition,* either gives directions about how to do something (directive) or provides information on how something happened (informative).

Proofreading (32, 33–34), an essential part of *rewriting,* is a thorough, careful review of the final draft of an *essay* that ensures that all errors have been eliminated.

Purpose (27, 41, 44, 494–495, 499) in an *essay* refers to its overall aim or intention: to entertain, inform, or persuade a particular *audience* with reference to a specific topic (to persuade an audience that America's tendency to read less will eventually lead to an inability to think clearly, as Mitchell Stephens argues in "The Death of Reading"). See also *dominant impression*.

Refutation is the process of discrediting the *arguments* that run counter to your *thesis statement*.

Revision (30–32, 33–34), meaning "to see again," takes place during the entire writing process as you change words, rewrite sentences, and shift *paragraphs* from one location to another in your *essay*. It plays an especially vital role in the *rewriting* stage of the composing process.

Rewriting (30–32, 33–34) is a stage of the composing process that includes *revision, editing,* and *proofreading*.

Rhetoric is the art of using language effectively.

Rhetorical questions are intended to provoke thought rather than bring forth an answer. See, for example, Shelby Steele's *rhetorical questions* in "Affirmative Action: The Price of Preference": "Given that unfairness cuts both ways, doesn't it only balance the scales of history that my children now receive a preference over whites? Doesn't this repay, in a small way, the systematic denial under which their grandfather lived out his days?"

Rhetorical strategy or mode is the plan or method whereby an *essay* is organized. Most writers choose from methods discussed in this book, such as *narration, example, comparison/contrast, definition,* and *cause/effect*.

Sarcasm is a form of *irony* that attacks a person or belief through harsh and bitter remarks that often mean the opposite of what they say. See, for example, Jessica Mitford's sarcastic praise of the funeral director in "Behind the Formaldehyde Curtain": "He has relieved the family of every detail, he has revamped the corpse to look like a living doll, he has arranged for it to nap for a few days in a slumber room, he has put on a well-oiled performance in which the concept of *death* has played no part whatsoever. . . . He has done everything in his power to make the funeral a real pleasure for everybody concerned." See also *satire*.

Satire is a literary technique that attacks foolishness by making fun of it. Most good satires work through a "fiction" that is clearly transparent. Judy Brady claims she wants a wife, for example, yet she obviously does not; she simply uses this satiric "pose" to ridicule the stereotypical male view of wives as docile, obedient creatures who do everything possible to please their husbands.

Setting refers to the immediate environment of a *narrative* or *descriptive* piece of writing: the place, time, and background established by the author.

Simile (45–46, 498) is a *comparison* between two dissimilar objects that uses the words *like* or *as*. See, for example, Ray Bradbury's description of the women in "Summer Rituals," who appear "like ghosts hovering momentarily behind the door screen." See also *metaphor*.

Slang (254) is casual conversation among friends; as such, it is inappropriate for use in formal and informal writing, unless it is placed in quotation marks and introduced for a specific rhetorical purpose: "Hey dude, what's up?" See also *colloquial expressions*.

Spatial order (103, 161) is a method of *description* that begins at one geographical point and moves onward in an orderly fashion. See, for example, the opening of John McPhee's "The Pines," which first describes the front yard of Fred Brown's house, then moves through the vestibule and into the kitchen, and finally settles on Fred himself, who is seated behind a porcelain-topped table in a room just beyond the kitchen.

Specific: See *general*.

Style is the unique, individual way in which each author expresses his or her ideas. Often referred to as the "personality" of an *essay, style* is dependent on a writer's manipulation of *diction*, sentence structure, *figurative language, point of view, characterization, emphasis, mood, purpose, rhetorical strategy*, and all the other variables that govern written material.

Subjective: See *objective*.

Summary (571) is a condensed statement of someone else's thoughts or observations.

Syllogism (498) refers to a three-step *deductive argument* that moves logically from a major and a minor *premise* to a *conclusion*. A traditional example is "All men are mortal. Socrates is a man. Therefore, Socrates is mortal."

Symbol refers to an object or action in literature that metaphorically represents something more important than itself. In Annie Dillard's "Living Like Weasels," for example, the weasel symbolizes a type of instinctive fierceness, freedom, and commitment that the author wishes she had in her own human life.

Synonyms are terms with similar or identical *denotative* meanings, such as *aged, elderly, older person,* and *senior citizen.*

Syntax describes the order in which words are arranged in a sentence and the effect that this arrangement has on the creation of meaning.

Thesis statement or thesis (27) is the principal *focus* of an *essay.* It is usually phrased in the form of a question to be answered, a problem to be solved, or an assertion to be argued. The word *thesis* derives from a Greek term meaning "something set down," and most good writers find that "setting down" their thesis in writing helps them tremendously in defining and clarifying their topic before they begin to write an outline or a rough draft.

Tone (108, 498) is a writer's *attitude* or *point of view* toward his or her subject. See also *mood.*

Topic sentence is the central idea around which a *paragraph* develops. A *topic sentence* controls a *paragraph* in the same way a *thesis statement* unifies and governs an entire essay. See also *induction* and *deduction.*

Transition (108) is the linking together of sequential ideas in sentences, paragraphs, and essays. This linking is accomplished primarily through word repetition, pronouns, parallel constructions, and such transitional words and phrases as *therefore, as a result, consequently, moreover,* and *similarly.*

Understatement, the opposite of *hyperbole,* is a deliberate weakening of the truth for comic or emphatic purpose. Commenting, for example, on the great care funeral directors take to make corpses look lifelike for their funerals, Jessica Mitford explains in "Behind the Formaldehyde Curtain," "This is a rather large order, since few people die in the full bloom of health."

Unity (161) exists in an *essay* when all ideas originate from and help support a central *thesis statement*.

Usage (31–32, 33) refers to the customary rules that govern written and spoken language.

Vantage point (46, 108).) is the frame of reference of the narrator in a story: close to the action, far from the action, looking back on the past, or reporting on the present. See also *person* and *point of view*.

CREDITS

INDEX OF AUTHORS AND TITLES